Microsoft

Materials excerpted from:

Managing and Maintaining a Microsoft® Windows Server™ 2003 Environment (70-290)

Craig Zacker

and

Implementing, Managing and Maintaining a Microsoft® Windows Server™ 2003 Network Infrastructure (70-291)

Greg Bott

Textbook

To order books or for customer service, please call 1(800)-CALL-WILEY (225-5945).

Printed in the United States of America.

ISBN   978-0-470-24723-5

10 9 8 7 6 5 4 3 2 1

The content of this text has been taken from

Microsoft® Official Academic Course
70-290 Managing and Maintaining a Microsoft®
Windows Server™ 2003 Environment, ISBN 0-7356-2031-8

and

Microsoft® Official Academic Course
70-291 Implementing, Managing, and Maintaining a Microsoft®
Windows Server™ 2003 Network Infrastructure, ISBN 0-7356-2030-X

Since this custom text is based on excerpts of the full Microsoft® Official Academic Course
textbooks for 70-290 and 70-291, it is not intended to cover the entire objective domain for these two
Microsoft® certification exams. In that way, this custom text is not meant to be a preparatory text for
these two Microsoft® certification exams.

CONTENTS

Microsoft® Official Academic Course
**70-290 Managing and Maintaining a Microsoft® Windows Server™ 2003
Environment** Textbook

Microsoft® Official Academic Course 70-291
**Implementing, Managing and Maintaining a Microsoft® Windows Server™ 2003
Network Infrastructure** Textbook

Microsoft

Managing and Maintaining a Microsoft® Windows Server™ 2003 Environment (70-290)

Textbook

Craig Zacker

PUBLISHED BY
Microsoft Press
A Division of Microsoft Corporation
One Microsoft Way
Redmond, Washington 98052-6399

Library of Congress Cataloging-in-Publication Data
Zacker, Craig.
    Managing and Maintaining a Microsoft Windows Server 2003 Environment / Craig Zacker, Mark Fugatt.
        p. cm.
    Includes index.
    ISBN 0-7356-2031-8
    1. Microsoft Windows server.   2. Operating systems (Computers).   I. Title.

    QA76.76.O63Z345   2004
    005.4'47682--dc22   2003064855

Printed and bound in the United States of America.

1 2 3 4 5 6 7 8 9   QWT   8 7 6 5 4 3

A CIP catalogue record for this book is available from the British Library.

Microsoft Press books are available through booksellers and distributors worldwide. For further information about international editions, contact your local Microsoft Corporation office or contact Microsoft Press International directly at fax (425)
936-7329. Visit our Web site at www.microsoft.com/learning. Send comments to *moac@microsoft.com*.

Program Managers: Linda Engelman, Hilary Long
Project Editor: Lynn Finnel
Technical Editor: Eric Dettinger
Indexer: Bill Meyers

Sub Assy Part No. X10-35339
Body Part No. X10-23991

CONTENTS AT A GLANCE

CONTENTS

PART 2: MANAGING AND MAINTAINING USERS, GROUPS, AND COMPUTERS

ABOUT THIS BOOK

Welcome to *Managing and Maintaining a Microsoft Windows Server 2003 Environment (70-290)*, a part of the Microsoft Official Academic Course (MOAC) series. Through lectures, discussions, demonstrations, textbook exercises, and classroom labs, this course teaches students the skills and knowledge necessary to take Microsoft certification exam 70-290: Managing and Maintaining a Microsoft Windows Server 2003 Environment and to become a Microsoft Certified Professional (MCP), a Microsoft Certified Systems Engineer (MCSE) on Windows Server 2003, or a Microsoft Certified Systems Administrator (MCSA) on Windows Server 2003.

This course is for anyone who wants to learn how to install, configure, administer, and support the primary services in the Windows Server 2003 operating system, as well as those seeking Microsoft certification. The course begins by examining basic system administration procedures. Subsequent chapters are devoted to creating and managing Windows Server 2003 user, group, and computer accounts; sharing system resources; and installing and maintaining system hardware.

TARGET AUDIENCE

Students in this course typically aspire to careers as Windows Server 2003 system administrators or support technicians, and they want an objective assessment and certification of their skills. The audience for this book consists of IT professionals who work in the typically complex computing environment of medium-size to large companies. Students should have 6 to 12 months of experience administering client and network operating systems in environments with the following characteristics:

- 250 to 5000 or more users

- Three or more physical locations

- Three or more domain controllers

- Network services and resources such as messaging, database, file and print, proxy server, firewall, Internet, intranet, remote access, and client computer management

- Connectivity requirements such as connecting branch offices and individual users in remote locations to the corporate network and connecting corporate networks to the Internet

PREREQUISITES

There are no official prerequisites for taking the 70-290 exam, but students taking this course should have the following background:

- CompTIA A+ certification or equivalent knowledge and skills

- CompTIA Network+ certification or equivalent knowledge and skills

THE TEXTBOOK

The textbook content has been crafted to provide a meaningful learning experience to students in an academic classroom setting.

Key features of the Microsoft Official Academic Course (MOAC) textbooks include the following:

- Learning objectives for each chapter that prepare the student for the topic areas covered in that chapter

- Chapter introductions that explain why the content is important

- An inviting design with screen shots, diagrams, tables, bulleted lists, and other graphical formats that makes the book easy to comprehend and supports a number of different learning styles

- Clear explanations of concepts and principles, and frequent exposition of step-by-step procedures

- A variety of reader aids that highlight a wealth of additional information, including:

  - Note – Real-world application tips and alternative procedures, and explanations of complex procedures and concepts

  - Caution – Warnings about mistakes that can result in loss of data or are difficult to resolve

  - Important – Explanations of essential setup steps before starting a procedure, and other instructions

- Short, optional, hands-on exercises that break up lectures and provide a warm-up for more complex lab exercises.

- End-of-chapter review questions that assess knowledge and can serve as homework, quizzes, and review activities before or after lectures. Answers to the textbook questions are available from your instructor.

- Chapter summaries that distill the main ideas in a chapter and reinforce learning.

- Case scenarios, approximately two per chapter, that provide students with an opportunity to evaluate, analyze, synthesize, and apply information learned during the chapter.

- Comprehensive glossary that defines key terms introduced in the book.

THE SUPPLEMENTAL COURSE MATERIALS CD-ROM

This book comes with a Supplemental Course Materials CD-ROM, which contains a variety of informational aids to complement the book content:

- An electronic version of this textbook (eBook). For information about using the eBook, see the section titled "eBook Setup Instructions" later in this introduction.

- The Microsoft Press Readiness Review Suite from MeasureUp. This suite of practice tests and objective reviews contains questions of varying complexity and offers multiple testing modes. You can assess your understanding of the concepts presented in this book and use the results to develop a learning plan that meets your needs.

- Installation scripts and example files for performing the hands-on exercises in the Lab Manual. These include files that demonstrate key concepts and illustrate a specific point, as well as files included for your convenience, such as scripts that can be used to reduce the amount of time you spend setting up your system to perform a particular exercise.

- An eBook of *Microsoft Encyclopedia of Networking*, Second Edition.

- Microsoft PowerPoint slides based on textbook chapters, for note taking.

- Windows System Resource Manager, a feature of Microsoft Windows, that allows administrators to control how CPU and memory resources are allocated to applications, services, and processes. For more information or to install Windows System Resource Manager, open the Readme.htm file in the \WSRM folder.

- Microsoft Word Viewer and PowerPoint Viewer

- A second CD contains a 180-day evaluation edition of Windows Server 2003 Enterprise Edition.

    CAUTION The 180-day evaluation edition of Windows Server 2003 Enterprise Edition provided with this book is not the full retail product; it is provided only for the purposes of training and evaluation. Microsoft Technical Support does not support this evaluation edition.

Readiness Review Suite Setup Instructions

The Readiness Review Suite includes a practice test of 300 sample exam questions and an objective review with an additional 125 questions. Use these tools to reinforce your learning and to identify areas in which you need to gain more experience before taking the exam.

▶ **Installing the Practice Test**

1. Insert the Supplemental Course Materials CD into your CD-ROM drive.

    NOTE If AutoRun is disabled on your machine, refer to the Readme.txt file on the Supplemental Course Materials CD.

2. On the User Interface menu, select Readiness Review Suite and follow the prompts.

eBook Setup Instructions

The eBook is in Portable Document Format (PDF) and must be viewed using Adobe Acrobat Reader.

▶ **Using the eBook**

1. Insert the Supplemental Course Materials CD into your CD-ROM drive.

    NOTE If AutoRun is disabled on your machine, refer to the Readme.txt file on the CD.

2. On the User Interface menu, select Textbook eBook and follow the prompts. You also can review any of the other eBooks provided for your use.

NOTE   You must have the Supplemental Course Materials CD in your CD-ROM drive to run the eBook.

THE LAB MANUAL

The Lab Manual is designed for use in a combined lecture and lab situation, or in a separate lecture and lab arrangement. The exercises in the Lab Manual correspond to textbook chapters and are intended for use in a classroom setting under the supervision of an instructor. However, they are also suitable for independent study under the supervision of an instructor.

The Lab Manual presents a rich, hands-on learning experience that encourages practical solutions and strengthens critical problem-solving skills:

- Lab Exercises teach procedures by using a step-by-step format. Questions interspersed throughout Lab Exercises encourage reflection and critical thinking about the lab activity.

- Lab Review Questions appear at the end of each lab and ask questions about the lab. They are designed to promote critical reflection.

- Lab Challenges are review activities that ask students to perform a variation on a task they performed in the Lab Exercises, but without detailed instructions.

- Troubleshooting Labs appear after a number of regular labs and consist of mid-length review projects based on true-to-life scenarios. These labs challenge students to think like an expert to solve complex problems.

- Labs are based on realistic business settings and include an opening scenario and a list of learning objectives.

Students who successfully complete the Lab Exercises, Lab Review Questions, Lab Challenges, and Troubleshooting Labs in the Lab Manual will have a richer learning experience and deeper understanding of the concepts and methods covered in the course. They will be better able to answer and understand the testbank questions, especially the knowledge application and knowledge synthesis questions. They will also be better prepared to pass the associated certification exams if they choose to do so.

NOTATIONAL CONVENTIONS

The following conventions are used throughout this texbook and the Lab Manual:

- Characters or commands that you type appear in **bold** type.
- Terms that appear in the glossary also appear in **bold** type.

- *Italic* in syntax statements indicates placeholders for variable information. *Italic* is also used for book titles and terms defined in the text.

- Names of files and folders appear in Title caps, except when you are to type them directly. Unless otherwise indicated, you can use all lowercase letters when you type a filename in a dialog box or at a command prompt.

- Filename extensions appear in all lowercase.

- Acronyms appear in all uppercase.

- Monospace type represents code samples, examples of screen text, or entries that you might type at a command prompt or in initialization files.

- Square brackets [ ] are used in syntax statements to enclose optional items. For example, [*filename*] in command syntax indicates that you can type a filename with the command. Type only the information within the brackets, not the brackets themselves.

- Braces { } are used in syntax statements to enclose required items. Type only the information within the braces, not the braces themselves.

KEYBOARD CONVENTIONS

- A plus sign (+) between two key names means that you must press those keys at the same time. For example, "Press ALT+TAB" means that you hold down ALT while you press TAB.

- A comma (,) between two or more key names means that you must press the keys consecutively, not at the same time. For example, "Press ALT, F, X" means that you press and release each key in sequence. "Press ALT+W, L" means that you first press ALT and W at the same time, and then you release them and press L.

COURSE COVERAGE OF EXAM OBJECTIVES

The title is intended to support your efforts to prepare for the 70-290 exam. The following table correlates the exam objectives with the textbook chapters and Lab Manual lab exercises.

> **NOTE** The Microsoft Learning Web site describes the various MCP certification exams and their corresponding courses. It provides up-to-date certification information and explains the certification process and the course options. See *http://www.microsoft.com/learning/learning/mcp* for up-to-date information about MCP exam credentials about other certification programs offered by Microsoft.

Textbook and Lab Manual Coverage of Exam Objectives

Objective	Textbook Chapter	Lab Items
Managing and Maintaining Physical and Logical Devices		

(continued)

Textbook and Lab Manual Coverage of Exam Objectives

Objective	Textbook Chapter	Lab Items
■ Manage basic disks and dynamic disks.	12	Lab 12, Exercises 1 to 5
■ Monitor server hardware. Tools might include Device Manager, the Hardware Troubleshooting Wizard, and appropriate Control Panel items.	11	Lab 11, Exercises 1 to 3
■ Optimize server disk performance.	12	Lab 12, Lab Challenge 1
■ Install and configure server hardware devices.	11	Lab 11, Exercises 1 to 3
Managing Users, Computers, and Groups		
■ Manage local, roaming, and mandatory user profiles.	6	Lab 6, Exercise 9
■ Create and manage computer accounts in an Active Directory environment.	8	Lab 8, Exercises 1 to 3
■ Create and manage groups.	7	Lab 7, Exercises 2 to 7
■ Create and manage user accounts.	6	Lab 6, Exercises 1 to 8
■ Troubleshoot computer accounts.	8	Troubleshooting Lab B
■ Troubleshoot user accounts.	6	Troubleshooting Lab A
■ Troubleshoot user authentication issues.	6	Troubleshooting Lab A
Managing and Maintaining Access to Resources		
■ Configure access to shared folders.	9	Lab 9, Exercise 1
■ Troubleshoot Terminal Services.	2	Troubleshooting Lab A
■ Configure file system permissions.	9	Lab 9, Exercise 5
■ Troubleshoot access to files and shared folders.	9	Troubleshooting Lab B
Managing and Maintaining a Server Environment		
■ Monitor and analyze events. Tools might include Event Viewer and System Monitor.	3	Lab 3, Exercises 1, 3, and 4
■ Manage software update infrastructure.	5	Lab 5, Exercises 3 and 5
■ Manage software site licensing.	5	Lab 5, Exercises 6 and 7
■ Manage servers remotely.	2	Lab 2, Exercises 4 and 5, and Lab Challenge 1
■ Troubleshoot print queues.	10	Lab 10, Exercises 5 and 6
■ Monitor system performance.	3	Lab 3, Exercise 2
■ Monitor file and print servers. Tools might include Task Manager, Event Viewer, and System Monitor.	3	Lab 10, Exercise 6

(continued)

Textbook and Lab Manual Coverage of Exam Objectives

Objective	Textbook Chapter	Lab Items
■ Monitor and optimize a server environment for application performance.	3	
■ Manage a Web server.	9	Lab 9, Exercise 7, and Lab Challenge 1
■ Manage Internet Information Services (IIS).	9	Lab 9, Exercise 7, and Lab Challenge 1
■ Manage security for IIS.	9	Lab 9, Exercise 7, and Lab Challenge 1
Managing and Implementing Disaster Recovery		
■ Perform system recovery for a server.	4	
■ Manage backup procedures.	4	Lab 4, Exercises 1 to 4, and Lab Challenge 1
■ Recover from server hardware failure.	4	
■ Restore backup data.	4	Lab 4, Exercises 1 to 3
■ Schedule backup jobs.	4	Lab 4, Exercise 4

THE MICROSOFT CERTIFIED PROFESSIONAL PROGRAM

The MCP program is the best way to prove your proficiency with current Microsoft products and technologies. The exams and corresponding certifications are developed to validate your mastery of critical competencies as you design and develop, or implement and support, solutions using Microsoft products and technologies. Computer professionals who become Microsoft certified are recognized as experts and are sought after industrywide. Certification brings a variety of benefits to the individual and to employers and organizations.

> **MORE INFO** For a full list of MCP benefits, go to http://www.microsoft.com/learning/itpro/.

Certifications

The MCP program offers multiple certifications, based on specific areas of technical expertise:

- **Microsoft Certified Professional (MCP)** In-depth knowledge of at least one Windows operating system or architecturally significant platform. An MCP is qualified to implement a Microsoft product or technology as part of a business solution for an organization.

- **Microsoft Certified Systems Engineer (MCSE)** Qualified to effectively analyze the business requirements for business solutions and design and implement the infrastructure based on the Windows and Windows Server 2003 operating systems.

- **Microsoft Certified Systems Administrator (MCSA)**   Qualified to manage and troubleshoot existing network and system environments based on the Windows and Windows Server 2003 operating systems.

- **Microsoft Certified Database Administrator (MCDBA)**   Qualified to design, implement, and administer Microsoft SQL Server databases.

MCP Requirements

Requirements differ for each certification and are specific to the products and job functions addressed by the certification. To become an MCP, you must pass rigorous certification exams that provide a valid and reliable measure of technical proficiency and expertise. These exams are designed to test your expertise and ability to perform a role or task with a product, and are developed with the input of industry professionals. Exam questions reflect how Microsoft products are used in actual organizations, giving them real-world relevance.

- Microsoft Certified Professional (MCP) candidates are required to pass one current Microsoft certification exam. Candidates can pass additional Microsoft certification exams to validate their skills with other Microsoft products, development tools, or desktop applications.

- Microsoft Certified Systems Engineer (MCSE) candidates are required to pass five core exams and two elective exams.

- Microsoft Certified Systems Administrator (MCSA) candidates are required to pass three core exams and one elective exam.

- Microsoft Certified Database Administrator (MCDBA) candidates are required to pass three core exams and one elective exam.

ABOUT THE AUTHORS

Craig Zacker, the author of the textbook, is a writer, editor, and networker whose computing experience began in the days of teletypes and paper tape. After making the move from minicomputers to PCs, he worked as an administrator of Novell Net-Ware networks and as a PC support technician while operating a freelance desktop publishing business. After earning a masters degree in English and American literature from New York University, Craig worked extensively on the integration of Windows NT into existing internetworks, supported fleets of Windows workstations, and was employed as a technical writer, content provider, and Webmaster for a large software company. Since devoting himself to writing and editing full time, Craig has authored or contributed to many books on networking topics, operating systems, and PC hardware, including *MCSE Self-Paced Training Kit (Exam 70-293): Planning and Maintaining a Microsoft Windows Server 2003 Network Infrastructure*, and *MCSA Training Kit: Managing a Microsoft Windows 2000 Network Environment*. He has also developed educational texts for college courses and online training courses for the Web, and he has published articles in top industry publications. For more information on Craig's books and other works, see *http://www.zacker.com*.

Mark Fugatt, the author of the Lab Manual, is a Microsoft Certified Trainer and the owner of Pentech Office Solutions, Inc., a consulting/training organization specializing in delivering certified technical training to small- and medium-sized business,

Mark has been delivering certified training since 1995 and holds MCSE, MCSA, and MCT certifications and is also a Microsoft Exchange MVP.

Drew Bird, the author of the Pretest and Testbank questions and the PowerPoint slides, has been working in the IT industry for over 14 years. In addition to his 400-plus days of classroom teaching as a Microsoft Certified Trainer and Master Certified Novell Instructor, he has performed the roles of network manager, network system analyst, and networking consultant to some of the world's most prestigious organizations. Drew is the author of numerous certification study guides, including Microsoft's *Faster Smarter A+ Certification*. He is also a contributor to a number of technical Web sites and journals, with over 100 articles published.

MOAC SUPPORT

If you have any problems regarding the use of this book's CD-ROM, you should first consult with your instructor. If you are using the CD-ROM at home or at your place of business and need additional help with the practice files, contact Wiley Technical Support at:

http://higheredwiley.custhelp.com

where you can view our Knowledge Base of frequent questions, Chat live with an Agent, or submit a question. Please note that product support is not offered through the above address.

EVALUATION EDITION SOFTWARE SUPPORT

The 180-day evaluation edition of Windows Server 2003 Enterprise Edition provided with this textbook is not the full retail product and is provided only for training and evaluation purposes. Microsoft and Microsoft Technical Support do not support this evaluation edition. For information about issues relating to the use of the evaluation edition, go to the Support section of the Microsoft Learning Web site (*http://www.microsoft.com/learning/support/*).

For online support information relating to the full version of Windows Server 2003 Enterprise Edition that might also apply to the evaluation edition, go to *http://www.microsoft.com/learning/support/*. For information about ordering the full version of any Microsoft software, call Microsoft Sales at (800) 426-9400 or visit *http://www.microsoft.com*.

> **CAUTION** The evaluation edition of Windows Server 2003 Enterprise Edition should not be used on a primary work computer.

PART 1
MANAGING AND MAINTAINING THE OPERATING SYSTEM

CHAPTER 1
INTRODUCING MICROSOFT WINDOWS SERVER 2003

The purpose of this course is to teach you to manage and maintain a Microsoft Windows Server 2003 environment and to prepare you for the 70-290 certification examination. The course assumes that you have some experience with Microsoft Windows, but the Windows Server 2003 family might be new to you. The goal of this chapter, therefore, is to introduce you to the various editions of Windows Server 2003 so you can identify the key differences among them and select the appropriate product to satisfy the needs of your organization.

The chapter then guides you through the process of installing Windows Server 2003 on a computer and configuring it to function as an Active Directory domain controller. Your instructor might not require you to install the operating system on your classroom computer, but if you want to work with Windows Server 2003 at home or elsewhere outside of class, you must be familiar with this installation and configuration process.

Upon completion of this chapter, you will be able to:

- Identify the key differences among the Windows Server 2003 editions
- Install Windows Server 2003
- Create a domain controller
- Identify the logical components and concepts of Active Directory

THE WINDOWS SERVER 2003 FAMILY

Windows Server 2003 is the latest incarnation of the Windows server operating system and provides substantial improvements over previous versions: it is more secure, more reliable, and easier to administer. This section provides a brief overview of the Windows Server 2003 family, focusing on the similarities and differences among the four product editions: Web Edition, Standard Edition, Enterprise Edition, and Datacenter Edition.

Windows Server 2003 Editions

Windows Server 2003 is an update to the platform and technologies introduced in Windows 2000. If you are coming to Windows Server 2003 with experience from Windows 2000 servers, you will find the transition to be relatively easy. If your only experience is with Windows NT 4, your learning curve will be much steeper.

Although the basic appearance of Windows Server 2003 is similar to that of Windows 2000, the operating system includes a great many improvements and new features that add security and reliability and enhance the administrative toolset. When you consider an upgrade or migration to Windows Server 2003, you might be drawn to the significant new features and improvements in Active Directory, the new tools to support **group policy objects (GPOs)**, the enhancements to enterprise security, the improvements to Terminal Services, or a number of other enhanced capabilities of the new operating system.

> **MORE INFO**   New Features in Windows Server 2003   For a complete list of new features and capabilities in the Windows Server 2003 platform, see the Microsoft Web site at http://www.microsoft.com/windowsserver2003.

The different editions of Windows Server 2003 are designed to support various hardware platforms and server roles. In addition to the four basic editions of Windows Server 2003—Web, Standard, Enterprise, and Datacenter—the operating system is also available in versions that support 64-bit processor platforms and embedded systems. The following sections discuss the editions in greater detail.

System Requirements

The four main operating system editions differ in the hardware they support. Table 1-1 lists the system requirements for each, as well as hardware recommendations.

Table 1-1   **Windows Server 2003 System Requirements**

	Web Edition	Standard Edition	Enterprise Edition	Datacenter Edition
Minimum Processor Speed	133 MHz	133 MHz	133 MHz	400 MHz
Recommended Processor Speed	550 MHz	550 MHz	733 MHz	733 MHz
Minimum RAM	128 MB	128 MB	128 MB	512 MB
Recommended Minimum RAM	256 MB	256 MB	256 MB	1 GB
Maximum RAM	2 GB	4 GB	32 GB	64 GB

Table 1-1   **Windows Server 2003 System Requirements**

	Web Edition	Standard Edition	Enterprise Edition	Datacenter Edition
Symmetric Multiprocessing (SMP) Support	Up to 2 processors	Up to 4 processors	Up to 8 processors	Up to 32 processors
Minimum Disk Space	1.5 GB	1.5 GB	1.5 GB	1.5 GB

Web Edition

To position Windows Server 2003 more competitively against other Web servers, Microsoft has released a special-purpose edition of Windows Server 2003 that was designed specifically to function as a Web server. The Web Edition is a subset of the standard operating system that enables customers to deploy Web sites, Web applications, and Web services with a minimum of expense and administrative overhead. The operating system supports a maximum of 2 GB of memory and up to two processors—half the capacity of the Standard Edition.

The Web Edition does not contain any features that are not found in the other Windows Server 2003 editions, but it does omit some of the components that are typically not needed on a Web server, such as the following:

- A computer running the Web Edition can be a member of an Active Directory **domain**, but it cannot function as a domain controller.

- The standard Client Access License model does not apply to computers running the Web Edition. The operating system supports an unlimited number of Web connections, but it is limited to 10 simultaneous Server Message Block (SMB) connections. This means that no more than 10 internal network users can access the server's file and print resources at any one time.

- The Internet Connection Firewall (ICF) and Internet Connection Sharing (ICS) features are not included with the Web Edition, which prevents the computer from functioning as an Internet gateway.

- A computer running the Web Edition cannot function as a Dynamic Host Configuration Protocol (DHCP) server, fax server, Microsoft SQL Server, or terminal server, although Remote Desktop for Administration is supported.

- The Web Edition cannot run non–Web serving applications.

However, the Web Edition does include all of the standard components that a Web server would need, including Microsoft Internet Information Services (IIS) 6, Network Load Balancing (NLB), and Microsoft ASP.NET.

Obviously, the Web Edition is not a suitable platform for a general purpose network server, nor is it intended to be one. However, it does enable organizations to deploy dedicated Web servers without having to provide support for a lot of components that the computer doesn't need to fulfill its role.

NOTE   **Purchasing the Web Edition**   The Web Edition is not sold through retail channels. The product is available only to Microsoft customers with Enterprise and Select licensing agreements, to service providers with a service provider licensing agreement (SPLA), and through Microsoft original equipment manufacturers (OEMs) and System Builder partners.

Standard Edition

The Standard Edition is a multipurpose server platform that can provide directory, file, print, application, multimedia, and Internet services for small to medium-sized businesses. Among the many features included with the operating system are:

- **Directory services**   The Standard Edition includes full Active Directory support, enabling the computer to function as a member server or a domain controller. Administrators can therefore use the tools included with the operating system to deploy and manage Active Directory objects, group policies, and other Active Directory–based services.

- **Internet services**   The Standard Edition includes IIS 6, which provides Web and FTP services as well as other components used by Web server deployments, such as NLB, which enables multiple Web servers to host a single Web site, sharing the incoming client requests among up to 32 servers and providing fault tolerance.

- **Infrastructure services**   The Standard Edition includes the Microsoft DHCP Server, Domain Name System (DNS) Server, and Windows Internet Name Service (WINS) server, which provide important services for internal network and Internet clients.

- **TCP/IP routing**   A computer running the Standard Edition can function as a router in a variety of configurations, including local area network (LAN) and wide area network (WAN) routing, Internet access routing, and remote access routing. To facilitate these roles, the operating system's Routing and Remote Access service (RRAS) also includes support for network address translation (NAT), Internet Authentication Service (IAS), Routing Information Protocol (RIP), and the Open Shortest Path First (OSPF) routing protocol.

- **File and print services**   Users on the network can access shared drives, folders, and printers on a Standard Edition server. A Client Access License (CAL) is needed for each client that attempts to access server shares. The Standard Edition is typically sold with a package of 5, 10, or more CALs. To add more users, you must purchase additional CALs.

- **Terminal Server**   A computer running the Standard Edition can function as a terminal server, enabling computers and other devices to access the Windows desktop and applications running on the server. Terminal Server is essentially a remote control mechanism that enables clients to access a Windows session on the server. All application execution takes place on the server, and only keyboard, mouse, and display information is transmitted over the network. Terminal Server clients require a license that is separate from the standard Windows Server 2003 CAL, although Standard Edition does include a two-user license for Remote Desktop for Administration, which is a Terminal Server–based remote administration tool.

- **Security services**   The Standard Edition includes a variety of security features that administrators can deploy as needed, including Encrypting File System (EFS), which protects files on server drives by storing them in an encrypted format, IP Security extensions (IPsec), which digitally sign and encrypt data before transmitting them over the network, ICF, which regulates the traffic admitted onto the network from the Internet, and the Public Key Infrastructure (PKI), which provides security based on public key encryption and digital certificates.

Enterprise Edition

The Enterprise Edition is designed to be a powerful server platform for medium- to large-sized businesses. The Enterprise Edition differs from the Standard Edition primarily in terms of degree. For example, the Enterprise Edition supports up to eight processors, compared to the Standard Edition's four, and up to 32 GB of memory, compared to the Standard Edition's 4 GB.

The Enterprise Edition also includes some important additional features that are not supplied with the Standard Edition, including the following:

- **Microsoft Metadirectory Services (MMS)**   A *metadirectory* is essentially a directory of directories—a means of integrating multiple information sources into a single, unified directory. MMS makes it possible to combine Active Directory information with other directory services, to create a unified view of all available information about a given resource. The Enterprise Edition includes support only for MMS, not the actual MMS software, which you must obtain from a Microsoft Consulting Service (MCS) or via an MMS partner engagement.

- **Server clustering**   A *server cluster* is a group of servers that function as a single entity, providing high availability for a particular set of applications. High availability in this case means that application processing is distributed among the servers in the cluster, reducing the load on each computer and providing fault tolerance if any of the servers fails. The servers in a server cluster, which are called *nodes*, have shared access to a common data source, usually in the form of a storage area network (SAN), enabling all of the nodes to maintain a current information base. The Enterprise Edition supports server clusters of up to eight nodes.

- **Hot Add Memory**   The Enterprise Edition includes software support for a hardware feature called Hot Add Memory, which enables administrators to add or replace memory in the computer without powering it down or restarting. To use this capability, the computer must have the appropriate hardware support.

- **Windows System Resource Manager (WSRM)**   This feature enables administrators to allocate system resources to specific applications or processes, based on the needs of the computer's users, and maintain accounting records of the resources used by those applications or processes. This enables businesses to set resource limits for specific processes or to bill customers based on their resource usage.

Datacenter Edition

The Datacenter Edition is designed for high-end, high-traffic application servers that require huge amounts of system resources. The Datacenter Edition is nearly identical to the Enterprise Edition in its feature set but provides even greater hardware scalability, supporting up to 64 GB of RAM and up to 32 processors. The Datacenter Edition does omit a few Enterprise Edition features, such as ICS and ICF, primarily because a high-end server such as those supporting the Datacenter Edition are not expected to serve in the roles that use these features.

> **NOTE Purchasing the Datacenter Edition**   Like the Web Edition, the Datacenter Edition is not available through standard retail channels. You can obtain the operating system only through an OEM as part of a high-end server hardware package.

64-Bit Editions

Both the Enterprise Edition and the Datacenter Edition are available in versions that support computers equipped with Intel Itanium processors. Itanium is a processing platform that provides 64-bit addressing (while Intel's standard x86 processors are 32-bit), a greatly enlarged virtual address space and paged pool area, and enhanced floating point performance. It is specifically designed for processor-intensive tasks, such as massive database applications, scientific analysis, and heavily accessed Web servers.

The system requirements for the Itanium versions of the Enterprise Edition and the Datacenter Edition are slightly different from those of the x86 versions, as summarized in Table 1-2. Also, some features of the x86 editions are not available in the Itanium editions. Most notably, the Itanium editions do not support 16-bit Windows applications, real-mode applications, POSIX applications, or print services for Apple Macintosh clients.

Test your knowledge of the Windows Server 2003 operating system versions by doing Exercise 1.1, "Selecting an Operating System," now.

Table 1-2   **Special System Requirements for Windows Server 2003 Itanium Versions**

	Enterprise Edition	Datacenter Edition
Minimum Processor Speed	733 MHz	733 MHz
Maximum RAM	64 GB	512 GB
Minimum Disk Space	2 GB	2 GB

INSTALLING WINDOWS SERVER 2003

Before you can learn to manage and maintain Windows Server 2003, you must be able to install the operating system and configure it to perform the tasks demanded of it. Although this course does not cover advanced topics such as Active Directory design, it does cover the administration of Active Directory objects, such as users, computers, and groups. Before you can perform some of the exercises in this textbook and in the accompanying Lab Manual, you must have a computer with Windows Server 2003 installed that is configured to function as an Active Directory domain controller.

Installation Phases

If you have experience installing Windows 2000, the Windows Server 2003 installation process will be familiar. It has two distinct phases:

- **Text mode**   The initial phase of the installation begins when the computer boots from the Windows Server 2003 distribution CD and runs the Winnt.exe program. Unlike Windows 2000 and earlier, there is no support for starting the installation using floppy disks in Windows Server 2003. The Winnt.exe program loads the Windows Server 2003 operating system files from the CD. This is a limited, character-based version of the operating system because the files needed for the graphical user interface (GUI) have not been installed yet. The program then formats the partition that will become the system drive, creates the system root directory structure, and copies the operating system files from the temporary directories to their final locations. The program also begins to build the registry during this phase, creating keys containing basic operating system information, as well as information about the hardware detected in the computer thus far. The computer then restarts.

■ **Graphical mode**   When the system starts for the second time, it uses the boot and operating system files, which are now in their final, permanent locations on the system drive. The familiar Windows interface appears for the first time, using a low-resolution VGA display driver. After the system starts, the graphical mode phase begins, with the operating system executing its primary hardware detection routine. When the hardware is detected and drivers installed, the program begins to gather information from the user that is needed to complete the installation and installs various nonessential operating system components. If a network interface adapter is detected, the installation program installs the required networking components and binds them to the network adapter driver. Finally, the program builds the Start menu, sets system security parameters, deletes any temporary files it has created, and saves the system configuration before restarting the computer for the final time.

Installation Procedure

This section contains a detailed account of the Windows Server 2003 installation process. It assumes that you are using a computer that meets the Windows Server 2003 system requirements, that you are installing the operating system from the original distribution CD, and that the computer's primary hard drive is completely empty.

NOTE   **Installation Variations**   This installation procedure assumes the use of a computer with a basic hardware configuration. The presence of certain hardware devices in the computer can cause variations in the installation process (such as additional configuration steps) that are not mentioned here.

▶ **Windows Server 2003 Installation**

To install Windows Server 2003, use the following procedure:

1. Insert the Windows Server 2003 installation CD into the CD-ROM drive and restart the computer.

   If you are prompted to do so, press a key to boot from the CD.

2. After the computer starts, a brief message appears, stating that Setup is inspecting your computer's hardware configuration. The Windows Setup screen appears.

3. If your computer requires special mass storage drivers that are not part of the Windows Server 2003 driver set, press F6 when prompted and provide the appropriate drivers.

4. The system prompts you to press F2 if you want to perform an Automated System Recovery (ASR). Do not press F2 at this time. The setup continues.

NOTE   Automated System Recovery   ASR is a new feature in Windows Server 2003 that replaces the Emergency Repair Disk feature of previous Windows versions. For more information on using ASR, see Chapter 4 in this textbook.

The gray status bar at the bottom of the screen indicates that Setup is loading files. This is required to start a minimal version of the operating system. At this point, the hardware in the computer has not been specifically identified, so after loading the operating system kernel, the setup program loads a series of drivers that support a wide range of mass storage, keyboard, pointer, and video devices, in an attempt to create a functional input/output (I/O) configuration that will allow the installation to proceed.

NOTE   Locating Storage Drivers   If appropriate drivers for your mass storage devices are not included with Windows Server 2003, you must obtain them, restart the installation, and press F6 to supply them to the setup program.

5. If you are installing an evaluation version of Windows Server 2003, the Setup Notification screen appears, informing you of this. Read the Setup Notification message, and then press ENTER to continue. The Welcome To Setup screen appears.

```
Windows Server 2003, Standard Edition Setup

   Welcome to Setup.

   This portion of the Setup program prepares Microsoft(R)
   Windows(R) to run on your computer.

        •   To set up Windows now, press ENTER.

        •   To repair a Windows installation using
            Recovery Console, press R.

        •   To quit Setup without installing Windows, press F3.












   ENTER=Continue   R=Repair   F3=Quit
```

6. Read the Welcome To Setup message, and then press ENTER to continue.
The License Agreement screen appears.

```
Windows Licensing Agreement

    END-USER LICENSE AGREEMENT FOR 180-DAY
    EVALUATION OF MICROSOFT SOFTWARE

    MICROSOFT WINDOWS SERVER 2003, STANDARD EDITION
    EVALUATION VERSION
    MICROSOFT WINDOWS SERVER 2003, ENTERPRISE EDITION
    EVALUATION VERSION

    PLEASE READ THIS END-USER LICENSE AGREEMENT
    ("EULA") CAREFULLY.  BY INSTALLING OR USING
    THE SOFTWARE THAT ACCOMPANIES THIS EULA
    ("SOFTWARE"), YOU AGREE TO THE TERMS OF THIS
    EULA.  IF YOU DO NOT AGREE, DO NOT USE THE
    SOFTWARE AND, IF APPLICABLE, RETURN IT TO THE
    PLACE OF PURCHASE.

    THE SOFTWARE CONTAINS FUNCTIONALITY THAT
    IS TIME-SENSITIVE AND DESIGNED TO CEASE
    FUNCTIONING AFTER A CERTAIN PERIOD.  PLEASE
    REFER TO SECTION 2.e FOR DETAILS.

    THIS SOFTWARE DOES NOT TRANSMIT ANY
    PERSONALLY IDENTIFIABLE INFORMATION FROM YOUR
    SERVER TO MICROSOFT COMPUTER SYSTEMS WITHOUT
    YOUR CONSENT.

      1. GENERAL.  This EULA is a legal agreement between you (either
  F8=I agree   ESC=I do not agree   PAGE DOWN=Next Page
```

7. Read the license agreement and press F8 to accept it. A screen appears,
containing a list of the partitions on the computer's available disk drives
as well as any unpartitioned space. From this screen, you can also create
and delete partitions on the computer's drives as needed. Selecting an
Unpartitioned Space entry in the list creates a new partition using all of
that space. If you want to create a partition using only part of the unpartitioned space, press C and specify the size of the partition you want to
create. To complete the exercises in this book, a partition of at least 3 GB
is recommended. In addition, you must leave at least 1 GB of unpartitioned space on the drive for exercises that involve the creation of new
partitions.

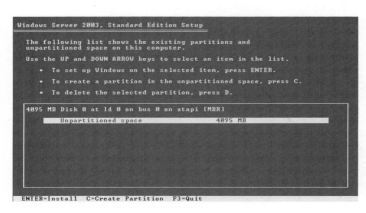

8. Select an area of unpartitioned disk space at least 4 GB in size, and then press C and specify 3072 as the size of the new partition. Then press ENTER.

9. A screen appears, prompting you to select the file system to use when formatting the selected partition. Select the Format The Partition Using The NTFS File System option and press ENTER to continue.

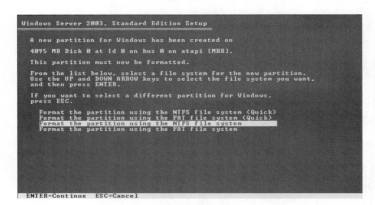

Setup formats the partition using NTFS, examines the hard disk for physical errors that might cause the installation to fail, and begins copying files from the CD to the hard disk. This process takes several minutes.

10. Setup initializes the Windows configuration and then displays a screen with a red status bar that counts down for 15 seconds before the computer restarts and enters the GUI mode phase of the installation process.

Windows Setup launches and produces a graphical user interface that tracks the progress of installation in the left pane. The Collecting Information, Dynamic Update, and Preparing Installation options are selected, indicating these steps have been completed. Collecting Information was completed before the GUI appeared, and Dynamic Update is not used when starting from the CD.

The Preparing Installation step occurred when the Setup program copied the operating system files to the local disk drive. The Installing Windows step begins with Setup's hardware detection process, which might take several minutes. Unlike the text mode hardware detection routine, which identifies hardware components by loading drivers using trial and error, this process identifies the specific components in the computer, writes information about them to the registry, and configures the operating system to load the correct drivers for the hardware. Eventually, the Windows Setup Wizard loads and the Regional And Language Options page appears.

11. Modify the default regional and language option settings if necessary, by clicking the Customize button or the Details button. Then click Next. The Personalize Your Software page appears.

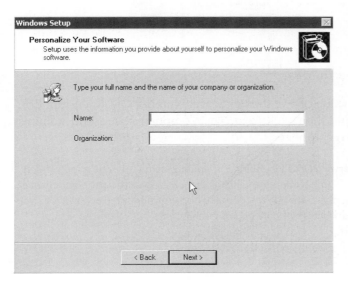

12. In the Name text box, type your name; in the Organization text box, type the name of an organization, and then click Next. The Your Product Key page appears.

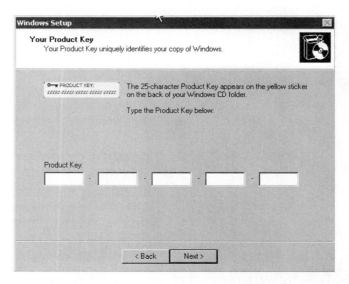

13. Enter the product key included with your Windows Server 2003 installation CD in the Product Key text boxes, and then click Next. The Licensing Modes page appears.

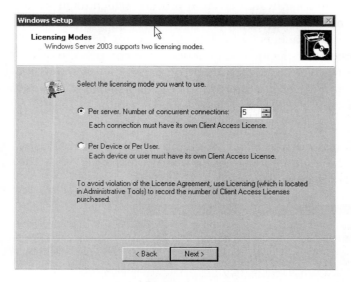

14. Leave the default value of 5 in the Per Server Number Of Concurrent Connections option, and then click Next. The Computer Name And Administrator Password page appears.

NOTE **Windows Server 2003 Licensing** If you are using an evaluation version of Windows Server 2003, the default value of 5 servers is sufficient to complete this course. However, if you are using a licensed copy of Windows Server 2003, you should specify a legal number of concurrent connections based on the actual licenses that you own.

15. In the Computer Name text box, type **Server*xx*,** where ***xx*** is a unique number assigned to you by your instructor.

CAUTION   Avoiding Name Conflicts   If your computer is connected to a LAN, check with the network administrator before assigning a name to your computer.

16. In the Administrator Password text box and the Confirm Password text box, type a password for the Administrator account, and then click Next. The Date And Time Settings page appears.

IMPORTANT   Specifying a Password   In a manual installation, Windows Server 2003 will not let you progress to subsequent steps until you enter an Administrator password that meets complexity requirements. By default, Windows Server 2003 requires complex passwords that are at least seven characters long. A complex password is one that contains at least three of the following four component elements: uppercase letters, lowercase letters, numbers, and symbols. You are allowed to enter a blank password, although this practice is strongly discouraged.

17. Specify the correct date and time, and select the correct time zone for your location. Then click Next. After a brief delay, the Network Settings page appears.

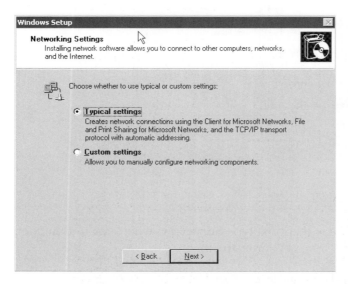

18. Leave the default Typical Settings option selected, and then click Next. The Workgroup Or Computer Domain page appears.

NOTE   Typical Networking Settings   Selecting the Typical Settings option on the Network Settings page causes the setup program to install the Client for Microsoft Networks, Network Load Balancing, File and Printer Sharing for Microsoft Networks, and Internet Protocol (TCP/IP) components (although the Network Load Balancing module is disabled) and configure TCP/IP to obtain an IP address from a DHCP server. If you are connected to a network with no DHCP server, you must obtain an IP address and other TCP/IP configuration settings from your network administrator and select the Custom Settings option to apply them before your computer can communicate with the LAN.

19. Leave the default No option selected and the default workgroup name of WORKGROUP in place, and then click Next.

The setup program installs and configures the remaining operating system components by copying files, installing Start menu items, registering components, saving settings, and removing temporary files. When the installation is complete, the computer restarts automatically and the Welcome To Windows dialog box appears.

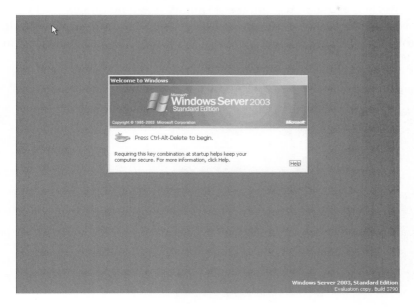

In a business environment, such as a large enterprise network, the operating system installation process is often substantially different from this procedure. Network administrators who are responsible for large fleets of computers usually do not have the time to perform lengthy manual operating system installations such as the one described here. They can use a number of methods to streamline or automate the Windows Server 2003 installation process, including the following:

■ **Answer files**   An *answer file* is a script that contains settings for all of the options presented to the user during a Windows Server 2003 installation. With a properly configured answer file, it is possible to start an operating system installation and let it proceed unattended, with responses to all prompts supplied by the answer file. The main drawback of using answer files for a mass operating system deployment is that each computer requires its own file. Some of the settings supplied during the installation must be unique, such as computer names and IP addresses.

■ **Disk images**   When you deploy a large number of identical computers, you can bypass much of the operating system installation process by using a *disk image*. A disk image is a bit-for-bit copy of the hard drive in a computer that has the operating system already installed. Transferring the image to another computer with the same hardware configuration enables the operating system to run on that computer with no interactive installation. Windows Server 2003 includes a tool called Remote Installation Services that administrators can use to deploy disk images to other computers over the network.

Practice logging on to Windows Server 2003 for the first time by doing Exercise 1.2, "Logging On

to Windows,"
now.

Activating Windows Server

Some editions of Windows Server 2003, including the evaluation edition provided with this book, require that you activate the operating system after installation. Depending on the version you are using, you might have 14 days or 30 days to activate Windows Server 2003. Activation is a simple, one-time process that can be completed over the Internet or by telephone. To begin the activation process, click Start, point to All Programs, and click Activate Windows. The Let's Activate Windows page of the Activate Windows Wizard appears (as shown in Figure 1-1).

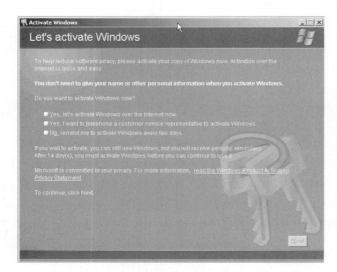

Figure 1-1   The Let's Activate Windows page of the Activate Windows Wizard

> **NOTE**   **Volume Licensing**   If you acquired your Windows Server 2003 license through one of the Microsoft volume licensing programs, you are not required to activate the license.

To activate Windows over the Internet, you must have your computer connected to the Internet when you begin the activation procedure. This means that the computer must either be equipped with a modem and configured to connect to an Internet service provider (ISP) or be configured with appropriate TCP/IP configuration parameters (including IP Address, Subnet Mask, Preferred DNS Server, and Default Gateway settings) and connected to a LAN that provides Internet access. If the computer cannot access the Internet, you must activate Windows by telephone.

CONFIGURING WINDOWS SERVER 2003

After installing and activating Windows, you can configure the server using the Manage Your Server page, as shown in Figure 1-2. This page launches after you log on, or you can launch it at any time by selecting Manage Your Server from the Start menu. This page enables you to install specific services, tools, and configurations based on the roles that the server can perform.

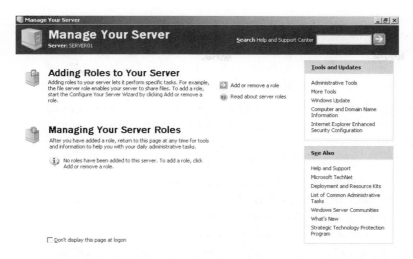

Figure 1-2   The Manage Your Server page

When you click the Add Or Remove A Role hyperlink, the Configure Your Server Wizard appears. After scanning for network connections, the wizard enables you to select any of the following server roles:

- **File Server**   Provides centralized access to files and folders for individual users, departments, and entire organizations. Choosing this role enables you to manage user disk space by enabling and configuring disk quotas and to provide improved file system search performance by enabling the Indexing service.

- **Print Server**   Provides centralized and managed access to printing devices by serving shared printers and printer drivers to client computers. Choosing this role starts the Add Printer Wizard, enabling you to install printers and their associated Windows printer drivers. Selecting the Print Server role also installs IIS 6, configures the Internet Printing Protocol (IPP), and installs the Web-based printer administration tools.

- **Application Server (IIS, ASP.NET)**   Provides infrastructure components required to support the hosting of Web applications. Selecting this role installs and configures IIS 6 as well as Microsoft ASP.NET and COM+.

- **Mail Server (POP3, SMTP)**   Installs Post Office Protocol version 3 (POP3) and Simple Mail Transfer Protocol (SMTP) so the server can function as an incoming and outgoing e-mail server for network clients.

- **Terminal Server**   Provides multiple network clients with access to server applications and resources as if those applications and resources were installed on their own computers. Users connect to the server with the Terminal Services client or the Remote Desktop client.

- **Remote Access / VPN Server**   Provides multiple-protocol routing and remote access services for dial-in, LAN, and WAN connections. Virtual private network (VPN) connections enable remote sites and users to connect securely and inexpensively to the network using the Internet as a network medium.

- **Domain Controller (Active Directory)**   Provides directory services to clients on the network. Choosing this role runs the Active Directory Installation Wizard, which configures the server to function as a domain controller for a new or existing domain and, if there is not already a DNS server on the network, installs the Microsoft DNS Server service.

- **DNS Server**   Provides host name resolution by translating host names to IP addresses (forward lookups) and IP addresses to host names (reverse lookups). Choosing this role installs the Microsoft DNS Server service and then starts the Configure A DNS Server Wizard.

- **DHCP Server**   Provides automatic IP addressing services to clients configured to use dynamic IP addressing. Choosing this role installs the DHCP Server service and then starts the New Scope Wizard so you can define one or more IP address scopes in the network.

- **Streaming Media Server**   Choosing this role installs Windows Media Services (WMS), which enables the server to stream multimedia content over an intranet connection or the Internet. Content can be stored and delivered on demand or delivered in real time.

- **WINS Server**   Provides computer name resolution by translating NetBIOS names to IP addresses. It is not necessary to install WINS unless you are supporting legacy operating systems such as Windows 95 or Windows NT, which are based on NetBIOS names. The Windows Server 2003, Windows 2000, and Windows XP operating systems do not require WINS, although legacy applications on those platforms might very well require NetBIOS name resolution. Choosing this option installs the WINS service.

CREATING A DOMAIN CONTROLLER

To complete the exercises in this book and in the Lab Manual, you must have a Windows Server 2003 computer that is configured as a domain controller.

▶ **Active Directory Installation**

To configure your Server01 computer to function as a domain controller, use the following procedure:

> **NOTE**   **Active Directory Installation Options**   When the Active Directory Installation Wizard runs, the prompts that the wizard displays differ depending on whether it detects another domain on the network. The steps presented below assume that you are running the wizard on an isolated network. If you are connected to a network with another domain, the steps might vary, and you might have to modify your selections or disconnect from the network before performing the exercise.

1. Log on to Windows Server 2003 as Administrator.

2. If it is not already open, open the Manage Your Server page from the Administrative Tools program group.

3. Click the Add Or Remove A Role hyperlink. The Configure Your Server Wizard loads and the Preliminary Steps page appears.

4. Verify that all of the steps listed on the page have been completed, and then click Next. After a brief delay while the wizard scans the network, the Server Role page appears.

5. Select Domain Controller (Active Directory) from the list of server roles and click Next. The Summary Of Selections page appears.

6. Click Next. The Active Directory Installation Wizard launches.

7. Click Next to bypass the Welcome page. The Operating System Compatibility page appears.

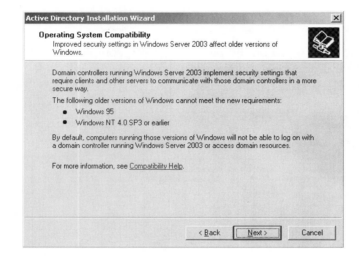

8. Read the information on the page and click Next. The Domain Controller Type page appears.

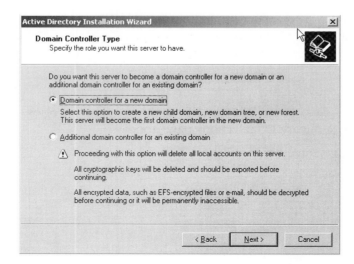

9. Leave the default Domain Controller For A New Domain option selected, and click Next. The Create New Domain page appears.

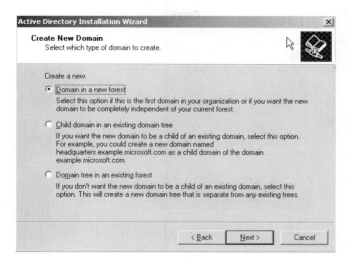

10. Leave the default Domain In A New Forest option selected, and click Next. The New Domain Name page appears.

11. In the Full DNS Name For New Domain text box, type **contosoxx.com,** where *xx* is a number assigned to you by your instructor, and then click Next. The NetBIOS Domain Name page appears.

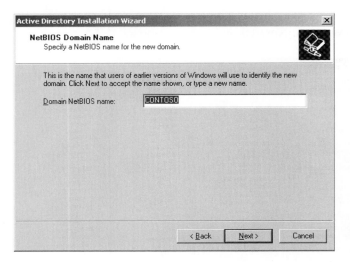

12. Verify that the Domain NetBIOS Name text box reads *CONTOSOXX*, and then click Next. The Database And Log Folders page appears.

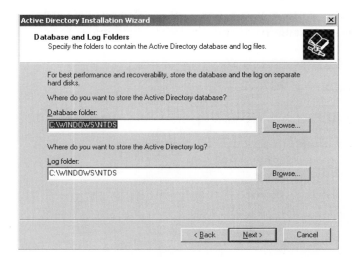

13. Click Next to accept the default database and log folder locations. The Shared System Volume page appears.

14. Click Next to accept the default shared system volume location. The DNS Registration Diagnostics page appears.

At this time, the wizard attempts to connect to the DNS servers specified in the computer's TCP/IP configuration to determine whether they are capable of hosting the records required for an Active Directory domain.

15. Select the Install And Configure The DNS Server On This Computer option, and then click Next. The Permissions page appears.

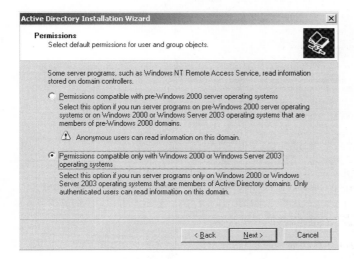

16. Click Next to accept the default permissions option, and then click Next. The Directory Services Restore Mode Administrator Password page appears.

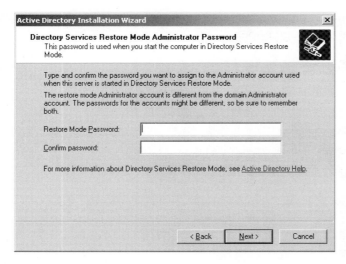

17. Type an appropriate password in the Restore Mode Password and Confirm Password text boxes, and then click Next. The Summary page appears.

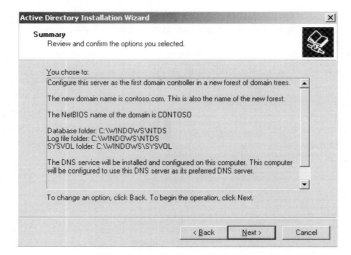

18. Review the options you have selected in the wizard, and then click Next. The wizard proceeds to install the Active Directory and DNS Server services.

19. When the configuration process is finished, the Completing The Active Directory Installation Wizard page appears. Click Finish.

20. An Active Directory Installation Wizard message box appears, prompting you to restart the computer. Click Restart Now.

21. After the system has restarted, log on as Administrator. The Configure Your Server Wizard reappears, displaying the This Server Is Now A Domain Controller page.

22. Click Finish.

AN ACTIVE DIRECTORY PRIMER

Although the Active Directory directory service is not the primary focus of this course, some exposure to Active Directory is unavoidable for every Windows Server 2003 system administrator. The upcoming chapters will not cover advanced topics such as Active Directory design and schema administration, but you will work with the Active Directory management tools supplied with Windows Server 2003 and learn to manipulate the properties of Active Directory objects, such as users, groups, and computers.

> **NOTE**   **Active Directory**   To study the more advanced Active Directory topics, consider taking the course for exam 70-294: Planning, Implementing, and Maintaining a Microsoft Windows Server 2003 Active Directory Infrastructure.

What Is a Directory Service?

The first commercial local area networking products that appeared in the early 1990s were geared toward small collections of computers, commonly called *work-groups*. A workgroup network enabled a handful of users working together on the same project to share resources such as documents and printers. As the value of data networking was recognized by the business world, networks grew larger. Today it is not uncommon for organizations to have networks consisting of thousands of nodes.

As networks grew larger, so did the number of shared resources available on them, and it became increasingly difficult to locate and keep track of the available resources. When you work in a company with 12 employees, it is usually not a problem to memorize everyone's telephone extension. However, when you work for a company with 1200 employees, memorizing everyone's extension is virtually impossible. To find out the number of the person you want to reach, most large companies provide a list of employees and their numbers—that is, a directory. A **directory service** is a digital resource that functions in exactly the same way, except that it contains a list of the resources available on a data network.

A directory service can contain information about the computers on the network, the network users, and other hardware and software devices, such as printers and applications. By storing the information in a central directory, it is available to anyone at any time.

Domains and Domain Controllers

Windows networks support two directory service models: the workgroup and the domain, with the domain model being far more common in organizations implementing Windows Server 2003. The workgroup directory service is a flat database of computer names, designed to support a small network. This is the original directory service that was introduced in Windows NT 3.1 in the early 1990s.

The domain model is a hierarchical directory of enterprise resources—Active Directory—that is trusted by all systems that are members of the domain. These systems can use the user, group, and computer accounts in the directory to secure their resources. Active Directory thus acts as an identity store, providing a single trusted Who's Who list for the domain.

Active Directory itself is more than just a database, though. It is also a collection of supporting components, including transaction logs and the system volume, or Sysvol, that contains logon scripts and group policy information. It is the services that support and use the database, including Lightweight Directory Access Protocol (LDAP), the Kerberos security protocol, replication processes, and the File Replication Service (FRS). Finally, Active Directory is a collection of tools that administrators use to manage the directory service.

The Active Directory database and its services are installed on one or more **domain controllers**. A domain controller is a server that has been promoted by running the Active Directory Installation Wizard, as described earlier in the "Creating a Domain Controller" section. Once a server has been promoted to a domain controller, it hosts a copy, or replica, of the Active Directory database.

Because Active Directory is such a vital network resource, it is critical that it be available to users at all times. For this reason, Active Directory domains typically have at least two domain controllers, so that if one fails, the other can continue to support clients. These domain controllers continually replicate their information with each other, so that each one has a database containing current information. When an administrator makes a change to an Active Directory database record on any domain controller, the change is replicated to all of the other domain controllers within the domain. This is called multiple-master replication, because it is possible to make changes to any one of the domain controllers.

> **NOTE Single-Master Replication**   Windows NT's domain model uses a technique called single-master replication, in which all changes to the domain records have to be made to a primary domain controller (PDC), which then replicates them to one or more backup domain controllers (BDCs). Multiple-master replication is better suited to a large enterprise network because administrators can update the Active Directory database from any domain controller, not just a designated PDC.

Domains, Trees, and Forests

The domain is the fundamental administrative unit of the Windows Server 2003 directory service. However, an enterprise might have more than one domain in its Active Directory. Multiple domain models create logical structures called **trees** when they share contiguous DNS names. For example, contoso.com, us.contoso.com, and europe.contoso.com share contiguous DNS namespaces and would together be considered a tree (as shown in Figure 1-3). The contoso.com domain is the parent in which the child domains are created and is therefore called the *root domain*.

contoso.com

us.contoso.com   europe.contoso.com

Figure 1-3   An Active Directory tree

If domains in an Active Directory do not share a common root domain, they exist as multiple trees. An Active Directory that consists of multiple trees is naturally called a **forest** (as shown in Figure 1-4). The forest is the largest structure in an Active Directory. When you promote the first domain controller on a Windows Server 2003 network, you create a forest, a tree within that forest, and a domain within that tree, all at the same time. A forest might contain multiple domains in multiple trees, or just one domain.

contoso.com   adatum.com

us.contoso.com   europe.contoso.com   ny.adatum.com   chicago.adatum.com

Figure 1-4   An Active Directory forest

When an Active Directory installation consists of more than one domain, a component of Active Directory called the global catalog enables clients in one domain to find information in other domains. The *global catalog* is essentially a subset of the information in all of the domain databases combined. When you search for a user in another domain, for example, the global catalog might not contain all of the available information about the user, but it will contain enough information to tell you where to look for greater detail.

Objects and Attributes

All databases are made up of records, and in Active Directory the records are called **objects**. An object is a component that represents a specific network resource. An Active Directory can contain objects representing physical resources, such as computers and printers; human resources, such as users and groups; software resources, such as applications and DNS zones; and administrative resources, such as organizational units (OUs) and sites. After promoting a server to a domain controller, administrators can populate the domain by creating objects.

The most commonly used Active Directory objects are as follows:

- **Domain**   The root object that contains all of the other objects in the domain.

- **Organizational unit**   A **container object** that is used to create logical groupings of computer, user, and group objects.

- **User**   Represents a network user and functions as a repository for identification and authentication data.

- **Computer**   Represents a computer on the network and provides the machine account needed for the system to log on to the domain.

- **Group**   A container object representing a logical grouping of users, computers, and/or other groups that is independent of the Active Directory tree structure. Groups can contain objects from different OUs and domains.

- **Shared Folder**   Provides Active Directory–based network access to a shared folder on a Windows computer.

- **Printer**   Provides Active Directory–based network access to a shared printer on a Windows computer.

Every Active Directory object consists of a set of **attributes**, which are pieces of information about that object. A user object, for example, contains attributes specifying the user's account name, password, address, telephone number, and other identifying information. A group object has an attribute containing a list of the users who are members of that group. Administrators can use Active Directory to store virtually any information about the organization's users and other resources. In addition to purely informational attributes, objects also have attributes that perform administrative functions, such as an access control list (ACL) that specifies who has permission to access each object.

View the objects created in an Active Directory domain by default by doing Exercise 1.3, "Viewing Active Directory Objects," now.

The Active Directory component that specifies what types of objects administrators can create and what attributes each object has is called the *schema*. By default, the Active Directory schema contains a large collection of object types and attributes, but it is sometimes necessary to add new object types or new attributes to existing object types. This is possible because the Active Directory schema is extensible. Administrators can extend the schema manually using the Active Directory Schema snap-in, or applications can automatically extend the schema to create object types or attributes specific to their needs. For example, when you install Microsoft Exchange, the application modifies the schema to add additional attributes to every user object in the Active Directory database.

Containers and Leaves

Active Directory is capable of hosting millions of objects, and consequently there must be a means of organizing those objects into units smaller than the domain. To make this organization possible, Active Directory uses a hierarchical structure. A domain is called a **container object** because other objects can exist beneath it in the hierarchy. OUs are another type of container that administrators can use to create a hierarchy of objects within a domain. An object that cannot contain another object, such as a user or computer, is called a **leaf object**.

One of the more complicated tasks in Active Directory administration is creating an effective hierarchy of OUs. Administrators use various organizational structures when designing the OU hierarchy, such as geographical locations, departmental divisions, or a combination of the two. For example, Figure 1-5 shows an Active Directory hierarchy in which the first layer of OUs represents the cities in which the organization has branch offices, and the second layer represents the departments in each branch. By creating a logical Active Directory hierarchy, users and administrators can locate the objects they need more easily.

Figure 1-5   An Active Directory OU hierarchy

Group objects are also containers, but they are not elements of the hierarchy because they can contain members located anywhere in the domain. In addition to their purely organizational function, container objects also perform a crucial role in object administration. As in a file system, permissions flow downward in the Active Directory hierarchy. If you grant an OU object permission to access a specific share, for example, all of the objects in that container will inherit that permission. This is one of the fundamental characteristics that makes a hierarchical directory service so useful to administrators. Instead of granting rights and permissions to individual users, administrators are more likely to grant them to containers and let them flow down to the leaf objects in the container.

Group Policies

Because of the way objects inherit settings from their parent containers, administrators typically use OUs to collect objects that are configured similarly. Just about any configuration setting that you can apply to an individual Windows computer can also be managed centrally using a feature of Active Directory called *group policies*. Group policies enable you to specify security settings, deploy software, and configure operating system and application behavior on a computer without ever having to touch it directly. Instead, you implement the desired configuration settings in a special Active Directory object called a **group policy object** (GPO) and then link the GPO to an Active Directory object containing the computers or users you want to configure.

GPOs are collections of hundreds of possible configuration settings, from user logon rights and privileges to the software that is allowed to be run on a system. You can link a GPO to any domain, site, or OU container object in Active Directory, and all the users and computers in that container will receive the settings in the GPO. In most cases, administrators design the Active Directory hierarchy to accommodate the configuration of users and computers using GPOs. By placing all of the computers performing a specific role into the same OU, for example, you can assign a GPO containing role-specific settings to that OU and configure all of the computers at once.

SUMMARY

- Windows Server 2003 is available in four main editions—Web Edition, Standard Edition, Enterprise Edition, and Datacenter Edition—which differ primarily in the hardware they support and the features they provide.

- The Enterprise Edition and Datacenter Edition are available in 64-bit as well as 32-bit versions.

- Windows Server 2003 retail and evaluation versions require a product key and product activation within 14 or 30 days of installation.

- The Manage Your Server page and the Configure Your Server Wizard enable you to configure a computer running Windows Server 2003 to perform specific roles.

- Active Directory is a domain-based enterprise directory service that consists of objects, which are themselves composed of attributes.

- The Active Directory hierarchy is made up of forests, trees, domains, and organizational units. Permissions, rights, and group policy settings all flow downward in the hierarchy.

- To install Active Directory, you promote one or more servers to be domain controllers, using the Active Directory Installation Wizard. A domain controller stores a copy of the Active Directory database and is responsible for responding to requests for Active Directory information from clients.

EXERCISES

Exercise 1-1: Selecting an Operating System

For each of the Windows Server 2003 versions in the left column, specify which description (or descriptions) in the right column apply.

1. Web Edition	a. Supports 512 GB of memory
2. Standard Edition	b. Supports eight-node server clusters
3. Enterprise Edition	c. Cannot run 16-bit Windows applications
4. Datacenter Edition	d. Supports 32-node NLB clusters
5. Datacenter Edition (64-bit)	e. Supports computers with four processors

Exercise 1-2: Logging On to Windows

Once you have completed the Windows Server 2003 operating system installation, the computer restarts and displays the Welcome To Windows dialog box. To log on to the computer for the first time, use the following procedure:

1. In the Welcome To Windows dialog box, press CTRL+ALT+DELETE. The Log On To Windows dialog box appears.

2. In the Password text box, type the password you specified for the Administrator account in the operating system installation procedure. The Windows desktop appears.

Exercise 1-3: Viewing Active Directory Objects

When you create a new Active Directory domain, the operating system creates a number of container and leaf objects by default. To view some of these objects, use the following procedure:

1. Log on to a Windows Server 2003 domain controller as Administrator.

2. Click Start, point to Administrative Tools, and click Active Directory Users And Computers. The Active Directory Users And Computers console appears.

3. Expand the contoso*xx*.com domain icon in the scope pane (on the left) and select the Users container beneath the domain. The user and group objects in the Users container appear in the details pane (on the right).

REVIEW QUESTIONS

1. You are planning the deployment of Windows Server 2003 computers for a department of 250 employees. The server will host the home directories and shared folders for the department, and it will serve several printers to which departmental documents are sent. Which edition of Windows Server 2003 will provide the most cost-effective solution for the department? Explain your answer.

2. Which of the following versions of Windows Server 2003 require product activation? (Select all that apply.)

    a. Standard Edition, retail version

    b. Enterprise Edition, evaluation version

    c. Enterprise Edition, Open License version

    d. Standard Edition, Volume License version

3. What is the primary distinction between an Active Directory tree and an Active Directory forest?

4. Which of the following types of Active Directory objects are not container objects?

    a. User

    b. Group

    c. Computer

    d. Organizational unit

5. Which of the following is true about setup in Windows Server 2003? (Select all that apply.)

    a. Setup can be launched by booting from the CD.

    b. Setup can be launched by booting from setup floppy disks.

    c. Setup requires an Administrator password that is not blank to meet complexity requirements.

    d. Setup requires you to activate the product license before it installs the operating system.

CASE SCENARIOS

Scenario 1-1: Windows Server 2003, Web Edition Capabilities

You are a network administrator who has been assigned the task of deploying the Windows Server 2003 servers for your company's new e-commerce Web site, which is being designed by an outside consultant. The site will require four Web servers, configured as a four-node NLB cluster, and a single database server, running SQL Server. The consultant's deployment plan calls for the use of Windows Server 2003 Web Edition on all five of the servers. Which of the following statements regarding this proposed deployment is true?

1. The Web Edition is a suitable operating system for all five servers.

2. The Web Edition is a suitable operating system for the database server, but not for the Web servers, because it does not support NLB clusters.

3. The Web Edition is a suitable operating system for the Web servers, but not for the database server, because it cannot run SQL Server.

4. The Web Edition is not a suitable operating system for either the database or the Web servers.

Scenario 1-2: Selecting a Windows Server 2003 Edition

You are planning the deployment of Windows Server 2003 computers for a new Active Directory domain in a large corporation that includes multiple separate Active Directories maintained by each of the corporation's subsidiaries. The company has decided to roll out Exchange Server 2003 as a unified messaging platform for all the subsidiaries and plans to use Microsoft Metadirectory Services (MMS) to synchronize appropriate properties of objects throughout the organization. Which edition of Windows Server 2003 will provide the most cost-effective solution for this deployment? Explain your answer.

CHAPTER 2
ADMINISTERING MICROSOFT WINDOWS SERVER 2003

A large part of a Windows Server 2003 system administrator's daily work consists of configuring Active Directory objects, modifying computer software and service settings, installing new hardware and software, and performing many other tasks, using tools supplied with the operating system. As the computing environment expands to include more computers, the amount of work to be done increases as well. Microsoft Management Console (MMC) is the primary Windows Server 2003 system administration tool. MMC makes it possible to consolidate your most commonly used tools into a single interface and use them to manage Windows computers anywhere on the network. Understanding the capabilities of MMC is essential to efficient system administration.

When more comprehensive control of a computer at a remote location is required, beyond what can be accomplished remotely using MMC, two other key tools make administration of remote computers possible: Remote Desktop for Administration and Remote Assistance. Remote Desktop for Administration is a client/server application that displays the local console of a remote server in a window on your desktop, enabling you to control the keyboard and mouse functions as if you were logged on to that computer locally. Remote Assistance is similar in function but is designed to enable a Windows Server 2003 or Windows XP user to request help from another user on the network. Once the user issues a request for assistance, an expert elsewhere on the network can establish a remote connection to the user's desktop.

Upon completion of this chapter, you will be able to:

- Use a preconfigured MMC console

- Create a new MMC console

- Administer both local and remote computers using an MMC console

- Troubleshoot Terminal Services

- Configure a server to enable Remote Desktop for Administration

- Enable a computer to accept requests for Remote Assistance

- Use one of the available methods to request and establish a Remote Assistance session

USING MICROSOFT MANAGEMENT CONSOLE

MMC is a shell application that Windows Server 2003 uses to provide access to most of its system and network management tools. MMC provides a standardized, common interface for one or more application modules (called **snap-ins**) that are used to configure your system environment. These snap-ins are individualized to specific tasks and can be combined, ordered, and grouped within the MMC shell to your administrative preference. An instance of MMC with one or more snap-ins installed is referred to as a *console*. Most of the primary administrative tools in Windows Server 2003 are MMC consoles with collections of snap-ins installed that are suited to a specific purpose. With only a few exceptions, all of the shortcuts in the Administrative Tools program group on a computer running Windows Server 2003 are links to preconfigured MMC consoles.

For example, when you promote a Windows Server 2003 computer to a domain controller, the Active Directory Installation Wizard creates shortcuts to the following three primary management tools for Active Directory:

- Active Directory Domains and Trusts
- Active Directory Sites and Services
- Active Directory Users and Computers

Each of these shortcuts opens an MMC console containing a single snap-in, as shown in Figure 2-1. The Active Directory Users and Computers snap-in, for example, is specifically designed to administer the user, group, and computer objects in a domain. It is the snap-ins within the MMC shell, not MMC itself, that provide the administrative tools you use.

Figure 2-1   The Active Directory Users and Computers console

The three Active Directory consoles listed earlier all consist of a single snap-in, but an MMC console is not limited to using one snap-in at a time. When you open the Computer Management console found in the Administrative Tools program group on any Windows Server 2003 computer, you see a console containing many snap-ins, all combined into a single, convenient interface, as shown in Figure 2-2.

Figure 2-2   The Computer Management console

NOTE   MMC Interoperability   MMC consoles can run on Windows Server 2003, Windows XP, Windows 2000, Windows NT 4, and Windows 98.

Using the MMC Interface

MMC uses a two-pane design, much like Windows Explorer. The left pane, called the **scope pane**, contains a hierarchical list of the snap-ins installed in the console and any subheadings that the snap-ins provide. This hierarchy is sometimes called the **console tree**. You can expand and contract the elements in the scope pane to display more or less information, just as you can expand and contract folders in Windows Explorer. Selecting an element in the scope pane displays its contents in the console's right pane, called the **details pane**. What you see in the details pane is wholly dependent on the function of the snap-in you are using.

Using MMC Menus

Above the two panes, MMC has a standard Windows menu and toolbar. The commands on the menus and the tools on the toolbar vary depending on the snap-in that is currently selected in the scope pane. For example, when you open the Computer Management console and click each snap-in in the scope pane in turn, you see the contents of the toolbar change with each one, as well as some of the menu contents.

The primary menu for context-specific functions in an MMC console is the Action menu. When you select a snap-in element in either the scope or the details pane, the Action menu changes to include commands specific to that element. Most Action menus contain an All Tasks submenu that lets you select any of the possible tasks to perform on the selected element (as shown in Figure 2-3). It is also common to find a New submenu under Action, which enables you to create subelements beneath the selected element. In most cases, the Action menu commands for a selected element are also available from a context menu, which is accessible by clicking the secondary mouse button on the element.

Figure 2-3   The Action menu in an MMC console

Although the Action menu changes most frequently, other MMC menus can contain context-specific elements as well, particularly the View menu, which often contains commands that control how the snap-in displays information. For example, several MMC snap-ins display a subset of their available information by default. When an Advanced Features command appears on the View menu, selecting it switches the console to the full display (as shown in Figure 2-4).

Figure 2-4   The Active Directory Users and Computers console with Advanced Features displayed

Using Multiple Windows

If you look carefully at the upper-right corner of one of the predefined MMC consoles, you'll see two sets of window manipulation buttons, because the snap-ins installed in that console are actually in a separate window that is maximized by default. When you click the Restore Down button (the middle one of the three), the snap-ins revert to a floating window, as shown in Figure 2-5.

This leads to one of the most powerful MMC features, which is the ability to create customized consoles containing whatever snap-ins you want to use. You can combine one or more snap-ins or parts of snap-ins in a single console to create a single interface in which you can perform all of your administrative tasks. By creating a custom MMC, you do not have to switch between different programs or individual consoles. Customized consoles can contain any of the Windows Server 2003 snap-ins, whether or not they are already included in a preconfigured console, as well as any third-party snap-ins you might have.

The executable file for MMC is Mmc.exe. When you run this file from the Run dialog box or a command prompt, an empty console appears, as shown in Figure 2-7. This is a console with no snap-ins, so the menus and toolbar buttons have their default MMC functions at this point. The only element in the console window is the console root object in the scope pane, which is a placeholder representing the top of the console hierarchy. Before you can perform any administrative tasks using the console, you must add one or more snap-ins to it.

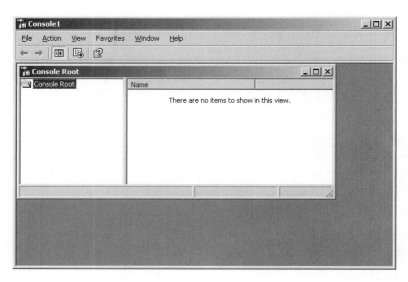

Figure 2-7   A blank MMC console

Adding Snap-Ins

There are two types of MMC snap-ins, as follows:

- **Standalone**   A standalone snap-in is a single tool that you can install directly into an empty MMC console. Stand-alone snap-ins appear in the first level directly beneath the console root in the console's scope pane.

- **Extension**   An extension snap-in provides additional functionality to specific stand-alone snap-ins. You cannot add an extension snap-in to a console without adding an appropriate stand-alone snap-in first. Extension snap-ins appear beneath the associated stand-alone snap-in in the console's scope pane.

Some snap-ins offer both stand-alone and extension functionality. For example, the Event Viewer snap-in is used to display the contents of a computer's event logs. In the Computer Management console, the Event Viewer snap-in appears as an extension, beneath the System Tools object in the scope pane. However, you can also add the Event Viewer snap-in to a custom console as a stand-alone snap-in, so that it appears directly beneath the console root.

To add snap-ins to a custom console, you select Add/Remove Snap-in from the File menu to display the Add/Remove Snap-in dialog box (as shown in Figure 2-8). By default, the Standalone tab in this dialog box is selected, and you click Add to display a list of the available stand-alone snap-ins on the computer.

Figure 2-8   The Add/Remove Snap-in dialog box

You can select and add as many stand-alone snap-ins to a console as you like. Once you have added a stand-alone snap-in, you can select it in the Add/Remove Snap-in dialog box and click the Extensions tab to display a list of the extension snap-ins associated with the stand-alone snap-in you selected (as shown in Figure 2-9). After clearing the Add All Extensions check box, you can select which extensions you want to appear in the console. Using the Snap-ins Added To drop-down list, you can specify whether an extension snap-in is added to the console root or to a lower element in the tree.

Figure 2-9   The Extensions tab of the Add/Remove Snap-in dialog box

Creating a Taskpad

Create a custom MMC console by doing Exercise 2.2, "Creating a Custom MMC Console," now.

Once you have added snap-ins to your custom console, you can create a customized taskpad, if you wish. The taskpad is an area of the details pane for a particular snap-in that contains links to frequently used functions from that snap-in (as shown in Figure 2-10). To create a taskpad, you select a snap-in in the scope pane and then select New Taskpad View from the Action menu. The New Taskpad View Wizard then takes you through the process of specifying how and where you want the taskpad to appear. After creating the taskpad view, you can run the New Task Wizard to create links in the taskpad.

Figure 2-10   A custom MMC console with a taskpad

Setting Console Options

Once you add the snap-ins you want to have appear in your custom MMC console, you can set options that determine what changes other users can make to the console's configuration. Select Options from the File menu to display the Options dialog box, in which you can specify the name that should appear in the console's title bar, and select the console mode.

By default, all new consoles you create are configured to use Author mode, which provides full access to all console functions. The available modes you can choose from are as follows:

- **Author Mode**   Provides full console access, including adding or removing snap-ins, creating windows, creating taskpad views and tasks, viewing portions of the console tree, changing the options on the console, and saving the console.

- **User Mode: Full Access**   Allows users to navigate between snap-ins and between open windows and to access all portions of the console tree. Prevents users from adding or removing snap-ins or changing console properties.

- **User Mode: Limited Access, Multiple Windows**   Allows users to create new windows and view multiple windows in the console, but prevents them from closing existing windows.

- **User Mode: Limited Access, Single Window**   Prevents users from opening new windows and allows them to view only one window in the console.

Console modes enable you to create consoles for other users that have limited capabilities and that the users cannot alter. Console mode settings are why you can't add snap-ins to the preconfigured consoles supplied with Windows Server 2003.

Saving MMC Consoles

Once you have configured a custom console the way you want it, you must save it as a file so you can access it again later. MMC console files have an .msc extension, which is associated with the Mmc.exe application, so executing a console file launches MMC with that console module. By default, consoles are saved in the Administrative Tools folder in the users' profiles and therefore appear as shortcuts in the Start menu's Administrative Tools program group.

> **NOTE**   **Console Shortcuts**   The shortcuts for your custom consoles appear only in the All Programs/Administrative Tools program group, not in the Administrative Tools group on the Start menu itself.

Connecting to Remote Computers

The MMC consoles that appear on the Start menu of a computer running Windows Server 2003 are all configured to manage resources on the local system. However, with most of the snap-ins supplied with Windows Server 2003, you can manage other Windows computers on the network as well. This is one of MMC's most useful features because it enables administrators to manage computers anywhere on the network from their own desktops.

> **NOTE   Exam Objectives**   The objectives for Exam 70-290 state that a student should be able to "manage servers remotely" and "manage a server by using available support tools."

You can access a remote computer using an MMC snap-in in two ways:

- Redirect an existing snap-in to another system
- Create a custom console with snap-ins directed to other systems

To connect to and manage another system using an MMC snap-in, you must launch the console with an account that has administrative credentials on the remote computer. The exact permissions required depend on the functions performed by the snap-in. If your credentials do not provide the proper permissions on the target computer, you will be able to load the snap-in but you will not be able to read information from or modify settings on the target computer.

> **NOTE   Using Run As**   If you know that the credentials you are currently using do not have the permissions needed to manage a remote computer, you can use Run As, or secondary logon, to launch a console with credentials other than those with which you are currently logged on.

Redirecting a Snap-In

A snap-in that is directed at a specific system has a Connect To Another Computer command on its Action menu. Selecting this command opens a Select Computer dialog box (as shown in Figure 2-11), in which you can type the name of or browse to another computer on the network. Once you specify the name of the computer you want to manage and click OK, the snap-in element in the scope pane changes to reflect the name of the computer you selected.

Figure 2-11   The Select Computer dialog box

Not every snap-in has the ability to connect to a remote computer because some do not need it. The Active Directory management consoles, for example, automatically locate a domain controller on the network and access the Active Directory database there. There is no need to specify a computer name.

Creating a Remote Console

Connecting to a remote computer by redirecting an existing console is convenient for impromptu management tasks, but it is limited by the fact that you can access only one computer at a time. You also have to open the console and redirect it every time you want to access the remote system. A more permanent solution is to create a custom console with snap-ins that are already directed at other computers.

When you add a snap-in to a custom console by selecting it in the list of available snap-ins and clicking the Add button, you might see a dialog box in which you can select what computer you want to manage with that snap-in, as shown in Figure 2-12. This adds a whole new dimension to MMC's functionality. Not only can you create custom consoles containing a variety of tools, but you can also create consoles containing tools for a variety of computers. For example, you can create a single console containing multiple instances of the Computer Management snap-in, with each one pointing to a different computer. This enables you to manage Windows Server 2003, Windows XP, and Windows 2000 computers all over the network from a single console.

Figure 2-12   The Computer Management dialog box

MANAGING SERVERS WITH REMOTE DESKTOP FOR ADMINISTRATION

In Windows 2000, Terminal Services was a separate component that had to be installed manually. Now it is an integral part of Windows Server 2003 that is installed by default with the operating system. By purchasing and configuring the appropriate licenses, you can configure a computer running Windows Server 2003 to host Terminal Services clients, providing them with access to the Windows desktop and applications running on the server.

Terminal Services has functions other than supporting Terminal Services clients, however. You can also use the Terminal Services engine to access a remote computer for administrative purposes, without the application-sharing capabilities. Windows Server 2003 calls this feature Remote Desktop for Administration. The operating system allows two concurrent Remote Desktop connections without the need for any additional licensing and with little additional system overhead.

> **NOTE   Exam Objectives**   The objectives for Exam 70-290 state that a student should be able to "manage a server by using Terminal Services remote administration mode."

Using MMC consoles, you can connect to a remote computer and perform many administrative tasks, but sometimes an administrator needs full access to the computer. Terminal Services in Windows Server 2003 enables a client program called Remote Desktop Connection running on another computer to connect to the server and access virtually any part of the system. The client window shows the server's desktop, making it possible for the user to access all of the standard controls and tools and even run applications on the server (as shown in Figure 2-13).

Figure 2-13   A Remote Desktop session

Enabling and Configuring the Remote Desktop Server

Because all of the components needed to support Remote Desktop for Administration connections are installed by default with the Windows Server 2003 operating system, activating the server side of the application is simplicity itself. In the Remote tab of the System Properties dialog box (accessible using the System icon in Control Panel), select the Allow Users To Connect Remotely To This Computer check box (as shown in Figure 2-14). By default, members of the local Administrators group are granted remote access permission. To allow other users to access the computer using Remote Desktop, you must click Select Remote Users and add them to the list of remote desktop users.

Figure 2-14   The Remote tab of the System Properties dialog box

Practice
enabling
Remote
Desktop for
Administratio
n on your
computer by
doing Exercise
2.3, "Enabling
Remote
desktop for
Administratio
n," now.

Selecting this one check box is all you have to do to enable the Remote Desktop server in Windows Server 2003. However, you can also configure the Remote Desktop server properties using the Terminal Services Configuration snap-in for MMC (as shown in Figure 2-15).

> **NOTE**   **Terminal Services and Domain Controllers**   By default, Windows Server 2003 domain controllers are configured to accept Terminal Services connections only from members of the Administrators group. Even users you have explicitly added to the Remote Desktop Users group are not permitted access. To override this behavior, you must change the effective value of the Allow Log On Through Terminal Services group policy, which lists the Administrators group only, by default. To do this, you can either modify the domain controller's local computer policy or define the same policy in the group policy object (GPO) for an Active Directory object containing the computer, such as the Default Domain Controllers Policy GPO.

Figure 2-15   The Terminal Services Configuration snap-in

To configure the Remote Desktop server properties, add the Terminal Services Configuration snap-in to an MMC console. Click the Connections folder in the scope pane, select the RDP-Tcp connection listed in the details pane, and, from the Action menu, select Properties. The RDP-Tcp Properties dialog box appears.

Using the tabs in this dialog box, you can configure various properties of the server, as follows:

■ **General**   Sets the encryption level and authentication mechanism for connections to the server.

- **Logon Settings**   Enables you to specify static credentials to be used by Remote Desktop connections rather than those provided by the client.

- **Sessions**   Contains settings that override the client values, specifying when to end a disconnected session, session time limits and idle time-outs, and whether reconnection is allowed.

- **Environment**   Overrides the client and user profile settings for starting a program upon connection to the server.

■ **Remote Control**   Specifies whether remote control of a Remote Desktop Connection session is possible and, if it is, whether the user must grant permission at the initiation of the remote control session. Additional settings can restrict the remote control session to viewing only or allow full interactivity with the Remote Desktop client session.

■ **Client Settings**   Overrides client settings for color depth and resource mapping.

■ **Network Adapter**   Specifies which network interface adapters on the server can accept Remote Desktop for Administration connections.

■ **Permissions**   Specifies permissions for Remote Desktop connections.

Installing and Configuring Remote Desktop Connection

For a computer to connect to a Remote Desktop server, it must run a client program called Remote Desktop Connection. This client program is installed by
default with the Windows Server 2003 and Windows XP operating systems, but it
can also run on any other 32-bit version of Windows. Windows Server 2003
includes the Remote Desktop Connection files on the installation CD and also copies them to the *Systemroot*\System32\Clients\Tsclient\Win32 folder. You can
install the client on another computer from either location by using the following
procedures:

■ **From the CD**   Insert the Windows Server 2003 CD into the drive. When
the Welcome to Microsoft Windows Server 2003 screen appears, click the
Perform Additional Tasks hyperlink, and then click Set Up Remote Desktop Connection. Follow the instructions displayed by the Remote Desktop Connection – InstallShield Wizard.

■ **From the network**   Create a share out of the *Systemroot*\System32\Cli-
ents\Tsclient\Win32 folder. Connect to the share from the client computer and run the Setup.exe file. Follow the instructions displayed by the
Remote Desktop Connection – InstallShield Wizard.

> **TIP** **Client Updates**   It is recommended that you update computers running
> previous versions of the Terminal Services client to the latest version of Remote
> Desktop Connection to take advantage of improvements such as a revised user
> interface, 128-bit encryption, and alternate port selection.

Once the client is installed, you connect to a server by running the program using
the Remote Desktop Connection shortcut in the Start menu and configuring the client using the Remote Desktop Connection dialog box. The tabs in this dialog box
enable you to configure client parameters, as follows:

> **NOTE** **Viewing Client Options**   Click the Options button to display the entire
> Remote Desktop Connection dialog box.

- **General**   Allows you to specify the computer to which the client should connect, the credentials the client should use to log on, and whether to save the configuration settings for the connection.

- **Display**   Allows you to specify the size of the Remote Desktop client window, its color depth, and whether the connection bar is available in full-screen mode.

- **Local Resources**   Allows you to specify whether the client should bring the server's sound events to the local computer, how Windows key combinations should be interpreted by the remote computer, and whether local disk, printer, and serial port connections should be available within the remote session. For example, selecting the Disk Drives option causes the local drives on the client computer to appear in the Remote Desktop session as if they were local drives on the server.

- **Programs**   Allows you to specify the name and the starting folder for an application to launch as soon as a connection with the server is established.

- **Experience**   Allows you to specify the speed of the connection between the client and the server and to disable the display of certain server desktop characteristics to conserve bandwidth and increase the client/server response time.

> **NOTE** **Remote Desktop and Terminal Services**   *Remote Desktop for Adminis-*
> *tration and Terminal Services use many of the same components. With the appro-*
> *priate licenses in place, network users can run the same client to access a*
> *terminal server for application-sharing purposes that they use for Remote Desk-*
> *top for Administration.*

Terminal Services Troubleshooting

When you use Remote Desktop for Administration, you create a connection
between a client program and a server. Remote Desktop for Administration uses
the same type of connection as a Terminal Services connection used for application
sharing, and the possible causes of a connection failure are the same as well. In the
event of a failed connection or problematic session, some of the potential causes
that you should investigate are as follows:

> **NOTE** **Exam Objectives**   *The objectives for Exam 70-290 state that a student*
> *should be able to "troubleshoot Terminal Services," "diagnose and resolve issues*
> *related to Terminal Services security," and "diagnose and resolve issues related to*
> *client access to Terminal Services."*

- **Network failures**   With any application that relies on client/server communications, failures are commonly caused by network problems, such
  as incorrectly configured TCP/IP settings, name resolution failures, routing problems, or networking hardware malfunctions. You can check for
  network communication problems by testing to see if other network
  applications are functioning, trying to connect using an IP address instead
  of a DNS name, and determining whether other users are experiencing
  the same problem. Check to see that the TCP/IP configuration settings on
  the client and server are correct, that DNS servers are operating properly,
  and that networking hardware is intact.

- **Port settings**   Terminal Services uses TCP and UDP port number 3389
  for all of its client/server communications, by default. If either the client
  or the server has been configured to use a different port number, or if that
  port is somehow being blocked (such as by a firewall), a Terminal Services client/server connection will not be possible.

- **Credentials**   Users must belong to the Administrators or Remote Desktop Users group to successfully connect to the server using Remote Desktop for Administration. In addition, you can block client access for a
  specific user or group by enabling the Deny Logon Through Terminal
  Services user right, either on the local system or by using group policies.

- **Number of connections**   If client sessions have been disconnected
  without the users logging off, the server might consider the connections
  still open and might reach its concurrent connection limit even though
  two human users are not connected at the time. Remote Desktop for
  Administration allows only two concurrent connections.

USING REMOTE ASSISTANCE

Remote Desktop is designed to provide administrative access to a computer, but
end users can sometimes benefit from this capability as well. Many users, but particularly those without much technical expertise, have configuration problems or
usage questions that are difficult for a support professional or even a friend or family member to diagnose and fix over the telephone. Remote Assistance is another

permutation of the Terminal Services model that enables a user to request help from another user at a remote location and receive that help in the form of on-screen guidance or demonstration, with neither party having to travel to the other. Remote Assistance enables helpers (or, as the application refers to them, experts) to offer technical support, troubleshooting help, and even training to users whenever they need it, with minimal expense and delay.

> **NOTE** *Exam Objectives* *The objectives for Exam 70-290 state that a student should be able to "manage a server by using Remote Assistance."*

Enabling Remote Assistance

Before you can receive remote assistance, you must enable the feature, in one of the following ways:

- **Using Control Panel** Open the System Properties from Control Panel and select the Remote tab. Select the Turn On Remote Assistance And Allow Invitations To Be Sent From This Computer check box. By clicking the Advanced button, you can specify whether to let the expert take control of the computer or simply view activities on the computer, as well as specify the amount of time that the invitation for remote assistance will remain valid.

- **Using group policies** Use the Group Policy Object Editor console (gpedit.msc) to open a GPO for a domain or organizational unit object containing the client computer. Browse to the Computer Configuration\Administrative Templates\System\Remote Assistance container and enable the Solicited Remote Assistance policy. This policy also enables you to specify the degree of control the expert will receive over the client computer, the duration of the invitation, and the method for sending e-mail invitations. The Offer Remote Assistance policy enables you to specify the names of users or groups that can function as experts and whether those experts can perform tasks or just observe.

Creating an Invitation

To receive remote assistance, a client must issue an invitation and send it to a particular expert. The client can send the invitation using any of the following methods:

- **Microsoft Windows Messenger** To use the Windows Messenger service for your Remote Assistance connection, you must have the expert's Windows Messenger username in your contact list and make the request from a Windows Messenger client. Remote Assistance can be requested directly only when the expert is online.

- **E-mail** To send an invitation using e-mail, both computers must be using a MAPI-compliant e-mail client.

- **File** When you save the invitation to a file, you can use any method to send it to an expert, such as a non-MAPI e-mail message, an FTP transfer, or a floppy disk.

To issue an invitation, you select Help And Support from the Start menu to open the Help and Support Center screen and then click the Remote Assistance hyperlink to display the screen shown in Figure 2-16.

Figure 2-16   The Remote Assistance screen

When you click the Invite Someone To Help You link, you see the interface shown in Figure 2-17. You then follow the instructions for the contact method of your choice.

Figure 2-17   The Remote Assistance page of the Help And Support Center

> **TIP**   **Using Passwords**   When users create invitations, they can specify a password that experts have to supply to connect to their computers. You should urge your users to always require passwords for Remote Assistance connections and instruct them to supply the expert with the correct password using a different medium from the one they are using to send the invitation.

The expert who receives the invitation can invoke it to launch the Remote Assistance application, which enables the expert to connect to the remote computer, as shown in Figure 2-18. Using this interface, the user and the expert can talk or type messages to each other and, by default, the expert can see everything that the user is doing on the computer. If the client computer is configured to allow remote control, the expert can also click the Take Control button and operate the client computer interactively.

Figure 2-18   The expert's Remote Assistance interface

Securing Remote Assistance

Because an expert offering remote assistance to another user can perform virtually any activity on the remote computer that the local user can, this feature can be a significant security hazard. An unauthorized user who takes control of a computer using Remote Assistance can cause almost unlimited damage. However, Remote Assistance is designed to minimize the dangers. Some of the protective features of Remote Assistance are as follows:

- **Invitations**   No person can connect to another computer using Remote Assistance unless that person has received an invitation from the client. Clients can configure the effective lifespan of their invitations in minutes, hours, or days to prevent experts from attempting to connect to the computer later.

- **Interactive connectivity**   When an expert accepts an invitation from a client and attempts to connect to the computer, a user must be present at the client console to grant the expert access. You cannot use Remote Assistance to connect to an unattended computer.

- **Client-side control**   The client always has ultimate control over a Remote Assistance connection. The client can terminate the connection at any time by pressing the Esc key or clicking Stop Control (ESC) in the client-side Remote Assistance page.

- **Remote control configuration**   Using the System Properties dialog box or Remote Assistance group policies, users and administrators can specify whether experts are permitted to take control of client computers. An expert who has read-only access cannot modify the computer's configuration in any way using Remote Access. The group policies also enable administrators to grant specific users expert status so no one else can use Remote Access to connect to a client computer, even with the client's permission.

■ **Firewalls**   Remote Assistance uses Transmission Control Protocol (TCP) port number 3389 for all its network communications. For networks that use Remote Assistance internally and are also connected to the Internet, it is recommended that network administrators block this port in their firewalls to prevent users outside the network from taking control of computers that request remote assistance. However, it is also possible to provide remote assistance to clients over the Internet, which would require leaving port 3389 open.

NOTE   **Using Windows Messenger**   If you elect to use Windows Messenger to send Remote Assistance invitations, port 1863 must be left open as well, to permit Windows Messenger communications.

SUMMARY

- Microsoft Management Console is the primary system administration tool for Windows Server 2003.

- MMC is a shell application that you use to run snap-ins, which are individual tools that load into an MMC console.

- There are two types of snap-ins, stand-alone and extension, with extensions appearing and behaving within the MMC based on the context of their placement.

- Some snap-ins can be used to configure both local and remote computers; others are limited to local computer access only.

- MMC consoles can be saved in either Author mode, granting users full access to the console configuration, or User mode, granting limited access.

- Remote Desktop for Administration allows you to administer a remote server as if you were logged on locally to the server as an administrator.

- Remote Assistance is a tool that enables users to request assistance from an expert, who can then connect to the user's computer and either view the user's actions or take over operation of the system.

- Remote Assistance is a mutual arrangement: the user can ask an expert for help, or the expert, if properly configured through Group Policy, can initiate a help session. In either case, the user must actively agree to the establishment of the connection and is always in control of the session. At no time can the expert take control of the user's desktop unannounced.

- The Remote Desktop Connection client, a default component of Windows XP and Windows Server 2003, can be installed on any 32-bit Windows platform from the Windows Server 2003 installation CD or (after sharing the directory) from any Windows Server 2003 computer.

- Both Remote Desktop for Administration and Remote Assistance use the Terminal Services service for their communications, but neither requires a special Terminal Services license.

EXERCISES

Exercise 2-1: Opening an MMC Window

In this exercise, you open a second window in an MMC console.

1. Click Start, point to Administrative Tools, and click Computer Management. The Computer Management console appears.

2. From the Window menu, select New Window. A second window appears on top of the first one.

3. From the Window menu, select Tile Horizontally. The console display changes to show both windows at once. Notice that you can navigate in each window independently.

Exercise 2-2: Creating a Custom MMC Console

In this exercise, you create a new, custom MMC console.

1. Click Start, and then click Run. The Run dialog box will appear.

2. In the Open text box, type **mmc** and click OK. A Console1 window appears.

3. From the File menu, select Add/Remove Snap-in. The Add/Remove Snap-in dialog box appears.

4. Click Add. The Add Standalone Snap-in dialog box appears.

5. In the Available Standalone Snap-ins list, select Device Manager and then click Add. The Device Manager dialog box appears.

6. Click Finish to accept the default settings, click Close, and then click OK. The Device Manager snap-in now appears in the console's scope pane.

7. From the File menu, select Save As, and save the console in the default Administrative Tools folder using the filename DevMgr.msc.

Exercise 2-3: Enabling Remote Desktop for Administration

In this exercise, you configure your client computer to accept Remote Desktop connections.

1. Click Start, point to Control Panel, and then click System. The System Properties dialog box appears.

2. Select the Remote tab, and then select the Allow Users To Connect Remotely To This Computer check box.

3. Click OK.

REVIEW QUESTIONS

1. What is the default mode when you create a new MMC console? *the console has no snap in's, just the console root object in the scope pane*

2. Can a snap-in have focus on both the local computer and a remote computer simultaneously? *no*

3. What credentials are required for administration of a remote computer using MMC? *you need administrative credentials on the remote computer*

4. Can an existing MMC snap-in be changed from local to remote context, or must a snap-in of the same type be loaded into the console for a remote connection? *yes, an existing MMC snap-in can be changed from local to remote context*

5. Are all of the functions in a snap-in always available for use when you are connected to a remote computer? *no*

6. How many simultaneous connections are possible to a terminal server running in Remote Administration mode? Why? *2, to avoid connection failure*

7. What tool is used to enable Remote Desktop on a server?

    a. Terminal Services Manager

    b. Terminal Services Configuration

    c. System Properties in Control Panel

    d. Terminal Services Licensing

CASE SCENARIOS

Scenario 2-1: Using Remote Assistance

Your company has enabled Remote Assistance on each computer in the enterprise. The company's sales representatives travel frequently and use laptops to perform their work while on the road. On your internal network, you use Windows Messenger for spontaneous communication with your clients and for Remote Assistance. However, you disallow Instant Messenger traffic across the Internet by closing port 1863 at the firewall. You want to perform Remote Assistance for your remote users, but you cannot connect to them with Windows Messenger to determine whether they are online. Describe two alternative methods that traveling sales representatives can employ to send a Remote Assistance invitation to an expert in the home office.

Scenario 2-2: Using Remote Desktop Connection

You are trying to connect to a Windows Server 2003 server in your environment with Remote Desktop Connection, but you consistently get the following message when you attempt to connect:

You have checked settings on the server and confirmed the following:

■ You are a member of the Remote Desktop Users group.

■ You are not a member of the Administrators group.

■ You are able to connect to share points on the Terminal Server computer, and the computer responds affirmatively to a ping.

What other settings should you check on the Terminal Server computer to troubleshoot this problem?

CHAPTER 3
MONITORING MICROSOFT WINDOWS SERVER 2003

Keeping the network servers running smoothly and efficiently is one of the primary jobs of a system administrator, and Microsoft Windows Server 2003 includes a collection of tools that enable you to do this. Although a server might be running at peak capacity immediately after installation, performance can degrade over time for a variety of reasons. A good system administrator must monitor the server's performance on a regular basis to identify trends and detect problems that can affect performance. Learning to use the Windows Server 2003 monitoring tools properly is an important skill to acquire so you can recognize changes in a server's performance before the situation turns into a catastrophe.

Upon completion of this chapter, you will be able to:

- Use Event Viewer to monitor system logs
- Configure Task Manager to display performance data
- Use System Monitor to display real-time performance data
- Create counter logs and alerts

SERVER MONITORING PRACTICES

The performance monitoring tools included with Windows Server 2003 enable an administrator to examine a variety of system parameters in a number of ways. How you use the tools depends on the resources that you want to monitor as well as your personal preferences. The two basic types of system monitoring are as follows:

- **Real-time monitoring**   Real-time monitoring uses tools that display a continuous stream of statistics about what the system is doing right now. The statistics can be displayed numerically or in the form of a graph. Obviously, this method provides the most current information, but few system administrators have the time or the inclination to watch a graph of system performance parameters all day long.

- **Logged monitoring**   Logged monitoring typically produces the same information as real-time monitoring but stores it on a permanent medium instead of (or in addition to) displaying it immediately. This method enables administrators to observe trends that develop over longer periods of time than those observed in a typical real-time monitoring session. When using logged monitoring, administrators must be sure to provide sufficient storage space for the captured data, and, of course, they must examine the captured information on a regular basis.

The uses of real-time and logged monitoring are not mutually exclusive. Each method has its value, and indeed some of the Windows Server 2003 monitoring tools support both.

Monitoring Subsystems

Windows Server 2003 system performance can be broken down into four basic subsystems, each of which must function properly for the computer to perform satisfactorily. These four subsystems are as follows:

- **Processor**   A computer's microprocessor performs millions of individual computations using clock cycles, with each computation devoted to a particular task. The processor's available clock cycles are divided between the many different processes running on the computer. The faster the processor, the more clock cycles there are to go around in a given period of time. Monitoring processor performance typically involves checking the burden on the processor as it performs its regular tasks. If the processor's clock cycle utilization consistently approaches 100 percent, system performance might be suffering due to insufficient processing power.

- **Memory**   Random access memory (RAM) is the temporary storage space that a computer uses as a staging area for the data passing to and from the processor. When insufficient RAM is available to complete a particular task, Windows uses hard disk space instead of RAM, in a process called memory paging. Because accessing hard disks is much slower than accessing RAM, performance degrades when too much paging occurs. Monitoring memory performance is a matter of ensuring that the computer has sufficient memory to complete its designated tasks.

- **Disk**   The computer's hard disk drives provide permanent storage for operating system and application files, as well as for the data used and produced by the applications. Monitoring disk storage subsystem performance typically involves checking the number of disk access requests that are waiting to be processed at a given time. If large amounts of data are waiting to be read from or written to the disks, the overall performance of the computer can suffer.

- **Network**   Network subsystem monitoring differs slightly from that of the other three subsystems because the performance of the network can be affected by external factors as well as internal ones. A large number of queued network transmission requests can degrade a server's performance as perceived by its users on the network, even though the computer itself is functioning properly.

Determining which subsystems in the computer require the most careful monitoring depends on the applications that the computer is running. Different applications require different degrees of performance from each subsystem, and a problem with one particular subsystem can have a different effect on various applications.

Establishing a Baseline

When you monitor a server's performance characteristics, the actual subsystem performance values themselves are not as important as the changes that occur in the performance values over time. For example, if you examine the processor performance of a server that was first installed a year ago and discover that processor utilization is at 100 percent, you have no way of knowing whether this has always been the case or something has changed recently to affect the processor's performance.

For this reason, one of the most important parts of monitoring server performance is establishing a baseline of performance levels that you can refer to later. This is why the introduction to this chapter states that you should learn to use the Windows Server 2003 monitoring tools before something goes wrong. A **baseline** is a collection of performance levels taken when the computer is functioning normally, preferably soon after it is fully installed and configured. By comparing later levels with the baseline, you can determine whether the performance of the various subsystems is degrading. You'll learn more about creating a baseline later in this chapter, in the discussions of the various Windows Server 2003 monitoring tools.

USING EVENT VIEWER

Windows Server 2003 maintains a variety of logs that contain information about its ongoing processes. To view these logs, you use the Event Viewer MMC snap-in. Event Viewer can function as either a standalone or an extension snap-in. The Windows Server 2003 Administrative Tools program group has a shortcut to an Event Viewer console, but the snap-in is also included with many other tools in the Computer Management console.

> **NOTE   Exam Objectives**   The objectives for the 70-290 exam state that a student should be able to "monitor and analyze events. Tools might include Event Viewer and System Monitor."

Event Viewer Logs

When you launch Event Viewer (shown in Figure 3-1), the scope pane contains a list of the logs maintained by the system. The three base logs that appear on all Windows Server 2003 computers are as follows:

- **Application**   Contains information about specific programs running on the computer, as determined by the application developer.

- **System**   Contains information about events generated by Windows Server 2003 components, such as services and device drivers. For example, a failure of a service to start or a driver to load during system startup is recorded in the System log. The types of events recorded in this log are preconfigured by the operating system and cannot be changed. This is the primary Windows Server 2003 log; you should always view this log first when looking for information about system problems.

- **Security**   Can contain information about security-related events, such as failed logons, attempts to access protected resources (such as shares and file system elements), and success or failure of audited events. Windows Server 2003, in its default configuration, does not record information in the Security log. The events recorded in this log are determined by audit policies, which you can enable using either local computer policies or group policies. By default, only members of the Administrators group can view this log.

Figure 3-1   The Event Viewer console

When the computer is promoted to a domain controller, the following two logs are added to Event Viewer:

- **Directory Service**   Contains information about the Active Directory directory service, such as irreconcilable object replications or other significant events within the directory.

- **File Replication Service**   Contains information about the success or failure of the replication activities that occur between Active Directory domain controllers.

Finally, when the computer has the Microsoft DNS Server service installed, Event Viewer contains one more log:

- **DNS Server**   Contains information about the status and operations of the DNS Server service.

Although Event Viewer contains the most important Windows Server 2003 logs, it does not contain all of them. A number of services are included with the operating system that maintain their own separate logs. In nearly all cases, these logs are simple text files that you can open with any text editor, such as the Windows Notepad application. Some of the separate logs you might find on a computer running Windows Server 2003 are as follows:

- DHCP auditing

- Dr. Watson (program errors)

- Fax activity

- Internet Connection Firewall (ICF)

- Microsoft Internet Information Services (IIS)

- Windows Media Services clients

- WINS database transactions

Understanding Event Types

When you select one of the logs listed in the scope pane of the Event Viewer snap-in, you see a list of individual events in the details pane. The most immediately apparent element in each event is its type, which is identified with an icon. The type indicates the importance of the event, and whether it is the result of a normal process or a problem of some sort. The event types used in the Event Viewer snap-in are listed in Table 3-1. Obviously, errors and warnings are the most significant types of events to a system administrator, because they indicate that a significant event has occurred.

Table 3-1   **Windows 2000 Event Types**

Event Type	Icon	Description
Error		A significant problem, such as loss of data or loss of functionality
Warning		An event that might not be significant but might indicate a future problem
Information		An event that describes the successful operation of an application, driver, or service
Success audit		An audited security access attempt that succeeds
Failure audit		An audited security access attempt that fails

Double-clicking an entry in the Event Viewer's details pane displays an Event Properties dialog box like the one shown in Figure 3-2. This dialog box contains more information about the event, including:

- **Date**   The date on which the event occurred

- **Time**   The time at which the event occurred

- **Type**   The type of event that occurred (error, warning, information, success audit, or failure audit)

- **User**   The name of the user account associated with the process that generated the event

- **Computer**   The name of the computer on which the event occurred

- **Source**   The software module that generated the event

- **Category**   A classification of the event, as defined by the source process

- **Event ID**   A unique value identifying this particular event

- **Description**   A text message describing the nature of the event, generated by the source process

- **Data**   Binary data generated by the event

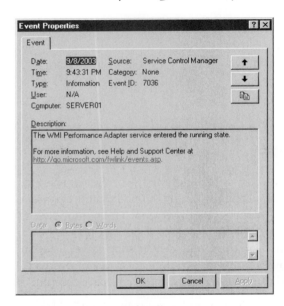

Figure 3-2   An Event Properties dialog box

Configuring Event Viewer Logs

Practice using Event Viewer by doing Exercise 3.1, "Using Event Viewer," now.

Each log in the Event Viewer snap-in has its own Properties dialog box, which you can use to configure the log's retention parameters and control what information is displayed in the log. These settings are discussed in the following sections.

Event Log Retention Settings

On the general tab of each log's Properties dialog box (shown in Figure 3-3), you can specify the maximum size of the log and its behavior when the log reaches its maximum size. The available log retention options are as follows:

- **Overwrite Events As Needed**   The log erases the oldest individual entries as needed once the log file has reached the specified maximum size.

- **Overwrite Events Older Than X Days**   The log retains all entries for the number of days (from 1 to 365) specified by this option and overwrites older entries as needed. If the log reaches its specified maximum size and there are no entries older than the number of days specified, the system stops writing new events to the log.

- **Do Not Overwrite Events (Clear Log Manually)**   The system retains all log entries until they are manually erased by an administrator. Once the log reaches its specified maximum size, the system stops writing new events to the log.

Figure 3-3   The General tab of the System event log's Properties dialog box

The default settings for the event logs on a Windows Server 2003 domain controller running the Microsoft DNS Server service are shown in Table 3-2. The Directory Service and File Replication Service logs have small maximum sizes (512 KB) because entries to these logs are relatively rare. The Security log, however, has an extremely large maximum size (128 MB). This is because the computer has been promoted to a domain controller, and part of the default configuration for Windows Server 2003 domain controllers is the activation of several audit policies, which cause large numbers of events to be written to the Security log. The default maximum size for the Security log on a Windows Server 2003 computer that is not a domain controller is 16 MB.

Table 3-2   Default Event Log Retention Settings

Event Log	Maximum Log Size	Log Retention Setting
Application	16,384 KB (16 MB)	Overwrite events as needed
Directory Service	512 KB	Overwrite events as needed
DNS Server	16,384 KB (16 MB)	Overwrite events older than 7 days
File Replication Service	512 KB	Overwrite events as needed
Security	131,072 KB (128 MB)	Overwrite events as needed
System	16,384 KB (16 MB)	Overwrite events as needed

NOTE   Configuring Retention Settings Using Group Policies   In addition to configuring the retention settings for the event logs manually by using the Event Viewer snap-in, you can configure the same parameters for the Application, System, and Security logs by enabling the Event Log policies in a group policy object (GPO) and applying it to an individual computer or to an Active Directory container object.

On a domain controller, leaving the default setting of Overwrite Events As Needed on the Security log could overwrite important resource access or other security-related data if an administrator does not archive the log entries on a regular basis. To ensure that no Security log entries are lost, Windows Server 2003 has a drastic measure available in the form of a Security Option group policy called Audit: Shut Down System Immediately If Unable To Log Security Audits.

Using Filters

When you first start Event Viewer, the snap-in displays all of the events that are recorded in the selected log, chronologically. Depending on the size of the log and the retention settings, the list could be extremely lengthy. However, many of the event entries are of the Information type, which result from normal, everyday activities. To locate specific entries in the list, you can modify its order by clicking one of the column headings, or you can limit the display of what appears in the log to focus on the important events, by using the Filter or the Find command.

To implement a filter on a log in Event Viewer, from the View menu, select Filter to display the Filter tab of the event log's Properties dialog box, as shown in Figure 3-4. In this dialog box, you can specify the event types you want to display and select other event criteria to reduce the event list to a manageable size.

Figure 3-4   The Filter tab of an event log's Properties dialog box

To search for specific items in the event list, you can select Find from the View menu to display the Find dialog box (shown in Figure 3-5).

Both the Filter tab and the Find dialog box enable you to select from the event criteria listed in "Windows 2000 Event Types," earlier in this chapter, to locate specific entries.

Figure 3-5   Event Viewer's Find dialog box

Accessing Remote Event Logs

As with many MMC snap-ins, you can use Event Viewer to view the logs on other Windows computers as well as the computer on which you are working. To perform this task, in the scope pane, select the Event Viewer (Local) object and select Connect To Another Computer from the Action menu. In the Select Computer dialog box, specify the name of the computer whose event logs you want to see.

Archiving Event Logs

The Event Viewer snap-in can save logs to files in several formats, including tab-delimited text (.txt) files, comma-delimited (.csv) files, and an Event Log format with an .evt extension, which can be opened by the snap-in. Once you save a log to a file, you have a permanent record of the entries and you can safely clear the log. Archiving on a regular basis ensures that the log files never grow too large, causing entries to be lost.

USING TASK MANAGER

Task Manager is an important Windows application that you can use to display information about the computer's current performance levels as well as manage the programs and processes running on the system. You can open Task Manager by right-clicking an open area of the taskbar and then selecting Task Manager from the context menu, or by pressing Ctrl+Alt+Del and then clicking the Task Manager button. The Windows Task Manager dialog box contains five tabs by default:

- Applications
- Processes
- Performance
- Networking
- Users

The functions found on these tabs are described in the following sections.

NOTE   Exam Objectives   *The objectives for the 70-290 exam state that a student should be able to "monitor file and print servers. Tools might include Task Manager, Event Viewer, and System Monitor."*

Working with Applications

The Applications tab (shown in Figure 3-6) shows the status of the user-level programs currently running on the computer. Services and system applications running in different contexts from the logged-on user are not displayed. For each application listed, the Status column indicates whether the application is running or not responding.

Figure 3-6   Task Manager's Applications tab

By selecting an application from the list and clicking Switch To, you can make the selected application the active window, leaving Task Manager open in the background. You can also select an entry in the list and click End Task to close the application.

NOTE   Ending Tasks   *Closing applications by using Task Manager is not a recommended practice unless the application has a status of Not Responding and cannot be terminated any other way. When you end a task in this way, you usually lose any data that has not been saved to disk.*

When you right-click an application in the list and select Go To Process from the context menu, the dialog box switches to the Processes tab and highlights the process associated with the application. This is a helpful feature when you are trying to locate the process for a particular application and the process name is less than intuitive.

When you click the New Task button, a Create New Task dialog box appears, in which you can enter or browse for the name of any standard executable file or command. This dialog box is the functional equivalent of the Run dialog box, which is accessible from the Start menu.

Monitoring Processes

The Processes tab (shown in Figure 3-7) lists all of the current user's processes running on the computer. When you select the Show Processes From All Users check box, the list includes all services and other system processes, in addition to user-level applications. By default, the list includes the following information about each process:

- **Image Name**   The name of the executable file for the process

- **User Name**   The user account that owns the process

- **CPU**   The current processor utilization percentage for the process

- **Mem Usage**   The amount of memory utilized by the process

Figure 3-7   Task Manager's Processes tab

By selecting Select Columns from the View menu, you open the Select Columns dialog box (shown in Figure 3-8), which you can use to add or remove data columns from the display. Task Manager provides a large selection of counters, enabling you to display detailed information about the processor, memory, and I/O utilization of each process in the list. You can also sort the list using any of the displayed counters by clicking the column heading.

Figure 3-8   The Select Columns dialog box

In addition to simply monitoring information about system processes, you can also manipulate them with Task Manager. By right-clicking any process in the list, you can perform any of the following actions:

- **Set Priority**   Modifies the amount of processor time allocated to the process in relation to the other processes running on the system.

- **Set Processor Affinity**   Specifies which processor on a multiprocessor computer you want to use to run the process.

- **End Process**   Halts the process immediately. All unsaved data is lost.

- **End Process Tree**   Halts the process and any child or related processes immediately. All unsaved data is lost.

- **Debug**   Causes an exception to halt a process and attach it to the debugger, if one is installed on the system.

> **WARNING**   **Manipulating Processes**   Changing the settings of a process such as priority or processor affinity can have an adverse effect on the performance of other applications running on the computer. Ending a process, and especially a process tree, should be done only after normal termination procedures have failed. Windows Server 2003 safeguards its operating system processes from termination through Task Manager, but they are still susceptible to resource starvation through inappropriate priority adjustment of other processes.

Monitoring Performance Levels

The Performance tab (shown in Figure 3-9) displays a real-time view of the computer's processor and memory utilization. There are graphs displaying the current usage for each processor and the memory page file usage, as well as historical graphs for both statistics. Double-clicking one of the graphs expands it vertically to show the values with greater precision. Numerical displays show physical, kernel, and **commit memory** utilization, as well as the number of handles, threads, and active processes.

Figure 3-9   Task Manager's Performance tab

Monitoring Network Activity

The Networking tab (shown in Figure 3-10) shows all active network connections by name, with their connection speed, bandwidth utilization percentage, and operational status. There is also a graph displaying the bandwidth utilization for the currently selected network connection. Here again, double-clicking the graph displays a larger version with more precise y-axis gradations.

Figure 3-10   Task Manager's Networking tab

Monitoring Users

The Users tab (shown in Figure 3-11) lists all of the users who are currently logged on to the computer. Logged-on users can be working locally at the computer's console or remotely connected over the network. Using the controls on this tab, you can log off a user, forcibly disconnect a user from the computer, or send a message to a user.

Figure 3-11   Task Manager's Users tab

USING THE PERFORMANCE CONSOLE

Practice using
Task Manager
by doing
Exercise 3.2,
"Using Task
Manager,"
now.

The Performance console is one of the most powerful monitoring tools in Windows Server 2003. The console consists of the following two snap-ins:

- **System Monitor** Displays real-time performance data as collected from configurable components called **performance counters**

- **Performance Logs and Alerts** Records data from performance counters over a period of time and executes specific actions when counters reach a certain value

Performance is an MMC console that is accessible from a shortcut in the Administrative Tools program group. You can also add the individual snap-ins to custom consoles. By default, the Performance console monitors the current computer, but you can configure the snap-ins to monitor the performance of any computer on the network for which you have the appropriate permissions.

> **MORE INFO** Using MMC Snap-Ins For more information on creating custom MMC consoles, see Chapter 2 in this textbook.

> **NOTE** Exam Objectives The objectives for the 70-290 exam state that a student should be able to "monitor system performance."

Using System Monitor

When you open the Performance console, the System Monitor snap-in appears by default, as shown in Figure 3-12. The details pane of the snap-in contains a line graph, updated in real time, showing the current levels for the following three performance counters:

- **Memory: Pages/Second** The rate at which pages are read from or written to disk to resolve hard page faults. This counter is a primary indicator of the kinds of faults that cause system-wide delays.

- **PhysicalDisk(_Total): Average Disk Queue Length** The Length counter average number of read and write requests queued for the selected disk during the sample interval.

Figure 3-12 The default System Monitor display

■ **Processor(_Total): % Processor Time**   The percentage of elapsed time that the processor spends to execute a nonidle thread. This counter is the primary indicator of processor activity and displays the average percentage of busy time observed during the sample interval.

Modifying the Graph View

The legend beneath the graph specifies the line color for each of the three counters, the scale of values for each counter, and other identifying information about the counter. When you select one of the counters in the legend, its current values appear in numerical form at the bottom of the graph. Click the Highlight button in the toolbar (or press Ctrl+H) to change the selected counter to a broad, white line that is easier to distinguish in the graph (as shown in Figure 3-13).

Figure 3-13   A System Monitor graph with a highlighted counter

If your computer is otherwise idle, you will probably notice that the lines in the default graph are all hovering near the bottom of the scale, making it difficult to see their values. You can address this problem by modifying the scale of the graph's y (vertical) axis. Click the Properties button on the toolbar (or press Ctrl+Q) to display the System Monitor Properties dialog box, and then select the Graph tab (as shown in Figure 3-14). In the Vertical Scale box, you can reduce the maximum value for the y axis, thereby using more of the graph to display the counter data.

Figure 3-14   The Graph tab of the System Monitor Properties dialog box

In the General tab of the System Properties dialog box, you can also modify the sample rate of the graph. By default, the graph updates the counter values every 1 second, but you can increase this value to display data for a longer period of time on a single page of the graph. This can make it easier to detect long-term trends in counter values.

> **NOTE**   **Modifying Graph Properties**   The System Monitor Properties dialog box contains a number of other controls that you can use to modify the appearance of the graph. For example, on the Graph tab, you can add axis titles and gridlines, and in the Appearance tab, you can control the graph's background color and select a different font.

Using Other Views

In addition to the line graph, System Monitor has two other views of the same data: a histogram view and a report view. You can change the display to one of these views by clicking the View Histogram or View Report toolbar button, or by pressing Ctrl+B or Ctrl+R. To change back to the original line graph view, click View Graph or press Ctrl+G.

The histogram view is a bar graph with a separate vertical bar for each counter, as shown in Figure 3-15. In this view, it is easier to monitor large numbers of counters because the lines do not overlap.

Figure 3-15   The System Monitor histogram view

The report view (as shown in Figure 3-16) displays the numerical value for each of the performance counters.

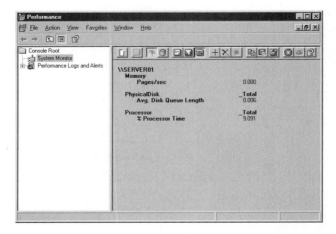

Figure 3-16   The System Monitor report view

As with the line graph, the histogram and report views both update their counter values at the interval specified in the General tab of the System Properties dialog box. The main drawback of these two views, however, is that they do not display a history of the counter values, only the current value. Each new sampling overwrites the previous one in the display, unlike the line graph, which displays the previous values as well.

Adding Counters

The three performance counters that appear in System Monitor by default are useful gauges of the computer's performance, but the snap-in includes dozens of other counters that you can add to the display. To add counters to the System Monitor details pane, click the Add button in the toolbar or press Ctrl+I to display the Add Counters dialog box (as shown in Figure 3-17).

Figure 3-17   The Add Counters dialog box

> **NOTE**   **Accessing System Monitor Functions**   Unlike most MMC snap-ins, System Monitor does not insert its most commonly used functions into the MMC console's Action menu. The only methods of accessing System Monitor functions are the toolbar buttons, hotkey combinations, and the context menu that appears when you right-click the display.

In this dialog box, you have to specify the following four pieces of information to add a counter to the display:

- **Computer**   The name of the computer you want to monitor with the selected counter. Unlike with most MMC snap-ins, you cannot redirect the entire focus of System Monitor to another computer on the network. Instead, you specify a computer name for each counter you add to the display. This enables you to create a display showing counters for various computers on the network, such as a single graph of processor activity for all of your servers.

- **Performance object**   A category representing a specific hardware or software component in the computer. Each **performance object** contains a selection of performance counters related to that component.

- **Performance counter**   A statistic representing a specific aspect of the selected performance object's activities.

■ **Instance**   An element representing a specific occurrence of the selected performance counter. For example, on a computer with two network interface adapters, each counter in the Network Interface performance object would have two instances, one for each adapter, enabling you to track the performance of each adapter individually. Some counters also have instances such as Total or Average, enabling you to track the performance of all instances combined or the median value of all instances.

Once you have selected a computer name, a performance object, a performance counter in that object, and an instance of that counter, click Add to add the counter to the display. The dialog box remains open so you can add more counters. Click Close when you are finished.

> **NOTE**   **Understanding Counters**   Clicking the Explain button opens an Explain Text message box that contains a detailed description of the selected performance counter.

The performance objects, performance counters, and instances that appear in the Add Counters dialog box depend on the computer's hardware configuration, the software installed on the computer, and the computer's role on the network. For example, installing the DNS Server service on the computer adds the DNS performance object, which consists of a collection of counters enabling you to track the DNS server's activities.

Creating an Effective Display

In most cases, when users first discover the System Monitor snap-in, they see the embarrassment of riches that the hundreds of available performance counters provide, and they proceed to create a graph containing dozens of different counters. In most cases, the result is a graph that is crowded and incoherent. The number of counters you can display effectively depends on the size of your monitor and the resolution of your video display.

Consider the following tips when selecting counters:

■ **Limit the number of counters**   Too many counters make the graph more difficult to understand and negatively affect system performance. To display a large number of statistics, you can display multiple windows in the console and select different counters in each window, or use the histogram or report view to display a large number of counters in a more compact form (as long as you are willing to give up the value history shown in the graph view).

■ **Modify the counter display properties**   Depending on the size and capabilities of your monitor, the default colors and line widths that System Monitor uses in its graph might make it difficult to distinguish counters from each other. In the Data tab of the System Monitor Properties dialog box for each counter, you can modify the color, style, and width of that counter's line in the graph to make it easier to distinguish.

■ **Choose counters with comparable values**   System Monitor imposes no limitations on the combinations of counters you can select for a single graph, but some statistics are not practical to display together because of their disparate values. When a graph contains a counter with a typical value that is under 20 and another counter with a value in the hundreds, it is

Practice creating a System Monitor console by doing Exercise 3.3, "Creating a System Monitor Console," now.

difficult to arrange the display so that both counters are readable. Choose counters with values that are reasonably comparable so you can display them legibly. Here again, if you must display counters with different value ranges, you might use the report view instead of graph view.

Saving a System Monitor Console

Once you are satisfied with the display you have created, you can save it as a console file by selecting Save As from the File menu and specifying a filename with an .msc extension. Launching this console file opens the Performance console and displays the System Monitor snap-in, with all of the counters and display properties you configured before saving it.

Monitoring Server Performance

Once you understand how to use System Monitor, the next step is to decide which of the hundreds of performance counters you should choose to monitor your server's performance most efficiently. There is, of course, no single answer to this question. You might want to create several consoles to monitor different aspects of server performance or the same performance aspects on several different computers. The best practice is to create a server-monitoring strategy as soon as possible after the computer is fully installed and configured. This way, you can establish a performance-level baseline for the server in normal, idle, and peak performance states. When problems occur during later monitoring, measurement against the baseline can help you to find a solution.

> **NOTE** *Monitoring Overhead* It is important to remember that in some cases, the performance levels measured by System Monitor include resources utilized by the monitoring process itself. For example, the System Monitor snap-in utilizes some memory and processor time, just like any other program, and if you are monitoring counters on another computer, the process generates some network traffic as well. Be sure to account for this overhead when you are interpreting your System Monitor results.

The primary reasons for monitoring server performance using System Monitor are to ensure that the applications running on the server are functioning properly and to detect system bottlenecks that are affecting server efficiency. It is not uncommon for system administrators to be faced with server performance problems that are not immediately attributable to an obvious cause, such as a service failure. Users might complain that a server is slow at certain times of the day or that performance has been declining gradually over the course of weeks or months. When this occurs, one of the most common causes is a bottleneck somewhere in the path between the client and the data on the server that the client needs to use.

A **bottleneck** is a component that is not providing an acceptable level of performance compared to the other components in the system. For example, users might complain that their file server performance is slow, and you might spend a great deal of time and money upgrading your local area network (LAN) from 10Base-T to 100Base-TX, expecting to see a dramatic improvement. However, if your server is an old computer using a first-generation Pentium processor, the improvement is likely to be minimal because it is probably the server's processor, not the LAN technology, that is the bottleneck. All the other components are running well, but the processor cannot keep up with the data flow provided by the new, faster network.

> **NOTE** **Exam Objectives**   The objectives for the 70-290 exam state that a student should be able to "monitor server hardware for bottlenecks" and "monitor and optimize a server environment for application performance" by monitoring memory, network, processor, and disk performance objects.

Bottlenecks can appear for a variety of reasons, including the following:

- **Increased server load**   A server might function adequately in a particular role at first, but as you increase the server's load by adding more users or more tasks, the inadequacy of one or more components might become more pronounced. For example, a Web server might be sufficient for a company's Web site at first, but then the company introduces a new product and traffic to the site triples. Suddenly, you find that the Web server's disk performance is insufficient to handle the additional traffic.

- **Hardware failure**   Hardware failures do not always manifest themselves as catastrophic stoppages. A component might malfunction intermittently for a long period of time, causing degraded server performance that is maddeningly inconsistent. For example, a faulty network cable connecting a server to a hub can cause occasional traffic interruptions that show up as degraded performance in the server.

- **Changed server roles**   Different applications have different resource requirements. You might have a computer that functions adequately as a Web server, but when you change the computer's role to that of a database server, you find that the processor is not fast enough to handle the load that the new application places on it.

Locating a bottleneck that is hindering performance can be a complicated task, but monitoring the correct performance counters in System Monitor is usually a good way to begin. In many cases, the cause of the bottleneck can be narrowed down to one of the four major subsystems listed at the beginning of this chapter (processor, memory, disk, or network).

When you monitor server performance levels, the best practice is to start from the top down—that is, you start with the broadest monitoring configuration for each subsystem to determine which one is the most likely cause of the problem. Once you have determined the general problem area, you can then look at the particular services and applications that make the heaviest use of that subsystem, and at protocol and thread levels, if needed. Usually, the problem is caused by either one device or one application, or a global lack of resources on the system. Single devices can be reconfigured or replaced, and global resources can be augmented (such as by adding more memory or an additional processor) as appropriate.

The following sections discuss the problems to look for and the performance counter to use when monitoring each of the four main subsystems.

Monitoring Processor Performance

An inadequate or malfunctioning processor array can cause a server to queue incoming client requests, preventing the server from fulfilling them promptly. For general monitoring of the processor subsystem, use the following performance counters:

> **NOTE** **Locating Counters**   The performance counters in this and the following sections are notated using the format *performance object: performance counter.*

- **Processor: % Processor time**   Specifies the percentage of time that the processor is busy. This value should be as low as possible, with anything below 85 percent being acceptable. If this value is consistently too high, you should attempt to determine which process is using too much processor time, upgrade the processor, or add another processor, if possible.

- **System: Processor Queue Length**   Specifies the number of program threads waiting to be executed by the processor. This value should be as low as possible, with values less than 10 being acceptable. If the value is too high, upgrade the processor or add another processor.

- **Server Work Queues: Queue Length**   Specifies the number of requests waiting to use a particular processor. This value should be as low as possible, with values less than 4 being acceptable. If the value is too high, upgrade the processor or add another processor.

- **Processor: Interrupts/sec**   *for baseline*   Specifies the number of hardware interrupts the processor is servicing each second. The value of this counter can vary greatly and is significant only in relation to an established baseline. A hardware device that is generating too many interrupts can monopolize the processor, preventing it from performing other tasks. If the value increases precipitously, examine the various other hardware components in the system to determine which one is generating too many interrupts.

Monitoring Memory Performance

An inadequate amount of memory in a server can prevent the computer from caching frequently used data aggressively enough, causing processes to rely on disk reads more than memory reads and slowing down the entire system. Memory is the single most important subsystem to monitor because memory problems can affect all of the other subsystems. For example, when a memory condition causes excessive disk paging, the system might appear to have a problem in the storage subsystem when memory is actually the culprit.

One of the most common conditions that can cause memory-related problems is a memory leak. A **memory leak** is the result of a program allocating memory for use but not freeing up that memory when it is finished using it. Over time, the computer's free memory can be totally consumed, degrading performance and ultimately halting the system. Memory leaks can be fast, causing an almost immediate degradation in overall server performance, but they can also be slow and difficult to detect, gradually degrading system performance over a period of days or weeks. In most cases, memory leaks are caused by third-party applications, but operating system leaks are not unheard of.

To monitor basic memory performance, use the following counters:

- **Memory: Page Faults/Sec**   Specifies the number of times per second that the code or data needed for processing is not found in memory. This value should be as low as possible, with values below 5 being acceptable. This counter includes both soft faults (in which the required page is found elsewhere in memory) and hard faults (in which the requested page must be accessed from a disk). Soft faults are generally not a major problem, but hard faults can cause significant delays because disk accesses are much slower than memory accesses. If this value is too high, you should determine whether the system is experiencing an inordinate number of hard faults by examining the Memory: Pages/Sec counter. If the number of hard page faults is excessive, you should either determine what process is causing the excessive paging or install more random access memory (RAM) in the system.

- **Memory: Pages/Sec**   Specifies the number of pages per second that were not in RAM and had to be accessed from disk or that had to be written to disk to make room in RAM. This value should be as low as possible, with values from 0 to 20 being acceptable. If the value is too high, you should either determine what process is causing the excessive paging or install more RAM in the system.

- **Memory: Available Bytes**   Specifies the amount of available physical memory in bytes. (Other counters are available that show the same value in kilobytes and megabytes.) This value should be as high as possible and should not fall below 5 percent of the system's total physical memory, as this might be an indication of a memory leak. If the value is too low, consider installing additional RAM in the system.

- **Memory: Committed Bytes**   Specifies the amount of virtual memory that has space reserved on the disk-paging files. This value should be as low as possible and should always be less than the amount of physical RAM in the computer. If the value is too high, this could be an indication of a memory leak. Consider installing additional RAM in the system.

- **Memory: Pool Non-Paged Bytes**   Specifies the size of an area in memory used by the operating system for objects that cannot be written to disk. This value should be a stable number that does not grow without a corresponding growth in server activity. If the value increases over time, this could be an indication of a memory leak.

Monitoring Disk Performance

A storage subsystem that is overburdened with read and write commands can slow down the rate at which the system processes client requests. The server's hard disk drives carry a greater physical burden than the other three subsystems because in satisfying the I/O requests of many clients, the drive heads must continually move to different locations on the drive platters. The drive head mechanism can move only so fast, however, and once the drive reaches its maximum read/write speed, additional requests can begin to pile up in the queue, waiting to be processed. For this reason, the storage subsystem is a prime location for a bottleneck.

- **PhysicalDisk: Disk Bytes/sec**   Specifies the average number of bytes transferred to or from the disk each second. This value should be equivalent to the levels established in the original baseline readings or higher. A decrease in this value could indicate a malfunctioning disk that could eventually fail. If this is the case, consider upgrading the storage subsystem.

- **PhysicalDisk: Avg. Disk Bytes/Transfer**   Specifies the average number of bytes transferred during read and write operations. This value should be equivalent to the levels established in the original baseline readings or higher. A decrease in this value indicates a malfunctioning disk that could eventually fail. If this is the case, consider upgrading the storage subsystem.

- **PhysicalDisk: Current Disk Queue Length**   Specifies the number of pending disk read or write requests. This value should be as low as possible, with values less than 2 being acceptable per disk spindle. High values for this counter can indicate that the drive is malfunctioning or that it is incapable of keeping up with the activities demanded of it. If this is the case, consider upgrading the storage subsystem.

- **PhysicalDisk: % Disk Time**   Specifies the percentage of time that the disk drive is busy. This value should be as low as possible, with values less than 80 percent being acceptable. High values for this counter can indicate that the drive is malfunctioning, that it is incapable of keeping up with the activities demanded of it, or that a memory problem is causing excess disk paging. Check for memory leaks or related problems and, if none are found, consider upgrading the storage subsystem.

- **LogicalDisk: % Free Space**   Specifies the percentage of free space on the disk. This value should be as high as possible, with values greater than 20 percent being acceptable. If the value is too low, consider adding more disk space.

Most storage subsystem problems, when not caused by malfunctioning hardware, are resolvable by upgrading the storage system. These upgrades can include any of the following measures:

- Install faster hard disk drives.

- Install additional hard disk drives and split your data among them, reducing the I/O burden on each drive.

- Replace standalone drives with a RAID (redundant array of independent disks) array.

- Add more disk drives to an existing RAID array.

Monitoring Network Performance

Monitoring network performance is more complicated than monitoring the other three subsystems because many factors outside the computer can affect network performance. You can use the following counters to try to determine if a network problem exists, but if you suspect one, you should begin looking for causes external to the computer:

- **Network Interface: Bytes Total/sec**   Specifies the number of bytes sent and received per second by the selected network interface adapter. This value should be equivalent to the levels established in the original baseline readings or higher. A decrease in this value could indicate malfunctioning network hardware or other network problems.

- **Network Interface: Output Queue Length**   Specifies the number of packets waiting to be transmitted by the network interface adapter. This value should be as low as possible, and preferably zero, although values of two or less are acceptable. If the value is too high, the network interface adapter could be malfunctioning or another network problem might exist.

- **Server: Bytes Total/Sec**   Specifies the total number of bytes sent and received by the server over all of its network interfaces. This value should be no more than 50 percent of the total bandwidth capacity of the network interfaces in the server. If the value is too high, consider migrating some applications to other servers or upgrading to a faster network.

The bandwidth of the network connections limits the amount of traffic reaching the server through its network interfaces. If these counter values indicate that the network itself is the bottleneck, there are two ways to upgrade the network, and neither one is a simple fix:

- **Increase the speed of the network**   This means replacing the network interface adapters in all the computers, hubs, routers, and other devices on the network, and possibly replacing the cabling as well.

- **Install additional network adapters in the server and redistribute the network**   If traffic frequently saturates the network interfaces already in the server, the only way to increase the network throughput without increasing the network's speed is to install more network interfaces. However, connecting more interfaces to the same network will not permit any more traffic to reach the server. Instead, you must create additional subnets on the network and redistribute the computers among them, so that there is less traffic on each subnet.

Monitoring Server Roles

When you monitor server performance and look for bottlenecks, it is important that you understand the implications of the roles that the server is performing. Applications and services make different demands on system resources, and your monitoring strategy for each server should concentrate on the performance objects and counters for the resources that are most heavily affected on that server. Table 3-3 lists some of the most common server roles, the resources most important to each role, and the performance objects you should monitor.

Table 3-3   **Server Roles and Objects to be Monitored**

Server Role	Resources Used	Performance Objects to Monitor
Application server	Memory, network, and processor	Memory, Processor, Network Interface, and System
Backup servers	Processor and network	System, Server, Processor, and Network Interface
Database servers	Storage, network, and processor	PhysicalDisk, LogicalDisk, Processor, Network Interface, and System
Domain controllers	Memory, processor, network, and disk	Memory, Processor, System, Network Interface, protocol objects (network-dependent, but can include TCPv4, UDPv4, ICMP, IPv4, NBT Connection, NWLink IPX, NWLink NetBIOS, and NWLink SPX), PhysicalDisk, and LogicalDisk
File and print servers	Memory, disk, and network components	Memory, Network Interface, PhysicalDisk, LogicalDisk, and Print Queue
Mail/messaging servers	Processor, disk, network, and memory	Memory, Cache, Processor, System, PhysicalDisk, Network Interface, and LogicalDisk
Web servers	Disk, cache, and network components	Cache, Network Interface, PhysicalDisk, and LogicalDisk

Using Performance Logs and Alerts

As useful as the System Monitor snap-in is, few system administrators have the time or inclination to sit around watching a graph crawl across their screens, looking for signs of trouble on their servers. Performance Logs and Alerts eliminates the need to do this. Performance Logs and Alerts is an MMC snap-in that provides logged monitoring capabilities using the same performance objects and counters as System Monitor. With this snap-in, you can collect performance data automatically from local or remote computers, store it in a variety of formats, and generate alerts when a particular counter level reaches a specified threshold.

When you select the Performance Logs And Alerts snap-in in the Performance console, you see three subheadings, as follows:

- **Counter Logs**   Enables the Performance console to capture statistics for specific counters to a log file at regular intervals over a specified time

- **Trace Logs**   Enables the Performance console to record information about system applications when certain events occur, such as disk I/O operations or page faults

- **Alerts**   Enables the Performance console to monitor the values of a specific counter at regular intervals and perform an action when the counter reaches a specified value

One of the main benefits of Performance Logs and Alerts is that it enables you to capture performance counter information for later study. The snap-in supports a variety of file formats that enable you to import the captured information into spreadsheet and database programs. You can use counter logs to establish a baseline for network performance, and then periodically check the logs for deviation from that baseline. You can also create alerts to warn you when specific network conditions deviate too far from the norm.

> **NOTE**   **Unattended Logging**   Performance Logs and Alerts runs as a service. This means that you can configure the snap-in to monitor certain performance counters, and the service will load during system startup and continue to operate even if no user is logged on to the system.

Creating a Counter Log

To create a counter log in the Performance Logs and Alerts snap-in, you select the Counter Logs object in the scope pane and select New Log Settings from the Action menu. After you specify a name for the new log, you see a dialog box (shown in Figure 3-18) in which you specify the following information:

- **Performance objects and counters**   The same performance objects and counters, and the same interface you use to select them, as those for System Monitor.

- **Sample interval**   The time interval at which the snap-in should log the values of the counters you selected. Keep in mind that short sample intervals produce larger log files and also generate more system overhead. The value you choose should depend largely on how long you plan to let the counter log run.

- **Run As credentials**   A user name and password that the Performance Logs and Alerts service will use to log on to the system before capturing information to the counter log.

- **Log file type**   The file format you want to use for the counter log and the folder you want to save it in. You can choose to save the log as a comma- or tab-delimited text file, a regular or circular binary file (viewable in System Monitor), or a SQL database file. You can also specify a maximum size for the log file and a naming convention for the file.

> **NOTE**   **Using Circular Files**   A circular binary file is one in which the snap-in continuously logs information to the same file, overwriting the oldest data as it does so.

■ **Scheduling information**   You can configure the counter log to start and stop at particular dates and times, or you can choose to start and stop the logging process manually from the snap-in.

■ **Close command**   Enables you to specify a command that the snap-in should run when the log file closes.

Figure 3-18   A counter log's configuration dialog box

Once you configure the counter log, it appears in the snap-in scope pane with an icon, the color of which indicates the log's current status. A red icon is stopped and a green icon is running.

Creating a Trace Log

The process of creating a trace log is similar to that of creating a counter log, except that instead of selecting performance counters, you select the system events that you want to monitor, using the interface shown in Figure 3-19.

Figure 3-19   A trace log's configuration dialog box

Viewing a Counter Log

When you choose to save a counter log as a binary file, it appears in its destination folder with a .blg extension. To open one of these files and view its contents, you go to the System Monitor snap-in and click the View Log Data toolbar button or press Ctrl+L. In the System Monitor Properties dialog box that appears (as shown in Figure 3-20), you must configure the following elements:

- **Data source**   In the Source tab, click the Log Files option and select the log file you want to display.

- **Time range**   In the Source tab, click the Time Range button to display a slider bar containing the time period during which data was captured to the log. You can use the slider to select all or part of the log for display.

- **Counters**   In the Data tab, click Add and select the counters you want to display. In this case, the Add Counters dialog box contains only the performance objects and counters that you selected for inclusion in the log.

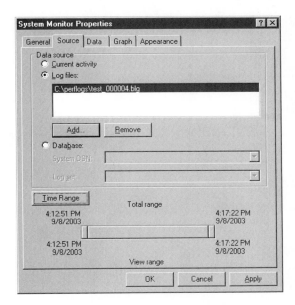

Figure 3-20   The System Monitor Properties dialog box, configured to display a log file

When you click OK to close the dialog box, the System Monitor line graph displays the data captured in the log. You can manipulate the appearance of the graph in the same way as you can when it displays the system's current activity.

Creating Alerts

Alerts enable a Windows Server 2003 computer to inform you when performance levels reach a specified threshold. To create an alert, you select the Alerts object in the scope pane of the Performance Logs and Alerts snap-in and select New Alert Settings from the Action menu to display a dialog box (as shown in Figure 3-21) in which you specify the following information:

- **Counters**   The performance object and counters that you can select for an alert, and the interface you use to select them, are the same as those for System Monitor.

- **Counter value limits**   For each counter you select, you must specify a value limit and whether you want the alert to trigger when the counter value is over or under the limit.

- **Sample interval**   The time interval at which the snap-in should monitor the values of the counters you selected.

- **Run As credential**   A username and password that the Performance Logs and Alerts service will use to log on to the system before monitoring the selected counters.

- **Action**   The action that you want the snap-in to perform when one of your selected counters reaches the limit you specified. The snap-in can create an event log entry, send a network message to a specified user, begin logging performance data for the counter, or execute a specified program or command.

- **Scheduling information**   You can configure the snap-in to start and stop monitoring the selected counters at particular dates and times, or you can choose to start and stop the monitoring process manually from the snap-in.

Figure 3-21   An alert's configuration dialog box

SUMMARY

- Event Viewer is an MMC snap-in that displays logs maintained by the computer. Every Windows Server 2003 computer has Application, System, and Security logs; domain controllers have two additional Directory Service and File Replication Service logs, and DNS servers have a DNS Server log.

- Individual event log entries can contain information, warnings, error messages, or auditing results.

- Task Manager displays real-time performance data for the computer's processor and memory, lists of the applications and processes running on the computer, and network and user activity information. You can also use Task Manager to end applications and processes, set process priorities, and disconnect users.

- The Performance console consists of two snap-ins: System Monitor and Performance Logs and Alerts.

- System Monitor shows real-time performance data for system hardware and software components, using graph, histogram, and report views.

- To monitor specific system characteristics using System Monitor, you choose a performance object representing a specific component, a performance counter that represents a specific aspect of the selected object, and in some cases an instance, which is a specific occurrence of the selected object.

- Performance Logs and Alerts records performance counter information to counter logs and operating system events to trace logs over scheduled periods of time, enabling you to capture large data samples for later examination.

- Performance Logs and Alerts can also monitor specific counters and perform an action when the counter values reach a specified threshold.

EXERCISES

Exercise 3-1: Using Event Viewer

In this exercise, you use the Event Viewer console to examine the computer's System log.

1. Log on to the computer as Administrator.

2. Click Start, point to Administrative Tools, and click Event Viewer. The Event Viewer console appears.

3. In the console's scope pane, click the System object. A list of System log entries appears in the details pane.

4. Double-click one of the entries in the details pane to display the Event Properties dialog box.

Exercise 3-2: Using Task Manager

In this exercise, you use Task Manager to start an application and identify its process.

1. Log on to the computer as Administrator.

2. Right-click an open section of the taskbar, and select Task Manager from the context menu. The Windows Task Manager window appears.

3. On the Applications tab, click New Task. Type **notepad**, and then click OK.

   An Untitled-Notepad window appears, and an Untitled-Notepad entry appears in the Task Manager's Applications tab.

4. In Task Manager's Applications tab, right-click the Untitled-Notepad entry and select Go To Process from the context menu. Task Manager switches to the Processes tab, with the Notepad.exe process highlighted.

Exercise 3-3: Creating a System Monitor Console

In this exercise, you create a new System Monitor console.

1. Log on to the computer as Administrator.

2. Click Start, point to Administrative Tools, and click Performance. The Performance console appears.

3. In the details pane, click the Add button in the toolbar. The Add Counter dialog box appears.

4. Leaving the default Processor object selected, click the % Idle Time counter and then click Add. Then add the % Interrupt Time and Interrupts/Sec counters in the same way, and then click Close.

5. From the File menu, select Save As. The Save As dialog box appears.

6. Save the console using the name procmon.msc.

CHAPTER REVIEW

1. You do not want data in the Security log to be overwritten, but you also do not want your Windows Server 2003 computer to stop serving the network at any time. What settings should you configure on your server?

2. Your goal is to monitor all your Windows Server 2003 servers so that they can be defragmented on a regular schedule, and as efficiently as possible. The disk defragmentation program that you use requires at least 20 percent free disk space on each volume to defragment properly. What should you do?

3. The computer that you are using to monitor the other systems on your network is overburdened with the task, so you must lighten its monitoring load. What should you do to lighten the monitoring computer's load while maintaining as much monitored data as possible?

4. You are running a database application on a computer with two processors. You want the database application to run on the second processor. How can you use Task Manager to do this?

5. Which of the following statements is true if System Monitor shows a value greater than 2 for the PhysicalDisk: Current Disk Queue Length counter on a non-RAID system?

   a. You need more disk space.

   b. You need a faster disk drive.

   c. You need additional information to determine whether the disk is the problem.

   d. You have a memory problem, not a disk problem.

6. Which of the following logs are available using Event Viewer on a member server functioning as an application server? (Choose all correct answers.)

   a. Application

   b. Directory Service

   c. System

   d. Security

   e. File Replication Service

7. Why do System Monitor performance counters sometimes have multiple instances?

8. What are two possible remedies for a disk subsystem that is the bottleneck in a server's performance?

CASE SCENARIOS

Scenario 3-1: Detecting a Bottleneck

You are a network administrator for Fabrikam, Inc., a high-technology company that has recently landed a lucrative government contract. As a result of the contract, the company will be undergoing a dramatic expansion over the next 12 months. The number of users accessing the company's client database is expected to double, and the IT director has instructed you to determine if the database server in its current configuration can keep up with the increased load, and if not, what improvements need to be made.

To accomplish this task, your first course of action is to implement a plan to monitor the server for performance bottlenecks. As the first step in the plan, you establish a baseline by using the Performance Logs and Alerts snap-in to create a counter log that tracks the values for critical counters in the Processor, Memory, PhysicalDisk, and Network Interface performance objects. After establishing the normal operational values for the counters, what should you do next to configure the Performance console to detect a bottleneck?

a. Leave the counter log running at all times and check the values of the counters at regular intervals.

b. Using System Monitor, create a graph of the same counters and configure the snap-in to sound an alarm when any counter value exceeds the maximum baseline value.

c. In the Performance Logs And Alerts snap-in, create a series of alerts that send a message to your workstation when any baseline counter exceeds a certain value.

d. In the Performance Logs And Alerts snap-in, create a trace log using the same counters as the baseline.

Scenario 3-2: Eliminating a Bottleneck

You are a network administrator who has been given the task of determining why the Windows Server 2003 file and print server on a particular LAN is performing poorly. You must also implement a remedy for the problem. After monitoring server performance counters using the Performance console, you have determined that the network itself is the bottleneck preventing peak performance. Which of the following solutions would enable you to achieve the goal of increasing the performance level of the file and print server? (Choose all correct answers.)

a. Install a second network interface adapter in the server, and connect it to the same network.

b. Increase the speed of the network by replacing the 10Base-T network interface adapters in the computers on the network and the hub to which the computers are connected with 100Base-TX equipment.

c. Split the network into two separate LANs with an equal number of computers on each. Then install a second network interface adapter in the file and print server and connect the server to both LANs.

d. Replace the network interface adapter in the file and print server with a model that has a larger memory buffer.

CHAPTER 4
BACKING UP AND RESTORING DATA

The most common analogy used to describe the relationship between a hard disk drive's platters (where the data is stored) and its heads (which read and write the data to the platters) is that of a 747 airliner flying at 600 miles an hour, five feet above the ground. When you consider this, it is amazing that hard drives work as well and as long as they do. Someday, you are going to lose a hard drive containing essential data. It might not happen today or tomorrow, but it will happen someday. The drive might be stolen along with the computer, destroyed in a fire or other catastrophe, or simply fail. Whatever the cause, the data will be gone, and it might be up to you to get it back. The day this occurs is the day you will thank yourself for all the effort you took to set up a backup strategy. If you don't have a backup strategy in place, that might be the day you start working on your résumé.

Performing regular backups is one of the most basic functions of the system and network administrator. Unlike most of the key components in a computer, hard drives have parts that move at high speeds, working at very close tolerances. As a result, hard drive failures are relatively common, and you must prepare for them by regularly saving your data on another storage medium.

Upon completion of this chapter, you will be able to:

- Describe the various types of hardware used to perform backups
- Understand the capabilities of network backup software products
- Understand the difference between full, incremental, and differential backup jobs
- List the capabilities of the Microsoft Windows Server 2003 Backup program
- Back up and restore an Active Directory database
- Use volume shadow copies

UNDERSTANDING BACKUPS

Backups are simply copies of your data that you make on a regular basis so that if a storage device fails or is damaged, and the data stored there is lost, you can restore it in a timely manner. A backup is the ultimate fault-tolerance measure. Even if you have other storage technologies in place that provide fault tolerance, such as a redundant array of independent disks (RAID) or clustered servers, you still need a backup solution.

Networks both complicate and simplify the process of making regular backups. A backup strategy for a stand-alone computer consists of a backup drive installed in the system. The network backup process is more complicated because you have data, stored on multiple devices, that must be protected, and it is not practical to install and maintain a separate backup drive for each one. However, the network backup process is simplified by the fact that you can use the network to access the devices that need backing up, enabling you to use one backup drive to protect multiple computers.

A network backup strategy specifies what data you back up, how often you back it up, and what medium you use to store the backups. The decisions you make regarding the backup hardware, software, and administrative policies you will use depend on how much data you have to back up, how much time you have to back it up, and how much protection you want to provide.

A network backup solution consists of the following two elements:

- One or more backup drives
- A backup software product

An effective backup plan specifies how to use the capabilities provided by these two items to provide the degree of protection that the organization needs. The criteria you should use when evaluating backup hardware and software products are discussed in the following sections.

> **NOTE**   **Exam Objectives**   The objectives for the 70-290 examination state that students should be able to "manage backup procedures."

Backup Hardware

You can perform backups using any type of storage device, although a device that uses removable media is the norm. The three main criteria used to evaluate backup hardware devices are:

- **Capacity**   One of the main objectives in developing an effective backup strategy should be to automate as much of the process as possible. Although you can back up a gigabyte of data onto 1.44-MB floppy disks, you probably don't want to be the person sitting around feeding 712 disks into a floppy drive. Therefore, you should select a device that is capable of storing as much of your data as possible without your having to change media. The ideal situation is one in which an entire backup job fits on a single tape cartridge or other medium. This enables you to schedule backup jobs to run completely unattended. This does not mean, however, that you have to purchase a drive that can hold all of the data stored on all of your network's computers. You can be selective about which data you want to back up. But it's therefore important to determine just how much of your data needs protecting, and how often, before you decide on the capacity of your backup device.

- **Speed** Another important criterion to use when selecting a backup device is the speed at which the drive writes data to the medium. Backup drives are available in many speeds, and, not surprisingly, the faster ones are generally more expensive. It is typical for backup jobs to run during periods when the network is not otherwise in use. This ensures that all of the data on the network is available for backup. The amount of time that you have to perform your backups is sometimes called the *backup window*. The backup device that you choose should depend in part on the amount of data you have to protect and the amount of time in which you have to back it up. If, for example, you have 10 GB of data to back up and your company closes down from 5 P.M. until 9 A.M. the next morning, you have a 16-hour backup window—plenty of time to copy your data using a medium-speed backup device. However, if your company operates three shifts and leaves you only one hour, from 7 A.M. to 8 A.M., to back up 100 GB of data, you have to use a much faster device or, in this case, several devices.

- **Cost** Cost is always a factor in selecting a hardware product. You can purchase a low-end backup drive for $100 to $200, which is suitable for backing up a home computer, where speed and capacity are not major factors. However, when you move up to the drives that have the speed and capacity that make them suitable for network backups, the prices increase dramatically. High-end backup drives can command prices that run into five figures. When you evaluate backup devices, you must be aware of the product's extended costs as well. Backup devices use a removable medium, such as a tape or disk cartridge. This enables you to store copies of your data offsite, such as in a bank's safe deposit vault. If the building where your network is located is destroyed by a fire or other disaster, you still have your data, which you can use to restart operations elsewhere. Therefore, in addition to purchasing the drive, you must purchase storage media as well. Some products might seem at first to be economical because the drive is inexpensive, but in the long run they might not be because the media are so expensive. One of the most common methods of evaluating a backup device is to determine the cost per megabyte (or gigabyte) of the storage it provides. Divide the price of the medium by the number of megabytes (or gigabytes) it can store, and use this figure to compare the relative media cost of various devices. Of course, in some cases you might need to sacrifice economy for speed or capacity.

Some of the removable storage devices used as backup drives are examined in the following sections.

CD-ROM and DVD-ROM Drives

The popularity of writable CD-ROM drives, such as compact disc-recordable (CD-R) drives and compact disc-rewritable (CD-RW) drives, has led to their increasing use as backup devices. Although the capacity of a CD is limited to approximately

650 MB, the low cost of the media can make CDs appear to be an economical solution, even if the disks can only be used once, as is the case with CD-Rs. Now that prices for DVD-ROM drives are coming down, DVD-ROMs are more suitable than CD-ROMs because of their greater capacity (over 4 GB). The biggest factor in favor of using CD-ROMs or DVD-ROMs for backup is that many computers already have the drives installed for other purposes, eliminating the need to purchase a dedicated backup drive.

For network backups, CD-ROMs are usually inadequate because most networks have many gigabytes' worth of data to back up, which would require many disc changes. DVD-ROMs reduce the number of media changes, and might be suitable for smaller networks, but they still do not have the capacity required for efficient backups of a large enterprise network. In addition, CD-ROM and DVD-ROM drives are usually not recognized by network backup software products. Although these drives often come with software that provides its own limited backup capabilities (intended for relatively small, single-system backups), this software usually does not provide the features needed to back up a network effectively.

Cartridge Drives

Another commonly used storage device that can be easily used for backups is the removable cartridge drive. Products such as Iomega's Zip and Jaz drives provide performance that approaches that of a hard disk drive, but they use removable cartridges. These drives mount into a computer's file system, which means that you can assign them a drive letter and copy files to them, just as you can with a hard drive.

Zip cartridges hold no more than 750 MB, which makes them only slightly more practical than CDs for backups. However, Jaz drives are available in 1-GB and 2-GB versions, which is sufficient for a backup device, even on a small network. The drawback of using this type of drive for backup purposes is the extremely high cost of the media. A 2-GB Jaz cartridge can cost as much as $125, which is more than 6 cents per megabyte—far more than virtually any other storage device.

Magnetic Tape Drives

The most commonly used hardware device for backing up data is the magnetic tape drive, like the one shown in Figure 4-1. Unlike hard disk, floppy disk, and CD-ROM drives, tape drives are not random access devices. This means that the drive can't move its heads to read any particular file on a tape without spooling through all of the files before it. As with other types of magnetic tape drives, such as audio and video, the drive unwinds the tape from a spool and pulls it across the heads until it reaches the point in the tape where the data you want is located. As a result, you can't mount a tape drive in a computer's file system, assign it a drive letter, and copy files to it, as you can with a hard disk drive. A special software program is required to address the drive, send the data you select to it for storage, and restore the data later. This also means that tape drives are useless for anything other than backups, whereas other types of removable storage media, such as writable CD-ROMs, can be used for other things.

Figure 4-1   An external magnetic tape drive

Magnetic tape drives are well-suited for backups. They're fast, they can hold a lot of data, they can archive that data nearly indefinitely, and their media cost per megabyte is low—often less than one-half cent per megabyte. There are many different types of magnetic tape drives that differ greatly in speed, capacity, and price. The general rule with magnetic tape drives is that you trade speed and capacity for cost. At the low end are quarter-inch cartridge (QIC) drives, which can cost as little as $200. There are many different QIC formats, with the capacity of a single QIC tape cartridge ranging from 150 MB to 20 GB. At the high end of the market are digital linear tape (DLT) and linear tape-open (LTO) drives, which can cost many thousands of dollars and store hundreds of gigabytes on a single tape. The most common magnetic tape technologies used for backups are listed in Table 4-1.

Table 4-1   **Magnetic Tape Drive Types**

Type	Tape Width	Cartridge Size	Capacity (uncompressed)	Speed
QIC, Travan	.25 inch	4 × 6 × 0.625 inches (data cartridge); 3.25 × 2.5 × 0.6 inches (minicartridge)	50 GB	600 MB/min
DAT	4 mm	2.875 × 2.0625 × 0.375 inches	20 GB	360 MB/min
8 mm	8 mm	3.7 × 2.44 × 0.59 inches	100 GB	1400 MB/min
DLT, Super DLT	.50 inch	4.16 × 4.15 × 1 inches	160 GB	960 MB/min
LTO, Ultrium	.50 inch	4.0 × 4.16 × 0.87 inches	200 GB	Up to 3600 MB/min

NOTE   Magnetic Tape Compression   The capacities of magnetic tape drives are generally specified using two figures, such as 40 GB to 80 GB. These numbers refer to the capacity of a tape without compression and with compression. Most tape drives have hardware-based data compression capabilities built into them, but the additional capacity that you achieve when using compression is based on the type of data you are storing. The capacity figures cited by drive manufacturers assume an average compression ratio of 2:1, which is the typical amount of compression achieved with executables and other types of application files. Some file types, such as image files that use uncompressed BMP or TIF formats, can compress at much higher ratios, as high as 8:1. However, files that are already compressed, such as GIF and JPG image files or ZIP archives, cannot be compressed further and are stored at a 1:1 compression ratio.

Autochangers

In some cases, even the highest-capacity magnetic tape drive isn't sufficient to back up a large network with constantly changing data. A network might have an extraordinarily large amount of data to back up or an extremely small backup window to work with. To create an automated backup solution with a greater capacity than that provided by a single drive, you can purchase a device called an **autochanger**.

An *autochanger* (shown in Figure 4-2) is a hardware device that contains one or more drives (usually magnetic tape drives, but optical disk and CD-ROM autochangers are also available), a media array, and a robotic mechanism that swaps the media in and out of the drives. Sometimes these devices are called jukeboxes or tape libraries. When a backup job fills one tape (or other storage medium), the robotic mechanism extracts it from the drive and inserts another, after which the job continues. The autochanger also retains a memory of which tapes are available, commonly called an *index*, and can automatically load the appropriate tape needed to perform a restore job.

Figure 4-2   A magnetic tape autochanger

Some autochangers are small devices with a single drive and an array of four or five tapes, whereas others are enormous devices with four or more drives and an array of 100 tapes or more. If you purchase a large enough autochanger, you can create a long-term backup strategy that enables backups to run completely unattended for weeks at a time. However, before you solidify your plans to get a refrigerator-size autochanger and never load a tape into a drive by hand again, be aware that the cost of these devices can be astonishingly high, reaching well into six figures in some cases.

Drive Interface Selection

Backup devices can use any of the standard computer interfaces, such as Integrated Device Electronics (IDE), universal serial bus (USB), and Small Computer System Interface (SCSI), plus the newest interface to hit the mainstream, IEEE 1394 (FireWire). Some backup drives even connect to the computer's parallel port, although this is just a form of SCSI that uses a different port. The most common interface used in high-end network backup solutions is SCSI.

SCSI devices operate more independently than those using IDE, which means that the backup process, which might entail reading from one device while writing to another on the same interface, is more efficient. When two IDE devices share a channel, only one operates at a time. Each drive must receive, execute, and complete a command before the other drive can receive its next command. On the other hand, SCSI devices can maintain a queue of commands that they have received from the host adapter, and execute them sequentially and independently.

Magnetic tape drives, in particular, require a consistent stream of data to write to the tape with maximum effectiveness. If there are constant interruptions in the data stream, as can be the case with the IDE interface, the tape drive must repeatedly stop and start the tape (called *shoeshining*), which reduces its speed and its overall storage capacity. A SCSI drive can often operate continuously, without pausing to wait for the other devices on the channel.

A SCSI backup device is usually more expensive than a comparable IDE alternative because the drive requires additional electronics, and because you must have a SCSI host adapter installed in the computer. Most SCSI devices are available as internal or external units. The latter have their own power supplies, which also adds to the cost. However, the additional expense for SCSI is worth it for a fast, reliable network backup solution.

Backup Software

Apart from the hardware, the primary component in a network backup solution is the software that you use to perform the backups. Storage devices designed for use as dedicated backup solutions are not treated like the other storage subsystems in a computer; a specialized software product is required to gather the data that you want to back up, and to send it to the drive. Windows Server 2003 includes a backup software program that provides basic functionality for single-system backups, but as with most operating system backup programs, it lacks the advanced features that are required to effectively back up a complex network environment.

The primary functions of a good backup software product are examined in the following sections.

Target Selection

The most basic function of a backup software program is to let you select what you want to back up, which is sometimes called the *target*. A good backup program enables you to do this in many ways. In most cases, you can select:

- Entire computers
- Specific drives on a computer
- Specific folders on a drive
- Specific files in a folder

Using Tree Selection   Most backup programs provide a tree display that you can use to select the targets for a backup job. Figure 4-3 shows the interface that the Windows Server 2003 Backup program uses to select backup targets.

Figure 4-3   The Backup tab in the Windows Server 2003 Backup program

In nearly all cases, it is not necessary to back up all of the data on a computer's drives. If a hard drive is completely erased or destroyed, you are likely to have to reinstall the operating system before you can restore files from a backup tape, so it might not be worthwhile to back up all of the operating system files each time you run a backup job. The same is true for applications. You can reinstall an application from the original distribution media, so you might want to back up only your data files and configuration settings for that application. In addition, most operating systems today create temporary files as they run, which you do not need to back up. Windows, for example, creates a memory paging file that can be hundreds or thousands of megabytes in size. Because this file is automatically created, you can save space on your backup tapes by omitting it and files like it from your backup jobs. Judicious selection of backup targets can mean the difference between fitting an entire backup job onto one tape or staying late after work to insert a second tape into the drive.

Practice
selecting files
for backup
by doing
Exercise 4-1,
"Selecting
Backup
Targets," now.

Using Filters   Individually selecting the files, directories, and drives that you want to back up can be quite tedious on a large network installation, so many backup programs provide other ways to specify targets. One common method is to use filters that enable the software to evaluate each file and folder on a drive and decide whether to back it up. Backup software products that support filtering typically enable you to use the filters inclusively or exclusively; that is, a filter can identify the files you want to back up or the files you want to exclude from the backup.

A good backup program provides a variety of filters that enable you to select targets based on any of the following criteria:

- **File and folder name**   Specifying individual file and folder names using filters is not easier than using a tree display, but the ability to use wildcard characters in file and folder names makes this a powerful feature. You can use the standard question mark (?) and asterisk (*) to represent single characters and multiple characters, respectively. For example, creating an exclude filter using the file mask *.tmp would exclude all files with a .tmp extension (which is commonly used for temporary files) from the backup job.

- **File size**   Filtering based on file size enables you to exclude zero-length files from your backups or exclude extremely large files, such as the Pagefile.sys memory paging file.

- **File dates/times**   All file systems maintain at least one date and time for each file stored, typically specifying when the file was most recently modified. Some file systems, such as the Windows NTFS file system, include multiple dates and times for each file, such as when the file was created, when it was last accessed, and when it was last modified. Filtering based on these dates enables you to back up only the files that have changed since a given date and time, or only the files that are older than a certain date.

- **File attributes**   Attributes are 1-bit flags attached to files that specify characteristics about them. Most file systems support the four standard MS-DOS attributes, which are *H* for hidden, *R* for read-only, *S* for system, and *A* for archive, but some file systems include other attributes as well. Most backup programs rely primarily on archive attribute filtering for performing backups, which enables them to back up only the files that have changed since the last backup. This type of filter is the basis for **incremental** and **differential backup** jobs.

  NOTE   Windows Server 2003 Backup Filtering   The Windows Server 2003 Backup program enables you to create custom file and folder name filters to exclude specific files from a backup job, but it does not support inclusive filters or size, date/time, and attribute filters other than those provided in the standard backup job types.

Understanding Backup Job Types   Most, if not all, backup software products include a collection of standard backup job types that are actually preset filter combinations. For example, the Windows Server 2003 Backup program enables you to select from the following five job types (as shown in Figure 4-4):

- **Normal**   Backs up all files to the storage medium and resets each file's **archive bit** to indicate that the file has been backed up

- **Copy**   Backs up all files to the storage medium and does not reset their archive bits

- **Differential**   Backs up only the files that have changed since the last normal backup and does not reset their archive bits

- **Incremental**   Backs up only the files that have changed since the last normal or incremental backup and resets their archive bits

- **Daily**   Backs up only the files that were created or modified today and does not reset their archive bits

Figure 4-4   The Backup Type tab in the Windows Server 2003 Backup program's Options dialog box

The most basic type of backup job is a *full backup* (called a *normal job* by Windows Server 2003 Backup), which copies the entire set of selected targets to the tape or other backup medium. You can perform a full backup every day, if you want to, or each time that you back up a particular computer. However, this practice can be impractical for any of the following reasons:

- **There is too much data to back up.**   The hard drives that are typically included in today's computers hold more data than ever, and on a large network, total storage capacity can easily add up to thousands of gigabytes. Unless you want to spend an enormous amount of money on tape drive and autochanger hardware, it is not feasible to back up all of the data in every computer every day.

- **There is not enough time to perform the backups.**   Most network administrators schedule network backup jobs to occur at night or when-ever the organization is closed. Backing up during off hours makes it less likely for the backup to skip files because they are locked open, and it minimizes the impact of the network traffic generated by remote backup processes. For some organizations, the amount of time available to per-form backups is insufficient to back up the entire network unless multiple high-speed drives are used.

- **There is too much redundant data.**   Much of the data stored on a typical computer's hard drive is static; it does not change every day. Application and operating system files never change, and some document files can go for long periods without users changing them. Backing up files such as these every day means saving the same data to tape over and over, which is a waste of time and media.

    TIP   **Server-Based Storage**   Ease of backup is one of the primary reasons that many network administrators insist that users store their data files on servers rather than on their local hard drives. By giving each user a home directory on a server, it is possible to back up everyone's data files with a single server backup rather than having to configure the backup software to connect to each individual workstation every day.

To save tape and shorten the backup time, many administrators perform full backups only once a week or even less frequently. In between the full backups, they perform special types of filtered jobs that back up only the files that have recently been modified. These types of jobs are called incremental backups and differential backups. An incremental backup is a job that backs up only the files that have changed since the last backup job of any kind. A differential backup is a job that backs up only the files that have changed since the last full backup. The backup software filters the files for these jobs using the archive attribute, also known as the *archive bit*, which every file on the computer possesses.

The archive bit does not actually modify a file's functionality, as the read-only and hidden attributes do; it is simply a marker that backup software uses to determine whether to back up each file. The state of the archive bit during a typical sequence of backup jobs is as follows:

1. When a file is written to a computer's hard disk for the first time, its archive bit is activated, meaning that it is set to a value of 1.

2. During the first full backup you perform on the computer, the software backs up the entire contents of the computer's drive and also resets (that is, sets to a value of 0) the archive bit on all of the files. At this point, you have a complete backup of the drive on tape, and none of the files on the drive has an active archive bit.

3. Whenever a file on the drive is modified by any application or process, the file system reactivates the archive bit.

4. For the next backup, you perform an incremental or differential job. The backup software scans the archive bits of all the files on the drive and backs up only the files with active bits. At this point, you have a full backup of the entire drive and a backup of all the files that have changed since that full backup. If a disaster occurs, causing the entire contents of the drive to be lost, you can return it to its current state by performing a restore from the full backup tape and then restoring the incremental or differential tape, allowing the changed versions of the files to overwrite the original versions.

Because incremental and differential jobs back up only part of the drive's contents, they run faster and take up less tape than full backups. A typical network backup strategy consists of a full backup on one day of the week and an incremental or differential job on the other days. With this arrangement, you can always restore the drive to a state no more than 24 hours old.

The difference between an incremental job and a differential job lies in the behavior of the backup software when it either resets or does not reset the archive bits of the files it copies to tape. Incremental jobs reset the archive bits, and differential jobs do not. Running incremental or differential jobs is often what makes it possible to automate your backup regimen without spending too much on hardware. If your full backup job totals 50 GB, for example, you might be able to purchase a 20-GB drive. You'll have to manually insert two additional tapes during your full backup jobs, once a week, but you should be able to run incremental or differential jobs the rest of the week using only one tape for each one, which means that the jobs can run unattended.

Using Incremental Backups   This means that when you run an incremental job, you're backing up only the files that have changed since the last backup, whether it was a full backup or an incremental backup. Performing incrementals between your full backups uses the least amount of tape, but it also lengthens the restore process. If you have to restore an entire computer, you must first perform a restore from the last full backup tape, and then you must restore each of the incremental jobs you performed since the last full backup.

For example, consider the backup schedule shown in Table 4-2.

Table 4-2   Sample Incremental Backup Schedule

Day	Job Type	Files Included in Job
Sunday	Full	Data1.txt, Data2.txt, Data3.txt
Monday	Incremental	Data1.txt
Tuesday	Incremental	Data1.txt, Data3.txt
Wednesday	Incremental	Data1.txt, Data2.txt
Thursday	Incremental	Data1.txt, Data3.txt
Friday	Incremental	Data1.txt
Saturday	Incremental	Data1.txt

The Sunday backup is the only complete copy of the computer's drive, and each of the incrementals consists of only the files that have changed during the previous 24 hours. Because Data1.txt changes every day, it appears in every one of the incremental backups. The file's archive bit is activated each time it changes, and each incremental backup resets the bit again. Data2.txt changes only once, on Wednesday, so it appears only in the full backup job and in Wednesday's incremental. Data3.txt changes twice, on Tuesday and Thursday, so it appears in the full backup and in Tuesday's and Thursday's incrementals.

If the computer's drive were to malfunction on Friday, causing all of its data to be lost, you would begin the restoration process by restoring the most recent Sunday full backup, and then you would restore the Monday, Tuesday, Wednesday, and Thursday incrementals that followed the full backup, in that order. The results of the restorations on the three data files would be as follows:

- **Data1.txt**   The original copy from the full restore would be overwritten by a newer copy during each incremental restore, leaving the newest (Thursday) version on the drive when the restoration process is complete.

- **Data2.txt**   The original copy from Sunday's full restore would remain on the drive until the restoration of the Wednesday incremental tape, at which time the newest (Wednesday) version would overwrite the Sunday version. The Wednesday version would be left on the drive when the restoration process is complete.

- **Data3.txt**   The original copy from Sunday's full restore would be overwritten twice, first by the version on the Tuesday incremental tape and then by the Thursday version, leaving the latest (Thursday) version on the drive when the restoration process is complete.

NOTE   Restoring Incrementals   When you restore from incrementals, the order of the tapes you restore is crucial. You must restore the incrementals in the order they were written, or you might end up with old versions of files overwriting the newer versions.

Using Differential Backups   If you were to perform the same sequence of backups using differential jobs instead of incrementals, the results would be like those in Table 4-3.

Table 4-3   **Sample Differential Backup Schedule**

Day	Job Type	Files Included in Job
Sunday	Full	Data1.txt, Data2.txt, Data3.txt
Monday	Differential	Data1.txt
Tuesday	Differential	Data1.txt, Data3.txt
Wednesday	Differential	Data1.txt, Data2.txt, Data3.txt
Thursday	Differential	Data1.txt, Data2.txt, Data3.txt
Friday	Differential	Data1.txt, Data2.txt, Data3.txt
Saturday	Differential	Data1.txt, Data2.txt, Data3.txt

Because the Data1.txt files changes every day, it appears in every differential job, just as it appeared in every incremental. However, because differential jobs do not reset the archive bits on the files they back up, once a file appears in a differential, it appears in every subsequent differential until the next full backup. Therefore, the Data2.txt file that first appears in the Wednesday incremental is also backed up on Thursday, Friday, and Saturday because its archive bit is still active. In the same way, the Data3.txt file that first appears in Tuesday's differential also appears in all of the subsequent differentials, but starting on Thursday, it is a newer version that is backed up each night. The archive bits for all three files are not reset until the next full backup, on the following Sunday.

When you use differential backups, the jobs take a bit longer and they use a bit more tape because in some cases you are backing up the same files several days in a row. However, restoring from differentials is simpler and faster because you only have to restore the last full backup and the most recent differential. If the drive in this example were to fail on a Saturday, you would only have to restore the full backup from the previous Sunday and the previous day's (Friday's) differential. The Friday tape would have the Data1.txt, Data2.txt, and Data3.txt files on it. The version of Data1.txt would be Friday's, Data2.txt would be Wednesday's version, and Data3.txt would be Thursday's version.

Test your understanding of incremental and differential backups by doing Exercise 4-2, "Incremental and Differential Backups," now.

Using Copy Jobs and Daily Jobs   All backup software programs enable you to perform full, incremental, and differential backups, but Windows Server 2003 Backup includes two additional job types that are not necessarily found in all other software products. A daily job uses a filter based on the date rather than the archive bit to back up only the files that were created or changed on the day the job is run. A copy job is identical to a full backup job except that the software does not modify the archive bits of the files it copies to tape. You can use copy jobs to perform additional full backups at any time, such as for offsite storage, without disturbing your regular sequence of full and incremental or differential jobs.

> **NOTE** **Backup Job Names** Just as the Windows Server 2003 Backup program refers to full backups as normal jobs, it is not unusual for other backup software programs to use different names when referring to the basic job types.

Job Scheduling

All backup products enable you to create a backup job and execute it immediately, but the key to automating a backup routine is being able to schedule jobs to execute unattended. Not all of the backup programs supplied with operating systems or designed for standalone computers support scheduling, but all network backup software products do.

> **NOTE** **Exam Objectives** The objectives for the 70-290 examination state that students should be able to "schedule backup jobs."

Most organizations perform incremental or differential backups daily, and a full backup once a week. This arrangement provides a good compromise between sufficient protection and the amount of time and media devoted to backups. The ideal situation for a backup administrator is having each daily incremental or differential job fit on a single tape. This enables the administrator to schedule the job to run unattended when the office is closed and the network is idle. As a result, all resources are available for backup and user productivity is not compromised by the sudden surge of network traffic caused by the backup process, and there is no need to have someone change media. Once you have created the backup schedule, you can simply insert the correct tape into the drive each day. Full backups might require more than one tape, so someone might have to be there to change media.

> **TIP** **Selecting Backup Hardware** The ability to create an unattended backup schedule is a key factor to consider when you evaluate backup hardware products. Before selecting a drive, you should estimate the amount of data you will have to back up each day (allowing some leeway for growth) and look at drives that can store at least that much data on a single tape.

Backup programs use various methods to automatically execute backup jobs. The Windows Server 2003 Backup program adds its jobs to the operating system's Scheduled Tasks list; other programs supply their own program or service that runs continuously and triggers the jobs at the appropriate times. Some of the higher-end network backup products can use a directory service such as Microsoft's Active Directory or Novell's eDirectory for scheduling. These programs modify the directory schema (the code that specifies the types of objects that can exist in the directory) to create an object representing a queue of jobs waiting to be executed.

No matter which mechanism the backup software uses to launch jobs, the process of scheduling them is usually the same. You specify whether you want to execute the job once or repeatedly at a specified time each day, week, or month, using an interface like the one from the Windows Server 2003 Backup program (shown in Figure 4-5). The idea of the scheduling feature is for the network administrator to create a logical sequence of backup jobs that execute by themselves at regular intervals. After the administrator does this, the only action required is to change the tape in the drive each day. If you have an autochanger, you can even eliminate this part of the job and create a backup job sequence that runs for weeks or months without any attention at all.

Figure 4-5   The Windows Server 2003 Backup program's Schedule Job dialog box

Maintaining Backup Logs

When a backup job runs, the software accesses the specified targets and feeds the data to the backup drive in the appropriate manner. Because of the nature of the media typically used for backups, it is important for the data to arrive at the storage device in a consistent manner and at the proper rate of speed. The software, therefore, must be designed to address specific drives in the manner appropriate for that device.

As the software feeds the data to the drive, it also keeps track of the software's activities. Most backup software products can maintain a log of the backup process as it occurs. You can often specify a level of detail for the log, such as whether it should contain a complete list of every file backed up or just record the major events that occur during the job. The Backup program in Windows Server 2003 uses the interface shown in Figure 4-6 to specify whether the program should keep a detailed log, a summary, or no log at all.

Figure 4-6   The Backup Log tab in the Windows Server 2003 Backup program's Options dialog box

In most cases, a detailed log of your backup jobs is not necessary. This type of log typically contains a list of every file that the program has backed up (as shown in Figure 4-7), and since backup jobs can consist of many thousands of files, a detailed log can be very long and the pertinent entries (such as errors) difficult to find. It is also important to keep an eye on the size of your log files, particularly when you configure them to maintain a high level of detail. These files can grow huge very quickly and can consume all of the available disk space on the drive on which they are stored.

Figure 4-7   A Windows Server 2003 backup log

Periodically checking the logs is an essential part of administering a network backup program. The logs tell you when selected files are skipped for any reason, such as when the files are locked open by an application or the computers on which they are stored are unreachable. The logs also let you know when errors occur on either the backup drive or one of the computers involved in the backup process. Some software products can generate alerts when errors occur, notifying you by sending a status message to a network management console, by sending you an e-mail message, or by other methods.

> **NOTE   Exam Objectives**   The objectives for the 70-290 examination state that students should be able to "verify the successful completion of backup jobs."

Cataloging

In addition to logging their activities, backup software programs also catalog the files they back up, thus facilitating the process of restoring files later. The catalog is essentially a list of every file that the software has backed up during each job. To restore files from the backup medium, you browse through the catalog and select the files, folders, or drives that you want to restore. Different backup software products store the catalog in different ways. Lower-end backup programs, such as those intended for stand-alone computers, store the catalog for each tape on the tape itself. The problem with this method is that you have to insert a tape into the drive to read the catalog and browse the files on that tape.

More elaborate network backup software programs take a different approach by maintaining a database of the catalogs for all of your backup media on the computer where the backup software is installed. This database enables you to browse through the catalogs for all of your tapes and select any version of any file or folder for restoration. In some cases, you can view the contents of the database in several different ways, such as by the computer, drive, and folder where the files were originally located, by the backup job, or by the tape or other media name. After you make your selection, the program specifies which tape contains the file or folder; you insert it into the drive, and the restore job proceeds.

The database feature can use a lot of the computer's disk space and processor cycles, but it greatly enhances the usability of the software, particularly in a network environment.

> **NOTE   Backup Databases**   Backup software products that rely on a database typically store a copy of the database on your tapes as well as on the computer's hard drive. This is done so that if the computer you use to run the backups suffers a drive failure, you can restore the database later. Many products also enable you to rebuild the database on a computer by reading the contents of a tape and assimilating its index into a new database file.

Media Rotation

Some fastidious administrators use new tapes for every backup job and store them all permanently. However, this practice can be extremely expensive. It is more common for administrators to reuse backup tapes. To do this properly, however, you must have a carefully planned media rotation scheme so that you don't inadvertently overwrite a tape you might need later. You can always create such a scheme yourself, but some backup software products do it for you.

> **NOTE   Exam Objectives**   The objectives for the 70-290 examination state that students should be able to "manage backup storage media."

One of the most common media rotation schemes is called the Grandfather-Father-Son method. In this method, the terms *grandfather*, *father*, and *son* refer to monthly, weekly, and daily tapes, respectively. For daily backups, you have one set of "son" tapes that you reuse every week. For the weekly full backup, you have "father" tapes that you reuse every month. Then, every month, you perform an additional full backup to tapes in your "grandfather" set, which you reuse every year. This method enables you to perform a complete restore at any time and maintains a year's history of your files. There are also other schemes that vary in complexity and utility, depending on the software product.

When the software program implements the rotation scheme, it provides a basic schedule for the jobs (which you can modify to have the jobs execute at specific times of the day), tells you what name to write on each tape as you use it, and once you begin to reuse tapes, tells you which tape to put in the drive for each job. The end result is that you maintain a perpetual record of your data while using the minimum number of tapes and without fear of overwriting a tape you need.

Device Configuration

Because dedicated backup drives are accessible only using specialized programs, most backup software products include an interface that enables you to manipulate the drive directly, to perform tasks such as the following:

- **Tape formatting**   All tapes must be formatted before a backup software program can write to them. Most backup software products automatically format new tapes at the beginning of a backup job, but it is also possible to format them manually. Different types of magnetic tape cartridges require different types of formatting. Some formats require the entire tape to be overwritten, while others require only a new header at the beginning of the tape. Formatting overwrites any existing data on the tape.

- **Tape erasing**   Erasing a tape is sometimes simply a matter of reformatting it because the reformatting process overwrites the entire length of the tape in the cartridge. For other types of tapes, reformatting is just the replacement of a header, which leaves the rest of the data on the tape intact. Most network backup software products enable you to erase the data from any tape, for security purposes, by overwriting its entire length. This does not necessarily mean that the data is unrecoverable by any means, but the backup software itself can't read the erased data from the tape.

- **Tape retensioning**   Some types of magnetic tapes can benefit from retensioning, in which the drive runs the tape all the way to its end and back again, to ensure that the entire length of the tape is wound onto the spool with a consistent amount of tension. Software products that are capable of retensioning tapes typically do so only for the types of tape that can benefit from the process.

- **Drive compression**   Most magnetic tape drives manufactured today include data compression capabilities implemented in their hardware, and backup software programs frequently provide the capability to select whether the drive's hardware compression circuitry is turned on or off. Some backup programs also have their own software-based compression routines for use with devices that do not support hardware compression. However, the use of hardware compression is always preferable to software compression because software compression places an additional burden on the computer's processor.

Performing Restores

Restoring data from your backups is, of course, the sole reason for making the backups in the first place. The ease with which you can locate the files you need to restore is an important feature of any backup software product. It is absolutely essential that you perform periodic test restores from your backup tapes or other media to ensure that you can get back any data that is lost. Even if all your jobs seem to complete successfully and your log files show that all of your data has been backed up, there is no more reliable test of a backup system than an actual restore. There are plenty of horror stories about administrators who dutifully performed their backups every day, only to find out when disaster struck that all their carefully labeled tapes were blank due to a malfunctioning drive.

> **NOTE**   **Exam Objectives**   *The objectives for the 70-290 examination state that students should be able to "restore backup data."*

Although performing regular backups is usually thought of as protection against a disaster that causes you to lose an entire hard drive, the majority of the restore jobs you will perform in a network environment are of one or a few files that a user has inadvertently deleted. As mentioned earlier, your backup software's cataloging capability is a critical part of the restoration process. If a user needs to have one particular file restored and you have to insert tape after tape into the drive to locate it, everyone's time is wasted. A backup program with a database that lets you search for that particular file makes your job much easier and enables you to restore any file in minutes.

Restore jobs are similar to backup jobs in that you select the files or folders that you want to restore, using an interface like that shown in Figure 4-8. When you create a restore job, a good backup software product typically enables you to configure the following parameters:

- **File selection**   You should be able to select any combination of files, folders, or drives on any tape. Some software products enable you to switch between a media view, which displays the contents of each tape in the library, and a disk view, which displays your backup targets and a list of the multiple versions of each file available on your various tapes.

- **Restore location**   You should be able to restore your selected files to their original locations automatically or specify an alternative location; you should also be able to re-create the original directory tree or dump all the files into a single folder.

- **Overwrite options**   When restoring files to their original locations, you should be able to specify rules for overwriting existing files with the same names, based on their dates or using other criteria.

Figure 4-8   The Windows Server 2003 Backup program's Restore And Manage Media tab

Optional Network Backup Features

When you are developing a backup solution for a network, it is particularly important that you choose a backup software product that is designed for network use. The primary difference between network backup software and an application designed for standalone systems is that the former can back up other computers on the network. This means you can purchase one backup drive and use it to protect your entire network. Many standalone backup products can access drives on networked computers, but a fully functional network backup product can also back up important operating system features on other computers, such as the Windows registry and directory service databases. This type of remote backup might require you to install an additional software component on the target computer.

In many cases, network backup products also have additional components that enable you to perform specialized backup tasks, such as backing up live databases or computers running other operating systems. Some of these components are described in the following sections.

> **NOTE   Add-On Components**   In many cases, network backup software packages include only the basic components described in the previous sections. To add the greater functionality described in the following sections, you must purchase the other components as separate add-on modules that work together with the main backup engine.

Remote Backup Agents

Virtually all backup software products can back up shared drives on computers other than the one running the software, but this does not mean that they should be considered network backup software products. A true backup is one that can restore a drive that has been completely erased back to its previous state. Accessing a remote Windows computer through a drive or folder share theoretically enables you to back up everything that appears in the file system, but you cannot access elements such as the Windows registry or an Active Directory database in this way. Therefore, a backup of the share would be incomplete and could not be used to restore the remote computer to its original state.

In the Windows Server 2003 Backup program, you select a target called the System State (as shown in Figure 4-9) to back up the following elements on the local computer:

- System boot files
- System files under Windows File Protection
- Windows registry
- COM+ Class Registration database
- Active Directory directory service (domain controllers only)
- Sysvol directory (domain controllers only)
- Cluster service information (cluster nodes only)
- Internet Information Services (IIS) metadirectory (IIS servers only)
- Certificate Services database (certification authorities only)

> **NOTE   Backing Up and Restoring the System State**   You can back up and restore the System State only as a single object. You cannot, for example, restore only the Windows registry database from a System State backup and not the other elements in the object, such as the system boot files.

Figure 4-9   Backing up the System State object

However, in Windows Server 2003 you cannot back up the System State object on a computer other than the one running the Backup program.

Using most network backup software products, you can back up these system elements on remote computers, but in most cases, you must install a software component—typically called an *agent*—on them first. The agent enables the backup server to establish contact with the remote system and download the operating system elements needed to perform a complete backup of the computer's drives.

> **NOTE   Purchasing Agents**   Backup products can differ in the remote backup agents they include with the base product. For example, when you buy a product that runs the main backup engine on a Windows Server 2003 computer, the product might include the agent needed to back up other Windows computers on the network. However, if you have computers running other operating systems, you might have to purchase agents for those platforms separately.

Open File Backup

In many cases, when an application opens a document file, the file is locked open so that no other application or process can access it. This is to prevent another program from modifying the disk copy of a file that is currently in memory. One of the main reasons why administrators prefer to perform backups after hours is to prevent files from being skipped over because they are locked open by users. However, if a user leaves an application running with a file open, the backup can still fail to protect that file. To address this problem, some backup software products have open file capabilities that make it possible to back up certain types of files even when another application has them open.

Database Backup

Databases are a common backup problem, both because they often contain vital data that needs protection and because they frequently have to be left running around the clock. Databases that are running typically lock their data files open like any other application, enabling standard backup jobs to protect the database program files (that are easily replaceable) but skip the databases themselves.

▶ Backing Up a Database

To back up a database, you have to shut it down to unlock the open data files. In cases where shutting down the application is impossible because the database must remain available to users, many backup software products have specialized database agents that make it possible to back up the database using a procedure like the following:

1. The agent creates a temporary copy of the database file called a *delta file*.

2. The agent redirects all client requests for database information to the delta file.

3. The agent closes the original database file.

4. The agent communicates with the backup server and transmits the contents of the database file for backup to tape.

5. After the backup is complete, the agent copies any changes made to the delta file by clients back to the original database file.

6. The agent reopens the database file.

7. The agent directs the incoming client requests back to the original database file.

8. The agent deletes the delta file.

Disaster Recovery

As with any application, a backup software product requires an operating system in order to run. If the system drive of your backup server fails, you might have a full backup of the drive, but how do you restore it? Under normal conditions, you would have to reinstall the operating system and then reinstall the backup software before you could restore the drive back to its original condition. For an organization in which server down time means lost revenue, this delay might be intolerable.

> **NOTE**   **Exam Objectives**   *The objectives for the 70-290 examination state that students should be able to "perform system recovery for a server" and "recover from server hardware failure."*

Some backup software products can circumvent this problem by providing a disaster recovery feature. Disaster recovery software is designed to enable administrators to perform a complete restore of a computer's system drive in as little time as possible. The software creates a full backup in combination with a boot disk that contains only the operating system files needed to run the backup program and perform a restore. After booting from the disk, you can perform the restore, and the computer is back to its original condition much more quickly than if you had to install the operating system manually.

The Windows Server 2003 Backup program contains a disaster recovery feature called Automated System Recovery (ASR). The Automated System Recovery Preparation Wizard (as shown in Figure 4-10) backs up the System State data, system services, and all disks associated with the operating system components. It also creates a floppy disk, which contains information about the backup, the disk configurations (including basic and dyanmic volumes), and how to accomplish a restore.

Figure 4-10   The Automated System Recovery Preparation Wizard

> **NOTE**   **Exam Objectives**   *The objectives for the 70-290 examination state that students should be able to "implement Automated System Recovery (ASR)."*

Backup Security

Backups contain copies of the same data you have stored on your hard drives, so you should take the same pains to secure the backups that you do with the original files. Network backup programs enable you to specify an account name and password that the software should use to access the backup targets. The best practice is to create a special account for this purpose that has only the privileges needed to perform the backups rather than use the Administrator account or some other, more comprehensive credentials. You can easily provide a user account with these privileges by adding it to the built-in Backup Operators group in Active Directory. This prevents unauthorized users from penetrating the security of the network using the backup software.

> **NOTE**   **Exam Objectives**   *The objectives for the 70-290 examination state that students should be able to "configure security for backup operations."*

To keep your data secure, you must also protect the files on the backup tapes themselves. Network backup software products typically enable you to password-protect your backup tapes. You specify a password during the creation of the backup job, and you must then use that same password to restore files from the backup. When password-protecting your tapes, you should use the same password requirements that you have imposed on your network, such as passwords of a specified length and complexity.

You should also physically secure your backup tapes, not only for data security but also for safekeeping. Password protection might prevent the casual intruder from restoring data on your tapes using the backup software, but the data still exists on the tape in an unprotected format, and someone with sufficient skill and equipment could still access the files. Therefore, you should always keep your backup tapes locked up, preferably in a fireproof safe or other secure storage area. You should also be sure to store copies of your backups offsite so that a theft or a disaster doesn't cause your backup tapes to be lost along with your computers.

USING WINDOWS SERVER 2003 BACKUP

The Backup program included with Windows Server 2003 is not a full-featured network backup software package as described earlier in this chapter, but it is certainly sufficient for backing up the server itself. With the Backup program, you can perform the following tasks:

- Back up local drives, network shares, and the local System State object
- Select backup targets using a tree display
- Perform normal, incremental, differential, copy, or daily backup jobs
- Exclude specific file masks from a backup job
- Back up files to a tape drive or to a file on a local disk, which you can then transfer to a CD-ROM, DVD-ROM, or other medium
- Schedule backups to occur at a specific time or at regular intervals
- Verify backups by comparing the image on the backup medium to the original target
- Restore backed-up files to their original locations or to alternate locations
- Specify when and if restored files should overwrite existing ones

Some of the other backup-related features that Windows Server 2003 provides are discussed in the following sections.

Using Volume Shadow Copy

Volume shadow copy is a Windows Server 2003 feature that maintains a library containing multiple versions of selected files. Although not a replacement for system backups, volume shadow copy enables users to access saved versions of files they have accidentally damaged or deleted. This eliminates one of the most onerous chores of the backup administrator: performing single file restores for users who have inadvertently deleted their own files.

> **NOTE   Exam Objectives**   The objectives for the 70-290 examination state that students should be able to "restore data from shadow copy volumes."

To enable volume shadow copy for a volume on your server, you display the Local Disk Properties dialog box for the volume and select the Shadow Copies tab (as shown in Figure 4-11). When you select a volume in the list and click Enable, Windows Server 2003 makes a copy of all the files in shared folders on that volume and stamps the copies with the current date and time. As long as shadow copying is enabled for that volume, Windows Server 2003 continues to make two copies of these files each weekday and saves them until the amount of space designated for volume shadow copies is full. You can modify both the frequency with which the Windows operating system makes copies and the size of the space used to store the copies.

IMPORTANT   *Volume Shadow Copy Limitations*   *Volume shadow copy only protects the files on the volume that are stored in shared folders, and that volume must use the NTFS file system.*

Figure 4-11   The Shadow Copies tab in a volume's Local Disk Properties dialog box

Only computers running Windows Server 2003 and Windows XP can access the shadow copies of files on your designated volumes. On Windows XP workstations, you must first install the client software that makes this possible. Then, a user can access shadow copies by displaying the Properties dialog box for a file in a shadow volume and selecting the Previous Versions tab (as shown in Figure 4-12).

Figure 4-12   The Previous Versions tab in a file's Properties dialog box

NOTE   *Volume Shadow Copy Clients*   *Windows Server 2003 includes the client software for volume shadow copy in its Systemroot\System32\Clients\Twclient folder. You can deploy the software by installing it manually on the Windows XP clients or by using an automated method, such as group policies.*

In addition to providing users with access to multiple versions of their files, volume shadow copy also functions as an open file backup mechanism for the Windows Server 2003 Backup program. By default, Backup uses volume shadow copies of files that are locked open when performing backups. This enables the program to back up files that are in use by an application at the time the backup is performed. You can prevent Backup from using volume shadow copy during a particular backup job by selecting the Disable Volume Shadow Copy check box in the Advanced Backup Options dialog box (as shown in Figure 4-13).

Figure 4-13   The Advanced Backup Options dialog box

Backing Up and Restoring Active Directory

As mentioned earlier in this chapter, you can back up the Active Directory database on a Windows Server 2003 domain controller using the Backup program by selecting the System State object as one of the backup targets. However, restoring Active Directory to a domain controller is not so simple. Before you can restore the Active Directory database from a System State backup, you must start the computer in Directory Services Restore Mode. You do this by pressing F8 as the system starts and selecting Directory Services Restore Mode from the Windows Advanced Options menu. This starts the computer with the Active Directory database closed, so that it is accessible to the Backup program and can be restored from a tape.

> **NOTE** **Logging On**   When you restart the computer in Directory Services Restore Mode, you must log on as an Administrator by using a valid Security Accounts Manager (SAM) account name and password, *not* the Active Directory Administrator's name and password. This is because Active Directory is offline, and account verification cannot occur. The SAM accounts database is used to control access to Active Directory while Active Directory is offline. You specified this password when you set up Active Directory.

Once the computer is started in Directory Services Restore Mode, you can run the Backup program and restore the System State object from your tape or other medium. The Windows Server 2003 Backup program supports two types of Active Directory restores:

- **Nonauthoritative restore**   The objects in the Active Directory database are restored exactly as they appear in the System State object, with their

Practice enabling volume shadow copy on your Windows Server 2003 computer by doing Exercise 4-3, "Enabling Volume Shadow Copies," now.

original update sequence numbers intact. Because these sequence numbers are the same values the objects had when the backup was performed, they are outdated, and the Active Directory replication process will overwrite the objects with the newer versions from other domain controllers. You use a nonauthoritative restore when you want to rebuild a domain controller that has been damaged with the latest Active Directory information from your other domain controllers. Windows Server 2003 Backup performs nonauthoritative restores by default.

- **Authoritative restore**   The objects in the Active Directory database are restored with updated sequence numbers that prevent them from being overwritten during the next replication pass. You use an authoritative restore when you want to use a System State backup to recover Active Directory objects that have been accidentally deleted.

To perform a nonauthoritative restore, you simply restore the System State object using the Backup program while in Directory Services Restore Mode.

To perform an authoritative restore, you first perform a nonauthoritative restore, and then before restarting the computer, you use a command-line utility called Ndsutil.exe to mark specific Active Directory objects as authoritative. The Ntdsutil.exe utility can be found in the *Systemroot*\System32 folder. Marking objects as authoritative changes the update sequence number of an object so it is higher than any other update sequence number in the Active Directory replication system. This ensures that any replicated or distributed data that you have restored is properly replicated throughout your organization.

When the restored domain controller is online and connected to the network, normal replication brings the restored domain controller up-to-date with any changes from the additional domain controllers that were not overridden by the authoritative restore. Replication also propagates the authoritatively restored object(s) to other domain controllers in the forest. The deleted objects that were marked as authoritative are replicated from the restored domain controller to the additional domain controllers. Because the objects that are restored have the same object properties, security remains intact and object dependencies are maintained.

For example, suppose you back up the system on Monday and then create a new user called Jeff Smith on Tuesday, which replicates to other domain controllers in the domain. Then, on Wednesday, you accidentally delete Nancy Anderson's user object. To authoritatively restore the Nancy Anderson user without reentering information and without losing the Jeff Smith account, you perform a nonauthoritative restore of the domain controller with the backup created on Monday. Then, using Ntdsutil.exe, you mark Nancy Anderson's user object as authoritative and restart the domain controller. The result is that Nancy Anderson's object is restored without any effect on Jeff Smith.

NOTE Exam Objectives   The objectives for the 70-290 examination state that students should be able to "back up files and System State data to media."

SUMMARY

- A network backup solution consists of backup hardware, backup software, and a plan for using them.

- When you evaluate backup hardware, higher speed and greater capacity nearly always mean higher price.

- Magnetic tape is the most popular storage medium for backups because it is fast, inexpensive, and holds a lot of data. Tape drives are available in a variety of speeds, capacities, and price ranges to suit the needs of different installations.

- The primary function of the backup software is to enable the administrator to select the targets for backup and then send them to the tape drive or other device.

- Incremental and differential backup jobs save tape by backing up only the files that have changed since the last backup, based on the status of each file's archive bit.

- A good backup software program enables you to schedule jobs to execute at any time, and it maintains both a tape version and a hard disk version of a catalog of all of the files that have been backed up.

- Network backup software enables you to back up data from computers anywhere on the network, and it might also provide optional features such as live database backups.

- To back up the Windows registry, the Active Directory database, and other system resources, you must back up the System State object.

- Volume shadow copy is a Window Server 2003 feature that enables users to access multiple copies of files that they have accidentally deleted or damaged.

- When you restore the System State data in nonauthoritative mode, any component of the System State data that is replicated with another domain controller, such as the Active Directory database, is brought up-to-date by replication after you restore the data.

- When you restore the System State data in authoritative mode, changes that were made since the last backup operation are not restored; the deleted objects are recovered and replicated. To perform an authoritative restore, you use the Ntdsutil.exe command-line utility.

EXERCISES

Exercise 4-1: Selecting Backup Targets

In this exercise, you practice using the Backup program's tree display to select backup targets.

1. Log on to Windows Server 2003 as Administrator.

2. Click Start, point to All Programs, point to Accessories, point to System Tools, and click Backup. The Welcome To The Backup Or Restore Wizard page appears.

3. Click the Advanced Mode hyperlink. The Backup Utility window appears.

4. Select the Backup tab.

5. Expand the Local Disk (C:) object and select the check box for the Windows folder.

6. Select the System State check box.

7. From the Job menu, select Exit.

Exercise 4-2: Incremental and Differential Backups

1. If you back up your network by performing a full backup every Wednesday at 6 P.M. and differential backups in the evening on the other six days of the week, how many jobs would be needed to completely restore a computer with a hard drive that failed on a Tuesday at noon?

2. If you back up your network by performing a full backup every Wednesday at 6 P.M., how many jobs would be needed if you performed incremental backups in the evening of the other six days of the week and a hard drive failed on a Tuesday at noon?

3. For a complete restore of a computer that failed at noon on Tuesday, how many jobs would be needed if you performed full backups at 6 A.M. every Wednesday and Saturday and incremental backups at 6 A.M. every other day?

Exercise 4-3: Enabling Volume Shadow Copies

In this exercise, you enable the volume shadow copy feature for your computer's C: drive.

1. Log on to Windows Server 2003 as Administrator.

2. Click Start, point to All Programs, point to Accessories, and click Windows Explorer. The Windows Explorer window appears.

3. Expand the My Computer object in the scope pane, select Local Disk (C:), and from the File menu, select Properties. The Local Disk (C:) Properties dialog box appears.

4. Select the Shadow Copies tab, and then click Enable. The Enable Shadow Copies message box appears.

5. Read the warning message and click Yes. After a brief delay, the date and time appear in the Shadow Copies Of Selected Volume list, indicating that the system has created the first shadow copy.

REVIEW QUESTIONS

1. Why is it best to perform backups when the organization is closed?

2. Which of the following backup job types does not reset the archive bits on the files that it copies to the backup medium? (Choose all correct answers.)

    a. Full

    b. Incremental

    c. Differential

    d. Copy

3. Which of the following tape drive devices has the greatest capacity?

    a. LTO

    b. QIC

    c. DAT

    d. DLT

4. Which of the following is the criterion most commonly used to filter files for backup jobs?

    a. Filename

    b. File extension

    c. File attributes

    d. File size

5. How does an autochanger increase the overall storage capacity of a backup solution?

6. What are the three elements of the Grandfather-Father-Son media rotation system?

    a. Hard disk drives, CD-ROM drives, and magnetic tape drives

    b. Incremental, differential, and full backup jobs

    c. Monthly, weekly, and daily backup jobs

    d. QIC, DAT, and DLT tape drives

7. Network backup devices most commonly use which drive interface?

    a. IDE

    b. SCSI

    c. USB

    d. Parallel port

8. How does Windows Backup verify the data written to the backup medium?

9. When you restart the computer in Directory Services Restore Mode, what logon must you use? Why?

CASE SCENARIO

You are designing a backup solution for your company network. To make it easier to back up valuable company data, you have supplied each of the network's 125 users with a home folder on a shared server drive and have instructed the users to store all their data files in their home folder. You have also created disk quotas granting each user a maximum of 1 GB of storage space.

Because of this arrangement, you will be backing up only the network servers, not user workstations. In addition to the file servers hosting the users' home folders, there are also six Web servers, each with a 40-GB drive containing the home page files, a database server with an 80-GB drive hosting approximately 10 GB of database files, and an e-mail server with 25 GB of mail archives.

Based on this information, answer the following questions:

1. What is the approximate total amount of regularly changing data that you might have to back up each day?

    a. 60 GB

    b. 160 GB

    c. 360 GB

    d. 480 GB

2. Assuming that you decide to perform a weekly full backup and daily incremental backups, approximately how much data from the six Web servers can you expect to find on each incremental backup tape? Explain your answer.

3. Based on the information shown earlier in Table 4-1, which type of magnetic tape drive would best be suited for this network, assuming that you want to use only a single tape for your daily incremental backups?

    a. DLT

    b. 8 mm

    c. QIC

    d. DAT

CHAPTER 5
MAINTAINING THE OPERATING SYSTEM

All viable software products are in a constant state of development, and the manufacturers periodically release updates and upgrades. Operating systems are no exception, and it is important to keep your Microsoft Windows Server 2003 systems up to date. Updating a single computer is a simple task, but updating a large fleet of computers in a timely and efficient fashion is much more complicated. In this chapter, you learn about the types of operating system updates that Microsoft releases, and about some of the methods you can use to apply those updates.

Upon completion of this chapter, you will be able to:

- Understand the difference between service packs and hotfixes

- Deploy service packs using Windows Update, Automatic Updates, and group policies

- Integrate service packs and hotfixes into a Windows Server 2003 operating system installation

- Use Microsoft Baseline Security Analyzer

- Install and configure a Microsoft Software Update Services server

- Understand Per Server and Per Device or Per User licensing modes

- Configure licenses using the Choose Licensing Mode tool in Control Panel and the Licensing administrative tool

- Create license groups

WINDOWS OPERATING SYSTEM UPDATES

At one time, updating software was a relatively simple matter. If a problem arose in an application or operating system, the manufacturer released an update in the form of a patch that users applied to their computers. An *update* is a minor revision to a software product that is usually intended to address specific performance issues rather than add new features. When it came time to produce the next version of the software, the manufacturer incorporated all of the patches into an upgrade release. An *upgrade* is a major revision that might include new features as well as all of the existing patches for the previous version of the product.

> **NOTE**   **Exam Objectives**   *The objectives for the 70-290 exam require students to be able to "manage [a] software update infrastructure."*

As software products grew more complex, the number of programming problems tended to increase as well, and so did the number of patches. Some products, particularly operating systems, could have dozens of patch releases between upgrades. Updating applications and operating systems therefore became increasingly problematic for several reasons, including the following:

- **Number of patches**   When there are a large number of patches for a software product, it becomes difficult to keep track of which patches have been applied and which versions of the product files are being used in a particular installation.

- **Patching order**   When patches are applied in different orders, the resulting software configurations can be different, particularly if a product has multiple patches containing different versions of the same files.

The result of these problems is a nightmare for technical support people trying to troubleshoot an installation of the software. Determining which patches have been applied and the order in which they were applied is the only way to ascertain what versions of the program files are actually in use.

Service Packs

When faced with the hundreds of patches required for its modern operating systems, Microsoft eventually chose to use a different method of releasing its updates. Instead of many small patch releases, Microsoft creates larger interim releases called service packs. A **service pack** is a collection of patches and other updates that are tested and packaged as a single unit. A single installation program applies all of the updates at once, producing a consistent software configuration on every computer to which the service pack is applied.

Service packs simplify the update process for everyone involved. For Microsoft, releasing updates in a service pack means that it can test the entire package as a whole rather than having to test many different patch combinations. For system administrators and end users, the installation process is reduced to running a single program rather than performing many separate patch installations. For technical support personnel, the troubleshooting process is simplified because they do not have to deal with large numbers of patch releases that might have been installed in any order. It is easy to determine what service packs have been installed on a Windows 2000, Windows XP, or Windows Server 2003 computer by looking at the General tab in the System Properties dialog box (as shown in Figure 5-1).

Figure 5-1   The System Properties dialog box

Microsoft service pack releases are cumulative, meaning that every service pack for a particular product contains all of the updates since the last major release of the product, including all previous service packs. Therefore, when you perform a new installation of a Windows operating system or other Microsoft product, you only have to apply the most recent service pack.

Service Pack Releases

Microsoft releases operating system service packs in three forms:

- **CD-ROM**   Service packs are available on CD-ROM directly from Microsoft for a nominal fee. The CD contains the service pack installation files and an installation program called Update.exe. The disk also contains the service pack documentation, deployment tools, and updated support tools, which aren't included as part of a downloaded installation.

- **Express download**   The express download consists only of the few files needed to begin the service pack download process. When you run the installation program, the software examines your system, accesses the Microsoft Web site, and downloads the files needed to complete the update. Because the installation program checks to see what service packs are already installed on the computer, it can download only the files it needs, which can significantly reduce the size of the download. To run an express installation, the computer must have access to the Internet.

- **Network download**   The network download option consists of the entire service pack in the form of a single executable archive file. It is intended for network administrators who have to deploy the service pack on large fleets of computers. Once you perform the initial download, you can launch the executable to install the service pack on any computer running the operating system. No additional Internet access is needed. However, because this version contains all of the service pack files, the download can be extremely large, often 100 MB or more.

One-Time Installation

When you install a service pack on a computer running one of the Windows operating systems, the installation program applies only the updates for the components installed on the system. For example, if you have Microsoft Internet Information Services (IIS) and Certificates Services installed on a computer running Windows Server 2003, installing a service pack will apply any updates for those two components but not updates for other components that are not installed.

At one time, if you modified the hardware or software configuration on a computer running Windows NT, you had to reapply the latest service pack to install the updated software for the components you just installed. However, starting with Windows 2000, this is no longer necessary. The service pack installation program now stores the location of a cabinet (.cab) file containing all of the updated drivers to the computer, as well as an information file called Layout.inf. This ensures that whenever you install a new operating system component, whether it is a device driver, an application, or a service, the system uses the latest version of the files from the service pack release.

Hotfixes

Although the schedule for service pack releases is fluid, the updates appear relatively infrequently, usually no more than once a year. However, it is not unusual for operating system issues to arise that require immediate attention and cannot wait for the next service pack release. For these occasions, Microsoft also releases individual patches, which it calls hotfixes. A **hotfix** is a software update that addresses one specific issue. Like service packs, hotfixes are released as a single executable file that installs the patch on the computer on which you run it. Microsoft typically releases hotfixes in conjunction with a Knowledge Base article that explains the problem and the circumstances in which users or administrators should apply the update.

> **MORE INFO**   **Microsoft Knowledge Base**   The Microsoft Knowledge Base is a library of articles providing support information for all Microsoft products. You can access the Knowledge Base at *http://support.microsoft.com*.

Unlike service packs, which Microsoft recommends that you install on all computers, hotfixes are often intended only for systems experiencing a particular problem or running a particular hardware or software configuration. You should always familiarize yourself with the function of a hotfix and the conditions of its use before installing it on a computer.

When to Update?

The question of when to apply service packs and hotfixes has been hotly debated among system administrators over the years. Not every update release has turned out to be rock solid, and some administrators are leery of applying them until they are shown to be stable. In fact, some people prefer to wait for Service Pack 3 to be released before they install Service Pack 2.

While this prudence might have once been practical, today it is not. Service packs and particularly hotfixes are often released to address specific security issues such as new viruses or other threats, and it is often important to deploy these updates in a timely fashion. However, this is not to say that everyone should immediately install every update as soon as it is released.

For a stand-alone computer, the Windows Update Web site makes the process of downloading and applying updates easy, and in most cases you can uninstall Microsoft updates when necessary. Therefore, most users can safely apply updates as they are released. However, in a network environment, the decision about which updates to install and when to install them should not be left up to the individual user. Administrators must be responsible for obtaining updates when they are released, and for deploying them on the network in a timely manner. However, network administrators should not immediately install every update that appears. It is important to test the update releases first, and this is one of the reasons why an enterprise should have a set of well-defined update policies in place.

Software update policies are designed to aid the network administrator in performing the following tasks:

- **Remain aware of new update releases.**   Microsoft frequently releases software updates that might or might not be applicable to the systems on your network. Network administrators must be aware of new releases when they occur and must understand the specific issues each release addresses.

- **Determine which computers need to be updated.**   In some cases, a new update release might apply only to computers performing a specific function, using a specific application or feature, or containing a particular hardware device. Network administrators must understand each release's specific function and determine which computers require the update.

- **Test update releases on multiple system configurations.**   A software update that causes a malfunction might be just an annoyance on a single computer, but on a large network, it can be a catastrophe. Network administrators must perform their own tests of all updates before deploying them on the entire network.

- **Deploy update releases on large fleets.**   Manually installing software updates on hundreds or thousands of computers requires enormous amounts of time, effort, and expense. To deploy updates on a large network efficiently, the process must be automated.

Microsoft offers tools that help the administrator accomplish these tasks, such as those discussed in the following sections.

Testing Security Updates

Before you deploy software updates on a network, you must test them to make sure they are compatible with all your system configurations. The amount and type of testing depends on the nature of the updates and the complexity of your network. For a major update such as a service pack, testing should be extensive. You might want to test the release on an isolated lab network first, and then do a pilot deployment on a part of your production network before proceeding with the general deployment. For smaller, minor updates, a pilot deployment might be sufficient testing, followed by a general deployment if no problems occur.

Uninstalling Service Packs

When you install a service pack, the installation program always gives you the opportunity to save backup copies of all the operating system files that the service pack replaces. This makes it possible to uninstall the service pack at a later time and restore the original system configuration, if necessary.

USING MICROSOFT BASELINE SECURITY ANALYZER

Microsoft Baseline Security Analyzer (MBSA) is a graphical tool (shown in Figure 5-2) that can check for common security lapses on a single computer or multiple computers running various Windows operating system versions. These lapses are typically due to incorrect or incomplete configuration of security features and failure to install security updates. The security faults that MBSA can detect are as follows:

- **Missing security updates**   Using a list of current update releases obtained from a Microsoft Internet server or from a local Microsoft Software Update Services (SUS) server, MBSA determines whether all the required service packs and security updates have been installed on the computer; if not, it compiles a list of the updates that need to be installed.

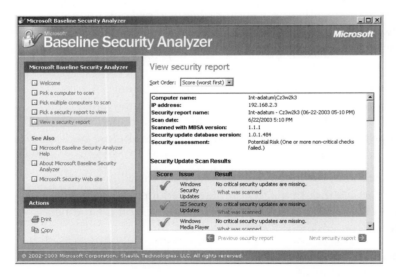

Figure 5-2   The Microsoft Baseline Security Analyzer interface

> **NOTE   Hfnetchk.exe**   MBSA replaces an earlier Microsoft update checking utility called Hfnetchk.exe, which operates from the command line and only checks computers for missing updates. MBSA includes all the functionality of Hfnetchk.exe, including the command-line interface, which you can activate by running the Mbsacli.exe executable with the /hf parameter. This enables administrators to continue using batch files and scripts, incorporating Htnetchk.exe commands with a minimum of modification.

- **Account vulnerabilities**   MBSA checks to see if the Guest account is activated on the computer, whether more than two accounts have Administrator privileges, whether anonymous users have too much access to system information, and whether the computer is configured to use the Autologon feature.

- **Improper passwords**   MBSA checks the passwords on all the computer's accounts to see if they are configured to expire, are blank, or are too simple. This check is not performed on domain controllers.

- **File system vulnerabilities**   MBSA checks to see whether all the disk drives on the computer are using the NTFS file system.

- **IIS and SQL vulnerabilities**   If the computer is running Internet Information Services (IIS) or Microsoft SQL Server, MBSA examines these applications for a variety of security weaknesses.

In addition, MBSA displays other information about security on the computer, such as a list of shares, the Windows operating system version number, and whether auditing is enabled.

> **NOTE Downloading MBSA**   MBSA is not included with Windows Server 2003, but it is available without charge for download from the Microsoft Web site.

MBSA is an informational tool that can display security information about a computer, but it cannot do anything to remedy the vulnerabilities that it finds. You can use MBSA to determine which security updates to install on specific computers, but to develop effective update policies, you must implement a system to keep track of which security updates have been installed on every computer in the enterprise.

USING WINDOWS UPDATE

Windows Update is a Web site, maintained by Microsoft, that enables computers running Windows Server 2003 and most other versions of Microsoft Windows to locate and download the latest operating system and driver updates and patches. When you access the Windows Update site—by clicking Start, pointing to All Programs, and selecting Windows Update, or by using the URL *http:// windowsupdate.microsoft.com*—the computer downloads an application that examines the computer's current configuration and compiles a list of all the updates and patches the system might need (as shown in Figure 5-3), in the following categories:

- Critical updates and service packs

- Version-specific Windows updates

- Driver updates

The user can then select from the list of updates, download them, and install them all at once, thereby simplifying the maintenance process.

Practice using Windows Update by doing Exercise 5.1, "Using Windows Update," now.

Figure 5-3   The Windows Update Web site interface

For a single user running a home computer, the Windows Update Web site is a great way to keep a computer current, but it is generally not suitable for use on networks, for the following reasons:

- **Bandwidth**   Each time a computer receives an update release using Windows Update, it downloads the software from a Microsoft server on the Internet. On a large network, this would mean that hundreds or thousands of computers would be downloading the same files. For small updates, this might not be a problem, but Windows service packs are usually more than 100 MB, and downloading the same file for every computer could monopolize an enormous amount of the network's Internet bandwidth.

- **Testing**   Although Microsoft tests its updates carefully before releasing them, it cannot possibly test every combination of configuration settings and software products. Therefore, it is possible for a particular update to cause problems with some or all of the computers on your network. Here again, for a single computer, this might not be a major issue, but if an update causes a problem on all a network's computers, the loss of productivity and the added burden on technical support personnel could be catastrophic.

NOTE   **Windows Update and Software Update Services**   The drawbacks listed here to using Windows Update assume that the computer is configured to access the Windows Update Web site on the Internet. However, it is also possible to configure Windows Update to access software updates from an SUS server on the local network. This practice eliminates potential for bandwidth and testing issues. You'll learn more about SUS later in this chapter.

Using Automatic Updates

Although you can always access the Windows Update Web site manually, using Internet Explorer, it is also possible to configure Windows Server 2003 to automatically download and install software updates as they become available. This feature is called Automatic Updates, and it is available in Windows Server 2003, Windows XP with Service Pack 1 installed, and Windows 2000 with Service Pack 3 installed.

> **NOTE   Obtaining Automatic Updates**   For clients running earlier releases of the supported operating systems, you can download Automatic Updates as a standalone client from the Microsoft SUS Web site at *http://go.microsoft.com/fwlink/?LinkID=6930*.

By default, the Automatic Updates client in Windows Server 2003 is configured to connect automatically to a Windows Update server and download updates, and then prompt the user to install them. You can modify this default behavior by opening the System Properties dialog box from Control Panel and selecting the Automatic Updates tab (as shown in Figure 5-4), or by launching the Automatic Updates Setup Wizard by clicking the Stay Current With Automatic Updates icon in the taskbar tray. You can also configure Automatic Updates using a group policy object (GPO), as described in "Configuring Automatic Updates" later in this chapter.

Figure 5-4   The Automatic Updates tab of the System Properties dialog box

When you configure Automatic Updates, you can select from the following three options:

- **Notify Me Before Downloading Any Updates And Notify Me Again Before Installing Them On My Computer**   When new updates are available, the computer creates an entry in the System log (which you can access using Event Viewer) and notifies the system's administrators by means of a balloon in the taskbar tray.

- **Download The Updates Automatically And Notify Me When They Are Ready To Be Installed**   The computer downloads updates from the Windows Update site as they become available, using the Background Intelligent Transfer Service (BITS) to perform the file transfer using idle network bandwidth. BITS ensures that network performance is not affected by the file transfers. The Automatic Updates client then confirms the Microsoft digital signature on the downloaded files, examines the cyclical redundancy check (CRC) on each package, and notifies the system's administrators of their presence, using a System log entry and a balloon in the taskbar tray. The administrator can then select the updates to install from a list of those downloaded.

Practice using
Automatic
Updates
by doing
Exercise 5-2,
"Configuring
Automatic
Updates," now.

- **Automatically Download The Updates, And Install Them On The Schedule That I Specify**   The computer downloads updates from the Windows Update site as they become available, using BITS, and installs them at a specific time each day or each week. If an administrator is logged on at the scheduled time, a countdown message appears prior to the installation, and the administrator has the option to delay the installation until the next scheduled time. If a nonadministrator is logged on, a warning dialog box appears, but the user cannot delay the installation. If no user is logged on, installation occurs automatically. If the installed updates require that the system be restarted, a five-minute countdown notification appears, informing users of the impending restart. Only an administrator can cancel the restart.

DEPLOYING UPDATES ON A NETWORK

A network administrator who decides not to have users download their own operating system updates from the Internet can use a variety of alternative methods of delivering the updates to the individual computers on the network, as described in the following sections.

Installing Service Packs Manually

When you purchase a service pack CD, you receive a disk containing all of the service pack files in expanded form. To install the service pack, you run the Update.exe program in the Update folder. This launches the Service Pack Setup Wizard (shown in Figure 5-5), which takes you through the process of installing the service pack. After you agree to the supplemental end user license agreement, the wizard prompts you to specify whether you want to create archive copies of the files the service pack replaces so you can uninstall the service pack later, if needed. After the installation is completed, you are prompted to restart the computer.

Figure 5-5   The Windows XP Service Pack 1 Setup Wizard

When you download the network version of a service pack, you receive a single executable archive file with a name that specifies the operating system for which the update is intended and the number of the service pack release. For example, the archive file for Windows XP Service Pack 1 is Xpsp1.exe. When you run the executable, the computer expands all of the files in the archive, writes them to a temporary directory on the system's drive, and then executes the Update.exe file, so the installation proceeds just as with the CD version. You can put the archive file on a network share and run it from any computer on the network. The archive program always copies the installation files to the local drive and runs the installation program from there.

The service pack's Update.exe file and the network download archive also support command-line switches that you can use to affect the installation process. You can run the executable with these switches from a command prompt or from the Run dialog box. The switches, which are the same for both Update.exe and the archive file, are as follows:

- **/D:*foldername***   By default, the installation program creates backup copies of all the files it overwrites to a folder called $ntservicepackuninstall$. This switch enables you to specify an alternate folder name for the backup files.

- **/F**   Causes the installation program to close all open applications without saving data when it restarts the computer after the installation is completed.

- **/L**   Displays a list of all hotfixes installed on the computer.

- **/N**   Prevents the installation program from creating backup copies of the files overwritten during the installation.

- **/O**   Causes the installation program to overwrite original equipment manufacturer (OEM) files during the installation without notifying the user.

- **/Q**   Runs the installation in quiet mode. In this mode, the installation program uses the default values for all options but does not display a progress indicator or any error messages.

- **/S:*foldername***   Incorporates the service pack distribution files with the operating system distribution files to create an integrated installation. This process is also known as *slipstreaming*. The foldername placeholder lets you specify the path to the operating system distribution files.

- **/U**   Runs the installation in unattended setup mode. In this mode, the installation program uses the default values for all options and displays a progress indicator, but only critical error messages stop the installation process.

- **/X**   Causes the archive executable to expand all of the files in the archive and store them in an i386 directory structure on the local drive without executing the Update.exe program.

- **/X:*foldername***   Causes the archive executable to expand all of the files in the archive and store them in the folder you specify on the local drive without executing the Update.exe program.

- **/Z**   Prevents the installation program from restarting the computer after the installation is completed. This option is most commonly used when you plan to install hotfixes immediately after the service pack and want to defer the system restart until after the hotfix installations.

Practice expanding a service pack archive by doing Exercise 5-3, "Expanding a Service Pack," now.

Installing Hotfixes Manually

As with service packs, users can download and install hotfixes through the Windows Update Web site, but it is also possible to download them as individual executables. This enables network administrators to deploy hotfixes to large numbers of computers without having to perform redundant Internet downloads. A hotfix distribution file is an executable archive file, much like the network download file for a service pack, but much smaller. The filename uses the following format:

***OperatingSystem*-KB*KnowledgeBase#-Platform-Language*.exe**

For example, one particular security update for Windows Server 2003 is named WindowsServer2003-KB823980-x86-ENU.exe. The number 823980 is that of the Knowledge Base article describing the issue the hotfix addresses, x86 is the processor platform for which the hotfix is intended, and ENU indicates that the hotfix is for the U.S. English version of Windows Server 2003.

> **NOTE   Hotfix File Replacement**   Unlike service packs, hotfixes update only the software that is actually installed on the computer when you run the installation program. If you remove an operating system component and later reinstall it, you must also reinstall any hotfixes that apply to that component.

Running a hotfix executable extracts the files in the archive to a temporary folder on the local system and runs the Update.exe installation program, just as with a service pack. Hotfixes always make backup copies of overwritten files for uninstall purposes by default, saving them to a hidden folder beneath the system root called $NtUninstallKB######$, where ###### is the hotfix's Knowledge Base article number.

To modify the default behavior of the hotfix installation program, you can run it with any of the following switches:

- **/F**   Causes the installation program to close all open applications without saving data when it restarts the computer after the installation is completed.

- **/L**   Displays a list of all hotfixes installed on the computer.

- **/N**   Prevents the installation program from creating backup copies of the files overwritten during the installation.

- **/Q**   Runs the installation in quiet mode. In this mode, the installation program uses the default values for all options but does not display a progress indicator or any error messages.

- **/U**   Runs the installation in unattended setup mode. In this mode, the installation program uses the default values for all options and displays a progress indicator, but only critical error messages stop the installation process.

- **/X**   Causes the archive executable to expand all of the files in the archive and store them in a directory structure on the local drive without executing the Update.exe program.

- **/Z**   Prevents the installation program from restarting the computer after the installation is completed.

> **NOTE** Hotfix Checks   When you attempt to install a hotfix, the installation
> program always checks to see what service packs have been installed on the com-
> puter. If the hotfix you are installing is older than the system's currently installed
> service pack, the installation halts because the hotfix was already applied as part
> of that service pack. If the hotfix is newer than the currently installed service
> pack, the installation proceeds.

Chaining Hotfixes

Starting with the Windows 2000 Service Pack 3 release, all hotfixes include a program called Qchain.exe that makes it possible to install multiple hotfixes one
after the other without restarting the computer after each one. If you install multiple hotfixes that include different versions of the same file, Qchain.exe ensures
that the system is using the correct version of that file when the installation is
completed.

To chain hotfix installations, you run the hotfix installation programs with the /Z
command-line switch, which prevents the programs from restarting the computer.
However, you must remember to restart the system after the last hotfix is installed
so the hotfixes can take effect. To automate the process of installing multiple hotfixes, you can create a batch file like the following:

```
WindowsServer2003-KB8239809-x86-ENU.exe /Z /U
WindowsServer2003-KB8239810-x86-ENU.exe /Z /U
WindowsServer2003-KB8239811-x86-ENU.exe /U
```

Notice that the first two hotfix installation commands in the batch file include
the /Z switch, preventing a restart, while the last command omits this switch
so the computer will restart after all of the hotfixes are installed. All three
commands include the /U switch, which prevents the installations from pausing
for user input.

You can also incorporate a service pack installation into the batch file, thus automating the entire postinstallation update process, as follows:

```
Update.exe /Z /U
WindowsServer2003-KB8239809-x86-ENU.exe /Z /U
WindowsServer2003-KB8239810-x86-ENU.exe /Z /U
WindowsServer2003-KB8239811-x86-ENU.exe /U
```

Slipstreaming

When you install new computers on a network, the operating system installation is
not necessarily the end of the process. You might have to install a service pack and
numerous hotfixes as well. While it is certainly possible to install each component
separately, it is often preferable to incorporate the service pack and the hotfixes
into the operating system installation. This process is called **slipstreaming**.

Slipstreaming a Service Pack
To slipstream a service pack into the Windows Server 2003 operating system installation, you must first create a distribution folder on a network share and copy the
i386 folder from the Windows Server 2003 installation CD to that folder. Then, from

the folder containing the service pack installation files, you run the Update.exe program or the archive executable with the /S switch, specifying the location of the distribution folder you created, as in the following examples:

```
Update.exe /s:distfolder
W2k3sp1.exe /s:distfolder
```

The installation program extracts the service pack files from the archive to a temporary directory (if necessary) and then copies the files to the appropriate places in the distribution folder. You can then start the operating system installation from the distribution folder, and the service pack files will be installed at the same time.

Using Group Policies

Another method of automating service pack installations is to use the combination of Windows Installer and the Software Installation policy in a GPO. Windows Installer is a program that installs software that has been saved as a Windows Installer Package file with an .msi extension. Service pack releases include a Windows Installer Package version of the installation program called Update.msi. Update.msi is located in the update folder on a service pack CD. If you have downloaded the network version of the service pack, you must expand the archive file by running it with the /X switch before you can use Update.msi.

To deploy a service pack using its Update.msi file and group policies, you must select an Active Directory object containing the computers you want to update. If all of the computers on your network are running the same version of Windows, you can configure the Software Installation policy in the default domain GPO associated with your Active Directory domain object. If you have computers running various versions of Windows, you can create an organizational unit (OU) object for each version and then create a GPO containing the correct Windows Installer Package for each OU, or you can create multiple Windows Installer Packages in the default domain GPO and use permissions to specify which computers should receive each package.

> **MORE INFO** **Using GPOs**   For more information on using group policy objects, see the course for exam 70-294, "Planning, Implementing, and Maintaining a Microsoft Windows Server 2003 Active Directory Infrastructure."

▶ **Adding a Windows Installer Package**

To add the Windows Installer Package to your default domain GPO, use the following procedure:

1. Log on to Windows Server 2003 as Administrator.

2. Expand the service pack archive to a distribution folder on a network share.

3. Click Start, point to Administrative Tools, and click Active Directory Users And Computers. The Active Directory Users And Computers console appears.

4. Select the domain icon in the scope pane and, from the Action menu, select Properties. The Properties dialog box for your domain object appears.

5. Select the Group Policy tab, and then click Edit. The Group Policy Object Editor console appears.

6. In the scope pane, expand the Computer Configuration/Software Settings folder and select the Software Installation icon.

   The User Configuration heading also has a Software Settings folder and a Software Installation icon, but you cannot use them to install service packs. You must use the Computer Configuration heading.

7. On the Action menu, point to New and select Package. An Open dialog box appears.

8. Type the full path to the Update.msi Windows Installation Package file in the Update subfolder of your distribution folder. A Deploy Software dialog box appears.

   Be sure to use a Universal Naming Convention (UNC) name for the path to the package file, not a drive letter. For example, you can use \\Server01\d$\sp1\i386\update\update.msi, but not D:\sp1\i386\update\update.msi.

9. Click OK to accept the default Assigned option. The installation package for the service pack appears in the details pane (as shown in Figure 5-6).

Figure 5-6 The Group Policy Object Editor console with a service pack installation package

The next time the computers in the domain restart, they will download the service pack installation files from the specified share and install them.

USING MICROSOFT SOFTWARE UPDATE SERVICES

Deploying any software on a large network is a complicated task, and operating system updates are no exception. What might be a simple task on a single computer turns into a major project when you have hundreds or thousands of computers. SUS is a free product that notifies administrators when new security updates are available, downloads the updates, and then deploys them to the computers on the network (as shown in Figure 5-7).

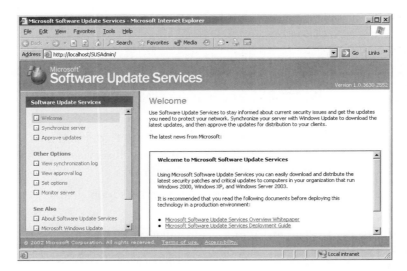

Figure 5-7   The SUS administration interface

MORE INFO   *Obtaining SUS*   SUS with Service Pack 1 (SP1) is not included with Windows Server 2003 or any of the Windows operating systems, but it is available as a free download from Microsoft's Web site at *http:// www.microsoft.com/windowsserversystems/SUS/default.mspx.*

As mentioned earlier in this chapter, having users download and install their own operating system updates using the Windows Update Web site can be a waste of time and bandwidth. SUS is essentially an intranet version of the Windows Update Web site that eliminates the need for each computer to download software updates from the Internet and prevents administrators from having to manually deploy the updates on multiple computers. Administrators can control which updates are applied to the computers on the network, and when, automating the process so that it is completely invisible to the users.

SUS consists of the following components:

- **Synchronization server**   One computer, running SUS, functions as a synchronization server, downloading software updates from the Windows Update Web site as they are released. The administrator can allow the downloads to occur as needed, schedule them to occur at specific times (such as off-peak hours), or trigger them manually. Once SUS downloads the updates, it stores them on the server. This eliminates the need for the administrator to continually check the Windows Update Web site for new releases.

- **Intranet Windows Update server**   Once the SUS server has downloaded the updates, the administrator must decide whether the server should deploy them immediately to the network or save them for testing and later deployment. When updates are ready for deployment, SUS functions as the Windows Update server for the computers on the network, except that this server is on the intranet and does not require the clients to access the Internet.

- **Automatic Updates** Automatic Updates is a Windows operating system feature that enables computers to download and install software updates with no user intervention. You can configure this feature on your client computers so that they retrieve the updates from an SUS server on the local network rather than from the Windows Update Web site, thereby restricting the updates to those approved by the network administrator.

    PLANNING **SUS Operating System Requirements** SUS runs only on Windows Server 2003 and Windows 2000 Server with Service Pack 2 or later. SUS clients must be running Windows Server 2003, Windows 2000, or Windows XP.

▶ Deploying SUS

The process of deploying SUS consists of the following basic steps:

1. **Install an SUS server.** SUS is a series of Web pages and intranet applications providing client and administrator access to the service. You must have IIS installed on the server before you install SUS.

2. **Synchronize the server.** Synchronization is the process by which the SUS server downloads updates from the Windows Update Web site on the Internet and stores them on the local drive.

3. **Approve updates.** Before clients can access the updates stored on an SUS server, they must be approved, either manually by an administrator or automatically. Administrators might choose to put new updates through a testing regimen before approving them for client access.

4. **Configure Automatic Updates clients.** Using group policies, you can configure the Automatic Updates feature on your client computers to obtain updates from your SUS server rather than from the Windows Update Web site.

Installing SUS *—read through this in the lab book*

Because SUS uses Web sites for both client and administrative access, you must install IIS on your server before you install SUS. Windows Server 2003 includes the IIS software but does not install it by default. To install IIS, open Add Or Remove Programs in Control Panel, click Add/Remove Windows Components, and select Internet Information Services (IIS) from the list of Application Server components.

Once you have installed IIS, you can execute the SUS installation program you downloaded from the Microsoft Web site, which launches the Microsoft Software Update Services Setup Wizard. After you agree to the terms of the software's end-user license agreement, the wizard leads you through configuration of the following parameters:

- **File Locations** Each Windows Update patch consists of two components: the patch file itself and metadata that specifies the platforms and languages to which the patch applies. SUS always downloads the metadata, which you use to approve updates and which clients on your intranet retrieve from the SUS server. You can choose whether to download the files themselves and, if so, where to save the updates. If you elect to maintain the update files on Microsoft Windows Update servers, your clients will connect to the SUS server to obtain the list of approved updates but will then connect to the Windows Update Web site to download the files. If you select to store the updates locally, you must use a folder on an NTFS drive. A minimum of 6 GB of free disk space is recommended.

■ **Language Settings**   Specifies the languages for which you want to store updates on the server. If all of your clients use the English-language version of Windows, you can choose the English Only option. If you have clients using languages other than English, you can download updates in all available languages or choose specific languages. This parameter is configured only if you have selected to store updates locally.

■ **Update Approval Settings**   When SUS downloads a new version of an update that has already been approved, this setting specifies whether the new version should be approved automatically or wait for manual approval.

> **NOTE   SUS URLs**   When the wizard concludes, it displays the URL for the SUS server's administrative interface and the URL that clients must use to retrieve updates from the server. Take note of these URLs because you will need them to administer the server and when configuring your clients.

The Microsoft Software Update Services Setup Wizard installs the following three components on the server:

■ The Software Update Synchronization Service, which downloads content to the SUS server

■ An IIS Web site that services update requests from Automatic Updates clients

■ An SUS administration Web page, from which you can synchronize the SUS server and approve updates

When the installation is completed, Internet Explorer displays the SUS administration Web page.

> **NOTE   Internet Explorer Enhanced Security Configuration**   You might need to add your server to the Local Intranet trusted site list to access the site. Open Internet Explorer and select Internet Options from the Tools menu. Select the Security tab, select Trusted Sites, and click Sites. Add your server name to the trusted site list.

Synchronizing SUS

The two main administrative tasks for SUS are synchronizing the server and approving the updates. When you click the Synchronize Server hyperlink on the administrative home page, you see the interface shown in Figure 5-8. On this page, you can schedule synchronizations to occur on a regular schedule or trigger them manually.

Figure 5-8   The SUS Synchronize Server page

To schedule synchronizations, you click the Synchronization Schedule button to display the Schedule Synchronization dialog box (shown in Figure 5-9). During the synchronization process, the server connects to the Windows Update Web site and downloads a catalog of all available updates. Then, depending on the settings you specified during the installation, SUS either downloads all of the new updates or incorporates the metadata into its own catalog of updates.

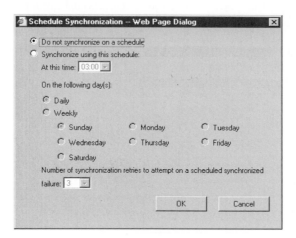

Figure 5-9   The Schedule Synchronization dialog box

Approving Updates

When the synchronization process is complete, you are taken to the Approve Updates page, shown in Figure 5-10. Here, an administrator can view the list of synchronized updates and select the ones that should be made available to clients.

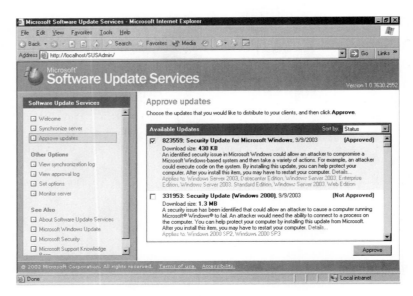

Figure 5-10   The SUS Approve Updates page

Each of the entries in the list of updates has a Details hyperlink that displays an Update Details page like that shown in Figure 5-11. This page provides information about the selected update, including the platforms for which it is intended, the languages for which it is available, its date and size, and the setup parameters that the update will use when it is installed on a client computer. The Update Details page also contains a link to the Knowledge Base article (on Microsoft's support Web site) associated with the update and a link to the update executable itself so administrators can access the updates for testing purposes.

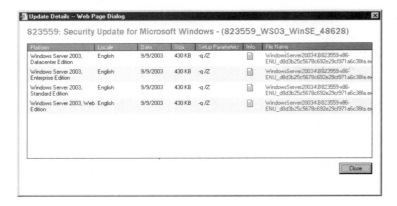

Figure 5-11   The SUS Update Details page

Configuring Automatic Updates

Once the SUS server is installed and operational, the next step is to configure the clients to make use of it. Earlier in this chapter, you learned about the Automatic Updates feature available in Windows Server 2003, Windows XP, and Windows 2000. By default, Automatic Updates downloads the update files from the Windows Update Web site, but you can also configure this client to obtain updates from an

SUS server instead. To do this, you must configure the Automatic Updates client using group policies.

To deploy these or any group policies, you must select an Active Directory domain, site, or OU object, open its Properties dialog box, select the Group Policy tab, and launch the Group Policy Object Editor console by selecting a group policy and clicking Edit. In the Group Policy Object Editor console, expand the Computer Configuration, Administrative Templates, and Windows Components folders, and then select Windows Update to display the four policies shown in Figure 5-12.

Figure 5-12   The Windows Update policies in the Group Policy Object Editor console

The policies are as follows:

- **Configure Automatic Updates**   Specifies the default behavior of the Automatic Updates client using the following three options: Notify For Download And Notify For Install, Auto Download And Notify For Install, and Auto Download And Schedule The Install. These are the same options that you can configure in the Automatic Updates tab of the client machine's System Properties dialog box.

- **Specify Intranet Microsoft Update Service Location**   Identifies the server from which the client will access Windows updates. This is the policy that enables you to redirect Automatic Updates clients to a server running SUS rather than the Windows Update Web site. In the Set The Intranet Update Service For Detecting Updates text box, you enter the client URL for your SUS server that the Microsoft Software Update Server Setup Wizard supplied to you during the installation. By default, the client logs its interactions on the SUS server from which it obtains updates. However, this policy also enables you to point clients to another IIS server for statistics logging. This makes it possible for clients to obtain updates from a local SUS server while logging their activities to a single central server for easier retrieval and analysis of the log data. The IIS logs are located in the *systemroot*\System32\Logfiles\W3svc1 folder.

- **Reschedule Automatic Updates Scheduled Installations**   If installations are scheduled and the client computer is turned off at the scheduled time, the default behavior is to wait for the next scheduled time. This policy, if set to a value between 1 and 60, causes Automatic Updates to reschedule the installation to occur the specified number of minutes after the next system startup.

■ **No Auto-Restart For Scheduled Automatic Updates Installations**   Causes Automatic Updates to forego a restart required by an installed update when a user is logged on to the system. Instead, the user is notified that a restart is required for installation to complete.

Once you configure the GPO and the policies take effect, the Automatic Updates clients poll their SUS server every 22 hours, minus a random offset (to prevent a surge in network traffic). After clients have downloaded the approved updates from the SUS server, they are installed and configured—manually or automatically— at the scheduled time. If an approved update is later unapproved by an administrator, that update is not uninstalled, but it will not be installed by any additional clients. Updates installed through SUS can be uninstalled manually, however, using Add Or Remove Programs in Control Panel.

> **NOTE   Critical Updates**   In some cases, an update addressing a critical security problem might be so important that you do not want to wait for your clients to poll, download, and install patches. In these cases, you should still install updates manually.

Building an SUS Topology

A single SUS server might be sufficient for a small organization, but for a large enterprise, you might want to have more than one. When you install multiple SUS servers on a network, you can configure them to interact using any one of the following topologies:

■ **Multiple server topology**   Each SUS server synchronizes its content from the Windows Update Web site and manages its own list of approved updates. This topology enables the administrator of each server to control that server's list of approved updates, and it also enables an organization to maintain a variety of patch and update configurations.

■ **Strict parent/child topology**   A parent SUS server synchronizes content from the Windows Update Web site and stores the updates in a local folder. The SUS administrator then approves the updates to be deployed to clients. Other SUS servers in the enterprise synchronize from the parent and are configured to synchronize both the update files and the list of approved updates. Clients can then retrieve updates from the closest SUS server. In this topology, administrators of child SUS servers cannot approve or disapprove updates; that task is performed on the parent SUS server only.

■ **Loose parent/child topology**   A parent SUS server synchronizes content from Windows Update and stores updates in a local folder. Other SUS servers in the enterprise synchronize from the parent. Unlike the strict configuration, these additional SUS servers do not synchronize the list of approved updates, so the administrator of each server can approve or disapprove updates independently. Although this topology increases administrative overhead, it is helpful when an organization wants to minimize Internet exposure and requires distributed power of update approval or a variety of client patch and update configurations.

SUS uses the multiple-server topology by default. To implement one of the parent/child topologies, you access the Set Options page in the SUS server's administrative site and configure the Select Which Server To Synchronize Content From option. For a parent/child topology, you leave the default setting in place on the parent server and configure the child servers with the Synchronize From A Local Software Update Services Server option and the name of the parent server. For a strict parent/child topology, you also select the Synchronize List Of Approved Items Updated From This Location check box; for a loose parent/child topology, you leave the check box cleared.

SUS Monitoring

The Monitor Server page of the SUS administration Web site displays statistics that reflect the number of updates available for each platform, and the date and time of the most recent update. The information is summarized from the Windows Update metadata that is downloaded during each synchronization. Metadata information is written to disk and stored in memory to improve performance as systems request platform-appropriate updates.

You can also monitor SUS and Automatic Updates using the following logs:

- **Synchronization Log**   You can retrieve information about current or past synchronizations and the specific packages that were downloaded by clicking View Synchronization Log in the left navigation bar.

- **Approval Log**   For information about packages that have been approved, click View Approval Log in the left navigation bar.

- **Windows Update Log**   The Automatic Updates client logs activity in the *systemroot*\Windows Update.log file on the client's local hard disk.

- **Wutrack.bin**   The client's interaction with SUS is logged to the specified statistics server's IIS logs, which are typically stored in the *systemroot* \System32\Logfiles\W3svc1 folder.

SUS System Events

The synchronization service generates event log messages for each synchronization performed by the server and when updates are approved. These messages can be viewed in the System log using Event Viewer. The events relate to the following scenarios:

- **Unable to connect**   Automatic Updates could not connect to the update service (Windows Update or the computer's assigned SUS server).

- **Install ready—no recurring schedule**   Updates listed in the event were downloaded and are pending installation. An administrator must click the notification icon and click Install.

- **Install ready—recurring schedule**   Updates listed in the event are downloaded and will be installed at the date and time specified in the event.

- **Installation success**   Updates listed in the event were installed successfully.

- **Installation failure**   Updates listed in the event failed to install properly.

- **Restart required—no recurring schedule**   An update requires a restart. If installation behavior is set for notification, the restart must be performed manually. Windows cannot search for new updates until the restart has occurred.

- **Restart required—recurring schedule**   When Automatic Updates is configured to automatically install updates, an event is registered if an update requires restart. Restart will occur within five minutes. Windows cannot search for new updates until after the restart has occurred.

Troubleshooting SUS

SUS on a Windows Server 2003 computer might require the following trouble-shooting steps:

- **Reloading the memory cache**   If no new updates appear since the last time you synchronized the server, it is possible that no new updates are available. However, it is also possible that memory caches are not loading new updates properly. From the SUS administration site, click Monitor Server and then click Refresh.

- **Restarting the synchronization service**   If you receive a message that the synchronization service is not running properly or if you cannot modify settings in the Set Options page of the SUS administration Web site, open the Services console from the Administrative Tools program group, right-click the Software Update Services Synchronization Service, and select Restart.

- **Restarting IIS**   If you cannot connect to the administration site or if clients cannot connect to the SUS server, restart the World Wide Web Publishing Service using the Services console.

ADMINISTERING SOFTWARE LICENSES

The End-User License Agreement (EULA) is more than just a nuisance that you must click through to begin installing a new operating system, update, or application. The EULA is a binding contract that gives you the legal right to use a piece of software. In an enterprise environment, managing software licenses is critically important, and Windows Server 2003 includes licensing tools that you use to register and monitor licenses and compliance.

> **NOTE** Evaluation Editions   The Evaluation Edition of Windows Server 2003 included on a supplemental CD-ROM with this book does not support licensing. You cannot follow along with the examples in this lesson without purchasing the full retail version of the product.

Obtaining a Client Access License

The server license for Windows Server 2003 enables you to install the operating system on a computer, but you need a **Client Access License (CAL)** before a user or device is legally authorized to connect to the server. CALs are typically obtained in bundles and might be included in your purchase of the operating system. For example, it is common to see Windows Server 2003 sold with a 5- or 10-user license package. However, if the operating system does not include any CALs, you must purchase them separately. Keep copies of your CAL certificates and your EULAs on file in the event that your organization is audited for licensing compliance.

> **NOTE   Upgrading Licenses**   When you upgrade a server from Windows NT 4 or Windows 2000 to Windows Server 2003, you must purchase CAL upgrades as well.

You must have a CAL for any connection to a Windows Server 2003 computer that uses server components, which include file and print services or authentication. Very few server applications run so independently that the client/server connection does not require a CAL. The most significant exception to the CAL requirement is unauthenticated access conducted through the Internet. Where there is no exchange of credentials during Internet access, such as Internet users browsing your Web site anonymously, no CAL is required. CALs are therefore not required for the Web Edition of Windows Server 2003.

There are two types of CALs: Windows Device CALs, which allow a device to connect to a server regardless of the number of users who might use that device, and Windows User CALs, which allow a user to connect to a server from a number of devices. Windows Device CALs are advantageous for an organization with multiple users per device, such as shift workers. Windows User CALs make most sense for an organization with employees who access the network from multiple or unknown devices.

> **NOTE   User and Device CALs**   The licensing tools and the user interface do not yet distinguish between Windows User and Windows Device CALs. A device CAL is registered indirectly, using license groups.

The number of CALs you require, and how you track those licenses, depends on which client access licensing mode you pursue. There are two licensing modes: Per Server licensing and Per Device or Per User licensing.

Per Server Licensing

Per Server Licensing requires a Windows User or Windows Device CAL for each concurrent connection. If a server is configured with 1,000 CALs, the 1,001st concurrent connection will be denied access. CALs are designated for use on a particular server, so if the same 1,000 users require concurrent connections to a second server, you must purchase another 1,000 CALs.

Per Server Licensing is advantageous only in limited-access scenarios, such as when a subset of your user population accesses a server product on very few servers. Per Server Licensing is less cost-effective in a situation where multiple users access multiple resources on multiple servers. If you are unsure which licensing mode is appropriate, select Per Server. The license agreement allows a no-cost, one-time, one-way conversion from Per Server to Per Device or Per User licensing when it becomes appropriate to do so.

Per Device or Per User Licensing

The **Per Device** or **Per User** licensing mode varies from the Per Seat scheme in previous versions of Windows. In this new mode, each device or user that connects to a server requires a CAL, but with that license the device or user can connect to a number of servers in the enterprise. Per User or Per Device mode is generally the mode of choice for distributed computing environments in which multiple users access multiple servers.

For example, a developer who uses a laptop and two desktops would require only one Windows User CAL. A fleet of 10 Tablet PCs that are used by 30 shift workers would require only 10 Windows Device CALs.

The total number of CALs equals the number of devices or users, or a mixture thereof, that access servers. CALs can be reassigned under certain conditions. For example, a Windows User CAL can be reassigned from a permanent employee to a temporary employee while the permanent employee is on leave. A Windows Device CAL can be reassigned to a loaner device while a device is being repaired.

The Per Server and Per Device or Per User licensing modes are illustrated in Table 5-1.

Table 5-1   CAL Licensing Modes

Per Server	Per User or Per Device
■ Traditionally licensed in Per Server mode when there are few servers and they require limited access.	■ Traditionally licensed in Per User or Per Device mode when there are many servers and they require frequent and widespread access.
■ The number of CALs needed is determined by the number of concurrent connections that are required.	■ Usually more economical when the number of CALs needed is determined by the number of users or devices, or both, that require access to the servers.

> **NOTE** **Terminal Services Licenses**   Windows Server 2003 includes Terminal Services, which includes a two (concurrent) connection license for administrators to connect to a remote server. To have Terminal Services perform as an application server, permitting nonadministrative users to connect to hosted applications, you must acquire Terminal Services CALs, which are included in Windows XP Professional.

Licensing Tools

There are two utilities you can use to track and manage software licensing:

- **Licensing in Control Panel**   The Choose Licensing Mode tool found in Control Panel, shown in Figure 5-13, manages licensing requirements for a single computer running Windows Server 2003. You can use Licensing to add or remove CALs for a server running in Per Server mode, change the licensing mode from Per Server to Per Device or Per User, or configure licensing replication.

Figure 5-13   The Choose Licensing Mode tool in Control Panel

■ **Licensing in Administrative Tools**   The Licensing administrative tool, discussed in the next section, enables you to manage licensing for an enterprise by centralizing the control of licensing and license replication in a site-based model.

Administering Site Licensing

The License Logging service, which runs on each Windows Server 2003 computer, assigns and tracks licenses when clients access server resources. To ensure compliance, licensing information is replicated to a centralized licensing database on a server at the site. This server is called the site license server. A site administrator, or an administrator for the site license server, can then use the Licensing tool in the Administrative Tools program group to view and manage licensing for the entire site. This new license tracking and management capability incorporates licenses not just for file and print services, but also for IIS, Terminal Services, and other Microsoft products (such as Exchange and SQL Server).

The Site License Server

The site license server is typically the first domain controller created in a site. To find out what server is the license server for a site, open Active Directory Sites And Services, expand to select the Site node, and then right-click Licensing Site Settings and select Properties. The current site license server is displayed, as shown in Figure 5-14.

Figure 5-14   Identifying and changing the site license server with Active Directory Sites and Services

To assign the site license server role to another server or domain controller, click Change and select the desired computer. To retain the licensing history for your enterprise, you must stop the License Logging service on the new license server immediately after transferring the role, and then copy the following files from the old to the new licensing server:

- *Systemroot*\System32\Cpl.cfg, which contains the purchase history for your organization

- *Systemroot*\Lls\Llsuser.lls, which contains user information about the number of connections

- *Systemroot*\Lls\Llsmap.lls, which contains license group information

After all files have been copied, restart the License Logging service.

Administering Site Licenses

Once you have identified the site license server for a site, you can view the licensing information on that server by opening Licensing from the Administrative Tools program group. The Server Browser tab in Licensing (shown in Figure 5-15) enables you to manage licensing for an entire site or enterprise.

Figure 5-15   The Server Browser tab of the Microsoft Licensing administrative tool

The Server Browser tab of Licensing enables you to manage any server in any site or domain for which you have administrative authority. You can locate a server and, by right-clicking it and selecting Properties, manage that server's licenses. For each server product installed on that server, you can add or remove per-server licenses. You can also, where appropriate, convert the licensing mode. Remember that Per Server licensing mode issues a license when a user connects to the server product. When a user disconnects from the server product, the License Logging service makes the license available to another user.

The server properties also enable you to configure license replication, which you can configure on a server using its Licensing properties in Control Panel. By default, license information is replicated from a server's License Logging service to the site license server every 24 hours, and the system automatically staggers replication to avoid burdening the site licensing server. If you want to control replication schedules or frequency, you must manually vary the Start At time and Start Every frequency of each server replicating to a particular site license server.

To manage Per Device or Per User licensing, click Licensing from the Administrative Tools program group, and then select the New License command from the License menu. In the New Client Access License dialog box, select the server product and the number of licenses purchased. Licenses are added to the pool of licenses. As devices or users connect to the product anywhere in the site, they are allocated licenses from the pool, with one license for each device or user. After a pool of licenses is depleted, license violations occur when additional devices or users access the product.

The Purchase History tab in Licensing (shown in Figure 5-16) provides a historical overview of licenses purchased for a site, as well as the quantity, date, and administrator associated with the addition or removal of licenses.

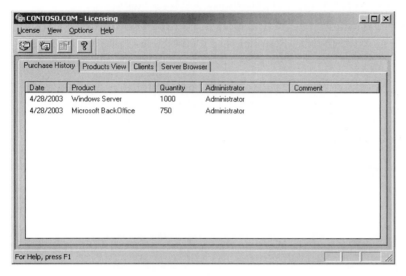

Figure 5-16   The Purchase History tab of the Microsoft Licensing administrative tool

To view cumulative information about licensing and compliance, select the Products View tab. This tab shows how many licenses have been purchased and allocated to users or devices (in Per Device or Per User mode) or the number of licenses purchased for all servers in the site and the peak connections reached to date (in Per Server mode). You can also determine compliance using the licensing status symbols shown in Table 5-2.

Table 5-2   **Licensing Status Symbols**

Symbol	Licensing Status
	The product is in compliance with legal licensing requirements. The number of connections is less than the number of licenses purchased.
	The product is not in compliance with legal licensing requirements. The number of connections exceeds the number of licenses purchased.
	The product has reached the legal limit. The number of connections equals the number of licenses purchased. If additional devices or users will connect to the server product, you must purchase and log new licenses.

License Groups

Per Device or Per User licensing requires one CAL for each device. However, the License Logging service assigns and tracks licenses by username. When multiple users share one or more devices, you must create license groups, or else licenses will be consumed too rapidly. A **license group** is a collection of users who share one or more CALs. When a user connects to the server product, the License Logging service tracks the user by name but assigns a CAL from the allocation assigned to the license group. The concept is easiest to understand with examples such as the following:

- **10 users share a single handheld device for taking inventory.**   You create a license group with the 10 users as members. The license group is assigned one CAL, representing the single device they share.

- **100 students occasionally use a computer lab with 10 computers.**   You create a license group with the 100 students as members and allocate 10 CALs to the group.

To create a license group, click the Options menu and, from the Advanced menu, select New License Group. Enter the group name and allocate one license for each client device used to access the server. The number of licenses allocated to a group should correspond to the number of devices used by members of the group.

> **NOTE** **Exam Objectives**   The objectives for the 70-290 exam require students to be able to "manage software site licensing."

SUMMARY

- Microsoft releases operating system updates in the form of service packs and hotfixes.

- A service pack is a collection of updates that have been tested together and approved for installation on all computers.

- A hotfix is a patch that addresses a single issue that is explained in an accompanying Microsoft Knowledge Base article. Hotfixes are not necessarily meant to be installed on all systems; some are intended only for computers performing certain tasks or experiencing a particular problem.

- Service packs can be obtained from Microsoft on CD for a small fee or downloaded free of charge. If the service pack is a single file, it can be extracted by executing the file with the /X switch.

- Service packs can be deployed manually on each computer, integrated into an operating system installation (slipstreamed), and automatically installed using group policies.

- Microsoft Software Update Services enables you to centralize and manage the approval and distribution of Windows critical updates and Windows security rollups. One or more SUS servers host lists of approved updates and, optionally but typically, the update files themselves. Automatic Updates clients are configured, usually through GPOs, to obtain updates from intranet SUS servers rather than directly from Microsoft Windows Update.

- Tracking and managing licenses and compliance is an important part of an administrator's job. Windows Server 2003 enables you to assign licenses based on concurrent connections to a specific server or to maintain a license for each device or user that connects to any number of servers in your enterprise.

- Licenses are replicated between servers' License Logging service and the site license server. The site license server can be identified using Active Directory Sites And Services, but site licensing is administered using the Licensing tool in the Administrative Tools programs group.

- A license group enables users to share one or more devices. The number of Windows Device CALs is assigned to the license group.

EXERCISES

Exercise 5-1: Using Windows Update

In this exercise, you use Windows Update to download the latest hotfixes for Windows Server 2003.

1. Log on to a Windows Server 2003 computer with Internet access as Administrator.

2. Connect to the Internet (if necessary).

3. Click Start, point to All Programs, and select Windows Update. The Windows Update site appears. Then a Security Warning dialog box appears, asking if you want to download and install the Windows Update application.

4. Review the security warning to ensure that the content is signed by Microsoft and then click Yes to continue.

5. Click the Scan For Updates link.

6. Click the Review And Install Updates link.

7. Review the updates listed and click Install Now. A Microsoft Windows Update dialog box appears, containing the license agreement for the updates.

8. Click Accept to agree to the terms of the license agreement. A Windows Update dialog box appears, containing a progress indicator.

9. When the installation is completed, if the installed updates require a restart, a Microsoft Internet Explorer message box appears, prompting you to restart the system. Click OK to restart the computer.

Exercise 5-2: Configuring Automatic Updates

In this exercise, you configure Automatic Updates to download updates at a scheduled time.

1. Log on to Windows Server 2003 as Administrator.

2. Click Start, point to Control Panel, and click System. The System Properties dialog box appears.

3. Select the Automatic Updates tab.

4. In the Settings box, select the Automatically Download The Updates, And Install Them On The Schedule That I Specify option.

5. In the scheduling drop-down lists, select Every Sunday and 6:00 A.M. Then click OK.

Exercise 5-3: Expanding a Service Pack

In this exercise, you expand the network version of a service pack into its component directory structure.

1. Log on to your computer as Administrator.

2. Open Windows Explorer and create a new folder on your drive C called temp.

3. Obtain a service pack for Windows Server 2003 or Windows XP from the Microsoft Web site or from your instructor and copy it to the temp folder you created on your computer.

4. Click Start, point to All Programs, point to Accessories, and click Command Prompt. A command prompt window appears.

5. In the command prompt window, type **cd\temp**. A C:\temp> prompt appears.

6. At the prompt, type the full name of the downloaded service pack file followed by a space and the /X switch, as in the following example. Then press Enter.

   xpsp1.exe /X

   A Choose Directory For Extracted Files dialog box appears.

7. Click OK to accept the default C:\temp folder. The installation program creates an i386 parent directory in the C:\temp folder containing the expanded service pack installation files.

8. Close the Command Prompt window.

REVIEW QUESTIONS

1. You are configuring a Software Update Services infrastructure using the loose parent/child topology. One server is synchronizing metadata and content from Windows Update. Other servers (one in each site) are synchronizing content from the parent SUS server. Which of the following steps is required to complete the SUS infrastructure? (Choose all correct answers.)

   a. Configure Automatic Updates clients using Control Panel on each system.

   b. Configure GPOs to direct clients to the SUS server in their sites.

   c. Configure a manual content distribution point.

   d. Approve updates using the SUS administration page on the child servers.

2. You are configuring SUS for a group of Web servers. You want the Web servers to update themselves nightly based on a list of approved updates on your SUS server. However, once in a while an administrator is logged on, performing late-night maintenance on a Web server, and you do not want the update installation and potential restart to interfere with those tasks. What Windows Update policy configuration should you use in this scenario?

   a. Notify For Download And Notify For Install

   b. Auto Download And Notify For Install

   c. Auto Download And Schedule The Install

   d. Auto Download And Install Immediately

3. You want all network clients to download and install updates automatically during night hours, and you have configured scheduled installation behavior for Automatic Updates. However, you discover that some users are turning off their machines at night and updates are not being applied. Which group policy enables you to correct this situation without changing the installation schedule?

   a. Specify Intranet Microsoft Update Service Location

   b. No Auto-Restart For Scheduled Automatic Updates Installations

   c. Reschedule Automatic Updates Scheduled Installations

   d. Configure Automatic Updates

4. What command should you use to unpack the single-file download of a service pack?

    a. Setup.exe -u

    b. Update.exe -x

    c. Update.msi

    d. *Servicepackname*.exe –x

5. What are the valid licensing modes in Windows Server 2003? (Choose all correct answers.)

    a. Per User

    b. Per Server

    c. Per Seat

    d. Per Device or Per User

6. You are hiring a team to tackle a software development project. There will be three shifts of six programmers. Each programmer uses four computers to develop and test the software, which authenticate against a Windows Server 2003 computer. What is the minimum number of CALs required if the servers involved are in Per Device or Per User licensing mode?

    a. 6

    b. 4

    c. 18

    d. 24

7. What tool enables you to identify the site license server for your site?

    a. Active Directory Domains And Trusts

    b. Licensing tool in Control Panel

    c. Active Directory Sites And Services

    d. DNS

8. You manage the network for a team of 500 telephone sales representatives. You have 550 licenses configured in Per Device or Per User licensing mode. A new campaign is launched, and you will hire another shift of 500 reps. What do you need to do to most effectively manage license tracking and compliance?

    a. Revoke the licenses from the existing clients.

    b. Delete the existing licenses, and then add 500 licenses.

    c. Create license groups.

    d. Convert to Per Server licensing.

CASE SCENARIOS

Scenario 5-1: Deploying Microsoft SUS

You are the systems administrator for a medium-sized organization that is considering implementing SUS on all Windows XP Professional workstations and Windows Server 2003 systems companywide. Before the companywide rollout can proceed, a pilot program will be implemented. You have been assigned a lab with 10 Windows XP Professional workstations, a Windows Server 2003 member server running SUS, a Windows Server 2003 domain controller, and a standalone Windows Server 2003 system. You want to configure all of the computers except the SUS server to automatically connect to the SUS server each morning at 7 A.M. to download and install new updates. Which of the following steps should you take to accomplish this goal? (Choose all correct answers.)

a. Use the Automatic Updates tab in the System Properties dialog box on every Windows XP Professional workstation computer to set the update server to the address of the SUS server. Set the Windows XP workstations to automatically download and install updates at 7 A.M. each day.

b. Use the Automatic Updates tab in the System Properties dialog box on each Windows Server 2003 system except the SUS server to set the update server to the address of the SUS server. Set these servers to automatically download and install updates at 7 A.M. each day.

c. Place the Windows XP Professional workstations and the Windows Server 2003 domain controller in a separate OU named SUStest. Edit a GPO's Windows Update properties for the SUStest OU, specifying the address of the update server as the SUS server in the Specify Intranet Microsoft Update Service Location policy. Set Configure Automatic Updates Policy to Automatic Download And Schedule The Install, and set the scheduled install day to Every Day and the time to 7 A.M. Apply this GPO to the SUStest OU.

d. On the standalone Windows Server 2003 system, edit the local GPO's Windows Update properties, specifying the address of the update server as the SUS server in the Specify Intranet Microsoft Update Service Location policy. Set Configure Automatic Updates Policy to Automatic Download And Schedule The Install, and set the scheduled install day to Every Day and the time to 7 A.M. Apply this GPO to the SUStest OU.

e. On the SUS server, edit the local GPO's Windows Update properties, specifying the address of the update server as the SUS server in the Specify Intranet Microsoft Update Service Location policy. Set Configure Automatic Updates Policy to Automatic Download And Schedule The Install, and set the scheduled install day to Every Day and the time to 7 A.M. Apply this GPO to the SUStest OU.

Scenario 5-2: Deploying a Service Pack

Fred is the systems administrator for an academic department at the local university. The department has 40 Windows XP Professional workstations and 2 Windows Server 2003 servers. One of these servers is configured as a domain controller, the other as a file and print server. All department computers are members of a single Windows Server 2003 domain. Microsoft has recently released a service pack for Windows XP and, after testing it, Fred feels confident enough to deploy it to the Windows XP Professional workstations in his department. He extracts the service pack to a directory on the file server called \\Fileshare\newsrvpk. Which of the following methods can he use to install the service pack on all Windows XP Professional workstations? (Choose all correct answers.)

a. He can visit each Windows XP Professional workstation and manually install the service pack from the file share.

b. He can create a group called Xpwkstn and put all the Windows XP Professional workstation computer accounts in this group. He can then create a GPO in which he sets up a new package in the Computer Configuration\Software Settings node using the location of the service pack .msi file on the \\Fileshare\newsrvpk share. In the Deploy Software dialog box, he should select Assign, and then apply this GPO to the Xpwkstn group.

c. He can create a group called Xpusrs and put all who use Windows XP Professional workstations in this group. He can then create a GPO in which he sets up a new package in the Computer Configuration\Software Settings node using the location of the service pack .msi file on the \\Fileshare\newsrvpk share. In the Deploy Software dialog box, he should select Assign, and then apply this GPO to the Xpusrs group.

d. He can create an OU called Xpwkstn and put all the Windows XP Professional workstation computer accounts in this OU. He can then create a GPO in which he sets up a new package in the Computer Configuration \Software Settings node using the location of the service pack .msi file on the \\Fileshare\newsrvpk share. In the Deploy Software dialog box, he should select Assign, and then apply this GPO to the Xpwkstn OU.

PART 2

MANAGING AND MAINTAINING USERS, GROUPS, AND COMPUTERS

CHAPTER 6
WORKING WITH USER ACCOUNTS

Before any user can access a computer running Microsoft Windows Server 2003 from the console or over the network, that user must be authenticated. Authentication is the process by which the user is identified and the user's credentials are verified. In most cases, the authentication process requires the user to supply an account name and a password, which the server verifies against its records before granting the user access. Managing these user accounts and passwords is one of the most common tasks performed by network administrators. In this chapter, you learn how to create, manage, and troubleshoot user accounts, both individually and collectively.

Upon completion of this chapter, you will be able to:

■ Understand the differences between local user accounts and domain user accounts

■ Plan user account creation

■ Create and manage local user accounts

■ Create and manage domain user accounts

■ Create and manage user accounts with templates, importation, and command-line tools

■ Manage user profiles

■ Understand the differences between local, roaming, and mandatory profiles

■ Troubleshoot user authentication issues

UNDERSTANDING USER ACCOUNTS

A Microsoft Windows network can be based on one of two organizational schemes, commonly referred to as the *workgroup* and the *domain*. Both of these schemes require users to have user accounts for authentication purposes, but the nature of the accounts and the tools that you use to create and manage them are slightly different. The differences between the local user accounts used by workgroups and domain user accounts are summarized in Table 6-1.

Table 6-1   Local and Domain User Name Characteristics

	Local User Names	Domain User Names
Management Tool	Local Users And Groups	Active Directory Users And Computers
Account Location	Security Account Manager on each local computer	Active Directory database
Logon Location	The local computer	Active Directory domain
Provides Access To	Local computer resources only	Domain and network resources
Name Restrictions	Must be unique on the computer	Must be unique in the directory

Workgroups

A workgroup is a collection of computers that interact on an informal basis, with no centralized authority. Every computer in the workgroup has its own set of local user accounts that are stored in a local, flat-file database called the Security Accounts Manager (SAM). The computer uses these accounts to authenticate users and grant them access to resources on that computer only. If a user requires access to resources on more than one computer in a workgroup, the user must have a separate account on each computer and be authenticated by each computer before access is granted.

However, just because each computer in a workgroup has to perform its own authentications does not necessarily mean that a user has to manually supply an account name and password to connect to each computer. If every computer has an account for that user with the same account name and password, all authentications after the first one occur automatically and in the background.

To create local user accounts, you use an MMC snap-in called Local Users And Groups. To log on with a local user account, in the Log On To Windows dialog box, you specify an account name and password in the text boxes provided, and select This Computer in the Log On To drop-down list.

Although the process of creating a local user account is simple, the primary drawback of the workgroup model is the additional administrative effort required to maintain accounts for the same users on multiple computers. If, for example, a user has an account on 10 different computers, you must modify each account individually to change that user's password. For this reason, the workgroup model is impractical on anything other than a small network.

Domains

The domain model used by Windows Server 2003, Microsoft Windows XP, and Microsoft Windows 2000 is based on Microsoft's Active Directory directory service. In Chapter 1, you learned about the architecture and functions of Active Directory. Active Directory user accounts take the form of user objects, which are stored, as with all Active Directory information, on domain controllers, where they are accessible from anywhere in the domain. When users log on with domain accounts, they are actually being authenticated by a domain controller, not by the computer on which they are working or by the computer they are trying to access.

A domain user account consists of a logon name and password, as well as a unique **security identifier (SID)**. During logon, Active Directory authenticates the username and password entered by the user. The security subsystem can then build a security access token that represents that user. The access token contains the user account's SID, as well as the SIDs of groups to which the user belongs. That token can then be used to verify user rights assignments, including the right to log on locally to the system and to authorize access to resources secured by access control lists (ACLs).

In the domain model, each user has only one domain account, which greatly simplifies the task of the network administrator. This one account can be used to grant the user access to any resource on the network. Because the Active Directory database is (usually) replicated among multiple domain controllers, the user accounts are nearly always available to authenticate the user's access to a new resource. Administrators create domain user objects using the Active Directory Users And Computers MMC snap-in. To log on using a domain user account, you specify the account name and password in the Log On To Windows dialog box and then select the domain in which the account was created in the Log On To drop-down list, as shown in Figure 6-1.

Figure 6-1   The Log On To Windows dialog box

> **NOTE**   **Logging On to a Domain Controller**   When a Windows Server 2003 computer is functioning as a domain controller, there is no other choice but to log on to the domain. Local user accounts and the Local Users And Groups snap-in are not used.

PLANNING USER ACCOUNTS

Before you begin actually creating local or domain user accounts, you should consider a number of planning issues. This is particularly true when you are working with a large and complex network. Although the task of creating an account for each one of your users might seem simple at first, some preparation regarding the names you choose for the accounts, the passwords you are going to allow, and the structure of the Active Directory hierarchy can save you a great deal of trouble later.

Account Naming

When you create a user account, either local or domain, you specify the user's first and last name, but the actual name that the user employs when logging on or authenticating is the account name. Local and domain user account names can be as long as 20 characters, but for the convenience of users they are usually much shorter. The names are not case sensitive (although Windows Server 2003 does preserve the case you enter) and cannot use any of the following characters:

" / \ [ ] : ; | = , + * ? < > @

> **NOTE**   **Account Names and E-Mail Addresses**   When you create account names that will also be used for the users' e-mail addresses, be sure to consider the character limitations of your e-mail software. Some e-mail systems cannot use names that contain spaces or parentheses, even though Windows Server 2003 will accept them.

To form an account name, many organizations use some combination of the user's first or last name and one or more initials. For example, the user Mark Lee might have the account name mlee or markl. However, for an organization of any substantial size, using first names can be impractical because you can easily have two users called Mark and possibly even two Marks with surnames beginning with L.

Whatever form you choose for your account names, the most important thing is to create a set of rules for forming the names and then to stick to it. Assigning account names inconsistently or using obscure nicknames and user preferences only leads to confusion when other administrators have to determine the account name for a particular user. Your rules should specify a standard combination of first or last names and initials, as well as a standardized method for dealing with users for whom the rules produce identical account names. An administrator should be able to hear a user's name for the first time and guess the user's account name with a reasonable degree of certainty.

Choosing Passwords

Security is a pervasive influence on virtually all network administration tasks today, and creating user accounts is no exception. When you create a new account, you must specify a password for it, and what policies you use to control the account passwords should depend on the degree of security your organization needs.

By default, when you create a new domain user account in Windows Server 2003, you must specify a complex password at least seven characters long. These restrictions are imposed by group policy settings that the operating system configures in the default domain policy group policy object (GPO). Local user accounts are not subject to these restrictions. You can modify these requirements and other default password assignment rules by altering the settings of the following password policies using the Group Policy Object Editor console:

- **Enforce Password History**   Specifies the number of unique passwords that users have to supply before the operating system permits them to reuse an old password. The default value is 24.

- **Maximum Password Age**   Specifies how long a single password can be used before the operating system forces the user to change it. The default value is 42 days.

- **Minimum Password Age**   Specifies how long a single password must be used before the operating system permits the user to change it. The default value is one day.

- **Minimum Password Length**   Specifies the minimum number of characters the operating system permits in user-supplied passwords. The default value is seven.

Practice altering password policies by doing Exercise 6-1, "Changing Password Policy Settings," now.

- **Password Must Meet Complexity Requirements**   Specifies criteria for passwords, such as length of at least six characters; no duplication of all or part of the user's account name; and inclusion of characters from at least three of the following four categories: uppercase letters, lowercase letters, numbers, and symbols. By default, the Windows operating system enables this policy.

The default settings for a new user object also enable the User Must Change Password At Next Logon setting. This setting assumes that users will be responsible for supplying their own passwords and changing them at regular intervals. The administrator creating the account, therefore, only has to supply a temporary password for a user's first logon.

Whether you want users to supply their own passwords is another security decision you must make before you start creating accounts. Generally speaking, it is preferable to have users specify their passwords, both because it will be easier for them to remember passwords they created themselves and because changing all of the users' passwords every 42 days would be a severe burden on the network administrators. The default password policy settings force users to change their passwords and also prevent them from reusing the same passwords too often.

Depending on your network's security requirements, you might want to impose on your users other password policies that are not enforceable using software, such as the following:

- Do not share passwords with coworkers or anyone inside or outside the organization.

- Do not write down passwords and leave them where they can easily be found.

■ Do not create passwords using commonly held information such as birthdays or names of spouses, children, or pets.

■ Refer all telephone or e-mail inquiries regarding passwords to network administrators or security officers.

Designing an Active Directory Hierarchy

Because local user accounts are not intended for use on large networks, they are stored in a simple flat-file (nonhierarchical) database. The SAM is really little more than a list of user (and group) accounts with a few basic attributes for each account. Therefore, no design issues are associated with creating this type of account. Domain user accounts, however, are part of an Active Directory hierarchy, and the design of this hierarchy is a critical part of the network infrastructure planning process.

As you learned in Chapter 1, the basic structure of an Active Directory domain is tree-like and similar to the directory structure of a file system. The domain object is at the top of the tree (which is known, somewhat confusingly, as the root) and one or more levels of organizational unit (OU) objects are located beneath. The actual task of designing the hierarchy is best left to the network's architects, but the administrators responsible for creating user accounts must be familiar with the hierarchy and the basic paradigms used to construct it.

To create a domain user object, you must first decide what OU to put it in. This decision should be based on the functions of the OUs created in the hierarchy. An Active Directory tree design can be based on the political divisions of the organization, such as departments and workgroups, or it can be based on geographical locations, such as buildings, floors, wings, and offices, or a combination of these and other factors. The point of having a directory hierarchy is to simplify the process of locating objects in the tree and to facilitate the dissemination of attributes to large numbers of objects by assigning them to an OU and letting them flow downward through the tree.

Placing new user objects in their correct locations in the hierarchy enables them to receive the settings they need without individual configuration and prevents you from having to move them around later.

WORKING WITH LOCAL USER ACCOUNTS

Local accounts enable users to access the resources of the computer on which you create the accounts, either by logging on at the console or by connecting over the network. By default, Windows Server 2003 always creates the following three local user accounts:

■ **Administrator**   This account is required for the first system logon, using a password supplied during the operating system installation. The Administrator user is a member of the Administrators group, which gives him or her complete access to all areas of the operating system. This access includes the ability to create new local user accounts, specify permissions and rights for local user accounts, and install new hardware and software.

The local Administrator account is always needed, even on an Active Directory network, because certain tasks require local Administrator access to the computer.

- **Guest**   This account is intended for use by temporary users who need only limited access to the system. The account is created during the operating system installation, but is left in a disabled state and with no password. You must first enable the account before anyone can use it to log on. The Guest account is a member of the Guests group and has limited access to the operating system. In most cases, it is recommended that you leave the Guest account disabled and create new, individual accounts for specific users rather than letting them all log on using the Guest account.

- **SUPPORT_*number***   This account was created for use by Microsoft technical support personnel when they connect to the system using the Remote Assistance feature. The account is disabled by default and must be enabled before a Microsoft technician can access the computer.

If the computer is connected to a domain, there is no need to create any additional local user accounts because users will log on using their domain accounts and be able to access system resources that way. However, if the computer is part of a workgroup, you can create new local user accounts using the Local Users And Groups snap-in. On non-domain controllers, this snap-in is incorporated into the Computer Management console (as shown in Figure 6-2), which you can access from the Administrative Tools program group on the Start menu.

Figure 6-2   The Local Users And Groups snap-in

Creating a Local User Account

To create a local user account, you select the Users folder in the scope pane of the snap-in and, from the Action menu, select New User to display the New User dialog box (as shown in Figure 6-3). In this dialog box, you specify the following information:

- **User Name**   The account name that the user employs while logging on to the computer (required).

- **Full Name**   The user's full name (optional).

- **Description**   Text describing the user or the function of the user account (optional).

- **Password**   A password of up to 127 characters used to authenticate the account (optional).

- **Confirm Password**   Reenter the same password to ensure that you have typed it correctly. If the two passwords do not match, you are prompted to enter them again.

- **User Must Change Password At Next Logon**   Select this check box if you want the user to change the password after logging on for the first time. You cannot select this option if you have selected the Password Never Expires check box. Selecting this option automatically clears the User Cannot Change Password option.

- **User Cannot Change Password**   Select this check box if you have more than one person using the same domain user account or to maintain control over user account passwords. This option is commonly used to manage service account passwords. You cannot select this option if you have selected the User Must Change Password At Next Logon option.

- **Password Never Expires**   Select this check box if you never want the password to expire. You cannot select this option if you have selected the User Must Change Password At Next Logon option. This option is commonly used to manage service account passwords.

- **Account Is Disabled**   Select this check box to disable the user account, such as when you create an object for a newly hired employee who does not yet need access to the network.

Figure 6-3   The New User dialog box

Managing Local User Accounts

Local user accounts have a relatively small number of attributes. When you select an account in the Users folder of the Local Users And Groups snap-in and select Properties from the Action menu, the user's Properties dialog box appears (as shown in Figure 6-4). This dialog box enables you to modify the Properties you specified while creating the user account, except for the username and the password, which you can change by using the Rename and Set Password commands on the Action menu, respectively. In addition, the dialog box provides access to the other user account parameters found on the following tabs:

■ General

■ Member Of

■ Profile

■ Environment

■ Sessions

■ Remote Control

■ Terminal Services Profile

■ Dial-in

Figure 6-4   A local user's Properties dialog box

The settings on these tabs are identical to those found on the tabs of the same names in a domain user's Properties dialog box. For more information about the specific settings on each tab, see "Managing Domain User Accounts" later in this chapter.

WORKING WITH DOMAIN USER ACCOUNTS

Working with domain user accounts is similar to working with local user accounts, except that domain accounts are capable of containing a lot more information about the user. When you create an Active Directory domain by promoting the first domain controller, Windows Server 2003 creates the following user accounts by default:

■ **Administrator**   The domain Administrator account is a member of the domain's Administrators group and performs basically the same function as the local Administrator account: it provides the account needed for the initial domain logon and provides complete access to all domain functions and features. It is critical to understand that the domain Administrator account is a completely separate entity from the local Administrator account. The two can have different passwords, permissions, and other capabilities. On a Windows Server 2003 computer that is a member of a domain (but not a domain controller), it is possible to log on using either the local or the domain Administrator account, depending on the setting in the Log On To drop-down list in the Log On To Windows dialog box.

■ **Guest**   As with the local Guest account, the domain Guest account is disabled by default and intended for users requiring temporary access to the domain.

> **NOTE**   **Exam Objectives**   *The objectives for the 70-290 exam specify that students should be able to "create and manage user accounts."*

Windows Server 2003 also creates other built-in accounts by default when you install certain services on the computer. For example, promoting a server to a domain controller creates a hidden user object called *krbtgt* to function as the security principal for the Key Distribution Center service. When you install Microsoft Internet Information Services (IIS), two users are created, IUSR_*computername*, which anonymous users use to connect to the server, and IWAM_*computername*, which IIS uses to start out-of-process applications.

The built-in user objects in a domain are all located in a container object called *Users*. Although you can create new user objects in this or any container, or even directly in the domain itself, it is best to always create user objects in an OU so you can manage them later using group policies. You can only link a GPO to a domain, site, or OU object, and the Users container is none of these. Therefore, your Active Directory installation should have appropriate OUs in it, in accordance with your organization's Active Directory design, before you begin creating user objects.

> **NOTE**   **Container Objects**   *The Users, Builtin, Computers, and ForeignSecurity-Principals objects belong to a special object class called a container. In directory services parlance, the term container is mostly used generically, to refer to any objects that can have other objects subordinate to them. However, in the case of the four objects listed here, each is literally an object type called a container. You cannot apply GPOs to these four container objects, nor can you delete them or create new objects of the same type. You can, however, move the subordinate objects from those containers to OU objects of your own creation, which are more manageable.*

On a Windows Server 2003 domain controller, you create domain user objects by using the Active Directory Users And Computers snap-in (as shown in Figure 6-5), which is accessible from the Administrative Tools program group on the Start Menu. To create user objects, you must be a member of the Enterprise Admins, Domain Admins, or Account Operators groups, or you must have been delegated the administrative permissions necessary to create user objects.

> **NOTE**   **Installing Consoles**   *Although the Active Directory management consoles appear in the Administrative Tools program group only on domain controllers, you can run them from Windows Server 2003 member servers and even Windows XP workstations. To install the Administrative Tools package on another computer, run the Adminpak.msi file from the i386 folder of the Windows Server 2003 installation CD.*

Figure 6-5   The Active Directory Users And Computers console

Creating a Domain User Account

To create a user object, select from the console's scope pane the container in which you want to create the object and, from the Action menu, point to New and select User to display the New Object – User wizard. Unlike the New User dialog box that you use to create local user objects, the New Object – User wizard has two pages of configuration parameters that are presented wizard-style.

The first page of the wizard (shown in Figure 6-6) contains the following parameters:

- **First Name**   The user's first name (optional).
- **Initials**   The user's middle initials (optional).
- **Last Name**   The user's last name (optional).

Figure 6-6   The first page of the New Object – User wizard

- **Full Name**   The user's full name (required). If you enter values for the first or last name, the full name field is populated automatically, but you can modify the suggested value. The value entered here generates several user object properties: the common name (CN), the distinguished name (DN), the name, and the displayName properties. Because the CN property must be unique within a container, the name entered here must be unique relative to all other objects in the OU (or other container) in which you create the user object.

- **User Logon Name**   The account name that the user will use to log on (required). This value is used to form the user principal name (UPN), which consists of a logon name and a UPN suffix that is, by default, the Domain Name System (DNS) name of the domain in which you are creating the object. The entire UPN, in the format *logon-name@UPN-suffix*, must be unique within the Active Directory forest. A sample UPN would be *someone@contoso.com*. The UPN can be used to log on to any computer in the domain running Windows Server 2003, Windows XP, or Windows 2000.

- **User Logon Name (Pre–Windows 2000)**   The account name that the user will use when logging on to down-level clients (required). Down-level clients are computers running Windows 95, Windows 98, Windows Millennium Edition (Windows Me), or Microsoft Windows NT. The wizard automatically populates this field with up to 20 characters from the User Logon Name value you supplied. This field must be unique within the domain.

Once you have entered the values in the first page of the New Object – User wizard, click Next. The second page of the wizard, shown in Figure 6-7, contains the following parameters:

- **Password**   A password of up to 127 characters used to access the account. The value you enter for the password must conform in length and complexity to the password policy settings currently in force in the domain.

- **Confirm Password**   Reenter the same password to ensure that you have typed it correctly. If the two passwords do not match, you are prompted to enter them again.

Figure 6-7   The second page of the New Object – User wizard

- **User Must Change Password At Next Logon**   Select this check box if you want the user to change the password after logging on for the first time. You cannot select this option if you have selected the Password Never Expires check box. Selecting this option automatically clears the User Cannot Change Password option.

- **User Cannot Change Password**   Select this check box if you have more than one person using the same domain user account or to maintain control over user account passwords. This option is commonly used to manage service account passwords. You cannot select this option if you have selected the User Must Change Password At Next Logon check box.

- **Password Never Expires**   Select this check box if you never want the password to expire. This option automatically clears the User Must Change Password At Next Logon check box. This option is commonly used to manage service account passwords.

- **Account Is Disabled**   Select this check box to disable the user account, such as when you create a template account or an object for a newly hired employee who does not yet need access to the network.

Some of these account options have the potential to contradict group policy settings that the user object will inherit from the domain or other container objects. For example, the default domain policy GPO specifies that passwords for all user accounts in the domain must be changed every 42 days. However, if you enable the Password Never Expires option in a user object, it overrides the group policy setting and the user will not be prompted to change the password.

Once you have entered the values in the second page of the New Object – User wizard, click Next to display a final summary page. Clicking Finish closes the wizard and creates the new user object in the selected container.

Practice creating domain user accounts by doing Exercise 6-2, "Creating a Domain User Object," now.

Managing Domain User Accounts

Once you have created a user object, you can use the Active Directory Users And Computers console to manage its properties. By selecting a user object and clicking the Action menu, you can perform a variety of tasks, such as the following:

- **Add To A Group**   Makes the user object a member of an existing group.

- **Disable Account**   Causes the account to be rendered inoperable, preventing users from logging on with the account. To reenable the account, you must open the user object's Properties dialog box, select the Account tab, and clear the Account Is Disabled check box in the Account Options list.

- **Reset Password**   Enables an administrator to specify a new password for the account without knowing the old password.

- **Open Home Page**   Opens a Microsoft Internet Explorer window and connects to the Uniform Resource Locator (URL) specified in the Web Page text box on the General tab in the user object's Properties dialog box.

- **Send Mail**   Using the computer's default e-mail client application, opens a new mail message with the address specified in the E-mail text box on the General tab in the user object's Properties dialog box.

- **Delete**   Permanently deletes the user object from Active Directory.

- **Rename**   Modifies the value of the user object's Full Name field and opens a Rename User dialog box, in which you can also modify the First Name, Last Name, Display Name, User Logon Name, and User Logon Name (Pre–Windows 2000) text box values.

> **NOTE** **Exam Objectives**   The objectives for the 70-290 exam specify that students should be able to "create and modify user accounts by using the Active Directory Users And Computers MMC snap-in."

When you create a new domain user account, you specify values for only the most basic user object properties. By far, the most powerful management tool for a user object is its Properties dialog box, which you open by selecting the user object and, from the Action menu, selecting Properties. By default this dialog box has 13 tabs, which contain dozens of user object properties, which you can use to control the account's capabilities and populate with information about the user. These tabs can be divided into the categories shown in Table 6-2.

> **NOTE** **Active Directory Schema and Object Properties**   In some cases, you might notice that the user objects' Properties dialog boxes on a particular network have more than 13 tabs or have additional fields on some of the default tabs. This is because the Active Directory schema, specifying which properties each object type in the directory service has, is extensible. Administrators can extend the schema manually by adding properties to an object type (although Microsoft does not recommend this), or the schema can be automatically extended by the installation of software products. For example, installing Microsoft Exchange extends the schema to create Exchange General, Exchange Features, and E-mail Addresses tabs in each user's Properties dialog box.

Table 6-2   Categories of User Properties Dialog Box Tabs

Category	Dialog Box Tabs
Personal information	■ General
	■ Address
	■ Telephones
	■ Organization
Account properties	■ Account
User configuration management	■ Profile
Group membership	■ Member Of
Terminal Services	■ Terminal Services Profile
	■ Environment
	■ Remote Control
	■ Sessions
Remote Access	■ Dial-in
Applications	■ COM+

The settings on each tab are discussed in the following sections.

The General Tab

The General tab contains basic information about the user, such as the first and last names you specified when creating the object. There are also fields in which you can specify a display name, office location, and a text description for the user, plus the user's telephone numbers, Web page addresses, and e-mail address.

Many of the fields in the General, Address, Telephones, and Organization tabs are purely informational in nature. The use of these fields is optional, and their values are not directly related to the operation of the user object or Active Directory services; they provide only background information about the user. Providing values for these fields enables administrators to locate domain user accounts by searching the directory using whatever information they have about the user they need to find. Other people on the network can also look up a specific user to find contact information for them or other data.

The Address Tab

The Address tab contains informational fields that enable administrators to enter the user's mailing address information into Active Directory.

The Telephones Tab

The Telephones tab contains informational fields in which administrators can record the user's various telephone numbers. Although fields such as these are purely informational in the default Active Directory configuration, this is not to say that applications cannot make use of them. For example, it would be possible to create a telephone dialer application that enabled you to search for another user's account in Active Directory and automatically dial a telephone number specified on this tab in that user's object.

The Organization Tab

The Organization tab contains informational fields in which administrators can specify information about the user's place in the organization, including a field in which you select the account of the user's manager from the Active Directory.

The Account Tab

The Account tab contains the User Logon Name, UPN Suffix, and User Logon Name (Pre–Windows 2000) fields, with the values you specified when creating the user object, along with the four check boxes from the Create Object – User wizard. The tab also includes a number of other account options, including the following:

- **Logon Hours** Displays the Logon Hours dialog box, in which administrators can specify which times of day and which days of the week the user is permitted to log on to the domain. By default, this feature only prevents the user from logging on. If the user is already logged on when the allowed logon time ends, service is not interrupted. However, a security option is available in group policy objects called Network Security: Force Logoff When Logon Hours Expire, which enables an administrator to automatically disconnect the user. Logon hours restrictions apply only to domain logons, not local logons.

- **Log On To** Displays the Logon Workstations dialog box, in which administrators can specify the names of specific computers on the network that can use this user object to log on. This feature is called Computer Restrictions in other parts of the user interface. You must have NetBIOS over TCP/IP enabled on your network to use this feature because it restricts logons based on NetBIOS computer names.

- **Account Is Locked Out**   Disabled by default, this check box is activated and selected when the user account is locked by too many failed logon attempts. You can configure the object's account lockout behavior by defining values for the Account Lockout Duration, Account Lockout Threshold, and Reset Account Lockout Counter After group policies. For example, an Account Lockout Threshold value of 3 causes the account to be locked after three failed logon attempts. When an account is locked out, an administrator can reopen it by clearing this check box.

- **Store Password Using Reversible Encryption**   Causes Active Directory to store the object's password using a reversible encryption algorithm, rather than the stronger, non-reversible algorithm it usually uses. This option is designed to support applications that require a reversible password, such as the original Challenge Handshake Authentication Protocol (CHAP). In all other instances, the option should be left disabled. It is also possible to enable or disable this same option using group policies. When this check box is selected, the setting overrides a conflicting group policy value.

- **Account Is Disabled**   Enables administrators to disable and reenable the user account.

- **Smart Card Is Required For Interactive Logon**   Causes the user object to require a smart card to log on. A smart card is a credit card-sized hardware device that contains identification information for the user, typically in the form of a digital certificate and private encryption key. For a user to log on with a smart card, the computer must be equipped with card reader hardware and the appropriate software, and the user must have the correct personal identification number (PIN) for the card. This option is used only for accounts requiring exceptional security. Because the use of a smart card eliminates the need for a password, selecting this check box changes the account password to a complex, random value and enables the Password Never Expires option.

- **Account Is Trusted For Delegation**   This option enables a service running under a user account (called a *service account*) to impersonate a client to access computer resources on behalf of other user accounts on the network. This option is rarely, if ever, selected in user objects representing actual users.

- **Account Is Sensitive And Cannot Be Delegated**   Delegation enables administrators to grant others control over a particular user account, typically one intended for temporary use, such as the Guest account. Selecting this option prevents the account from being delegated by another account.

- **Use DES Encryption Types For This Account**   Causes Active Directory to use Data Encryption Standard (DES) encryption algorithms for this user object.

- **Do Not Require Kerberos Preauthentication**   Causes Active Directory to omit the Kerberos preauthentication procedure when authenticating this user. This option is for accounts using an alternate implementation of the Kerberos authentication protocol; this alternate implementation does not support preauthentication. Omitting preauthentication reduces the security provided by the protocol, so this option should not be enabled unless there is specific reason for it.

- **Account Expires**   Enables administrators to specify a date on which the user account will be automatically disabled, using the following interface:

The Profile Tab

The Profile tab contains fields in which you can specify the location of the user's profile, home folder, and a logon script that should execute whenever the user logs on.

> **MORE INFO**   For more information about user profiles, see "Managing User Profiles" later in this chapter.

The Member Of Tab

The Member Of tab lists the groups of which the user is a member and enables administrators to modify the user's group memberships. By default, new users are made members of the Domain Users group.

> **NOTE**   For more information about Active Directory groups, see Chapter 7, "Working With Groups."

The Terminal Services Profile Tab

The Terminal Services Profile tab enables administrators to enable the user to connect to terminal servers and also to specify the locations of the user profile and home folder that apply when the user is connected to a terminal server.

The Environment Tab

The Environment tab enables administrators to specify an application that should run as soon as the user connects to a terminal server, to specify whether the user should connect to the mapped client drives and printers immediately at logon, and to specify whether to automatically print to the client's default printer.

The Remote Control Tab

The Remote Control tab contains settings that enable you to configure the Terminal Services remote control settings for the user object. These options specify whether the user's session can be accessed using the remote control feature of Terminal Services, whether the user's permission is required for this access, and whether the auditor can merely observe the user's session or actually take part in it. These options can also be configured using the Terminal Services Configuration console, or with group policies; in the event of a conflict, the group policy settings take precedence.

The Sessions Tab

The Sessions tab enables an administrator to configure the user's Terminal Services disconnection behavior, using the following controls:

■ **End A Disconnected Session**   Specifies the amount of time that the user's Terminal Services session remains open on the server after the user is disconnected.

■ **Active Session Limit**   Specifies the maximum duration for the user's Terminal Services sessions. When a session reaches the limit, it is disconnected.

■ **Idle Session Limit**   Specifies the maximum amount of idle time permitted during a Terminal Services session before the server disconnects.

■ **When A Session Limit Is Reached Or Connection Is Broken**   Specifies whether a terminal server should disconnect or end the session when a session limit is reached or the connection broken. The user can reestablish a disconnected session but cannot reconnect to the session if the server has ended it.

■ **Allow Reconnection**   Specifies whether the user should be permitted to reconnect to a terminal server from any client or from the client where the session originated only.

The Dial-in Tab

The Dial-in tab contains controls that enable administrators to specify the user's remote access capabilities. These controls are as follows:

- **Remote Access Permission (Dial-In Or VPN)** Specifies whether remote access should be explicitly allowed, explicitly denied, or determined by remote access policy settings. If access is explicitly allowed, remote access policy conditions, user account properties, or profile properties can still cause the connection attempt to be denied.

- **Verify Caller ID** Causes the remote access server to verify the number from which the user is connecting using caller ID. If the user's number cannot be verified or does not match the specified telephone number, the connection attempt is denied.

- **Callback Options** Enables an administrator to specify whether the user should employ the callback feature when connecting to a remote access server. If this feature is enabled, the server disconnects during the connection establishment process and calls the user back at a telephone number that is either specified by the user or configured by the network administrator on this tab. The callback feature can be an economy measure, placing the bulk of the connection charges on the company lines, or a security measure, in which only callers at specific telephone numbers are permitted remote access to the network.

- **Assign A Static IP Address** Enables an administrator to specify the IP address that the remote access server should always assign to this user.

- **Apply Static Routes** Enables administrators to specify static routes that are to be added to the remote router's routing table when a demand-dial connection is established.

The COM+ Tab

The COM+ tab contains a single control that enables administrators to assign a specific COM+ partition set to the user. A COM+ partition set is a collection of COM+ partitions, which is where COM+ applications are stored. Selecting a COM+ partition set on this tab enables the user to access the applications in the various COM+ partitions that comprise the set.

Managing Multiple Users

When you manage domain user accounts, there will likely be times when you have to make the same changes to multiple user objects and modifying each one individually would be a tedious chore. In these instances, it is possible to modify the properties of multiple user accounts simultaneously, using the Active Directory Users And Computers console. You simply select several user objects by holding down the Ctrl key as you click each user in the details pane, and then select Properties from the Action menu. A Properties On Multiple Objects dialog box then appears, as shown in Figure 6-8.

Figure 6-8   The Properties On Multiple Objects dialog box

> **NOTE   Modifying Object Classes**   When you select multiple objects to modify, you get the best results when the objects are all of the same class. For example, you can select multiple user objects and modify a variety of properties, but if you select a user object and a computer object, the only property you can modify is Description.

The Properties On Multiple Objects dialog box is slightly different from the standard user object Properties dialog box. The former dialog box contains only a limited subset of the object's properties—the ones that are likely to apply to multiple objects. The tabs in the dialog box and the properties on each tab are summarized in Table 6-3.

Table 6-3   **Properties Available for Multiple User Object Modification**

Tab	Properties
General	■ Description
	■ Office
	■ Telephone Number
	■ Fax
	■ Web Page
	■ E-mail
Account	■ UPN Suffix
	■ Logon Hours
	■ Computer Restrictions
	■ Account Options
	■ Account Expires

(continued)

Table 6-3   **Properties Available for Multiple User Object Modification**

Tab	Properties
Address	■ Street
	■ P.O. Box
	■ City
	■ State/Province
	■ Zip/Postal Code
	■ Country/Region
Profile	■ Profile Path
	■ Logon Script
	■ Home Folder
Organization	■ Title
	■ Department
	■ Company
	■ Manager

Moving User Objects

Although it is a good idea to have the organization's Active Directory hierarchy design when you create your user objects, so that you can create them in the correct containers, it is still possible to move them after creation. This capability also enables you to accommodate personnel transfers and business reorganizations.

To move a user object (or any object), you select it and, from the Action menu, select Move to display the Move dialog box (shown in Figure 6-9). Then you select the desired destination container and click OK. You can also move objects by dragging and dropping them.

Figure 6-9   The Move dialog box

To practice moving objects, do Exercise 6-3, "Moving a User Object," now.

NOTE   Deleting Objects   When you move objects around in the Active Directory hierarchy, be careful not to delete them accidentally. The SID associated with a user object is a unique value that is assigned when the object is created. When you delete an object accidentally and then re-create it with the exact same name and property settings, the SID is still different. This is not a big issue for newly created objects, but if you delete an older object, you must then reconfigure all of the user's permissions because these are referenced using the object's SID.

CREATING MULTIPLE USER OBJECTS

At times, network administrators are required to create multiple user objects quickly, to accommodate the arrival of a group of new hires or a new class of incoming students. For these times, there are methods that you can use to facilitate or automate the user object creation process so that you do not have to create each account individually. The Active Directory Users And Computers console is a tool that is designed primarily for individual object creation and management. However, Windows Server 2003 also includes other tools that can streamline the object creation process by using techniques such as importation and command-line scripting.

Using Object Templates

It is common for Active Directory objects of the same class to share similar properties. For example, all of the members of a particular department probably are members of the same groups, are allowed to log on to the network during the same hours, and have home folders and roaming profiles on the same server. In such cases, it can be helpful when creating a new user account to start out with an object that is prepopulated with common properties. You can accomplish this by creating a generic user object—called a *template*—and then copying that object to create new users.

To create a user object template, create a new user object, assign it an identifying name, such as UserTemplate, and configure the properties that are likely to be common to all of the new users you create, just as you would when configuring an object for an individual user. The properties that are copied to a new object are summarized in Table 6-4. After you have configured the properties, be sure to disable the template object so that no one can use it to access network resources.

Table 6-4   **Properties Copied to New User Objects**

Tab	Properties Copied
General	None
Address	All, except Street Address
Telephones	None
Organization	All, except Title
Account	All, except User Logon Name and User Logon Name (Pre–Windows 2000), which are specified during the copy process
Profile	All, including Profile Path and Local Path, which are modified to reflect the new user's logon name
Member Of	All
Terminal Services Profile	None
Environment	None
Remote Control	None
Sessions	None
Dial-in	None
COM+	None

> **NOTE** **Creating Multiple Templates** Depending on the size of your organization and the complexity of your user object configurations, you might want to create multiple templates at various locations in your Active Directory tree. For example, creating a separate user object template in each of your OUs would enable you to configure each one with property values specific to that OU.

Once the template is in place, you can use it to create a new user account by selecting it and, from the Action menu, selecting Copy. A Copy Object – User wizard appears that is nearly identical to the New Object – User wizard you used earlier in this chapter. The wizard walks you through the process of configuring the object properties that must have unique values, such as the user's first and last names, initials, logon names, password, and account options. When the wizard finishes, the new user object is created, with the template values for properties listed in the table.

> **EXAM TIP** **Object Copying and Permissions** A user that has been generated by copying a template has the same group memberships as the template, so the permissions and rights assigned to those groups apply to the new user as well. However, permissions or rights assigned explicitly to the template user object are not copied to new objects or adjusted, so the new user will not have those permissions or rights.

Importing User Objects Using CSV Directory Exchange

CSV Directory Exchange (Csvde.exe) is a command-line utility that imports objects to or exports them from Active Directory using comma-delimited text files. A comma-delimited text file (also known as a CSV, or comma-separated value, file), is a plain-text listing of database information with each record forming a separate line and commas separating the different fields in each record.

> **NOTE** **Exam Objectives** The objectives for the 70-290 exam specify that students should be able to "import user accounts."

Creating a CSV File

The most difficult part of using CSV Directory Exchange to create user objects is the format of the CSV file itself. The first line of a CSV file, called the header, must contain a list of the attributes that will be included in all of the subsequent lines. You list the attributes using the names assigned to them in Lightweight Directory Access Protocol (LDAP), which is the standard Active Directory communication protocol. A typical CSV header line might appear as follows:

```
DN,objectClass,sAMAccountName,sn,givenName,userPrincipalName
```

In this line, the field names stand for the following attributes:

- **DN** The object's distinguished name (DN), which specifies not only the name of the object itself but also its place in the Active Directory tree hierarchy. A DN consists of the user's common name (CN) followed by the names of all the containers above the user object, all the way to the root of the tree.

- **objectClass** Specifies the type of object.

- **sAMAccountName**   Specifies the object's pre–Windows 2000 logon name.

- **sn**   Specifies the user's surname.

- **givenName**   Specifies the user's first name.

- **userPrincipalName**   Specifies the user's full UPN, including the domain name.

Every subsequent line following this header must specify a value for each of the attributes listed in the header. An example of a record in the CSV file is as follows:

```
"CN=Scott Bishop,OU=Employees,DC=contoso,DC=com",
    user,sbishop,Bishop,Scott,scott.bishop@contoso.com
```

This file, when imported, creates a user object in the Employees OU called Scott Bishop. The logon names, first name, and last name are configured by the file. This is a simple example of a CSV file with only a few attributes. The header can be much longer and contain any of the attributes normally found in an object.

> **NOTE   Creating Blank Attributes**   When creating the records in a CSV file, you can leave the value for a particular attribute blank, but you must still account for it in the field layout. For example, to omit the user's first name from this sample record, you would use the following format:
>
> ```
> "CN=Scott Bishop,OU=Employees,DC=contoso,DC=com",
>     user,sbishop,Bishop,,scott.bishop@contoso.com
> ```
>
> The number of commas remains the same, so the givenName field is accounted for, but it contains no value.

The best way to create your own CSV file is to use an existing one as an example. You can use CSV Directory Exchange to export your entire Active Directory database to a CSV file by typing the following command in a command prompt window:

```
csvde -f outputFileName
```

You can then open the output file in any text editor, such as Notepad, and use it to determine the LDAP names for the attributes you want to use and the proper format for each record.

Importing a CSV File

Once you have created a properly formatted CSV file containing the information for multiple Active Directory objects, you can import them all into your directory at once by running the Csvde.exe program from the Windows command line with the name of the CSV file, using the following syntax:

```
csvde -i -f FileName -k
```

The functions of the command line switches are as follows:

- **-i**   Switches the program into import mode. If not specified, the default mode is export.

- **-f *filename***   Specifies the name of the CSV file to be imported.

- **-k**   Causes the program to ignore errors, such as "object already exists," "constraint violation," and "attribute or value already exists," during the import operation and continue processing.

Creating User Objects with Dsadd.exe

Dsadd.exe is a Windows Server 2003 program that enables you to create new Active Directory objects, complete with attribute values, from the command prompt. When you have a large number of user objects to create, the advantage of using Dsadd.exe is that you can create a batch file containing multiple commands and create as many objects as you need at one time.

> **NOTE Exam Objectives** *The objectives for the 70-290 exam specify that students should be able to "create and modify user accounts by using automation."*

The basic syntax for creating user objects with Dsadd.exe is as follows:

```
dsadd user UserDN [parameters]
```

> **NOTE Creating Other Object Types** *You can use Dsadd.exe to create any type of Active Directory object by replacing the user parameter with the name of any object class the directory supports, and by supplying additional parameters appropriate to that object class.*

The *UserDN* parameter is one or more distinguished names for the new user object(s). The DN uses the same format as it does in CSV files, as discussed earlier in this chapter. If a DN includes a space, you must surround the entire DN with quotation marks. When using Dsadd.exe interactively from the command prompt, you can supply the *UserDN* parameter in any one of the following ways:

- By typing each DN on the command line, separated by spaces.
- By piping a list of DNs from another command, such as Dsquery.exe.
- By leaving the DN parameter empty, at which point you can type the DNs, one at a time, at a prompt presented by the program. Press Enter after each DN, and press Ctrl+Z and Enter after the last DN.

In addition to the *UserDN* parameter, you can include any of the following parameters on the Dsadd user command line to specify values for other object attributes:

- **-samid** *SAMName*
- **-upn** **UPN**
- **-fn** *FirstName*
- **-mi** *Initial*
- **-ln** *LastName*
- **-display** *DisplayName*
- **-empid** *EmployeeID*
- **-pwd** {*Password* | *}, where * will cause you to be prompted for a password
- **-desc** *Description*
- **-memberof** *GroupDN*
- **-office** *Office*

- **-tel** *PhoneNumber*
- **-email** *Email*
- **-hometel** *HomePhoneNumber*
- **-pager** *PagerNumber*
- **-mobile** *CellPhoneNumber*
- **-fax** *FaxNumber*
- **-iptel** *IPPhoneNumber*
- **-webpg** *WebPage*
- **-title** *Title*
- **-dept** *Department*
- **-company** *Company*
- **-mgr** *ManagerDN*
- **-hmdir** *HomeDirectory*
- **-hmdrv** *DriveLetter*
- **-profile** *ProfilePath*
- **-loscr** *ScriptPath*
- **-mustchpwd** {yes | no}
- **-canchpwd** {yes | no}
- **-reversiblepwd** {yes | no}
- **-pwdneverexpires** {yes | no}
- **-acctexpires** *NumberOfDays*
- **-disabled** {yes | no}

You can also add the *-s*, *-u*, and *-p* parameters to specify the domain controller against which Dsadd.exe will run and the username and password that will be used to execute the command.

- **{-s** *Server* | **-d** *Domain*}
- **-u** *UserName*
- **-p** {*Password* | *}

The special variable *$username$* (case-insensitive) can be used to supply the user's SAM account name in the value of the *-email*, *-hmdir*, *-profile*, and *-webpg* parameters. For example, if a SAM account name is Denise, the *-hmdir* parameter can be written in either of the following formats:

```
-hmdir\users\Denise\home
-hmdir\users\$username$\home
```

To create an object for the Scott Bishop user from the earlier example, you would use the following Dsadd.exe command line:

```
dsadd user "CN=Scott Bishop,OU=Employees,DC=contoso,DC=com" -samid sbishop
   -ln Bishop -fn Scott -upn scott.bishop@contoso.com
```

Modifying User Objects with Dsmod.exe

Dsmod.exe is another Windows Server 2003 command-line tool that you can use to modify existing Active Directory objects. The syntax and command-line switches for modifying user objects with Dsmod.exe are exactly the same as those for Dsadd.exe, as follows:

```
dsmod user UserDN [parameters]
```

The only exceptions are that you cannot use the *–samid* switch to modify an object's User Logon Name property, and you cannot use the *–memberof* parameter to change the user's group memberships. You can, however, modify group memberships by using the Dsmod group command.

MANAGING USER PROFILES

A *user profile* is a collection of folders and data that stores the user's current desktop environment, application settings, and personal data. A user profile also contains all of the user's Start menu items and mapped drives to network servers. User profiles maintain consistency by providing users with the same desktop environment that they had the last time they logged on to the computer.

> **NOTE   Exam Objectives**   The objectives for the 70-290 exam specify that students should be able to "manage local, roaming, and mandatory user profiles."

On computers running Windows Server 2003, user profiles automatically create and maintain the desktop settings for each user's work environment on the local computer. The system creates a new user profile for each user logging on to the computer for the first time.

User profiles provide several advantages to users:

- Multiple users can work on the same computer, with all users maintaining their own desktop settings each time they log on.

- When users log on to their workstations, they receive the same desktop settings that they had when they logged off.

- Customization of the desktop environment by one user does not affect another user's settings.

- User profiles can be stored on a server so that they can follow users to other computers on the network. Server-based profiles are called **roaming user profiles**.

- Applications that are certified for Windows 2000 and later operating systems store their settings in user profiles.

- As an administrative tool, user profiles provide the following options:
  - ❏ You can create a default user profile that is appropriate for the user's tasks.
  - ❏ You can set up a **mandatory user profile**, which is a profile that does not change, enforcing a particular system configuration for all users.
  - ❏ You can specify the default user settings to be included in all of the individual user profiles.

User Profile Contents

A user profile contains configuration preferences and options for a specific user, forming a snapshot of a user's desktop environment. Table 6-5 lists the settings contained in a user profile.

Table 6-5   **Settings Contained in a User Profile**

Parameters Saved	Source
All user-definable settings for Windows Explorer	Windows Explorer
User-stored documents	My Documents
User-stored image files	My Pictures
Shortcuts and cookies for favorite locations on the Internet	Favorites/Cookies
User-created mapped network drives	Mapped network drive
Links to other computers on the network	My Network Places
Items stored on the desktop and in the taskbar, and shortcut elements	Desktop contents
All user-definable screen colors and display text settings	Screen colors and fonts
Application data and user-defined configuration settings	Application data and registry
Network printer connections	Printer settings
All user-defined settings in Control Panel	Control Panel
Per-user program settings for applications designed to track program settings	Programs certified for use with Windows 2000 and later operating systems
Certificates	Certificate store

User Profile Directory Structure

Local user profiles are stored on the computer's system drive in the Documents And Settings folder. When a user logs on for the first time, Windows Server 2003 creates a subfolder in Documents And Settings, named with the user's logon name, and also a new user profile. Figure 6-10 shows the directory structure of a user profile.

Figure 6-10   The user profile directory structure

The functions of the folders in a user profile are as follows:

- **Application Data**   A hidden folder that contains program-specific data, such as a custom dictionary. Application developers decide which data to store in this folder.

- **Cookies**   Contains Web site user information and preferences stored by Internet Explorer.

- **Desktop**   Contains desktop icons, including shortcuts to files and folders.

- **Favorites**   Contains shortcuts to favorite locations on the Internet.

- **Local Settings**   A hidden folder that contains the Application Data folder and History folder, as well as additional folders for the storage of temporary files.

- **My Documents**   Contains user-stored document files.

- **My Recent Documents**   Hidden folder that contains shortcuts to the most recently used documents and most recently accessed folders.

- **NetHood**   Hidden folder that contains shortcuts to My Network Places items.

- **PrintHood**   Hidden folder that contains shortcuts to printer folder items.

- **SendTo**   Hidden folder that contains shortcuts to document-handling utilities.

- **Start Menu**   Contains shortcuts to executables and other files that form the Start menu.

- **Templates**   Contains user template items.

In addition to these folders, a user profile also contains a copy of the Ntuser.dat file, which is the Windows Server 2003 registry file where user-specific settings are stored. Among other things, these settings include many of the options you can configure in Control Panel.

Using Local Profiles

The use of local user profiles on a computer running Windows Server 2003 is completely invisible to the average user. The operating system automatically creates the user profile for each user logging on for the first time. When that user logs on again, Windows Server 2003 loads the settings from the correct profile.

Users change their local user profiles without even knowing it, simply by changing their desktop settings, saving new favorites, or changing screen colors. When the user modifies the desktop environment while logged on, Windows Server 2003 incorporates the changes into the user profile stored on the computer the next time the user logs off. Thus, a user logging on to a computer running Windows Server 2003 always receives the desktop settings and connections as they were at the end of the previous session. When multiple users share the same computer, each user maintains and receives a separate profile.

Using Roaming Profiles

To support users who work at multiple computers, network administrators can set up roaming user profiles. A roaming user profile is simply a copy of a local user profile that is stored on a network share (to which the user has appropriate permissions) so that the user can access it from any computer on the network. No matter which computer a user logs on from, the user always receives the desktop settings and connections from the profile stored on the server, in contrast to a local user profile, which resides on only one client computer.

To enable a user to access a roaming user profile, rather than a local profile, you must open the user's Properties dialog box and specify the location of the roaming profile in the Profile Path text box on the Profile tab. Then, the next time the user logs on, Windows Server 2003 accesses the roaming user profile in the following manner:

1. During the user's first logon, the computer copies the entire contents of the roaming profile to the appropriate subfolder in the Documents And Settings folder on the local drive.

   Having the roaming user profile contents stored on the local drive enables the user to log on and access the profile, even if the server containing the roaming profile is not available.

2. The computer applies the roaming user profile settings to the computer.

3. As the user works, any changes made to the user profile are saved to the copy on the local drive.

4. When the user logs off, the computer replicates any changes that were made to the local copy of the user profile back to the server where the roaming profile is stored.

5. The next time the user logs on to the same computer, the system compares the contents of the locally-stored profile with the roaming profile stored on the server.

6. The computer copies only the roaming profile components that have changed to the copy on the local drive, which makes the logon process shorter and more efficient.

You should create roaming user profiles on a file server that you frequently back up so that you have copies of the most recent profiles for your users. To improve logon performance for a busy network, place the users' roaming profiles folder on a member server instead of a domain controller. Copying roaming user profiles between the server and client computers can consume a lot of system resources, such as network bandwidth and processor cycles. If the profiles are on a domain controller, the domain user authentication processes can be delayed.

> **NOTE Shared Profile Cautions** When you create a single roaming profile for multiple clients, be sure to consider the potential ramifications of having different hardware configurations on systems using the same profile. For example, if desktop shortcuts are arranged assuming a 1024x768 screen resolution and the user logs on to a system with a display adapter capable of only 800x600 resolution, some shortcuts might not be visible. Profiles are also not fully cross-platform. A profile designed for Windows 98 will not function properly on a Windows Server 2003 system. You will even encounter inconsistencies when roaming between Windows Server 2003 systems and computers running Windows XP or Windows 2000.

Using Mandatory Profiles

A mandatory user profile is a read-only roaming user profile. Users receive desktop settings as they would with any roaming profile, and they can modify the desktop settings of the computer while they are logged on, but none of these changes is saved when they log off. The next time the user logs on, the profile is the same as that of the previous logon. Windows Server 2003 downloads the mandatory profile settings to the local computer each time the user logs on. You can assign one mandatory profile to multiple users who require the same desktop settings, such as a group of users who all do the same job. Because the profile never changes, you do not have to worry about one user making changes that affect all of the other users. Also, a mandatory profile makes it possible to modify the desktop environment for multiple users by changing only one profile.

To create a mandatory user profile, you rename the Ntuser.dat file in the folder containing the roaming profile to Ntuser.man. The Ntuser.dat file is a hidden file that consists of the Windows Server 2003 system registry settings that apply to the individual user account and contains the user environment settings, such as desktop appearance. Renaming this file with a .man extension makes it read-only, preventing the client computers from saving changes to the profile when a user logs off.

MONITORING AND TROUBLESHOOTING USER AUTHENTICATION

Once you have configured user objects and users are authenticating against those accounts, you expose yourself to two additional challenges: security vulnerabilities, which if unaddressed could compromise the integrity of your enterprise network, and social engineering challenges, as you work to make the network authentication process friendly and reliable for users. Unfortunately, these two dynamics are at odds with each other—the more secure a network is, the less user-friendly it becomes.

Implementing the Windows Server 2003 features that provide security for the user authentication process frequently results in users having trouble logging on, and part of the network administrator's job is to troubleshoot these problems as they occur. The following sections examine some of the most common causes of user authentication problems and the tools that you can use to detect and address them.

Using Password Policies

Earlier in this chapter, in "Choosing Passwords," you learned about the password policies that Windows Server 2003 provides, which enable you to specify the length, complexity, and age of the passwords supplied by users for their accounts. The basic goals of these policies are to compel users to specify effective passwords and to force them to change the passwords at regular intervals.

It is easy to use these password policies to enforce the use of extremely secure passwords, but requiring each user to supply a new 15-character complex password every week is likely to cause more problems than it solves. The network support staff will probably start receiving a rash of forgotten password calls, but even worse, users will be more likely to write down their passwords and store them in unsafe places. You must design a password policy that is sufficiently daunting to attackers while being sufficiently convenient for users, so that they do not forget their passwords or have to write them down.

> **NOTE   Specifying Password Lengths**   When you implement password policies, keep in mind that while Windows Server 2003, Windows XP Professional, and Windows 2000 support 127-character passwords, Windows 95, Windows 98, and Windows Me only support passwords up to 14 characters long.

The five password policies listed earlier in this chapter are available in Active Directory group policy objects, which you configure using the Group Policy Object Editor console, by browsing to the Computer Configuration\Windows Settings \Security Settings\Account Policies\Password Policy node. However, you can also define the same policies for local user accounts using the Local Security Policy console, which is available in the Administrative Tools program group on any Windows Server 2003 member server.

> **NOTE   Changing Password Policies**   Configuring password length and complexity requirements does not affect existing passwords. These changes affect only new accounts and passwords that change after the policy is applied.

Using Account Lockout Policies

Account lockout happens when, after several failed logon attempts by a single user, the system assumes that an attacker is attempting to compromise the account by discovering its password, and locks the account so no further logons can be attempted. Domain account lockout policies determine how many invalid logon attempts can be made in a given period of time before the account is locked out. These policies also determine whether an administrator must be contacted to unlock the account, or if it simply becomes unlocked after a specified period of time.

> **NOTE   Exam Objectives**   The objectives for the 70-290 exam specify that students should be able to "diagnose and resolve account lockouts."

The group policies you use to control account lockouts are as follows:

■ **Account Lockout Threshold**   Specifies the number of invalid logon attempts that will trigger an account lockout. Possible values range from 0 to 999. A value that is too low (3, for example) might cause lockouts due to normal user error during logon. A value of 0 prevents accounts from ever being locked out.

■ **Account Lockout Duration**   Determines the period of time that must pass after a lockout before Active Directory will automatically unlock a user's account. The policy is not set by default because it is useful only in conjunction with the Account Lockout Threshold policy. Possible values range from 0 to 99,999 minutes (about 10 weeks). A low setting (5 to 15 minutes) is sufficient to reduce attacks significantly without unreasonably affecting legitimate users who are mistakenly locked out. A value of 0 requires the user to contact an administrator to unlock the account manually.

■ **Reset Account Lockout Counter After** Specifies the period of time that must pass after an invalid logon attempt before the lockout counter resets to 0. Possible values range from 1 to 99,999 minutes and must be less than or equal to the value of the Account Lockout Duration.

As with password policies, you configure account policies in the Group Policy Object Editor console, in the Computer Configuration\Windows Settings\Security Settings\Account Policies\Account Lockout Policy node. Account lockout policies are also available in the Local Security Policy console.

When you implement an account lockout policy on your network, you are all but guaranteed to receive a certain number of technical support calls from users who have unknowingly locked themselves out from their accounts. These calls might be reported as something else, such as lost passwords or other malfunctions, but savvy help desk technicians should be conscious of the account lockout policies in place on the network and of the procedure for unlocking a locked account.

> **NOTE** **Exam Objectives** *The objectives for the 70-290 exam specify that students should be able to "troubleshoot user accounts" and "troubleshoot user authentication issues."*

Active Directory Clients

When you run a heterogeneous network, you must keep in mind that not all operating systems, and not even all Windows operating systems, support Active Directory right out of the box. Active Directory was first introduced in Windows 2000, and only the Windows 2000, Windows XP, and Windows Server 2003 operating systems include Active Directory client capabilities.

Computers running Windows 95, Windows 98, Windows Me, and Windows NT 4 can function as Active Directory clients, but first you must download the Active Directory client software from Microsoft's Web site and install it. This client enables those platforms to participate in many of the Active Directory features available to Windows Server 2003, Windows XP, and Windows 2000 systems, including the following:

■ **Site-awareness** A computer running the Active Directory Client will attempt to log on to the closest domain controller on the network rather than to the primary domain controller (PDC).

■ **Active Directory Service Interfaces (ADSI)** Enables the use of scripting to manage Active Directory.

■ **Distributed File System (Dfs)** Enables the client to access Dfs shared resources on servers running Windows Server 2003 and Windows 2000.

■ **NT LAN Manager (NTLM) version 2 authentication** The client uses the improved authentication features in NTLM version 2.

- **Active Directory search capability**   The client can search for Active Directory objects using the Find or Search feature. Users with proper permissions can also use the Windows Address Book (WAB) property pages to modify the properties of objects.

The following types of functionality, supported on Windows 2000 Professional and Windows XP Professional, are *not* provided by the Active Directory client on Windows 95, Windows 98, and Windows NT 4:

- Kerberos V5 authentication

- Group Policy or Change And Configuration Management support

- Service principal name (SPN) or mutual authentication

- Internet Protocol Security (IPSec) or Layer 2 Tunneling Protocol (L2TP) support

In addition, you should be aware of the following issues in mixed environments:

- Without the Active Directory client, users on systems running versions of Windows prior to Windows 2000 can change their passwords only if the system has access to the domain controller functioning as the primary domain controller (PDC) emulator. To determine which system is the PDC emulator in a domain, open Active Directory Users And Computers, select the domain node, select the Operations Masters command from the Action menu, and then select the PDC tab. If the PDC emulator is unavailable (that is, if it is offline or on the distant side of a downed network connection), the user cannot change her password.

- As you learned earlier in this chapter, user objects maintain two user logon name properties. The Pre–Windows 2000 logon name, or SAM name, is equivalent to the username in Windows 95, Windows 98, or Windows NT 4. When users log on, they enter their username and must select the domain from the Log On To drop-down list. In other situations, the username can be entered in the format *DomainName\UserLogonName*. Users logging on using Windows 2000 or later platforms can log on in the same way, or they can log on using the more efficient UPN. The UPN takes the format *UserLogonName@UPN Suffix*, where the UPN suffix is, by default, the DNS domain name in which the user object resides. It is not necessary to select the domain from the Log On To box when using UPN logon. In fact, the box becomes disabled as soon as you type the @ symbol.

Auditing Authentication

If you are concerned that attacks might be taking place to discover user passwords, or if you want more information to troubleshoot authentication problems, you can configure an auditing policy that creates entries in the Security log that might prove illuminating. The following audit policies are located in the Computer Configuration \Windows Settings\Security Settings\Local Policies\Audit Policy node of both the Group Policy Object Editor console and the Local Security Policy console. You can configure auditing for successful or failed events.

- **Audit Account Logon Events** Audits each successful or failed user logon event. For domain controllers, this policy is defined in the Default Domain Controllers Policy GPO. Enabling the policy creates a Security log entry on a domain controller each time a user logs on interactively or over the network using a domain account. To evaluate fully the results of the auditing, you must examine the Security logs on all domain controllers because user authentication is distributed among the domain controllers in a site or domain.

- **Audit Account Management** Configures auditing of administrative activities, including the creation, deletion, or modification of user, group, or computer accounts, as well as password resets.

- **Audit Logon Events** Logon events include logon and logoff, interactively or through network connection. If you have enabled the Audit Account Logon Events policy for successes on a domain controller, workstation logons will not generate logon audits. Only interactive and network logons to the domain controller itself generate logon events. Account logon events are generated on the local computer for local accounts and on the domain controller for network accounts. Logon events are generated wherever the logon occurs.

> **NOTE** **Exam Objectives** The objectives for the 70-290 exam specify that a student should be able to "diagnose and resolve issues related to user account properties."

Once you have configured the auditing policies, the Security logs will begin to fill with event messages. You can view these messages using the Event Viewer console.

> **MORE INFO** For more information on using the Event Viewer console, see Chapter 3, "Monitoring Microsoft Windows Server 2003."

SUMMARY

- Computers running Windows Server 2003 can have local user accounts and domain user accounts. Local user accounts are stored on the local system and can provide users with access only to local resources. Domain user accounts are stored on Active Directory domain controllers and can provide users with access to resources all over the network.

- To create domain user accounts, you must be a member of the Enterprise Admins, Domain Admins, or Account Operators groups, or you must have been delegated administrative permissions to create user objects.

- User objects include the properties typically associated with a user "account," including logon names, password, and the unique SID for the user. They also include a number of properties related to the individuals they represent, including personal information, group membership, and administrative settings. Windows Server 2003 enables you to change some of these properties for multiple user objects simultaneously.

- A user object template is an object that is copied to produce new users. If the template is not a "real" user, it should be disabled. Only a subset of user properties is copied from templates.

- CSV Directory Exchange enables you to import directory objects from a comma-delimited text file.

- Windows Server 2003 includes command-line tools that you can use to create and manage Active Directory objects, including Dsadd.exe and Dsmod.exe

- A user profile is a collection of folders and files that make up the desktop environment for a specific user. User profiles include the user's personal documents, desktop icons, Start menu shortcuts, and Control Panel settings, such as those that control the screen colors.

- Windows Server 2003 generates an individual user profile for each person who logs on to the system. Profiles are stored, by default, on the local system in *Systemdrive*\Documents and Settings*Username*.

- A local user profile is one that is stored on the local drive, whereas a roaming user profile is one that is stored on a network server. Roaming profiles provide users with the same profile from any computer on the network.

- A mandatory user profile is one that never changes, providing the same desktop configuration each time the user logs on.

- Auditing for authentication generates events in each domain controller's security logs.

EXERCISES

Exercise 6-1: Changing Password Policy Settings

In this exercise, you modify the default password policy settings on your computer.

1. Log on to a Windows Server 2003 domain controller as Administrator.

2. Click Start, point to Administrative Tools, and click Active Directory Users And Computers. The Active Directory Users And Computers console appears.

3. Select the domain object and, from the Action menu, select Properties. The domain's Properties dialog box appears.

4. In the Group Policy tab, select Default Domain Policy and click Edit. The Group Policy Object Editor console appears.

5. Under Computer Configuration, expand the Windows Settings, Security Settings, and Account Policies nodes. Then select the Password Policy node.

6. Double-click the Minimum Password Length policy. The Minimum Password Length Properties dialog box appears.

7. Change the minimum password length setting to 8 characters, and then click OK.

8. Double-click the Maximum Password Age policy. The Maximum Password Age Properties dialog box appears.

9. Change the maximum password age setting to 7 days, and then click OK.

10. Close the Group Policy Object Editor console.

11. Click OK to close the domain's Properties dialog box.

12. Close the Active Directory Users And Computers console.

Exercise 6-2: Creating a Domain User Object

In this exercise, you create a new user object in an Active Directory container.

1. Log on to a Windows Server 2003 domain controller as Administrator.

2. Click Start, point to Administrative Tools, and click Active Directory Users And Computers. The Active Directory Users And Computers console appears.

3. Expand the domain object in the scope pane and select the Users container. On the Action menu, point to New and click User. The New Object – User wizard appears.

4. In the Full Name text box, type **Mark Lee**.

5. In the User Logon Name text box, type **mlee**, and then click Next.

6. In the Password and Confirm Password text boxes, type **rabbit!runs4all**, and then click Next.

7. Click Finish to create the new object.

8. Close the Active Directory Users And Computers console.

Exercise 6-3: Moving a User Object

In this exercise, you move a user object to a different container.

1. Log on to a Windows Server 2003 domain controller as Administrator.

2. Click Start, point to Administrative Tools, and click Active Directory Users And Computers. The Active Directory Users And Computers console appears.

3. Expand the domain object in the scope pane and select the Users container. In the details pane, select the Guest user object. On the Action menu, select Move. The Move dialog box appears.

4. Select the Computers container, and then click OK. The Guest object is moved to the Computers container.

5. Select the Computers container in the scope pane.

6. In the details pane, click the Guest user object and drag it to the Users container in the scope pane. The Guest object is moved back to the Users container.

REVIEW QUESTIONS

1. You are using the Active Directory Users And Computers console to configure user objects in your domain, and you are able to change the address and telephone number properties of the user object representing yourself. However, the New User command is unavailable to you. What is the most likely explanation? *you dont have the rights to create new users*

2. Which of the following properties can be configured simultaneously on more than one user object?

   a. Password Never Expires

   b. Direct Reports

   c. User Must Change Password At Next Logon

   d. Last Name

   e. Logon Hours

   f. Computer Restrictions (Logon Workstations)

   g. User Logon Name

   h. Title

3. Of the three methods for creating multiple user objects discussed in this chapter, which method would be most efficient for generating 100 new user objects, all with identical Profile Path, Home Folder, Title, Web Page, Company, Department, and Manager settings?

Creating user objects with Dsadd.exe

4. What variable can be used with the Dsadd.exe and Dsmod.exe program commands to create user-specific home folders and profile folders?

   a. *%Username%*

   b. *$Username$*

   c. *CN=Username*

   d. *<Username>*

5. How do you make a roaming profile mandatory?

   a. Configure the permissions on the folder's Security property sheet to deny write permission.

   b. Configure the permissions on the folders Sharing property sheet to allow only read permission.

   c. Modify the attributes of the profile folder to specify the Read Only attribute.

   d. Rename Ntuser.dat to Ntuser.man.

6. What is the difference between a local user profile and a roaming user profile?

7. What do you do to ensure that a user on a computer running Windows Server 2003 has a roaming user profile?

8. You have enabled the Password Must Meet Complexity Requirements in your domain. Describe the requirements for passwords and when those requirements will take effect. *p.169*

CASE SCENARIOS

Scenario 6-1: Configuring User Object Properties

You are creating a number of user objects for a team of your organization's temporary workers. They will work daily from 9 A.M. to 5 P.M. on a contract that is scheduled to begin in one month and end two months later. They will not work outside of that schedule. Which of the following properties should you configure initially to ensure maximum security for the objects?

a. Password

b. Logon Hours

c. Account Expires

d. Store Password Using Reversible Encryption

e. Account Is Trusted For Delegation

f. User Must Change Password At Next Logon

g. Account Is Disabled

h. Password Never Expires

Scenario 6-2: Managing Account Lockouts

A user has forgotten his or her password and attempts to log on several times with an incorrect password. Eventually, the user receives a logon message indicating that the account is either disabled or locked out. The message suggests that the user contact an administrator. What must the administrator do?

a. Delete the user object and recreate it.

b. Rename the user object.

c. Enable the user object.

d. Unlock the user object.

e. Reset the password for the user object.

CHAPTER 7
WORKING WITH GROUPS

In Chapter 6, you learned how user objects provide network users with access to resources on an Active Directory network. Another important tool for administrators is the group object. Using groups, administrators can simplify the process of assigning access permissions to users. In this chapter, you learn about the various types of groups that Active Directory supports, how to create them, and how to use them effectively.

Upon completion of this chapter, you will be able to:

- Understand the functions of groups and how to use them

- Understand the difference between local groups and domain groups

- Identify the two group types and three group scopes and their proper use

- List the predefined and built-in groups included in Microsoft Windows Server 2003

- Understand the difference between groups and special identities

- Create, manage, and delete groups

UNDERSTANDING GROUPS

For users to be able to access resources on an Active Directory network, they must have the appropriate permissions. Shared folders and drives, printers, and virtually all other resources on a network have an *access control list (ACL)*. An ACL is a list of objects that are permitted to access the resource, along with the degree of access that each object is permitted. In Windows Server 2003, ACLs are displayed in the Security tab of most any Properties dialog box, as shown in Figure 7-1. The objects in an ACL are referred to as *security principals*. You can use user objects as security principals to grant the user access to all of the resources they need, because a user object establishes the identity of the user through the authentication process.

Figure 7-1   The Security tab in a folder's Properties dialog box

Theoretically, administrators can create all permission assignments by adding user objects to ACLs, but on all but the smallest of networks, this process is incredibly time- and labor-intensive. Imagine hiring a group of 250 new employees and, after creating user objects for them, having to grant each one access to a dozen or more resources scattered around the network. Even worse, suppose a server fails and you have to quickly install a substitute server and then change the permissions for 250 users so they can access the new server.

To prevent nightmares like these, network administrators use groups. A group is simply a list of users that functions as a security principal. In Active Directory, group objects can contain user objects, computers, contacts, and, under certain conditions, even other groups. When you use a group object as a security principal by adding it to an ACL, all of the group's members receive the permissions that you assigned to the group (as shown in Figure 7-2). If you add new members to the group later, they also receive the permissions. If you remove members, their permissions are removed.

In the examples cited earlier, you can create a group object and assign it all of the permissions that new hires need. When a new employee arrives, all you have to do is create a new user object and add it to the group. To simplify the process of deploying a substitute server, you create a group containing all of the users of the original server. If the server fails and you have to switch to a new one, all you do is grant the group object permission to access the new server, and all of the users are instantly switched over. On a network with a well-designed system of groups, network administrators rarely, if ever, have to assign permissions to individual users.

Figure 7-2   As a security principal, one group is equivalent to multiple users.

Groups also make it possible to assign user rights to multiple users at once. In Windows Server 2003, rights are distinctly different from permissions. A *user right* grants a user or group the ability to perform a particular system task, such as access the computer from the network, change the system time, or take ownership of files and other objects. In addition, you can also use groups to create e-mail distribution lists.

Using Groups and Group Policies

In Chapter 6, you learned that the structure of the Active Directory hierarchy is a critical part of the domain user account creation process because rights and permissions granted to a container object are inherited by the objects they contain, including user objects. Group inheritance works in much the same way, with the members receiving the settings assigned to the group. The main difference between a group and a container is that the group is not restricted by the structure of the Active Directory tree. You can create groups with members anywhere in the domain, and even in other domains, and grant them all privileges in one quick step.

Group policies, despite their name, are as closely associated with containers as they are with groups. Group policy objects (GPOs) can be assigned only to Active Directory domain, site, and organizational unit (OU) objects, and their settings are passed down through the Active Directory tree. You cannot assign a group policy object to a group, although in many cases you can configure particular group policy settings to configure an operating system feature on all the members of the group.

For example, you can create an OU object in your Active Directory tree containing all the workstation computer objects in your domain and assign a GPO to that OU. The computers in the OU will all inherit the group policy settings from that GPO, and one of those policy settings might enable the Manage Auditing And Security Log user right, granting that right to a group object containing the users comprising the IT technical support staff. In this case, the computers in the OU receive policy settings from a GPO, and those same group policies grant rights to specific group objects.

Understanding Domain Functional Levels

One of the more widely misunderstood Active Directory concepts is that of the functional level. Administrators are sometimes daunted by the prospect of changing the functional level of a domain or forest because it is one of the few decisions in Windows Server 2003 that is irrevocable. Once you change the functional level, you cannot change it back.

Simply put, the different versions of Windows have slightly different capabilities built into their Active Directory implementations. Each successive version has some new features that are not usable when some of the domain controllers in a domain are running older versions of Windows. Changing the **domain functional level** informs the operating system that all of the domain controllers are compatible and that it is safe to activate the version-specific features.

In Windows Server 2003, four domain functional levels are available: Windows 2000 mixed, Windows 2000 native, Windows Server 2003 interim, and Windows Server 2003. These functional levels support domain controllers running various combinations of operating systems, and they provide various additional features, several of which apply to the functionality of group objects in the domain. The characteristics of the domain functional levels are as follows:

> **NOTE**   Domain Functional Levels and Member Servers   Raising the domain functional level does not prevent computers running older versions of Windows from joining the domain. The functional level refers only to the Windows version on the domain controllers. A domain running at the Windows Server 2003 functional level can still support member servers and workstations running Windows 2000, Windows NT, Windows XP, Windows Me, Windows 98, and Windows 95, as long as they have the correct Active Directory client software installed.

- **Windows 2000 mixed**   The default functional level of a Windows Server 2003 domain controller.
  - ❑ Supports domain controllers running Windows Server 2003, Windows 2000, and Windows NT 4.
  - ❑ Supports universal **distribution groups** but not universal **security groups**.
  - ❑ Global groups cannot have other groups as members (group nesting).
  - ❑ No group conversion allowed.
- **Windows 2000 native**   Supports domain controllers running Windows Server 2003 and Windows 2000.
  - ❑ Supports universal security and distribution groups.
  - ❑ Allows groups to be members of other groups.
  - ❑ Allows conversions between security groups and distribution groups.
  - ❑ Allows migration of security principals from one domain to another (security identifier [SID] history).

■ **Windows Server 2003 interim**   Supports domain controllers running Windows Server 2003 and Windows NT 4. This functional level is used only when upgrading domain controllers in Windows NT 4 domains to Windows Server 2003 domain controllers.

   ❑ Provides no additional features.

■ **Windows Server 2003**   Supports domain controllers running Windows Server 2003 only.

   ❑ Supports universal security and distribution groups.

   ❑ Allows groups to be members of other groups (group nesting).

   ❑ Allows conversions between security groups and distribution groups.

   ❑ Allows migration of security principals from one domain to another (SID history).

> **NOTE**   **Domain Functional-Level Features**   The previous lists contain only the Active Directory features of the functional levels that pertain to group objects and their operations. Raising the domain functional level also activates other features, such as the ability to rename domains. Additional Active Directory features are activated when you raise the **forest functional level** on your network, when all the domain controllers in the entire forest are running Windows Server 2003. None of these features affects the use of group objects, however.

To manage the functional level in Windows Server 2003, you use the Active Directory Domains And Trusts console, which is accessible from the Administrative Tools program group. To view the current functional levels of your domain and forest, select the domain object in the scope pane and, from the Action menu, select Properties. The Properties dialog box for the domain displays the current functional levels on the General tab, as shown in Figure 7-3.

Figure 7-3   A domain's Properties dialog box

To change the functional level, select the domain object and, from the Action menu, select Raise Domain Functional Level to display the dialog box shown in Figure 7-4. In the Select An Available Domain Functional Level drop-down list, choose the functional level you want to use and click Raise. As stated earlier, you cannot lower the functional level after you raise it, except by reinstalling Active Directory on all of your domain controllers, so the program cautions you to be sure before committing yourself. Once the functional level is raised on that one domain controller, the change is replicated to all of the other domain controllers in the domain.

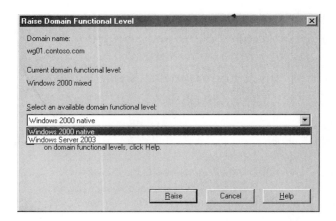

Figure 7-4   The Raise Domain Functional Level dialog box

> **NOTE**   **Raising the Forest Functional Level**   To raise the forest functional level, select the Active Directory Domains and Trusts object in the scope pane and, from the Action menu, select Raise Forest Functional Level.

USING LOCAL GROUPS

In Chapter 6, you learned that Windows Server 2003 supports both local user accounts and domain user accounts. The same is true for groups. Windows Server 2003 supports **local groups** and domain groups.

A *local group* is a collection of local user accounts on a particular computer. Local groups perform the same basic function as all groups: they enable you to assign permissions to multiple users in one step. You create local groups using the Local Users And Groups snap-in, which is integrated into the Computer Management console (which is accessible from the Administrative Tools program group), as shown in Figure 7-5. When you create a local group, the system stores it in the local Security Accounts Manager (SAM) database.

Local groups are subject to restrictions, just as local users are. The local group restrictions are as follows:

- You can use local groups only on the computer where you create them.

- Only local users from the same computer can be members of local groups.

- When the computer is a member of a domain, local group members can include users and **global groups** from the domain or any trusted domain.

- Local groups cannot have other local groups as members.

- Local group permissions provide access only to resources on the computer where you created the local group.

- You cannot create local groups on a Windows Server 2003 computer that is functioning as a domain controller.

Figure 7-5   The Local Users And Groups snap-in

USING ACTIVE DIRECTORY GROUPS

Active Directory groups are characterized by their type and their scope. There are two types of Active Directory groups, each with three distinct scopes. Understanding the constructions of these groups within the correct scope ensures the best use of administrative resources when you create, assign, and manage access to resources. The possibilities of group construction also depend on the functional level of the domain in which the groups are created. Windows Server 2003 comes with a large number of groups created, and you can create as many additional groups as you need.

Active Directory groups, no matter what their type or scope, take the form of objects in the Active Directory database, just as user accounts and containers are objects. Compared to user objects, group objects are quite simple. Instead of the dozens of attributes you find in a user object, a group object consists of only a few attributes, the most important of which is its member list. As the name implies, the member list is simply a list of objects, such as users, other groups, computers, and contacts, that are members of the group. All permissions and rights assigned to the group are inherited by every object in the member list.

You create and manage all Active Directory groups using the Active Directory Users And Computers console, which is accessible from the Administrative Tools program group in Windows Server 2003, as shown in Figure 7-6. As with any Active Directory object, to create and manage groups you must have the appropriate permissions for the containers where the groups are located.

Figure 7-6   The Active Directory Users And Computers console

Active Directory Group Types

There are two types of Active Directory group objects: security groups and distribution groups.

Security Groups

Security groups are the ones you use to assign access permissions for network resources. When someone speaks of a group in relation to Windows Server 2003 or Active Directory, they are usually speaking of a security group. Programs that are designed to work with Active Directory can also use security groups for nonsecurity-related purposes, such as retrieving user information for use in a Web application.

> **NOTE**   **Windows Server 2003 Uses Only Security Groups**   Security groups can be used as distribution groups, but distribution groups cannot be used as security groups. Windows Server 2003 itself can only make use of security groups, but because security groups have all the capabilities of distribution groups, this is not a shortcoming.

Distribution Groups

Distribution groups are intended for use by applications as lists for nonsecurity-related functions. You use distribution groups when the only function of the group is not security-related, such as sending e-mail messages to a group of users at the same time. You cannot use distribution groups to assign rights and permissions. Only applications that are designed to work with Active Directory can use distribution groups. For example, Microsoft Exchange uses distribution groups as mailing lists for sending e-mail messages.

Active Directory Group Scopes

Group scopes define how permissions are assigned to the group members. All Active Directory groups, both security and distribution groups, can be classified into one of three scopes: domain local, global, and universal.

Domain Local Groups

Domain local groups are most often used to assign access permissions to resources, either directly or by adding a global group to a domain local group. Domain local groups have the following characteristics:

- Domain local groups are available in all functional levels: Windows 2000 mixed, Windows 2000 native, Windows Server 2003 interim, and Windows Server 2003.

- You can use a domain local group to grant access permissions to resources only in the same domain where you create the domain local group.

- When you use the Windows 2000 mixed or Windows 2003 interim functional level, domain local group members can include user and computer accounts and global groups from any domain in the forest. No other group nesting is permitted.

- When you use the Windows 2000 native or Windows Server 2003 functional level, domain local group members can include user and computer accounts, global and **universal groups** from any domain in the forest, and other domain local groups from the same domain. Domain local groups can be converted to the universal scope as long as they do not have other domain local groups as members.

    NOTE   Local Groups and Domain Local Groups   Because Active Directory groups with a domain local scope are sometimes referred to as local groups, be sure to distinguish between a local group on a particular computer (sometimes called a *machine local group*) and an Active Directory group with a domain local scope.

Domain local groups are most commonly used to control access to resources within a single domain. For example, you might create a domain local group with permissions that grant members access to a particular printer. Then you can add users in the domain directly to the domain local group, or you can create a global group containing users that need printer access and make the global group a member of the domain local group.

Global Groups

Global groups are used primarily to provide categorized membership in domain local groups for individual security principals or for direct permission assignment (particularly in the case of a network using the Windows 2000 mixed or Windows Server 2003 interim domain functional level). Often, global groups are used to collect users or computers in the same domain that share the same job, role, or function or that have similar network access requirements. Global groups have the following characteristics:

- Global groups are available in all functional levels: Windows 2000 mixed, Windows 2000 native, Windows Server 2003 interim, and Windows Server 2003.

- Global groups can only include members from within their domain.

■ When you use the Windows 2000 native or Windows Server 2003 functional level, global group members can include user and computer accounts as well as other global groups from the same domain.

■ Global groups can be converted to universal groups as long as the group is not a member of any other global group.

■ When you use the Windows 2000 mixed functional level, global group members can include user and computer accounts from the same domain only.

■ Global groups can be members of machine local or domain local groups.

■ Global groups can be granted access permissions for resources in any domain in the forest, and in trusted domains in other forests.

Global groups are most commonly used to manage permissions for directory objects, such as user and computer accounts, that require frequent maintenance. On a network consisting of multiple domains, the main advantage of using global groups for this purpose rather than universal groups is that global groups are not replicated outside of their domain. This minimizes the amount of replication traffic to the *global catalog*, which is a directory of resources for the entire forest. Global groups are preferable to domain local groups when you assign permissions for any objects replicated to the global catalog.

Universal Groups

Universal groups are used primarily to grant access to related resources in multiple domains. Universal groups have the following characteristics:

■ Universal groups are available only in the Windows 2000 native and Windows Server 2003 functional levels.

■ Universal group members can include user and computer accounts, global groups, and other universal groups from any domain in the forest. Universal groups can be converted to domain local groups or to global groups as long as they do not have other universal groups as members.

■ When you use the Windows 2000 mixed functional level, you cannot create universal groups.

■ Universal groups can be granted access permissions for resources in any domain in the forest and in domains in other trusted forests.

The primary function of universal groups is to consolidate groups that span multiple domains. Universal groups are generally not needed on single-domain networks. To use universal groups effectively, the best practice is to create a global group in each domain, with user or computer accounts as members, and then make the global groups members of a universal group. This enables you to create a single universal group that is usable throughout the enterprise, but with a membership that does not change frequently.

This method is preferable to adding users and computers to the universal group directly because every change to the universal group's membership causes the entire membership to be replicated to the global catalog, throughout the forest. Managing the users and computers in the global groups does not affect the universal group's membership and therefore generates no additional replication traffic.

Universal groups are also useful when you want to grant users access to resources that are located in more than one domain. Unlike domain local groups, you can assign permissions to universal groups for resources in any domain on your network. For example, if executives need access to printers throughout your network, you can create a universal group for this purpose and assign it permissions enabling its members to use all of the printers in all of your domains.

Nesting Groups

As you learned in the previous sections, the ability to make groups members of other groups is one of the most powerful features of Active Directory's group object implementation. This practice is called *group nesting*. Nesting groups enables you to manage resource permissions efficiently for an entire enterprise without generating inordinate amounts of replication traffic. As mentioned earlier, your domain must be using the Windows 2000 native or Windows Server 2003 functional level to take full advantage of Active Directory's group nesting capabilities, and even then, there are restrictions on the nesting of the various group scopes. These nesting restrictions, along with all membership restrictions for the three group scopes, are summarized in Table 7-1.

Table 7-1 Group Scope Membership Rules

Group Scope	Members Allowed in Windows 2000 Mixed or Windows Server 2003 Interim Functional Level	Members Allowed in Windows 2000 Native or Windows Server 2003 Functional Level
Domain Local	User and computer accounts and global groups from any domain	User and computer accounts, universal groups, and global groups from any domain; other domain local groups from the same domain
Global	User and computer accounts from the same domain	User and computer accounts and other global groups from the same domain
Universal	Not available	User and computer accounts, other universal groups, and global groups from any domain

The membership rules in this table are an essential element of proper group management. If you encounter a situation where you cannot add a particular member to a group or use a group to provide access to a particular resource, the troubleshooting process should begin with an examination of the group's scope and the domain's functional level, to determine if you are actually supposed to be able to perform the task you are attempting.

Although group nesting is a valuable tool, administrators should be careful not to get carried away with its capabilities. While it is possible to nest groups many layers deep, this practice can make it difficult to keep track of the group memberships and how permissions are being disseminated throughout the network. As a general rule, a single level of nesting is sufficient for most environments and is easier to maintain.

Converting Groups

When you create a group, you must specify its type and its scope. However, in a domain using the Windows 2000 native or Windows Server 2003 functional level, you can convert groups to different scopes at any time, subject to certain membership restrictions. Table 7-2 summarizes the group scope conversions that are allowable and the conditions under which you can perform the conversion.

Table 7-2 **Active Directory Group Scope Conversion Restrictions**

	To Domain Local	To Global	To Universal
From Domain Local	Not applicable	Not permitted	Permitted only when the domain local group does not have other domain local groups as members
From Global	Not permitted	Not applicable	Permitted only when the global group is not a member of another global group
From Universal	No restrictions	Permitted only when the universal group does not have other universal groups as members	Not applicable

Planning Global and Domain Local Groups

It is a good idea to have a group strategy in place before you begin to create Active Directory groups. Creating groups of the wrong type or with the wrong scope can result in a failure of the groups to perform as expected. For most network installations, the most common method of deploying groups is to use global and domain local groups in the following manner:

■ **Create domain local groups for resources to be shared** Identify the resources, such as shared folders or printers, to which users need access, and then create one or more domain local groups for those resources. For example, if you have a number of color printers in your company, create a domain local group called Color Printers.

■ **Assign resource permissions to the domain local group** Assign the permissions needed for access to the resources to the appropriate domain local group. For example, you should assign the permissions needed to use the color printers to the Color Printers group.

■ **Create global groups for users with common job responsibilities** Identify users with common job responsibilities and add their user objects to a global group. For example, in an accounting department, add the user objects for all of the accountants to a global group called Accounting.

■ **Add global groups that need access to resources to the appropriate domain local group** Identify all global groups that require access to a particular resource, and make the global groups members of the appropriate domain local group. For example, to provide the accountants with access to the color printers, add the Accounting global group to the Color Printers domain local group. Users in the Accounting group then receive the permissions granted to the Color Printers group.

Once you have created your groups in this manner, you modify the domain local group permissions when resource requirements change and modify the global group memberships when there are personnel changes.

It might seem as though using both domain local groups and global groups is unnecessary. After all, it would be possible just to create a single domain local or global group, grant it the permissions needed to access resources, and add the user objects of the people needing those resources as members. However, there are distinct drawbacks to this strategy, whether you use domain local groups or global groups.

- **Placing user objects in domain local groups and assigning permissions to the domain local groups**   This strategy does not enable you to assign permissions for resources outside of the domain, which reduces the flexibility of your group strategy when your network grows.

- **Placing user accounts in global groups and assigning permissions to the global groups**   This strategy can complicate administration when you are using multiple domains. If global groups from multiple domains require the same permissions, you have to assign permissions for each global group.

WINDOWS SERVER 2003 DEFAULT GROUPS

Windows Server 2003 automatically creates a large number of groups in which it places its built-in user accounts. You can use these groups as they are, modify them as needed (in some cases), or create new groups of your own. There are four default group types in Windows Server 2003: built-in local groups, which exist only on computers that are not domain controllers, and three types of default groups in Active Directory—predefined groups, built-in groups, and special identities. These default groups are discussed in the following sections.

Built-In Local Groups

Windows Server 2003 standalone servers and member servers all have built-in local groups. Domain controllers do not have local groups (or local users) because their SAM is converted for Active Directory use. *Built-in local groups* give users the rights to perform system tasks on a single computer, such as backing up and restoring files, changing the system time, and administering system resources. The built-in local groups are located in the Groups folder in the Local Users And Groups snap-in.

The Windows Server 2003 built-in local groups and their capabilities are as follows. Except where noted, no initial members exist in these groups.

- **Administrators**   Members have complete and unrestricted access to the computer and the domain, enabling them to perform all administrative tasks. By default, the computer's built-in Administrator local user account is a member. When the computer joins a domain, Windows Server 2003 adds the Domain Admins predefined global group to the local Administrators group.

- **Backup Operators**   Members have user rights that enable them to override security restrictions for the sole purpose of backing up and restoring files.

- **Guests**   Members can perform only tasks for which you have specifically granted rights and can access only resources for which you have assigned permissions; members cannot make permanent changes to their desktop environment. By default, the computer's built-in Guest local user account is a member. When the computer joins a domain, Windows Server 2003 adds the Domain Guests predefined global group to the local Guests group.

- **Network Configuration Operators**   Members of this group have limited administrative privileges enabling them to make changes to TCP/IP settings, and to renew and release IP addresses.

- **Performance Log Users**   Members of this group are granted privileges enabling them to manage performance counters, logs, and alerts on the computer, both locally and from remote locations.

- **Performance Monitor Users**   Members of this group are granted privileges enabling them to monitor performance counters on the computer, both locally and from remote locations.

- **Power Users**   Members can create local user and group accounts on the computer and modify the users and groups they have created. They can also add or remove users from the Power Users, Users, and Guests local groups, create share resources, and administer the shared resources they have created. Power Users cannot take ownership of files, back up or restore folders, load or unload device drivers, or manage security logs.

- **Print Operators**   Members can manage printers and print queues on the computer.

- **Remote Desktop Users**   Members can log on to the computer remotely using Terminal Services.

- **Replicator**   This group is intended to support directory replication functions. The only member should be a domain user account used to log on to the Replicator services of the domain controller. Do not add the accounts of actual users to this group.

- **Users**   Members can perform tasks such as running applications, using local and network printers, and locking the server. Users cannot share directories or create local printers. All new local user accounts created on the computer are automatically added to the local Users group. When the computer joins a domain, Windows Server 2003 adds the Domain Users, Authenticated Users, and Interactive groups to the local Users group. As a result, all domain user accounts become members of this group as well.

In most cases, the privileges possessed by these local groups are granted by the assignment of user rights to the group. Table 7-3 lists the user rights assigned to the built-in local groups. (Groups not listed have no default user rights assigned to them.)

Table 7-3   Default User Rights Assigned to Built-In Local Groups

Local Group	Default User Rights
Administrators	■ Access This Computer From The Network ■ Adjust Memory Quotas For A Process ■ Allow Log On Locally ■ Allow Log On Through Terminal Services ■ Back Up Files And Directories ■ Bypass Traverse Checking ■ Change The System Time ■ Create A Pagefile ■ Debug Programs ■ Force Shutdown From A Remote System ■ Increase Scheduling Priority ■ Load And Unload Device Drivers ■ Manage Auditing And Security Log ■ Modify Firmware Environment Variables ■ Perform Volume Maintenance Tasks ■ Profile Single Process ■ Profile System Performance ■ Remove Computer From Docking Station ■ Restore Files And Directories ■ Shut Down The System ■ Take Ownership Of Files Or Other Objects
Backup Operators	■ Access This Computer From The Network ■ Allow Log On Locally ■ Back Up Files And Directories ■ Bypass Traverse Checking ■ Restore Files And Directories ■ Shut Down The System
Power Users	■ Access This Computer From The Network ■ Allow Log On Locally ■ Bypass Traverse Checking ■ Change The System Time ■ Profile Single Process ■ Remove Computer From Docking Station ■ Shut Down The System
Remote Desktop Users	■ Allow Log On Through Terminal Services
Users	■ Access This Computer From The Network ■ Allow Log On Locally ■ Bypass Traverse Checking

Predefined Active Directory Groups

All Active Directory domains have a collection of *predefined groups*. These are security groups, most with a global scope, that are intended to group together common types of domain user accounts. By default, Windows Server 2003 automatically adds members to some predefined global groups. You can add user objects to these predefined groups to provide additional users with the privileges and permissions assigned to the group.

When you create an Active Directory domain, Windows Server 2003 creates the predefined global groups in the domain's Users container, as shown in the Active Directory Users and Computers console in Figure 7-7. By default, these predefined groups do not have any inherent rights or permissions. You can assign rights or permissions to them by adding the predefined global groups to domain local groups or by explicitly assigning rights or permissions to the predefined global groups.

Figure 7-7 The Users folder of an Active Directory domain containing predefined global groups

The predefined global groups that Windows 2000 creates and their members include the following:

- **CertPublishers** Members are granted permission to publish certificates for users and computers. Unlike most of the other predefined groups, this is a domain local group.

- **Domain Admins** Members have full administrative control over the domain. The domain Administrator user is a member of this group by default. When a computer joins the domain or is promoted to a domain controller, the Domain Admins group is made a member of the computer's local Administrators group. This enables domain administrators to have full access to all of the computers in the domain.

- **Domain Computers** This group has as its members all computers in the domain (except domain controllers). By default, all new computer objects created in the domain (except those of domain controllers) become members of this group.

- **Domain Controllers**   This group has as its members the computer objects for all domain controllers in the domain. By default, the computer objects for all domain controllers added to the domain become members of this group.

- **Domain Guests**   By default, the domain Guest object is a member of this group, and Windows Server 2003 automatically adds the Domain Guests global group to the Guests built-in domain local group.

- **Domain Users**   This group is intended to represent all users in the domain. Windows Server 2003 automatically adds all domain User objects to this group and also adds the Domain Users global group to the Users built-in domain local group.

- **Enterprise Admins**   The Enterprise Admins group appears only in the forest root domain (the first domain created in the forest); its members have full administrative control over all domains in the forest. By default, the Enterprise Admins group is a member of the Administrators domain local group and the domain Administrator user object is a member of Enterprise Admins.

- **Group Policy Creator Owners**   Members are permitted to modify group policy settings in the domain. By default, the domain Administrator account is a member of this group.

- **RAS and IAS Servers**   Servers that are members of this group are permitted to access the remote access properties of users.

- **Schema Admins**   The Schema Admins group appears only in the forest root domain, and its members are permitted to modify the Active Directory schema. By default, the domain Administrator account is a member of this group.

> **NOTE**   **Enterprise Admins and Schema Admins**   The scopes of the Enterprise Admins and Schema Admins predefined groups are dependent on the functional level of their domain. In a domain running at the Windows 2000 mixed or Windows Server 2003 interim functional level, these are global groups. In a domain running the Windows 2000 native or Windows Server 2003 functional level, Enterprise Admins and Schema Admins are universal groups.

In addition to the groups listed here, other predefined groups are created when you install specific Windows Server 2003 software components on a computer, such as DnsAdmins and DnsUpdateProxy (which are created when the DNS Server service is installed), and IIS_WPG (which is created when Microsoft Internet Information Services [IIS] is installed).

As with the built-in local groups, some of the predefined Active Directory groups have privileges granted to them through the assignment of user rights. In this case, however, this is true only for the Domain Admins and Enterprise Admins groups. The user rights assigned to these groups by default are listed in Table 7-4.

Table 7-4   **Default User Rights Assigned to Predefined Active Directory Groups**

Local Group	Default User Rights
Domain Admins and Enterprise Admins	■ Access This Computer From The Network ■ Adjust Memory Quotas For A Process ■ Back Up Files And Directories ■ Bypass Traverse Checking ■ Change The System Time ■ Create A Pagefile ■ Debug Programs ■ Enable Computer And User Accounts To Be Trusted For Delegation ■ Force Shutdown From A Remote System ■ Increase Scheduling Priority ■ Load And Unload Device Drivers ■ Allow Log On Locally ■ Manage Auditing And Security Log ■ Modify Firmware Environment Values ■ Profile Single Process ■ Profile System Performance ■ Remove Computer From Docking Station ■ Restore Files And Directories ■ Shut Down The System ■ Take Ownership Of Files Or Other Objects

Built-In Active Directory Groups

Every Active Directory domain has a Builtin container in which the system creates another series of security groups, all of which have a domain local scope. These groups provide users with user rights and permissions to perform tasks on domain controllers and in the Active Directory tree. Built-in domain local groups provide these predefined rights and permissions to user accounts when you add user objects or global groups as members.

The built-in domain local groups and the capabilities granted to their members are as follows:

■ **Account Operators**   Members can create, delete, and modify user, computer, and group objects in the Users and Computers containers and in all OUs except Domain Controllers. Members do not have permission to modify the Administrators or Domain Admins groups, nor can they modify the accounts for members of those groups. Members of this group can log on locally to domain controllers in the domain and shut them down.

■ **Administrators**   Members have full administrative access to all domain controllers and to the domain itself. By default, the Domain Admins and Enterprise Admins groups and the domain Administrator are members of this group.

- **Backup Operators**   Members have user rights enabling them to back up and restore files on all domain controllers in the domain, even when they do not have individual permissions for the files. Members can also log on to domain controllers and shut them down.

- **Guests**   Members have no default user rights. By default, the Domain Guests global group and the domain Guest user object are members of this group.

- **Incoming Forest Trust Builders**   Members can create one-way, incoming forest trusts to the forest root domain.

- **Network Configuration Operators**   Members can modify TCP/IP settings and renew and release TCP/IP addresses on domain controllers in the domain.

- **Performance Log Users**   Members of this group are granted privileges enabling them to manage performance counters, logs, and alerts on domain controllers in the domain, both locally and from remote locations.

- **Performance Monitor Users**   Members of this group are granted privileges enabling them to monitor performance counters on domain controllers in the domain, both locally and from remote locations.

- **Pre-Windows 2000 Compatible Access**   Members of this group have read access for all user and group objects in the domain. This group is provided for backward compatibility for computers running Windows NT 4 and earlier. When you select the Permissions Compatible With Pre-Windows 2000 Server Operating Systems option in the Active Directory Installation Wizard, the Everyone special identity is made a member of this group.

- **Print Operators**   Members can manage, create, share, and delete printers connected to domain controllers in the domain and also manage Active Directory printer objects. Members can also log on locally to domain controllers in the domain and shut them down.

- **Remote Desktop Users**   Members can remotely log on to domain controllers in the domain using Terminal Services.

- **Replicator**   This group is intended to support directory replication functions. The only member should be a domain user account used to log on to the Replicator services of the domain controller. Do not add the accounts of actual users to this group.

- **Server Operators**   On domain controllers, members of this group can log on, create and delete shared resources, start and stop some services, back up and restore files, format the hard disk, and shut down the computer.

- **Terminal Server License Servers**   Members of this group have access to Terminal Server License Servers, which are used to supply licenses to Terminal Services clients on the network.

- **Users**   Members of this group can perform most common tasks, such as running applications, using local and network printers, and locking the server. By default, the Domain Users group and the Authenticated Users and Interactive special identities are members of this group. Therefore, any user account created in the domain becomes a member of this group.

- **Windows Authorization Access Group**   Members have access to the computed *tokenGroupsGlobalAndUniversal* attribute on domain User objects.

  NOTE   Built-In Local Groups and Domain Local Groups   Several of the built-in domain local groups, such as Backup Operators, Network Configuration Operators, and Remote Desktop Users, are virtual duplicates of the built-in local groups with the same names on Windows Server 2003 standalone and member servers. These groups are intended to perform the same functions as their local group counterparts for domain controllers, which do not have local groups of their own.

The default user rights that grant the built-in domain local groups their privileges are listed in Table 7-5.

Table 7-5   Default User Rights Assigned to Built-In Active Directory Groups

Local Group	Default User Rights
Account Operators	■ Allow Log On Locally ■ Shut Down The System
Administrators, domain local	■ Access This Computer From The Network ■ Adjust Memory Quotas For A Process ■ Back Up Files And Directories ■ Bypass Traverse Checking ■ Change The System Time ■ Create A Pagefile ■ Debug Programs ■ Enable Computer And User Accounts To Be Trusted For Delegation ■ Force Shutdown From A Remote System ■ Increase Scheduling Priority ■ Load And Unload Device Drivers ■ Allow Log On Locally ■ Manage Auditing And Security Log ■ Modify Firmware Environment Values ■ Profile Single Process ■ Profile System Performance ■ Remove Computer From Docking Station ■ Restore Files And Directories ■ Shut Down The System ■ Take Ownership Of Files Or Other Objects
Backup Operators, domain local	■ Back Up Files And Directories ■ Allow Log On Locally ■ Restore Files And Directories ■ Shut Down The System

(continued)

Table 7-5   Default User Rights Assigned to Built-In Active Directory Groups

Local Group	Default User Rights
Pre–Windows 2000 Compatible Access	■ Access This Computer From The Network ■ Bypass Traverse Checking
Print Operators	■ Allow Log On Locally ■ Shut Down The System
Server Operators	■ Back Up Files And Directories ■ Change The System Time ■ Force Shutdown From A Remote System ■ Allow Log On Locally ■ Restore Files And Directories ■ Shut Down The System

Special Identities

Special identities exist on all computers running Windows Server 2003. These are not really groups because you cannot create them, delete them, or directly modify their memberships. Special identities do not appear in the Local Users And Groups snap-in or the Active Directory Users and Computers console, but you can use them like groups, by adding them to the ACLs of system and network resources, as shown in Figure 7-8.

Figure 7-8   Special identities in an ACL

Special identities are essentially placeholders for one or more users. When you add a special identity to an ACL, the system substitutes the users that conform to the identity at the moment the ACL is processed. Special identities represent different users at different times, depending on how users access a computer or resource. For example, the Authenticated Users special identity includes all users that are currently logged on, having successfully been authenticated by a computer or domain controller. At any given moment, the list of users represented by the Authenticated Users special identity can change, as users log on and log off.

The exact list of users substituted for the Authenticated Users placeholder is determined at the time a resource is accessed and its ACL processed, not at the time the special identity is added to the ACL.

The special identities included in Windows Server 2003 are as follows:

- **Anonymous Logon** Includes all users who have connected to the computer without authenticating.

- **Authenticated Users** Includes all users with a valid local or domain user account whose identities have been authenticated. The Authenticated Users special identity does not include the Guest user even if the Guest account has a password.

- **Batch** Includes all users who are currently logged on through a batch facility such as a task scheduler job.

- **Creator Owner** Includes the account for the user who created or took ownership of a resource.

- **Creator Group** Includes the primary group of the user who created or took ownership of the resource.

- **Dialup** Includes all users who are currently logged on through a dial-up connection.

- **Everyone** On computers running Windows Server 2003, Everyone includes the Authenticated Users special identity plus the Guest user account. On computers running earlier versions of Windows, Everyone includes Authenticated Users, the Guest account, and the Anonymous Logon special identity.

- **Interactive** Includes all users who are currently logged on locally or through a Remote Desktop connection.

- **Network** Includes all users who are currently logged on through a network connection.

- **Service** Includes all security principals that have logged on as a service.

- **Terminal Server Users** Includes all users who are currently logged on to a Terminal Services server that is in Terminal Services version 4 application compatibility mode.

CREATING AND MANAGING GROUP OBJECTS

Once you have determined how you intend to use groups on your network and have studied the guidelines and restrictions for the various group types and scopes, you are ready to begin actually creating the groups you need. Fortunately, the process of creating groups is far easier than learning about them and their capabilities. The following sections describe some of the most common group administration activities that system and network administrators have to perform on a regular basis.

> **NOTE** **Exam Objectives** *The objectives for exam 70-290 require that students be able to "create and manage groups."*

▶ **Creating Local Groups**

To create local groups in Windows Server 2003, you must be working on a computer that is a standalone or member server because domain controllers do not have local groups. You must also be logged on with a user account that is a member of the Administrators or Power Users local group (or the Domain Admins group in a domain, which is itself a member of the local Administrators group).

To create a local group, use the following procedure:

1. Log on to the computer as Administrator (or use another account with the appropriate privileges).

2. Click Start, point to Administrative Tools, and select Computer Management. The Computer Management console appears.

3. Expand the Local Users And Groups node in the scope pane, and then select the Groups folder.

   In the Local Users And Groups snap-in, users and groups have their own separate folders; they are not mixed together in containers as in Active Directory.

4. From the Action menu, select New Group. The New Group dialog box appears.

5. In the Group Name text box, type a name for the group you are creating.

6. Click Add. The Select Users dialog box appears.

7. Type the name of a local user or special identity in the Enter The Object Names To Select text box, and then click OK. The user or identity is added to the Members list.

   You can also click Advanced to search for local users and special identities.

8. Click Create.

   The snap-in creates the new group in the Groups folder, and it clears the New Group dialog box so that you can create another group.

9. Click Close.

After creating a local group, you can select it and, from the Action menu, select Properties to open the group's Properties dialog box, as shown in Figure 7-9. Here you can add members to or remove them from the group at any time.

Figure 7-9   A local group's Properties dialog box

You can also manage local group memberships from the Properties dialog boxes of user accounts, as shown in Figure 7-10. Every local user's Properties dialog box contains a Member Of tab that you can use to add the local groups of which you want the user to be a member.

Figure 7-10   The Member Of tab in a local user's Properties dialog box

Working with Active Directory Groups

Although Active Directory groups are more complicated than local groups, because of the various types and scopes available, the procedures for creating and managing them are still rather simple. In the following sections, you learn how to use the Active Directory Users and Computers console to create new groups, manage their memberships, and modify their properties.

NOTE   Exam Objectives   *The objectives for exam 70-290 require that students be able to "create and modify groups by using the Active Directory Users and Computers Microsoft Management Console (MMC) snap-in."*

Creating Security Groups

Unlike the Local Users And Groups console, which forces you to create your groups in a specific folder, the Active Directory Users and Groups console lets you create group objects anywhere you want. You can create your groups in the Users container with the predefined global groups, in the Builtin container with the built-in domain local groups, in any OU object of your own creation, and even directly beneath the domain object. As with the creation of any Active Directory object, the location you select for the object should be based on the design of your directory tree.

If you plan on using groups to disseminate user rights to your users, you will probably want to create appropriate OU objects in which to put the groups. As you learned in Chapter 6, the Users and Builtin containers are not OUs and you cannot assign group policy objects to them. To assign user rights to a group in one of these containers, you must use a GPO applied to the domain or site object, and the policies will be inherited by all of the objects in the domain or site.

To create a group object, you select a container object in the scope pane of the Active Directory Users and Computers console and, from the Action menu, point to New and select Group. The New Object – Group dialog box appears, shown in Figure 7-11.

Figure 7-11   The New Object – Group dialog box

In this dialog box, you specify the following information:

- **Group Name**   The name you want to assign to the group object. The name you select can be up to 64 characters long and must be unique in the domain.

- **Group Name (Pre–Windows 2000)**   As you type the Group Name value, the object's pre–Windows 2000–compatible name appears in this text box.

- **Group Scope**   Select the option corresponding to the scope you want to use for the group: domain local, global, or universal. The scopes available to you depend on your domain's functional level, as described earlier in this chapter. The Active Directory Users And Computer console does not allow you to create groups that are not allowed in your current functional level.

- **Group Type**   Select the option corresponding to the type of group you want to create: security or distribution. In the vast majority of cases, you will want to create a security group.

Once you click the OK button, the console creates your new group object in the container you selected.

Practice creating groups by doing Exercise 7-1, "Creating a Security Group," now.

Managing Group Membership

Unlike the Local Users And Groups snap-in, which enables you to specify a group's members as you create it, in Active Directory Users and Computers, you must create the group object first, and then add members to it. To add members to a group, you select it in the console and, from the Action menu, select Properties to open the group's Properties dialog box, as shown in Figure 7-12.

> **NOTE   Exam Objectives**   The objectives for exam 70-290 require that students be able to "manage group membership."

Figure 7-12   A group object's Properties dialog box

Every group object's Properties dialog box has a Members tab and a Member Of tab, which you can use to add members to the group or make the group a member of another group, respectively. To add members to the group, select the Members tab and then click Add. This produces a standard Select Users, Contacts, Computers, Or Groups dialog box, as shown in Figure 7-13.

Figure 7-13   The Select Users, Contacts, Computers, Or Groups dialog box

In this dialog box, you can type the name of the object you want to add as a member of the group, or you can click Advanced to display the dialog box shown in Figure 7-14, in which you can search for the objects you want to add.

Figure 7-14   The advanced version of the Select Users, Contacts, Computers, Or Groups dialog box

Once you enter or find the object you want to add, clicking OK in the Select Users, Contacts, Computers, Or Groups dialog box adds the object to the group's Members list. Once you have added all the member objects you need, click OK to close the Properties dialog box. At this point, you should be able to open the Properties dialog box for the object you just added to the group and see the group object in its Member Of tab, as shown in Figure 7-15.

Figure 7-15   The Member Of tab in a user object's dialog box

Practice managing group members hips by doing Exercise 7-2, "Adding Members to a Group," now.

Nesting Groups

As you learned earlier in this chapter, the ability to nest group objects depends on your domain's functional level and on the types and scopes of the groups you are using. Review Table 7-1 if you are not sure whether your domain functional level supports the group nesting you want to perform.

You cannot nest groups in Active Directory Users and Computers by creating a new group inside an existing group. Instead, you must create both groups separately, using the process you learned earlier, and then add one group to the other as a member. Active Directory Users and Computers will not enable you to create a nesting arrangement that your domain does not support.

Practice nesting groups by doing Exercise 7-3, "Nesting Groups," now.

Changing Group Types and Scopes

As group functions change, you might need to change a group object from one type to another. For example, you might have created a distribution group that contains 100 members from multiple departments working on the same project for the purpose of sending e-mail messages. As the project progresses, members might need to access a common database. By converting the distribution group to a security group and assigning permissions to the group, you can provide the project members with access to the common database without having to create a new group and add 100 members to it all over again. You can change the group type only when the domain is using the Windows 2000 native or Windows Server 2003 functional level.

> **NOTE Exam Objectives**   The objectives for exam 70-290 require that students be able to "identify and modify the scope of a group."

To change the type of a group, open the group's Properties dialog box in the Active Directory Users and Computers console, as shown in Figure 7-16. On the General tab, you see the Group Type options. Click the unselected option and then click OK.

The process for changing the group's scope is exactly the same, except that you select one of the Group Scope options on the General tab. The console only enables you to perform permissible scope changes. In this figure, for example, you see that the Domain Local option is disabled because you cannot change a global group to a domain local group. Consult Table 7-2 for information on the scope changes that are permitted.

Figure 7-16   The General tab in a group object's Properties dialog box

Deleting a Group

As with user objects, each group object that you create in Active Directory has a unique, nonreusable SID. Windows Server 2003 uses the SID to identify the group and the permissions assigned to it. When you delete a group, Windows Server 2003 does not use the same SID for that group again, even if you create a new group with the same name as the one you deleted. Therefore, you cannot restore the access permissions you assigned to resources by re-creating a deleted group object. You must add the newly re-created group as a security principal in the resource's ACL all over again.

When you delete a group, you delete only the group object and the permissions and rights specifying that group as the security principal. Deleting a group does not delete the objects that are members of the group.

> **NOTE   Group Deletion Failures**   You cannot delete a group if one of the group's members has the group set as its primary group. Apart from inhibiting group deletions, primary groups are relevant only on Macintosh clients and in POSIX-compliant applications. To change a user's primary group, open the user object's Properties dialog box, and, in the Member Of tab, select a different group and then click Set Primary Group.

To delete a group, you select it in the Active Directory Users And Computers console and, from the Action menu, select Delete. An Active Directory message box appears, prompting you to confirm your decision. Clicking Yes causes the group to be deleted.

AUTOMATING GROUP MANAGEMENT

Although the Active Directory Users and Computers console is a convenient tool for creating and managing groups individually, it is not the most efficient method for creating large numbers of security principals. The Active Directory command-line tools included with Windows Server 2003 enable you to create and manage groups in large numbers using batch files or other types of scripts, just as you learned to do with users in Chapter 6. Some of these tools are discussed in the following sections.

> **NOTE   Exam Objectives**   *The objectives for exam 70-290 require that students be able to "create and modify groups by using automation."*

Creating Group Objects Using Dsadd.exe

You used the Dsadd.exe tool in Chapter 6 to create new user objects; you can use the same program to create group objects as well.

The basic syntax for creating group objects using Dsadd.exe is as follows:

```
dsadd group GroupDN [parameters]
```

The *GroupDN* parameter is a distinguished name (DN) for the new group object you want to create. The DNs use the same format as those in CSV files, as discussed in "Importing User Objects Using CSV Directory Exchange" in Chapter 6. If the DN includes a space, you must surround the entire DN with quotation marks. When you use Dsadd.exe interactively from the command prompt, you can supply the *GroupDN* parameter in any one of the following ways:

- By typing DNs on the command line, separated by spaces.
- By piping a list of DNs from another command, such as Dsquery.exe.
- By leaving the DN parameter empty, at which point you can type the DNs, one at a time, at a prompt presented by the program. Press Enter after each DN, and press Ctrl+Z and Enter after the last DN.

By default, Dsadd.exe creates global security groups, but you can use command-line parameters to create groups with other types and scopes, as well as to specify members and memberships for the groups and other group object properties. The most commonly used command-line parameters are as follows:

- **-secgrp {*yes* | *no*}**   Specifies whether the program should create a security group (*yes*) or a distribution group (*no*). The default value is *yes*.
- **-scope {*l* | *g* | *u*}**   Specifies whether the program should create a domain local (*l*), global (*g*), or universal (*u*) group. The default value is *g*.
- **-samid *SAMName***   Specifies the SAM name for the group object, to be used by pre–Windows 2000 systems.
- **-desc *description***   Specifies a description for the group object.
- **-memberof *GroupDN***   Specifies the DNs of one or more groups of which the new group should be made a member.
- **-members *GroupDN***   Specifies the DNs of one or more objects that should be made members of the new group.

You can also add the *-s*, *-u*, and *-p* parameters to specify the domain controller against which Dsadd.exe will run, and the username and password that will be used to execute the command:

- {**-s** *Server* | **-d** *Domain*}
- **-u** *UserName*
- **-p** {*Password* | *}

> **NOTE** Specifying Passwords Using Dsadd.exe Including an asterisk with the *-p* switch instead of a password causes the program to prompt you for a password before it executes the command.

For example, to create a new group called Sales in the Users container and make the Administrator user a member, you would use the following command:

```
dsadd group "CN=Sales,CN=Users,DC=contoso,DC=com" -members
  "CN=Administrator,CN=Users,DC=contoso,DC=com"
```

Managing Group Objects Using Dsmod.exe

Dsmod.exe enables you to modify the properties of existing group objects from the Windows Server 2003 command prompt. Using this program, you can perform tasks such as adding members to a group, removing them from a group, and changing a group's type and scope. The basic syntax for Dsmod.exe is as follows:

```
dsmod group GroupDN [parameters]
```

The most commonly used command-line parameters are as follows:

- **-secgrp** {*yes* | *no*} Sets the group type to security group (*yes*) or distribution group (*no*).
- **-scope** {*l* | *g* | *u*} Sets the group scope to domain local (*l*), global (*g*), or universal (*u*).
- **-addmbr** *members* Adds members to the group. Replace *members* with the DNs of one or more objects.
- **-rmmbr** *members* Removes members from the group. Replace *members* with the DNs of one or more objects.
- **-chmbr** *members* Replaces the complete list of group members. Replace *members* with the DNs of one or more objects.

For example, to add the Administrator user to the Guests group, you would use the following command:

```
dsmod group "CN=Guests,CN=Builtin,DC=contoso,DC=com" -addmbr
  "CN=Administrator,CN=Users,DC=contoso,DC=com"
```

Finding Objects Using Dsget.exe

Once an Active Directory installation begins to grow, it can quickly get to a size where working with individual objects using consoles like Active Directory Users and Computers is time consuming and difficult. When this happens, many administrators turn to the Active Directory command-line tools. One such tool, the

Dsget.exe program, enables you to locate and display information about any object in the Active Directory database.

Dsget.exe uses a syntax similar to that of Dsadd.exe and Dsmod.exe, in which you specify an object class, the DN of one or more objects, and parameters indicating the information you want to display, as follows:

```
dsget objectclass ObjectDN [parameters]
```

The values for the *objectclass* variable include the following:

- computer
- contact
- subnet
- group
- ou
- server
- site
- user
- quota
- partition

Each of these object classes has a set of parameters particular to that class, which enables you to display the values of the properties for that type of object. For the *dsget user* command, some of the available parameters are as follows:

- **–dn**   Shows the DN of the user
- **–samid**   Shows the SAM account name of the user
- **–sid**   Shows the user's security ID
- **–upn**   Shows the principal name of the user
- **–fn**   Shows the first name of the user
- **–ln**   Shows the last name of the user
- **–display**   Shows the display name of the user
- **–tel**   Shows the telephone number of the user
- **–email**   Shows the e-mail address of the user
- **–memberof**   Displays the immediate groups of which the user is a member
- **–expand**   Displays a recursively expanded list of groups of which the user is a member

For example, to display a list of the groups of which a user is a member, use the following command:

```
dsget user "CN=Administrator,CN=Users,DC=contoso,DC=com" -memberof
```

> **NOTE   Exam Objectives**   *The objectives for exam 70-290 require that students be able to "find domain groups in which a user is a member."*

SUMMARY

- A group is an object that consists of a list of users. You can assign security permissions to a group by adding it to an ACL, just as with any other security principal, such as a user or computer. All permissions assigned to the group are inherited by its members.

- Windows Server 2003 supports local groups and Active Directory domain groups in the same way that it supports local and domain users.

- An Active directory domain's functional level determines which group types and scopes you can use, what groups can be nested, and what group conversions you can perform.

- In Active Directory, there are two types of groups: security and distribution; there are also three group scopes: domain local, global, and universal.

- Security groups can be assigned permissions, while distribution groups are used for query containers, such as e-mail distribution groups, and cannot be assigned permissions to a resource.

- Domain local groups are for assigning permissions to resources. Global groups are for gathering together users with similar resource requirements. Universal groups are used primarily to grant access to related resources in multiple domains.

- To create and manage local groups, you use the Local Users And Groups snap-in. To create and manage Active Directory groups, you use the Active Directory Users And Computers console.

- You can create domain groups in any container or OU in the Active Directory tree.

- Group nesting means making one group a member of another group.

- You can create and modify groups from the command line using tools such as Dsadd.exe, Dsmod.exe, and Dsget.exe.

EXERCISES

Exercise 7-1: Creating a Security Group

In this exercise, you create a new Active Directory group in your domain.

1. Log on to a Windows Server 2003 domain controller as Administrator.

2. Click Start, point to Administrative Tools, and click Active Directory Users And Computers. The Active Directory Users And Computers console appears.

3. Select the Users container in the scope pane, and, on the Action menu, point to New and click Group. The New Object – Group dialog box appears.

4. In the Group Name textbox, type **Accountants**.

5. In the Group Scope box, select the Global option, and then click OK.

6. Create a second security group object using the Global scope with the name Development.

Exercise 7-2: Adding Members to a Group

In this exercise, you add user objects to a group as members.

1. Log on to a Windows Server 2003 domain controller as Administrator.

2. Click Start, point to Administrative Tools, and click Active Directory Users And Computers. The Active Directory Users And Computers console appears.

3. Select the Users container in the scope pane.

4. In the details pane, select the Domain Users group and, from the Action menu, select Properties. The Domain Users Properties dialog box appears.

5. Select the Members tab and then click Add. The Select Users, Computers, Contacts, Or Groups dialog box appears.

6. In the Enter The Object Names To Select box, type **Guest**, and then click OK. The Guest user object is added to the Members list.

7. Click OK to close the Domain Users Properties dialog box.

Exercise 7-3: Nesting Groups

1. In this exercise, you create nested groups by adding one group to another as a member. Log on to a Windows Server 2003 domain controller as Administrator.

2. Click Start, point to Administrative Tools, and click Active Directory Users And Computers. The Active Directory Users And Computers console appears.

3. Select the Users container in the scope pane, and, on the Action menu, point to New and click Group. The New Object – Group dialog box appears.

4. In the Group Name textbox, type **Printers**.

5. In the Group Scope box, select the Domain Local option, and then click OK.

   At this point, you would grant the Printers group the permissions needed to access the printers on the network.

6. Create a second security group object using the Global scope with the name Sales.

7. Select the Printers group object you created, and, from the Action menu, select Properties. The Printers Properties dialog box appears.

8. Select the Members tab, and then click Add. The Select Users, Computers, Contacts, Or Groups dialog box appears.

9. In the Enter The Object Names To Select box, type **Sales**, and then click OK. The Sales group object is added to the Members list.

10. Click OK to close the Domain Users Properties dialog box.

    At this point, the Sales group would inherit all the permissions granted to the Printers group and pass them on to its members.

REVIEW QUESTIONS

1. What type of domain group is most like the local group on a member server? How are they alike?

2. In a domain running in Windows Server 2003 domain functional level, what security principals can be a member of a global group? (Choose all correct answers.)

   a. Users

   b. Computers

   c. Universal groups

   d. Global groups

3. In the properties of a group, which tab do you access to add users to the group?

4. You want to nest the IT Administrators group responsible for the Sales group inside the Sales group so that its members will have access to the same resources (set by permissions in an ACL) as the Sales group. From the Properties page of the IT Administrators group, what tab do you access to make this setting?

5. If your environment consists of two domains, one Windows Server 2003 and one Windows NT 4, what group scopes can you use for assigning permissions on any resource on any domain member computer?

6. Which of the following group scope modifications are not permitted? (Choose all correct answers.)

   a. Global to universal

   b. Domain local to universal

   c. Universal to global

   d. Domain local to local

   e. Global to domain local

7. What tool do you use to create local groups on a Windows 2000 computer that is not a domain controller?

8. You are attempting to delete a global security group in the Active Directory Users And Computers console, and the console will not let you complete the task. Which of the following could be causes of the failure? (Choose all correct answers.)

   a. There are still members in the group.

   b. One of the group's members has the group set as its primary group.

   c. You do not have the proper permissions for the container in which the group is located.

   d. You cannot delete global groups from the Active Directory Users And Computers console.

9. Why shouldn't you use local groups on a computer after it becomes a member of a domain?

CASE SCENARIOS

Scenario 7-1: Using Group Scopes

You are the administrator of a Windows Server 2003 domain that is currently running at the Windows 2000 mixed domain functional level. Your Windows 2003 domain, contoso.com, has an external trust established with a Windows NT 4 domain, contoso_north, which makes contoso_north a trusted domain. You are planning the use of groups in your domain and need to determine what group scopes can be used in any domain in your forest. What group scope can be used in this context as a security principal?

   a. Domain local

   b. Global

   c. Universal

   d. Domain local with a nested global group

Scenario 7-2: Creating Groups Using Dsadd.exe

You are a network administrator who is building an Active Directory on a new network for a company called Fabrikam, Inc., and you have to create user objects for the 75 users in the Inside Sales department. You have already created the fabrikam.com domain and an OU called Inside Sales for this purpose. The human resources department has provided you with a list of the users' names and has instructed you to create the account names by using the first initial and the last name. Each user object must also have the value *Inside Sales* in the *Department* property and *Fabrikam, Inc.* in the *Company* property. Using the first name in the list, Mark Lee, as an example, which of the following command-line formats would enable you to create the 75 user objects, with the required property values?

   a. `dsadd "Mark Lee" -company "Fabrikam, Inc." -dept "Inside Sales"`

   b. `dsadd user CN=Mark Lee,CN=Inside Sales,DC=fabrikam,DC=com -company`
        `Fabrikam, Inc. -dept Inside Sales`

   c. `dsadd -company "Fabrikam, Inc." -dept "Inside Sales"`
        `"CN=Mark Lee,CN=Inside Sales,DC=fabrikam,DC=com"`

   d. `dsadd user "CN=Mark Lee,CN=Inside Sales,DC=fabrikam,DC=com" -company`
        `"Fabrikam, Inc." -dept "Inside Sales"`

CHAPTER 8
WORKING WITH COMPUTER ACCOUNTS

In the previous two chapters, you learned a lot about Microsoft Active Directory objects such as users, groups, and organizational units (OUs), which are logical constructs that enable people to access computer network resources. However, there are also Active Directory objects that represent concrete, physical resources, and one of the most important of these is the **computer object**. Without computer objects, users might have permission to access resources, but they have no physical mechanism to provide that access. In this chapter, you learn how to create and manage computer objects on an Active Directory network.

Upon completion of this chapter, you will be able to:

■ Describe the process of adding a computer to an Active Directory domain

■ Create and manage computer objects

■ Troubleshoot computer accounts

247

UNDERSTANDING COMPUTER OBJECTS

In the default configuration of Windows Server 2003 and all other Windows operating systems, the computer belongs to a workgroup. As you learned in Chapter 6, workgroup computers authenticate users with accounts stored on the local system. If a user wants to access a resource on a workgroup computer, the person must have a user account on that computer, as shown in Figure 8-1. Even though you can connect to a workgroup computer over a network, each system is responsible for its own security and access control. Therefore, on a workgroup, there is never any question about what computer you are using because you must be authenticated using an account on that same computer.

Figure 8-1   Workgroup user account storage

Most Windows networks with more than a handful of computers, however, do not use the workgroup model—they use domains, which are implemented in Windows Server 2003 by the Active Directory directory service. In Active Directory, users have accounts in a domain rather than on individual computers. Administrators can use one domain account to grant a user access to resources on computers all over the network. Because domain user accounts are stored in a centralized directory on servers called domain controllers, a user can log on to the domain from any computer on the network and be authenticated by a domain controller.

Because a Windows domain network uses a centralized directory, there has to be some means of tracking the actual computers that are part of the domain. To do this, Active Directory uses computer accounts, which take the form of computer objects in the Active Directory tree (as shown in Figure 8-2). You might have a valid Active Directory user account and a password, but if your computer is not represented by a computer object, you cannot log on to the domain.

Computer objects are stored in the Active Directory hierarchy just as user and group objects are, and they possess many of the same capabilities, such as the following:

■ They consist of properties that specify the computer's name, where it is located, and who is permitted to manage it.

■ They inherit group policy settings from container objects such as domains, sites, and OUs.

- They can be members of security and distribution groups and inherit permissions from group objects.

Figure 8-2   Active Directory domain computer account storage

When a user attempts to log on to an Active Directory domain, the client computer establishes a connection to a domain controller to authenticate the user's identity. But before the user authentication occurs, the two computers perform a preliminary authentication using their respective computer objects to ensure that both systems are part of the domain. The NetLogon service running on the client computer connects to the same service on the domain controller, and then each one verifies that the other system has a valid computer account. When this validation is completed, the two systems establish a secure communications channel between them, which they can then use to begin the user authentication process.

The computer account validation between the client and the domain controller is a genuine authentication process using account names and passwords, just as when a user authenticates to the domain. The difference is that the passwords used by the computer accounts are generated automatically and kept hidden. Administrators can reset a computer account, but they do not have to supply passwords for them.

> **NOTE   Windows Operating Systems and Computer Objects**   Computers running Windows NT–based operating systems, such as Windows Server 2003, Windows XP, Windows 2000, and Windows NT, have native domain support and are always represented by computer objects in Active Directory. The MS-DOS–based Windows operating systems, including Windows Millennium Edition (Me), Windows 98, and Windows 95, can participate in a domain through the installation of an Active Directory client, but they use a domain name specified during the client installation and do not have computer objects in the domain.

ADDING COMPUTERS TO A DOMAIN

What all this means for Windows network administrators is that, in addition to creating user and group accounts in the domain, they also have to make sure that the network computers are part of the domain. Adding a computer to an Active Directory domain consists of two steps:

- **Creating a computer account**   You create a computer account by creating a new computer object in Active Directory and assigning it the name of an actual computer on the network.

■ **Joining the computer to the domain**   When you join a computer to the domain, the system contacts a domain controller, establishes a trust relationship with the domain, locates (or creates) a computer object corresponding to the computer's name, alters its security identifier (SID) to match that of the computer object, and modifies its group memberships.

How these steps are performed, and who performs them, depends on how the computers are deployed on a network. There are many ways to create new computer objects, and how administrators choose to do this depends on several factors, including the number of objects they need to create, where they will be when creating the objects, and what tools they prefer to use.

Generally speaking, you create computer objects when you deploy new computers in the domain. Once a computer is represented by an object and joined to the domain, any user in the domain can log on from that computer. For example, you do not have to create new computer objects or rejoin computers to the domain when employees leave the company and new hires start using their computers. However, if you reinstall the operating system on a computer, you must create a new computer object for it (or reset the existing one) because the computer will have a different SID after the reinstallation.

The joining of a new computer to a domain must always be performed at the computer itself, either by an administrator or by the end user. However, the creation of the computer object can occur either before or during the joining process. Administrators are often responsible for creating the computer objects, but it is also possible for end users to create the objects themselves under certain conditions.

> **NOTE**   **Exam Objectives**   *The objectives for exam 70-290 require students to be able to "create and manage computer accounts in an Active Directory environment."*

Creating Computer Objects

The creation of a computer object must always occur before the corresponding computer can actually join the domain, although it sometimes does not appear that way. There are two basic strategies for creating Active Directory computer objects:

■ Create the computer objects in advance using an Active Directory tool so the computers can locate the existing objects when they join the domain.

■ Begin the joining process first, and allow the computer to create its own computer object.

In each case, the computer object exists before the joining takes place. In the second strategy, the joining process appears to begin first, but the computer creates the object before the actual joining process begins.

When you have a number of computers to deploy, particularly in different locations, most administrators prefer to create the computer objects in advance. For large numbers of computers, it is even possible to automate the computer object creation process by using command-line tools and batch files. The following sections examine the tools you can use for computer object creation.

Creating Computer Objects Using Active Directory Users And Computers

As with the user and group objects you studied in the previous chapters, the primary Windows Server 2003 utility for creating computer objects is the Active Directory Users And Computers console, as shown in Figure 8-3.

Figure 8-3   The Active Directory Users And Computers console

To create computer objects in an Active Directory domain using the Active Directory Users And Computers console or any other utility, you must have the appropriate permissions for the container in which the objects will be located. By default, the Administrators group has permission to create objects anywhere in the domain, and the Account Operators group has the Create Computer Objects and Delete Computer Objects special permissions needed to create computer objects in and delete them from the Computers container, as well as from any new OUs you create. The Domain Admins and Enterprise Admins groups are members of the Administrators group, so members of those groups can also create computer objects anywhere. An administrator can also explicitly delegate control of containers to particular users or groups, enabling them to create computer objects in those containers.

> **MORE INFO**   Ordinary users are also permitted to create a limited number of computer objects. For more information, see "Joining Computers to a Domain" later in this chapter.

The process of creating a computer object in Active Directory Users And Computers is similar to that of creating a user or group object. You select the container in which you want to place the object and, from the Action menu, point to New and select Computer. The New Object – Computer wizard appears, as shown in Figure 8-4.

In the first page of this wizard, you can configure the following properties of the computer object:

- **Computer Name**   Specifies a name up to 63 characters long, to be assigned to the computer object. This name must match the name of the computer joined with the object.

- **Computer Name (Pre–Windows 2000)**   When you enter the Computer Name, the first 15 characters appear in this field. This is the computer name that pre–Windows 2000 computers on the network will use.

- **User Or Group**   Specifies the user or group that is permitted to join the computer to the domain. The default value is the Domain Admins group. To change the default, click Change to open a standard Select User Or Group dialog box.

- **Assign This Computer Account As A Pre–Windows 2000 Computer** Select this check box if the computer to be joined to the domain using this object is running Windows NT 4.0.

- **Assign This Computer Account As A Backup Domain Controller** Select this check box if the computer to be joined to the domain using this object is functioning as a Windows NT 4.0 backup domain controller (BDC).

Figure 8-4   The New Object – Computer wizard

After completing this page, click Next to display the Managed page, shown in Figure 8-5. On this page, you can specify whether the computer to be joined to this object is a managed computer that you will install using Remote Installation Services (RIS). If you select this check box, you must supply a globally unique identifier (GUID) or a universally unique identifier (UUID) for the computer.

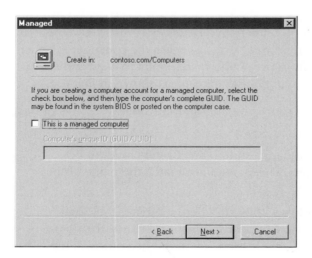

Figure 8-5   The Managed page of the New Object – Computer wizard

Clicking Next displays a summary page, and clicking Finish creates the computer object in the container you selected.

Practice creating computer objects by doing Exercise 8-1, "Creating a Computer Object Using Active Directory Users and Computers," now.

Creating Computer Objects Using Dsadd.exe

As with users and groups, the Active Directory Users And Computers console is good for creating and managing single objects, but many administrators turn to the Active Directory command-line tools included with Windows Server 2003 when they have to create multiple objects.

The Dsadd.exe utility enables you to create computer objects from the command line, just as you created user and group objects in the previous chapters. You can create a batch file of Dsadd.exe commands to generate multiple objects in one process. The basic syntax for creating a computer object with Dsadd.exe is as follows:

```
dsadd computer ComputerDN [parameters]
```

The *ComputerDN* parameter is a distinguished name for the new group object you want to create. The DNs use the same format as those in comma-separated value (CSV) files, as discussed in Chapter 6. If the DN includes a space, you must surround the entire DN with quotation marks. When using Dsadd.exe interactively from the command prompt, you can supply the *ComputerDN* parameter in any one of the following ways:

- By typing DNs on the command line, separated by spaces.

- By piping a list of DNs from another command, such as Dsquery.exe.

- By leaving the DN parameter empty, at which point you can type the DNs, one at a time, at a prompt presented by the program. Press Enter after each DN, and press Ctrl+Z and Enter after the last DN.

You can also add any of the following parameters to the Dsadd.exe command line, to define values for certain computer object properties:

- **-samid *SAMName***   Specifies the Security Accounts Manager (SAM) name for the computer object, to be used by pre–Windows 2000 systems

- **-desc *description***   Specifies a description for the computer object

- **-loc *location***   Specifies the location of the computer associated with the computer object

- **-memberof *GroupDN***   Specifies the DNs of one or more groups of which the new computer should be made a member

You can also add the *-s*, *-u*, and *-p* parameters to specify the domain controller against which Dsadd.exe will run, and the username and password that will be used to execute the command, as shown here:

- {**-s *Server*** | **-d *Domain***}

- **-u *UserName***

- **-p {*Password*** | ***}**   , where * causes you to be prompted for a password

For example, to create a new computer object called webserver1 in the Computers container, you would use the following command:

```
dsadd computer "CN=webserver1,CN=Computers,DC=contoso,DC=com"
```

Practice creating computer objects from the command line by doing Exercise 8-2, "Creating a Computer Object Using Dsadd.exe," now.

Creating Computer Objects Using Netdom.exe

Netdom.exe is another command-line tool that you can use to create computer objects as well as perform many other domain account and security tasks. The advantage of using Netdom.exe instead of Dsadd.exe is that you do not have to specify the name of the computer object you want to create as a DN. A simple command such as the following creates a computer object in the default Computers container:

```
netdom add webserver1
```

> **NOTE** *Obtaining Netdom.exe* Netdom.exe is included with Windows Server 2003, but it is not installed with the operating system. You can install Netdom.exe with the Windows Support Tools, by running Suptools.msi from the Support\Tools folder on the Windows Server 2003 installation CD.

The full syntax of Netdom.exe, when you use the add subcommand, is as follows:

```
netdom add computername [/Domain:DomainName] [/UserD:User/PasswordD:UserPassword]
    [/OU:OUDN]
```

The functions of the command-line parameters are as follows:

- ■ ***computername***   Specifies the common name for the computer object to be created.

- ■ **/Domain:*DomainName***   Specifies the name of the domain in which to create the computer object. When this is omitted, the program creates the object in the domain in which the current user is logged on.

- ■ **/UserD:*User***   Specifies the name of the user account that the program should use to create the computer object. When this is omitted, the program uses the account of the currently logged-on user.

- ■ **/PasswordD:*UserPassword***   Specifies the password associated with the user account indicated by the */UserD* parameter. This parameter must be included when the command line includes the */UserD* parameter. The wildcard character (*) can be used to cause a prompt for the password.

- ■ **/OU:*OUDN***   Specifies the DN of the OU in which the computer object should be created. When this is omitted, the program creates the object in the Computers container.

Joining Computers to a Domain

The process of actually joining a computer to a domain must occur at the computer itself and be performed by a member of the computer's local Administrators group. After logging on, you join a computer running Windows Server 2003 to a domain from the Computer Name tab in the System Properties dialog box (which is accessible from the System icon in Control Panel), as shown in Figure 8-6.

Figure 8-6   The Computer Name tab in the System Properties dialog box

On a computer that is not joined to a domain, the Computer Name tab displays the name assigned to the computer during the operating system installation and the name of the workgroup to which the system currently belongs (which is WORKGROUP by default). To join the computer to the domain, click Change to display the Computer Name Changes dialog box (shown in Figure 8-7).

Figure 8-7   The Computer Name Changes dialog box

In this dialog box, the Computer Name text box enables you to change the name assigned to the computer during installation. Depending on whether you have already created a computer object, observe the following precautions:

- If you want to join a domain in which you have already created a computer object for the system in Active Directory, the name entered in this text box must match the name of the object exactly.

- If you intend to create a computer object during the joining process, the name in this text box must not already exist in the domain.

Next, select the Domain option and enter the name of the domain the computer will join, and then click OK. When the computer establishes contact with a domain controller for the domain, a second Computer Name Changes dialog box appears, as shown in Figure 8-8, prompting you for the username and password of a domain user account with permission to join the computer to the domain.

Figure 8-8   The Computer Name Changes authentication dialog box

> **NOTE   Domain Controller Communications**   If you see a message box informing you that the computer was unable to locate a domain controller for the domain you specified, the problem is most likely due to a network configuration error. Most likely, the Preferred DNS Server address in the computer's TCP/IP configuration is incorrect. Windows Server 2003 relies on the Domain Name System (DNS) to locate domain controllers, and if the computer does not have access to a DNS server that is hosting the domain, communication with the domain controller is not possible.

Once you have authenticated with the domain controller, the computer is welcomed to the domain and you are instructed to restart the computer.

Joining a Domain Using Netdom.exe

You can also use the Netdom.exe command-line utility to join a computer to a domain. The syntax for the command is as follows:

```
netdom join computername /Domain:DomainName [/UserD:User /PasswordD:UserPassword]
    [/UserO:User /PasswordO:UserPassword] [/OU:OUDN] [REBoot:seconds]
```

The functions of the command-line parameters are as follows:

- **computername**   Specifies the name of the computer to be joined.

- **/Domain:DomainName**   Specifies the name of the domain the computer will join.

- **/UserD:User**   Specifies the name of the domain user account that the program should use to join the computer to the domain.

- **/PasswordD:UserPassword**   Specifies the password associated with the domain user account indicated by the /UserD parameter.

- **/UserO:User**   Specifies the name of the local user account that the program should use to access the computer.

- **/PasswordO:***UserPassword*   Specifies the password associated with the local user account indicated by the */UserO* parameter.

- **/OU:***OUDN*   Specifies the DN of the OU in which the program should create a computer object. When this is omitted, the program creates the object in the Computers container.

- **/REBoot:***seconds*   Specifies that the computer should automatically shut down and reboot after it is joined to the domain. You can also specify the number of seconds that should elapse before the restart. The default value is 20 seconds.

Creating Computer Objects While Joining to a Domain

You can join a computer to a domain whether or not you have already created a computer object for it. Once the computer authenticates to the domain controller, the domain controller scans the Active Directory database for a computer object with the same name as the computer. If it does not find a matching object, the domain controller creates one in the Computers container, using the name supplied.

For the computer object to be created automatically in this manner, one would expect that the user account you specify when connecting to the domain controller must have object creation privileges for the Computers container, such as membership in the Administrators group. However, this is not always the case. Domain users can also create computer objects themselves through an interesting, indirect process. The Default Domain Controllers Policy group policy object (GPO) grants a user right called Add Workstations To Domain to the Authenticated Users special identity, as shown in Figure 8-9. This means that any user who is successfully authenticated to Active Directory is permitted to join up to 10 workstations to the domain and create 10 associated computer objects, even if they do not possess explicit object creation permissions.

Figure 8-9   The Default Domain Controllers Policy user rights assignments

The important thing to remember about the Add Workstations To Domain user right, however, is that *workstations* is the operative word. Authenticated users can add up to 10 workstations to the domain, but not servers. This means that the computers must be running Windows XP Professional, Windows 2000 Professional, or one of the down-level Active Directory clients. Authenticated users cannot join computers running Windows Server 2003 or Windows 2000 Server to the domain.

Joining a Domain During Operating System Installation

Although you can join an existing Windows Server 2003 computer to a domain at any time, you can also perform the join during the operating system installation. When the Windows Setup wizard displays the Workgroup Or Computer Domain page, as shown in Figure 8-10, you can specify the name of the domain the computer is to join. You are prompted for a domain user account and password to authenticate to the domain controller, and the joining process proceeds as described earlier.

Figure 8-10   The Workgroup Or Computer Domain page of the Windows Setup wizard

Locating Computer Objects

By default, every new Active Directory domain has two containers, which are called Computers and Domain Controllers, as shown in Figure 8-11. When you create the domain by promoting your first domain controller, the Active Directory Installation wizard creates these two containers and then creates a computer object for the new domain controller in the Domain Controllers container.

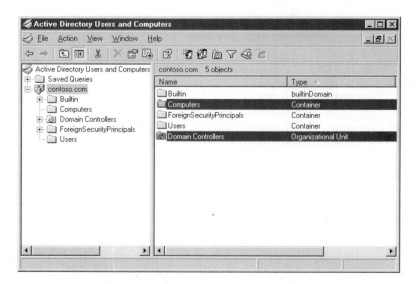

Figure 8-11   The Computers and Domain Controllers containers in an Active Directory domain

Locating Domain Controller Computer Objects

The Domain Controllers container is an OU object. You never have to create computer objects for domain controllers because the Active Directory Installation wizard creates them for you and puts them in the Domain Controllers OU. This container must be an OU because there is a GPO applied to it called the Default Domain Controllers Policy GPO. This GPO contains group policy settings that are essential for the security of the domain controllers. In most Active Directory installations, the computer objects for domain controllers can remain where they are. If you move them, be sure to apply the Default Domain Controllers Policy GPO to the OU at their new location, or create an equivalent GPO containing settings specific to the domain controller role.

Locating Other Computer Objects

The Computers container is the default location for all other computer objects that are created by automatic means, such as when a computer joins a domain and there is no computer object there for it already. Using the Active Directory Users And Computers console, you can manually create computer objects in any container, manage them, and move them around at will.

Oddly enough, the Computers container is not an OU; it is one of those strange objects whose object class literally is a container, like the Users, Builtin, and Foreign-SecurityPrincipals containers. As you learned in Chapter 6, you cannot create or delete these containers, and you cannot apply GPOs to them, which makes it impossible to deploy group policy settings to the computer objects stored there in one step. For this reason, it is usually a good idea to create at least one OU and move the computer objects from the Computers container there.

Many Active Directory networks create multiple OUs for computer objects, either to implement an organizational or geographical hierarchy in the Active Directory tree or to create separate containers for the different roles performed by the computers. For example, you might create an OU for your workstation computers and a series of OUs for the roles performed by your member servers. This would enable you to deploy a GPO containing different policy settings for each OU, thereby creating a different system configuration for each computer role.

Redirecting Computer Objects

Although you can create computer objects in the Computers container and manually move them to any location you want, it is also possible to configure Windows Server 2003 to place its automatically created computer objects in another container. This is generally preferable because it enables you to place the new computer objects into the proper OU before the computer actually joins the domain. This ensures that the computer is governed by the policies applied to the OU immediately upon joining the domain.

To redirect new computer objects, your domain must be using the Windows Server 2003 domain functional level. Open a Command Prompt window and, from the command line, run a utility called Redircmp.exe, which is supplied with Windows Server 2003, specifying the distinguished name (DN) of the OU or other container you want to be the location of your new computer objects, as in the following example:

```
redircmp ou=workstations,DC=contoso,dc=com
```

MORE INFO   *For more information on domain functional levels and how they affect the creation and management of Active Directory objects, see "Understanding Domain Functional Levels" in Chapter 7.*

MANAGING COMPUTER OBJECTS

Once you have created objects for your computers and joined them to the domain, you can manage the objects and the computers from the Active Directory Users and Computers console. Some of the management functions you can perform are described in the following sections.

Modifying Computer Object Properties

As with all other objects in Active Directory, computer objects consist of properties, which contain various pieces of information about the system the object represents. To modify the properties of a computer object, you select it in the Active Directory Users and Computers console and, from the Action menu, select Properties to display the object's Properties dialog box, as shown in Figure 8-12.

Figure 8-12   A computer object's Properties dialog box

The dialog box has seven tabs:

- **General**   On this tab, you can enter descriptive text for the computer represented by the object. The other text boxes (Computer Name [Pre–Windows 2000], DNS Name, and Role) contain information that is automatically supplied when the computer joins the domain.

- **Operating System**   Contains the name, version, and service pack level of the operating system running on the computer represented by the object. This information is supplied automatically when the computer joins the domain. There are no user-definable properties on this tab.

- **Member Of**   Enables you to specify the groups of which the computer object is a member. By default, all new computer objects that are not domain controllers are added to the Domain Computers global group.

- **Delegation**   Enables you to grant services running under the computer account permission to send service requests to other network computers on behalf of a user. You can permit the object to request any service or create a list of specific services that it can request, using another account's credentials.

- **Location**   Contains a text box that you can use to specify the location of the computer represented by this object.

- **Managed By**   Enables you to specify a user object that is responsible for the management of the computer represented by the object. When you do this, pertinent informational properties from the selected user object appear on this tab, as shown in Figure 8-13. This information is retrieved dynamically from the user object; only the name of the user is stored as part of the computer object.

- **Dial-In**   Enables you to specify values for properties controlling remote dial-in access to the computer represented by the object, such as whether access should be permitted or denied and whether features such as caller ID and callback should be used.

Figure 8-13   The Managed By tab in a computer object's Properties dialog box

Deleting, Disabling, and Resetting Computer Objects

Under normal usage conditions, computer objects require no maintenance and no attention from administrators. However, in some situations administrators might have to manipulate computer objects, such as to prevent them from being abused, or to accommodate changes in the physical computer itself.

Deleting Computer Objects

Deleting a computer object in the Active Directory Users and Computers console is simply a matter of selecting the object and, from the Action menu, selecting Delete. After you confirm your action, the object is permanently deleted. However, before you begin deleting computer objects, be sure you fully understand the ramifications of your actions.

As with user and group objects, computer objects have a unique SID value that is lost when the object is deleted. Creating a new object with the same name and property value will not re-create the same SID, and any permissions and group memberships granted to the original, deleted computer object will be irretrievably lost. You should therefore not delete computer objects (or any objects, for that matter) unless you are absolutely sure you will not need them again. You can prevent an object from being used by disabling it instead.

> **TIP   Disjoining Computers**   When a computer is removed from a domain, by being joined to a workgroup or to a different domain, the system attempts to delete its computer object. If the computer cannot delete the object because of networking problems, insufficient permissions, or any other reason, the account remains in Active Directory. It might appear, immediately or eventually, as disabled. If the object is no longer needed in that domain, it must be deleted manually.

Disabling Computer Objects

If you plan to have a computer offline for an extended period of time, the best practice is not to delete it, but to disable it. One of the most basic security principles is to keep identity stores as small as possible, allowing authentication only of the minimum number of accounts needed to service the organization. When you disable a computer object, its SID and all of its property values remain intact, so that when you enable it again, the object is ready for use with no modification.

To disable a computer object in the Active Directory Users And Computers console, select it and, from the Action menu, select Disable Account. A red X appears in the object's icon to indicate that it is disabled, as shown in Figure 8-14. While the object is disabled, the computer cannot establish a secure channel with the domain. Users who have not previously logged on to the computer, and who therefore do not have cached credentials on the computer, cannot log on until you reestablish the secure channel by enabling the account.

Figure 8-14   A disabled computer account

To reenable the object, use the same procedure, selecting Enable Account from the Action menu.

Practice
managing
computer
objects by doing
Exercise 8-3,
"Disabling and
Enabling a
Computer
Object," now.

Resetting a Computer Object

Sometimes an administrator might want to replace a computer on the network, to upgrade hardware or for other reasons, but still continue to use the original computer object, along with its group memberships and permission assignments. Once a computer is joined to a domain and associated with a particular computer object, you cannot join a different computer to that same object, nor can you disjoin the computer from the domain and rejoin another computer with the same name without re-creating the object and losing the object's SID, as well as its associated group memberships and permissions.

However, you can reuse the same computer object for two different computers by resetting the object. Resetting a computer object resets its password but maintains all of its properties. With a reset password, the object is rendered available for use again. Any appropriately named computer can join the domain using that object. To reset a computer object using the Active Directory Users And Computers console, select the object and, from the Action menu, select Reset Account. After confirming your action, a message box appears stating that the account was successfully reset. You can also reset computer accounts from the command line using the Netdom.exe utility.

> **NOTE** **Exam Objectives** *The objectives for exam 70-290 require students to be able to "reset computer accounts."*

Managing Remote Computers

In addition to manipulating computer objects, the Active Directory Users And Computers console also enables you to access the computer itself. When you select a computer object and, from the Action menu, select manage, a new Computer Management console opens, with the focus on the selected Computer. You can then perform any of the standard functions provided by that console on the selected computer (permissions permitting).

Managing Computer Objects from the Command Line

All of the computer object management tasks you learned about in the previous sections are also possible using the command-line tools included with Windows Server 2003. The following sections examine the use of these tools.

Managing Computer Object Properties with Dsmod.exe

The Dsmod.exe tool can modify the properties of computer objects, just as it can for user and group objects. In addition, you can use Dsmod.exe to disable, enable, and reset computer objects (but not delete them). The syntax for computer object modifications with the tool is as follows:

```
dsmod computer ComputerDN [parameters]
```

The functions of the command-line parameters are as follows:

■ ***ComputerDN*** Specifies the DN of the computer object to be modified.

■ **-desc *Description*** Specifies a value for the computer object's *Description* property.

- **-loc *Location***   Specifies a value for the computer object's *Location* property.

- **-disabled [yes | no]**   Disables or enables the specified computer object.

- **-reset**   Resets the password of the specified computer object.

- **-s *Server***   Specifies the name of the domain controller that the program will use to access the computer object. When this is omitted, the program defaults to a domain controller in the domain to which the user is currently logged on.

- **-d *Domain***   Specifies the name of the domain in which the computer object is located. When this is omitted, the program defaults to the domain to which the user is currently logged on.

- **-u *UserName***   Specifies the name of the user account the program will use to access the domain. When this is omitted, the program defaults to the user account with which the system is currently logged on to the domain.

- **-p [*Password* | *]**   Specifies the password associated with the user account identified in the *-u* parameter. Including an asterisk (*) causes the program to stop and prompt the user for a password.

To disable a computer account, use a command like the following:

```
dsmod computer CN=webserver1,CN=Computers,DC=contoso,DC=com -disabled yes
```

To reset a computer account, use a command like the following:

```
dsmod computer CN=webserver1,CN=Computers,DC=contoso,DC=com -reset
```

Deleting Computer Object Properties with Dsrm.exe

Dsmod.exe can modify computer objects but not delete them. To delete computer objects, you must use the Dsrm.exe utility. You specify the DN of the object you want to delete on the Dsrm.exe command line, using the following syntax:

```
Dsrm ObjectDN
```

Once you confirm your request, the program deletes the object. An example of a Dsrm.exe command follows:

```
dsrm CN=webserver1,CN=Computers,DC=contoso,DC=com
```

TROUBLESHOOTING COMPUTER ACCOUNTS

Active Directory treats computer objects as security principals. This means that a computer, just like a user, has properties, such as a name, a password, and an SID, that enable it to be added to the access control lists (ACLs) of other objects. Computer accounts, and the secure relationships between computers and their domain, are generally robust. However, like user accounts, computer accounts sometimes require maintenance and troubleshooting. In the rare circumstance that an account or secure channel breaks down, the symptoms of failure are generally obvious.

The most common signs of computer account problems are as follows:

- Messages at logon that indicate that a domain controller cannot be contacted, that the computer account might be missing, or that the trust (another way of referring to the secure channel) between the computer and the domain has been lost. A sample of such an error message, from a Windows XP client, is shown in Figure 8-15.

- Error messages or entries in an event log that indicate similar problems or suggest that passwords, trusts, secure channels, or relationships with the domain or a domain controller have failed.

- A computer account is missing in Active Directory.

Figure 8-15   A Windows XP logon message indicating a possible computer account problem

> **NOTE   Exam Objectives**   The objectives for exam 70-290 require students to be able to "troubleshoot computer accounts" and "diagnose and resolve issues related to computer accounts by using the Active Directory Users and Computers MMC snap-in."

If one of these situations occurs, you must troubleshoot the computer account. You learned earlier how to delete, disable, and reset a computer account and how to join a computer to the domain. The rules that govern the troubleshooting of a computer account when one of these events occurs are as follows:

1. If the computer account exists in Active Directory, you must reset it.

2. If the computer account is missing from Active Directory, you must create a computer account.

3. If the computer still belongs to the domain, you must remove it from the domain by changing its membership to a workgroup. The name of the workgroup is irrelevant.

4. Rejoin the computer to the domain. Alternatively, join another computer to the domain, but the new computer must have the same name as the computer account.

To troubleshoot any computer account problem, apply all four of these rules. They can be carried out in any order, except that rule 4, rejoining the computer to the domain, must always be the final step. The following two scenarios illustrate the use of these rules:

- A user complains that when she attempts to log on, the system presents error messages indicating that the computer account might be missing. Applying rule 1, you open Active Directory Users And Computers and find that there is a computer account for the system in the domain. You reset the object. Rule 2 does not apply—the object does exist. Then, using rule 3, you remove the system from the domain and, following rule 4, rejoin it to the domain.

- A computer account is reset by accident, so rule 1 has already been completed. Although the reset is accidental, you must continue to recover by applying the remaining three rules. Rule 2 does not apply because the computer object exists in the domain. Follow rules 3 and 4, removing the computer from the domain and then rejoining it.

SUMMARY

- For users to log on to an Active Directory domain, they must have not only user objects, but also objects representing their computers. A computer object represents a specific system on the network and contains properties with information about the system.

- Computer objects can function as security principles. You can add them to groups and grant them permissions.

- To add a computer to a domain, you must create a computer object for it in Active Directory and then join the physical computer to the domain. The computer object can be created ahead of time, or it can be created as part of the join process.

- You must be logged on as a member of the local Administrators group to change the domain membership of a computer.

- To create computer objects, you can use the Active Directory Users And Computers console, the Dsadd.exe utility, or the Netdom.exe utility. The Administrators and Account Operators groups have sufficient permissions to create new computer objects, and you can also delegate the appropriate permissions to other users or groups.

- Computer objects for non–domain controllers are placed in the Computers container by default. You cannot apply group policies to this container, so it is usually preferable to locate the computer objects in an OU instead.

- To join a computer to a domain, you use the Computer Name tab in the System Properties dialog box or the Netdom.exe utility. If a computer object for the computer does not exist when you attempt to join it to the domain, the system creates the object (assuming you have the necessary permissions).

- Using the Active Directory Users and Computers console and the Dsmod.exe and Dsrm.exe utilities, you can manage the properties of computer objects, as well as delete, disable, and reset them.

- Computer objects have an SID that Active Directory uses to reference the computer in its group memberships and other permissions. Accidentally deleting a computer object causes its SID to be irretrievably lost, forcing you to create the permission. Be careful about deleting computer objects; disabling them instead makes it possible to enable the objects again, with no loss of information.

- The typical steps for troubleshooting a computer object problem include creating or resetting the object, removing the computer from the domain, and rejoining it to the domain.

EXERCISES

Exercise 8-1: Creating a Computer Object Using Active Directory Users And Computers

In this exercise, you create a new computer object using the Active Directory Users and Computers console.

1. Log on to a Windows Server 2003 domain controller as Administrator.

2. Click Start, point to Administrative tools, and select Active Directory Users And Computers. The Active Directory Users And Computers console appears.

3. In the scope pane, select the Computers container and, on the Action menu, point to New and select Computer. The New Object – Computer wizard appears.

4. In the Computer Name text box, type **Computer1**, and then click Next.

5. Click Next again, and then click Finish. The Computer1 computer object appears in the Computers container.

Exercise 8-2: Creating a Computer Object Using Dsadd.exe

In this exercise, you create a new computer object using the Dsadd.exe utility.

1. Log on to a Windows Server 2003 domain controller as Administrator.

2. Click Start and select Command Prompt. A command prompt appears.

3. At the command prompt, type the following command (where *xx* is your student number) and press Enter:

```
dsadd computer "CN=Computer2,CN=Computers,DC=contosoxx,DC=com" -desc
    "Mark Lee's Workstation"
```

4. Click Start, point to Administrative tools, and select Active Directory Users And Computers. The Active Directory Users And Computers console appears.

5. In the scope pane, select the Computers container. Confirm that the Computer2 computer object appears in the container and that the description "Mark Lee's Workstation" appears in the object's Properties dialog box on the General tab.

Exercise 8-3: Disabling and Enabling a Computer Object

In this exercise, you disable and reenable a computer object using the Active Directory Users And Computers console.

1. Log on to a Windows Server 2003 domain controller as Administrator.

2. Click Start, point to Administrative tools, and select Active Directory Users And Computers. The Active Directory Users and Computers console appears.

3. In the scope pane, select the Computers container. Then select the Computer1 computer object you created in Exercise 8-1 and, on the Action menu, select Disable Account. An Active Directory message box appears, prompting you to confirm your command to disable the object.

4. Click Yes. Another Active Directory message box appears, confirming that the Computer1 object has been disabled.

5. Click Yes. The Computer1 icon in the console appears with a red X.

6. Select the same Computer1 computer object and, on the Action menu, select Enable Account. An Active Directory message box appears, informing you that the object has been enabled.

7. Click Yes. The Computer1 icon appears without the red X.

REVIEW QUESTIONS

1. What are the minimum group memberships necessary to create a Windows Server 2003 computer account in an OU in a domain? Consider all steps of the process, and assume that the computer object for the system does not yet exist in Active Directory. (Choose all correct answers.)

   a. Domain Admins

   b. Enterprise Admins

   c. Administrators on a domain controller

   d. Account Operators on a domain controller

   e. Server Operators on a domain controller

   f. Account Operators on the computer

   g. Server Operators on the computer

   h. Administrators on the computer

2. Which of the following command-line tools can create a computer object in Active Directory?

   a. Dsmod.exe

   b. Dsrm.exe

   c. Netdom.exe

   d. Dsadd.exe

   e. Net.exe

3. Which of the following Windows platforms are capable of joining to a computer object in an Active Directory domain?

   a. Windows 95

   b. Windows NT 4

   c. Windows 98

   d. Windows 2000

 e. Windows Me

 f. Windows XP

 g. Windows Server 2003

4. When you open the Properties dialog box for a computer object in the Active Directory Users And Computers console, you discover that no properties are displayed in the Operating System tab. What causes these properties to be absent? *It is not joined to a domain*

5. After a period of expansion, your company created a second domain. Last weekend, a number of machines that had been in your domain were moved to the new domain. When you open Active Directory Users And Computers, the objects for those machines are still in your domain and are displayed with a red X icon. What is the most appropriate course of action?

 a. Enable the objects

 b. Disable the objects

 c. Reset the objects

 d. Delete the objects

6. A user reports that during a logon attempt, he received a message stating that the computer cannot contact the domain because the domain controller is down or the computer account might be missing. You open Active Directory Users And Computers and discover that the account for that computer is missing. What steps should you take? *you must create an account*

7. A user reports that during a logon attempt, he received a message stating that the computer cannot contact the domain because the domain controller is down or the computer account might be missing. You open Active Directory Users And Computers and see that the computer's account appears normal. What steps should you take? *reset the account, remove it from the domain, rejoin it to the domain*

CASE SCENARIOS

Scenario 8-1: Resetting a Computer Object

In your Windows Server 2003 domain contoso.com, you have a computer object for a member server called Pserver01 in an OU called Pservers. This object represents a print server that has been offline for a lengthy period and is not communicating with other computers in the domain to accept print jobs. You have determined that the password on this computer's account within the domain needs to be reset. Which command can you issue to correctly reset the computer account?

 a. dsmod CN=pserver01,CN=PSERVERS,DC=contoso,DC=com –reset

 b. dsmod computer pserver01.contoso.com –reset

 c. dsmod contoso\pserver01 –reset

 d. dsmod computer CN=pserver01,CN=PSERVERS,DC=contoso,DC=com –reset

Scenario 8-2: Computer Object Troubleshooting

After a consultant performs maintenance on the computers in the east branch office over the weekend, users complain of trouble logging on. You examine the event log on one of the branch office computers and discover the following entry:

There seems to be a problem with the computer account. Specify which of the following steps you should perform to correct the problem, in the correct order.

a. Delete the computer accounts.

b. Reset the user accounts.

c. Join the computers to a workgroup.

d. Disable the computer accounts.

e. Reset the computer accounts.

f. Enable the computer accounts.

g. Create new computer accounts.

h. Join the computers to the domain.

PART 3
MANAGING AND MAINTAINING SHARED RESOURCES

CHAPTER 9
SHARING FILE SYSTEM RESOURCES

One of the primary reasons for the existence of data networks is the ability to share files among users working on different computers. On a small network, file sharing is often an informal process performed by trusted end users with little thought given to security. On a large network, however, and particularly in organizations dealing with sensitive data, it is the job of the network administrator to ensure that the appropriate files are shared, that they are protected from accidental or deliberate damage, and that they are accessible only by the people who should be authorized to work with them. In this chapter, we review the concepts and skills required to share data files with network users effectively and securely.

Upon completion of this chapter, you will be able to:

■ Create and manage file system shares and work with share permissions

■ Use NTFS file system permissions to control access to files

■ Manage file sharing using Microsoft Internet Information Services (IIS)

UNDERSTANDING PERMISSIONS

One of the most fundamental concepts of Microsoft Windows Server 2003 system administration is that of permissions. As the name implies, a permission is a privilege granted to a particular entity, such as a user, group, or computer, enabling that entity to perform a particular action or access a particular resource. Windows Server 2003 and all of the other Windows operating systems use permissions in a variety of ways to control access to various elements of the operating system.

Windows Server 2003 has many types of permissions, the most prominent of which are as follows. Each of these permission types is completely separate from the others, although some can be applied to the same system elements.

- **File system permissions**   Controls access to files and folders on NTFS drives. All users require permissions to access NTFS files and folders, whether they are working on the network or on the computer where the data is stored.

- **Share permissions**   Controls access to file system and printer shares. Users must have permissions to access shared resources over the network.

- **Active Directory permissions**   Controls access to Microsoft Active Directory objects. Users must have some access to Active Directory objects to log on to the network to access network resources. Administrators need greater access to maintain the object properties and the Active Directory tree structure.

- **Registry permissions**   Controls access to registry keys. To modify registry keys, administrators must have the appropriate permissions.

Some of these systems require more maintenance than others. A typical network administrator might work with file system permissions every day but never have to manually modify registry permissions. In Chapters 6, 7, and 8, you learned something about the Active Directory permissions that administrators need to create and manage objects, such as users, groups, and computers. In many cases, Active Directory permissions are delegated to specific groups of administrators once and need not be adjusted again unless a dramatic reorganization tales place.

Access Control Lists

The functionality of these permission systems is based on the concept of the **access control list (ACL)**. Most Windows elements, including files, shares, Active Directory objects, and registry keys, have an ACL. An ACL is simply a list of permissions specifying who has access to that particular element and what degree of access they have. The ACL for a particular element consists of **access control entries (ACEs)**. An ACE specifies the name of a *security principal* (that is, the user, group, or computer being granted permissions) and the specific permissions granted to that security principal.

NOTE **Where Is the ACL?** It is critical for the system administrator to understand that the ACL is always stored with the element being controlled, not with the security principal being granted access to the element. For example, a particular folder on an NTFS drive has an ACL containing a list of users or groups that have permission to access that folder. If you look at a particular user or group object, you will not find a list of the folders to which that user or group has access. This is a particularly important point when you move elements to different locations or back them up to another storage medium. Moving files from an NTFS drive to a FAT drive, for example, causes the permissions to be lost because the FAT file system cannot store the ACLs.

Working with ACLs is relatively simple because all of the permissions systems in Windows Server 2003 use a similar interface. Virtually all system elements protected by permissions have a Properties dialog box that contains a Security tab, like the one shown in Figure 9-1. The upper list box in the tab displays a list of ACEs (that is, security principals), and the lower list box specifies the permissions allocated to the ACE selected in the upper list box. You can add and remove ACEs as needed and specify the permissions granted or denied to each one.

Figure 9-1 The Security tab in a Properties dialog box

Permissions

The permissions specified in the ACEs are designed to provide granular access control over the elements to which they are applied. When you grant a user permission to access a folder, for example, the access is not simply a yes-or-no proposition. You have a great many options as to how much access the user receives. Each of the permissions systems listed earlier has its own list of individual permissions that are specific to the types of resources they control. When you create an ACE, you select a security principal, and then you select the individual permissions that you want to grant that security principal.

For example, NTFS permissions enable you to specify that a particular user be able to read the files in a folder but not modify them, or you can provide the user with however much additional access he needs. Depending on the resource you are working with, you might have dozens of permissions available, which you can combine in any way you wish.

In many cases, the sheer number of permissions involved can make the ACL administration process rather complicated. To simplify matters, Windows Server 2003 uses two levels of permissions, standard permissions and special permissions. **Standard permissions** are the permissions you see on the Security tab of a Properties dialog box. These are the permissions you will probably work with every day because they provide basic control over various aspects of the element being protected.

However, standard permissions are actually combinations of even more detailed permissions called **special permissions**. (You learn more about how to use special permissions for the NTFS file system later in this chapter.) To access special permissions, you click the Advanced button on the Security tab to display an Advanced Security Settings dialog box, as shown in Figure 9-2.

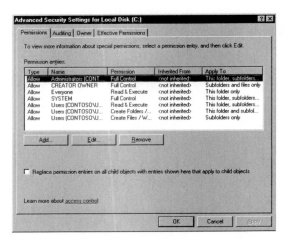

Figure 9-2   An Advanced Security Settings dialog box

In this dialog box, you can control access to a resource with much greater specificity, by selecting from a complete list of special permissions in a Permission Entry dialog box, as shown in Figure 9-3. This is often not necessary on a typical network, but some of the default permission settings created by Windows Server 2003 during the operating system installation rely on individual special permission assignments.

Figure 9-3   A Permission Entry dialog box

NOTE   You work with all the Windows Server 2003 permissions systems in much the same way, except that the standard and special permissions can be different, depending on the resource being protected.

Inheritance

One of the key features of the permissions systems in Windows Server 2003 is that, by default, subordinate objects inherit the permissions possessed by their parent objects. Permissions always flow downstream through a file system hierarchy, Active Directory hierarchy, or registry structure. When you grant a security principal permission to access an NTFS folder or share, an Active Directory object, or a registry key, that principal also receives the same permission to access the subfolders beneath the specified NTFS folder or share, the objects beneath the specified Active Directory object, or the keys subordinate to the specified key, respectively.

For example, granting a user permissions for the root of an NTFS drive means that the user receives the same permissions for all of the files and subfolders on that entire drive. In most cases, this permission inheritance is beneficial because it prevents administrators from having to create separate permissions for every subfolder, subordinate object, or subkey. In fact, for most administrators, it is second nature to take this inheritance into account when designing their directory structures, share strategies, and Active Directory trees.

However, sometimes inheritance is not desirable, and in these cases, there are two ways to counteract the default behavior of permissions:

- **Turn off inheritance**   When you are working with special permissions, you can control whether the permissions you assign to a particular element are inherited by some or all of its subelements.

- **Deny permissions**   All of the permissions systems enable you to explicitly deny a security principal specific permissions, counteracting the effect of any permissions the principal might have inherited from parent elements.

Effective Permissions

Because the security principals used to assign permissions can be users, groups, or computers, it is possible for a single principal to receive permissions from multiple sources, and in some cases those permissions can conflict. For this reason, there are rules that specify how the permissions from various sources interact. All of the permissions that the security principal receives individually, by inheritance, and through group memberships, are subject to these rules and are combined to create the user's **effective permissions**.

The rules forming a security principal's effective permissions are as follows:

- **Allowed permissions are cumulative.**   All of the allowed permissions granted to a security principal, no matter what their source, are combined to form the principal's effective permissions. For example, a specific user might be explicitly granted permissions providing full access to a particular folder on an NTFS drive. At the same time, the user might be a member of a group that also has permissions for that folder, but the group has read-only access to the folder. In addition, the user inherits read and write permissions from the folder's parent folder. In this case, all of the user's permissions, whether explicit or inherited from any source, are combined.

- **Denied permissions override allowed permissions.** Explicitly denying permissions to a security principal overrides the allowed permissions the principal receives from any other source. For example, if a user receives full access permissions to a folder by inheritance and also receives full access from a group membership, permissions you create that explicitly deny the user all access to that folder override all of the permissions inherited from parents and groups. Therefore, in this case, the user's effective permissions provide no access at all to the folder.

- **Explicit permissions take precedence over inherited permissions.** When a security principal inherits permissions from a parent or a group, you can override those permissions by explicitly assigning different permissions to the principal itself. The inherited permissions form a rule, and the explicit permissions are an exception to that rule. Therefore, explicitly allowed permissions override inherited denied permissions.

SHARING FOLDERS

When you sit down at a computer running Windows Server 2003, you can access the files and folders on its drives from the system console, assuming that you have the appropriate credentials. You can also allow users elsewhere on the network access to the computer's files and folders, but to do so, you must first create a share specifying what files the users can access.

> **MORE INFO** You can actually create two types of shares on computers running Windows: file system shares and printer shares. This chapter deals exclusively with file system shares. To learn about creating printer shares, see Chapter 10.

The ability to create shares in Windows Server 2003 is based on two services that run on every Windows computer: the Workstation service and the Server service. These two services are implemented by the Client For Microsoft Networks module and the File And Printer Sharing For Microsoft Networks module, respectively, both of which appear in the Local Area Connection Properties dialog box for every network interface adapter installed on the computer, as shown in Figure 9-4. The Server service is responsible for making shared system resources available on the network, and the Workstation service enables other computers to access those shared resources.

> **NOTE** **Workstations and Servers** Despite the names of its various versions and editions, Windows is a peer-to-peer operating system, meaning that every computer is capable of functioning both as a client and as a server simultaneously. Even computers that are not running an operating system with Server in its name can still run the Server service.

Figure 9-4   A Local Area Connection Properties dialog box

Administrative Shares

Windows Server 2003 has some file system shares even before you create any of your own. By default, the Windows Server 2003 installation program creates the following administrative file system shares (as shown in Figure 9-5):

Figure 9-5   Administrative shares in the Shared Folders snap-in

- **Drive shares**   Every volume on the computer's hard drives has a default administrative share at its root, which is named using its drive letter in uppercase, plus a dollar sign (as in C$). The inclusion of the dollar sign causes these shares to be hidden from view in My Network Places, although it is still possible to access them directly by using the Shared Folders snap-in for Microsoft Management Console (MMC), by creating a network place shortcut or by using Windows Explorer. The default share permissions for these administrative shares grant full control to the Administrators group; these permissions cannot be changed, nor can you delete the shares.

- **Admin$**   The system root folder, C:\Windows by default, is automatically shared with the name Admin$. This, too, is a hidden share, and it enables members of the Administrators group to exercise full control over the system root without having to know exactly where it is located.

- **IPC$**   A share that provides remote access to the computer's named pipes, which are portions of memory used to pass information from one process to another. This share is required to perform remote administration tasks on the computer over the network.

In addition, Windows Server 2003 creates other administrative shares when you install specific operating system elements:

- **Print$**   When you install the first shared printer on the computer, Windows Server 2003 creates a hidden share out of the *systemroot*\System32\Spool \Drivers folder with the name Print$. This share is designed to provide other systems on the network with access to the drivers for the printers installed on the computer. The Administrators, Print Operators, and Server Operators groups all have full control over this share; the Everyone special identity group has only the Read permission.

- **faxclient**   When you install Fax Services on the computer, Windows Server 2003 creates a share of the C:\WINDOWS\system32\clients\faxclient folder with the name faxclient. This share provides network users with access to the fax client software on the server. The Everyone special identity has the Read permission for this share.

- **FxsSrvCp$**   When you install Fax Services on the computer, Windows Server 2003 creates a hidden share of the C:\Documents and Settings \All Users\Application Data\Microsoft\Windows NT\MSFax\Common Coverpages folder with the name FxsSrvCp$. This share enables fax clients to access cover pages stored on the server. The Administrators group has full control of the share, while the Everyone special identity has only Read permission.

- **SYSVOL**   When you promote a Windows Server 2003 computer to a domain controller, the system shares the *systemroot*\SYSVOL\sysvol folder, giving it the name SYSVOL. The SYSVOL share is used by domain controllers to store group policy objects (GPOs) and scripts that are replicated to other computers in the domain. The Administrators and Authenticated Users groups have full control of the share, while the Everyone special identity has only the Read permission.

- **NETLOGON**   When you promote a Windows Server 2003 computer to a domain controller, the system shares the *systemroot*\SYSVOL\sysvol\ *domainname*\SCRIPTS folder, giving it the name NETLOGON. NETLOGON is a share, created for backward compatibility purposes, that provides the same basic function as SYSVOL for Windows NT 4 domain controllers. The Administrators group has full control of the share, while the Everyone special identity has only the Read permission.

NOTE   Hiding Shares   The hidden nature of the administrative shares is not limited to these particular shares. You can hide any share by using a dollar sign as the last character of the share name. This practice does not prevent anyone from accessing the shares; it only prevents them from browsing to the shares in Windows Explorer.

Preparing to Create File System Shares

To create a file system share, you must have the following privileges:

- **On a domain controller**   On a computer functioning as a domain controller, you must be logged on as a member of the Administrators or Server Operators group to create file system shares. Because the Enterprise Admins and Domain Admins groups are members of the Administrators group, these groups can also create file system shares.

- **On a domain member server or workstation**   On a member server or a domain workstation, you must be logged on as a member of the Administrators, Server Operators, or Power Users group to create file system shares.

- **On a workgroup or standalone computer**   On a computer that is not a member of a domain, you must be logged on as a member of the Administrators or Power Users group to create file system shares.

- **On an NTFS drive**   If the folder you plan to share is on an NTFS drive, you must be logged on as a user with at least the NTFS Read permission for the folder.

As with many tasks in Windows Server 2003, you can create file system shares in several ways. The following sections examine some of the tools that you can use to create and manage shares.

NOTE   Exam Objectives   The objectives for exam 70-290 require students to be able to "configure access to shared folders."

Creating a File System Share Using Windows Explorer

The most common method of creating a file system share is to use Windows Explorer to select a folder and then enable sharing for that folder. You can share any folder on any drive in the computer, creating as many shares as you need. When network users browse the shares on the computer, the shares appear as isolated folders with no context. Unless you tell users somehow, they have no way of knowing which drives the shares are on or where the folders are that you have shared.

To share a folder in Windows Explorer, you right-click it and select Sharing And Security to display the dialog box shown in Figure 9-6. You can also access this dialog box by selecting a folder and, from the File menu, selecting Properties, and then selecting the Sharing tab.

Figure 9-6   The Sharing tab of a folder's Properties dialog box

When you select the Share This Folder option, you activate the other controls in the Sharing tab, enabling you to configure the following parameters:

- **Share Name**   Specifies the name by which the share will be visible on the network. By default, the name of the folder appears in the text box, but you can supply any name up to 80 characters. This field is required.

- **Description**   Enables you to specify a description of the share's purpose, its contents, or any other information. This field is optional.

- **User Limit**   Enables you to specify how many users are permitted to access the shared folder at one time. You can use this feature to prevent system resources from being monopolized by too many clients accessing the share simultaneously.

- **Permissions**   Enables you to specify who has access to the share and to what degree. For more information, see "Managing Share Permissions" later in this chapter.

- **Offline Settings**   Enables you to specify whether network users are permitted to cache the shared folder contents on their computers. For more information, see "Controlling Offline Storage" later in this chapter.

Once you have configured the properties in the Sharing tab, clicking OK creates the share. You can tell that the share has been created in several ways, including the following:

- In Windows Explorer, under My Computer, the icon for the folder has an open hand affixed to it, metaphorically sharing its contents with the network.

- In Windows Explorer, under My Network Places, the new share appears beneath the icon for the computer on which you created it.

Practice
creating shares
with Windows
Explorer
by doing
Exercise 9-1,
"Creating a
Share Using
Windows
Explorer," now.

At this point, users on the network with the appropriate permissions can access the share and the files and folders inside.

Sharing a Volume Using Windows Explorer

You can create a file system share out of an entire volume using Windows Explorer, but the procedure is slightly different, to account for the existence of the administrative share already present on every volume. When you select a volume root in Windows Explorer and access its Sharing tab, you see the interface shown in Figure 9-7.

Figure 9-7   A shared volume root

Here you can see that the Share This Folder option is already selected, and the name of the administrative share appears in the Share Name text box. If you want to grant network users access to the entire volume without compromising the security of the administrative share, you have to create a second share in the root of the volume. To do this, you click New Share to display the New Share dialog box, as shown in Figure 9-8.

Figure 9-8   The New Share dialog box

In this dialog box, you specify the name for the new share, a description, a user limit, and share permissions, just as you did earlier when creating a folder share. When you click OK, the new share is created and is added to the Share Name drop-down list in the Sharing tab. Now you can select any of the volume root shares for management from the drop-down list. Whichever share you choose, this is the one controlled by the User Limit, Permissions, and Offline Settings controls.

Creating a File System Share Using the Shared Folders Snap-In

Using Windows Explorer is usually the most convenient way to create file system shares, but it does have one distinct drawback: you can create shares only on the computer where you are working. You cannot select a folder on another computer and share it. Windows Server 2003 includes a tool that provides this capability, however—an MMC snap-in called Shared Folders.

The Shared Folders snap-in is integrated into the Windows Server 2003 Computer Management console, as shown in Figure 9-9. As always, you can also create a custom MMC console containing Shared Folders and any other snap-ins you wish. Clicking the snap-in's Shares subfolder displays a list of the currently existing shares on the local computer, including the hidden shares that are not visible in Windows Explorer.

Figure 9-9   The Shared Folders snap-in

> **NOTE**   **Managing Remote Shares**   *To manage another computer on the network, select the Computer Management (Local) icon at the root of the scope pane and, on the Action menu, select Connect To Another Computer. Then enter or browse to the name of the computer you want to manage, and click OK. You can then create and manage shares on the other computer, just as you would on the local system.*

To create a new share, select the Shares subfolder and, on the Action menu, select New Share to launch the Share A Folder Wizard. This wizard contains three pages:

■ **Folder Path**   Specify the path to the folder you want to share, using drive letter notation.

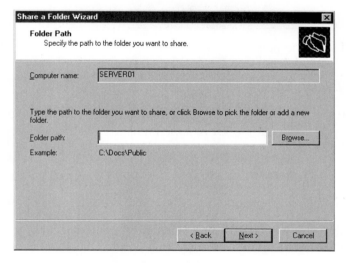

■ **Name, Description, And Settings**   Specify a name and description for the share. You can also click Change to configure the offline settings for the share.

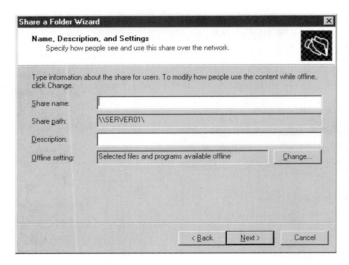

■ **Permissions**   Select the permissions that you want to assign to the share.

Practice
creating shares
with the Shared
Folders snap-in
by doing
Exercise 9-2,
"Using the
Shared Folders
Snap-In," now.

Completing the wizard adds the new share to the list.

Creating a File System Share Using Net.exe

In Windows Server 2003, it is also possible to create a share from the command line, using the Net.exe program with the *share* subcommand. The syntax is as follows:

```
net share sharename=drive:\path [parameters]
```

The additional parameters you can include on the command line are as follows:

■ **/grant:*principal*,[read | change | full]**   Assigns the specified security principal the Read, Change, or Full Control permission for the share

■ **/users:*number***   Specifies the maximum number of users that are permitted to access the share

- **/unlimited** Specifies that an unlimited number of users are permitted to access the share

- **/cache:[manual|documents|programs|none]** Configures offline settings for the share

The following example creates a share called Documents out of the C:\Docs folder and assigns the users group the Read permission:

```
net share documents=c:\docs /grant:users,read
```

MANAGING SHARED FOLDERS

Once you have created file system shares, you can manage them at any time using Windows Explorer by accessing the same Sharing tab of the folder's Properties dialog box that you used to create the share. You can also select the share in the Shared Folders snap-in and, on the Action menu, select Properties to display the dialog box shown in Figure 9-10.

Figure 9-10 A share's Properties dialog box in the Shared Folders snap-in

In addition to modifying the share properties you set during the share's creation, such as its user limit and description, you can also configure the features described in the following sections.

Controlling Offline Storage

Security is often a critical aspect of file system sharing. You want the files stored on the shares to be made available to the right users, and only those users. Administrators can use permissions to control who accesses the shares, but they do not have as much control over what happens to the files after the network users access them. One way of exercising control of file system shares after they are accessed is to limit the Offline Files capabilities of the users who access the shares.

When you click Offline Settings in a share's Properties dialog box, you see the dialog box shown in Figure 9-11. Here you can specify whether the client computers accessing the share are permitted to cache its contents using the Windows Offline Files feature.

Figure 9-11   The Offline Settings dialog box

Offline Files is a mechanism in Windows Server 2003, Microsoft Windows XP, and Microsoft Windows 2000 that maintains local copies of files that users access over the network. If the client computer's connection to the server is lost or interrupted, the user can continue working with the cached copy of the files. When the connection is restored, the client computer replicates any changes made to the offline copies of the files back to their original locations on the share.

The problem with Offline Files with respect to security is that the file copies stored on client computers do not have the same permission protection as the copies on the source share. Sensitive files that are carefully protected on the share might be stored on client computers all over the network, with no protection at all. The options in the Offline Settings dialog box enable administrators to specify whether clients can cache the files in a share using Offline Files. The options are described below.

> **NOTE   Using Net.exe**   You can also configure the offline settings from the command line, using the Net.exe program with the share subcommand. The command-line parameters corresponding to the options in the Offline Settings dialog box are listed in the following descriptions.

- **Only The Files And Programs That Users Specify Will Be Available Offline**   Enables users to select which documents and executables to store offline on their client computers. The corresponding command-line parameter for Net.exe is */cache:manual*.

- **All Files And Programs That Users Open From The Share Will Be Automatically Available Offline**   Automatically stores all shared documents offline on client computers. Selecting the Optimized For Performance check box automatically caches all programs for local execution on the client computer. The corresponding command-line parameters for Net.exe are */cache:documents* and */cache:programs*.

- **Files And Programs From The Share Will Not Be Available Offline**
  Prevents all documents and executables from being stored offline on
  client computers. The corresponding command-line parameter for
  Net.exe is */cache:none*.

Publishing File System Shares in Active Directory

When you click the Publish tab of a share's Properties dialog box in the Shared
Folders snap-in, you see the controls shown in Figure 9-12, which you can use to
publish the folder in Active Directory. Publishing shared folders in Active Directory
does not actually store the shared files in the Active Directory database, but it does
create a shared folder object that points to the location of the share. Once a shared
folder is published, users can search for it in Active Directory, using the same tools
they would use to locate users and other resources.

Figure 9-12   The Publish tab of a shared folder's Properties dialog box

To publish a shared folder in Active Directory, you must select the Publish This
Share In Active Directory check box and supply the name of the share's owner.
You can also supply keywords describing the contents of the share, to facilitate
searches for the information it contains.

Managing Share Permissions

As mentioned earlier in this chapter, shares have their own system of permissions,
which you can use to control who is allowed to access them. To specify permissions for a shared folder, you use one of the following interfaces:

- In Windows Explorer, open the folder's Properties dialog box and, in the
  Sharing tab, click Permissions.

- In the Shared Folders snap-in, open the share's Properties dialog box and
  select the Share Permissions tab.

> **NOTE   Exam Objectives**   The objectives for exam 70-290 require students to be able to "manage shared folder permissions."

Whichever method you use, you see an interface like that shown in Figure 9-13.

Figure 9-13   The Share Permissions tab in a shared folder's Properties dialog box

The permissions system for shares is the simplest one in Windows Server 2003. In this case, there is no distinction between standard permissions and special permissions; there are only the following three simple permissions:

- **Read**   Users can display folder names, file names, file data, and attributes. Users can also execute program files and access other folders within the shared folder.

- **Change**   Users can create folders, add files to folders, change data in files, append data to files, change file attributes, delete folders and files, and perform actions permitted by the Read permission.

- **Full Control**   Users can change file permissions, take ownership of files, and perform all tasks allowed by the Change permission.

To set permissions, you click Add, select a security principal (such as a user, group, or computer), and specify the permissions you want to allow or deny that principal. You can select a principal already present in the Group Or User Names list to modify its permissions as needed.

Using Share Permissions

Share permissions are a form of access control that provides only limited protection to shared files. Some of the limitations of share permissions are as follows:

- **Limited scope**   Share permissions apply only to files and folders accessed over the network. Share permissions do not prevent users from accessing the shared files while working at the system console or when accessing the computer by other network means, such as Web, FTP, Telnet, and Terminal Server applications.

- **Lack of flexibility**   Share permissions are not granular; they provide a single template containing only three possible permissions, which apply to every file and folder beneath the shared folder. You cannot modify permissions for particular folders or files beneath the shared folder.

- **No replication**   Share permissions are not replicated by the File Replication service (FRS).

- **No resiliency**   Share permissions are not included in a backup or restore of a data volume.

- **Fragility**   Share permissions are lost if you move or rename the folder that is shared.

- **No auditing**   You cannot configure auditing based on share permissions.

The only real advantages of using share permissions are the simplicity of the system and the fact that share permissions are available on any file system supported by Windows Server 2003. On a drive using the FAT file system, for example, share permissions are the only way to control access to the drive.

On a small network with few security requirements, share permissions might be an acceptable solution, but in most cases, network administrators prefer to use the more flexible and robust permissions provided by the NTFS file system. If you choose to do this, however, you must be conscious of the following facts:

- The share permissions system is still in place, whether you use NTFS permissions or not.

- The share permissions system is completely separate from the NTFS permissions system.

- Both share permissions and NTFS permissions can apply to the same elements.

Therefore, the best practice when you use NTFS permissions for access control is to grant all users (in the form of the Everyone special identity) the Full Control share permission for all shared folders. This prevents conflicts and confusion between the two permission systems. In other words, you should use either share permissions or NTFS permissions to protect your files, but not both.

If you do not do this, the effective permissions realized by your network users are a combination of the most restrictive settings imposed by both permission systems. For example, if your share permissions grant the Read permission to the Users group, you can give the same group the Full Control NTFS permission, but the users will still be subject to the limitations imposed by the share permissions. This factor, combined with the previously described complications provided by inheritance, group memberships, and denied permissions, can result in a nightmarish web of conflicting influences that is incredibly difficult to understand and maintain.

> **NOTE   Exam Objectives**   The objectives for exam 70-290 require students to be able to "troubleshoot access to files and shared folders."

One of the most common causes of problems with accessing file system shares is a conflict between share permissions and NTFS permissions. When you trouble-shoot problems like these, be sure to check both permission systems to make sure that users have appropriate access to the files they need.

> **MORE INFO**   The advantages and capabilities of the NTFS permissions system are described later in this chapter.

Share Permission Defaults

In all Windows operating systems up to and including Windows 2000, the default share permissions for a new file system share grant Full Control permission to the Everyone special identity. This leaves the share wide open from a security stand-point, which is a convenience to administrators who plan to use NTFS permissions, but a hindrance to those who want to provide some protection with share permis-sions. Beginning with the Windows XP release, the default permissions for new file system shares have changed. Windows XP and Windows Server 2003 grant the Everyone special identity only the Read permission and give the Administrators group the Full Control permission. This means that if you plan to rely on NTFS per-missions for access control, you must remember to modify the permissions for your shares to grant full control to everyone.

Creating a File System Sharing Strategy

The most obvious file system sharing strategy is simply to share the root of each volume on every networked computer. There are two main reasons why this is a bad idea:

- **Confusion**   When users are faced with a dozen different shares repre-senting the disk drives on a dozen different computers, it can be difficult for them to figure out where the files they need are located. They might have to search through the shares on several different systems before they locate their files. Even a single large drive shared from its root can present a large and complicated directory structure.

- **Security**   Sharing an entire drive, particularly a system drive, grants users access to many files and folders that they would be better off not seeing. Users typically do not need access to operating system and application files on other computers, and they can cause damage if they inadvertently delete a required file or directory.

The solution to this problem is to create shares from specific folders and not from entire volumes. In fact, the Shared Folders snap-in even displays a message box when you try to share an entire volume, warning you that root sharing is not rec-ommended for security reasons. The files that users are most likely to access over the network are documents and data files. Therefore, you should organize the directory structure of your systems in such a way as to store documents and other shared files in logically named folders, and then create shares out of those folders.

Sharing Removable Drives

One exception to this practice should be when you are sharing files on removable drives, such as CD-ROM, DVD-ROM, or cartridge drives. While nothing prevents you from sharing a specific folder on these types of drives, keep in mind that the share will be usable only when the disk or cartridge containing that folder is in the drive. Sharing the root of the drive enables you to swap media as needed and still have the share remain available.

Nesting Shares

As mentioned earlier, you can share any folder on a volume, even one that is already included in another share higher in the directory. For example, you can share the root of drive D, calling the share D, and then create a separate share out of the D:\docs folder, calling it Docs. These two shares can even have different permissions. However, you must remain conscious of the fact that even though the shared folders are nested in Windows Explorer, to network users they are two separate and completely independent shares. What's more, the permissions for the two shares are separate as well. If, for example, you give users full control of the D share and then give them read-only access to the Docs share, their limited access to the D:\docs folder through the Docs share does not affect the full control they have when they access the exact same folder using the D share.

USING NTFS PERMISSIONS

Windows Server 2003 supports two main file systems: FAT and NTFS. The file allocation table (FAT) file system is a holdover from the MS-DOS operating system that provides basic functionality but few of the features required for network storage. The only advantage to using FAT drives is that you can start a computer with an MS-DOS boot disk and still access the drives. NTFS is a file system first introduced in Microsoft Windows NT 3.1 that includes a number of features beneficial to network administrators. Chief among these is the system of permissions that provides detailed access control for all of the individual files and folders on a drive.

> **NOTE   Exam Objectives**   *The objectives for exam 70-290 require students to be able to "configure file system permissions."*

Every file and folder on an NTFS drive has an ACL containing ACEs that list the security principals that have been granted permissions for that file or folder. When a user attempts to access a file or folder, the system compares the user's security access token, which contains the security identifiers (SIDs) of the user's account and those of the groups to which the user belongs, to the SIDs in the ACEs of the ACL. Once the system authorizes the user, access is granted to the file or folder.

Compared to the share permissions discussed earlier in this chapter, NTFS permissions have many distinct advantages, including the following:

- **Scope**   NTFS permissions apply to files and folders no matter how they are accessed. Users at the system console or connecting over the network by any means are subject to the same permissions.

- **Flexibility**   NTFS provides a long list of special permissions, which are combined into standard permissions, either of which you can apply to any file or folder on a drive, with complete control over permission inheritance.

- **Replication**   NTFS permissions are replicated by the FRS.

- **Resilience**   NTFS permissions are included in a backup or restore of a data volume.

- **Less fragile**   NTFS permissions are not lost if you move or rename the file or folder to which the permissions are applied (as long as the file or folder remains on an NTFS volume).

- **Auditing**   You can audit access to NTFS files or folders based on the security principals who have permission to access them.

Working with NTFS permissions is understandably more complex than using share permissions, but the additional protection provided is usually worth the trouble to network administrators.

Managing Standard Permissions

Most of the time, administrators work with NTFS standard permissions because they usually provide enough flexibility to control access to shared files and folders. In Windows Explorer, every file and folder on an NTFS volume has a Properties dialog box with a Security tab, as shown in Figure 9-14, which you use to assign standard permissions for that file or folder, as well as access the more advanced permission controls discussed later in this chapter.

Figure 9-14   The Security tab for an NTFS folder

> **NOTE**   **Remote NTFS Administration**   Windows Explorer is capable of configuring NTFS permissions for any file or folder on the network, as long as the user has the appropriate privileges. This is in contrast to Windows Explorer's share permission capabilities, which are limited to the local system.

The process of assigning standard permissions to an NTFS file or folder is similar to that of assigning share permissions. You select a security principal in the Group Or User Names list box or click Add to specify a new security principal, and then, in the Permissions list box, you select the appropriate Allow or Deny check boxes for the permissions you want to apply. The standard permissions for the NTFS file system and the tasks that can be performed with each permission are listed in Table 9-1.

> **NOTE** **File and Folder Permissions** There are slight differences when a particular permission is applied to a file as opposed to a folder. One permission, List Folder Contents, is not applicable to files.

Table 9-1 NTFS Standard Permissions

Standard Permission	When Applied to a Folder, Enables a Security Principal to:	When Applied to a File, Enables a Security Principal to:
Read	■ See the files and subfolders contained in the folder ■ View the ownership, permissions, and attributes of the folder	■ Read the contents of the file ■ View the ownership, permissions, and attributes of the file
Read and Execute	■ Navigate through restricted folders to reach other files and folders ■ Perform all actions associated with the Read and List Folder Contents permissions	■ Perform all actions associated with the Read permission ■ Run applications
Write	■ Create new files and subfolders inside the folder ■ Modify the folder attributes ■ View the ownership and permissions of the folder	■ Overwrite the file ■ Modify the file attributes ■ View the ownership and permissions of the file
Modify	■ Delete the folder ■ Perform all actions associated with the Write and the Read & Execute permissions	■ Modify the file ■ Delete the file ■ Perform all actions associated with the Write and the Read & Execute permissions
List Folder Contents	■ View the names of the files and subfolders contained in the folder	■ Not applicable
Full Control	■ Modify the folder permissions ■ Take ownership of the folder ■ Delete subfolders and files contained in the folder ■ Perform all actions associated with all of the other NTFS folder permissions	■ Modify the file permissions ■ Take ownership of the file ■ Perform all actions associated with all of the other NTFS file permissions

Practice creating NTFS permissions by doing Exercise 9-3, "Configuring NTFS Permissions," now.

> **NOTE** **Inherited Permissions** When a check box in the Security tab is selected and shaded gray, this indicates that the permission has been inherited from a parent folder.

Using Advanced Security Settings

This basic interface in the Security tab enables administrators to perform common permissions assignment tasks quickly and easily, but it does not provide a great deal of information, nor does it provide full access to all of the features provided by the NTFS permissions system. Clicking the Advanced button displays the Advanced Security Settings dialog box, as shown in Figure 9-15, which is as close as you can get to viewing the file or folder's actual ACL in the Windows graphical user interface.

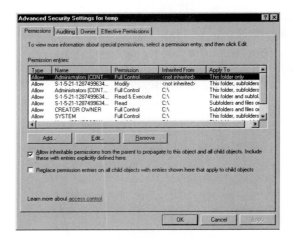

Figure 9-15   The Advanced Security Settings dialog box

The default Permissions tab of the Advanced Security Settings dialog box contains a Permission Entries list, which is essentially a list of the individual ACEs in the file or folder's ACL. Each entry in the list contains the following information:

- **Type**   Specifies whether the entry allows or denies the permission.

- **Name**   Specifies the name of the security principal receiving the permission.

- **Permission**   Specifies the standard permission being assigned to the security principal. If the ACE is used to assign special permissions, the word *Special* appears in this field.

- **Inherited From**   Specifies whether the permission is inherited and, if so, where it is inherited from.

- **Apply To**   Specifies whether the permission is inherited by subordinate objects and, if so, by which ones.

The Permission Entries list might contain multiple entries for a particular security principal, indicating that there are permissions originating from more than one source, such as one explicitly assigned permission and one inherited permission, or that the principal has both Allow and Deny permission types assigned to it. When this is the case, each entry in the list is managed separately.

To work with one of the entries in the list, you select it and click Edit to open a Permission Entry dialog box. Other than this, the only active controls in the Advanced Security Settings dialog box are the two following options:

- **Allow Inheritable Permissions From The Parent To Propagate To This Object And All Child Objects**   Specifies whether the file or folder should inherit permissions from parent objects. This check box is selected by default. Clearing it causes a Security message box to appear, in which you can choose to remove all of the inherited ACEs from the list or copy the inherited permissions from the parents to the file or folder. If you choose the latter, the effective permissions stay the same but the file or folder is no longer dependent on the parents for permission inheritance. If you change the permissions on the parent objects, the file or folder remains unaffected.

- **Replace Permission Entries On All Child Objects With Entries Shown Here That Apply To Child Objects**   Causes child objects to inherit permissions from this folder, to the exclusion of all permissions explicitly assigned to the child objects. This check box is available on folders only.

Managing Special Permissions

Editing one of the permission entries in the Advanced Security Settings dialog box or adding a new entry in that dialog box displays a Permission Entry dialog box, like the one shown in Figure 9-16. Here, for the first time, you have direct access to the special permissions that form the underlying fabric of the NTFS permissions system.

Figure 9-16   A Permission Entry dialog box

NTFS has 14 special permissions, the functions of which are as follows. In cases where the special permissions are presented in pairs, separated by a slash, the first permission applies to folders and the second to files.

- **Traverse Folder/Execute File**   The Traverse Folder permission allows or denies security principals the ability to move through folders that they do not have permission to access, so they can reach files or folders that they do have permission to access. This permission applies to folders only. The Execute File permission allows or denies security principals the ability to run program files. This permission applies to files only.

- **List Folder/Read Data**   The List Folder permission allows or denies security principals the ability to view the file and subfolder names within a folder. This permission applies to folders only. The Read Data permission allows or denies security principals the ability to view the contents of a file. This permission applies to files only.

- **Read Attributes**   Allows or denies security principals the ability to view the NTFS attributes of a file or folder.

- **Read Extended Attributes**   Allows or denies security principals the ability to view the extended attributes of a file or folder.

- **Create Files/Write Data**   The Create Files permission allows or denies security principals the ability to create files within the folder. This permission applies to folders only. The Write Data permission allows or denies security principals the ability to modify the file and overwrite existing content. This permission applies to files only.

- **Create Folders/Append Data**   The Create Folders permission allows or denies security principals the ability to create subfolders within a folder. This permission applies to folders only. The Append Data permission allows or denies security principals the ability to add data to the end of the file but not to modify, delete, or overwrite existing data in the file. This permission applies to files only.

- **Write Attributes**   Allows or denies security principals the ability to modify the NTFS attributes of an existing file or folder.

- **Write Extended Attributes**   Allows or denies security principals the ability to modify the extended attributes of an existing file or folder.

- **Delete Subfolders and Files**   Allows or denies security principals the ability to delete subfolders and files, even if the Delete permission has not been granted on the subfolder or file.

- **Delete**   Allows or denies security principals the ability to delete the file or folder.

- **Read Permissions**   Allows or denies security principals the ability to read the permissions for the file or folder.

- **Change Permissions**   Allows or denies security principals the ability to modify the permissions for the file or folder.

- **Take Ownership**   Allows or denies security principals the ability to take ownership of the file or folder.

- **Synchronize**   Allows or denies different threads of multithreaded, multiprocessor programs the ability to wait on the handle for the file or folder and synchronize with another thread that might signal it.

The Permission Entry dialog box for an ACE displays the individual special permissions that are the functional equivalent of the standard permission specified in the Advanced Security Settings dialog box. The special permissions that make up the six standard permissions are listed in Table 9-2.

Table 9-2   **NTFS Standard Permissions and Their Special Permission Equivalents**

Standard Permission	Special Permissions
Read	■ List Folder/Read Data ■ Read Attributes ■ Read Extended Attributes ■ Read Permissions ■ Synchronize
Read and Execute	■ List Folder/Read Data ■ Read Attributes ■ Read Extended Attributes ■ Read Permissions ■ Synchronize ■ Traverse Folder/Execute File
Modify	■ Create Files/Write Data ■ Create Folders/Append Data ■ Delete ■ List Folder/Read Data ■ Read Attributes ■ Read Extended Attributes ■ Read Permissions ■ Synchronize ■ Traverse Folder/Execute File ■ Write Attributes ■ Write Extended Attributes
Write	■ Create Files/Write Data ■ Create Folders/Append Data ■ Read Permissions ■ Synchronize ■ Write Attributes ■ Write Extended Attributes
List Folder Contents	■ List Folder/Read Data ■ Read Attributes ■ Read Extended Attributes ■ Read Permissions ■ Synchronize ■ Traverse Folder/Execute File

(continued)

Table 9-2   **NTFS Standard Permissions and Their Special Permission Equivalents**

Standard Permission	Special Permissions
Full Control	■ Change Permissions
	■ Create Files/Write Data
	■ Create Folders/Append Data
	■ Delete
	■ Delete Subfolders and Files
	■ List Folder/Read Data
	■ Read Attributes
	■ Read Extended Attributes
	■ Read Permissions
	■ Synchronize
	■ Take Ownership
	■ Traverse Folder/Execute File
	■ Write Attributes
	■ Write Extended Attributes

When you edit a permission entry, you can change any of the following parameters:

■ **Name**   Specifies the name of the security principal that receives the permission assignment. When you want to switch permissions from one principal to another, rather than create an entirely new ACE, you can use this interface to change the name of the assignee.

■ **Apply Onto**   Specifies which objects should receive the permission assignment, using the options shown in Figure 9-17. This selector provides the most complete control over the inheritance of the assigned permissions available; you can limit inheritance to any combination of files, folders, subfolders, and child files.

Figure 9-17   The Apply Onto options

■ **Permissions**   Specifies the special permissions to be assigned to the security principal. The Permissions list box includes all of the applicable special permissions listed earlier, plus the Full Control standard permission.

NOTE   Using the Apply Onto Option   When you use the Apply Onto selector to limit the targets for permission inheritance, all of the child folders and files still receive the ACE from the parent. Excluding certain child objects from inheritance just prevents those objects from enforcing the permissions in the ACE. In situations where the ACE is inherited by a large number of child objects, possibly causing network performance problems, using the Apply Onto option to limit the inheritance of the permissions is no help.

Viewing Effective Permissions

Considering the complexities of the NTFS permission system, it is fortunate that Windows Server 2003 includes a mechanism for viewing a security principal's effective permissions for a particular file or folder. To view effective permissions, you open the Advanced Security Settings dialog box for a file or folder and select the Effective Permissions tab, as shown in Figure 9-18. When you click Select and specify the name of a security principal in the Select User, Computer, Or Group dialog box, the check boxes in the Effective Permissions list change to reflect the cumulative permissions assigned to that principal.

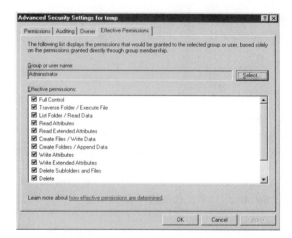

Figure 9-18   The Effective Permissions tab of an Advanced Security Settings dialog box

NOTE   Exam Objectives   The objectives for exam 70-290 require students to be able to "verify effective permissions when granting permissions."

While the Effective Permissions tab is useful for troubleshooting shared file access problems, it is not perfect. The effective permissions displayed in this interface are compiled by factoring together the following:

■ Permissions explicitly assigned to the security principal

■ Permissions the security principal inherits from parent objects

■ Permissions the security principal inherits from local and domain group memberships

However, the Effective Permissions list does not account for share permissions or for permissions inherited from special identities that depend on the security principal's logon status.

For example, the Effective Permissions tab might show that a particular group has the Full Control permission for a folder on a shared drive. However, if the default share permissions are still in place, granting the Everyone special identity only the Read permission, the group is actually limited to read-only access, despite what the Effective Permissions display says.

In the same way, the Effective Permissions cannot anticipate the logon status of a security principal at any given time. Windows Server 2003 makes it possible to assign permissions based on special identities, such as Anonymous Logon, Dialup, and Interactive. As you learned in Chapter 7, these identities are determined based on the way in which a user logs on to the system or the network. A user who accesses the network using a dial-up connection, for example, is a part of the Dialup special identity for the duration of that connection. Because security principals need not be logged on when you view their effective permissions, there is no way for the system to know which identities will have an effect on the principals when they do log on.

> **NOTE**   **Effective Permissions Workaround**   *To account for the permissions assigned to special identities that might affect your users, you can use the Effective Permissions tab to display the effective permissions for a particular special identity, and then you can factor those results into your users' effective permissions.*

Resource Ownership

Every file and folder in the NTFS file system (as well as every object in Active Directory) has an owner. By default, the owner is the user who created the file or folder. In the case of files and folders created by the operating system, the Administrators group is the owner. However, the ownership of any file or folder can be taken at any time by a member of the Administrators group, or by any user who possesses the Take Ownership special permission for the file or folder.

> **NOTE**   **Exam Objectives**   *The objectives for exam 70-290 require students to be able to "change ownership of files and folders."*

File or folder ownership has two main purposes:

- **Owners can modify ACLs.**   No matter what other permissions the owner of a file or folder has, the owner can still modify the file or folder's ACL. Ownership therefore functions as a fallback mechanism, in case someone locks all users out of a file or folder. If, for example, you create a new file and accidentally revoke all of your permissions to that file, your ownership enables you to modify the ACL for the file again and restore your permissions.

- **Disk quotas are determined by ownership.**   Disk quotas enable administrators to track and control how much server disk space each user is occupying. These quotas work by adding up the sizes of all the files owned by a particular user. You learn more about disk quotas in Chapter 12.

In addition to the Take Ownership permission, there are also two user rights that provide the ability to manage the ownership of NTFS files and folders:

- **Take Ownership Of Files Or Other Objects** Users or groups possessing this user right can take ownership of any NTFS file or folder. By default, the Administrators group receives this user right from the Default Domain Controllers Policy GPO.

- **Restore Files And Directories** Users or groups possessing this user right can take ownership of any NTFS file or folder or assign ownership to any other user or group. By default, the Default Domain Controllers Policy GPO grants this user right to the Administrators, Backup Operators, and Server Operators groups.

To view or take ownership of a file or folder, open its Advanced Security Settings dialog box and select the Owner tab, as shown in Figure 9-19. This tab lists the file or folder's current owner. If you have the Take Ownership special permission for the file or folder or the Take Ownership Of Files Or Other Objects user right, you can select your user account in the Change Owner To box and click Apply or OK to take ownership of the object. If you have the Restore Files And Directories user right, you can also click Other Users Or Groups to select another security principal and give it ownership of the object.

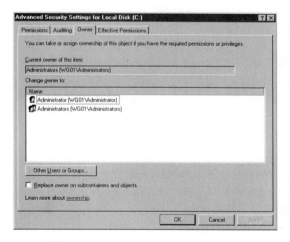

Figure 9-19 The Owner tab of the Advanced Security Settings dialog box

If you are the current owner of a file or folder and you want to pass ownership to another user, but you lack the Restore Files And Directories user right, you can still modify the ACL for the object and grant the other user the Take Ownership permission. The other user can then use the procedure described in the previous paragraph to take ownership of the file or folder.

ADMINISTERING INTERNET INFORMATION SERVICES

So far in this chapter, you have learned how to provide network users with access to the files on a computer running Windows Server 2003 by publishing shares with the Server service, which are accessible by clients running the Workstation service.

However, this is not the only way to share files using Windows Server 2003. You can also use Internet services, such as those provided by Microsoft Internet Information Services (IIS), even when your clients are on the local network.

> **NOTE** **Exam Objectives**   *The objectives for exam 70-290 require students to be able to "manage Internet Information Services (IIS)."*

IIS is a Windows Server 2003 application that can publish files and applications using Internet standard protocols such as Hypertext Transfer Protocol (HTTP), which is the standard protocol for Web communications, and File Transfer Protocol (FTP). Compared to file system shares, IIS in its default configuration is a limited method of publishing files. For security reasons, IIS is installed in a secure, locked mode that enables the server to supply only static content to clients. Users can retrieve files from an IIS server to their local systems and work on them there, but they cannot open files directly from the server drives and save modified versions back to their original locations, as they can with a file system share. However, even in its locked-down state, IIS does provide a means of disseminating files easily and securely.

In the following sections, you learn how to install and configure IIS on a computer running Windows Server 2003 and manage the security of an IIS server.

Installing IIS

Unlike Windows 2000, Windows Server 2003 does not install IIS with the operating system by default. This is to prevent a potential security breach in the operating system. Earlier versions of Windows installed IIS by default, activated the World Wide Web Publishing Service, and created a default Web page. In cases where administrators did not use the service and neglected to shut it down, this provided a potential entry point for unauthorized users. In Windows Server 2003, you must install IIS manually, after the operating system installation is completed.

To install IIS, open Add Or Remove Programs in Control Panel and select Add/Remove Windows Components to launch the Windows Components Wizard. In this wizard, you select Application Server, click Details, and then select Internet Information Services (IIS). You can click Details again to specify which IIS components to install. By default, the wizard installs the following components:

- **Common Files**   Installs required IIS program files.

- **Internet Information Services Manager**   Installs the Internet Information Services (IIS) Manager snap-in for MMC. You use this snap-in to manage the IIS services and configure site security.

- **World Wide Web Service**   Installs the service providing HTTP connectivity with TCP/IP clients on the network.

> **NOTE** **Installing Additional Components**   *Although they are not needed for the functions described in this chapter, you can select additional IIS components to provide greater functionality to your server, but do not omit any of the default components listed here.*

When you complete the wizard, Windows Server 2003 installs the components you selected and activates the World Wide Web Publishing Service.

Managing an IIS Web Site

When IIS is installed, a default Web site is created, enabling you to implement a Web environment quickly and easily. Initially, the default site has no content (except for an Under Construction message). By adding your own files to the home directory for the default site, you can create a home page that provides clients with access to whatever files, folders, and other information you want to publish.

> **NOTE   Exam Objectives**   The objectives for exam 70-290 require students to be able to "manage a Web server."

To manage the Web sites on an IIS server, you use the Internet Information Services (IIS) Manager snap-in, as shown in Figure 9-20, which is accessible from the Start menu's Administrative Tools program group. This snap-in enables you to create and manage as many separate Web sites as your server hardware is capable of running.

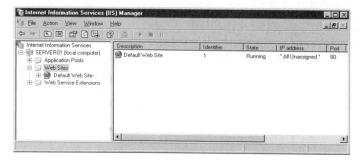

Figure 9-20   The Internet Information Services (IIS) Manager snap-in

Initially, there is only one Web site on the server, called Default Web Site. To view the sites on the server, expand the server node in the scope pane and then expand the Web Sites folder. By selecting one of the listed sites and, from the Action menu, selecting Properties, you open the Properties dialog box for that site. This dialog box contains a wealth of controls that enable you to configure this Web site's parameters. The following sections examine some of the most critical controls in this important dialog box.

Using the Web Site Tab

The Web Site tab of the Properties dialog box, shown in Figure 9-21, contains settings that specify how clients are able to access the Web site. IIS is able to host a virtually unlimited number of Web sites on a single computer, but for clients to access them, there must be a way to differentiate one site from another.

Figure 9-21   The Web Site tab of a Web site's Properties dialog box

Web servers typically use techniques such as the following to host multiple sites:

- **Different IP addresses**   By configuring the computer with multiple IP addresses and assigning a different IP address to each Web site, the Web server can direct incoming requests to the appropriate site, based on the IP address specified in the request.

- **Different port numbers**   By default, the HTTP protocol uses the well-known port number 80 for its TCP/IP communications. When you connect to a Web site, your browser assumes the use of port 80 unless you specify otherwise, using a Uniform Resource Locator (URL) like *http://www.contoso.com:81*. By assigning different port numbers to Web sites, a server can direct incoming requests to the appropriate site based on the port number specified in the request.

- **Host headers**   Despite the fact that clients typically use names to access Web sites, TCP/IP communications are based on IP addresses. Domain Name System (DNS) servers are responsible for converting the names supplied by users into the correct IP addresses. A **host header** is an optional field in an HTTP request message that contains the name of the Web server specified in the URL. Requests with different host header values can then be directed to a single Web server using one IP address and one port number. The server can then direct incoming requests to the appropriate site based on the host header value. For example, a company might run two Web sites, www.adatum.com and www.contoso.com, using one Web server. The company's DNS server resolves both names into the same IP address, so the request messages destined for each site all end up at the same server. The server then distinguishes between the two destinations by examining the contents of the host header fields.

With the controls in the Web Site tab, you can use any one of these three methods to differentiate this particular Web site from others running on the server. The Default Web Site is configured to use port 80 and all of the computer's IP addresses that are not assigned to other Web sites. If you create additional Web sites on the server, you might want to change these values by selecting a specific IP Address value, changing the TCP Port value, or clicking Advanced to specify a host header name for the site.

This tab also enables you to specify a time limit before inactive users are disconnected from the server, and also to control the server's logging behavior for this site, by selecting a log format, specifying what information is to be logged, and configuring a logging schedule.

Using the Home Directory Tab

A Web site's home directory is the default location for its content files. When you specify a URL in a Web browser that contains only a site name (such as *www.contoso.com*), the server automatically supplies the content files in the site's home directory. In the Home Directory tab, shown in Figure 9-22, you specify the location of the home directory for this particular Web site. By creating different home directories for the various sites running on a single server, you can maintain separate content for each site.

Figure 9-22   The Home Directory tab of a Web site's Properties dialog box

IIS enables you to specify a home directory by selecting any one of the following three options:

- **A Directory Located On This Computer**   Uses standard drive letter notation to specify a home directory on one of the computer's local drives

- **A Share Located On Another Computer**   Uses **Universal Naming Convention** (**UNC**) notation to specify a home directory on a share that's elsewhere on the network

- **A Redirection To A URL**   Uses URL notation to specify a home directory on another Web server

The default Web site uses a local home directory, which the IIS installation creates in the C:\Inetpub\wwwoot folder by default. Initially, this folder contains no actual content except for the files producing the Under Construction page, but by placing your own content files in this folder, you make them immediately available to clients.

In addition to allowing you to specify the actual location of the home directory, this tab also enables you to configure the types of access that clients have to this directory. The following options are available when you specify a home directory on a local drive or a network share:

- **Script Source Access**   Enables clients to access script files in the directory, assuming that the Read or Write permission is set.

- **Read**   Enables clients to read and download files in the directory.

- **Write**   Enables clients to upload files to the directory or change the content of write-enabled files.

- **Directory Browsing**   Assuming the absence of a default document, enables users to view a hypertext listing of the files and folders in the directory.

- **Log Visits**   Assuming that logging is enabled for the site, causes visits to this directory to be recorded in the log.

- **Index This Resource**   Causes a full-text index of the directory to be created in the Microsoft Indexing Service. (You must install the Indexing Service by clicking Add/Remove Windows Components in the Add Or Remove Programs utility.)

- **Application Settings**   Enables you to specify the types of Web applications clients are permitted to run.

Using the Documents Tab

In the Documents tab, shown in Figure 9-23, you can specify the name of the content file that IIS delivers to clients by default. When a client enters a URL that does not contain a file name in a browser, the Web server delivers the file with the default name specified in the Enable Default Content Page box. If the first file name listed does not exist in the directory, the server checks each of the listed names and delivers the file with the highest name in the list. If none of the listed files exist in the directory, the server either displays a hypertext listing of the directory's contents (if the Directory Browsing option is enabled in the Home Directory tab) or an error message (if Directory Browsing is disabled).

Figure 9-23   The Documents tab of a Web site's Properties dialog box

The Enable Document Footer box enables you to supply the name of a footer file to be appended to all documents published by the Web site.

Using the Performance Tab

In the Performance tab, shown in Figure 9-24, you can limit the amount of network bandwidth used by this site, and also the number of users that are able to connect simultaneously. This enables you to prevent one Web site from monopolizing all of the system's bandwidth.

Figure 9-24   The Performance tab of a Web site's Properties dialog box

Creating Virtual Directories

When you specify a home directory for an IIS Web site, all of the files in that directory and its subdirectories are published by the server and made available to clients. However, if you have existing files and folders you want to publish, it is not necessary to move them all to the home directory structure. Instead, you can create a virtual directory. A **virtual directory** is a pointer to a folder at another location, which appears to clients as part of the Web site's directory structure.

To create a virtual directory on an IIS Web site, you select the site in the Internet Information Services (IIS) Manager's scope pane and, on the Action menu, point to New and select Virtual Directory. This launches the Virtual Directory Creation Wizard, in which you supply the following information:

- **Virtual Directory Alias**   Specifies the name by which the virtual directory will be known to clients. The alias you enter here will appear as a subdirectory of the Web site in client URLs. The alias you choose need not (and often should not) conform to the actual name of the folder you are publishing.

- **Web Site Content Directory**   Specifies the path to the directory you intend to share with the virtual directory. The path you specify can use drive letter or UNC notation and be located on a local drive or a network share.

- **Virtual Directory Access Permissions**   Specifies the permissions granted to clients accessing the virtual directory (such as Read, Run Scripts, Execute, Write, and Browse).

Once you have created the virtual directory, the files in the content directory you specified appear on the Web site in a subdirectory identified by the alias you specified.

Configuring IIS Security

Most Web servers on the Internet provide clients with anonymous access. When you configure an IIS Web site to use anonymous access, all clients connect to the server using a special account dedicated to this purpose. The default name of the account in Windows Server 2003 is IUSR_*servername*, where *servername* is the name of the computer. Technically, the clients are authenticated, but there is no exchange of secure credentials and clients are not restricted in their access to the Web site.

> **NOTE** **Exam Objectives**   *The objectives for exam 70-290 require students to be able to "manage security for IIS."*

However, if you want to restrict access to a Web site, you can increase the security level in several ways, including the following:

- **Authentication and Access Control**   Requires clients to supply a username and password for access to the site. IIS supports several types of encryption, with varying degrees of security.

- **IP Address and Domain Name Restrictions**   You can configure an IIS Web site to grant or deny specific clients access to the site, based on their IP addresses or domain names.

- **Secure Communications**   Requires clients to use a secured communications protocol or a digital certificate to gain access to the site.

You can configure all of these security mechanisms in the Directory Security tab of a Web site's Properties dialog box, as shown in Figure 9-25.

Figure 9-25   The Directory Security tab of a Web site's Properties dialog box

> **NOTE** **IIS and NTFS Permissions**   *In addition to the security mechanisms just mentioned, you can also use NTFS permissions to secure Web sites. As explained earlier in this chapter, NTFS permissions apply no matter how a user accesses the NTFS file system. This means that a user who accesses a Web site with content stored on an NTFS drive must have the appropriate permissions to access the content files. See "Using NTFS Permissions," earlier in this chapter, for more information.*

Configuring IIS Authentication

To configure an IIS Web site to use any form of authentication other than the default anonymous access option, you click the Edit button in the Authentication And Access Control group box on the Directory Security tab to display the Authentication Methods dialog box (shown in Figure 9-26).

Figure 9-26   The Authentication Methods dialog box

To prevent unauthenticated access to the Web site, you must clear the Enable Anonymous Access check box; otherwise, the other authentication options have no effect. You must also apply NTFS permissions to the files and folders you want to protect. Then you must select an alternative form of authentication from the following options:

- **Integrated Windows Authentication**   The server performs a cryptographic exchange with the client so that the username and password are transmitted in the form of a hash that prevents eavesdroppers from accessing the user's credentials. This form of authentication is not usable across proxy servers or firewalls.

- **Digest Authentication For Windows Domain Servers**   For clients with Active Directory accounts only, the server collects user credentials and stores them on the domain controller as an MD5 (Message Digest 5) hash.

- **Basic Authentication**   The client transmits the username and password to the server in clear text, creating a potential security breach. Use this option only when none of the more secure options is available.

- **.NET Passport Authentication**   Clients connect to the server using their existing .NET Passport accounts, which are authenticated by a central .NET Passport server on the Internet.

Configuring IP Address and Domain Name Restrictions

When you click the Edit button in the IP Address And Domain Name Restrictions group box, you see the IP Address And Domain Name Restrictions dialog box, as shown in Figure 9-27. Here you can specify individual IP addresses, network addresses, and domain names, and then grant or deny them access to the site.

Figure 9-27   The IP Address And Domain Name Restrictions dialog box

In the IP Address And Domain Name Restrictions dialog box, you first specify whether you want the addresses or names you select to be granted or denied access to the site, and then you click Add to open a Granted Access or Denied Access dialog box, in which you enter the IP address of a specific computer, a network address and subnet mask, or a domain name.

This type of restriction is computer-based, rather than user-based. When you grant a specific IP address access to the site, anyone working on the computer with that address can access the site unless other security mechanisms are in place. Because these restrictions are separate from the Web site's authentication requirements, you can use them instead of or in combination with authentication. For example, you might want to grant a specific user access to the site, but make sure that the user connects only from a specific workstation. By enabling authentication and configuring an IP address restriction, you can do both of these things.

Configuring Secure Communications

When you click the Edit button in the Secure Communications group box, the Secure Communications dialog box (shown in Figure 9-28) appears, in which you can configure the following options:

Figure 9-28   The Secure Communications dialog box

- **Require Secure Channel (SSL)** Requires clients to use an encrypted communications protocol when connecting to the Web server, such as the Secure Sockets Layer (SSL) protocol. You can also require clients to use 128-bit encryption for greater security.

- **Client Certificates** Specifies whether clients can, cannot, or must use digital certificates to access the Web site. To require certificates, you must select the Require Secure Channel (SSL) option.

- **Enable Client Certificate Mapping** Configures the server to authenticate clients logging on with valid certificates. Click Edit to map certificates to specific user accounts.

- **Enable Certificate Trust List** Configures the server to use a list of trusted certification authorities to validate user certificates. Users not possessing a certificate from one of the listed authorities are denied access.

SUMMARY

- Windows Server 2003 includes a number of independent permissions systems, including share permissions, NTFS permissions, Active Directory permissions, and registry permissions. Each of these systems enables you to control access to a specific type of system resource.

- Every object protected by permissions has an access control list (ACL), which is a list of access control entries (ACEs) that contain a security principal (such as a user, group, or computer) and the permissions assigned to that principal.

- File system shares enable network users to access files and folders on other computers. To create file system shares, you can use Windows Explorer, the Shared Folders snap-in, or the Net.exe command-line utility.

- Share permissions provide basic protection for file system shares, but they lack the granularity and flexibility of NTFS permissions. Share permissions also apply only to network access through the Server service. Files protected by share permissions are still accessible from the system console or through other network services, such as IIS and terminal servers.

- NTFS permissions can be allowed or denied, explicit or inherited. A Deny permission takes precedence over an Allow permission; and an explicit permission takes precedence over an inherited permission. The result is that an explicit Allow permission overrides an inherited Deny permission. The effective permissions for a file or folder are a composite of all the permissions assigned to the element, either explicitly or by inheritance.

- Access granted by NTFS permissions can be further restricted by share permissions and other factors, such as IIS permissions on Web sites. Whenever two permission types are assigned to a resource, such as share permissions and NTFS permissions, you must evaluate each set of permissions and then determine which of the two is more restrictive.

- Inheritance enables an administrator to control access to files and folders by applying permissions to a single parent folder and letting those permissions flow downward to the child objects beneath the parent.

- Every NTFS file and folder has an owner. The owner of a file or folder is always permitted to modify the file or folder's ACL, even without permissions.

- Any user with the Take Ownership permission or the Take Ownership Of Files Or Other Objects user right can take ownership of an object. A user with the Restore Files And Directories user right can assign ownership of any object to any user.

- IIS is a Windows Server 2003 application that makes it possible to share files and folders using Web and FTP server services. You can secure IIS sites by applying NTFS permissions and requiring user authentication, by restricting access to specific IP addresses or domain names, or by using encrypted communications protocols and digital certificates.

EXERCISES

Exercise 9-1: Creating a Share Using Windows Explorer

In this exercise, you share a folder on your computer using Windows Explorer.

1. Log on to Windows Server 2003 as Administrator.

2. Click Start and select Windows Explorer. The Windows Explorer window appears.

3. Expand the My Computer icon and Local Disk (C:).

4. Right-click the Documents And Settings folder and, from the context menu, select Sharing And Security. The Documents And Settings Properties dialog box appears, with the Sharing tab active.

5. Click Share This Folder and, in the Share Name text box, type **Test Share**. Click OK. The icon for the Documents And Settings folder is modified to indicate that it has been shared.

Exercise 9-2: Using the Shared Folders Snap-In

In this exercise, you use the Shared Folders snap-in to create a new share and configure permissions for it.

1. Log on to Windows Server 2003 as Administrator.

2. Click Start, point to Administrative Tools, and select Computer Management. The Computer Management console appears.

3. Expand the Shared Folders icon in the scope pane and select the Shares subfolder.

4. On the Action menu, select New Share. The Share A Folder Wizard launches.

5. Click Next to bypass the Welcome page. The Folder Path page appears.

6. In the Folder Path text box, type **C:\Windows**, and then click Next. The Name, Description, And Settings page appears.

7. In the Share Name text box, type **Test Share 2**, and then click Next. The Permissions page appears.

8. Select the Administrators Have Full Access; Other Users Have Read-Only Access option, and then click Finish. The Sharing Was Successful page appears.

9. Click Close.

Exercise 9-3: Configuring NTFS Permissions

In this exercise, you configure the NTFS permissions for a folder on your computer using Windows Explorer.

1.. Log on to Windows Server 2003 as Administrator.

2. Click Start, and select Windows Explorer. The Windows Explorer window appears.

3. Expand the My Computer icon and Local Disk (C:).

4. Right-click the Documents And Settings folder and, on the context menu, select Sharing And Security. The Documents And Settings Properties dialog box appears, with the Sharing tab active.

5. Select the Security tab, and then click Add. The Select Users, Computers, Or Groups dialog box appears.

6. In the Enter The Object Names To Select text box, type **Guests**, and then click OK. The Guests group is added to the Group Or User Names list box in the Security tab.

7. Select the Guests security principal, and in the Permissions For Guests list box, select the Modify and Write check boxes in the Allow column.

8. Click OK to apply the permissions and close the Documents And Settings Properties dialog box.

REVIEW QUESTIONS

1. Which of the following tools enables you to create a share on a remote server? (Choose all correct answers.)

    (a.) A custom MMC console containing the Shared Folders snap-in

    (b.) Windows Explorer running on the local machine, connected to the remote computer's ADMIN$ share

    (c.) Net.exe

    d. The Computer Management console

2. A folder is shared on a FAT volume. The Project Managers group is given the Allow Full Control permission. The Project Engineers group is given the Allow Read permission. Julie initially belongs to the Project Engineers group. Later, she is promoted and is added to the Project Managers group. What are her effective permissions for the folder after the promotion? *allow full control / allow change / allow read*

3. A folder is shared on an NTFS volume, with the default share permissions. The Project Managers group is given the Allow Full Control NTFS permission. Julie, a member of the Project Managers group, calls to report problems creating files in the folder. Why can't Julie create files? *because the share permissions system is still in place, and it's completely separate from the NTFS permissions system*

4. What are the minimum NTFS permissions required to allow users to open documents and run programs stored in a shared folder?

    a. Full Control

    b. Modify

    c. Write

    (d.) Read & Execute

    e. List Folder Contents

5. Bill complains that he is unable to access the spreadsheet document containing the departmental budget. You open the Security tab for the document, and you find that all permissions for the document are inherited from its parent folder. The Deny Read permission is assigned to a group called Acctg3, of which Bill is a member. Which of the following methods would enable Bill to access the plan? (Choose all correct answers.)

   a. Modify the permissions on the parent folder by adding the permission Bill:Allow Full Control.

   b. Modify the permissions on the parent folder by adding the permission Bill:Allow Read.

   c. Modify the permissions on the spreadsheet document by adding the permission Bill:Allow Read.

   d. Modify the permissions on the spreadsheet document by deselecting Allow Inheritable Permissions, selecting Copy, and removing the Deny permission.

   e. Modify the permissions on the spreadsheet document by deselecting Allow Inheritable Permissions, selecting Copy, and adding the permission Bill:Allow Full Control.

   f. Remove Bill from the group that is assigned the Deny permission.

6. You want to ensure the highest level of security for your corporate IIS intranet server without the added infrastructure of certificate services. The goal is to provide authentication that is transparent to users and to allow you to secure intranet resources with the group accounts existing in Active Directory. All users are within the corporate firewall. Which of the following authentication methods should you choose?

   a. Anonymous Access

   b. Basic Authentication

   c. .NET Passport Authentication

   d. Integrated Windows Authentication

7. You are configuring share permissions for a shared folder on a file server. You want all Authenticated Users to be able to save files to the folder, read all files in the folder, and modify or delete files that they own. What are the minimum permissions that you need to set on the shared folder to achieve your objective? (Choose all correct answers.)

   a. Authenticated Users: Full Control

   b. Authenticated Users: Read

   c. Creator Owner: Change

   d. Creator Owner: Read

CASE SCENARIOS

Scenario 9-1: Web Server Publishing

The content files for your corporate Web server are currently stored on drive D of a Windows Server 2003 computer with IIS installed. The server is called Web1 and its URL is *http://intranet.contoso.com*. You have been instructed to create an IIS solution that will enable the human resources department to publish documents containing company benefit and policy information from its own server. You have also been told that the URL to access the HR information should be *http://intranet.contoso.com/hr*. What must you do to fulfill the instructions?

  a. Install IIS on the HR server.

  b. Create a new Web site on Web1 called hr.

  c. Install the FTP service on Web1.

  d. Create a virtual directory on Web1 with the alias hr.

Scenario 9-2: Configuring Share Permissions

Acctg01 is a file server running Windows Server 2003 that is used by the accounting department to provide timesheet and expense report forms for employees. You are the network administrator responsible for configuring the share permissions on the file system shares, which must meet the following requirements:

  ■ Employee-specific forms are stored in the Forms folder, which is shared using the name Forms. These forms must be accessible by all employees.

  ■ Only Authenticated Users can access the forms.

  ■ Employees can upload completed forms to a folder called Forms\Reports *username* that is shared as *username*.

  ■ Users must be able to read their own forms, but not forms submitted by other users.

  ■ Supervisor-specific forms are stored in the Forms\Supervisors folder, which is shared using the name Supervisors. These forms must be accessible only by members of the Supervisors global group.

To accomplish these goals, you have created the share permission assignments shown in the following table:

Shared Folder	Share Permissions
Forms	Everyone: Allow Read
Supervisors	Supervisors: Allow Read
Username	*username*: Allow Change

Assuming that the NTFS permissions for all of the folders are set to Authenticated Users – Modify, which of the following requirements have you met with your permission assignments? (Choose all correct answers.)

a. All employees can download their forms.

b. All employees can upload completed forms to their folders.

c. Employees can read only their own submitted forms.

d. Only Authenticated Users can download forms.

e. Only Supervisors can download Supervisor-specific forms.

CHAPTER 10
WORKING WITH PRINTERS

In addition to file sharing, the primary motivation for the development of local area networks (LANs) was the ability to share printers. Printers are often the bane of a network administrator's existence because they involve not just electronic components but also dirty things such as ink and toner and mechanical processes such as paper feeding. Microsoft Windows Server 2003 provides a powerful feature set to support enterprise print services, and understanding how to use these features can help you minimize the frustrations of dealing with network printing problems. In this chapter, you learn how to install, administer, and troubleshoot local, network, and Internet printers.

Upon completion of this chapter, you will be able to:

- Understand the model and terminology used for Windows printing
- Install a logical printer on a print server
- Prepare a print server to host clients
- Connect a printer client to a logical printer on a print server
- Manage print queues and printer properties
- Troubleshoot printer failures

UNDERSTANDING THE WINDOWS SERVER 2003 PRINTER MODEL

Windows Server 2003 provides print services that are powerful, secure, and flexible. By using a computer running Windows Server 2003 to manage printers, administrators can make them available to applications running locally on the Windows Server 2003 computer or to users on any client platform, including previous versions of Windows as well as Novell NetWare, UNIX, and Macintosh OS.

Windows Server 2003 and previous versions of Windows support two types of printers:

- **Locally attached printers**   Printers that are connected to a physical port on a **print server**, typically a universal serial bus (USB) or parallel port.

- **Network-attached printers**   Printers connected directly to the network instead of to a physical port on a computer. A network-attached printer contains (or is connected to) a network interface adapter and functions as a node on the network. Computers communicate with the printer using a standard networking protocol such as Transmission Control Protocol/Internet Protocol (TCP/IP) or Data Link Control (DLC).

When you install a printer of either type on a computer that uses Microsoft Windows, the operating system creates a **logical printer**, which represents the physical printer device. The logical printer defines the characteristics and behavior of the printer; it contains the printer driver, printer settings, print setting defaults, and other properties that control the manner in which a print job is processed and sent to the physical printer. This virtualization of the printer by a logical printer enables administrators to exercise a great deal of creativity and flexibility in configuring enterprise print services.

Using Locally Attached Printers

When you install a **locally attached printer** in Windows Server 2003 (or any other version of Windows), the computer to which the printer is attached can, of course, use it to process print jobs. It is possible to share the printer with other computers on the network. When you create a printer share, the computer hosting the printer functions as a print server. A print server is a computer (or stand-alone device) that receives print jobs from network clients, stores the jobs in a **print queue**, and sends them one by one to the physical printer.

> **NOTE**   Printing Terminology   In the documentation for previous versions of Windows, the physical printer was referred to as a *print device* and the logical printer was referred to as a *printer*. Microsoft has altered this terminology in Windows Server 2003 in an attempt to eliminate the confusion this terminology causes. It now uses *printer* and *logical printer*.

Using Network-Attached Printers

When you are using a network-attached printer, there are two network printing models you can use, which are described in the following sections.

Create a Logical Printer on Every Client Computer

In this model, you install a logical printer on each client computer and connect those logical printers directly to the network-attached printer. There is no print server in this arrangement; each computer maintains its own print settings, processes its own print jobs, and stores the jobs in its own print queue. In a network environment, this model has distinct disadvantages, such as the following:

- When users examine the contents of the print queue, they see only their own jobs.

- Users have no way of knowing what jobs have been sent to the printer by other users.

- Administrators have no way of centrally managing the print queue.

- Administrators cannot implement advanced printing features such as printer pools.

- Error messages appear only on the computer that is printing the current job.

- All print job processing is performed locally on the client computer, rather than being offloaded to a print server.

This model might be practical for a small workgroup network, but for an enterprise, it provides virtually no centralized administrative capabilities. The only real advantage to this arrangement is that it is easy to set up, even by individual end users. Each client computer installs the printer in the normal manner and remains oblivious of the other clients (except when waiting for their print jobs to complete).

Create a Print Server

Because of the significant drawbacks just described, the most typical printing configuration for enterprise networks is the three-part model, which consists of the following components:

- The physical printer

- A print server containing a logical printer, which is connected to the physical printer

- Printer clients, which are connected to the server's logical printer

Printing with a print server provides the following advantages:

- The logical printer on the print server defines the printer settings and manages the printer drivers.

- The logical printer uses a single print queue that is visible to all client computers, so users and administrators can see a complete list of jobs waiting to be printed.

- Error messages, such as out-of-paper or printer-jam messages, are visible to all client computers, so users and administrators can be informed of printer problems.

- Most applications and most printer drivers can offload part of the print-job processing to the print server, which increases the responsiveness of the client computers. In other words, when a client prints a document, the job is sent quickly to the print server and control of the computer returns to the user, while the print server assumes the task of processing the job.

- Security, auditing, monitoring, and logging functions are centralized.

DEPLOYING A SHARED PRINTER

The process of deploying a shared printer using the print server model consists of the following three steps:

- Install the printer on the print server.

- Create a printer share on the print server.

- Connect the clients to the print server.

These steps are described in the following sections.

Installing a Windows Server 2003 Print Server

The first step in deploying a print server on a network is to install the printer on the computer that is to function as the print server. This process is no different from installing a printer for exclusive use by the local system. It is the act of sharing the printer that enables Windows Server 2003 to function as a print server.

In Windows Server 2003, you manage printers using the Printers And Faxes window, which is accessible from Control Panel or directly from the Start menu. Double-clicking the Add Printer icon launches the Add Printer Wizard. After clicking Next to bypass the Welcome page, you complete the wizard pages described in the following list.

> **NOTE**   **Using USB Printers**   Printers that connect to the computer using the universal serial bus (USB) do not require you to manually launch the Add Printer Wizard. Because USB devices are plug and play, the computer detects and installs them automatically. You might have to supply drivers for printers that are not supported by Windows, however.

- **Local Or Network Printer**   On this page, you specify whether you are installing a local printer or a **network printer**. In the context of this wizard, *local printer* refers to a physical printer that is either locally attached or network-attached but is not currently shared by another print server. *Network printer* refers to a printer shared by another computer on the network. Therefore, to install a print server, you always select Local Printer Attached To This Computer. If the printer is currently connected and ready, you can select the Automatically Detect And Install My Plug And Play Printer check box to attempt to install the printer automatically. However, it is also possible to install the logical printer without the physical printer actually being present.

- **Select A Printer Port**   On this page, you specify how the computer communicates with the printer. If the printer is connected to a parallel (LPT) or serial (COM) port in the computer, you select the Use The Following Port option and select the correct port from the drop-down list. If the printer is connected by some other means, you select Create A New Port and select one of the port types from the drop-down list. Network-attached printers, for example, typically require a TCP/IP port. When you select the Standard TCP/IP Port option, the Add Standard TCP/IP Printer Port Wizard appears, in which you specify the IP address you assigned to the printer and, if necessary, the type of network interface adapter connecting the printer to the network.

- **Install Printer Software**   If plug and play does not detect and install the correct printer driver, you can select your printer from a list of printer drivers included with Windows Server 2003, which is categorized by manufacturer and printer model. If your printer does not appear in the list, you can click Have Disk to install printer drivers supplied by the device manufacturer.

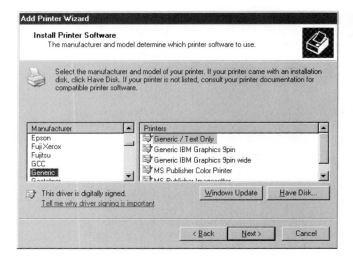

- **Name Your Printer**   On this page, you specify the name by which the printer will be known to the applications running on the computer. By default, the wizard supplies the manufacturer and model name associated with the printer driver it is installing, but you can modify the Printer Name to any value you want. For full application compatibility, you should limit printer names to no more than 31 characters. When other printers are installed, this page also enables you to specify whether you want to designate this printer as the default printer for the computer, which means that applications will print to this printer unless you select a different one. This setting applies only to applications running on the local system, not to network clients.

- **Printer Sharing**   On this page, you specify whether you want to share the printer, thereby causing the computer to function as a print server. To create a printer share, you select the Share Name option and specify the name by which the printer will be known on the network. By default, the wizard supplies the first eight nonblank characters of the printer name you supplied in the previous page, but you can use any share name you want. For compatibility reasons, it is best to stick with 8.3 printer names that do not contain spaces.

NOTE Sharing Printers The Printer Sharing page of the Add Printer Wizard provides only the most basic printer-sharing functionality. To configure other printer-sharing options, you must use the printer's Properties dialog box, as described in the next section.

- **Location And Comment** This page contains fields in which you can supply information about the printer's location or capabilities. This information is visible to users browsing the network and might help them to locate the correct printer.

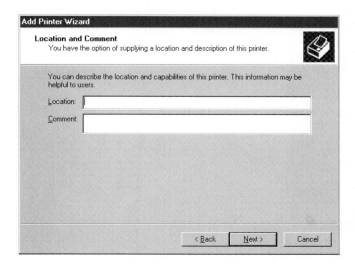

- **Print Test Page** This page enables you to print a test job to determine whether the computer can communicate with the printer.

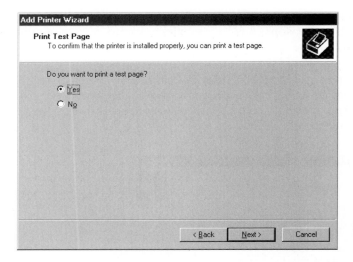

Practice
installing
a logical printer
by doing
Exercise 10-1,
"Creating a
Logical Printer,"
now.
When you complete the Add Printer Wizard, the system installs the appropriate printer driver and creates a logical printer icon for the printer in the Printers And Faxes window. You use this icon to access all of the configuration and maintenance tools for the printer. At this point, the printer is ready for use by the local system and, if you elected to share it, by clients on the network as well.

Sharing a Printer

It is possible to share a printer when you install it using the Add Printer Wizard, but you can get greater control over the share by using the Sharing tab of the printer's Properties dialog box (shown in Figure 10-1), which the wizard creates. To access this tab, select a printer icon in the Printers And Faxes window and, from the File menu, select Sharing.

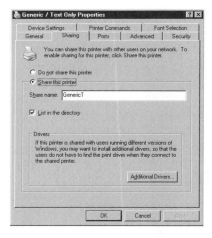

Figure 10-1   The Sharing tab of a printer's Properties dialog box

To share the printer (if it is not shared already), select the Share This Printer option and specify a name for the share in the Share Name text box. You can also select the List In The Directory check box to create a printer object for the printer in

Microsoft Active Directory. As with a shared folder object, a printer object is a pointer that enables users to locate a printer by searching Active Directory for its name or its capabilities. One benefit of specifying values for the Location field and similar properties is the ability to search for a printer based on these properties.

Click Additional Drivers to open the Additional Drivers dialog box, shown in Figure 10-2. When a client on the network accesses a shared printer, it can automatically download a printer driver from the Print$ share on the server, a capability that Windows calls Point And Print. This dialog box enables you to install printer drivers for other operating systems that your clients might be using. This is particularly beneficial if the printer uses drivers that are not included with Windows Server 2003. When you select other operating systems in this dialog box and click OK, the system installs the required drivers, prompting you to insert the manufacturer's driver disk, if needed.

Figure 10-2   The Additional Drivers dialog box

> **NOTE**   **Updating Printer Drivers**   Client computers running Microsoft Windows NT, Microsoft Windows 2000, Microsoft Windows XP, and Windows Server 2003 download the printer driver from the print server when they first connect to the shared printer. They also verify that they have the current printer driver each time they print, and if they do not, they download an updated driver from the server. For these client computers, you need only keep the printer drivers updated on the print server. Client computers running Microsoft Windows 95, Microsoft Windows 98, and Microsoft Windows Me can automatically download and install printer drivers when they first connect with the share, but they do not check for updated printer drivers after the initial installation. If you obtain an updated driver, you must manually install it on these clients as well as on the server.

Connecting Clients to a Print Server

Once the printer is installed on the print server and shared, it is available for access by clients. Clients can access a shared printer in several ways, as described in the following sections.

Using the Add Printer Wizard

The procedure for installing a print client using the Add Printer Wizard is similar to that of installing a print server, except that on the Local Or Network Printer page, you select the A Network Printer, Or A Printer Attached To Another Computer option. This takes you to a Specify A Printer page, shown in Figure 10-3, in which you are presented with the following ways to indicate the printer you want to use:

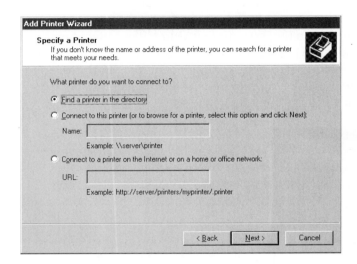

Figure 10-3   The Specify A Printer page of the Add Printer Wizard

- **Find A Printer In The Directory**   If the client computer is joined to an Active Directory domain, the Specify A Printer page displays this option, which causes the wizard to display a Find Printers dialog box that you can use to search for printers by name, location, or other criteria you have specified when creating the printer objects.

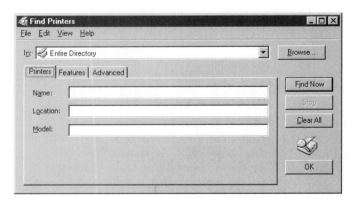

- **Browse For A Printer**   If the client computer is a member of a workgroup, the Specify A Printer page displays this option first. Selecting this option causes the wizard to display a Browse For Printer page, enabling you to browse in domains or workgroups for specific computers and select from the shared printers installed on each computer.

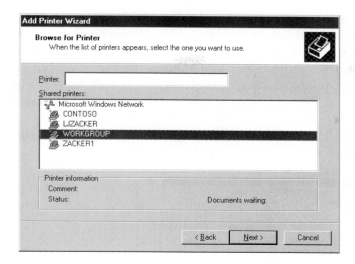

- **Connect To This Printer** Selecting this option enables you to specify the name of a printer share on the network, using Universal Naming Convention (UNC) notation, such as *servername\printershare*. Clicking Next without specifying a name produces the same Browse For Printer page that the Browse For A Printer option produces.

- **Connect To A Printer On The Internet Or On A Home Or Office Network** Selecting this option enables you to specify the name of a printer on the network or on the Internet using a Uniform Resource Locator (URL), such as *http://www.adatum.com/printers/printername*.

Once you identify the printer you want to install, the wizard installs the appropriate driver (presuming that one is available on the server or the client) and creates a logical printer in the Printers And Faxes window.

Browsing in Windows Explorer

You can also install a shared printer on a client simply by browsing in My Network Places using Windows Explorer. When you expand a computer icon in My Network Places, Windows Explorer displays a list of the shares on the computer. The printer shares are located in a container called Printers And Faxes, as shown in Figure 10-4. Select one of the shared printers and, from the File menu, select Connect to begin the process of installing the driver and logical printer.

Figure 10-4   Browsing for printers in Windows Explorer

Searching in Active Directory

For clients in Active Directory domains, the Add Printer Wizard provides the ability to search the directory for printer objects. You can search the directory for printers in other ways as well, such as from the Start menu's main Search page. When you select the Other Search Options, this page enables you to specify various search criteria, including a Printers, Computers, Or People option, as shown in Figure 10-5. Choosing to search for a printer on the network displays the same Find Printers dialog box that the Add Printer Wizard displays. This dialog box is accessible in many other ways throughout the Windows Server 2003 interface.

Figure 10-5   Searching for printers in Active Directory

CONFIGURING PRINTER PROPERTIES

After installing the logical printer on the print server, you can configure numerous properties by opening the printer's Properties dialog box, shown in Figure 10-6. Some of the controls in this dialog box are the same for all printers, but others that are provided by the printer driver can be specific to the printer. For example, a color printer might have color management controls that black-and-white printers don't need.

Figure 10-6   The General tab of a printer's Properties dialog box

The General tab enables you to configure the printer name, location, and comments, all of which were initially configured based on your responses to prompts in the Add Printer Wizard. The Sharing tab, as discussed earlier, enables you to specify whether the logical printer is shared and available to other clients on the network. Some of the other functions you can control in the Properties dialog box are discussed in the following sections.

Controlling Printer Security

Just as you can use permissions to secure file system shares, you can control printer usage and administration by assigning permissions through the Security tab of the printer's Properties dialog box, as shown in Figure 10-7.

Figure 10-7   The Security tab of a printer's Properties dialog box

The standard permissions that you can set for a printer are as follows:

- **Print**   Enables security principals to connect to a printer and submit print jobs to it. By default, this permission is assigned to the Everyone special identity. To restrict access to a printer, you can revoke the permission from the Everyone identity and assign it to other security principals, or you can deny the permission to specific security principals.

- **Manage Printers**   Enables security principals to perform all tasks associated with the Print permission, and also provides complete administrative control of the printer. Holders of this permission can modify printer properties, pause and restart the printer, control the printer's share status, adjust spooler settings, and modify printer permissions. By default, this permission is assigned to the Administrators and Power Users groups, and on domain controllers, the Server Operators and Print Operators groups.

- **Manage Documents**   Enables security principals to manipulate the documents in the print queue by pausing, resuming, restarting, canceling, and reordering them. However, this permission does not provide the ability to send documents to the printer or control the printer's status. By default, this permission is assigned to the Creator Owner special identity. Because a permission assigned to Creator Owner is inherited by the user who creates an object, this permission enables users to manage print jobs that they have created. The Administrators, Print Operators, and Server Operators groups are also assigned the Manage Documents permission, which means they can manage any document in the print queue. On computers that are not domain controllers, the Power Users group has this permission.

In addition to providing standard permissions, the Security tab also provides access to an Advanced Security Settings dialog box, as shown in Figure 10-8, which you can use to manage individual ACL entries and work with special permissions, just as you can with the NTFS permission system. Unlike with NTFS, however, the special permissions for printers include only three additional capabilities, enabling security principals to read permissions, change permissions, and take ownership of a printer.

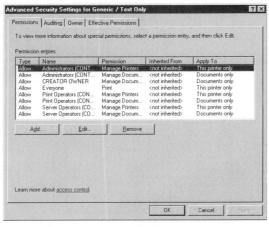

Practice working with printer permissions by doing Exercise 10-2, "Setting Printer Permissions," now.

Figure 10-8   The Advanced Security Settings dialog box

> **NOTE   For More Information**   See Chapter 9 for more information on using standard and special permissions to control access to system resources.

Assigning Forms to Paper Trays

If a print device has multiple trays that you use to hold different paper sizes, you can assign a form to a specific tray. A form defines a paper size. When users print a document of a particular paper size, Windows Server 2003 routes the print job to the paper tray that holds the correct form. Examples of forms include Legal, Letter, A4, Envelope, and Executive.

To assign a form to a paper tray, select the Device Settings tab of the printer's Properties dialog box, as shown in Figure 10-9. The number of trays shown in the Form To Tray Assignment section depends on the type of printer you have installed and the number of trays it supports. For each tray listed, you can select a different form. Further down the Device Settings tree are settings that specify the installation state of printer options, such as additional paper trays, paper handling units, fonts, and printer memory. These settings are all specific to the printer and depend on the capabilities of the printer and its driver.

Figure 10-9   The Device Settings tab of a printer's Properties dialog box

Setting Print Job Defaults

The General tab of the printer's Properties dialog box includes a Printing Preferences button, and the Advanced tab includes a Printing Defaults button. Both of
these buttons display a dialog box that lets you control the manner in which jobs
are printed by the logical printer, including page orientation (portrait or land-
scape), duplex (double-sided) printing (if supported), paper source, resolution,
and other document settings, as shown in Figure 10-10. These dialog boxes are
identical to each other and are also identical to the dialog box displayed when you
click Properties or Preferences in an application's Print dialog box.

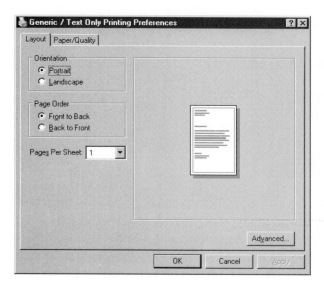

Figure 10-10   The Printing Preferences dialog box

The existence of three separate dialog boxes with identical controls is not an accident or simple redundancy. The Printing Defaults dialog box configures default settings for all users of the logical printer. If the printer is shared, these printing defaults become the default properties for all of the printer's clients as well. The Printing Preferences dialog box configures the user-specific, personal preferences for a printer. Any conflicting settings in the Printing Preferences dialog box override the printer's defaults. The Properties or Preferences dialog box provided by applications configures the properties for the specific print job the application is processing. These job-specific properties override both printing defaults and printing preferences.

Creating a Printer Pool

A printer pool is one logical printer that supports multiple physical printers. The physical printers can be attached to the server, to the network, or both. When you create a printer pool, the print server sends jobs submitted by clients to the first available printer. The logical printer representing the pool checks for an available port and forwards the job accordingly.

You configure printer pooling in the Ports tab of the printer's Properties dialog box. If you select the Enable Printer Pooling check box, you can specify multiple ports containing print devices that will be part of the pool. Figure 10-11 shows a printer pool connected to three network-attached printers.

Figure 10-11   The Ports tab of a printer's Properties dialog box, showing a three-printer pool

NOTE   Printer Pooling Hardware Requirements   Because a printer pool consists of multiple physical printers driven by a single logical printer, only one printer driver is installed. While the printers in the pool don't have to be completely identical, they must all be compatible with the driver installed in the logical printer.

Configuring Multiple Logical Printers for a Single Printer

While a printer pool is a single logical printer connected to multiple physical printers, the reverse structure—multiple logical printers connected to a single physical printer—is more common and more powerful. By creating more than one logical printer that directs jobs to the same physical printer, you can configure different properties, printing defaults, security settings, auditing, and monitoring for each logical printer.

For example, you might want to allow company executives to print jobs immediately, bypassing documents that are being printed by other users. To do so, you can create a second logical printer directed to the same physical printer as the other users, but with a higher priority.

To create this type of configuration, you simply use the Add Printer Wizard to create additional logical printers, using the same port as the first one. Each logical printer must have a unique name and share name. Then you configure the logical printers individually, with settings suitable for the clients that will have access to that logical printer.

To configure different priorities for the logical printers, you select the Advanced tab of the Properties dialog box, as shown in Figure 10-12, and specify a value for the Priority property in the range from 1 (lowest) to 99 (highest). If you assign the value 99 to the executives' logical printer and 1 to the logical printer used by all other users, documents sent to the executives' logical printer will print before documents queued in the users' logical printer. An executive's document will not interrupt a user's print job, but when the printer is free, it will accept jobs from the higher-priority logical printer before accepting jobs from the lower-priority logical printer. To prevent unauthorized users from printing to the executives' logical printer, you configure its ACL and remove the print permission assigned to the Everyone special identity, and instead allow only the executives the Print permission.

Figure 10-12   The Advanced tab of a printer's Properties dialog box

MONITORING PRINTERS

Once you have created, configured, and shared the logical printer on your print server, and once the network clients have been connected to those printers, you must begin to consider the administration tasks that inevitably result during the printing process. The following sections describe how you can use the various tools provided by Windows Server 2003 to monitor the network printing process and, when necessary, intervene.

> **NOTE** **Exam Objectives**   The objectives for exam 70-290 require students to be able to "monitor file and print servers. Tools might include Task Manager, Event Viewer, and System Monitor."

Monitoring Print Queues

Double-clicking a printer icon in the Printers And Faxes window opens another window, named for the printer, like the one shown in Figure 10-13. This is a print queue window, which lists all of the jobs currently waiting to be sent to the physical printer. Depending on the permissions they possess, users can manipulate the print queue and the individual jobs in it in various ways and to various degrees, using the menus in the window. Common tasks performed by users and administrators might include pausing, resuming, and canceling specific jobs in the queue, reordering jobs, and pausing and resuming the entire queue.

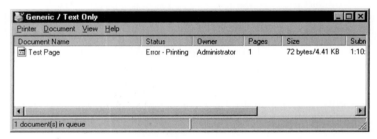

Figure 10-13   A print queue window

> **NOTE** **Exam Objectives**   The objectives for exam 70-290 require students to be able to "monitor print queues."

Practice working with queued print jobs by doing Exercise 10-3, "Canceling a Print Job," now.

Redirecting Print Jobs

If a printer is malfunctioning, you can send documents in the queue for that printer to another printer that is connected to a local port on the computer or is attached to the network. This is called *redirecting* print jobs. Redirection enables users to continue sending jobs to the same logical printer and prevents users with documents in the queue from having to resubmit the jobs.

To redirect a printer, you simply change the port to which the logical printer is sending the jobs. You do this by opening the printer's Properties dialog box, selecting the Ports tab, and selecting a different port or adding a new one. The check box of the port connecting the malfunctioning printer is immediately cleared—unless printer pooling is enabled, in which case you must manually clear the check box. Because the print jobs in the queue have already been prepared by the logical printer, the printer to which you redirect the jobs must be compatible with the driver used by the logical printer. All print jobs are redirected to the new port. (You cannot redirect individual documents, however, and any documents currently printing cannot be redirected.)

In most cases, print job redirection is most practical when you are using network-attached printers that are accessible through TCP/IP ports. When one printer malfunctions, you can change the port in its logical printer to the IP address of another physical printer on the network. This physical printer then services two logical printers until you fix the malfunctioning printer and change the port setting back again.

Using the Performance Console

The Performance console, accessible from the Administrative Tools program group in Windows Server 2003, contains two MMC snap-ins, System Monitor and Performance Logs And Alerts, that enable you to observe real-time performance of printers, log metrics for later analysis, or set alert levels and actions.

> **MORE INFO** **For More Information** To review the capabilities of and procedures for using the Performance console, see Chapter 3.

To configure System Monitor or Performance Logs And Alerts to monitor network printing activities, you typically select the Print Queue performance object in the Add Counters dialog box, as shown in Figure 10-14. This performance object provides an instance for each of the printers installed on the computer and a number of performance counters that you can use to monitor the printing process, including the following:

Figure 10-14 Selecting performance counters to monitor printer activity with the Performance console

- **Bytes Printed/Sec**   Specifies the number of bytes of raw data per second that are sent to the printer. Low values for this counter can indicate that a printer is underutilized, either because there are no jobs, print queues are not evenly loaded, or the server is too busy. This value varies according to the type of printer. Consult the printer documentation for acceptable printer throughput values.

- **Job Errors**   Specifies the number of job errors that have occurred since the spooler was last started. Job errors are typically caused by improper port configuration; check the port configuration for invalid settings. A printing job instance increments this counter only once, even if the error occurs multiple times.

- **Jobs**   Specifies the current number of jobs in the print queue. A high or constantly increasing value might indicate the printer is overworked or that jobs are not being printed properly.

- **Not Ready Errors**   Specifies the number of printer-not-ready errors that have occurred since the spooler was started.

- **Out Of Paper Errors**   Specifies the number of out-of-paper errors that have occurred since the spooler was started.

- **Total Jobs Printed**   Specifies the number of jobs sent to the printer since the spooler was started.

- **Total Pages Printed**   Specifies the number of pages printed since the spooler was started. This counter provides a close approximation of printer volume, although it might not be perfect, depending on the type of jobs and the document properties for those jobs.

> **NOTE**   **Using Performance Counters**   Some of the print queue performance counters are better suited for performance logging, such as those tracking the amount of printer activity, and others are best suited for alerts, such as the error counters. Using alerts, you can configure the system to notify administrators when a specific type of error occurs.

Using Event Viewer

Using Event Viewer, you can examine the Windows Server 2003 System log as a source of information on printer and print spooler activity. By default, the spooler registers events concerning printer creation, deletion, and modification. The log also contains events with information about printer traffic, hard disk space, spooler errors, and other maintenance issues.

To control or modify spooler event logging, open the Printers And Faxes folder and select Server Properties from the File menu. Select the Advanced tab to access the properties shown in Figure 10-15. In this tab, you can control printer event log entries and print job notifications. This is also the tab that enables you to move the print spooler folder—an important task when you configure an active print server or when an existing print spooler folder's disk volume becomes full.

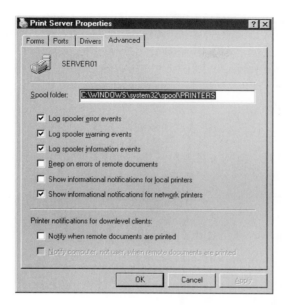

Figure 10-15   The Advanced tab of the Print Server Properties dialog box

Auditing Printer Access

Printer access, like file and folder access, can be audited. You can specify which groups or users and which actions to audit for a particular printer. After enabling the object access auditing policy, you can view the resulting audit entries in the Event Viewer console's Security log.

To configure auditing for a printer, open its Properties dialog box, select the Security tab, and then click Advanced. In the Advanced Security Settings dialog box, select the Auditing tab and add entries for specific groups or users. For each security principal you add to the audit entry list, you can configure auditing for successful or failed access based on the standard printer permissions, including Print, Manage Documents, and Manage Printers.

Next you must enable the Audit Object Access policy, which is located in the Group Policy Object Editor or Local Security Policy console under Computer Configuration\Windows Settings\Security Settings\Local Policies\Audit Policy. After the policy has taken effect, you can examine the Security event log to see and analyze entries made based on printer auditing.

> **TIP   When to Audit Printing**   Printer auditing creates dozens of log entries for a single print job, so it is useful only when you're troubleshooting specific problems. Do not use printer auditing to monitor printer use or to bill for printer usage. Instead, use performance counters such as Total Jobs Printed or Total Pages Printed.

TROUBLESHOOTING PRINTERS

Troubleshooting is an important part of printer management. This section can help you understand, identify, and address the types of incidents and problems that might occur in Windows Server 2003 printing.

NOTE   **Exam Objectives**   *The objectives for exam 70-290 require students to be able to "troubleshoot print queues."*

Remember when troubleshooting that printing includes multiple components, including the following:

- The application that is attempting to print
- The logical printer on the computer on which the application is running
- The network connection between the print client and the shared logical printer on the server
- The logical printer on the server—its spooler, drivers, security settings, and other components
- The connection between the print server and the printer
- The printer itself—its hardware, configuration, and status

An efficient way to solve most problems associated with printing is to troubleshoot each component logically and methodically.

Identify the Scope of Failure

If a user cannot print a job from one application on the computer but can print from another application on the same computer, the error is most likely related to the failed job's application rather than the computer, the network, the print server, or the printer hardware. However, in some cases, using a different driver or data type can solve an application's print errors.

If the user cannot print to the printer from any application, identify whether the user can print to other printers on the same print server or on other print servers. If all possibilities fail, and if other users can print to the printers on the network, the error is likely local to the user's computer.

If the printer is networked, try creating a local printer on the problematic system that points directly to the printer's port. In other words, bypass the print server. If this process succeeds, there is a problem on the print server or with the communication between the user's system and the print server.

Verify That the Print Client Can Connect to the Print Server

You can confirm connectivity between the print client and the print server by opening the print queue window from the Printers And Faxes folder on the client computer. If the print queue window opens and shows any documents in the print queue, the client is successfully connecting to the print server. An error opening the print queue window would indicate a potential networking, authentication, or permissions problem. If this is the case, you can use the Ping utility to test the connection to the print server's IP address, or click Start, select Run, and type **\\printserver**. If the ping test is successful or a window opens showing the Printers And Faxes folder and any shared folders, the client is connecting to the server. In that case, double-check security permissions on the logical printer.

Verify That the Printer Is Operational

Check the printer itself and ensure that it is in the ready state (ready to print). Check for depleted consumables, paper jams, and other obvious problems, and then print a test page from the printer console. Check the cable connecting the printer to the print server or the network. If the printer is network-attached, confirm that the network interface card light is on, indicating network connectivity.

Verify That the Printer Is Accessible from the Print Server

Some printers can display their IP address on the printer console or by printing out a configuration page. Confirm that the printer's IP address matches the IP address of the logical printer's port. The port's IP address can be seen in the printer's Properties dialog box, in the Ports tab. Ensure that it is possible to communicate with the printer over the network by pinging the printer's IP address.

Verify That the Print Server's Services Are Running

Using the Services console, check that the following print-related services are running properly:

- **Print Spooler**   Manages local and network print queues. If this service is not running, no printing will occur.

- **Remote Procedure Call (RPC)**   Required for standard network connections to shared printers.

You can also examine the volume on which the spool folder is stored to ensure that there is sufficient disk space for spooling. The spool folder location can be discovered and modified in the Server Properties dialog box, which you can access by selecting Server Properties from the File menu of the Printers And Faxes folder. By default, print jobs spool to the *Systemroot*\System32\Spool\Printers folder. For a high-volume print server, consider moving the spool folder to a partition other than the system or boot partition. If the partition where the spool folder resides fills to capacity with print jobs, printing will stop and, more importantly, the operating system might become unstable.

You should also look at the System log to see if the spooler has registered any error events, and, in the Printers And Faxes folder, make sure that the printer is not in Offline mode.

Attempt to print a job from an application on the print server. If you can print to the printer from the print server, the problem is not with the printer. If you cannot print to the printer from an application on the print server, create a new logical printer directed at the same port and attempt to print to the new printer. If that job succeeds, there is a problem with the configuration of the original logical printer. If that job is unsuccessful, there is a problem communicating with the printer, or with the hardware itself.

SUMMARY

- The printing architecture in Windows Server 2003 is modular, consisting of the physical printer itself, a print server with a shared, logical printer connected to the physical printer through a local or network port, and a logical printer on a client that connects to the shared, logical printer on the print server.

- A local printer is one that supports a printer directly attached to the computer or attached to the network. A network printer connects to a logical printer maintained by another computer, a print server.

- Shared printers are published to Active Directory by default, which enables users to easily search for printers based on location or other printer properties.

- To create a logical printer, you run the Add Printer Wizard and specify the printer driver and port to use.

- A single logical printer can direct jobs to more than one port, creating a printer pool.

- A single physical printer can be served by multiple logical printers, each of which can be configured with unique properties, drivers, settings, permissions, or monitoring characteristics.

- The print queue window, event logs, and performance counters enable you to monitor printers for potential signals of trouble and for utilization statistics.

- If a printer is to be taken offline or has already failed, you can redirect all its jobs not already in progress to another printer by adding or selecting the new printer's port in the properties of the original logical printer. The alternate port must represent a printer that is compatible with the driver in use by the original logical printer.

- Because the Windows Server 2003 printer model is modular, with the printer itself, the logical printer on a print server, and the logical printer on a client connected to the server's shared printer, you can methodically troubleshoot a printer failure by addressing each component and the links between those components.

EXERCISES

Exercise 10-1: Creating a Logical Printer

In this exercise, you install a logical printer on your computer.

1. Log on to Windows Server 2003 as Administrator.

2. Click Start, and select Printers And Faxes. The Printers And Faxes window appears.

3. Double-click the Add Printer icon. The Add Printer Wizard appears.

4. Click Next to bypass the Welcome page. The Local Or Network Printer page appears.

5. Select the Local Printer Attached To This Computer option. Be sure the Automatically Detect And Install My Plug And Play Printer check box is cleared, then click Next. The Select A Printer Port page appears.

6. In the Use The Following Port drop-down list, select LPT3: (Printer Port), and then click Next. The Install Printer Software page appears.

   Few, if any, computers have an LPT3 port. If your computer does, select a port that is unused by your computer, such as COM3 or COM4.

7. In the Manufacturer column, select Generic. In the Printers column, select Generic/Text Only, then click Next. The Name Your Printer page appears.

8. In the Printer Name text box, type **Test Printer**, and then click Next. The Printer Sharing page appears.

9. Click Next to accept the default sharing parameters. Click Next again to bypass the Location And Comment page. The Print Test page appears.

10. Select the No option, and then click Next. The Completing The Add Printer Wizard page appears.

11. Click Finish.

Exercise 10-2: Setting Printer Permissions

In this exercise, you configure permissions for your shared printer.

1. Log on to Windows Server 2003 as Administrator.

2. Install a logical printer, as described in Exercise 10-1.

3. Click Start, and select Printers And Faxes. The Printers And Faxes window appears.

4. Select the Test Printer icon for the logical printer you created and, from the File menu, select Properties. The Properties dialog box appears.

5. Select the Everyone security principal on the Security tab and then click Remove.

6. Click Add. The Select Users, Computers, Or Groups dialog box appears.

7. In the Enter The Object Names To Select text box, type **Users**, and then click OK. The Users group appears in the list of security principals.

8. Select the Allow check box for the Manage Documents permission, and then click OK.

Exercise 10-3: Cancelling a Print Job

In this exercise, you cancel a queued print job that has not completed.

1. Log on to Windows Server 2003 as Administrator.

2. Install a logical printer, as described in Exercise 10-1.

3. Click Start, and select Printers And Faxes. The Printers And Faxes window appears.

4. Right-click the Test Printer icon for the logical printer you created, and select Properties. The printer's Properties dialog box opens.

5. Click Print Test Page in the General tab to send a test page to the printer. A Test Printer message box opens. Click OK to close the message box, and click OK to close the printer's Properties dialog box.

6. Double-click the Test Printer icon for the logical printer you created. The Test Printer window appears.

7. Select the Test Page document in the list, and note its error status, which is due to no physical printer being connected to the selected port.

8. On the Document menu, select Cancel. A Printers message box appears, prompting you to confirm your decision to delete the print job.

9. Click Yes. The print job is deleted from the queue.

REVIEW QUESTIONS

1. You are installing a printer on a client computer. The printer will connect to a logical printer installed on a Windows Server 2003 print server. What type or types of information could you provide to set up the printer? (Choose all correct answers.)

   a. A TCP/IP printer port

   b. The physical printer's manufacturer and model

   c. The URL to the printer on the print server

   d. The UNC path to the printer share

   e. A printer driver

2. One of your networked printers is not working properly, and you want to prevent users from sending print jobs to the logical printer serving that device. What do you do?

   a. Stop sharing the printer

   b. Remove the printer from Active Directory

   c. Change the printer port

   d. Rename the share

3. You are administering a Windows Server 2003 computer configured as a print server. You want to perform maintenance on a physical printer connected to the print server. There are several documents in the print queue. You want to prevent the documents from being printed to the printer, but you don't want users to have to resubmit the documents to the printer. What is the best approach to take?

   a. Open the printer's Properties dialog box, select the Sharing tab, and select the Do Not Share This Printer option.

    b. Open the printer's Properties dialog box, and, in the Ports tab, select a port that is not associated with a print device.

    c. Open the print queue window, select the first document, and then select Pause from the Document window. Repeat the process for each document.

    d. Open the print queue window, and select Pause Printing from the Printer menu.

4. You are administering a Windows Server 2003 computer configured as a print server. Users in the Marketing group complain that they cannot print documents using a printer on the server. You view the permissions in the printer's Properties dialog box. The Marketing group is allowed Manage Documents permission. Why can't the users print to the printer?

    a. The Everyone group must be granted the Manage Documents permission.

    b. The Administrators group must be granted the Manage Printers permission.

    c. The Marketing group must be granted the Print permission.

    d. The Marketing group must be granted the Manage Printers permission.

5. You are setting up a printer pool on a Windows Server 2003 computer. The printer pool contains three print devices, all identical. You open the Properties dialog box for the printer and select the Enable Printer Pooling option in the Ports tab. What must you do next?

    a. Configure the LPT1 port to support three printers.

    b. Select or create the ports mapped to the three printers.

    c. In the Device Settings tab, configure the installable options to support two additional print devices.

    d. In the Advanced tab, configure the priority for each print device so that printing is distributed among the three print devices.

6. A Windows 2003 Server is configured as a print server. In the middle of the workday, the printer fuse fails and must be replaced. Users have already submitted jobs to the printer, which uses IP address 192.168.1.81. An identical printer uses address 192.168.1.217, and it is supported by other logical printers on the server. What actions do you take so that users' jobs can be printed without resubmission? (Choose all correct answers.)

    a. In the failed printer's Properties dialog box, select Enable Printer Pooling.

    b. In the failed printer's Properties dialog box, click Add Port.

    c. In the Printers And Faxes folder, right-click the failed printer and select Use Offline.

    d. In the failed printer's Properties dialog box, select the port 192.168.1.217.

7. Which of the following approaches gives you the clearest picture of printer utilization, allowing you to understand the consumption of printer toner and paper?

   a. Configure auditing for a logical printer, and audit for successful use of the Print permission by the Everyone system group.

   b. Export the System log to a comma-delimited text file, and use Microsoft Excel to analyze spooler events.

   c. Configure a performance log, and monitor the Total Pages Printed counter for each logical printer.

   d. Configure a performance log, and monitor the Jobs counter for each logical counter.

CASE SCENARIOS

Scenario 10-1: Updating Printer Drivers

The marketing department is complaining about print quality on its shared printer, which is called MarketingPrinter. When users print from their Windows XP desktops using Microsoft Office applications, documents print perfectly. But when they print from Adobe applications, the documents do not always reflect the desired results. The sales department, which has an identical shared printer called Sales-Printer and uses a mix of Windows 2000 and Windows XP workstations and Office, does not report any problems. As you consider the situation, it occurs to you that some applications produce different results depending on whether the printer is using PostScript or a non-PostScript driver. Where do you deploy the properly functioning printer driver so that the computers needing it are updated?

a. The Server Properties dialog box of the print server

b. The printer Properties dialog box of MarketingPrinter

c. The printer Properties dialog box of SalesPrinter

d. The printer Properties dialog box for the logical printers installed on the desktops of each marketing department user

Scenario 10-2: Enhancing Print Performance

You are the systems administrator for a law firm with a group of 20 legal assistants who provide administrative support to the attorneys. All of the assistants use a single, shared, high-speed laser printer installed on a Windows Server 2003 system. They must print large documents on a regular basis. Although the laser printer is fast, it is kept running almost constantly, printing documents. At times, the assistants have to wait 20 minutes or more after submitting a print job for their documents to reach the top of the queue. None of the assistants wants to scroll through a list of available printers to check which one has the fewest jobs before submitting a document. Which of the following options should you consider to minimize the amount of time that printers take to finish printing documents for all the assistants?

a. Install a second laser printer of the same make and model and create a printer pool.

b. Set different printer priorities for each legal assistant based on a list generated by the head of the group. The most important assistant should be set a priority of 1, and the least important a priority of 99.

c. Set different printer priorities for each legal assistant based on a list generated by the head of the group. The most important assistant should be set a priority of 99, and the least important a priority of 1.

d. Purchase three more identical laser printers, and install them with their own individual printer shares on the print server.

GLOSSARY

access control entry (ACE)   An entry in an access control list (ACL) that defines the permissions granted to a particular security principal.

access control list (ACL)   A collection of access control entries (ACEs) associated with a file, folder, Active Directory object, or other resource that defines the permissions that security principals, such as users, groups, and computers, have for accessing the resource.

ACE   *See* access control entry (ACE).

ACL   *See* access control list (ACL).

active partition   The partition on which the system's boot files are stored.

archive bit   A 1-bit flag included with every file on a drive that backup software programs use to determine which files to back up. Newly created files have their archive bits activated, and performing a full backup clears them. Whenever a file is modified, its archive bit is reactivated so that an incremental or differential backup can back up only the files that have changed.

attribute   A component element of an Active Directory object that contains information about that object. For example, a user object might consist of attributes such as the user's first name, last name, and e-mail address.

autochanger   A data storage hardware device that consists of one or more tape drives, a media array, and a robotic mechanism that inserts selected tapes into the drives. Autochangers make it possible for administrators to implement extended, unattended backup strategies.

baseline   A set of performance levels taken under normal conditions that is used for comparison with levels taken later, when problems occur.

bottleneck   A component that is not providing the same level of performance as the other components, causing a systemwide slowdown.

CAL   *See* Client Access License (CAL).

Client Access License (CAL)   A license that allows a user or device to connect to a server product for functionality that uses server components, including file and print service or authentication. Unauthenticated access through the Internet does not require a CAL.

commit memory   The amount of memory allocated to user programs and the operating system.

computer object   An Active Directory object representing a specific computer in a domain. The object includes a computer account that enables the system to establish a secure channel with a domain controller, as well as informational properties about the computer.

container object   Any Active Directory object that can act as a parent to other objects.

details pane   The right pane in a Microsoft Management Console (MMC) window, which displays information about whatever element is selected in the left (or scope) pane.

device driver   A set of software routines that implement device-specific functions for generic input/output (I/O) operations.

differential backup   A type of backup job that uses a filter so only the files that have changed since the last full backup job are backed up. The filter evaluates the state of each file's archive bit, which a full backup job clears. Creating or modifying a file sets its archive bit, and the differential job backs up only the files that have their archive bit set. The differential job does not modify the state of the bit, so the next differential job also backs up only the files that have changed since the last full backup. Differential jobs use more tape or other media than incremental jobs because they repeatedly back up the same files, but they're easier to restore in the event of a disaster. You have to restore only the last full backup and the most recent differential backup to completely restore a drive. *See also* incremental backup.

direct memory access (DMA) channel   A pathway used by a hardware device to transfer data directly to and from system memory.

directory service A database containing information about network entities and resources, which is used as a guide to the network and as an authentication resource by multiple users. Early network operating systems included basic flat-file directory services, such as Windows NT domains and the Novell NetWare bindery. Today's directory services, such as Microsoft's Active Directory and Novell's eDirectory, tend to be hierarchical and are designed to support large enterprise networks.

distribution group An Active Directory group type that cannot function as a security principal and is used primarily to create e-mail distribution lists.

DMA channel *See* direct memory access (DMA) channel.

domain A group of users, computers, and other resources for which information is stored in a directory service on a server called a domain controller.

domain controller A computer running Windows Server 2003, Windows 2000, or Windows NT that has been designated to store and process directory service information. Windows NT domains and the Windows Active Directory service store their directory service databases on domain controllers, which also authenticate users who want to access network resources.

domain functional level A setting that indicates which Active Directory features are available in the domain. The Active Directory implementations in the various versions of Windows have slightly different feature sets, and the domain functional level controls what group nesting and conversion tasks are possible.

domain local group An Active Directory group scope that is used primarily to provide access to resources in a single domain.

duplexing A disk-mirroring installation in which each physical disk is connected to a different host adapter. Duplexing provides increased performance and enables the volume to survive the failure of an adapter as well as a disk drive.

effective permissions A combination of allowed, denied, inherited, and explicitly assigned permissions that provides a composite view of a security principal's functional access to a resource.

forest A group of Active Directory trees that use different namespaces.

forest functional level A setting that indicates what Active Directory features are available in the forest. Raising the forest

functional level has no effect on Active Directory group activities.

fragmentation The tendency of a disk to contain files stored on clusters that are scattered all over the drive. Because the drive heads have to access clusters all over the disk to read a single file, overall performance decreases.

global group An Active Directory group scope that is most commonly used to manage permissions for directory objects that require frequent maintenance, such as user and computer accounts.

GPO *See* group policy object (GPO).

group policy object (GPO) A collection of group policy settings that can be applied to a domain, site, or organizational unit (OU) object.

host header A method of differentiating multiple Web sites running on a single server when the server uses only one IP address and port number. By specifying a Web server name in HTTP request messages, the Web server is able to forward each request to the appropriate site.

hotfix A patch or update for a Microsoft product that addresses a single issue that is explained in an accompanying Microsoft Knowledge Base article. Hotfixes might be recommended for installation only on computers that are performing certain tasks or are experiencing a specific problem.

incremental backup A type of backup job that uses a filter so only the files that have changed since the last backup job are backed up. The filter evaluates the state of each file's archive bit and backs up only the files with an archive bit that is set. Performing an incremental backup resets the archive bits (unlike a differential job, which does not reset the bits). Incremental jobs use the least amount of tape (or other medium), but they are more difficult to restore in the event of a disaster. To fully restore a drive, you must restore the last full backup job and all the incremental jobs performed since that last full backup, in chronological order.

interrupt request (IRQ) A signal sent from one component to another (typically from a peripheral device to the system processor) indicating that the sender requires the attention of the receiver.

I/O address A location in memory that is allocated for use by a particular hardware device, to exchange information with the system.

IRQ *See* interrupt request (IRQ)

leaf object   An Active Directory object that cannot act as a parent to other objects.

license group   Because the License Logging service allocates licenses based on username and not device name, Windows Device Client Access Licenses (CALs) are given to a license group. A license group has one or more users and is allocated licenses equivalent to the number of devices used by that group to connect to server products.

local group   A group account on a Windows Server 2003 standalone or member server. Local groups can have local users and domain global groups as members, but they provide access only to resources on the local system.

locally attached printer   A physical printer that is directly attached to a computer, typically using a parallel or USB port.

local user profile   A collection of folders and files that make up the desktop environment for a specific user, stored on a local drive.

logical printer   Represents a physical printer on a computer by sending print jobs out through a specific port. The logical printer includes the print queue, the printer driver, settings, permissions, and printing defaults that manage the creation of print jobs for the printer.

mandatory user profile   A read-only user profile that does not maintain modifications between sessions. Users can modify mandatory profiles, but their changes are not saved when they log off.

memory leak   The result of a program allocating memory for use but not freeing up that memory when it is finished using it.

mirrored volume   Two disks that contain identical copies of data. The only software RAID supported on the system volume. Good read and write performance; excellent fault tolerance; but costly in terms of disk utilization because 50 percent of the volume's potential capacity is used for data redundancy.

network-attached printer   A physical printer that is connected directly to the network rather than to a computer. Computers typically communicate with network-attached printers using IP addresses.

network printer   In the context of Windows, a logical printer that is a client of a shared logical printer on another computer. Not to be confused with a network-attached printer.

object   The fundamental building block of the Active Directory directory service.

Objects are elements that represent a network resource, such as a user, computer, domain, or group. Objects are composed of individual attributes, which contain information about the object. For example, the attributes of a user object might include the user's first name, last name, and e-mail address.

organizational unit (OU)   A type of Active Directory container object used within domains. OUs are logical containers in which you can place users, groups, computers, and other OUs. An OU can contain objects only from its parent domain. An OU is the smallest scope to which you can apply a group policy or delegate authority.

OU   *See* organizational unit (OU).

Per Device or Per User licensing mode   A licensing requirement that allows a single CAL to authorize a user (who might use more than one device) or a device (which might be used by more than one user) to connect to any number of servers.

performance counter   A data-reporting item associated with a performance object.

performance instance   An individual occurrence of a performance counter. If there are four processors in a server, there are four instances for each performance counter in the Processor object, numbered 0 through 3.

performance object   A logical collection of data-reporting items or counters connected with a resource, service, or application that can be monitored.

Per Server licensing mode   A licensing requirement that is allocated when a user or device connects to the server or product. When the user disconnects, the license is returned to the available license pool. This mode requires sufficient licenses to support the maximum number of concurrent connections on each individual server.

Plug and Play (PnP)   A standard that defines characteristics for computer components that enables the components to automatically detect and configure the hardware in a computer.

PnP   *See* Plug and Play (PnP).

print queue   A list of print jobs waiting to be submitted to a physical printer.

print server   A computer that is configured to share a printer with clients on a network. The print server queues the print jobs submitted by the clients and submits them to the physical printer.

RAID-5 volume   A volume on which data is written to multiple (from 3 to 32) physical disks at the same rate and that is interlaced with parity to provide fault tolerance for a single-disk failure. Has good read performance and good utilization of disk capacity, but is expensive in terms of processor utilization and write performance because parity must be calculated during write operations.

roaming user profile   A server-based user profile that is stored on a shared network drive, where the user can access it from any computer.

scope pane   The left pane in a Microsoft Management Console (MMC) window, which displays the snap-ins installed in the console.

security group   An Active Directory group type that is used as a security principal in access control lists (ACLs).

security identifier (SID)   A unique value assigned to every Active Directory object when it is created.

service pack   A collection of patches and updates for a Microsoft product that have been tested together and recommended for installation on all computers running the product.

SID   *See* security identifier (SID).

simple volume   The equivalent of a basic disk partition. Simple volumes exist on only one physical disk, so they are not fault tolerant.

slipstreaming   The process of integrating service packs and/or hotfixes into a Windows operating system installation.

snap-in   A special-purpose application module that runs within the Microsoft Management Console (MMC) shell. There are two types of snap-ins: standalone snap-ins, which you can add directly to an MMC console, and extension snap-ins, which must be associated with a specific standalone snap-in.

spanned volume   A volume that includes space on more than one physical disk.

Because their size tends to be greater and because multiple physical disks are involved, spanned volumes have a higher risk of failure and are not fault tolerant.

special permission   An element providing a security principal with a highly specific degree of access to a resource.

standard permission   A combination of special permissions used to provide a security principal with a frequently used level of access to a resource.

striped volume   A volume on which data is written to multiple (from 2 to 32) physical disks at the same rate. It offers maximum performance and capacity but no fault tolerance.

tree   A group of Active Directory domains sharing a contiguous namespace.

UNC   *See* Universal Naming Convention (UNC).

Uniform Resource Locator (URL)   A standard notation for identifying a resource on the Internet. For example, *http://www. adatum.com*. The most common way to use a URL is to enter it in a Web browser.

universal group   An Active Directory group scope that is typically used to grant access to related resources across multiple domains.

Universal Naming Convention (UNC)   A standard notation used to identify resources on a network. UNC uses the following format: \\Server\Share.

URL   *See* Uniform Resource Locator (URL).

virtual directory   An Internet Information Services (IIS) object that enables a folder on any local or remote volume to appear as a subfolder of a Web site.

volume shadow copy   A feature in Windows Server 2003 and Windows XP that maintains a library containing multiple versions of selected files. Users can select a version of a file to restore as needed, and the Backup program uses the shadow copies to back up open files.

INDEX

Number

64-bit server support, 8

A

access control lists. *See* ACLs (access control lists)
Account Operators group, 226, 228
accounts, computer. *See* computer accounts;
    computer objects
accounts, user. *See* user accounts
accounts, vulnerability of, checking for, 133
ACEs (access control entries)
    NTFS permissions with, 295
    permissions in, 277
    purpose of, 276
    special permissions, table of, 301–302
ACLs (access control lists)
    ACEs. *See* ACEs (access control entries)
    defined, 210
    displaying, 210
    editing, 277
    FAT file system with, 277
    groups in, 210
    NTFS permissions with, 295
    ownership of folders, 304
    purpose of, 276
    security principals, 210, 244, 276, 302
    special identities, 229–230
    storage of, 277
Action menu, MMC, 39
activating Windows Server, 18, 34
Active Directory
    attributes, 30
    authoritative restores, 121
    backups, 114, 120–121
    client OS compatibility, 201
    computer objects in. *See* computer objects
    container objects, 31, 34
    creating user objects, 205–206
    CSV for importing objects, 191–192
    directory services overview, 27–28
    domain controller server role, 20–21
    domain model, 28
    domain objects, 30
    Dsadd.exe, 193–194, 207
    features for legacy clients, 201–202
    forests, 29
    functional levels, 212–214
    global catalogs, 30
    group objects, 30
    group policy objects, 32
    groups. *See* Active Directory groups
    leaf objects, 31
    legacy OS issues, 202
    MMC consoles for, 38
    modifying objects with Dsmod.exe, 195
    moving user objects, 206
    multiple-master replication, 28

Ndsutil.exe, 121
nonauthoritative restores, 120
objects, 30
organizational unit objects, 30–31
OU hierarchy, 170
permissions, 31, 276
printer objects, 30
publishing shares, 291
purpose of, 27–28
replication, 28
restoring, 120–121, 124
schemas, 31
shared folder objects, 30
Standard Edition with, 6
Sysvol, 28
templates for user objects, 190–191
trees, 29
user accounts, hierarchy for, 170
user objects, 30, 205–206
viewing objects, 34
Web Edition with, 5
Active Directory Domains and Trusts console, 213
Active Directory groups
    Account Operators, 226, 228
    adding members, 235–236, 243, 244
    Administrators, 226, 228
    automating management of, 239–241
    Backup Operators, 227–228
    Builtin container, 226
    built-in domain local groups, 226–229
    CertPublishers, 224
    changing types, 237
    consoles for managing. *See* Active Directory
        Users and Computers console
    converting, 220
    creating, 234–235, 239–240, 242, 245
    defined, 215
    deleting, 238, 244
    distribution groups, 216
    Domain Admins, 224, 226
    Domain Computers group, 224
    Domain Controllers group, 225
    Domain Guests, 225
    domain local groups, 217, 220, 221, 244
    Domain Users, 225
    Dsadd.exe, 239–240, 245
    Dsget.exe, 240–241
    Dsmod.exe, 240
    Enterprise Admins, 225, 226
    finding with Dsget.exe, 240–241
    global groups, 217–218, 220
    Group Policy Creator Owners, 225
    Guests, 227
    management of, 235–236, 239–241
    nesting, 219, 237, 243
    Network Configuration Operators, 227
    Performance Log Users, 227
    Performance Monitor Users, 227

Implementing, Managing, and Maintaining a Microsoft® Windows Server™ 2003 Network Infrastructure (70-291)

Textbook

Greg Bott

PUBLISHED BY
Microsoft Press
A Division of Microsoft Corporation
One Microsoft Way
Redmond, Washington 98052-6399

Library of Congress Cataloging-in-Publication Data

Bott, Greg, 1966-
        ALS Implementing, Managing, and Maintaining a Microsoft Windows Server 2003
        Network Infrastructure / Greg Bott.
            p. cm.
        Includes bibliographical references and index.
        ISBN 0-7356-2030-x
        1. Computer networks--Planning.   2. Computer networks--Management.   3. Microsoft
Windows server.   I. Title.

TK5105.5B658   2004
004.6--dc22   2003071054

Printed and bound in the United States of America.

1 2 3 4 5 6 7 8 9   QWT   8 7 6 5 4 3

A CIP catalogue record for this book is available from the British Library.

Microsoft Press books are available through booksellers and distributors worldwide. For further information about international editions, contact your local Microsoft Corporation office or contact Microsoft Press International directly at fax (425) 936-7329. Visit our Web site at www.microsoft.com/mspress. Send comments to *moac@microsoft.com*.

Active Directory, BackOffice, Microsoft, Microsoft Press, MS-DOS, MSN, Outlook, Windows, the Windows logo, Windows Media, Windows NT, and Windows Server are either registered trademarks or trademarks of Microsoft Corporation in the United States and/or other countries. Other product and company names mentioned herein may be the trademarks of their respective owners.

The example companies, organizations, products, domain names, e-mail addresses, logos, people, places, and events depicted herein are fictitious. No association with any real company, organization, product, domain name, e-mail address, logo, person, place, or event is intended or should be inferred.

This book expresses the author's views and opinions. The information contained in this book is provided without any express, statutory, or implied warranties. Neither the authors, Microsoft Corporation, nor its resellers or distributors will be held liable for any damages caused or alleged to be caused either directly or indirectly by this book.

Program Managers: Hilary Long, Linda Engelman
Project Editor: Julie Miller
Technical Editor: Owen Fowler
Copy Editors: Ginny Bess, Christina Palaia (BookMasters, Inc.)
Indexer: Nancy Guenther (BookMasters, Inc.)
Instructional Designer: Emily Springfield

Sub Assy Part No. X10-36038
Body Part No. X10-23990

CONTENTS AT A GLANCE

CONTENTS

                 Update Services** **213**

What Does an Update Include? 214

Overview of SUS 214

SUS and Other Software-Distribution Technologies 215

Windows Update and Automatic Updates 215

    Windows Update 215

    Automatic Updates 216

Installing and Configuring SUS 218

    Hardware Requirements 218

    Software Requirements 218

How SUS Works 221

    SUS Distribution Points 221

Managing SUS 224

    Server Management 224

    Client Management 229

Monitoring SUS 234

    Monitor Server Page 234

    Synchronization Logs 234

    Approval Logs 235

    Server Event Log Messages 236

    Client Event Log Messages 236

Summary 237

Exercises 237

    Exercise 7-1: Using the Windows Update Web Site 237

    Exercise 7-2: Enabling Automatic Updates 238

Review Questions 238

Case Scenarios 240

    Case Scenario 7-1: Need for SUS 240

    Case Scenario 7-2: Stage and Test Updates 240

CHAPTER 8:   **Configuring Routing by Using Routing
                 and Remote Access** **241**

Overview of Windows Server 2003 Routing and Remote Access . . .242

    Routing Examples 243

Configuration Options for Remote Access Servers 245

    Configuring Dial-Up Remote Access .245

    Troubleshooting Dial-Up Remote Access Connections 246

    Configuring VPNs 247

    Components of a VPN 248

    Configuring NAT 249

Selecting a Routing Protocol 251

    Using Static Routes 251

    Using Dynamic Routes 253

ABOUT THIS BOOK

Welcome to *Implementing, Managing, and Maintaining a Microsoft Windows Server 2003 Network Infrastructure (70-291)*, a part of the Microsoft Official Academic Course (MOAC) series. Through lectures, discussions, demonstrations, textbook exercises, and classroom labs, this course teaches students the skills and knowledge necessary to configure, manage, and troubleshoot a Windows Server 2003 network infrastructure. The nine chapters in this book walk you through key concepts of Windows Server 2003 network management such as Dynamic Host Configuration Protocol (DHCP), Domain Name System (DNS), Routing and Remote Access, and Software Update Services (SUS).

TARGET AUDIENCE

This textbook was developed for information technology professionals who plan to implement, administer, and support Windows Server 2003 networks, as well as individuals preparing to take the 70-291 exam.

PREREQUISITES

This textbook requires that students meet the following prerequisites:

- 12–18 months of hands-on experience supporting, administering, or implementing a Windows network.

- A strong familiarity with the networking concepts

THE TEXTBOOK

The textbook content has been crafted to provide a meaningful learning experience to students in an academic classroom setting.

Key features of the Microsoft Official Academic Course textbooks include the following:

- Learning objectives for each chapter that prepare the student for the topic areas covered in that chapter.

- Chapter introductions that explain why the content is important.

- An inviting design with screen shots, diagrams, tables, bulleted lists, and other graphical formats that makes the book easy to comprehend and supports a number of different learning styles.

- Clear explanations of concepts and principles, and frequent exposition of step-by-step procedures.

- A variety of readeraids that highlight a wealth of additional information, including:

  - ❏ Note – Real-world application tips and alternative procedures, and explanations of complex procedures and concepts

  - ❏ Important – Explanations of essential setup steps before a procedure and other instructions

  - ❏ More Info – Cross-references and additional resources for students

- Short, optional, hands-on exercises that break up lectures and provide a warm-up for more complex lab exercises.

- End-of-chapter review questions that assess knowledge and can serve as homework, quizzes, and review activities before or after lectures. (Answers to the textbook questions are available from your instructor.)

- Chapter summaries that distill the main ideas in a chapter and reinforce learning.

- Case scenarios, approximately two per chapter, provide students with an opportunity to evaluate, analyze, synthesize, and apply information learned during the chapter.

- Comprehensive glossary that defines key terms introduced in the book.

THE LAB MANUAL

The Lab Manual is designed for use in a combined lecture and lab situation, or in a separate lecture and lab arrangement. The exercises in the Lab Manual correspond to textbook chapters and are intended for use in a classroom setting under the supervision of an instructor.

The Lab Manual presents a rich, hands-on learning experience that encourages practical solutions and strengthens critical problem-solving skills:

- Lab Exercises teach procedures by using a step-by-step format. Questions interspersed throughout Lab Exercises encourage reflection and critical thinking about the lab activity.

- Lab Review Questions appear at the end of each lab and ask questions about the lab. They are designed to promote critical reflection. (Answers to all Lab Manual questions are available from your instructor.)

- Lab Challenges are review activities that ask students to perform a variation on a task they performed in the Lab Exercises, but without detailed instructions.

- A Troubleshooting Lab, which appears after a number of regular labs and consists of mid-length review projects based on true-to-life scenarios. This lab challenges students to "think like an expert" to solve complex problems.

- Labs are based on realistic business settings and include an opening scenario and a list of learning objectives.

Students who successfully complete the Lab Exercises, Lab Review Questions, Lab Challenges, and Troubleshooting Lab in the Lab Manual will have a richer learning experience and deeper understanding of the concepts and methods covered in the course. They will be better able to answer and understand the testbank questions, especially the knowledge application and knowledge synthesis questions. They will also be much better prepared to pass the associated certification exams if they choose to take the exam.

NOTATIONAL CONVENTIONS

The following conventions are used throughout this texbook and the Lab Manual:

- Characters or commands that you type appear in **bold** type.

- Terms that appear in the glossary also appear in **bold** type.

- Italic in syntax statements indicates placeholders for variable information. *Italic* is also used for book titles and terms defined in the text.

- Names of files and folders appear in Title caps, except when you are to type them directly. Unless otherwise indicated, you can use all lowercase letters when you type a filename in a dialog box or at a command prompt.

- Filename extensions appear in all lowercase.

- Acronyms appear in all uppercase.

- Monospace type represents code samples, examples of screen text, or entries that you might type at a command prompt or in initialization files.

- Square brackets [ ] are used in syntax statements to enclose optional items. For example, [*filename*] in command syntax indicates that you can type a filename with the command. Type only the information within the brackets, not the brackets themselves.

- Braces { } are used in syntax statements to enclose required items. Type only the information within the braces, not the braces themselves.

KEYBOARD CONVENTIONS

- A plus sign (+) between two key names means that you must press those keys at the same time. For example, "Press ALT+TAB" means that you hold down ALT while you press TAB.

- A comma (,) between two or more key names means that you must press the keys consecutively, not at the same time. For example, "Press ALT, F, X" means that you presss and release each key in sequence. "Press ALT+W, L" means that you first press ALT and W at the same time, and then you release them and press L.

COVERAGE OF EXAM OBJECTIVES

This title is intended to support your efforts to prepare for the 70-291 exam. The following table correlates the exam objectives with the textbook chapters and Lab Manual lab exercises.

NOTE The Microsoft Learning Web site describes the various MCP certification exams and their corresponding courses. It provides up-to-date certification information and explains the certification process and the course options. See http://www.microsoft.com/learning/mcpexams/default.asp for up-to-date information about MCP exam credentials about other certification programs offered by Microsoft.

Table 1-1   Textbook and Lab Manual Coverage of Exam Objectives

Objective	Textbook Chapter	Lab Manual Content
Implementing, Managing, and Maintaining IP Addressing		
Configure TCP/IP addressing on a server computer.	Chapter 1	Lab 1, Exercise 1-4
Manage DHCP.		
■ Manage DHCP clients and leases.	Chapter 1	Lab 1, Exercise 1-4
■ Manage DHCP Relay Agent.	Chapter 1	Lab 1, Exercise 1-7
■ Manage DHCP databases.	Chapter 2	Lab 2, Exercise 2-1, Lab 2, Exercise 2-2
■ Manage DHCP scope options.	Chapter 1	Lab 1, Exercise 1-6
■ Manage reservations and reserved clients.	Chapter 1	Lab 1, Exercise 1-5
Troubleshoot TCP/IP addressing.		
■ Diagnose and resolve issues related to Automatic Private IP Addressing (APIPA).	Chapter 1 and Chapter 2	Lab 1, Exercise 1-1
■ Diagnose and resolve issues related to incorrect TCP/IP configuration.	Chapter 2	Lab 2, Exercise 2-5

Table 1-1   **Textbook and Lab Manual Coverage of Exam Objectives**

Objective	Textbook Chapter	Lab Manual Content
Troubleshoot DHCP.		
■ Diagnose and resolve issues related to DHCP authorization.	Chapter 1	Lab 1, Exercise 1-3
■ Verify DHCP reservation configuration.	Chapter 1	Lab 1, Exercise 1-5
■ Examine the system event log and DHCP server audit log file to find related events.	Chapter 2	Lab 2, Exercise 2-3
■ Diagnose and resolve issues related to configuration of DHCP server and scope options.	Chapter 2	Lab 2, Exercise 2-5
■ Verify that the DHCP Relay Agent is working correctly.	Chapter 1	Lab 1, Exercise 1-7
■ Verify DHCP database integrity.	Chapter 1	Lab 1, Exercise 1-7
Implementing, Managing, and Maintaining Name Resolution		
Install and configure the DNS Server service.	Chapter 3	Lab 3, Exercise 3-1
■ Configure DNS server options.	Chapter 3	Lab 3, Exercise 3-1
■ Configure DNS zone options.	Chapter 3	Lab 3, Exercise 3-2
■ Configure DNS forwarding.	Chapter 3	Lab 3, Exercise 3-4
Manage DNS.		
■ Manage DNS zone settings.	Chapter 3	Lab 3, Exercise 3-2
■ Mange DNS record settings.	Chapter 3	Lab 3, Exercise 3-3
■ Manage DNS server options.	Chapter 4	Lab 4, Exercise 4-4
Monitor DNS. Tools might include System Monitor, Event Viewer, Replication Monitor, and DNS debug logs.	Chapter 4	Lab 4, Exercise 4-3
Implementing, Managing, and Maintaining Network Security		
Implement secure network administration procedures.		
■ Implement security baseline settings and audit security settings by using security templates.	Chapter 5	Lab 5, Exercise 5-2
■ Implement the principle of least privilege.	Chapter 5	
Monitor network protocol security. Tools might include the IP Security Monitor MMC snap-in and Kerberos support tools.	Chapter 6	Lab 6, Exercise 6-2

Table 1-1   Textbook and Lab Manual Coverage of Exam Objectives

Objective	Textbook Chapter	Lab Manual Content
Troubleshoot network protocol security. Tools might include the IP Security Monitor MMC snap-in, Event Viewer, and Network Monitor.	Chapter 6	Lab 6, Exercise 6-4
Implementing, Managing, and Maintaining Routing and Remote Access		
Configure Routing and Remote Access user authentication.	Chapter 8	Lab 8, Exercise 8-3
■ Configure remote access authentication protocols.	Chapter 8	Lab 8, Exercise 8-3
■ Configure Internet Authentication Service (IAS) to provide authentication for Routing and Remote Access clients.	Chapter 8	Lab 8, Exercise 8-3
■ Configure Routing and Remote Access policies to permit or deny access.	Chapter 8	Lab 8, Exercise 8-4
Manage remote access.		
■ Manage packet filters.	Chapter 8	Lab 8, Exercise 8-6
■ Manage Routing and Remote Access routing interfaces.	Chapter 8	Lab 8, Exercise 8-2
■ Manage devices and ports.	Chapter 8	Lab 8, Exercise 8-2
■ Manage routing protocols.	Chapter 8	Lab 8, Exercise 8-2
■ Manage Routing and Remote Access clients.	Chapter 8	Lab 8, Exercise 8-3, Lab 8, Exercise 8-4
Manage TCP/IP routing.		
■ Manage routing protocols.	Chapter 8	Lab 8, Exercise 8-2
■ Manage routing tables.	Chapter 8	Lab 8, Exercise 8-2
■ Manage routing ports.	Chapter 8	Lab 8, Exercise 8-2, Lab 8, Exercise 8-6
Implement secure access between private networks.	Chapter 8	Lab 8, Exercise 8-2
Troubleshoot user access to remote access services.		
■ Diagnose and resolve issues related to remote access VPNs.	Chapter 8	Lab 8, Exercise 8-3
■ Diagnose and resolve issues related to establishing a remote access connection.	Chapter 8	Lab 8, Exercise 8-3
■ Diagnose and resolve user access to resources beyond the remote access server.	Chapter 8	
Troubleshoot Routing and Remote Access routing.		
■ Troubleshoot demand-dial routing.	Chapter 8	
■ Troubleshoot router-to-router VPNs.	Chapter 8	

Table 1-1   Textbook and Lab Manual Coverage of Exam Objectives

Objective	Textbook Chapter	Lab Manual Content
Maintaining a Network Infrastructure		
Monitor network traffic. Tools might include Network Monitor and System Monitor.	Chapter 9	Lab 9, Exercise 9-3
Troubleshoot connectivity to the Internet.	Chapter 9	Lab 9, Exercise 9-4
Troubleshoot server services.		
■ Diagnose and resolve issues related to service dependency.	Chapter 9	Lab 9, Exercise 9-5
■ Use service recovery options to diagnose and resolve service-related issues.	Chapter 9	Lab 9, Exercise 9-5

THE MICROSOFT CERTIFIED PROFESSIONAL PROGRAM

The MCP program is the best way to prove your proficiency with current Microsoft products and technologies. The exams and corresponding certifications are developed to validate your mastery of critical competencies as you design and develop, or implement and support, solutions using Microsoft products and technologies. Computer professionals who become Microsoft certified are recognized as experts and are sought after industry-wide. Certification brings a variety of benefits to the individual and to employers and organizations.

> **MORE INFO**   For a full list of MCP benefits, go to http://www.microsoft.com/learning/mcp/mcp/benefits.asp.

Certifications

The MCP program offers multiple certifications, based on specific areas of technical expertise:

- **Microsoft Certified Professional (MCP)**   In-depth knowledge of at least one Windows operating system or architecturally significant platform. An MCP is qualified to implement a Microsoft product or technology as part of a business solution for an organization.

- **Microsoft Certified Systems Engineer (MCSE)**   Qualified to effectively analyze the business requirements for business solutions and design and implement the infrastructure based on the Windows and Windows Server 2003 operating systems.

- **Microsoft Certified Systems Administrator (MCSA)**   Qualified to manage and troubleshoot existing network and system environments based on the Windows and Windows Server 2003 operating systems.

- **Microsoft Certified Database Administrator (MCDBA)**   Qualified to design, implement, and administer Microsoft SQL Server databases.

MCP Requirements

Requirements differ for each certification and are specific to the products and job functions addressed by the certification. To become an MCP, you must pass rigorous certification exams that provide a valid and reliable measure of technical proficiency and expertise. These exams are designed to test your expertise and ability to perform a role or task with a product, and are developed with the input of industry professionals. Exam questions reflect how Microsoft products are used in actual organizations, giving them "real-world" relevance.

- Microsoft Certified Professional (MCP) candidates are required to pass one current Microsoft certification exam. Candidates can pass additional Microsoft certification exams to validate their skills with other Microsoft products, development tools, or desktop applications.

- Microsoft Certified Systems Engineer (MCSE) candidates are required to pass five core exams and two elective exams.

- Microsoft Certified Systems Administrator (MCSA) candidates are required to pass three core exams and one elective exam.

- Microsoft Certified Database Administrator (MCDBA) candidates are required to pass three core exams and one elective exam.

ABOUT THE AUTHORS

The textbook, Lab Manual, pretest, testbank, and PowerPoint slides were written by instructors and developed exclusively for an instructor-led classroom environment.

Greg Bott is the author of the textbook. He is a husband, father, writer, golden retriever owner, and consultant. He resides in Dallas, Texas, where he has owned and operated his own consulting firm for six years. Greg's professional computer experience comes from working as a consultant for Price Waterhouse, as a program manager at Microsoft Corporation, and solving problems for a diverse client base. He is a Software Engineering Master's degree candidate at the University of Texas and has presented at technical conferences such as Fusion, Tech Ed Dallas, and Tech Ed Amsterdam. He has addressed audiences across the United States, South Korea, China, and Singapore. He has written several Microsoft Official Curriculum courses and contributed to the *Microsoft Windows 2000 Server Security Operations Guide* and co-authored the *Microsoft ASP.Net Security Operations Guide*.

Michael Hall is the co-author of the Lab Manual and the author of the testbank, pretest, and slides. He is the Director of Technical Training and a network administrator for the Georgia Department of Technical and Adult Education. He resides in Powder Springs, Georgia, with his wife and three daughters. In addition to his duties with the Georgia Department of Technical and Adult Education, he operates a technical consulting business that focuses on network design and implementation as well as courseware development and training. He has a Master's degree from Kennesaw State University and maintains several technical certifications from both Microsoft and Cisco Systems.

Tony Smith is the co-author of the Lab Manual and is a collaborating writer and technical editor of several technical manuals, books, and publications. He resides in Story, Wyoming, with his wife and three children. He is the owner of a technical consulting firm and for the past 10 years he has focused his efforts on assisting community colleges, universities, and state education programs in technical program development and the instruction of technology courses. He maintains several technical certifications from vendors including Microsoft, Novell, and Cisco. He has two master's degrees: one in Educational Program Curriculum and Development and the second in Science and Technology Programs Development. He is actively involved in technical consulting with corporations including Self-Test Software, MeasureUp, and Microsoft as a technical contributor and writer.

EVALUATION EDITION SOFTWARE SUPPORT

The 180-day evaluation edition of Windows Server 2003, Enterprise Edition provided with this textbook is not the full retail product and is provided only for training and evaluation purposes. Microsoft and Microsoft Technical Support do not support this evaluation edition. It differs from the retail version only in that Microsoft and Microsoft Technical Support do not support it, and it expires after 180 days.

For online support information relating to the full version of Windows Server 2003 Enterprise Edition that might also apply to the evaluation edition, go to *http://support.microsoft.com*. For information about ordering the full version of any Microsoft software, call Microsoft Sales at (800) 426-9400 or visit *http://www .microsoft.com*.

> **CAUTION**   The evaluation edition of Windows Server 2003, Enterprise Edition should not be used on a primary work computer.

CHAPTER 1
IMPLEMENTING DHCP

Upon completion of this chapter, you will be able to:

- Describe the purpose of the **Dynamic Host Configuration Protocol (DHCP)** and how it streamlines network administration.

- Explain the **Internet Protocol (IP)** address **DHCP lease** process.

- Authorize a **DHCP server** and explain how unauthorized DHCP servers are prevented from distributing incorrect addresses to **DHCP clients**.

- Explain the purpose of **multicasting**.

- Configure a DHCP server by defining a **scope** and a **superscope**, creating **DHCP client reservations**, and configuring **DHCP options**.

- Explain the purpose of, and configure, a **DHCP relay agent**.

Transmission Control Protocol/Internet Protocol (TCP/IP) hosts must be correctly configured to communicate with other TCP/IP hosts on a network. Each host must have an Internet Protocol (IP) address and a **subnet mask**, and if communicating outside the local subnet, each must also have a **default gateway**. Each IP address must be valid and unique within the host's **internetwork**. This requirement presents a challenge for network administrators. To ensure that each host has a unique IP address, the process of assigning, changing, and reassigning addresses must be carefully monitored. If it is done manually, accurate and timely records must be kept of each host that note where the host is located and what IP address and subnet mask have been assigned to it. This quickly becomes a daunting, tedious task. Organizations with large numbers of workstations requiring IP addresses would have great difficulty managing IP addressing manually. Dynamic Host Configuration Protocol (DHCP) simplifies the problem by automating the assigning, tracking, and reassigning of IP addresses.

BRIEF HISTORY OF DHCP

Since the advent of TCP/IP, several solutions have been developed to address the challenge of configuring TCP/IP settings for organizations with a large number of workstations. **Reverse Address Resolution Protocol (RARP)** was designed for diskless workstations that had no means of permanently storing their TCP/IP settings. RARP, as its name suggests, is essentially the opposite of **Address Resolution Protocol (ARP)**. ARP clients broadcast an IP address to discover the corresponding **Media Access Control (MAC) address** (an address unique to a piece of hardware). RARP clients broadcast the MAC address (as shown in Figure 1-1). (*Broadcasting* is a communication method for sending information to all components on a network of computers simultaneously.) A RARP server then responds by transmitting the IP address assigned to the client computer.

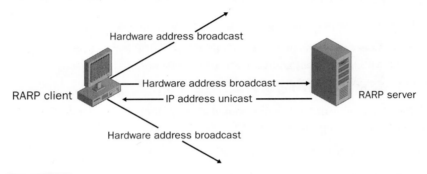

Figure 1-1   A workstation that uses RARP receives an IP address from a RARP server in response to a broadcast message containing the client's hardware address.

Because RARP failed to provide other much-needed settings to the client, such as a subnet mask and a default gateway, it gave way to another solution, the **Bootstrap Protocol (BOOTP)**.

BOOTP, which is still in use today, enables a TCP/IP workstation to retrieve settings for all the configuration parameters it needs to run, including an IP address, a subnet mask, a default gateway, and **Domain Name System (DNS)** server addresses. Using Trivial File Transfer Protocol (TFTP), a workstation also can download an executable boot file from a BOOTP server. The major drawback of BOOTP is that an administrator still must specify settings for each workstation on the BOOTP server. A better way to administer TCP/IP would be to automatically assign unique IP addresses while preventing duplicate address assignment and while providing other important settings such as the default gateway, subnet mask, DNS, **Windows Internet Naming Service (WINS)** server, and so on. Ideally, this would be accomplished without having to manually list every device on the network. Enter DHCP.

DHCP is based heavily on BOOTP, but rather than push preconfigured parameters to expected clients, DHCP can dynamically allocate an IP address from a pool of addresses and then reclaim it when it is no longer needed. Because this process is dynamic, no duplicate addresses are assigned by a properly configured DHCP server and administrators can move computers between subnets without manually configuring them. In addition, a large number of standard configuration and platform-specific parameters can be specified and dynamically delivered to the client.

WHAT IS DHCP?

DHCP is an open, industry-standard protocol that reduces the complexity of administering networks based on TCP/IP. It is defined by the **Internet Engineering Task Force (IETF)** Requests for Comments (RFCs) 2131 and 2132.

> **MORE INFO** **RFCs 2131 and 2132** RFCs 2131 and 2132 DHCP is an IETF standard based on the BOOTP protocol and is defined in RFCs 2131 and 2132, which can be looked up at http://www.rfc-editor.org/rfcsearch.html.

IP addressing is complex, in part because each *host* (a computer, printer, or other device with a network interface) connected to a TCP/IP network must be assigned at least one unique IP address and subnet mask in order to communicate on the network. Additionally, most hosts will require additional information, such as the IP addresses of the default gateway and the DNS servers. DHCP frees system administrators from manually configuring each host on the network. The larger the network, the greater the benefit of using DHCP. Without dynamic address assignment, each host has to be configured manually and IP addresses must be carefully managed to avoid duplication or misconfiguration.

Managing IP addresses and host options is much easier when configuration information can be managed from a single location rather than coordinating information across many locations. DHCP can automatically configure a host while it is booting on a TCP/IP network, as well as change settings while the host is connected to the network. All of this is accomplished using settings and information from a central DHCP database. Because settings and information are stored centrally, you can quickly and easily add or change a client setting (for example, the IP address of an alternate DNS server) for all clients on your network from a single location. Without a centralized database of configuration information, it is difficult to maintain a current view of the host settings or to change them.

All Microsoft Windows Server 2003 products (the Standard Edition, Enterprise Edition, Web Edition, and Datacenter Edition) include the DHCP Server service, which is an optional installation. All Microsoft Windows clients automatically install the DHCP Client service as part of TCP/IP, including Windows Server 2003, Microsoft Windows XP, Microsoft Windows 2000, Microsoft Windows NT 4, Microsoft Windows Millennium Edition (Windows Me), and Microsoft Windows 98.

In brief, DHCP provides four key benefits to those managing and maintaining a TCP/IP network:

- **Centralized administration of IP configuration** DHCP IP configuration information can be stored in one location and enables the administrator to centrally manage all IP configuration information. A DHCP server tracks all leased and reserved IP addresses and lists them in the DHCP console. You can use the DHCP console to determine the IP addresses of all DHCP-enabled devices on your network. Without DHCP, not only would you have to manually assign addresses, you would also have to devise a method of tracking and updating them.

- **Dynamic host configuration** DHCP automates the host configuration process for key configuration parameters. This eliminates the need to manually configure individual hosts when TCP/IP is first deployed or when IP infrastructure changes are required.

- **Seamless IP host configuration**   The use of DHCP ensures that DHCP clients get accurate and timely IP configuration parameters, such as the IP address, subnet mask, default gateway, IP address of the DNS server, and so on, without user intervention. Because the configuration is automatic, troubleshooting of misconfigurations, such as mistyped numbers, is largely eliminated.

- **Flexibility**   Using DHCP gives the administrator increased flexibility, allowing the administrator to more easily change IP configurations when the infrastructure changes.

- **Scalability**   DHCP scales from small to large networks. DHCP can service networks with 10 clients as well as networks with thousands of clients. For very small, isolated networks, **Automatic Private IP Addressing (APIPA)** can be used. (APIPA is discussed later in this chapter.)

HOW DHCP WORKS

The core function of DHCP is to assign addresses. As discussed previously, the key aspect of this process is that it is dynamic. What this means to the network administrator is that the network can be configured to allocate an IP address to any device that is connected anywhere on the network. This allocation of addresses is achieved by sending application layer messages to, and DHCP server and receiving application layer messages from, a DHCP server. All DHCP messages are carried in **User Datagram Protocol (UDP)** datagrams using the well-known port numbers 67 (at the server) and 68 (at the client).

> **MORE INFO**   **The Application Layer**   *The application layer is part of the Open Systems Interconnection (OSI) reference model defined by the International Organization for Standardization (ISO) and the Telecommunication Standards Section of the International Telecommunications Union (ITU-T). The model is used for reference and teaching purposes. It divides computer networking functions into seven layers. From top to bottom, the seven layers are application, presentation, session, transport, network, data-link, and physical. For more information about the OSI reference model, see the Network+ Certification Training Kit, Second Edition (Microsoft Press, 2001).*

Before learning how address allocation works, you should understand some terminology: DHCP clients, servers, and leases. These terms are defined in the following sections.

DHCP Clients and Servers

A computer that obtains its configuration information from DHCP is known as a *DHCP client*. DHCP clients communicate with a DHCP server to obtain IP addresses and related TCP/IP configuration information. The IP addresses and configuration information that the DHCP server makes available to the client are defined by the DHCP administrator.

DHCP Leases

A *DHCP lease* defines the duration for which a DHCP server loans an IP address to a DHCP client. The lease duration can be any amount of time between 1 minute and 999 days, or it can be unlimited. The default lease duration is eight days.

DHCP Message Types

The application layer messages in DHCP server/client communication must be one of the following eight types:

- **DHCPDISCOVER**   Sent by clients via broadcast to locate a DHCP server. Per RFC 2131, the DHCPDISCOVER message may include options that suggest values for the network address and lease duration.

- **DHCPOFFER**   Sent by one or more DHCP servers to a DHCP client in response to DHCPDISCOVER, along with offered configuration parameters.

- **DHCPREQUEST**   Sent by the DHCP client to signal its acceptance of the offered address and parameters. The client generates a DHCP-REQUEST message containing the address of the server from which it is accepting the offer along with the offered IP address. Because the client has not yet configured itself with the offered parameters, it transmits the DHCPREQUEST message as a broadcast. This broadcast notifies the server that the client is accepting the offered address and also notifies the other servers on the network that the client is rejecting their offers.

- **DHCPDECLINE**   Sent by a DHCP client to a DHCP server, informing the server that the offered IP address has been declined. The DHCP client will send a DHCPDECLINE message if it determines that the offered address is already in use. After sending a DHCPDECLINE, the client must begin the lease or renewal process again.

- **DHCPACK**   Sent by a DHCP server to a DHCP client to confirm an IP address and to provide the client with those configuration parameters that the client has requested and the server is configured to provide.

- **DHCPNACK**   Sent by a DHCP server to a DHCP client to deny the client's DHCPREQUEST. This might occur if the requested address is incorrect because the client was moved to a new subnet or because the DHCP client's lease expired and cannot be renewed. After receiving a DHCPNACK message, the client must begin the lease or renewal process again.

- **DHCPRELEASE**   Sent by a DHCP client to a DHCP server to relinquish an IP address and cancel the remaining lease. This message type is sent to the server that provided the lease.

- **DHCPINFORM**   Sent from a DHCP client to a DHCP server to ask only for additional local configuration parameters; the client already has a configured IP address. This message type is also used to detect unauthorized DHCP servers.

How Clients Obtain an Initial Lease

A DHCP client performs the initial lease process in the following situations:

- The very first time the client boots

- After releasing its IP address

- After receiving a DHCPNACK message, in response to the DHCP client attempting to renew a previously leased address

If successful, the initial lease process is accomplished using a series of exchanges between a DHCP client and DHCP server that utilize four messages: DHCP-DISCOVER, DHCPOFFER, DHCPREQUEST, and DHCPACK. This message exchange process is illustrated in Figure 1-2.

Figure 1-2   Messages exchanged with a DHCP server to obtain a lease

Locating a Server

The client broadcasts a DHCPDISCOVER message to find a DHCP server. Because the client does not already have an IP address or know the IP address of the DHCP server, the DHCPDISCOVER message is sent as a local area broadcast, with 0.0.0.0 as the source address and 255.255.255.255 as the destination address. The DHCP-DISCOVER message is a request for the location of a DHCP server and IP addressing information. The request contains the client's MAC address and computer name so that the DHCP servers know which client sent the request.

Receiving Address Offers

All DHCP servers that receive the DHCPDISCOVER message, and have a valid configuration for the client, broadcast a DHCPOFFER message with the following information:

- Source (DHCP server) IP address

- Destination (DHCP client) IP address

- An offered IP address

- Client hardware address

- Subnet mask

- Length of lease

- A server identifier (the IP address of the offering DHCP server)

As depicted in Figure 1-3, the DHCPDISCOVER and DHCPOFFER messages are broadcast.

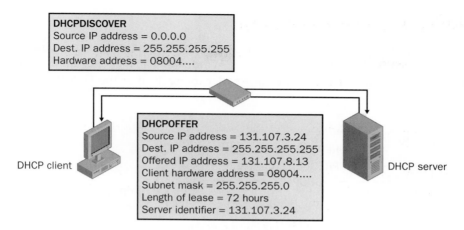

Figure 1-3 DHCPDISCOVER and DHCPOFFER messages are broadcast.

After broadcasting its DHCPDISCOVER message, the DHCP client waits 1 second for an offer. If an offer is not received, the client will not be able to initialize, and the client will rebroadcast the request three times (at 9-, 13-, and 16-second intervals, plus a random offset between 0 milliseconds and 1 second). If an offer is not received after four tries, the client continuously retries in five-minute intervals. If DHCP fails, Windows XP, Windows Server 2003, Windows 98, Windows Me, and Windows 2000 clients can use APIPA to obtain a dynamically assigned IP address and subnet mask. Windows XP and Windows Server 2003 can also use an alternate configuration, which dynamically assigns predefined settings if a DHCP server cannot be located. APIPA and alternate configurations are described in the "Automatic Client Configuration" section later in this chapter.

Responding to Address Offers

After the client receives an offer from at least one DHCP server, it broadcasts a DHCPREQUEST message to all DHCP servers. The broadcast DHCPREQUEST message contains the following information:

- The IP address of the DHCP server chosen by the client

- The requested IP address for the client

- A list of requested parameters (subnet mask, router, DNS server list, domain name, vendor-specific information, WINS server list, NetBIOS node type, NetBIOS scope)

When DHCP servers whose offers were not accepted receive the DHCPREQUEST message, they retract their offers.

Receiving Acknowledgement

The DHCP server with the accepted offer sends a successful acknowledgement to the client in the form of a DHCPACK message. This message contains a valid lease for an IP address, including the renewal times (T1 and T2, which are discussed in the following section, "How DHCP Renews a Lease") and the duration of the lease (in seconds).

How DHCP Renews a Lease

Because the IP lease has a finite lifetime, the client must periodically renew the lease after obtaining it. As Figure 1-4 illustrates, Windows DHCP clients attempt to renew the lease either at each reboot or at regular intervals after the DHCP client has initialized.

DHCP client — DHCPREQUEST (Broadcast) → — DHCPREQUEST (Unicast) → ← DHCPACK — DHCP server

Figure 1-4   DHCP messages exchanged during lease renewal

As Figure 1-4 shows, a lease renewal involves just two DHCP messages—DHCP-REQUEST (either broadcast or unicast) and DHCPACK. If a Windows DHCP client renews a lease while booting, these messages are sent through broadcast IP packets. If the lease renewal is made while a Windows DHCP client is running, the DHCP client and the DHCP server communicate using unicast messages. (In contrast with broadcast messages, *unicast messages* are point-to-point messages between two hosts.)

When a client obtains a lease, DHCP provides values for the configuration options that were requested by the DHCP client and are configured on the DHCP server. By reducing the lease time, the DHCP administrator can force clients to regularly renew leases and obtain updated configuration details. This can be useful when the administrator wants to change the scope's configuration or wants to keep more addresses available to DHCP clients by reclaiming them more quickly. A *DHCP scope* is a range of IP addresses that are available to be leased or assigned to DHCP clients by the DHCP service. A scope may also include one or more options. An *option* is a specific configuration item, such as a subnet mask or a default gateway IP address, that the DHCP administrator wants the DHCP server to provide to the DHCP client.

> **NOTE**   **When to Increase or Decrease DHCP Lease Times**   If your TCP/IP network configuration doesn't change often or if you have more than enough IP addresses in your assigned IP **address pool**, you can increase the DHCP lease considerably beyond its default value of eight days. However, if your network configuration changes frequently or if you have a limited pool of IP addresses that is almost used up, keep the reservation period short—perhaps one day. The reason is that if the pool of available IP addresses is used up, machines that are added or moved might be unable to obtain an IP address from a DHCP server and thus would be unable to participate in network communication.

A DHCP client first attempts to reacquire its lease at half the lease time, which is known as *T1*. The DHCP client obtains the value of T1 from the DHCPACK message that confirmed the IP lease. If the lease reacquisition fails at T1, the DHCP client attempts a further lease renewal at 87.5 percent of the lease time, which is known as *T2*. Like T1, T2 is specified in the DHCPACK message. If the lease is not reacquired before it expires (if, for example, the DHCP server is unreachable for an extended period of time), as soon as the lease expires, the client immediately releases the IP address and attempts to acquire a new lease.

Changing Subnets and DHCP Servers

If the DHCP client requests a lease through a DHCPREQUEST message that the DHCP server cannot fulfill (for example, when a portable computer is moved to a different subnet), the DHCP server sends a DHCPNACK message to the client. This informs the client that the requested IP lease will not be renewed. The client then begins the acquisition process again by broadcasting a DHCPDISCOVER message. Figure 1-5 illustrates the sequence of DHCP messages that occurs when a client boots in a new subnet.

Figure 1-5   DHCP messages exchanged when a DHCP client boots in a new subnet

When a Windows DHCP client boots in a new subnet, it broadcasts a DHCPREQUEST message to renew its lease. The DHCP renewal request is broadcast on the subnet so all DHCP servers that provide DHCP addresses will receive the request. This DHCP server responding on the new subnet is different from the server that provided the initial lease. When the DHCP server receives the broadcast, it compares the address the DHCP client is requesting with the scopes configured on the server and the subnet. If it is not possible to satisfy the client request, the DHCP server issues a DHCPNACK message, and the DHCP client then begins the lease acquisition process again.

If the DHCP client is unable to locate any DHCP server when rebooting, it issues an ARP broadcast for the default gateway that was previously obtained, if one was provided. If the IP address of the gateway is successfully resolved, the DHCP client assumes that it remains located on the same network from which it obtained its current lease and continues to use its lease. Otherwise, if the IP address of the gateway is not resolved, the client assumes that it has been moved to a network that has no DHCP services currently available (such as a home network), and it configures itself using either APIPA or an alternate configuration. Once it configures itself, the DHCP client tries to locate a DHCP server every 5 minutes in an attempt to renew its lease.

Using the DHCP Relay Agent

DHCP relies heavily on broadcast messages. Broadcast messages are generally limited to the subnet in which they originate and are not forwarded to other subnets. This poses a problem if a client is located on a different subnet from the DHCP server. A DHCP relay agent is either a host or an IP router that listens for DHCP (and BOOTP) client messages being broadcast on a subnet and then forwards those DHCP messages to a DHCP server. The DHCP server sends DHCP response messages back to the relay agent, which then broadcasts them onto the subnet for the DHCP client. Using DHCP relay agents eliminates the need to have a DHCP server on every subnet.

To support and use the DHCP service across multiple subnets, routers connecting each subnet should comply with the DHCP/BOOTP relay agent capabilities described in RFC 1542. To comply with RFC 1542 and provide relay agent support, each router must be able to recognize BOOTP and DHCP protocol messages and relay them appropriately. Because routers typically interpret DHCP messages as BOOTP messages, a router with only BOOTP relay agent capability relays DHCP packets and any BOOTP packets sent on the network.

The DHCP relay agent is configured with the address of a DHCP server. The DHCP relay agent listens for DHCPDISCOVER, DHCPREQUEST, and DHCPINFORM messages that are broadcast from the client. The DHCP relay agent then waits a previously configured amount of time and, if no response is detected, sends a unicast message to the configured DHCP server. The server then acts on the message and sends the reply back to the DHCP relay agent. The relay agent then broadcasts the message on the local subnet, allowing the DHCP client to receive it. This is depicted in Figure 1-6.

1. Client1 broadcasts a DHCPDISCOVER packet
2. Relay agent forwards DHCPDISCOVER packet to DHCP server
3. Server sends a DHCPOFFER packet to the DHCP relay agent
4. Relay agent broadcasts the DHCPOFFER packet
5. Client1 broadcasts a DHCPREQUEST packet
6. Relay agent forwards the DHCPREQUEST packet to the DHCP server
7. Server broadcasts a DHCPACK packet which is picked up by DHCP relay agent
8. Relay agent broadcasts the DHCPACK packet

Figure 1-6   DHCP messages are forwarded by a DHCP relay agent

Automatic Client Configuration

In most cases, DHCP clients find a server either on a local subnet or through a relay agent. To allow for the possibility that a DHCP server is unavailable, Windows Server 2003, Windows XP, Windows 2000, and Windows 98 provide APIPA. APIPA is a facility of the Windows TCP/IP implementation that allows a computer to determine IP configuration information without a DHCP server or manual configuration.

APIPA avoids the problem of IP hosts being unable to communicate if for some reason the DHCP server is unavailable. Figure 1-7 illustrates different IP address assignment outcomes when a DHCP client attempts to find a DHCP server. In the case where a DHCP server is not found and APIPA is configured and enabled, an APIPA address is assigned. APIPA is useful for small workgroup networks where no DHCP server is implemented. Because autoconfiguration does not support a default gateway, it works only with a single subnet and is not appropriate for larger networks.

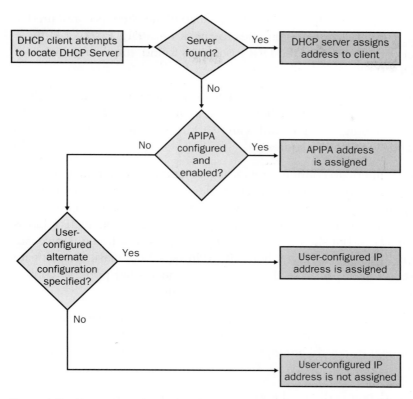

Figure 1-7   How IP addresses are assigned using APIPA or an alternate configuration

If the DHCP client is unable to locate a DHCP server and is not configured with an alternate configuration (as shown in Figure 1-8), the computer configures itself with an IP address randomly chosen from the Internet Assigned Numbers Authority (IANA)–reserved class B network 169.254.0.0 and with the subnet mask 255.255.0.0. The autoconfigured computer then tests to verify that the IP address it has chosen is not already in use by using a gratuitous ARP broadcast. If the chosen IP address is in use, the computer randomly selects another address. The computer makes up to 10 attempts to find an available IP address.

Figure 1-8   Alternate Configuration properties page

Once the selected address has been verified as available, the client is configured to use that address. The DHCP client continues to check for a DHCP server in the background every 5 minutes, and if a DHCP server is found, the configuration offered by the DHCP server is used.

Windows XP and Windows Server 2003 clients can be configured to use an alternate configuration, which the DHCP client uses if a DHCP server cannot be contacted. The alternate configuration includes an IP address, a subnet mask, a default gateway, DNS, and WINS server addresses.

One purpose of the alternate configuration is as a solution for portable computers that move between a corporate, DHCP-enabled network and a home network where static IP addressing is used. For example, Janice has a portable computer she uses at work and at home. At work, her portable computer obtains IP address information using DHCP, but she does not use a DHCP server at home. Janice can use alternate configuration to hold her home IP address, subnet mask, default gateway, and DNS server information so that when she connects her portable computer to her home network, it is configured automatically.

If you use DHCP with an alternate configuration, and the DHCP client cannot locate a DHCP server, the alternate configuration is used to configure the network adapter. No additional discovery attempts are made except under the following conditions:

- The network adapter is disabled and then enabled again
- Media (such as network cabling) is disconnected and then reconnected
- The TCP/IP settings for the adapter are changed, and DHCP remains enabled after these changes

If a DHCP server is found, the network adapter is assigned a valid DHCP IP address lease.

▶ **Displaying the Alternate Configuration Tab**

To display the Alternate Configuration tab shown in Figure 1-9, the network adapter must be configured to obtain an IP address automatically. To view the Alternate Configuration tab, follow these steps:

1. Open the Control Panel, and double-click Network Connections.

2. In the Network Connections window, right-click Local Area Connection, and then click Properties.

3. In the Local Area Connection Properties page, click Internet Protocol (TCP/IP), and then click Properties.

4. In the Alternate Configuration tab, specify your IP address settings.

Figure 1-9 The Alternate Configuration tab of the Internet Protocol (TCP/IP) properties page

AUTHORIZING A DHCP SERVER

In implementations of DHCP prior to Windows 2000, any user could create a DHCP server on the network, an action that could lead to conflicts in IP address assignments. For example, if a client obtains a lease from an incorrectly configured DHCP server, the client might receive an invalid IP address, which prevents it from communicating on the network. This can prevent users from logging on. In Windows Server 2000 and Windows Server 2003, an *unauthorized DHCP* server (also referred to as a *rogue* DHCP server) is simply a DHCP server that has not been explicitly listed in the **Active Directory** directory service as an authorized server. You must authorize a DHCP server in Active Directory before the server can issue leases to DHCP clients.

DHCP Server Authorization Process

At the time of initialization, the DHCP server contacts Active Directory to determine whether it is on the list of servers that are currently authorized to operate on the network. One of the following actions then occurs:

- If the DHCP server is authorized, the DHCP Server service starts.

- If the DHCP server is not authorized, the DHCP Server service logs an error in the system event log, does not start, and, of course, will not respond to client requests.

Let's examine two scenarios. In the first scenario, the DHCP server is part of a domain and is authorized. In the second scenario, the DHCP server is not in a domain and, consequently, not authorized. These scenarios are roughly represented by the right and left sides of Figure 1-10, respectively.

In the first scenario, the DHCP server initializes and determines if it is part of the directory domain. Since it is, it contacts the directory service to verify that it is authorized. The directory service confirms the server is authorized. After receiving this confirmation, the server broadcasts a DHCPINFORM message to determine if other directory services are available and repeats the authorization process with each directory service that responds. After this is completed, the server begins servicing DHCP clients accordingly.

In the second scenario, the server is *not* a part of a domain. When the server initializes, it checks for DHCP member servers. If no DHCP member servers are located, the server begins servicing DHCP clients and continues to check for member servers by sending a DHCPINFORM message every 5 minutes. If a DHCP member server is located, the server shuts down its DHCP service and, of course, stops servicing DHCP clients.

Active Directory must be present to authorize DHCP servers and block unauthorized servers. If you install a DHCP server on a network without Active Directory, no authorization will take place. If you subsequently add Active Directory, the DHCP server will sense the presence of Active Directory; however, if it has not been authorized, the server will shut itself down. DHCP servers are not authorized by default; they must be explicitly authorized.

Protecting Against Improper Use of Workgroup DHCP Servers

When a DHCP server that is not a member server of the domain (such as a member of a workgroup) initializes, the following happens:

- The server broadcasts a DHCPINFORM message on the network.

- Any other server that receives this message responds with a DHCPACK message and provides the name of the directory domain it is part of.

- If a workgroup DHCP server detects another member DHCP server of a domain on the network, the workgroup DHCP server assumes itself to be unauthorized on that network and shuts itself down.

- If the workgroup DHCP server detects the presence of another workgroup server, it ignores it; this means multiple workgroup servers can be active at the same time as long as there is no directory service.

Even when a workgroup server initializes and becomes authorized (because no other domain member server or workgroup server is on the network), it continues to broadcast DHCPINFORM every 5 minutes. If an authorized domain member DHCP server initializes later, the workgroup server becomes unauthorized and stops servicing.

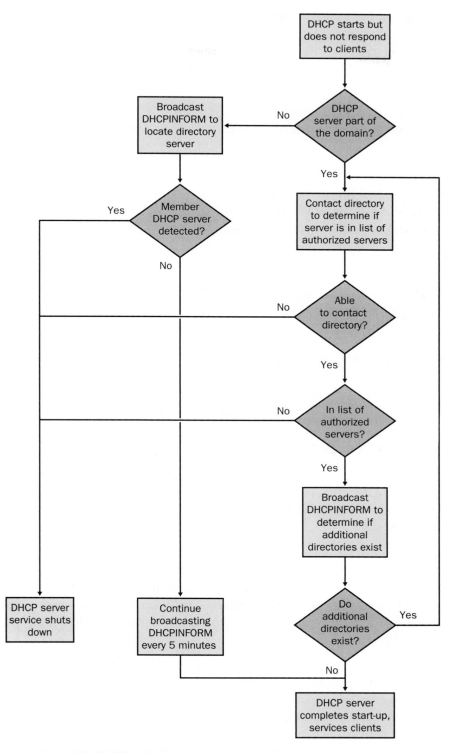

Figure 1-10   The DHCP initialization and authorization process

▶ **Authorizing the DHCP Server Service**

To authorize a DHCP server in Active Directory, perform the following steps:

1. Open the DHCP console from the Administrative Tools menu.

2. In the console tree, right-click DHCP, and then click Manage Authorized Servers.

3. In the Manage Authorized Servers dialog box, select Authorize.

4. In the Authorize DHCP Server dialog box, type the name or IP address of the DHCP server to be authorized, and then click OK.

5. The computer will list the IP and full computer name and then ask for confirmation. Click OK to continue.

   When authorization is complete, the arrow on the server icon in the DHCP console changes from red to green. You may need to refresh the console.

Practice authorizing a DHCP server by doing Exercise 1-1, "Installing and Authorizing a DHCP Server," now.

NOTE Who Can Authorize DHCP Servers   To authorize a DHCP server, a user must be a member of the Enterprise Admins group, which exists in the root domain of the forest.

CONFIGURING A DHCP SCOPE

Scopes determine which IP addresses are allocated to clients. You can configure as many scopes on a DHCP server as needed for your network environment.

What Is a DHCP Scope?

A DHCP scope, as mentioned previously, is a set of IP addresses and associated configuration information that can be supplied to a DHCP client. A scope must be defined and activated before DHCP clients can use the DHCP server for dynamic TCP/IP configuration.

A DHCP administrator can create one or more scopes on one or more Windows Server 2003 servers running the DHCP Server service. However, because DHCP servers do not communicate scope information with each other, the administrator must be careful to define scopes so that multiple DHCP servers are not assigning the same IP address to multiple clients or assigning addresses that are statically assigned to existing IP hosts.

The IP addresses defined in a DHCP scope must be contiguous and are associated with a subnet mask. If the addresses you want to assign are not contiguous, you must create a scope encompassing all the addresses you want to assign and then exclude specific addresses or address ranges from the scope. You can create only one scope per subnet on a single DHCP server. To allow for the possibility that some IP addresses in the scope might have been already assigned and are in use, the DHCP administrator can specify an *exclusion*—one or more IP addresses in the scope that are not handed out to DHCP clients.

Address Pools

Once a DHCP scope is defined and exclusion ranges are applied, the remaining addresses form what is called an *available address pool* within the scope. Pooled addresses can then be dynamically assigned to DHCP clients on the network.

Exclusion Ranges

An *exclusion range* is a limited sequence of IP addresses within a scope range that are to be excluded from DHCP service offerings. Where exclusion ranges are used, they ensure that any addresses within the defined exclusion range are not offered to clients of the DHCP server. You should exclude all statically configured IP addresses in the range.

▶ Configuring a DHCP Scope

To configure a DHCP scope, follow these steps:

1. Open the DHCP console from the Administrative Tools menu.

2. In the console tree, left-click, then right-click the DHCP server on which you want to create the new DHCP scope, and then click New Scope.

3. In the New Scope Wizard, click Next, type a name and description for the scope, and then click Next. You can use any name that you want, but it should be descriptive enough so that you can identify the purpose of the scope on your network. (For example, you could use a name such as "Administration Building Client Addresses.")

4. On the IP Address Range page, type the range of addresses that can be leased as part of this scope. (For example, use a range of IP addresses from a starting IP address of 10.1.1.50 to an ending address of 10.1.1.150.) Because these addresses are given to clients, they must all be valid addresses for your network and not currently in use. The default subnet mask that corresponds to your IP address range is provided. If you want to use a different subnet mask, type the new subnet mask, and then click Next.

5. On the Add Exclusions page, in the Start box, type the beginning of the IP address range you want to exclude, and in the End box, type the end of the IP address range you want to exclude. To exclude a single IP address, in the Start box, type the IP address.

6. Click Add and repeat step 5 until you have specified all the IP addresses to exclude. You should exclude any addresses statically assigned. Click Next.

7. On the Lease Duration page, type the number of days, hours, and minutes before an IP address lease from this scope expires. As discussed earlier, this determines how long a client can hold a leased address without renewing it. The default lease duration is eight days. Click Next.

8. On the Configure DHCP Options page, click Yes, I Want To Configure These Options Now to use the wizard to configure the most common DHCP options, such as the IP address of default gateways, DNS servers, and WINS settings. Click Next.

9. On the Router (Default Gateway) page, type the IP address for the default gateway that should be used by clients that obtain an IP address from this scope. Click Add to place the default gateway address in the list, and then click Next.

10. On the Domain Name And DNS Servers page, if you are using DNS servers on your network, type your organization's domain name in the Parent domain box.

11. On the Domain Name And DNS Servers page, type the name of your DNS server, and then click Resolve to ensure that your DHCP server can contact the DNS server and determine its address.

12. On the Domain Name And DNS Servers page, click Add to include the server in the list of DNS servers that are assigned to the DHCP clients. Click Next.

13. On the WINS Servers page, type the IP address of the WINS server(s) on your network and click Add. If you do not know the IP address, in the Server name box, type the name of the WINS server and click Resolve. After adding the WINS servers, click Next.

Practice configuring a DHCP scope by doing Exercise 1-2, "Configuring a DHCP Scope," now.

14. On the Activate Scope page, click Yes, I Want To Activate This Scope Now to activate the scope and allow clients to obtain leases from it, and then click Next.

15. On the Completing The New Scope Wizard page, click Finish.

Multicast Addressing

The Microsoft DHCP server has been extended to allow the assignment of multicast addresses, in addition to unicast addresses. A proposed IETF standard defines multicast address allocation. The proposed standard benefits network administrators by allowing multicast addresses to be assigned in the same fashion as unicast addresses, enabling complete utilization of the existing infrastructure.

Multicast address allocation is often used with conferencing or audio applications, which usually require users to specially configure multicast addresses. Unlike IP broadcasts, which must be readable by all computers on the network, a multicast address points to a group of computers, using the concept of group membership to identify those to whom the message is to be sent.

The multicast address allocation feature has two parts: (1) the server-side implementation to hand out multicast addresses and (2) the client-side application programming interfaces (APIs) that applications can use to request, renew, and release multicast addresses. To use multicast addresses, the administrator first configures the multicast scopes and the corresponding multicast IP ranges on the server through a snap-in. The multicast addresses are then managed like normal IP addresses. The client can call the APIs to request a multicast address from a scope. The underlying implementation uses DHCP protocol-style packet formats between the client and the server.

CONFIGURING A DHCP RESERVATION

Use reservations for DHCP-enabled hosts that need to have static IP addresses on your network. Examples of hosts that require static IP addresses are e-mail servers and application servers. File and print servers may also require static or reserved IP addresses if they are accessed by their IP addresses.

What Is a DHCP Reservation?

Reservations enable permanent address lease assignment by the DHCP server. Where reservations are used, they ensure that a specified hardware device on the subnetwork can always use the same IP address. Reservations must be created within a scope and must not be excluded from the scope. Excluded addresses are not available for assignment to clients even if reserved for a client. An IP address is set aside, or reserved, for a specific network device that has the MAC address associated with that IP address. Therefore, when creating a reservation, you must know the MAC address for each device for which you are reserving an address. For Windows 98, Windows 2000, Windows XP, and Windows Server 2003, the MAC address can be obtained by typing **ipconfig /all** at the command line, which will result in output similar to the following:

```
Ethernet adapter :
Description . . . . . . . . : DEC DC21140 PCI Fast Ethernet Adapter
Physical Address. . . . . . : 00-03-FF-F6-FF-FF
DHCP Enabled. . . . . . . . : Yes
IP Address. . . . . . . . . : 169.254.150.72
Subnet Mask . . . . . . . . : 255.255.0.0
Default Gateway . . . . . . :
DHCP Server . . . . . . . . : 255.255.255.255
Primary WINS Server . . . . :
Secondary WINS Server . . . :
Lease Obtained. . . . . . . : 07 12 03 6:11:42 PM
Lease Expires . . . . . . . :
```

The MAC address in this example is 00-03-FF-F6-FF-FF.

▶ **How to Configure a DHCP Reservation**

To configure a DHCP reservation, follow these steps:

1. Open the DHCP console.

2. In the console tree, click Reservations.

3. On the Action menu, click New Reservation.

   Figure 1-11 shows an example of a completed New Reservation properties page.

Figure 1-11   The DHCP New Reservation properties page

4. In the New Reservation dialog box, provide the following information and then click Add:

   a. Reservation name (for example, **MailServer01**)

   b. IP address

   c. MAC address

   d. Description (optional)

   e. Supported types (DHCP Only, BOOTP Only, Both).

   You can restrict the type of client that may utilize this reservation to DHCP or BOOTP or allow both. Some older client computers that are running a non-Microsoft operating system may use the older BOOTP instead of DHCP. Also, Windows 2000 Remote Installation Services (RIS) clients use the BOOTP when they initialize. Click Both, unless you want the client computers to be limited to a specific protocol to receive an IP address.

5. To add the client reservation to the scope, click Add.

6. Repeat the two previous steps for any other client reservations that you want to add, and then click Close.

Practice configuring a DHCP reservation by doing Exercise 1-3, "Configuring a DHCP Reservation," now.

CONFIGURING DHCP OPTIONS

DHCP options are additional client-configuration parameters that a DHCP server can assign when serving leases to DHCP clients. DHCP options are configured using DHCP console and can apply to scopes and reservations. For example, IP addresses for a router or default gateway, WINS servers, or DNS servers are commonly provided for a single scope or globally for all scopes managed by the DHCP server. Many DHCP options are predefined through RFC 2132, but the Microsoft DHCP server also allows you to define and add custom options. Table 1-1 describes some of the options that can be configured.

Table 1-1   **DHCP Scope Options**

Option	Description
Router (default gateway)	The addresses of any default gateway or router. This router is commonly referred to as the default gateway.
Domain name	A DNS domain name defines the domain to which a client computer belongs. The client computer can use this information to update a DNS server so that other computers can locate the client.
DNS and WINS servers	The addresses of any DNS and WINS servers for clients to use for network communication.

User and Vendor Classes

DHCP options can be assigned to all scopes, one specific scope, and to a specific machine reservation. There are four types of DHCP options in Windows Server 2003:

- **Server options**   Server options apply to all clients of the DHCP server. Use these options for parameters common across all scopes on the DHCP server.

■ **Scope options**   Scope options apply to all clients within a scope and are the most often used set of options. Scope options override server options.

■ **Class options**   Class options provide DHCP parameters to DHCP clients based on type—either **vendor classes** or **user classes**.

■ **Client options**   Client options apply to individual clients. Client options override all other options (server, scope, and class).

User classes are created at the discretion of the DHCP administrator. Vendor classes are defined by the machine's vendor and cannot be changed. Figure 1-12 shows the use of a vendor class to apply the 002 Microsoft Release DHCP Lease On Shutdown option to computers running Windows 2000. Using vendor and user classes, an administrator can then configure the DHCP server to assign different options, depending on the type of client receiving them. For example, an administrator can configure the DHCP server to assign different options based on type of client, such as desktop or portable computer. This feature gives administrators greater flexibility in configuring clients. If client class options are not used, default settings are assigned.

Figure 1-12   The DHCP Server Options properties page

> **MORE INFO**   *Vendor Class and Vendor Options*   *The vendor class and vendor options are described in RFC 2132 and can be looked up at http://www.rfc-editor.org/rfcsearch.html.*

CONFIGURING A DHCP RELAY AGENT

When the DHCP client and the DHCP server are on the same subnet, the DHCP-DISCOVER, DHCPOFFER, DHCPREQUEST, and DHCPACK messages are sent by means of MAC-level and IP-level broadcasts. When the DHCP server and DHCP client are not on the same subnet, the connecting router or routers must support the forwarding of DHCP messages between the DHCP client and the DHCP server, or a BOOTP/DHCP relay agent must be installed on the subnet. The BOOTP and DHCP protocols rely on network broadcasts to perform their work. Routers in normal routed environments do not automatically forward broadcasts from one interface to another.

Two methods enable you to work around this limitation. First, if the routers separating the DHCP server and clients are RFC 1542 compliant, the routers can be configured for BOOTP forwarding. Through BOOTP forwarding, routers forward DHCP broadcasts between clients and servers and inform servers on the originating subnet of the DHCP requests. This process allows DHCP servers to assign addresses to the remote clients from the appropriate scope.

The second way to allow remote communication between DHCP servers and clients is to configure a DHCP relay agent on the subnet containing the remote clients. DHCP relay agents intercept DHCPDISCOVER packets and forward them to a remote DHCP server whose address has been preconfigured. A *DHCP relay agent* is either a router or a host computer configured to listen for DHCP/BOOTP broadcast messages and direct them to a specific DHCP server or servers. Using relay agents eliminates the necessity of having a DHCP server on each physical network segment or having RFC 2131–compliant routers. Relay agents not only direct local DHCP client requests to remote DHCP servers, but also return remote DHCP server responses to the DHCP clients. Although the DHCP relay agent is configured through Routing And Remote Access, the computer hosting the agent does not need to be functioning as an actual router between subnets. RFC 2131–compliant routers (supercedes RFC 1542) contain relay agents that allow them to forward DHCP packets.

How Relay Agents Work

Figure 1-13 and the following numbered list shows how a DHCP client on Subnet 2 obtains a DHCP address lease from the DHCP server on Subnet 1.

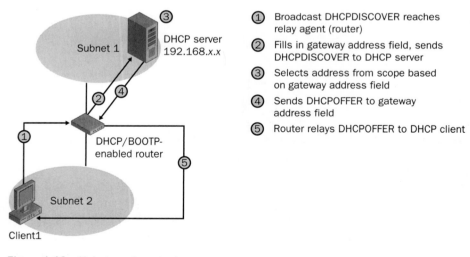

① Broadcast DHCPDISCOVER reaches relay agent (router)

② Fills in gateway address field, sends DHCPDISCOVER to DHCP server

③ Selects address from scope based on gateway address field

④ Sends DHCPOFFER to gateway address field

⑤ Router relays DHCPOFFER to DHCP client

Figure 1-13 Using a relay agent

1. The DHCP client broadcasts a DHCPDISCOVER message on Subnet 2 as a UDP datagram over UDP port 67, which is the port reserved and shared for BOOTP and DHCP server communication.

2. The relay agent, in this case a DHCP/BOOTP relay–enabled router, examines the gateway IP address field in the DHCP/BOOTP message header. If the field has an IP address of 0.0.0.0, the relay agent fills it with its own IP address and forwards the message to Subnet 1, where the DHCP server is located.

3. When the DHCP server on Subnet 1 receives the DHCPDISCOVER message, it examines the gateway IP address field for a DHCP scope to determine whether it can supply an IP address lease. If the DHCP server has multiple DHCP scopes, the address in the gateway IP address field identifies the DHCP scope from which to offer an IP address lease.

For example, if the gateway IP address field has an IP address of 192.168.45.2, the DHCP server checks its DHCP scopes for a scope range that matches the Class C IP network that includes the gateway IP address of the computer. In this case, the DHCP server checks to see which scope includes addresses between 192.168.45.1 and 192.168.45.254. If a scope exists that matches this criterion, the DHCP server selects an available address from the matched scope to use in an IP address lease offer (DHCPOFFER) response to the client.

4. The DHCP server sends a DHCPOFFER message directly to the relay agent identified in the gateway IP address field.

5. The router relays the address lease offer (DHCPOFFER) to the DHCP client as a broadcast since the client's IP address is still unknown.

After the client receives the DHCPOFFER, a DHCPREQUEST message is relayed from client to server, and a DHCPACK message is relayed from server to client, according to RFC 1542.

▶ **Installing a DHCP Relay Agent**

To install a DHCP relay agent, follow these steps:

1. On the Administrative Tools menu, open Routing And Remote Access.

2. In the console tree, expand the server icon, and then click IP Routing.

3. In the details pane, right-click General, and then click New Routing Protocol.

4. In the New Routing Protocol dialog box, click DHCP Relay Agent, and then click OK.

5. Open the Properties dialog box for the DHCP relay agent. In the Server Address box, type the IP address of a DHCP server, and then click Add.

Using Superscopes

A *superscope* is an administrative grouping of scopes that is used to support *multinets*, or multiple logical subnets (subdivisions of an IP network) on a single network segment (a portion of the IP internetwork bounded by IP routers). Multinetting commonly occurs when the number of hosts on a network segment grows beyond the capacity of the original address space. By creating a logically distinct second scope and then grouping these two scopes into a single superscope, you can double your physical segment's capacity for addresses. (In multinet scenarios, routing is also required to connect the logical subnets.) In this way, the DHCP server can provide clients on a single physical network with leases from more than one scope.

NOTE   Superscopes Only Contain List of Member Scopes   Superscopes contain only a list of member scopes or child scopes that can be activated together; they are not used to configure other details about scope use.

▶ **Creating a Superscope**

To create a superscope, you must first create a scope. After you have created a scope, you can create a superscope by completing the following steps:

1. Open the DHCP console.

2. In the console tree, select the applicable DHCP server.

3. From the Action menu, select New Superscope.

   This menu command appears only if at least one scope that is not currently part of a superscope has been created at the server.

4. On the Welcome To The New Superscope Wizard page, click Next.

5. On the Superscope Name page, in the Name box, type the name of your superscope, and then click Next.

6. On the Select Scopes page, in the Available Scopes box, select one or more scopes from the list to add to the superscope, and then click Next.

7. On the Completing The New Superscope Wizard page, click Finish.

Superscope Configurations for Multinets

The next sections show how a simple DHCP network consisting originally of one physical network segment and one DHCP server can be extended by means of superscopes to support multinet configurations.

Superscope Supporting Local Multinets   Figure 1-14 illustrates multinetting on a single physical network (Subnet A) with a single DHCP server.

Figure 1-14   Multinetting on a single network segment

To support this scenario, you can configure a superscope that includes as members the original scope (Scope 1) and the additional scopes for the logical multinets you need to support (Scopes 2 and 3).

> **NOTE**   *Connecting Two Logical Subnets*   When supporting two logical subnets on one physical segment, use a router to connect traffic from one subnet to another.

Superscope Supporting Remote Multinets   Figure 1-15 illustrates a configuration used to support multinets on a physical network (Subnet B) that is separated from the DHCP server. In this scenario, a superscope defined on the DHCP server, along with a relay agent configured on the router, combines subnets A and B into a multinet, where hosts on both subnets can communicate with the DHCP Server in Subnet A.

Superscope for Subnet A:
Scope 1: 192.168.1.1 – 192.168.1.254
Subnet mask: 255.255.255.0

Superscope added here with member scopes for Subnet B:
Scope 2: 192.168.2.1 – 192.168.2.254
Scope 3: 192.168.3.1 – 192.168.3.254
Subnet mask: 255.255.255.0

Figure 1-15   Routed multinetting

Superscopes Supporting Two Local DHCP Servers   Without superscopes, two DHCP server computers issuing leases on a single segment would create address conflicts. Figure 1-16 illustrates such a scenario.

Figure 1-16   Conflicts in a two-server subnet

In this configuration, DHCP Server A manages a different scope of addresses from that of DHCP Server B, and neither has any information about addresses managed by the other. A problem arises when a client that has previously registered with Server A, for example, releases its name during a proper shutdown and later reconnects to the network.

When the client (Client A) reboots, it tries to renew its address lease. However, if Server B responds to Client A's request before Server A does, Server B rejects the foreign address renewal request with a DHCPNACK message. As a result of this process, Client A's address resets, and Client A is forced to seek a new IP address. In the process of obtaining a new address lease, Client A might be offered an address that places it on an incorrect logical subnet.

Figure 1-17 shows how you can avoid these problems and manage two scopes predictably and effectively by using superscopes on both DHCP servers. In this configuration, both servers are still located on the same physical subnet. A superscope is included on both Server A and Server B that includes both scopes defined on the physical subnet as members. To prevent the servers from issuing leases in each other's scopes, each server excludes the full scope range belonging to the other server. This is illustrated in Figure 1-17.

Figure 1-17   Two servers using a superscope

SUMMARY

- DHCP is a simple, standard protocol that makes TCP/IP network configuration much easier for the administrator by dynamically assigning IP addresses and providing additional configuration information to DHCP clients automatically.

- Additional configuration information is provided in the form of options and can be associated with reserved IPs, to a vendor or user class, to a scope, or to an entire DHCP server.

EXERCISES

IMPORTANT *Complete All Exercises* If you plan to do any of the textbook exercises in this chapter, you must do all of the exercises to return the computer to its original state in preparation for the subsequent Lab Manual labs.

Exercise 1-1: Installing and Authorizing a DHCP Server

1. Click Start, and then click Manage Your Server.

2. On the Manage Your Server page, click Add Or Remove A Role.

3. On the Preliminary Steps page, click Next.

4. On the Server Role page, click DHCP Server, and then click Next.

5. On the Summary Of Selections page, click Next.

6. On the Welcome To The New Scope Wizard page, click Cancel. (You will create a scope in Exercise 1-2.)

7. On the Cannot Complete page, click Finish.

8. Click Start, point to Administrative Tools, and then click DHCP.

9. In the DHCP console, left-click and then right-click the DHCP server that you want to authorize, and then click Authorize.

10. Open the Event Viewer and examine the System log. Locate an information event whose source is DhcpServer, which indicates that the DHCP server has been successfully authorized

11. In the DHCP console, right-click the server you authorized, and then click Unauthorize. Click Yes to confirm the removal of the DHCP server from the directory and then refresh the console.

Exercise 1-2: Configuring a DHCP Scope

1. Open the DHCP console.

2. In the DHCP console, right-click the DHCP server for which you want to configure a scope, and then click New Scope.

3. On the Welcome page, click Next.

4. On the Scope Name page, type a name and description for the scope, and then click Next.

5. On the IP Address Range page, enter the following information and then click Next.

   a. Starting IP address: **10.1.1.50**

   b. Ending IP address: **10.1.1.100**

   c. Subnet mask: **255.255.0.0**

6. On the Add Exclusions page, exclude 10.1.1.70 through 10.1.1.75 from the range, and then click Next.

7. On the Lease Duration page, set the lease duration to **4 days** and click Next.

8. On the Configure DHCP Options page, click Yes, I Want To Configure These Options Now, and then click Next.

9. On the Router (Default Gateway) page, enter **10.1.1.1** as the router, and then click Next.

10. On the Domain Name and DNS Servers page, in the Parent domain box, type **contoso.com**, and in the IP address box, type **10.1.1.200**. Click Add, and then click Next.

11. On the WINS Servers page, in the IP address box, type **10.1.1.200**. Click Add, and then click Next.

12. On the Activate Scope box, click No, I Will Activate This Scope Later, click Next, and then click Finish.

13. In the DHCP console, examine the scope that you have just created.

Exercise 1-3: Configuring a DHCP Reservation

1. In the DHCP console, expand the scope you created in Exercise 1-2. Right-click Reservations, and then click New Reservation.

2. On the New Reservation properties page, type the following values, click Add, and then click Close.

   a. Reservation Name: **MailServer01**

   b. IP address: **10.1.1.71**

   c. MAC address: **00-53-45-0F-00-0A**

Exercise 1-4: Removing DHCP

In this exercise, you will undo the configuration changes you made in the previous exercises.

1. Click Start and then click Manage Your Server.

2. On the Manage Your Server page, click Add Or Remove A Role.

3. On the Preliminary Steps page, click Next.

4. On the Server Role page, click DHCP Server and then click Next.

5. Select the Remove The DHCP Server Role check box and then click Next.

6. On the DHCP Server Role Removed page, click Finish.

REVIEW QUESTIONS

1. Under what circumstances should network administrators use DHCP? *when there are many devices in many locations*

2. Place the following DHCP message types in the order in which a successful initial IP address assignment procedure uses them.

   a. DHCPACK *4*

   b. DHCPOFFER *2*

   c. DHCPREQUEST *3*

   d. DHCPDISCOVER *1*

3. How does a DHCP client respond when its attempt to renew its IP address lease fails and the lease expires? *the client immediately releases the IP address and attempts to acquire a new lease*

4. You have configured a scope with an address range of 192.168.0.11 through 192.168.0.254. However, your DNS server on the same subnet has already been assigned a static address of 192.168.0.200. With the least administrative effort, how can you allow for compatibility between the DNS server's address and DHCP service on the subnet? *specify an exclusion*

5. Within your only subnet, you want 10 specific DHCP clients (out of 150 total on the network) to use a test DNS server that is not assigned to any other computers through DHCP. How can you best achieve this objective? *set up DHCP reservations*

CASE SCENARIOS

Case Scenario 1-1: Obtaining an IP Address

Last month, a server was configured for DHCP and was functioning normally. Five days ago, a test server on the same network segment was promoted to be the first domain controller on the network. Today several users on the same subnet as the original DHCP server have complained that they are unable to obtain an IP address using DHCP. What is the most likely reason users are unable to obtain an IP address?

a. The user's IP address leases have expired.

b. A DHCP relay agent is missing or incorrectly configured.

c. There are duplicate IP addresses on the network.

d. The DHCP server must be authorized and is not.

Case Scenario 1-2: Maximizing Lease Availability

You are configuring DHCP scope options for Contoso, Ltd. The company has a limited number of IP addresses available for clients, and it wants to configure DHCP to maximize lease availability. Choose all of the following actions that will accomplish this objective:

a. Set long lease durations for IP addresses.

b. Set short lease durations for IP addresses.

c. Configure a DHCP option to automatically release an IP address when the computer shuts down.

d. Create DHCP reservations for all portable computers.

CHAPTER 2
MANAGING AND MONITORING DHCP

Upon completion of this chapter, you will be able to:

- Describe the importance and best practices of managing a **Dynamic Host Configuration Protocol** (DHCP) server.

- Manage a DHCP database by performing the following tasks: backing up and restoring, compacting a DHCP database, and reconciling a DHCP database.

- Monitor a DHCP database by creating and viewing a DHCP audit log, creating a DHCP performance baseline, viewing **DHCP server** and **scope** statistics, and creating DHCP performance alerts.

After you successfully install and configure DHCP on a Microsoft Windows Server 2003 server, you must manage and monitor the server on an ongoing basis. The more volatile your environment (volatility results from adding, removing, or repurposing servers), the more important it is that you manage and monitor your DHCP servers. Your network's level of volatility determines both the frequency of management and monitoring that you will have to do.

The purpose of managing and monitoring a DHCP server is to help prevent problems, to ensure the server is performing the functions for which you deployed it, and to verify that the server is performing its functions at an acceptable level of performance. Effective monitoring enables you to identify and remedy trends that may eventually lead to downtime or loss of performance. This chapter looks at how you manage and monitor a DHCP server.

MANAGING DHCP

DHCP plays a key role in an organization's network infrastructure. As discussed in Chapter 1, "Implementing DHCP," organizations use DHCP to provide mandatory connection settings (Internet Protocol [IP] address and subnet mask). DHCP servers also provide IP addresses of important resources such as **Domain Name System (DNS)** servers and **Windows Internet Naming Service (WINS)** servers. Without an accessible DHCP server, most clients completely lose network connectivity. Therefore, like any key resource in your organization, you must carefully manage the DHCP server. Proper management of a DHCP server helps prevent server downtime and aids in quick recovery after a server failure. Table 2-1 lists DHCP administrative tasks and when they are most often performed.

Table 2-1   **DHCP Administrative Tasks**

Administrative Task	When the Task Is Performed
Configure or modify scopes	At installation or when adding clients outside of current scopes
Configure or modify options	When adding or modifying network service servers
Configure the DHCP relay agent	When adding new subnets
Back up the DHCP database	Every hour, by default
Restore the DHCP database	When the database is corrupt
Compact the DHCP database	When it is necessary to manage DHCP database growth
Reconcile DHCP scopes	When inconsistencies are found

UNDERSTANDING DNS DYNAMIC UPDATES

Windows Server 2003 DNS supports the **DNS dynamic update** protocol **(RFC [Request for Comments]** 2136), which enables DNS clients to dynamically update their resource records in DNS **zones**. You can specify that the DHCP server in your network dynamically update DNS when it configures a **DHCP client** computer. This reduces the administration time that is necessary when manually administering zone records. You use the dynamic update feature in conjunction with DHCP to update resource records when a computer releases or updates its IP address.

On the DHCP server, you specify the DNS zone(s) that the DHCP server is responsible for automatically updating. On the DNS server, you specify the DHCP server as the only computer that is authorized to update the DNS entries.

If you use multiple Windows Server 2003 DHCP servers on your network and you configure your zones to allow secure dynamic updates only, you must use Active Directory Users And Computers to add your DHCP servers to the built-in DnsUpdateProxy security group. This enables your DHCP servers to perform updates on behalf of your DHCP clients.

You should include dynamic DNS updates from DHCP servers if

- The DNS client operating system is not Microsoft Windows 2000, Microsoft Windows XP, or Windows Server 2003.

- Assigning the permissions, which enable each computer, group, or user to update the respective DNS entries, becomes unmanageable.

- Allowing individual DNS clients to update DNS entries presents security risks that could potentially allow unauthorized computers to impersonate authorized computers.

Client computers running Windows 2000 or later attempt to update **address (A) resource records** directly, but they utilize the DHCP server to dynamically update their **pointer (PTR) resource records**, as shown in Figure 2-1 (note that steps 3 and 4 may be reversed). A records associate host names to IP addresses, while PTR records associate IP addresses to host names. When both are present, a DNS server may perform forward and reverse lookups.

Figure 2-1   Dynamic update process for Windows 2000 or later clients

DHCP-enabled client computers running earlier versions of Microsoft operating systems are unable to update or register their DNS resource records directly. These DHCP clients must use the DHCP service provided with Windows Server 2003 to register and update both their A and PTR resource records. Figure 2-2 shows this process.

Figure 2-2   Dynamic update process for clients that run pre–Windows 2000 Microsoft operating systems

You can modify this default behavior in various ways by configuring DNS update settings on the DHCP server. This is discussed in the next section.

Configuring DNS Dynamic Update Settings on the DHCP Server

To enable dynamic update, on the properties page of the DHCP server, select Enable DNS Dynamic Updates According To The Settings Below. This option and the Dynamically Update DNS A And PTR Records Only If Requested By The DHCP Clients option are both selected by default. When the defaults are selected and a DHCP client requests the DHCP server to update its PTR resource record, the DHCP server carries out only that request. To configure the DHCP server to update both the A and PTR resource records, use the DHCP Manager console to display the properties of the DNS server and modify the settings in the DNS tab as shown in Figure 2-3. To update DNS for clients running earlier versions of the Windows operating system, such as Microsoft Windows 98 and Windows NT 4, select the Dynamically Update DNS A And PTR Records For DHCP Clients That Do Not Request Updates option, which is also shown in Figure 2-3.

Figure 2-3   Enabling the DHCP server to update DNS A and PTR records

> **NOTE**   **Configuring Scope Properties**   DNS dynamic updates also are config-
> ured at the scope level by using the Scope Properties dialog box or for a host with
> a reserved IP address in the properties dialog box for that reservation.

If you are unable to secure dynamic updates, you may want to disable DNS dynamic updates. To prevent the DHCP server from attempting dynamic updates on behalf of Windows 2000, Windows XP, or Windows Server 2003 clients, clear the Enable DNS Dynamic Updates According To The Settings Below check box.

Generally, there is no reason to maintain a deleted client's DNS information. Selecting the Discard A And PTR Records When Lease Is Deleted check box removes the client's resource records from DNS when the DHCP address leases are deleted.

Practice configuring DNS dynamic updates by doing Exercise 2-1, "Configuring DNS Dynamic Update," now.

The final dynamic update setting you can configure in the DNS tab determines whether the DHCP server provides dynamic DNS update service on behalf of DHCP clients that are not capable of performing dynamic updates, such as computers running Microsoft Windows NT 4. By default, Windows Server 2003 DHCP servers do not attempt to perform dynamic updates on behalf of these clients. To enable the Windows Server 2003 DHCP server to perform updates on behalf of these clients, select Dynamically Update DNS A And PTR Records For DHCP Clients That Do Not Request Updates.

Using Secure Dynamic Updates

Although dynamic updates allow clients to update DNS resource records, this is not a secure method. A more secure way of updating DNS resource records is using secure dynamic updates. The server attempts the update only if the client can prove its identity and has the proper credentials to make the update. Secure dynamic updates are available only through Active Directory directory service and when Active Directory–integrated DNS is enabled. (For more information, see Chapter 3, "Implementing Name Resolution Using DNS".)

Configuring Secure Dynamic Update   By default, **Active Directory–integrated zones** only allow secure dynamic updates, and this setting can be modified when you create the zone. If you created the zone as a standard primary zone, and then you converted it into an Active Directory–integrated zone, it preserves the primary zone dynamic update configuration, which can be changed using the DNS console.

▶ Configuring Secure Dynamic Updates

This procedure uses the DNS console to verify a zone is using secure dynamic updates. To verify the dynamic update setting, follow these steps:

1. In the DNS console, right-click the zone that you want to configure for secure dynamic updates, and then click Properties.

2. In the Dynamic Updates drop-down list box, verify that Secure Only (see Figure 2-4) is selected.

Figure 2-4   DNS zone configured for secure updates only

By default, when the DHCP Client service registers resource records for a DNS name, it first attempts a standard dynamic update. If the dynamic update fails, the client attempts to negotiate a secure dynamic update. You also can configure the client to always attempt a standard dynamic update or secure dynamic update by adding the UpdateSecurityLevel registry entry to the following subkey:

```
HKEY_LOCAL_MACHINE\SYSTEM\CurrentControlSet\Services\Tcpip\Parameters
```

The value of UpdateSecurityLevel can be set to the decimal values 0, 16, or 256, which configure security as follows:

- **0**   Specifies the use of secure dynamic update when a standard dynamic update is refused. This is the default value.

- **16**   Specifies the use of standard dynamic update only.

- **256**   Specifies the use of secure dynamic update only.

Using the DnsUpdateProxy Security Group   Using secure dynamic updates can lead to situations in which records cannot be updated. When using secure dynamic updates, the registering client, and only the registering client, can modify that name. For example, consider a DHCP server that registered a record for a pre–Windows 2000 client. Later, that client is upgraded to Windows XP and now has the capability to update its own DNS resource records. Because secure dynamic updates require the owner (which is the DHCP server) of a resource record to update that record, the newly upgraded client is unable to update its own record. Similarly, if your secondary DHCP server registers a name and then goes offline, that name cannot be dynamically updated until the secondary server comes back online.

To remedy these issues, Windows Server 2003 Active Directory provides a built-in security group called *DnsUpdateProxy*. Objects created by this group are not secure. As a result, initially the object has no owner, so a DHCP server or client that did not create it, even in zones requiring secure updates, can update it. However, as with all records, as soon as the first DHCP server or client that is not a member of the DnsUpdateProxy security group modifies such a record, that server or client then becomes its owner. At this point, only the owner can update the record in zones requiring secure updates. Thus, if every DHCP server registering resource records for older clients is a member of this group, and the clients themselves are not members of the group, the problems discussed earlier are eliminated. To avoid problems, consider adding DHCP servers to the DnsUpdateProxy security group.

Adding Computer Objects to the DnsUpdateProxy Security Group   You can add computer objects to the DnsUpdateProxy security group through the Active Directory Users And Computers console.

▶ **Adding a DHCP Server to the DnsUpdateProxy Security Group**

To add a DHCP server to the DnsUpdateProxy security group, follow these steps:

1. Click Start, point to All Programs, point to Administrative Tools, and click Active Directory Users And Computers.

2. Expand contoso.com, and then click the Users container folder.

3. Right-click DnsUpdateProxy, and then click Properties.

4. In the Members tab, click Add.

5. In the Enter The Object Names To Select box, type the names of the member servers or domain controllers that host DHCP.

6. Click Check Names, and then close the property sheet by clicking OK.

> **NOTE**   **Adding DHCP Servers to the DnsUpdateProxy Security Group**   If you are using multiple DHCP servers for fault tolerance and secure DNS dynamic updates are required for zones serviced by these DHCP servers, be sure to add each of the computers operating a Windows Server 2003 DHCP server to the DnsUpdateProxy security group.

Security Concerns   Although adding all DHCP servers to this special built-in group, DnsUpdateProxy, helps resolve some concerns about maintaining secure DNS updates, this solution also introduces some additional security risks.

For example, any DNS domain names registered by the computer running the DHCP server are not secure. The A resource record for the DHCP server is an example of such a record. To protect against this risk, you can manually specify a different owner for any DNS records associated with the DHCP server.

However, a more significant issue arises if the DHCP server that is a member of the DnsUpdateProxy security group is installed on a domain controller. In this case, the service location (SRV), the host (A), and the **canonical name (CNAME) resource records** that are registered by the Netlogon service for the domain controller are not secure. To minimize this problem, you should not install a DHCP server on a domain controller when using dynamic updates.

> **CAUTION**   **Adding DHCP Servers to the DnsUpdateProxy Security Group**   For Windows Server 2003, the use of secure dynamic updates can be compromised by running a DHCP server on a domain controller when the Windows Server 2003 DHCP service is configured to perform registration of DNS records on behalf of DHCP clients. To avoid this problem, deploy DHCP servers and domain controllers on separate computers.

Troubleshooting Dynamic Update

On occasion, you might have problems with dynamic update or secure dynamic update. This section helps you identify and solve dynamic update problems.

If dynamic updates do not correctly register a name or an IP address, one or more of the following actions should aid you in diagnosing and solving the problem:

■ Check the system event log on the client for specific errors.

■ Force the client to renew its registration by typing **ipconfig /registerdns** at the command prompt.

■ Check to see whether or not dynamic updates are enabled for the zone that is authoritative for the name that the client attempts to update.

- To rule out other problems, check to see if the dynamic update client lists the primary DNS server for the zone as its preferred DNS server. To determine the preferred DNS server for the client, check the IP address configured in the **Transmission Control Protocol/Internet Protocol (TCP/IP)** properties of the network connection for the client, or, at the command prompt, type **ipconfig /all**.

- If the client lists a preferred server other than the primary DNS server for the zone, dynamic updates can still function correctly; however, other problems might cause the failure, such as a network connectivity problem between the two servers or a prolonged recursive lookup for the primary server of the zone.

- If the zone is Active Directory–integrated, any DNS server that hosts an Active Directory–integrated copy of the zone can process the updates.

- Check to see if the resource record's **access control list (ACL)** is configured to enable dynamic updates. If the zone is configured for secure dynamic updates, the update can fail if the record's security settings do not permit this client to make changes to the record, or the update can fail if this client does not own the name that it is updating. To determine whether the update failed for one of these reasons, check Event Viewer on the client.

Enabling secure dynamic updates can also prevent a client from creating, modifying, or deleting records depending on the ACL for the zone and the name. By default, secure dynamic updates prevent a client from creating, deleting, or modifying a record if the client is not the original creator of the name. For example, if two computers have the same name and both try to register their names in DNS, dynamic updates fail for the client that registers second.

If a client fails to update a name in a zone that is configured for secure dynamic updates, one of the following conditions might have caused the failure:

- The system time on the DNS client and the system time on the DNS server are not synchronized.

- You have modified the UpdateSecurityLevel registry entry to prevent the use of secure dynamic updates on the client.

- A zone is locked. A DNS server locks a zone before doing a large zone transfer. When the zone is locked, a client cannot update a name.

- The client does not have the appropriate rights to update the resource record. You can confirm this by checking the ACL associated with the updated name. If the client does not have the appropriate rights to update the resource record, check to see that the DHCP server registered the name of the client and that the DHCP server is the owner of the corresponding dnsNode object. If so, you might consider placing the DHCP server in the DnsUpdateProxy security group. However, recall that any object created by a member of the DnsUpdateProxy security group is not secure.

MANAGING A DHCP DATABASE

Your network is constantly changing. New servers are added and existing servers are changing roles or are removed from the network altogether. As discussed already, it is because your network is constantly changing that you must both monitor and manage the DHCP service to ensure it is meeting the needs of the organization. Specifically, you must manage the DHCP database by performing the following database functions:

- Backup and restore
- Reconciliation
- Compacting the database
- Removing the database

What Is a DHCP Database?

The DHCP server database is a *dynamic database*, which is a data store that is updated as DHCP clients are assigned or as they release their TCP/IP configuration parameters. Because the DHCP database is not a distributed database like the DNS server database, maintaining the DHCP server database is less complex. DNS is stored hierarchically across many different servers with each server containing a part of the overall database. DHCP, in contrast, is contained in a few files on one server.

The DHCP server database in the Windows Server 2003 family uses the Joint Engine Technology (JET) storage engine. When you install the DHCP service, the files shown in Table 2-2 are automatically created in the %systemroot%\System32\Dhcp directory.

Table 2-2   **DHCP Service Database Files**

File	Description
Dhcp.mdb	The DHCP server database file.
Temp.edb	A file used by the DHCP database as a temporary storage file during database index maintenance operations. This file sometimes resides in the %systemroot%\System32\Dhcp directory after a system failure.
J50.log and J50#####.log	A log of all database transactions. The DHCP database uses this file to recover data when necessary.
J50.chk	A *checkpoint file* indicates the location of the last information that was successfully written from the transaction logs to the database. In a data recovery scenario, the checkpoint file indicates where the recovery or replaying of data should begin. The checkpoint file is updated when data is written to the database file (Dhcp.mdb).
Res*.log	Reserved log files that are used to record the existing transactions if the system runs out of disk space.

> **CAUTION   Removing or Altering Database Files**   *The J50.log file, J50#####.log file, Dhcp.mdb file, and Dhcp.tmp file should not be removed or altered. Altering these files may cause your DHCP server to fail.*

There is no limit to the number of records a DHCP server stores. The size of the database is dependent upon the number of DHCP clients on the network. The DHCP database grows over time because clients join and leave the network. Microsoft suggests that a DHCP server service no more than 10,000 clients and 1,000 scopes.

The size of the DHCP database is not directly proportional to the number of active client lease entries. Over time, some DHCP client entries become obsolete or deleted. Space is not reclaimed and therefore some space remains unused.

To recover the unused space, the DHCP database is compacted. Dynamic database compaction occurs on DHCP servers as an automatic background process during idle time or after a database update.

Backing Up and Restoring DHCP Server Configuration

Windows Server 2003 DHCP servers support automatic and manual backups. To provide fault tolerance in the case of a failure, it is important to back up the DHCP database. This enables you to restore the database from the backup copy if the hardware fails. When you perform a backup, the entire DHCP database is saved, including the following:

- Scopes, including **superscopes** and **multicast** scopes
- Reservations
- Leases
- Options, including server options, scope options, reservation options, and **class** option

> **CAUTION   Security Credentials**   *Note that security credentials are not included in this list. Neither automatic nor manual processes back up security credentials. You must reconfigure them after restoring the DHCP database.*

Automatically Backing Up a DHCP Database

By default, the DHCP service automatically backs up the DHCP database and related registry entries to a backup directory on the local drive. This occurs every 60 minutes. By default, automatic backups are stored in the %systemroot%\System32\Dhcp\Backup directory. The administrator can also change the backup location. Automatic backups use only automatic restores (automatic restores are performed by the DHCP service when corruption is detected).

Manually Backing Up a DHCP Database

You can also back up the DHCP database manually. By default, manual backups are stored in the %systemroot%\System32\Dhcp\Backup\ directory. The administrator can also change the backup location. Manual backups use only manual restores. You can manually back up the DHCP database while the DHCP service is running. The backup destination must be on the local disk; remote paths are not

Practice backing up the DHCP database manually by doing Exercise 2-2, "Manually Backing Up a DHCP Database," now

allowed, and the backup directory is created automatically (if it does not already exist). The administrator can then copy the backed up DHCP files to an offline storage location (such as a tape or a disk).

Automatically Restoring the DHCP Database

When the DHCP service starts, if the original DHCP database is unable to load, the DHCP service automatically restores from a backup directory on the local drive.

If the DHCP database fails, the administrator can choose to either restore from the backup directory on the local drive or, if that's not available, restore from the offline backup location.

If the server hardware fails and the local backup is unavailable, the administrator can restore only from the offline backup location.

Manually Restoring a DHCP Database

You can restore the database from the backup directory on the local drive. If restoring the DHCP database from the backup directory on the local drive is unsuccessful, you must restore the DHCP database from an offline storage location.

▶ **Configuring a DHCP Database Backup Path**

To configure a DHCP database backup path, follow these steps:

1. In the DHCP console, in the console tree, select the appropriate DHCP server.

2. On the Action menu, click Properties.

3. In the Advanced tab, in the Backup Path field, type the appropriate backup path, and then click OK.

▶ **Manually Backing Up a DHCP Database**

To manually back up a DHCP database to the backup directory on a local drive, follow these steps:

1. In the DHCP console, in the console tree, select the appropriate DHCP server.

2. On the Action menu, click Backup.

3. In the Browse For Folder dialog box, select the appropriate folder to back up to, and then click OK.

▶ **Manually Restoring a DHCP Database**

To manually restore a DHCP database from the backup directory on a local drive, follow these steps:

1. In the DHCP console, in the console tree, select the appropriate DHCP server.

2. On the Action menu, click Restore.

3. In the Browse For Folder dialog box, select the folder where the backup resides, and then click OK.

4. In the DHCP dialog box, click Yes to stop and then restart the service.

5. If the status of the service does not update, press F5 to refresh the DHCP console.

Reconciling a DHCP Database

Reconciling is the process of verifying DHCP database values against DHCP registry values. You should reconcile your DHCP database in the following scenarios:

- The DHCP database values are configured correctly, but they are not displayed correctly in the DHCP console.

- After you have restored a DHCP database, but the restored DHCP database does not have the most recent values.

For example, assume your existing database was deleted and you have to restore an older version of the database. If you start DHCP and open the console, you will notice that the scope and options display, but the active leases do not. Reconciliation populates the client lease information from the registry to the DHCP database.

How a DHCP Database Is Reconciled

When you reconcile a server or a scope, the DHCP service uses both the summary information in the registry and the detailed information in the DHCP database to reconstruct the most current view of the DHCP service. You can choose to reconcile all scopes on the server by selecting the DHCP server, or you can reconcile one scope by selecting the appropriate scope.

Before using the Reconcile feature to verify client information for a DHCP scope from the registry, the server computer needs to meet the following criteria:

- You must restore the DHCP server registry keys, or they must remain intact from previous service operations on the server computer.

- You must generate a fresh copy of the DHCP server database file in the %systemroot%\System32\Dhcp folder on the server computer.

▶ **Generating a Fresh Copy of the DHCP Server Database**

You can generate a fresh copy of the DHCP server database by following these steps:

1. Verify you have a backup copy of the DHCP database, including all required files and subdirectories.

2. Stop the DHCP server.

3. Delete all the database files in the current database path folder.

4. Restart the DHCP server.

When the registry and database meet the previous criteria, you can restart the DHCP service. Upon opening the DHCP console, you might notice that scope information is present, but that there are no active leases displayed. To regain your active leases for each scope, use the Reconcile feature.

▶ **Reconciling All Scopes in a DHCP Database**

To reconcile all scopes in a DHCP database, follow these steps:

1. In the DHCP console, in the console tree, select the DHCP server.

2. On the Action menu, click Reconcile All Scopes.

3. In the Reconcile All Scopes dialog box, click Verify.

4. In the DHCP dialog box, click OK.

▶ **Reconciling One Scope in a DHCP Database**

To reconcile one scope in a DHCP database, follow these steps:

1. In the DHCP console, select the appropriate scope in the console tree.

2. On the Action menu, click Reconcile.

3. In the Reconcile dialog box, click Verify.

4. In the DHCP dialog box, click OK.

Practice reconciling a DHCP database by doing Exercise 2-3, "Reconciling a DHCP Database."

When viewing properties for individual clients displayed in the list of active leases, you might notice client information displayed incorrectly. When the scope clients renew their leases, the DHCP Manager corrects and updates this information.

Compacting a DHCP Database

To recover unused space, the DHCP database must be compacted. Windows Server 2003 dynamically compacts the database in an automatic background process during idle time after a database update. Although dynamic compacting greatly reduces the need for performing offline compaction, it does not fully eliminate it. Offline compaction reclaims the space more efficiently. You should perform it at least once a month for large, volatile networks that have 1,000 or more DHCP clients. For smaller networks, manual compaction is required only every few months.

Windows Server 2003 includes the Jetpack.exe utility, which manually compacts the DHCP and other Jet databases (such as WINS). Use Jetpack.exe to compact a Jet database periodically whenever the database grows beyond 30 megabytes or more in size. As mentioned previously, for Windows Server 2003, the DHCP Server service performs dynamic Jet compaction of the DHCP database while the server is online. This reduces, but does not eliminate the need to use Jetpack.exe for offline compaction.

Consider the following command that uses Jetpack.exe:

```
jetpack dhcp.mdb tmp.mdb
```

The syntax for this command is

```
Jetpack.exe <database name> <temp database name>
```

Practice compacting a DHCP database by doing Exercise 2-4, "Manually Compacting a DHCP Database." now

Using this command, Jetpack.exe uses Tmp.mdb for compaction. Tmp.mdb is a temporary database used by Jetpack.exe to compact Dhcp.mdb. Dhcp.mdb is the DHCP database file. Jetpack.exe compacts the DHCP database by copying database information to Tmp.mdb, deleting the original DHCP database file, Dhcp.mdb, and then renaming the temporary database file to the original file name, Dhcp.mdb.

Enabling Server-Based Conflict Detection

The Windows Server 2003 DHCP server provides the ability to enable server-based conflict detection, which pings an IP address before leasing it to ensure the IP address is not already in use. Windows Server 2003, Windows XP, and Windows 2000 automatically verify that the IP address offered by the DHCP server is available before accepting it, so conflict detection is useful only for pre–Windows 2000 clients. Server-Based Conflict Detection can be enabled on the Advanced tab of the DHCP server properties page. To avoid unnecessary network traffic, leave it disabled unless the assignment of duplicate IP addresses to pre–Windows 2000 clients becomes an issue.

Removing the DHCP Role

Removing the DHCP role from a server is also known as *decommissioning*. When you remove DHCP, the DHCP files are deleted from the server, except for the program files that are in use. To remove the program files, you must restart the system.

▶ **Removing the DHCP Role**

To remove or uninstall DHCP, follow these steps:

1. On the Start menu, click Manage Your Server.
2. On the Manage Your Server page, click Add Or Remove A Role.
3. On the Preliminary Steps page, click Next.
4. On the Server Role page, click DHCP Server, and then click Next.
5. On the Role Removal Confirmation page, click Remove The DHCP Server Role, and then click Next.
6. On the DHCP Server Role Removed page, click Finish.

Best Practices for Managing a DHCP Database

When backing up and restoring a DHCP database, apply the following best practices:

- Manually back up the DHCP database to a location other than %systemroot% \System32\Dhcp\Backup, which is the default location for the automatic backup. If you store a manually created copy of the DHCP database in the same location as the copy that is created automatically, the DHCP service will not function properly.

- Maintain a copy of the backed up DHCP database offline (for example, keep a copy on a tape or a disk). Because the DHCP service automatically backs up a copy of the DHCP database to a location on the local drive, you can lose both the original DHCP database and the backup DHCP database if the hardware fails.

MONITORING A DHCP DATABASE

Monitoring the DHCP service requires you to collect and view data about the DHCP service. You need to monitor both the DHCP clients and the DHCP server. You also might want to monitor related services, such as DNS and WINS. This section focuses on what is involved in monitoring the DHCP server.

Establishing a Performance Baseline

Effectively monitoring DHCP server performance requires quantifying acceptable and unacceptable performance of the DHCP server. To identify a drop in DHCP performance early, you already must have identified "normal" DHCP performance. Identifying normal performance for your environment and DHCP server requires that you establish a performance baseline. A *baseline* is the level of system performance that you decide is acceptable. You should establish or create the baseline when the server is handling a typical workload. When you have a performance baseline, it is easy to identify performance issues because you can compare metrics of key resources as they currently are against the performance baseline. Significant deviations from the baseline often indicate system problems.

Baselines are also valuable when planning for changes and additions to the network. Using performance baselines and data collected over time enables you to assess the throughput of a DHCP server, given a certain number of users. Based on the data from DHCP monitoring, you can extrapolate the result of adding additional users and estimate what additional resources are necessary, if any.

When monitoring a computer configured as a DHCP server, consider other functions the server may be performing, including the following:

- Is it a domain controller, a file and print server, or a mail server in addition to being a DHCP server?

- What is the total utilization of the server's resources? How would adding the DHCP server role impact the server's overall performance?

- Consider the time of day at which you are collecting data: Is it during peak logon times?

- Are other scheduled processes, such as backups, running at the same time?

- How many users accessed the server for functions other than DHCP while you were collecting data for your baseline?

The DHCP service uses memory, processor, disk, and network subsystems. Although these subsystems are important for the DHCP service to perform optimally, you can obtain the greatest benefit by monitoring the performance of the network subsystem.

Location of DHCP Data

Four tools provide DHCP data: the DHCP console, DHCP audit log, Event Viewer, and Performance console. Each tool provides information, as described in table Table 2-3.

Table 2-3   **DHCP Data Tools**

Tool	Description	Examples of Information Provided
DHCP console statistics	Use the DHCP console to display DHCP server statistics, which is data collected at either the server level or the scope level since the DHCP service was last started.	■ DHCP service start and stop times ■ Number of IP addresses available in a scope ■ Number of leases in use in a scope ■ Number of clients in use
DHCP audit log/Event Viewer	These two tools do the exact same thing. They provide information about DHCP events. Information includes significant occurrences either in the system or in an application that requires notification to the user or an additional entry to a log.	■ When the service is stopped or started, and by whom ■ DHCP service errors ■ DHCP service authorizations
Performance console	This tool provides DHCP performance data. The DHCP service includes a set of performance counters that the administrator can use to monitor various types of server activity.	■ Number of leases renewed for a period of time ■ Number of DHCPACK or DHCPNACK packets for a period of time ■ Amount of disk space that the DHCP database uses ■ Number of IP address conflicts

Using DHCP Statistics to Monitor a DHCP Server

DHCP statistics represent data collected at the server level or the scope level since the most recent start of the DHCP service.

Statistics provide a real-time view that you can use to check the status of your DHCP server or scopes. You can get statistics for a particular scope or at the server level; the latter shows the aggregate of all the scopes that the server manages.

Using the DHCP console, you can view the DHCP statistics, for both a server and a scope, as listed in Table 2-4.

Table 2-4   **DHCP Statistics**

DHCP Statistics	Description	Server Statistics	Scope Statistics
Start Time	When the DHCP service was started	X	
Up Time	Period of time the DHCP service has been active	X	
Discovers	Number of client DHCPDISCOVERs received	X	

(continued)

Table 2-4   **DHCP Statistics**

DHCP Statistics	Description	Server Statistics	Scope Statistics
Offers	Number of client DHCPOFFERs sent	X	
Requests	Number of client DHCPREQUESTs received	X	
Acks	Number of client DHCPACKs sent	X	
Nacks	Number of client DHCPNACKs sent	X	
Declines	Number of client DHCPDECLINEs received	X	
Releases	Number of client DHCPRELEASEs received	X	
Total Scopes	Total number of scopes on the DHCP server	X	
Total Addresses	Total number of IP addresses configured for clients	X	X
In Use	Number of IP addresses currently leased	X	X
Available	Number of IP addresses available for lease	X	X

Viewing DHCP Statistics

You can view DHCP statistics for both a server and a scope. For greater ease in viewing DHCP statistics, you can enable DHCP server statistics to refresh automatically, which also enables the DHCP scope statistics to refresh automatically.

▶ **Enabling Automatic Refresh of DHCP Statistics**

To enable automatic refresh of DHCP statistics, follow these steps:

1. In the DHCP console, in the console tree, select the appropriate DHCP server.

2. On the Action menu, click Properties.

3. In the General tab, select the Automatically Update Statistics Every check box, configure the Hours and Minutes fields appropriately, and then click OK.

▶ **Viewing DHCP Server Statistics**

To view DHCP server statistics, follow these steps:

1. In the DHCP console, in the console tree, select the appropriate DHCP server.

2. On the Action menu, click Display Statistics. Figure 2-5 is displayed.

Figure 2-5   DHCP server statistics

▶ **Viewing DHCP Scope Statistics**

To view DHCP scope statistics, follow these steps:

1. In the DHCP console, in the console tree, select the appropriate DHCP scope.

2. On the Action menu, click Display Statistics. Figure 2-6 is displayed.

Figure 2-6   DHCP scope statistics

Using the DHCP Audit Log to Monitor a DHCP Server

Logging DHCP server data enables you to gather information about the DHCP Server service operations on the network. You can view a single day's log file for information, or you can collect log files on a separate server for analysis of DHCP server data over a longer period. This information is helpful when deciding whether you need to add more DHCP servers or when troubleshooting problems with DHCP servers. It is important that you understand the audit log process because there are times when logging will cease and log files will be overwritten. Understanding the process will enable you to gather the DHCP statistics necessary to maintain optimal performance of your DHCP server.

A DHCP audit log gives the administrator a day-to-day collection of DHCP events. DHCP audit logs provide you with the information that you may need for monitoring your DHCP server. You can use DHCP audit logs to view activity for one specified day, or you can collect the log files to analyze DHCP server activity over longer periods.

DHCP Audit Log File

A *DHCP audit log file* is a log of service-related events, such as the following:

- The starting and stopping of the service

- The verification of authorizations

- Leasing, renewal, and denial of IP addresses

When you enable logging, the DHCP server creates log files named DhcpSrvLog-*day*.log, where *day* is a three-letter abbreviation that represents the day the log was created; for example, a log created on Sunday would be named DhcpSrvLog-Sun .log. The DHCP server stores these files in the DHCP database directory. Figure 2-7 shows a sample log file.

```
ID,Date,Time,Description,IP Address,Host Name,MAC Address
24,07/27/03,00:00:13,Database Cleanup Begin,,,,
25,07/27/03,00:00:13,0 leases expired and 0 leases deleted,,,,
25,07/27/03,00:00:13,0 leases expired and 0 leases deleted,,,,
24,07/27/03,07:47:01,Database Cleanup Begin,,,,
25,07/27/03,07:47:01,0 leases expired and 0 leases deleted,,,,
25,07/27/03,07:47:01,0 leases expired and 0 leases deleted,,,,
55,07/27/03,07:47:25,Authorized(servicing),,contoso01.com,,
10,07/27/03,07:52:25,Assign,10.1.1.90,Bott98,0003FF4398CA,
24,07/27/03,08:47:03,Database Cleanup Begin,,,,
25,07/27/03,08:47:03,0 leases expired and 0 leases deleted,,,,
25,07/27/03,08:47:03,0 leases expired and 0 leases deleted,,,,
24,07/27/03,09:47:05,Database Cleanup Begin,,,,
25,07/27/03,09:47:05,0 leases expired and 0 leases deleted,,,,
25,07/27/03,09:47:05,0 leases expired and 0 leases deleted,,,,
24,07/27/03,10:47:07,Database Cleanup Begin,,,,
25,07/27/03,10:47:07,0 leases expired and 0 leases deleted,,,,
25,07/27/03,10:47:07,0 leases expired and 0 leases deleted,,,,
24,07/27/03,11:47:09,Database Cleanup Begin,,,,
25,07/27/03,11:47:09,0 leases expired and 0 leases deleted,,,,
25,07/27/03,11:47:09,0 leases expired and 0 leases deleted,,,,
24,07/27/03,12:47:11,Database Cleanup Begin,,,,
25,07/27/03,12:47:11,0 leases expired and 0 leases deleted,,,,
25,07/27/03,12:47:11,0 leases expired and 0 leases deleted,,,,
24,07/27/03,13:47:13,Database Cleanup Begin,,,,
25,07/27/03,13:47:13,0 leases expired and 0 leases deleted,,,,
25,07/27/03,13:47:13,0 leases expired and 0 leases deleted,,,,
24,07/27/03,14:47:15,Database Cleanup Begin,,,,
25,07/27/03,14:47:15,0 leases expired and 0 leases deleted,,,,
25,07/27/03,14:47:15,0 leases expired and 0 leases deleted,,,,
24,07/27/03,15:47:17,Database Cleanup Begin,,,,
25,07/27/03,15:47:17,0 leases expired and 0 leases deleted,,,,
25,07/27/03,15:47:17,0 leases expired and 0 leases deleted,,,,
```

Figure 2-7   Sample DHCP audit log file

The log files are comma-delimitated text files that contain log entries representing a single line of text. A DHCP audit log file includes the fields shown in Table 2-5.

Table 2-5   DHCP Audit Log File Fields

Field	Description
ID	A DHCP server event ID code
Date	The date on which this entry was logged on the DHCP server
Time	The time at which this entry was logged on the DHCP server
Description	A description of this DHCP server event
IP Address	The IP address of the DHCP client
Host Name	The host name of the DHCP client
MAC Address	The Media Access Control (MAC) address that the network adapter hardware of the client uses

The DHCP server's audit log files use reserved event ID codes to provide information about the type of server event or activity logged. Table 2-6 describes the DHCP event ID codes that might appear in the log file.

Table 2-6   **DHCP Event IDs and Descriptions**

Event ID	Description
00	The log started.
01	The log stopped.
02	The log temporarily paused because of low disk space.
10	A client leased a new IP address.
11	A client renewed a lease.
12	A client released a lease.
13	An IP address was found in use on the network.
14	A lease request was not satisfied because the address pool of the scope was exhausted.
15	A lease was denied.
20	A client leased a Bootstrap Protocol (BOOTP) address.

How DHCP Audit Logging Works

The following process describes how audit logging starts, performs, and ends during a 24-hour day:

1. A new log file is created when one of the following events occurs: the DHCP server is started, or the local time passes 12:00 A.M.

2. Depending on whether the audit log file has been modified in the previous 24 hours, the following actions occur:

   a. If the file previously existed without modification for more than a day, it is overwritten.

   b. If the file existed but was modified within the previous 24 hours, it is not overwritten. Instead, new logging activity is appended to the end of the existing file. This is the case when either the system or the DHCP Server service is restarted.

3. The server writes a header message in the audit log file, which indicates that logging has started.

4. During audit logging, the DHCP server performs various logical disk checks to ensure disk space used by the log stays within boundaries set in the registry. Disk checks are performed at intervals of events and when the server computer reaches 12:00 A.M. in its local clock. By default, disks are considered full when the amount of free disk space falls below 20 megabytes or the current audit file is larger than one-seventh (1/7) of the maximum allotted space for the combined total space of all audit log files stored on the computer. The default maximum space is 70 megabytes.

5. If the disk check finds the disk is full, logging ceases, but disk checks continue. If more disk space becomes available, logging resumes.

6. At 12:00 A.M., the current day's log file is closed and the logging process begins again.

> **NOTE   Keeping Log Files Older Than Seven Days**   To keep the audit log infor-
> mation for a period greater than a week, remove audit log files from the directory
> before the next week's audit log overwrites it.

▶ **Enabling and Configuring DHCP Audit Logging**

To enable and configure DHCP audit logging, follow these steps:

1. In the DHCP console, in the console tree, select the appropriate DHCP server.

2. On the Action menu, click Properties.

3. In the General tab, verify that the Enable DHCP Audit Logging option is selected.

4. In the Advanced tab, in the Audit Log File Path field, type the appropriate audit log file path, and then click OK.

5. In the DHCP dialog box, click Yes to stop and then restart the service.

Practice viewing DHCP audit logging by doing Exercise 2-5, "Configuring and Viewing the DHCP Audit Log."

Viewing the DHCP Audit Log

Because DHCP audit logging is enabled by default, as soon as DHCP is installed and configured, you can view the DHCP audit logs to view the information that you need to monitor your DHCP server. Using Windows Explorer, go to the directory where you are storing the audit log file, and double-click the appropriate log file.

> **NOTE   Where the DHCP Service Stores Logs**   By default, the DHCP service
> stores audit logs in the %systemroot%\System32\Dhcp folder. An audit log file
> contains the event IDs and their meanings in the file. Audit logs are named
> DhcpSrvLog-day.log where day is the three-letter abbreviation for the day of
> the week. For example, the audit log for Wednesday is DhcpSrvLog-Wed.log.

Using the Performance Console to Monitor DHCP

There is an administrative utility, called the Performance console, that you can use to monitor DHCP server performance. When you open the Performance console, the console tree has two nodes. The first node is System Monitor, and the second node is Performance Logs And Alerts.

System Monitor

You can add performance objects and counters to any one of the System Monitor's three graphical views: graph, histogram, and report. To view any of the views individually, right-click the desired view and then click New Window From Here. You also can view logged data. If you add a counter that has more than one instance, you have the option to select the instance. For example, if the computer you are monitoring has two network interfaces, when you select the Network Interface performance object, you have the option of selecting one or both of the interfaces for monitoring. A *performance object* is a logical collection of counters that is associated with a resource or service that can be monitored. A *performance counter* is a data item that is associated with a performance object. For each counter selected,

System Monitor presents a value corresponding to a particular aspect of the performance defined for the performance object. A *performance object instance* is a term used to distinguish between multiple performance objects of the same type on a computer.

Common Performance Counters Table 2-7 provides a sampling of common performance counters, along with explanations of what the data might mean. (The performance object is the DHCP server.)

Table 2-7 **Common Performance Counters**

Performance Counter	What Data Is Collected	What the Data Means	What to Look for After a Baseline Is Established
Packets received/ second	This is the number of message packets that the DHCP server receives per second.	A large number indicates heavy, DHCP-related message traffic to the server.	Monitor for sudden increases or decreases, which could reflect problems, such as loss of connectivity, on the network.
Requests/second	This is the number of DHCP request messages that the DHCP server receives per second from clients.	A sudden or unusual increase in this number indicates a large number of clients trying to renew their leases with the DHCP server. This might indicate that scope lease durations are too short.	Monitor for sudden increases or decreases, which could reflect problems, such as loss of connectivity, on the network.
Active queue length	This is the current length of the internal message queue of the DHCP server. This number equals the number of unprocessed messages that the server has queued.	A large number might indicate that the DHCP server cannot keep up with the load of requests presented.	Monitor for both sudden increases and gradual increases, which could reflect increased load or decreased server capacity.
Duplicates dropped/second	This is the number of duplicated packets that the DHCP server drops per second.	This number can be affected by multiple DHCP relay agents or network interfaces that are forwarding the same packet to the server. A large number indicates that the server is not responding fast enough or that the relay agent's boot threshold time is not set high enough.	Monitor this counter for any activity that indicates that more than one request is being transmitted on behalf of clients. A large number indicates that either the client is timing out too quickly or the server is not responding fast enough.

Creating DHCP Performance Alerts

Practice
creating alerts
by doing
Exercise 2-6,
"Creating Alerts
for a DHCP
Server." now

The counters that are available for the DHCP server performance object are also available for creating alerts. If you know the acceptable level that a counter can rise above or fall below before an issue occurs, you can create an alert to both notify you and run a program or script. An *alert* is a feature that detects when a pre-defined counter value either rises above or falls below a specified setting. The specified setting on the counter is the *alert threshold*. For example, if in your baseline the DHCP active queue length is nearly always less than three, set an alert threshold for six or seven. A sudden increase in DHCP active queue length may indicate that the request load is too great for the DHCP server.

Best Practices for Creating DHCP Alerts

When you create alerts for a DHCP server, follow these recommended guidelines:

- Define the acceptable level that a DHCP counter can rise above or fall below before creating an alert. To do this, you log the DHCP counter for a specific time period to create a baseline. Using this baseline, you can ascertain the normal operating range for a given DHCP counter and then create alerts to notify you when the activity for this DHCP counter is outside of the normal operating range.

- Use scripts with your alerts. Use DHCP Netsh commands in a script to respond to the alert.

    MORE INFO   Using Netsh Commands   For more information on using Netsh commands, see Microsoft Knowledgebase article 242468, "How to Use the Netsh.exe Tool and Command-Line Switches." To find this article, go to *http://support.microsoft.com* and enter the article number in the Search The Knowledge Base text box.

Best Practices for Monitoring DHCP

Consider the following best practices when monitoring the performance of a DHCP server:

- **Create a baseline of performance data on the DHCP server.**   You can compare the baseline with counters that can indicate if the server hosting DHCP is overloaded, or if the network is failing to send DHCP requests to the server.

- **Check the standard counters for server performance (such as processor utilization, paging, disk performance, and network utilization).**   Because DHCP often is installed on a server that also hosts other services or applications, it is important to understand the total application and service load on the server and how the load on the server might affect the operation of the DHCP Server service.

- **Review DHCP server counters, such as Acks/sec, to look for significant drops or increases that indicate a change in DHCP traffic.**   A sudden increase in activity could result from the addition of new DHCP clients, or it could reflect a change to a shorter **DCHP lease**. A sudden decrease in activity could indicate a lengthening of the DHCP lease, a failure of the network to transmit DHCP requests, or a failure of the DHCP server to process the requests.

USING AUTOMATIC PRIVATE IP ADDRESSING

As discussed in Chapter 1, "Implementing DHCP," **Automatic Private IP Addressing (APIPA)** is an addressing feature for simple networks that consist of a single network segment. Whenever a computer running Windows Server 2003 has been configured to obtain an IP address automatically, and when no DHCP server or alternate configuration is available, the computer uses APIPA to assign itself a private IP address in the range of 169.254.0.1 to 169.254.255.254.

To determine whether APIPA is currently enabled and active, type **ipconfig /all** at a command prompt. The resulting text identifies your IP address and other information. If the Autoconfiguration Enabled line reads Yes and the IP address is in the 169.254.0.1 to 169.254.255.254 range, APIPA is active.

This automatic-addressing feature works only for computers on a network segment that cannot obtain an IP address through other means. If a DHCP server later becomes available to a **host** that has assigned itself an APIPA address, the computer changes its IP address to one obtained from the DHCP server. Computers using APIPA addresses can communicate only with other computers using APIPA addresses on the same network segment; they are not directly reachable from the Internet. Note also that through APIPA, you cannot configure a computer with a DNS server address, a default gateway address, or a WINS server address. If you want a computer to obtain an address automatically but want to specify such an address when no DHCP server is available, you can specify it by using an alternate configuration. For more information about alternate configurations, see Chapter 1, "Implementing DHCP."

APIPA is available on any computer running Windows 98, Microsoft Windows Millennium Edition (Me), Windows 2000, Windows XP, or Windows Server 2003.

Disabling APIPA

If you want to ensure that APIPA will not be used, you can either configure an alternate address in the connection's IP properties or disable the automatic-addressing feature by editing the registry. Note that to disable APIPA for one adapter and to disable APIPA for all adapters requires you to edit different registry keys.

▶ **Disabling APIPA on a Single Adapter**

To disable APIPA on a single adapter by editing the registry, complete the following steps:

1. Use the registry editor Regedit.exe to add the registry entry IPAutoconfigurationEnabled with a value of 0 (REG_DWORD data type) in the following subkey:

   ```
   HKEY_LOCAL_MACHINE\SYSTEM\CurrentControlSet\Services\Tcpip\Parameters\
   Interfaces\interface
   ```

2. Restart the computer.

▶ **Disabling APIPA on Multiple Adapters**

To disable APIPA for multiple adapters by editing the registry, complete the following steps:

1. Set the value of the IPAutoconfigurationEnabled entry to 0 (REG_DWORD data type) in the following registry subkey:

   `HKEY_LOCAL_MACHINE\SYSTEM\CurrentControlSet\Services\Tcpip\Parameters`

2. Restart the computer.

Troubleshooting APIPA

For computers running any version of the Windows operating system since Windows 98, APIPA addresses are default addresses. That is, they are assigned to connected hosts whose network configuration has not been altered since the operating system was installed. In certain small networks, you might want to leave the computers with these default APIPA addresses to simplify network communication and administration. If so, you can run the Ipconfig /all command on networked computers to determine whether the address assigned to each computer's local area connection falls within the APIPA range of 169.254.0.1 to 169.254.255.254.

If the Ipconfig /all command does not reveal an APIPA address, the output instead reveals one of three scenarios: no address with or without an error message, an all-zeros address, or a nonzero IP address outside of APIPA range.

When no IP address has been assigned to a host, an error message might provide the specific cause. For example, the Ipconfig /all output might inform you that the media (in other words, the network cable) has been disconnected. At this point, you can check the network cable attachments and then run the Ipconfig /renew command to obtain a new IP address through the APIPA feature. Should this strategy fail to provide the host with a new IP address, you should proceed to diagnose hardware problems such as faulty cables, hubs, and switches.

Sometimes the Ipconfig /all command output does not provide an explicit cause for the computer's failure to obtain an IP address. If so, suspect problems with the network adapter. Verify that the computer in question has a network adapter properly installed, along with the most recent version of the appropriate driver. Then run the Ipconfig /renew command to attempt to obtain an IP address again. If problems persist, you should proceed to diagnose hardware issues.

An all-zeros address typically means that TCP/IP has successfully initialized on the computer, but has not yet obtained an address from a DHCP server. For example, if your computer has successfully obtained an IP address from a DHCP server and you type **ipconfig /release** to release the address, your IP address will display 0.0.0.0.

For properly functioning computers in an environment not deliberately using APIPA for network configuration, a nonzero IP address outside of APIPA range is expected. Common examples of this type of address include the blocks of IP addresses reserved by IANA for private networks (10.0.0.0 through 10.255.255.255, 172.16.0.0 through 172.31.255.255, and 192.168.0.0 through 192.168.255.255).

SUMMARY

- You can configure DHCP to dynamically update DNS. If you choose to dynamically update DNS resource records, you should consider using secure dynamic updates.

- Because DHCP is a key component in your organization, you must manage and monitor it.

- DHCP management consists of backing up and restoring the database as well as reconciling, compacting, and, in some cases, removing the database.

- You can monitor DHCP by using Performance Monitor, the DHCP audit log file, Event Viewer, and DHCP server and scope statistics.

- APIPA is useful for providing addresses to single-segment networks that do not have a DHCP server.

EXERCISES

IMPORTANT **Completing All Exercises** *If you plan to do any of the textbook exercises in this chapter, you must do all of the exercises in the chapter to return the computer to it's original state for the associated Lab Manual labs. Note that the following exercises require DNS and DHCP to be installed, which is the state of the student computers after the completion of Lab Manual Lab 1.*

Exercise 2-1: Configuring DNS Dynamic Update

To configure DNS dynamic update, follow these steps:

1. Open the DNS console.

2. Right-click the zone for which you want to configure dynamic updates, and then click Properties.

3. In the General tab, in the Dynamic Updates list, select Nonsecure And Secure, and then click OK.

Exercise 2-2: Manually Backing Up a DHCP Database

To back up the DHCP database at the source server, complete the following steps:

1. Open the DHCP console.

2. In the console tree, select the DHCP server you want to back up.

3. On the Action menu, select Backup.

   The Browse For Folder dialog box opens.

4. Select the folder that will contain the backup DHCP database, and then click OK.

   You must choose a local drive for the DHCP database backup folder.

Exercise 2-3: Reconciling a DHCP Database

To reconcile a DHCP database, follow these steps:

1. Open the DHCP console.

2. Perform one of the following, and then click Verify:

    a. To reconcile a particular scope, right-click that scope, and click Reconcile.

    b. To reconcile all scopes, right-click the DHCP server, and then click Reconcile All Scopes.

3. If the reconciliation is successful, a DHCP dialog box appears stating that the database is consistent.

Exercise 2-4: Manually Compacting a DHCP Database

To manually compact a DHCP database, follow these steps:

1. At a DHCP server computer, open a command prompt.

2. To change to the DHCP directory, at the command prompt, type **cd%systemroot%\system32\dhcp**, and then press Enter.

3. To stop the DHCP service, at the command prompt, type **net stop dhcpserver**, and press Enter.

4. To compact the DHCP database, at the command prompt, type **jetpack dhcp.mdb tmp.mdb**, and press Enter.

    A message is displayed stating how long it took to compact the database, that the database was moved from the temporary file to Dhcp.mdb, and that the process completed successfully.

5. To start the DHCP service, at the command prompt, type **net start dhcpserver**, and press Enter.

Exercise 2-5: Configuring and Viewing the DHCP Audit Log

To configure and view the DHCP audit log, follow these steps:

1. Open the DHCP console.

2. In the console tree, click the DHCP server for which you want to enable audit logging.

3. On the Action menu, click Properties.

4. In the General tab, select the Enable DHCP Audit Logging check box, and then click OK.

5. In the Advanced tab, in the Audit Log File Path box, type **c:\textbook\exercises\chapter02**.

6. You are asked if you want to restart the DHCP service to apply the changes. Select Yes.

7. Navigate to the **c:\Textbook\Exercises\Chapter02** folder, and double-click DhcpSrvLog-*day*.log (where *day* is the three-letter abbreviation of today's log).

Exercise 2-6: Creating Alerts for a DHCP Server

To create an alert for a DHCP server, follow these steps:

1. In the Performance console, under Performance Logs And Alerts, select Alerts.

2. On the Action menu, click New Alert Settings.

3. In the New Alert Settings dialog box, in the Name box, type **DHCP Renew Alert**, and then click OK.

4. In the General tab, in the DHCP Renew Alert dialog box, in the Comment field, type **Alert When DHCP Client Renews IP Lease**, and then click Add.

5. In the Add Counters dialog box, in the Performance Object field, select DHCP Server, add the counter Acks/sec, and then click Close.

6. In the General tab, in the DHCP Renew Alert dialog box, in the Limit field, type **1**.

7. In the General tab, in the DHCP Renew Alert dialog box, in the Interval field, type **5**.

8. In the Action tab, select Send A Network Message To, and then type **Administrator**.

   When the alert is tripped, a dialog box will appear.

9. In the Schedule tab, under Start Scan, verify that Manually (Using The Shortcut Menu) is selected, and then click OK.

REVIEW QUESTIONS

1. You have a Windows NT 4 client for which you want to enable dynamic updates. You want the DHCP server to automatically update both the A record and PTR record. Which action will accomplish this?

   a. Take no action. Updating of the A record and PTR record happens automatically by default.

   b. In the DNS tab of the DHCP server properties dialog box, select Dynamically Update DNS A And PTR Records For DHCP Clients That Do Not Request Updates.

   c. In the DNS tab of the DHCP server properties dialog box, select Always Dynamically Update DNS A And PTR Records.

   d. Register the client as a dynamic host with the DHCP server.

2. You have not modified the default settings for DNS on the DHCP client or server. Which of the following client record or records will the DHCP server update in DNS? (Assume the clients are running Windows XP.)

   a. The PTR resource record

   b. The A resource record

   c. Both the PTR and A resource records

   d. Neither the PTR nor the A resource record

3. For a zone in which only secure dynamic updates are allowed, you have configured your DHCP server to perform dynamic updates on behalf of Windows NT 4 clients. Other dynamic DNS settings on the DHCP server have the default settings. After you migrate the clients to Windows XP, you find that their A resource records are no longer being updated. What is the most likely explanation for this problem?

4. True or False: If a DNS zone accepts only secure dynamic updates and the DHCP server is a member of the DnsUpdateProxy security group, the resource records created by the Netlogon service for the domain controller lack security? Explain your answer. *Secure dynamic updates require the owner of a resource record to update that record*

5. Automatic and manual backups of the DHCP database are successfully performed. You want to restore the following: all of the scopes, reservations, leases, options, and security credentials. What should you do?

   a. Restore from the automatic backup.

   b. Restore from the manual backup.

   c. Restore from an offline backup.

   d. Restore from the automatic or manual backup, and reconfigure security credentials manually.

6. You just completed a restoration of the DHCP database. You start the DHCP console to verify a successful restoration. You notice the scope and options are displayed, but active leases are not. What should you do to repopulate the active leases?

   a. The restoration failed. Perform the restoration again.

   b. The restoration failed because the backup was corrupt. Locate a valid backup and use it to restore the DHCP database.

   c. Using the DHCP console, perform reconciliation.

   d. Delete the Tmp.mdb file, and restart the DHCP service.

7. You are monitoring a DHCP server and you want to save the audit log that was created last Tuesday. Today is Monday. What should you do?

   a. Do nothing; the DHCP server automatically saves the log after writing to it.

   b. Remove the log file from the directory.

   c. Change the location of the log files.

   d. On Wednesday, stop and start the DHCP Server service.

8. You want to determine how many IP addresses are available for lease across all scopes. What tool should you use for this?

   a. System Event Log

   b. DHCP scope statistics

   c. DHCP server statistics

   d. DHCP audit log

CASE SCENARIOS

Case Scenario 2-1: Monitoring DHCP Requests

You have been monitoring DHCP server activity by using System Monitor. You have been viewing the Discovers/sec counter. You observe a sudden increase in the number of DHCP requests. Which of the following statements could explain the sudden increase?

a. A large number of clients are initializing simultaneously and attempting to locate a DHCP server.

b. A large number of clients are shutting down simultaneously and releasing their IP address leases.

c. Scope leases are too short, forcing an increase in DHCPNACK messages.

d. Two new DHCP servers have been initialized on the network and are querying the directory service for the enterprise root.

Case Scenario 2-2: Monitoring DHCP Network Traffic

Recently, users have complained that the network is slow at different periods throughout the week. You suspect heavy DHCP traffic is a contributing cause. When DHCP traffic is heavier than normal, you want notification of it. How can you accomplish this?

CHAPTER 3
IMPLEMENTING NAME RESOLUTION USING DNS

Upon completion of this chapter, you will be able to:

- Describe the process of **name resolution** and why it is important to your organization.

- Install and configure the **Domain Name System (DNS)**.

- Describe and configure **primary zones**, **secondary zones**, **in-addr.arpa zones**, and **stub zones**.

- Create an **Active Directory–integrated zone**, and explain the benefits of doing so.

- Describe the different types of **DNS servers** and the functions they perform.

- Explain the benefits of delegating a **zone**, and create a delegated zone.

- Describe the process of a **zone transfer**.

This chapter introduces fundamental concepts related to DNS name resolution in Microsoft Windows Server 2003. The chapter also explains key DNS concepts, such as the **DNS namespace**, **DNS zones**, types of DNS servers, DNS **resource records**, and DNS **resolvers**. Also discussed is the process of configuring DNS servers, the types and process of DNS queries, and forwarding. Because DNS plays such a key role in Windows Server 2003, it is critical that you have a strong grasp of its concepts, processes, and methods of configuration. Without DNS, your network will most likely not function—clients won't be able to resolve names to **Internet Protocol (IP)** addresses. In addition, **Active Directory** directory service clients use DNS to locate domain controllers; therefore, it is important that you understand key DNS concepts and how to properly configure DNS for your network.

OVERVIEW OF THE NAME RESOLUTION PROCESS

For network devices, such as computers and printers, to communicate on the Internet or within your organization's network, they must be able to locate one another. In a Windows Server 2003 network, the primary means of locating network devices and network services is through the use of DNS.

For example, in order for ComputerA to communicate with ComputerB using **Transmission Control Protocol/Internet Protocol (TCP/IP)**, ComputerA must obtain the IP address of ComputerB. The process of obtaining an IP address for a computer name (for example, "ComputerA") is called *name resolution*. DNS and Windows Internet Naming System (WINS) name resolution are separate software processes of translating between names that are easy for users to understand and numerical IP addresses, which are difficult for users but necessary for TCP/IP communications.

OVERVIEW OF DNS

Before the growth of the ARPANET into what we now know as the Internet, text files handled name resolution. The text file listed each name of the host and its corresponding IP address (the HOSTS.txt file). Whenever a new host was added to the network, the HOSTS.txt file was updated with the host name and IP address. Periodically, all ARPANET users would then download and use the updated HOSTS.txt file. Because the HOSTS.txt file was flat, rather than hierarchical, every host name on the ARPANET had to be unique. There was no method for creating namespaces such as domains.

Another problem was the size of the database and the inability to distribute the workload that resulted from parsing this file across multiple computers. Every HOSTS.txt file listed every available host, which meant that every computer that parsed the HOSTS.txt file did 100 percent of the work to resolve client names into IP addresses. Clearly, this was inefficient, and a better name resolution system had to be devised.

In 1984, when the number of hosts on ARPANET reached 1,000, DNS was introduced. Because DNS is designed as a distributed database with a hierarchical structure, it can serve as the foundation for host name resolution in a TCP/IP network of any size, including the Internet. The distributed nature of DNS enables the name resolution workload to be shared among many computers. Today, most internet-working software, such as electronic mail programs and Web browsers, uses DNS for name resolution.

Benefits of DNS

Although DNS is most commonly associated with the Internet, private networks also use DNS because of the following benefits:

- **Scalability** Because DNS is capable of distributing workload across several databases or computers, it can scale to handle any level of name resolution required.

- **Constancy** Host names remain constant even when associated IP addresses change, which makes locating network resources much easier.

- **Ease of use**   Users access computers using easy-to-remember names such as www.microsoft.com rather than a numerical IP address, such as 192.168.1.100.

- **Simplicity**   Users need to learn only one naming convention to find resources on either the Internet or an intranet.

What Is DNS?

To understand the importance of DNS and how it functions within a Windows Server 2003 networking environment, you must understand the following components of DNS:

- Domain namespace
- DNS zones
- Types of DNS name servers
- DNS resource records

The following sections discuss each of these components.

Domain Namespace

The *domain namespace* is a hierarchical, tree-structured namespace, starting at an unnamed root used for all DNS operations. In the DNS namespace, each **node** and **leaf object** in the domain namespace tree represents a named domain. Each domain can have additional child domains. Figure 3-1 illustrates the structure of an Internet domain namespace.

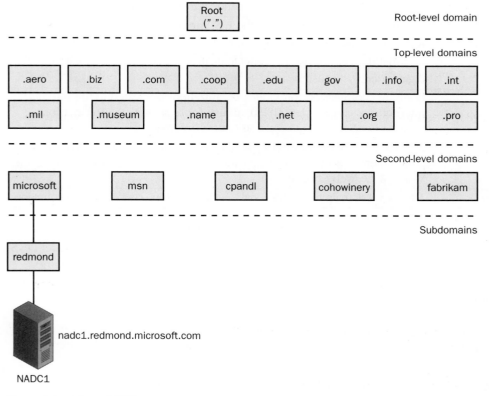

Figure 3-1   Internet DNS namespace

The DNS namespace has a hierarchical structure, and each **DNS domain** name is unique. In Figure 3-1, at the top of the Internet DNS namespace is the root domain. The root domain is represented by "." (a period). Under the DNS root domain, the **top-level domains**, or first-level domains, are organizational types such as .org, .com, and .edu. There are three types of top-level domains:

- **Generic**   See Table 3-1 for examples of generic, top-level domain names.

- **Country code**   Examples of country code domain names are .uk, .jp, and .us.

- **Infrastructure domain**   .arpa is the infrastructure domain name.

The Internet public created generic domains. Individual countries use code domains as necessary. The Internet Assigned Numbers Authority (IANA) assigns top-level domains. Table 3-1 lists the top-level domain names and their uses.

Table 3-1   **Generic Top-Level Domain Names**

Domain Name	Use
.aero	Exclusively reserved for the aviation community
.biz	A top-level domain that is aimed at large and small companies around the world
.com	Commercial organizations, such as microsoft.com for the Microsoft Corporation
.coop	A top-level domain for cooperatives
.edu	Educational institutions, now mainly four-year colleges and universities, such as wustl.edu for Washington University in St. Louis.
.gov	Agencies of the U.S. federal government, such as fbi.gov for the U.S. Federal Bureau of Investigation
.info	An unrestricted domain aimed at providing information for worldwide consumption
.int	Organizations established by international treaties, such as nato.int for NATO
.mil	U.S. military, such as af.mil for the U.S. Air Force
.museum	A domain restricted to museums and related organizations and individuals
.name	A global domain for use by individuals that possibly develops into a global digital identity for users
.net	Computers of network providers, organizations dedicated to the Internet, Internet service providers (ISPs), and so forth, such as internic.net for the Internet Network Information Center (InterNIC)
.org	A top-level domain for groups that do not fit anywhere else, such as non-governmental or nonprofit organizations (for example, w3.org, which is the World Wide Web Consortium)
.pro	A top-level domain for professionals, such as doctors, lawyers, and accountants

DNS uses the **fully qualified domain name (FQDN)** to map a host name to an IP address. An *FQDN* describes the exact relationship between a host and its DNS domain. For example, computer1.sales.microsoft.com represents a host name, computer1, in the sales domain, in the Microsoft second-level domain, and in the .com top-level domain. Figure 3-2 illustrates an FQDN.

Figure 3-2   Breakdown of an FQDN

Second-level DNS domains are registered to individuals or organizations, such as microsoft.com, the Microsoft Corporation domain; or wustl.edu, which is Washington University in the St. Louis domain; or gov.au, the domain for the Australian government. Second-level DNS domains can have many subdomains, and any domain can have hosts. A *host* is a specific computer or other network device within a domain, such as computer1 in the sales subdomain of the microsoft.com domain.

One benefit of the hierarchical structure of DNS is that it is possible to have two hosts with the same host names that are in different locations in the hierarchy. For example, two hosts named computer1—computer1.sales.microsoft.com and computer1.cpandl.microsoft.com—can both exist without conflict because they are in different locations in the namespace hierarchy.

As previously noted, another benefit of the DNS hierarchical structure is that workload for name resolution is distributed across many different resources.

DNS zones, name servers, and resource records are discussed later in this chapter.

INSTALLING DNS

To enjoy the benefits of DNS, you must, of course, install DNS. Before you install DNS, it is recommended that you configure your computer to use a static IP address. If the DNS server is assigned its IP address from Dynamic Host Configuration Protocol (DHCP), its IP address may change. If the DNS server's IP address changes, queries sent by DNS clients configured with the old IP address will fail. Windows Server 2003 provides several wizards and other tools to install DNS quickly and easily. One method of installing DNS is by using the Manage Your Server page. The Manage Your Server page enables you to add or remove server roles, such as file server, print server, DHCP server, and DNS server. The following procedure explains how to use the Manage Your Server page to add the DNS server role.

▶ **Adding the DNS Server Role**

To add the DNS server role, follow these steps:

1. Click Start, point to Control Panel, point to Administrative Tools, and then click Manage Your Server.

   The Manage Your Server page starts automatically by default when you log on.

2. On the Manage Your Server page, click Add Or Remove A Role.

3. On the Preliminary Steps page, click Next.

4. On the Server Role page, click DNS Server, and then click Next.

5. On the Summary Of Selections page, click Next.

6. On the Welcome To The Configure A DNS Server Wizard page, click Next.

7. On the Select Configuration Action page, click Configure Root Hints Only (Recommended For Advanced Users Only), and then click Next.

8. On the Completing The Configure A DNS Server Wizard page, click Finish.

9. On the This Server Is Now A DNS Server page, click Finish.

Practice adding a DNS server role by doing Exercise 3-1, "Adding the DNS Server Role," now.

DNS ZONES

For administrative purposes, DNS domains can be organized into zones. A zone is a collection of host name–to–IP address mappings for hosts in a contiguous portion of the DNS namespace, as shown in Figure 3-3. A zone can hold the resource records for one domain, or it can hold the resource records for multiple domains. A zone can host more than one domain only if the domains are contiguous—that is, connected by a direct parent-child relationship. One reason to divide a namespace into zones is to delegate authority for different portions of it. One very large domain could be difficult to administer.

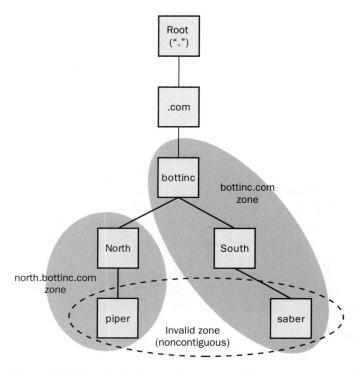

Figure 3-3   Two valid zones and one **noncontiguous namespace**, invalid zone

For each DNS domain name included in a zone, the zone becomes the authoritative source for information about that domain. When a zone is authoritative over a portion of the namespace, it means that it hosts the resource records for that portion of the namespace. It does not mean, however, that the server can update or modify the zone.

Zones are classified by where they are stored, whether they are writable, and by what information they receive and return. Zones can be stored either in text files or in Active Directory.

DNS servers are classified by the type of zones they host. A DNS server can host primary zones, secondary zones, stub zones, or no zones. A DNS server is called the **primary name server** for the primary zones it hosts and a **secondary name server** for the secondary zones it hosts. A caching-only server hosts no zones.

In brief, zone data is maintained on a DNS name server and is stored in one of two ways:

- As a flat zone file containing lists of mappings
- In an Active Directory database

With regard to types of queries, each zone can be either a **forward lookup zone** or a **reverse lookup zone**. In turn, a forward or reverse lookup zone can be one of three types:

- Primary
- Secondary
- Stub

When you configure a DNS server, you can configure it either with several zone types or with none at all, depending on the type of role that the DNS server has in the network.

By using different zones, you can configure your DNS solution to best meet your needs. For example, it is recommended that you configure a primary zone and a secondary zone on separate DNS servers to provide fault tolerance should one server fail. You can configure a stub zone if the zone is maintained on a separate DNS server.

The next two sections discuss the different ways in which zone data is stored: in standard zones and in Active Directory–integrated zones.

Standard Zones

There are numerous options for optimal configuration of the DNS server, based on network topology, administrative needs, and size of the namespace. Typical DNS server operation involves three standard zones (primary, secondary, and in-addr.arpa). Windows Server 2003 provides a fourth option, stub zones. Each of the standard zones is discussed in the following sections.

Standard Primary Zones

Practice adding a primary zone by doing Exercise 3-2, "Adding a Standard Primary Forward Lookup Zone," now.

A standard primary zone hosts a read/write copy of the DNS zone in which resource records are created and managed. Only one server can host and load the master copy of the zone, no additional primary servers for the zone are permitted, and only the server hosting the primary zone is allowed to accept dynamic updates and process zone changes. When setting up DNS servers to host the zones for a domain, the primary server normally is located where it will be accessible for administering the zone file.

Standard Secondary Zones

A copy of the zone file may be stored on one or more servers to balance network load, provide fault tolerance, or avoid forcing queries across a slow, wide area network (WAN) link. A standard secondary zone is a read-only copy of the standard primary DNS zone. Performing a zone transfer, which is done by simply copying the zone file from the primary server to a secondary server, creates a secondary zone. When a secondary zone is created, you must specify the IP address of one or more master DNS servers from which you want to copy the zone. These copies are referred to as secondary zone database files. The secondary zone database files are updated regularly from the primary zone database.

in-addr.arpa Zones

Most queries sent to a DNS server are *forward queries*; that is, they request an IP address based on a DNS name. DNS also provides a reverse lookup process, which enables a host to determine another host's name based on its IP address. For example, a query contains the equivalent of "What is the DNS domain name of the host at IP address 192.168.100.1?"

To answer this query, the **in-addr.arpa domain** is consulted in combination with the IP address in question. As you read the IP address from left to right, the network portion is some number of bits on the left, and the host portion is some number of bits on the right, based on the subnet mask. For example, 192.168.100.2, with a default subnet mask of 255.255.255.0, means the network portion is 192.168.100, and the host portion is 2. Because the higher-level portion of the address is on the right, it must be reversed when building the domain tree. In short, because FQDNs go from specific to general, and IP addresses go from general to specific, to facilitate reverse lookup, the IP address is reversed when concatenated with the in-addr.arpa domain. For example, the reverse lookup zone for the subnet 192.168.100.0 is 100.168.192.in-addr.arpa. The in-addr.arpa domain tree makes use of the **pointer (PTR) resource record**, which is used to associate the IP address with the host name. This lookup should correspond to an address (A) resource record for the host in a forward lookup zone.

Reverse lookup queries often are used by network applications for verification rather than identification or as a tool for monitoring and troubleshooting the DNS service.

> **NOTE   in-addr.arpa and IPv4-Based Networks**   The in-addr.arpa domain is used only for Internet Protocol version 4 (IPv4)-based networks. In the DNS console for Windows Server 2003, the DNS server's New Zone Wizard uses this domain when it creates a new reverse lookup zone. Internet Protocol version 6 (IPv6)-based reverse lookup zones are based on the domain ip6.arpa.

Reverse DNS zones have the same start of authority (SOA) and **name server (NS) resource records** as forward lookup zones. You also can configure reverse lookup zones to be standard primary or secondary zones or to be Active Directory–integrated. Active Directory–integrated reverse lookup zones replicate in the same manner as Active Directory–integrated forward lookup zones.

Stub Zones

A DNS server running Windows Server 2003 also supports a new type of zone called a stub zone. A *stub zone* is a copy of a zone that contains only those resource records necessary to identify the authoritative DNS servers for that zone. A stub zone is a pointer to the DNS server that is authoritative for that zone, and it is used to maintain or improve DNS resolution efficiency.

The stub zone contains a subset of zone data consisting of an SOA, an NS, and an A record. Like a standard secondary zone, resource records in the stub zone cannot be modified; they must be modified at the primary zone.

Stub zones enable a DNS server to perform recursion by using the stub zone's list of name servers without needing to query the Internet or internal root server for the DNS namespace. Using stub zones throughout your DNS infrastructure enables you to distribute a list of the authoritative DNS servers for a zone without using secondary zones. However, stub zones do not serve the same purpose as secondary zones and should not be considered when addressing redundancy and load sharing.

Active Directory–Integrated Zones

Storing zones in Active Directory is a Microsoft proprietary method of managing, securing, and replicating DNS zone information. An *Active Directory–integrated zone* is a DNS zone contained within Active Directory. Zones stored in text files are typically referred to as standard, or *file-backed zones*, and zones stored in Active Directory are referred to as *Active Directory–integrated zones*. Storing a zone in Active Directory has the following benefits:

■ **Fault tolerance**   Information is stored on multiple servers.

■ **Security**   DNS zones stored in Active Directory can take advantage of increased security by modifying the **discretionary access control list (DACL)**. The DACL enables you to specify which users and groups may modify the DNS zones.

■ **Zones are multimaster**   This means that zones can be updated in more than one location. All domain controllers where the zone is stored can modify the zone. Changes to the zone are then replicated to the other domain controllers that contain the zone file.

■ **Efficient replication**   Zone transfers are replaced by more efficient Active Directory replication. This can be especially important over networks with slow links because Active Directory compresses replication data that passes between sites.

■ **Secondary zones**   Zones stored in Active Directory can also be transferred to standard secondary servers to create secondary zones in the same way that file-backed zones are transferred.

Windows Server 2003 provides a more efficient method of replicating DNS zone information than does Microsoft Windows 2000 Server. In Microsoft Windows 2000, updates to Active Directory zones are replicated to all domain controllers in that domain, whether or not they are DNS servers. With Windows Server 2003, Active Directory–integrated zones can be replicated three different ways:

Practice changing standard primary zones into Active Directory–integrated zones by doing Exercise 3-3, "Changing a Zone to Active Directory–Integrated," now.

■ To all domain controllers in the domain (this is the same as Windows 2000)

■ To all domain controllers that are DNS servers in the local domain

■ To all domain controllers that are also DNS servers in the entire forest

You can create two types of Active Directory–integrated zones: forward lookup zones and reverse lookup zones. These are discussed in the following sections.

Forward Lookup Zones

An Active Directory–integrated *forward lookup zone* is similar to a standard primary zone. Outside of Active Directory, primary and secondary servers are necessary because they follow a single-master update model. Only one server contains a writable copy of the zone database. However, Active Directory–integrated zones follow a multimaster update model, meaning all Active Directory–integrated zones contain a read/write copy of the zone and can make changes to the zone information. Therefore, primary and secondary distinctions are not necessary. A forward lookup zone stores records to answer forward queries such as the one shown in Figure 3-4.

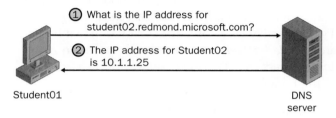

Figure 3-4   Forward lookup query

Reverse Lookup Zones

Practice creating reverse lookup zones by doing Exercise 3-4, "Creating a Reverse Lookup Zone," now.

A *reverse lookup zone* is used for resolving an IP address to a name and is similar to the standard in-addr.arpa zone. The reverse lookup zone is stored and updated in the same manner as the Active Directory–integrated forward lookup zone. A reverse lookup zone stores records to answer reverse lookup queries such as the one posed in Figure 3-5.

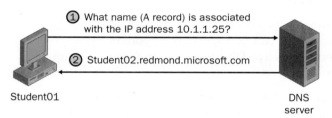

Figure 3-5   Reverse lookup zone

ROOT HINTS

DNS servers resolve DNS queries using local authoritative or cached data. But if the server does not contain the requested data and is not authoritative for the name in a query, it may perform **recursive resolution** or return a referral to another DNS server depending on whether the client requested recursion. The DNS Server service must be configured with the **root hints** to resolve queries for names that it is not authoritative for or for which it contains no delegations. Root hints contain the names and IP addresses of the DNS servers authoritative for the root zone. You can use the DNS console to manage the list of root servers as shown in Figure 3-6.

Figure 3-6   DNS root hints property page

By default, DNS servers use a root hints file, Cache.dns. The Cache.dns file is stored in the %systemroot%\System32\Dns folder on the server computer. When the server starts, Cache.dns is preloaded into server memory. By using root hints to find root servers, a DNS server is able to complete recursive queries. This process is designed to enable any DNS server to locate the servers that are authoritative for any other DNS domain name used at any level in the namespace tree.

When the Configure A DNS Server Wizard is used to configure a DNS server, it sends an NS query for the root domain (.) to the preferred and alternative DNS servers for the server. The query response is placed into the root hints of the DNS server. If no root servers are detected, the wizard sends the same query to the DNS servers specified in the Cache.dns file that correspond to the root servers on the Internet. If no root servers are detected, the wizard prompts the user to either make the server a root server or to manually specify root hints. Updating root hints enables the server to function more efficiently. You should update root hints whenever a new server is added or changed.

▶ **Updating Root Hints on the DNS Server**

To update root hints on the DNS server, follow these steps:

1. Open the DNS management console.

2. Right-click the applicable DNS server, and then click Properties.

3. Click the Root Hints tab.

4. Modify the server root hints as follows:

   ❏ To add a root server to the list, click Add, and then specify the name and IP address of the server to be added to the list of root servers.

   ❏ To modify a root server in the list, click Edit, and then specify the name and IP address of the server to be modified in the list.

   ❏ To remove a root server from the list, select it from the list, and then click Remove.

In addition to manually adding or deleting the list of root servers, you also can use the Copy From Server button, as shown previously in Figure 3-6. This enables you to specify the IP address of another DNS server from which your DNS server can copy the root hints.

You also can use the Dnscmd command to add or delete a server from root hints. Dnscmd is discussed in Chapter 4, "Managing and Monitoring DNS." In the following example, the server at 10.1.1.200 is added to the list of root servers at the name server ns1.eu.reskit.com:

```
C:\Windows>dnscmd ns1.eu.reskit.com. /RecordAdd /roothints @ ns 10.1.1.200
Command completed successfully.
```

> **MORE INFO** **The Dnscmd Command** Dnscmd is not installed by default; it must be added. Along with other tools, the Dnscmd command can be installed from the Microsoft Windows Server 2003 Installation CD from the following location: \Support\Tools\Suptools.msi.

In Windows Server 2003, for the DNS Server service running on a domain controller, root hints are stored in the domain-wide application directory partition.

> **NOTE** **Using Root Hints When Operating Internal Root Servers** If you have an internal DNS root in your DNS infrastructure, configure the root hints of internal DNS servers to point to only the DNS servers hosting your root domain and not the DNS servers hosting the Internet root domain. This will prevent your internal DNS servers from sending private information over the Internet when resolving names.

Removing the Root DNS Zone

A DNS server running Windows Server 2003 follows these specific steps in its name-resolution process: the DNS server first queries its cache, then checks its zone records, then sends requests to forwarders, and then tries resolution by using root servers.

By default, a Microsoft DNS server connects to the Internet to process DNS requests that require root resolution. When you use the Dcpromo tool to promote a server to a domain controller, the domain controller requires DNS. If you install DNS during the promotion process, a root zone is created. This root zone indicates to your DNS server that it is a root Internet server. Therefore, your DNS server does not use forwarders or root hints in the name-resolution process and may cause name resolution to fail. In order to fix this, remove the root zone on the DNS server.

▶ **Removing the DNS Root Zone**

1. Click Start, point to Administrative Tools, and then click DNS.

2. Expand *servername*, where *servername* is the name of the server, and then expand Forward Lookup Zones.

3. Right-click the "." zone, and then click Delete.

DNS SERVER TYPES

DNS server types are determined by the type of zone or zones they host and by the functions they perform. A DNS server may host either a primary or secondary zone or both. At the same time, a server may also be a *master name server*, which is a server that is responsible for updating other servers. If the server doesn't host any zones, it is a caching-only server. These four types of servers are supported in Windows Server 2003 and are discussed in the following sections.

Primary Name Server

Primary name servers contain one or more primary zones. When a change is made to the zone data, such as adding resource records to the zone, the changes must be made on the primary server for that zone. Changes are then propagated to secondary name servers. The primary name server also services client queries.

Secondary Name Server

The secondary name server hosts one or more secondary zone databases. Because a zone transfer is used to create a secondary zone, the primary name server and zone already must exist to create a secondary name server.

Master Name Server

A name server is a master name server when it is responsible for sending updated copies of the database to other name servers. A master name server can host either a primary or secondary copy of a zone database. This means that a master server can be either a primary name server or a secondary name server. In Figure 3-7:

- ns1.contoso.com is the primary and master server for ns2.contoso.com.

- ns2.contoso.com is a secondary server, receives updates from ns1, and is a master server to ns3.

- ns3.contoso.com is a secondary server and receives updates from ns2.

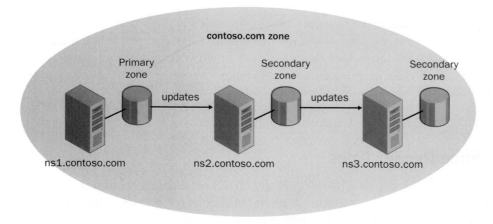

Figure 3-7   Primary and secondary zones acting as master name servers

Caching-Only Server

Caching-only servers do not host any zones and are not authoritative for a particular domain. Caching-only DNS servers start with an empty cache and add resource record entries as the server fulfills client requests. This information is then available from its cache when answering subsequent client queries. A caching-only DNS server is valuable at a site when DNS functionality is needed locally but when creating a separate domain or zone is not desirable.

DNS RESOURCE RECORDS

A *resource record* is information that is related to a DNS domain; for example, the host record defining a host IP address. Resource records are represented in binary form in packets when queries and responses are made using DNS. In DNS zone files, however, resource records are represented as text entries. Most resource records are represented as single-line text entries. If an entry is going to span more than one line, you can use parentheses to encapsulate the information. In many implementations of DNS, only the SOA record can be multiple lines in length. For readability, blank lines and comments often are inserted in the zone files and are ignored by the DNS server. Comments always start with a semicolon (;), and they end with a carriage return.

Resource records have the following syntax:

```
Owner [TTL] Class Type RDATA
```

Table 3-2 describes the common set of information in resource records.

Table 3-2   Typical Resource Record Fields

Name	Description
Owner	Identifies the host or the DNS domain to which this resource record belongs.
TTL (Time to Live)	A 32-bit integer representing the maximum time, in seconds, that a DNS server or client caches this resource record before it is discarded. This field is optional, and if it is not specified, the client uses the minimum TTL in the SOA record.
Class	Defines the protocol family in use, which is IN for the Internet system.
Type	Identifies the type of resource record. For example, A indicates that the resource record stores host address information.
RDATA (Resource Record Data)	Contains RDATA. The RDATA field is a variable-length field that represents the information being described by the resource record. For example, in an A resource record, the data contained in this field is the 32-bit IP address that represents the host identified by the owner.

Resource Record Types

The DNS database consists of resource records that relate different information about the names in the database. A resource record for a DNS name can identify a single resource within the network, such as the network host that uses that name, or that there is a service running on that network host, such as electronic mail.

Different types of resource records provide DNS data about computers on a TCP/IP network. The most common resource records are described in Table 3-3 and in detail in the following sections. This discussion includes resource records specific to Windows 2000 and Windows Server 2003 DNS implementations.

Table 3-3   Resource Record Types

Description	Class	TTL	Type	Data
Start of Authority	Internet (IN)	60 minutes	SOA	Owner name, primary name server FQDN, serial number, refresh interval, retry interval, expire time, and minimum TTL
Host	Internet (IN)	TTL of the SOA in the same zone	A	Owner name (host DNS name) and host IPv4 address
Name Server	Internet (IN)	TTL of the SOA in the same zone	NS	Owner name and DNS server name
Mail Exchanger	Internet (IN)	TTL of the SOA in the same zone	MX	Owner name, Mail Exchanger (MX) server DNS name, and preference number
Canonical Name (an alias)	Internet (IN)	TTL of the SOA in the same zone	CNAME	Owner name (alias name) and host DNS name

Start of Authority (SOA) Resource Record

Every zone contains an SOA resource record at the top of the zone file. An SOA resource record indicates the starting point or original point of authority for information stored in a zone. It contains all the zone-specific information for the DNS server to use when maintaining the zone. The SOA resource record is the first resource record that is created when creating a new zone.

The RDATA field for the SOA resource record contains the fields shown in Table 3-4.

Table 3-4   RDATA Fields for the SOA Resource Record

RDATA Fields	Description
Authoritative server	Contains the name of the primary DNS server authoritative for the zone.
Responsible person	Shows the e-mail address of the administrator who is responsible for the zone. This field takes a period (.) instead of an at (@) sign.
Serial number	Shows how many times the zone is updated. When a zone's secondary server contacts its master server to determine whether it needs to initiate a zone transfer, the zone's secondary server compares its own serial number with that of the master. If the serial number of the master server is higher, the secondary server initiates a zone transfer.
Refresh	Shows how often the secondary server for the zone checks to see whether the zone data is changed.
Retry	After sending a zone transfer request, shows how long (in seconds) the zone's secondary server waits before sending another request.
Expire	After a zone transfer, shows how long (in seconds) the zone's secondary server continues to respond to zone queries before discarding its own zone as invalid.

(continued)

Table 3-4   RDATA Fields for the SOA Resource Record

RDATA Fields	Description
Minimum TTL	Applies to all the resource records in the zone whenever a TTL value is not specified in a resource record or is shorter than the minimum TTL specified in the zone's SOA record. Whenever a DNS client queries the server, the server sends back resource records containing a record-specific TTL or the minimum TTL. Negative responses are cached for the minimum TTL of the SOA resource record of the authoritative zone.

The following output is an example of an SOA resource record:

```
na.contoso.com.  IN  SOA (
    nadc1.na.contoso.com.; authoritative server for the zone
    administrator.na.contoso.com. ; zone admin e-mail
                             ; (responsible  person)
    5099       ; serial number
    3600       ; refresh (1 hour)
    600        ; retry (10 mins)
    86400      ; expire (1 day)
    60    )    ; minimum TTL (1 min)
```

Name Server (NS) Resource Record

The name server (NS) resource record identifies a DNS server that is authoritative for a zone. The name of the DNS server that is authoritative for a zone is stored in the RDATA field. NS records are used to indicate both primary and secondary DNS servers for the zone specified in the SOA resource record and to indicate the DNS servers for any delegated zones. If a zone has multiple authoritative servers (for example, a primary server and one or more secondary servers), you need to have an NS record for each server. The Windows Server 2003 DNS Server service automatically creates the first NS record for a zone when the zone is created. You can add additional NS records by using DNS Manager or the Dnscmd command-line tool.

> **NOTE   Zones and NS Records**   Every zone must contain at least one NS record.

For example, if the administrator for contoso.com delegates authority for the na.contoso.com. subdomain to the nadc1.na.contoso.com server, the following line is added to the contoso.com and na.contoso.com zones:

```
na.contoso.com.  IN  NS  nadc1.na.contoso.com.
```

Host Address (A) Resource Record

The host address (A) resource record maps a FQDN to an IP address. For example, the following A resource record is located in the zone na.contoso.com and maps the FQDN of a server to its IP address:

```
nadc1.na.contoso.com.   IN   A  172.16.48.1
```

The A resource record contains the following fields:

- The Owner, TTL, Class, and Type fields, which are described in Table 3-2, "Typical Resource Record Fields," earlier in this chapter.

- The RDATA field is the IP address of the owner.

PTR Resource Record

The PTR resource record performs the reverse function of the A resource record by mapping an IP address to an FQDN. For example, the following PTR resource record maps the IP address 172.16.48.1 of nadc1.na.contoso.com to its FQDN:

```
1.48.16.172.in-addr.arpa.   IN   PTR   nadc1.na.contoso.com.
```

PTR resource records contain the following fields:

Practice
locating DNS
resource
records by doing
Exercise 3-5,
"Locating DNS
Resource
Records," now.

- The Owner, TTL, Class, and Type fields, which are described in Table 3-2, "Typical Resource Record Fields," earlier in this chapter.
- The RDATA field is the host name of the host with the IP address contained in the Owner field.

Canonical Name (CNAME) Resource Record

The canonical name (CNAME) resource record creates an alias for a specified FQDN. You can use CNAME records to hide the implementation details of your network from the clients that connect to it.

For example, if you want to put a File Transfer Protocol (FTP) server named ftp1.na.contoso.com on your na.contoso.com subdomain, but you know that in six months you might move it to a computer named ftp2.na.contoso.com and you do not want your users to have to know about the change, do the following: create an alias called ftp.na.contoso.com that points to ftp1.na.contoso.com. When you move your computer, you need change only the CNAME record to point to ftp2.na.contoso.com. For example, the following CNAME resource record creates an alias for ftp1.na.contoso.com:

```
ftp.na.contoso.com.   IN   CNAME   ftp1.na.contoso.com.
```

After a DNS client queries for the name for ftp.na.contoso.com, the DNS server finds the CNAME resource record, resolves the query for ftp1.na.contoso.com, and returns both the A and CNAME resource records to the client.

> **NOTE   CNAME and Aliases in a Zone**   If a CNAME resource record is present at a node (DNS name), no other resource records for the same name should be present in the zone. This ensures that the data for a CNAME and its aliases cannot be different. According to **Request for Comments (RFC)** 2181, an alias can have only one canonical name.

CNAME resource records contain the following fields:

- The Owner, TTL, Class, and Type fields. The Owner field for CNAME records is the alias.
- The RDATA field is the name of the host to which the alias points.

Mail Exchanger (MX) Resource Record

The mail exchanger (MX) resource record specifies a server that is willing to act as a mail server for a DNS name. The mail server identified by an MX record is a host that either processes or forwards mail for a DNS domain name. Processing the mail means either delivering it to the addressee or passing it to a different type of mail transport. Forwarding the mail means sending it to its final destination server, sending it by using Simple Mail Transfer Protocol (SMTP) to another mail exchange server that is closer to the final destination, or queuing it for a specified amount of time.

To improve the reliability of the mail service for a domain, you can designate secondary mail servers that can store mail for a domain. If the primary mail server stops responding, the secondary servers can hold the mail and then forward it when the mail server comes back into service. An SMTP *smart host* (a host capable of using MX records) uses multiple mail servers, provided you configure multiple MX resource records.

The following example shows MX resource records for the mail servers for the domain na.contoso.com:

```
@ IN  MX  5  mailserver1.na.contoso.com.
@ IN  MX  10 mailserver2.na.contoso.com.
@ IN  MX  20 mailserver3.na.contoso.com.
```

MX resource records contain the following fields:

- The Owner, TTL, Class, and Type fields, which are described in Table 3-2, "Typical Resource Record Fields," earlier in this chapter.

- The following data is stored in the RDATA field of the MX resource record:

  - The fourth field in the MX record is the mail server preference value. The preference value specifies the preference given to the MX record among other MX records. Records with lower priority numbers (which are higher priority) are preferred. Thus, when a mail client needs to send mail to a certain DNS domain, it first contacts a DNS server for that domain and retrieves all the MX records. It then contacts the mailer with the lowest preference value.

    MORE INFO Mail Routing and the Domain System For more information about how mail is routed in the domain system, see RFC 974, which can be looked up at http://www.rfc-editor.org/rfcsearch.html.

  - The final field is the name of the mail server to contact.

For example, suppose Holly Holt sends an e-mail message to loviatt@na.contoso .com on a day that mailserver1 is down, but mailserver2 is working. Her e-mail client tries to deliver the message to mailserver1 because it has the lowest preference value, but it fails because mailserver1 is down. In this case, Holly's e-mail client chooses mailserver2 because its preference value is the second lowest. If mailserver2 is operating, the mail is successfully delivered to mailserver2.

To prevent mail loops, if the e-mail client is on a host that is listed as an MX for the destination host, the e-mail client can deliver only to an MX with a lower preference value than its own host. If a mail server receives multiple MX records with equal priority, the choice of which MX record to use depends on implementation.

Service Locator (SRV) Resource Record

Service locator (SRV) resource records enable you to specify the location of servers that provide a specific network service over a specific protocol and in a specific domain. SRV records allow you to have several servers offering a network service and to move services between servers without changing the client configuration. For example, if you have two application servers in your domain, you can create SRV resource records in DNS that specify which hosts serve as application servers. Client applications that support SRV records will use DNS to retrieve the SRV resource records for the application servers.

Active Directory is an example of an application that relies on SRV resource records. An example of an application that supports SRV resource records is the Windows 2000 and Windows Server 2003 Net Logon service. On Windows 2000, Microsoft Windows XP, and Windows Server 2003, client computers use SRV resource records to locate domain controllers for a domain and join an Active Directory domain.

The format for an SRV record is as follows:

```
_Service_Protocol.Name [TTL] Class SRV Priority Weight Port Target
```

Table 3-5 outlines the SRV resource record fields.

Table 3-5 SRV Resource Record Fields

Field Name	Description
Service	Specifies the name of the service, such as http or telnet.
Protocol	Specifies the protocol, such as Transmission Control Protocol (TCP) or User Datagram Protocol (UDP).
Name	Specifies the domain name to which the resource record refers.
TTL	Uses a 32-bit integer to represent the maximum time, in seconds, that a DNS server or client caches this entry before it is discarded. This field is optional, and if it is not specified, the client uses the minimum TTL in the SOA record.
Class	Defines the protocol family in use, which is usually IN for the Internet system. The other value defined in RFC 1034 is CH for the Chaos system, which was used experimentally at the Massachusetts Institute of Technology.

Table 3-6 describes the data stored in the RDATA field of the SRV resource record.

Table 3-6 SRV Record RDATA Fields

Field Name	Description
Priority	Specifies the priority of the host. Clients attempt to contact the host with the lowest priority number.
Weight	Performs load balancing. When the Priority field is the same for two or more records in the same domain, clients must try records with higher weights more often, unless the clients support some other load-balancing mechanism.
Port	Shows the port for the service on this host.
Target	Shows the FQDN for the host providing the service.

The following example shows SRV records for two domain controller servers:

```
_ldap._tcp.contoso.com. IN  SRV 0  0  80  dc1.contoso.com.
_ldap._tcp.contoso.com. IN  SRV 10 0  80  dc2.contoso.com.
```

This example does not specify a TTL. Therefore, the DNS client uses the minimum TTL specified in the SOA resource record.

If a computer needs to locate a Lightweight Directory Access Protocol (LDAP) server in the contoso.com domain, the DNS client sends an SRV query for the following name:

```
_ldap._tcp.contoso.com.
```

The DNS server replies with the SRV records listed in the previous example. The DNS client then chooses between DC1 and DC2 by looking at their priority values. Because DC1 has the lowest priority value, the LDAP client chooses DC1. In this example, if the priority values were the same but the weight values were different, the client would choose a domain controller randomly with a probability proportional to the Weight field value.

Next, the DNS client requests the A record for DC1.contoso.com, and the DNS server sends the A record. Finally, the client attempts to contact the domain controller using the IP address in the A record.

Computers running Windows 2000, Windows XP, and Windows Server 2003 support RFC 2782, a DNS resource record for specifying the location of services (DNS SRV).

Other Resource Record Types

Table 3-7 shows additional resource records and the RFCs that define them. Many of these resource records are considered experimental and are rarely used. Windows Server 2003 family provides support for the definition, storage, and retrieval of these resource records. For more information about each resource record type, see the corresponding RFC. (See http://www.rfc-editor.org/rfcsearch.html for more information about each RFC.)

Table 3-7   Other Resource Record Types Supported by Windows Server 2003

Record Type	RFC
AAAA	1886
AFSDB	1183
HINFO	1035
ISDN	1183
KEY	2535
MB	1035
MG	1035
MINFO	1035
MR	1035
NXT	2535
OPT	2671
RP	1183

(continued)

Table 3-7 Other Resource Record Types Supported by Windows Server 2003

Record Type	RFC
RT	1183
SIG	2535
TXT	1035
WKS	1035
X25	1183

Resource Records Not Defined in RFCs

In addition to the resource record types listed in the RFCs, Windows Server 2003 uses the resource record types shown in Table 3-8.

Table 3-8 Resource Record Types Not Defined in RFCs but Supported by Windows Server 2003

Name	Description
WINS	The WINS resource record contains the IP addresses of the WINS servers that a DNS server must query to resolve A record queries. A Microsoft Windows NT, Windows 2000, or Windows Server 2003 DNS server can use a WINS server to look up the host portion of a DNS name that does not exist in the DNS zone that is authoritative for the name. If a DNS server is authoritative for a zone but does not contain the necessary A record, the DNS server queries only WINS.
WINSR	The WINS reverse lookup (WINSR) resource record is used in a reverse lookup zone to find the host portion of the DNS name for a specified IP address. A DNS server sends a NetBIOS adapter status query to the IP address specified in the query if the zone authoritative for the queried IP address does not contain the record and does contain the WINSR resource record.
ATMA	The Asynchronous Transfer Mode address (ATMA) resource record, which is defined by the ATM Forum, is used to map DNS domain names to ATM addresses.

Delegation and Glue Records

Delegation and glue records are resource records that you add to a zone to delegate a subdomain to a separate zone hosted on a different DNS server. A *delegation record* is represented by the NS record in the parent zone that lists the authoritative DNS server hosting the child zone for the delegated subdomain. A *glue record* is the A record in the parent zone for the authoritative DNS server hosting the child zone for the delegated subdomain.

For example, the DNS server that hosts the zone for the domain contoso.com will delegate authority for the subdomain na.contoso.com to the DNS server ns2.na .contoso.com, which is where a zone for the domain na.contoso.com is hosted. To create this delegation, the following records are added to the parent zone contoso.com:

```
na.contoso.com.     IN  NS  ns2.na.contoso.com
ns2.na.contoso.com. IN  A   172.16.54.1
```

When a DNS client submits a query for a name in the child zone to the DNS server that is authoritative for the parent zone, the authoritative DNS server for the parent zone checks its zone. The delegation resource records tell it which DNS server is authoritative for the child zone. The authoritative DNS server for the parent zone can then return a referral containing the delegation records to the DNS client.

A glue record is necessary in this example because ns2.na.contoso.com is a member of the delegated domain na.contoso.com. However, if it was a member of a different domain, such as microsoft.com, the DNS client can perform standard name resolution to resolve the name of the authoritative DNS server to an IP address, in which case a glue record is not required. Separate domain configurations are less common.

Incorrect delegations are a major source of name resolution failure for DNS because an incorrect delegation removes a branch of the DNS namespace tree, and the other nodes in the tree cannot locate the DNS names in and under the branch. For this reason, it is recommended that you verify delegations periodically and that administrators responsible for parent and child zones communicate any modifications that can affect delegation.

Wildcard Resource Records

In some DNS designs, you might need to use a large number of resource records in a zone; however, you might find it difficult to manually add the records. In such cases, you can define a wildcard DNS resource record.

The following is an example of a wildcard address from the contoso.com domain:

```
*    IN   A   172.16.54.1
```

If the preceding A record is in DNS, all queries for a host in the contoso.com domain not explicitly defined in the zone file receive a reply for 172.16.54.1. Windows 2000 and Windows Server 2003 DNS support wildcard resource records.

UNDERSTANDING THE DNS QUERY PROCESS

When a DNS client needs to look up a name to obtain its corresponding IP address, it forms a DNS query that contains the following information:

- DNS domain name stated as an FQDN
- Query type—specifies resource records to be returned (A, SRV, and so on)
- DNS domain name class, which is IN for the Internet system

The query is first passed to the local DNS resolver client service for resolution. If the query cannot be resolved locally, it is sent to the primary DNS server.

If the query does not match an entry in the cache, the resolution process continues with the client querying a DNS server to resolve the name. Queries from clients or servers can take one of two forms: iterative or recursive.

Iterative Queries

An **iterative query** is a DNS query sent to a DNS server in which the querying host requests it to return the best answer it can provide using its own information and without seeking further assistance from other DNS servers. For example, in Figure 3-8, a host queries the primary DNS server, which checks its records and refers the client to Server A. Server A checks its names cache, does not find an answer, and sends a referral to Server B instead. The host receives the response and submits a query to Server B, which responds with a referral to Server C. The host queries Server C and receives a response.

Figure 3-8   The iterative query process

As shown in Figure 3-8, the querying host is responsible for issuing additional queries until it obtains a definitive answer. In the example that follows, the host issues three queries before receiving the requested information. The process is as follows:

1. The first step of the query process is to convert a name request into a query and then pass it to the DNS Client service for resolution that uses locally cached information. If the query can be answered from the local cache, the process is complete. Otherwise, the client submits an iterative query to its primary DNS server.

2. The primary DNS server checks to see if it has authority for that domain. In this example, it does not have authority, but it does contain information that points to the .com top-level domain DNS servers. The primary server responds with a referral to .com top-level domain servers.

3. The DNS client submits an iterative query to DNS Server A.

4. DNS Server A responds with a referral to DNS Server B.

5. The client submits an iterative query to DNS Server B for sales.contoso.com.

6. DNS Server B responds with a referral to DNS Server C.

7. The client submits an iterative query to DNS Server C.

8. DNS Server C is authoritative for the sales.contoso.com domain and responds with a definitive answer to the client query (in this case, the A record for sales.contoso.com).

Iteration is used in the following situations:

- The client requests the use of recursion, but recursion is disabled on the DNS server.

- The client does not request the use of recursion when querying the DNS server.

- An iterative request from a client tells the DNS server that the client expects the best answer the DNS server can provide immediately, without contacting other DNS servers.

Recursive Queries

A *recursive query* is a DNS query sent to a DNS server in which the querying host asks the DNS server to provide a definitive answer to the query, even if that means contacting other servers to provide the answer. When sent a recursive query, the DNS server iteratively queries other DNS servers to obtain an answer. In Figure 3-9, the querying host issues only one query before receiving the requested information.

Figure 3-9   The recursive query process

To centralize the workload and reduce network traffic, host computers typically issue recursive queries to DNS servers. A network of 1,000 clients iteratively querying DNS servers is clearly less efficient than centralizing queries to a handful of DNS servers. Centralizing queries means each client sends a single recursive query rather than each client sending multiple iterative queries. DNS servers generally issue iterative queries against other DNS servers if they are unable to answer a recursive query from cached information. By using recursive queries, the workload of resolving DNS names can be concentrated to a few servers and thereby achieve much greater efficiency. Figure 3-9 illustrates the client submitting a recursive query and receiving a definitive answer. The process is as follows:

1. The first step of the query process is to convert a name request into a query and then pass it to the DNS Client service for resolution using locally cached information. If the query can be answered from the local cache, the process is complete. Otherwise, the query is passed to the local DNS server.

2. The local name server checks to see if it has authority for that domain. In this example, it does not have authority, but it does contain root hints. The local name server uses the root hints to begin a search for the name server that has authority for the domain sales.contoso.com. It then queries the root name server.

3. The root name server sends IP addresses of name servers for the .com top-level domain back to the local DNS server.

4. The local DNS server submits an iterative query to DNS Server A (.com) for sales.contoso.com.

5. DNS Server A responds with a referral to the contoso.com name server, DNS Server B.

6. The local DNS server submits another iterative query to DNS Server B, contoso.com.

7. DNS Server B responds with the IP address for the authoritative server, DNS Server C.

8. The local DNS server submits an iterative query to DNS Server C.

9. DNS Server C responds with a definitive answer (in this case, the A record).

10. The local DNS server responds to the DNS client with a definitive answer. The client can now establish a TCP/IP connection with sales.contoso.com. From the client's perspective, one request was submitted to and fulfilled by the local DNS server. The information obtained by the local DNS server is cached to answer subsequent queries.

Recursive Query Timings   By default, DNS servers use timings for retry intervals and time-out intervals. These are as follows:

- A recursion retry interval of 3 seconds. This is the length of time the DNS service waits before retrying a query made during a recursive lookup.

- A recursion time-out interval of 15 seconds. This is the length of time the DNS service waits before failing a recursive lookup that has been retried.

Under most circumstances, these parameters do not need adjustment. However, if you are using recursive lookups over a slow-speed WAN link, you might be able to improve server performance and query completion by making slight adjustments to these settings.

Disabling the use of recursion on a DNS server is generally done when DNS clients are limited to resolving names to a specific DNS server, such as one located on your intranet. Recursion also might be disabled when the DNS server is incapable of resolving external DNS names, and clients are expected to failover to another DNS server for resolution of these names.

You can disable the use of recursion by configuring the Advanced properties in the DNS console, as shown in Figure 3-10.

Figure 3-10   DNS Advanced properties page

> **NOTE**   **Disabling Recursion on a DNS Server**   If you disable recursion on the DNS server, you will not be able to use forwarders on the same server.

Query Responses

The two previous examples of DNS queries illustrate the process ending with a positive response returned to the client. However, queries can return other answers as well. Following are the most common answers:

- **An authoritative answer**   An authoritative answer is a positive answer returned to the client and delivered with the authority bit set in the DNS message to indicate the answer was obtained from a server with direct authority for the queried name.

- **A positive answer**   A positive answer can consist of the queried resource record or a list of resource records (also known as a resource record set) that fits the queried DNS domain name and record type specified in the query message. Positive answers may or may not be authoritative.

- **A referral answer**   A referral answer contains additional resource records not specified by the name or type in the query. This type of answer is returned to the client if the recursion process is not supported. The records are meant to act as helpful reference answers that the client can use to continue the query using iteration.

  A referral answer contains additional data, such as resource records, that are other than the type queried. For example, if the queried host name was "www" and no A resource records for this name were found in this zone, but a CNAME resource record for "www" was found instead, the DNS server can include that information when responding to the client.

If the client is able to use iteration, it can make additional queries using the referral information in an attempt to fully resolve the name.

- **A negative answer**   A negative answer from the server can indicate that one of two possible results was encountered while the server attempted to process and recursively resolve the query fully and authoritatively:

    - ❏ An authoritative server reported that the queried name does not exist in the DNS namespace.

    - ❏ An authoritative server reported that the queried name exists but no records of the specified type exist for that name.

The resolver passes the query response back to the requesting program and caches the response.

Name Server Caching

As DNS servers make recursive queries on behalf of clients, they temporarily cache resource records. Cached resource records contain information obtained from DNS servers that are authoritative for DNS domain names learned while making iterative queries to search and fully answer a recursive query performed on behalf of a client. Later, when other clients place new queries that request resource record information matching cached resource records, the DNS server can use the cached resource record information to answer them. Caching provides a way to speed the performance of DNS resolution for subsequent queries of popular names, while substantially reducing DNS-related query traffic on the network.

When information is cached, a TTL value applies to all cached resource records. As long as the TTL for a cached resource record does not expire, a DNS server can continue to cache and use the resource record again when answering queries by its clients that match these resource records. Caching TTL values used by resource records in most zone configurations are assigned the minimum (default) TTL, which is set in the zone's SOA resource record. By default, the minimum TTL is 3,600 seconds (1 hour) but can be adjusted, or, if needed, individual caching TTLs can be set at each resource record.

DELEGATING ZONES

Initially, a zone stores information about a single DNS domain name. As other domains are added, you must make a decision about whether or not the domain will be part of the same zone. If you choose to add the subdomain, you may

- Manage the subdomain as part of the original zone
- Delegate management of the subdomain to a different zone

For example, Figure 3-11 shows the contoso.com domain, which contains domain names for Contoso, Ltd. When the contoso.com domain is first created at a single server, it is configured as a single zone for all of the Contoso DNS namespace. If, however, the contoso.com domain needs to use subdomains, those subdomains must be included in the zone or delegated away to another zone.

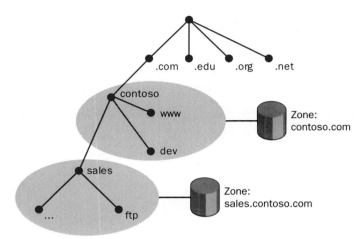

Figure 3-11   Using a subdomain to segment a zone

In this example, the contoso.com domain shows a new subdomain—the sales.contoso .com domain—delegated away from the contoso.com zone and managed in its own zone. However, the contoso.com zone needs to contain a few resource records to provide the delegation information that references the DNS servers that are authoritative for the delegated sales.contoso.com subdomain.

If the contoso.com zone does not use delegation for a subdomain, the data for the subdomain remains part of the contoso.com zone. For example, the subdomain dev.contoso.com is not delegated away but is managed by the contoso.com zone.

As previously discussed, namespaces can be divided into one or more zones. Zones can be stored, distributed, and replicated to other DNS servers. Before creating additional zones, determine if any of the following needs are true for your organization:

- Your organization has a need to delegate management of part of your DNS namespace to another location or department.

- You want to provide a more fault-tolerant DNS environment.

- You want to improve DNS name resolution performance by dividing one large zone into small zones, thereby distributing workload among several servers.

- Your organization has opened a new branch office or site and you need to extend the DNS namespace by adding numerous subdomains.

If any of these reasons are true for your organization, you could benefit from delegating zones. When structuring zones, use a plan that reflects the structure of your organization. Also, be aware that for each new zone you create, you will need delegation records in other zones that point to the authoritative DNS servers for the new zone. This is necessary both to transfer authority and to provide correct referral to other DNS servers and clients of the new servers being made authoritative for the new zone.

Figure 3-12 shows delegation from a parent zone to a new zone created for a subdomain, sales.contoso.com.

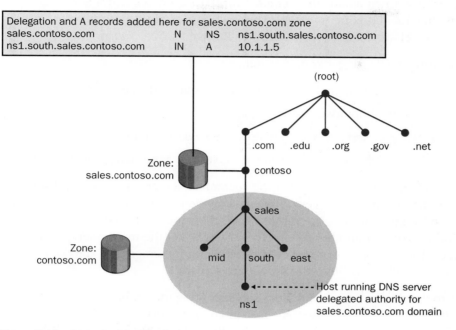

Figure 3-12   Delegating a subdomain to a new zone

In Figure 3-12, an authoritative DNS server computer for the newly delegated sales.contoso.com subdomain is named based on a derivative subdomain included in the new zone (ns1.south.sales.contoso.com). To make this server known to others outside of the newly delegated zone, two resource records are needed in the microsoft.com zone to complete delegation to the new zone:

- An NS resource record is necessary to effect the delegation. This resource record is used to advertise that the server named ns1.south.sales.contoso .com is an authoritative server for the delegated subdomain.

- An A resource record (glue record) is needed to resolve the name of the server specified in the NS resource record to its IP address. The process of resolving the host name in this resource record to the delegated DNS server in the NS resource record is sometimes referred to as *glue chasing*.

UNDERSTANDING ZONE TRANSFERS

Zone transfers are the complete or partial transfer of all data in a zone from the primary DNS server hosting the zone to a secondary DNS server hosting a copy of the zone. The copy of the zone hosted on a secondary DNS server is initially created using a zone transfer. When changes are made to the zone on a primary DNS server, the primary DNS server notifies the secondary DNS servers that changes have occurred and the changes are replicated to all the secondary DNS servers for that zone using zone transfers.

In the original DNS specifications, only one form of zone transfer was available, which was known as *full zone transfer*. RFC 1995 discusses an additional type of zone transfer, known as the *incremental zone transfer*. Windows Server 2003 supports incremental zone transfers. This section describes both types of zone transfers, as well as the notification process known as *DNS Notify*.

The following events trigger zone transfers:

- A transfer is manually initiated using the console at the secondary server.
- The zone refresh interval expires.
- The DNS Server service is started at the secondary server.
- The master server notifies the secondary server of a zone change or changes.

Zone transfers are always initiated at the secondary server for a zone and sent to their configured master servers, which act as their source for the zone. Master servers can be any other DNS server that loads the zone, such as either the primary server for the zone or another secondary server. When the master server receives the request for the zone, it can reply with either an incremental (IXFR) or full (AXFR) transfer of the zone to the secondary server.

In a full zone transfer, the primary DNS server hosting the primary zone transfers a copy of the entire zone database to the secondary DNS server hosting a copy of the zone. Whether a full or incremental transfer, the process shown in Figure 3-13 is followed:

1. When the value of the Refresh field in the SOA resource record for the zone hosted on the secondary DNS server expires, the secondary DNS server queries the primary DNS server for the SOA record of the primary zone.

2. The primary DNS server for the zone replies to the query with the SOA resource record.

3. The secondary DNS server for the zone compares the serial number in the returned SOA record to the serial number in the SOA record for the local copy of the zone. If the serial number sent by the primary DNS server for the zone is higher than the serial number for its local zone, the zone needs to be updated, and the secondary DNS server sends an AXFR request (a request for a full zone transfer) to the primary DNS server.

4. The primary DNS server receives the request for the zone transfer and sends the full zone database to the secondary DNS server, essentially re-creating the copy of the zone while maintaining any zone settings.

Figure 3-13   The zone transfer process

If the primary DNS server for the zone does not respond to the request for a zone transfer sent from the secondary DNS server, the secondary DNS server continues to retry after the interval specified in the Retry field in the SOA resource record for the zone. If there is still no answer after the interval specified in the Expire field in the SOA resource record for the zone expires, the secondary DNS server discards its zone.

Incremental Zone Transfer

Incremental zone transfers were designed to reduce the amount of network traffic generated by full zone transfers. Rather than sending a copy of the entire zone file, an incremental zone transfer sends only records that have changed since the last zone update. Both Windows 2000 and Windows Server 2003 support incremental zone transfers.

Although an incremental zone transfer saves network bandwidth, it uses additional disk space on the server to record the version history. The primary DNS server for the zone maintains a recent version history of the zone, which observes any record changes that occurred in the most recent version updates of the zone. To conserve disk space, DNS servers store only the most recent updates. The Windows Server 2003 DNS Server service stores these updates in a log file that resides in the %systemroot%\System32\Dns folder. The log file is named by using the name of the zone file with .log appended. For example, if the zone file for the contoso.com domain is stored in the file Contoso.com.dns, the log file is named Contoso.com.dns.log.

An incremental zone transfer uses the following process:

1. Initially, when a secondary server is first configured, it sends a full zone transfer request (AXFR) to its master DNS server. The master (source) server responds by sending a full copy of the zone to the secondary (destination) server.

2. Each zone delivery has a version indicated by a serial number in the properties of the SOA resource record and a refresh interval (by default, 900 seconds). The refresh interval indicates at what interval the secondary server should request another copy of the zone from the source server.

3. After the interval expires, the destination server submits an SOA query to request an incremental zone transfer.

4. The source server answers the query by sending its SOA record, which contains the aforementioned serial number.

5. The destination server compares the serial number from the SOA record to its current local serial number. If the numbers are equal, no transfer is requested, and the refresh interval is reset.

6. If the value of the serial number in the SOA response is higher than its current local serial number, records on the source are newer than the local records and an IXFR query is sent to the source server. This query contains the local serial number so the source server can determine which records the destination server needs.

7. Depending on several factors, the source server responds with either an incremental or full transfer of the zone. The primary DNS server for a zone is not required to perform an incremental zone transfer. It can choose to perform a full zone transfer under the following conditions:

❑ The primary DNS server does not support incremental zone transfers.

❑ The primary DNS server does not have all the necessary data for performing an incremental zone transfer.

❑ An incremental zone transfer uses more network bandwidth than a full zone transfer.

8. When the secondary DNS server receives an incremental zone transfer, it creates a new version of the zone and begins replacing outdated resource records with the updated resource records from the source server, applying oldest to newest. When all the updates are completed, the secondary DNS server replaces its old version of the zone with the new version of the zone.

DNS Notify

Windows-based DNS servers support DNS Notify, an update to the original DNS protocol specification that permits a means of initiating notification to secondary servers when zone changes occur (RFC 1996). Servers that are notified can then initiate a zone transfer as described previously to request zone changes from their master servers and update their local replicas of the zone. This process improves consistency of zone data.

The list of secondary DNS servers that a primary DNS server will notify is maintained in the *notify list*, which is a list of the IP addresses for those secondary servers. When the zone is updated, the primary DNS server for the zone notifies only DNS servers on the notify list. For secondary DNS servers to be notified by the DNS server acting as their configured source for a zone, each secondary server must first have its IP address in the notify list of the source server. In Windows Server 2003 DNS, you can use the DNS Notify dialog box, accessed through the DNS console, shown in Figure 3-14, to set the notify list.

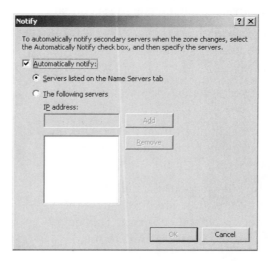

Figure 3-14   The DNS Notify dialog box

▶ **Creating a Notify List for a Zone**

To create a notify list for a zone, follow these steps:

1. Click Start, point to Administrative Tools, and then click DNS.

2. In the console tree, click the applicable zone.

3. On the Action menu, click Properties.

4. In the Zone Transfers tab, click Notify.

5. Verify that the Automatically Notify check box is checked.

6. Select the method to be used for creating a list for notifying other DNS servers when changes to the zone occur. Your options are as follows:

   a. Use the Servers Listed On The Name Servers tab option to permit only those servers that appear by IP address in the Name Servers tab to be included in the notify list.

   b. Select The Following Servers option if you want to specify a different notify list to be used instead.

7. If you selected The Following Servers option in the previous step, add or remove server IP addresses to form the notify list as needed:

   a. To add a server to the notify list, type its IP address in the IP Address field, and then click Add.

   b. To remove a server from the notify list, click the server IP address in the list box, and then click Remove.

In addition to notifying the listed servers, the DNS console permits you to use the contents of the notify list as a means to restrict or limit zone transfer access to only those secondary servers specified in the list. This can help prevent an undesired attempt by an unknown or unapproved DNS server to pull, or request, zone updates.

When the zone on a primary DNS server is updated, the following events occur:

- The Serial Number field in the SOA record is updated to indicate that a new version of the zone is written to a disk.

- The primary DNS server sends a notify message to the DNS servers that are specified in its notify list.

- A secondary DNS server for the zone that receives the notify message responds by sending an SOA-type query back to the notifying primary DNS server to determine if the zone on the primary DNS server is a later version than the copy of the zone currently stored on the secondary DNS server.

- If a notified secondary DNS server determines that the serial number specified in the SOA record of the zone on the primary DNS server is higher than the serial number specified in the SOA record for its current zone copy (the zone contains more recent updates), the notified secondary DNS server requests a zone transfer (AXFR or IXFR).

NOTE   DNS Notification in Active Directory–Integrated Zones   For replication of Active Directory–integrated zones, DNS notification is not needed. This is because DNS servers that load a zone from Active Directory automatically poll the directory (as specified by the SOA resource record's refresh interval) to update and refresh the zone. In these cases, configuring a notify list can actually degrade system performance by causing unnecessary, additional transfer requests for the updated zone.

UNDERSTANDING FORWARDING

A **forwarder** is a DNS server on a network used to forward DNS queries for external DNS names to DNS servers outside of that network. A *conditional forwarder* forwards queries according to specific domain names.

Standard Forwarding

As discussed previously, a DNS server on a network is designated as a forwarder by having the other DNS servers in the network forward the queries they cannot resolve locally to that DNS server. By using a forwarder, you can manage name resolution for names outside of your network, such as names on the Internet, and you improve the efficiency of name resolution for the computers in your network. For example, to use forwarders to manage the DNS traffic between your network and the Internet, configure the firewall used by your network to allow only one DNS server to communicate with the Internet. When you have configured the other DNS servers in your network to forward queries they cannot resolve locally to that DNS server, it will act as your forwarder.

Because external network traffic is going through a single DNS server, that server builds up a large cache of DNS data, which, over time, decreases Internet traffic and provides faster response times to clients.

Without having a specific DNS server designated as a forwarder, all DNS servers can send queries outside of a network using their root hints. As a result, a lot of internal, and possibly critical, DNS information can be exposed on the Internet. In addition to this security and privacy issue, this method of resolution can result in a large volume of external traffic that is costly and inefficient for a network with a slow Internet connection or a company with high Internet service costs.

A DNS server configured to use a forwarder will behave differently than a DNS server that is not configured to use a forwarder. A DNS server configured to use a forwarder behaves as follows:

1. When the DNS server receives a query, it attempts to resolve this query by using the primary and secondary zones that it hosts and by using its cache.

2. If the query cannot be resolved using this local data, it will forward the query to the DNS server designated as a forwarder.

3. The DNS server will wait briefly for an answer from the forwarder before attempting to contact the DNS servers specified in its root hints.

4. Rather than send the standard iterative query, when a DNS server forwards a query to a forwarder, by default, it sends a recursive query to the forwarder.

Conditional Forwarding

Conditional forwarding enables a DNS server to forward queries to other DNS servers based on the DNS domain names in the queries. With conditional forwarding, a DNS server could be configured to forward all the queries it receives for names ending with research.wingtiptoys.com to a specific DNS server's IP address or to the IP addresses of multiple DNS servers.

For example, when two companies, fabrikam.com and wingtiptoys.com, merge or collaborate, they may want to allow clients from the internal namespace of one company to resolve the names of the clients from the internal namespace of another company.

The administrators from one organization (fabrikam.com) may inform the administrators of the other organization (wingtiptoys.com) about the set of DNS servers that they can use to send DNS queries for name resolution within the internal namespace of the first organization. In this case, the DNS servers in the wingtiptoys.com organization will be configured to forward all queries for names ending with fabrikam.com to the designated DNS servers.

> **NOTE** **Authoritative DNS Servers' Forwarding Behavior** Authoritative DNS servers cannot forward queries according to domain names for which they are authoritative. For example, the authoritative DNS server for the zone widgets.microsoft.com cannot forward queries according to the domain name widgets.microsoft.com. If the DNS server were allowed to do this, it would nullify the server's capability to respond to queries for the domain name widgets.microsoft.com. The DNS server authoritative for widgets.microsoft.com can forward queries for DNS names that end with hr.widgets.microsoft.com, if hr.widgets.microsoft.com is delegated to another DNS server.

The conditional forwarder setting consists of the following:

- The domain names for which the DNS server will forward queries
- One or more DNS server IP addresses for each domain name specified

▶ **Configuring Forwarding**

To configure forwarding, follow these steps:

1. Open DNS.
2. In the console tree, click the applicable DNS server.
3. On the Action menu, click Properties.
4. In the Forwarders tab, for conditional forwarding, enter a domain name; for normal forwarding, choose All Other DNS Names.
5. Under Selected Domain's Forwarder IP Address list, type the IP address of a forwarder, and then click Add.

Forwarding Sequence

Each domain name used for forwarding on a DNS server is associated with the IP addresses of one or more DNS servers. A DNS server configured for forwarding will use its forwarders list after it has determined that it cannot resolve a query using its authoritative data (primary or secondary zone data) or cached data. If the server cannot resolve a query using forwarders, it may attempt recursion to the root hint servers.

The order of the IP addresses listed determines the sequence in which the IP addresses are used. After the DNS server forwards the query to the forwarder with the first IP address associated with the domain name, it waits a short period for an answer from that forwarder (according to the DNS server's time-out setting) before resuming the forwarding operation with the next IP address associated with the domain name. It continues this process until it receives an affirmative answer from a forwarder or until it has tried all addresses in the list.

When a DNS server configured to use conditional forwarding receives a query for a domain name, it compares that domain name with its list of domain name conditions and uses the longest domain name condition that corresponds to the domain name in the query. For example, a DNS server receives a query for www.qualitycontrol .research.wingtiptoys.com.

It compares that domain name with both wingtiptoys.com and research.wingtiptoys .com. The DNS server determines that research.wingtiptoys.com is the domain name that more closely matches the original query.

Forward-Only Server

A DNS server can be configured to not perform recursion after the forwarders fail; if it does not get a successful query response from any of the servers configured as forwarders, it sends a negative response to the DNS client.

The option to prevent recursion can be set for each conditional forwarder in Windows Server 2003. For example, a DNS server can be configured to perform recursion for the domain name research.wingtiptoys.com, but not to perform recursion for the domain name wingtiptoys.com.

> **NOTE**   **Disabling Recursion**   If you disable recursion in the Advanced tab in DNS server properties, you will not be able to use forwarders on the same server.

CONNECTING LOCAL NETWORKS TO THE INTERNET

Although it is possible to configure DNS servers inside your firewall to use the same DNS names as are used to access them from outside your firewall, this is not recommended. The recommended practice is to use a different namespace for your internal network, such applying the suffix ".local" to your domain name (for example contoso.local), than for your external namespace (for example, contoso.com).

We'll look at three ways that DNS names are resolved when the above recommendation is used: resolving a DNS name internal to the organization, resolving a DNS name external to the organization without using a proxy server, and resolving an external DNS name using a proxy server. In the following scenarios, Contoso, Ltd. has configured its external network to use contoso.com and its internal network uses contoso.local. The two zones are separated by a firewall and outside the firewall, DNS servers are provided by Contoso's ISP.

Resolving Internal Names

A client needs to access an internal Web site, *web.contoso.local.* The resolution process is as follows (see Figure 3-15):

1. The client sends a query for web.contoso.local to the internal DNS server.

2. The internal DNS server resolves web.contoso.local to an IP address and sends the result to the client.

   The client initiates a connection to web.contoso.local.

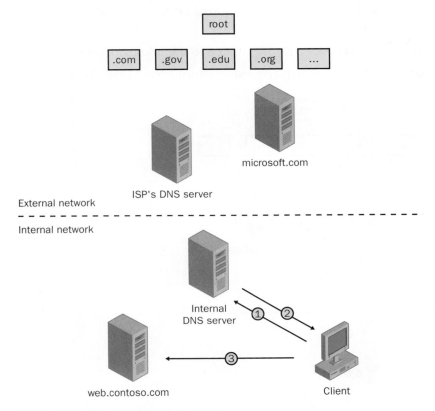

Figure 3-15 Resolving internal names

Resolving External Names Without a Proxy Server

Contoso's internal DNS servers are configured to forward requests for Internet addresses to the external DNS servers provided by the ISP. In this scenario, a client needs to access support.microsoft.com. The resolution process is as follows (see Figure 3-16).

1. The client sends the query for support.microsoft.com to the internal DNS server.

2. The internal DNS server forwards the query to the external DNS server provided by the ISP.

3. The external DNS server, not authoritative for this domain, checks its cache. If no entry exists for support.microsoft.com, it forwards the query to the top-level root domain.

4. The top-level root server replies to the external DNS server with a list of .com servers.

5. The external DNS server forwards the query for microsoft.com to a .com server.

6. The .com server replies to the external DNS server with the address of microsoft.com.

7. The external DNS server forwards the query for support.microsoft.com to the microsoft.com server.

8. The microsoft.com server replies to the external DNS server with the address of support.microsoft.com.

9. The external DNS server forwards the address to the internal DNS server.

10. The internal DNS server forwards requested information to the client.

Figure 3-16   Resolving external names

Resolving External Names Using a Proxy

To resolve support.microsoft.com using a proxy server, the query process is as follows (see Figure 3-17).

1. The proxy client sends a request for microsoft.com to the proxy server.

2. The proxy server determines this is an external address and forwards the request to its assigned external DNS server.

3. The external DNS server checks its cache for the address and, not finding it, sends a request to the top-level domain .com server.

4. The top-level domain .com server sends the address of the .com domain to the external DNS server.

5. The external DNS server forwards the request for microsoft.com to the .com domain.

6. The .com domain sends the address of microsoft.com to the external DNS server.

7. The external DNS server forwards the request to the microsoft.com DNS server.

8. The microsoft.com DNS server resolves the query and replies to the external DNS server.

9. The external DNS server forwards the reply to the proxy server.

10. After the proxy server receives the reply from the external DNS server, it queries microsoft.com directly for the address of support.microsoft.com.

11. The microsoft.com DNS server replies to the request and sends information to the proxy server.

12. The proxy server sends the response to the client.

Figure 3-17   Resolving external names using a proxy

SUMMARY

- DNS names and the DNS protocol are required for Active Directory domains and for compatibility with the Internet.

- The DNS namespace is hierarchical and based on a unique root that can have any number of subdomains. An FQDN is the name of a DNS host in this namespace that indicates the host's location relative to the root of the DNS domain tree. An example of an FQDN is host1.subdomain.microsoft.com.

- A DNS zone is a contiguous portion of a namespace for which a server is authoritative. A server can be authoritative for one or more zones, and a zone can contain one or more contiguous domains. A DNS server is authoritative for a zone if it hosts the zone, either as a primary or secondary DNS server. Each DNS zone contains the resource records it needs to answer queries for its portion of the DNS namespace.

- There are several types of DNS servers: primary, secondary, master name, and caching-only.

  - A DNS server that hosts a primary DNS zone is said to act as a primary DNS server. Primary DNS servers store original source data for zones. With Windows Server 2003, you can implement primary zones in one of two ways: as standard primary zones, in which zone data is stored in a text file, or as an Active Directory–integrated zone, in which zone data is stored in the Active Directory database.

  - A DNS server that hosts a secondary DNS server is said to act as a secondary DNS server. Secondary DNS servers are authoritative backup servers for the primary server. The servers from which secondary servers acquire zone information are called masters.

  - A master server can be the primary server or another secondary server.

  - A caching-only server forwards requests to other DNS servers and hosts no zones, but builds a cache of frequently requested records.

- Recursion is one of the two process types for DNS name resolution. A DNS client will request that a DNS server provide a complete answer to a query that does not include pointers to other DNS servers, effectively shifting the workload of resolving the query from the client to the DNS server. For the DNS server to perform recursion properly, the server needs to know where to begin searching for names in the DNS namespace. This information is provided by the root hints file, Cache.dns, which is stored on the server computer.

- A DNS server on a network is designated as a forwarder by having the other DNS servers in the network forward the queries they cannot resolve locally to that DNS server. Conditional forwarding enables a DNS server to forward queries to other DNS servers based on the DNS domain names in the queries.

EXERCISES

> **IMPORTANT** **Completing All Exercises** If you plan to do any of the textbook exercises in this chapter, you must do all of the exercises in the chapter to return the computer to its original state for the associated Lab Manual labs.

Exercise 3-1: Adding the DNS Server Role

In this exercise, you will use the Manage Your Server page to add the DNS server role.

1. Click Start, point to Control Panel, point to Administrative Tools, and then click Manage Your Server.

   Manage Your Server starts automatically by default when you log on.

2. On the Manage Your Server page, click Add Or Remove A Role.

3. On the Preliminary Steps page, click Next.

4. On the Server Role page, click DNS Server, and then click Next.

5. On the Summary Of Selections page, click Next.

6. On the Welcome To The Configure A DNS Server Wizard page, click Next.

7. On the Select Configuration Action page, click Configure Root Hints Only (Recommended For Advanced Users Only), and then click Next.

8. On the Completing The Configure A DNS Server Wizard page, click Finish.

9. On the This Server Is Now A DNS Server page, click Finish.

Exercise 3-2: Adding a Standard Primary Forward Lookup Zone

In this exercise, you will use the DNS console to add a standard primary forward lookup zone.

1. Click Start, point to Administrative Tools, and then click DNS.

2. In the console tree, click, then right-click *ComputerName* (where *Computer-Name* is the name of your computer), and then click New Zone.

3. On the Welcome To The New Zone Wizard page, click Next.

4. On the Zone Type page, click Primary Zone and clear the Store The Zone In Active Directory (Available Only If DNS Server Is A Domain Controller) option, and then click Next.

5. On the Forward Or Reverse Lookup Zone page, click Forward Lookup Zone, and then click Next.

6. On the Zone Name page, in the Zone Name box, type **computername .contoso.com**, and then click Next.

7. On the Zone File page, verify that Create A New File With This File Name is selected and *computername*.contoso.com.dns is displayed in the box, and then click Next.

8. On the Dynamic Update page, verify Do Not Allow Dynamic Updates is selected, and then click Next.

9. On the Completing The New Zone Wizard page, click Finish.

Exercise 3-3: Changing a Zone to Active Directory–Integrated

In this exercise, you will change a standard zone to an Active Directory–integrated primary zone.

1. Click Start, point to Administrative Tools, and then click DNS.

2. In the console tree, expand *ComputerName* (where *ComputerName* is the name of your computer), expand Forward Lookup Zones, right-click *computername*.contoso.com, and then click Properties.

3. In the General tab, click Change.

4. In the Change Zone Type window, select the Store The Zone In Active Directory (Available Only If DNS Server Is A Domain Controller), and then click OK.

5. When you are asked if you want this zone to become Active Directory–integrated, click Yes.

6. To close the *computername*.contoso.com Properties window, click OK.

7. In the console tree, click Forward Lookup Zones, and in the details pane, note that the type of zone for *computername*.contoso.com is now Active Directory–Integrated Primary.

Exercise 3-4: Creating a Reverse Lookup Zone

In this exercise, you will create a reverse lookup zone.

1. Click Start, point to Administrative Tools, and then click DNS.

2. In the console tree, expand *ComputerName* (where *ComputerName* is the name of your computer), right-click Reverse Lookup Zones, and then click New Zone.

3. On the Welcome To The New Zone Wizard page, click Next.

4. On the Zone Type page, verify the Primary Zone option is enabled and verify that the Store The Zone In Active Directory (Available Only If DNS Server Is A Domain Controller) option is selected, and then click Next.

5. On the Active Directory Zone Replication Scope page, verify that To All Domain Controllers In The Active Directory Domain Contoso.com is selected, and then click Next.

6. On the Reverse Lookup Zone Name page, in the Network ID box, type **10.1.1**, and then click Next.

7. On the Dynamic Update page, verify that Allow Only Secure Dynamic Updates (Recommended For Active Directory) is selected, and then click Next.

8. On the Completing The New Zone Wizard page, click Finish.

9. In the console tree, click Reverse Lookup Zones, and in the details pane, verify a zone named 10.1.1.x Subnet (where x is the number of your computer) with a type Active Directory–Integrated Primary is displayed.

Exercise 3-5: Locating DNS Resource Records

Exercise 3-5 teaches you how to use the DNS console to identify three different types of resource records.

1. Click Start, point to Administrative Tools, and then click DNS.

2. In the console tree, expand Forward Lookup Zones, and then click *domain*.contoso.com (where *domain* is the name of your domain).

3. Locate the SOA, NS, and A records in the details pane.

Exercise 3-6: Removing the DNS Server Role

To prepare for the labs associated with this chapter (Lab Manual Lab 3), this exercise shows you how to remove the DNS server role.

1. Click Start, point to Administrative Tools, and then click Manage Your Server.

   The Manage Your Server page starts automatically by default when you log on.

2. On the Manage Your Server page, click Add Or Remove A Role.

3. On the Preliminary Steps page, click Next.

4. On the Server Role page, click DNS Server, and then click Next.

5. On the Role Removal Confirmation page, click the Remove The DNS Server Role check box, and then click Next.

6. On the DNS Server Role Removed page, click Finish.

REVIEW QUESTIONS

1. Describe the process by which secondary servers determine whether a zone transfer should be initiated.

2. What is the difference between an IXFR query and an AXFR query?

3. You discover that an administrator has adjusted the default TTL value for your company's primary DNS zone to 5 minutes. Which of the following is the most likely effect of this change?

   a. Primary servers initiate a zone transfer every 5 minutes.

   b. DNS clients have to query the server more frequently to resolve names for which the server is authoritative.

   c. Secondary servers initiate a zone transfer every 5 minutes.

   d. DNS hosts reregister their records more frequently.

4. Relative to file-backed zones, storing DNS zones in Active Directory results in which of the following?

   a. Less frequent transfer of information

   b. Increased need for administration

   c. Less saturation of network bandwidth

   d. Ability to perform secure dynamic updates

5. You want to consolidate DNS traffic between your network and the Internet. How could you use a forwarder to accomplish this?

6. What are some reasons a source server might respond with an AXFR to an IXFR request?

7. True or False: A primary server always initiates a zone transfer?

CASE SCENARIOS

Case Scenario 3-1: Minimizing DNS Traffic and Administration

Contoso, Ltd., has a branch office connected to corporate headquarters with a slow WAN link. The company wants to minimize the amount of traffic generated by the local DNS server on this link and minimize DNS administration in the branch office.

How would you configure the DNS server to meet these requirements?

a. Disable round-robin and netmask ordering.

b. Reduce the refresh interval in the SOA resource record for the primary zone.

c. Do not configure any forward or reverse zones, but configure the server to use a forwarder.

d. Configure the forward lookup zone with a WINS lookup record, and decrease the cache time-out value.

Case Scenario 3-2: Troubleshooting Access to External Resources

You are the network administrator for Contoso, Ltd. Users are complaining that they cannot access resources external to the local network. You eliminate connectivity issues to the DNS server and narrow the problem to name resolution. Using Ping.exe, you are able to successfully resolve local hosts but cannot resolve names external to the local network. Which of the following is the most likely cause of this issue?

a. The local DNS server is not authoritative for the Internet DNS domains.

b. Iterative queries are disabled on the DNS servers.

c. Recursive queries are disabled on the DNS servers.

d. DNS root hints are missing or incorrectly configured.

CHAPTER 4
MANAGING AND MONITORING DNS

Upon completion of this chapter, you will be able to:

- Use management tools to configure the **Domain Name System (DNS)** including Nslookup, DNSLint, and Dnscmd.

- Define DNS and **Windows Internet Naming Service (WINS)** integration and explain how host names and the **network basic input/output system (NetBIOS)** names fit into DNS and WINS integration.

- Configure options available on the Advanced tab of the DNS Server Properties dialog box.

- Explain how outdated **resource records** are aged and scavenged and initiate the aging and scavenging process.

- Display and purge the DNS **resolver** cache.

- Secure DNS objects in **Active Directory** directory service.

- Use the Event Log, DNS debug log, and Active Directory replication monitor to monitor and troubleshoot DNS.

DNS is a key service in Microsoft Windows Server 2003 networks. If DNS fails, clients often lose connectivity to the Internet or to other clients and Active Directory fails. Effective management and monitoring procedures mitigate the possibility of **DNS server** failure.

This chapter introduces you to the tools, concepts, and procedures necessary to manage and monitor DNS **name resolution**. Topics in this chapter include securing DNS, monitoring and troubleshooting DNS with tools such as the DNS Events Log and DNS debug log, and using tools such as Nslookup, the Replication Monitor, and Dnscmd.

USING DNS MANAGEMENT TOOLS

Several tools are useful for managing and monitoring DNS services. These tools include the following:

■ The DNS console, which is part of Administrative Tools. The DNS console is the primary tool for configuring DNS. It is shown in Figure 4-1.

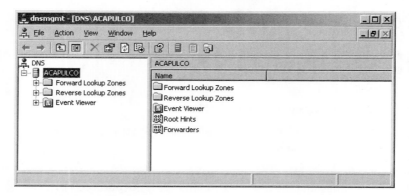

Figure 4-1   The DNS console

■ Nslookup, which can be used to query **DNS zone** information to verify existing and proper configuration of resource records.

■ DNSLint, which is a tool that verifies the consistency of a particular set of DNS records on multiple DNS servers.

■ Logging features, such as the DNS server log, which you can view with the DNS console or Event Viewer. File-based logs also can be used temporarily as an advanced debugging option to log and trace selected service events.

■ Dnscmd, which enables you to use the command line to perform most of the tasks you can perform using the DNS console.

Using the DNS Console to Monitor DNS Servers

You can use the DNS console to manually or automatically test DNS servers by submitting two different types of queries:

■ A simple query, or **iterative query**. The DNS resolver (client) on the server computer queries the local DNS servers, which are located on the same computer.

■ A **recursive query** to other DNS servers. The DNS resolver (client) on the server computer queries the local DNS server, but instead of submitting an iterative query, it submits a recursive query. Specifically, the client asks the server to use recursion to resolve a name server (NS)–type query for the root of the DNS **domain namespace**. This type of query typically requires additional recursive processing and can be helpful in verifying that server **root hints** or zone delegations are properly set.

These settings are accessed by clicking the Monitoring tab in the DNS server properties window. You can perform the test by clicking the Test Now button or specify an interval for performing the test.

Results of both manual and automatic tests are displayed in the Test Results list box shown in Figure 4-2. This information includes the following:

■ The date and time when each query was submitted

■ Additional status results of the specific test used, such as whether the simple or recursive query failed or succeeded

Figure 4-2   Test Results list box

Querying DNS with Nslookup

Nslookup is a command-line tool provided with **Transmission Control Protocol/Internet Protocol (TCP/IP)** available in Windows Server 2003 that performs DNS queries and enables examination of the content of zone files on local and remote servers. Nslookup often is used to verify the configuration of DNS zones and to diagnose and solve name resolution problems.

Nslookup can be run at the command prompt (in command prompt mode) or as a program that accepts serial commands and queries (in interactive mode). To look up a single host name, you would typically enter a single command at the command prompt. For example, executing the following command at the command prompt returns the Internet Protocol (IP) addresses associated with the **fully qualified domain name (FQDN)** www.microsoft.com (output results will vary):

```
C:\>nslookup www.microsoft.com
Server:  bottincdc1.bottinc.com
Address:  192.168.0.100

Non-authoritative answer:
Name:    www.microsoft.akadns.net
Addresses:  207.46.134.155, 207.46.134.190, 207.46.249.222, 207.46.249.27
         207.46.249.190
Aliases:  www.microsoft.com
```

To resolve the query, the Nslookup utility submits the name to the DNS server specified for the primary connection on the local client computer. This DNS server can then answer the query from its cache or through recursion.

If you submit a query for a host name that does not exist, you receive the following response:

```
C:\>nslookup thisdoesnotexist.bottinc.com
Server:  bottincdc1.bottinc.com
Address:  192.168.0.100

*** bottincdc1.bottinc.com can't find thisdoesnotexist.bottinc.com:
    Non-existent domain
```

If you troubleshoot a specific DNS server instead of the one specified for the primary connection on the local client computer, you can specify that DNS server using the Nslookup command. For example, the following command executed at the command prompt queries the DNS server at 207.46.138.20 for the name www.microsoft.com:

```
C:\>nslookup www.microsoft.com 207.46.138.20
```

You can also use Nslookup to resolve IP addresses to host names. For example, the following command executed at the command prompt returns the FQDN associated with the address 207.46.249.222, as shown in this output:

```
C:\>nslookup 207.46.249.222
Server:  localhost
Address:  127.0.0.1

Name:    www.microsoft.com
Address:  207.46.249.222
```

Nslookup Syntax

Use the following syntax for Nslookup in the command prompt mode:

```
nslookup [-opt  ...] [{Host| [Server]}]
```

The Nslookup command uses the following syntax:

- **-opt**   Specifies one or more Nslookup subcommands as a command-line option.

- **Host**   Looks up information for *Host* using the current default DNS name server (NS), if no other server is specified. To look up a computer not in the current **DNS domain**, append a period to the name.

- **Server**   Specifies to use this server as the DNS name server. If you omit *Server*, the default DNS name server is used.

Using Interactive Mode

When issuing multiple Nslookup commands, it is generally more efficient to use Nslookup in interactive mode. To enter interactive mode, open a command prompt, type **nslookup**, and press ENTER.

In interactive mode, Nslookup accepts commands that allow the program to perform a variety of functions, such as displaying the specific contents of messages included in DNS exchanges, simulating a **zone transfer**, or searching for records of a specific type on a given server. These commands can be displayed by typing the **help** or **?** command, as shown in Figure 4-3.

Figure 4-3   Nslookup commands

Exploring Nslookup Options

When you are in interactive mode, you can also use the Set command to configure Nslookup options that determine how the resolver carries out queries. One option is to use the Debug command. By default, Nslookup is set to Nodebug. Typing **set debug** while in interactive mode enters debug mode, which enables Nslookup to display the DNS response messages communicated from the DNS server as shown in Figure 4-4.

Figure 4-4   Nslookup in debug mode

NOTE   Nslookup Commands Are Case-Sensitive   Nslookup commands entered while in interactive mode are case-sensitive and must be typed in lowercase.

You can view the options currently configured for Nslookup by running the Set All command, as shown in Figure 4-5.

Figure 4-5   Displaying Nslookup options

Table 4-1 describes the most common options configured with the Set command.

Table 4-1   **Command-Line Options Available with the Set Command**

Option	Purpose	Example (Interactive Mode)
set all	Shows the configuration status of all options.	>set all
set [no]debug	Puts Nslookup in debug mode. With debug mode turned on, more information is printed about the packet sent to the server and the resulting answer.	>set debug Or >set nodebug
set [no]d2	Puts Nslookup in verbose debug mode so you can examine the query and response packets between the resolver and the server.	>set d2 Or >set nod2
set domain= *<domain name>*	Tells the resolver which domain name to append for unqualified queries (for example, sales is an unqualified query as opposed to sales.fabrikam.com), including all queried names not followed by a trailing dot.	>set domain=bottinc.com
set timeout= *<time-out value>*	Tells the resolver what time-out value to use, in seconds. This option is useful for slow links on which queries frequently time out and the wait time must be lengthened.	>set timeout=5
set type= *<record type>* or set querytype= *<record type>* or set q=*<record type>*	Tells the resolver which type of resource records to search for (for example, address [A], pointer [PTR], or service locator [SRV] records). If you want the resolver to query for all types of resource records, type **set type=all**.	>set type=A >set q=MX

The next section describes how to perform common tasks using Nslookup in interactive mode.

Looking Up Different Data Types

By default, names queried for in Nslookup return only matching host address (A) resource records. To look up different data types within the domain namespace, use the Set Type command or Set Querytype (Set Q) command at the command prompt. For example, to query for mail exchanger (MX) resource records only instead of A resource records, type **set q=mx**, as shown here:

```
C:\>nslookup
Default Server:  bottincdc1.bottinc.com
Address:  192.168.0.100

> set q=mx
> microsoft.com
Server:  bottincdc1.bottinc.com
Address:  192.168.0.100

Non-authoritative answer:
microsoft.com   MX preference = 10, mail exchanger = maila.microsoft.com
microsoft.com   MX preference = 10, mail exchanger = mailb.microsoft.com
microsoft.com   MX preference = 10, mail exchanger = mailc.microsoft.com

maila.microsoft.com      internet address = 131.107.3.124
maila.microsoft.com      internet address = 131.107.3.125
mailb.microsoft.com      internet address = 131.107.3.122
mailb.microsoft.com      internet address = 131.107.3.123
mailc.microsoft.com      internet address = 131.107.3.121
mailc.microsoft.com      internet address = 131.107.3.126
>
```

> **NOTE Querying a Record of Any Type**   To query for a record of any type,
> execute the Nslookup command Set q=any.

The first time a query is made for a remote name, the answer is authoritative, but subsequent queries are nonauthoritative. This pattern appears for the following reason: the first time a remote host is queried, the local DNS server contacts the DNS server that is authoritative for that domain. The local DNS server then caches that information so that subsequent queries are answered nonauthoritatively out of the local server's cache.

Querying Another Name Server Directly

To query another name server directly, use the Server or Lserver commands to switch to that name server. The Lserver command uses the local server to get the address of the server to switch to, whereas the Server command uses the current default server to get the address.

After you execute either of these commands, all subsequent lookups in the current Nslookup session are performed at the specified server until you switch servers again. The following syntax illustrates what you would type to initiate a server switch:

```
C:\> nslookup
Default Server:  nameserver1.contoso.com
Address:  10.0.0.1

> server nameserver2
Default Server:  nameserver2.contoso.com
Address:  10.0.0.2
```

Using Nslookup Subcommand Ls to View Zone Data

You can use the Nslookup subcommand Ls to list information for a DNS domain. When you issue an Nslookup command with the Ls subcommand, you effectively are requesting a zone transfer. The syntax for the Ls command is as follows:

```
ls [- a | d | t type] domain [> filename]
```

Table 4-2 lists valid options.

Table 4-2   Nslookup Ls Options

Option	Purpose	Example
-t *QueryType*	Lists all records of a specific type	>ls -t cname contoso.com
-a	Lists aliases of computers in the DNS domain (equivalent to -t CNAME)	>ls -a contoso.com
-d	Lists all records for the DNS domain (equivalent to -t ANY)	>ls -d contoso.com
-h	Lists central processing unit (CPU) and operating system information for the DNS domain (equivalent to -t HINFO)	>ls -h contoso.com
-s	Lists well-known services of computers in the DNS domain (equivalent to -t WKS)	>ls -s contoso.com

The following output demonstrates the use of the Ls command in interactive mode.

```
>ls contoso.com
[nameserver1.contoso.com]
nameserver1.contoso.com.  NS server = ns1.contoso.com
nameserver2.contoso.com   NS server = ns2.contoso.com
nameserver1               A    10.0.0.1
nameserver2               A    10.0.0.2
>
```

By default, the DNS Server service allows zone information to be transferred only to servers listed in the **name server (NS) resource records** of a zone. Although this is a secure setting, consider increasing security by allowing zone transfers only to specified IP addresses. You also have the option to allow zone transfers to any server. This is not recommended and can expose your DNS data to an attacker attempting to map your network for a larger attack. The following error message is returned if zone transfer security has been set:

```
*** Can't list domain <example>.: Query refused
```

Using DNSLint

DNSLint is a command-line DNS tool included with Windows Server 2003 that verifies the consistency of a particular set of DNS records on multiple DNS servers. It also can help diagnose and fix problems caused as a result of missing or incorrect DNS records. DNSLint compiles results into a Hypertext Markup Language (HTML) file named, by default, DNSLint.html. The file is stored in the same directory from which you executed the DNSLint command.

For example, DNSLint can help when clients experience problems resolving **NetBIOS names** or when verifying that the SRV records (which clients might use to find WINS servers) are available and accurate. DNSLint can help ascertain whether DNS is contributing to the problem.

You also can use DNSLint to troubleshoot DNS-related Active Directory replication issues. Specifically, use DNSLint to determine the following:

- Whether all DNS servers that are supposed to be authoritative for the root of an Active Directory forest actually have the necessary DNS records to successfully synchronize **directory partition replicas** among domain controllers in an Active Directory forest. DNSLint identifies which DNS records are missing from each authoritative DNS server.

- Whether a particular Active Directory domain controller can resolve the necessary DNS records to successfully synchronize partition replicas among domain controllers in an Active Directory forest. DNSLint identifies which DNS records cannot be resolved by the domain controller that is tested.

  MORE INFO   Using DNSLint to Troubleshoot Active Directory Replication Issues   See Microsoft Knowledge Base Article 321046, "HOW TO: Use DNSLint to Troubleshoot Active Directory Replication Issues." To find this article, go to http://support.microsoft.com and enter the article number in the Search The Knowledge Base text box.

In another scenario, you are able to send e-mail, but not receive it. One likely cause of this is incorrect DNS configuration. To determine whether DNS is misconfigured, use DNSLint to verify the DNS records on the DNS servers that are used to resolve the e-mail server's IP address.

DNSLint Syntax and Functions

The syntax for DNSLint is as follows:

```
dnslint /d domain_name | /ad [LDAP_IP_address] | /ql input_file
       [/c [smtp,pop,imap]] [/no_open] [/r report_name]
       [/t] [/test_tcp] [/s DNS_IP_address] [/v] [/y]
```

DNSLint performs one of three functions and then generates an HTML report.

- **/d**   The /d (domain name test) switch is used to test a particular DNS domain name. This switch is used to help diagnose "lame delegation" issues and other related DNS issues. *Lame delegation* occurs when either a zone is delegated to a server that has not been properly configured to be authoritative for the zone or a server that is authoritative for the zone has an NS record that points to another that is not authoritative for the zone.

- **/ad**   The /ad (Active Directory replication test) switch is used to test the DNS records that are responsible for Active Directory forest replication. Figure 4-6 shows the result section of the DNSLint report run using the Dnslint /ad /s localhost /v command.

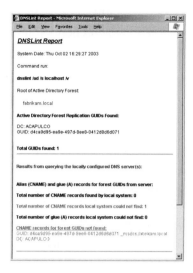

Figure 4-6   DNSLint result section

- **/ql**   The /ql (Query List test) switch is used to test the DNS records specified in a text input file.

> **MORE INFO   Using DNSLint**   See Microsoft Knowledge Base Article 321045, "Description of the DNSLint Utility." To find this article, go to http://support .microsoft.com and enter the article number in the Search The Knowledge Base text box.

The following procedure describes how to use the autocreate parameter with the /ql switch to generate an input file you can customize.

▶ Creating an Input File for DNSLint

To create the DNSLint report, follow these steps:

1. Open the command prompt.

2. Navigate to the directory containing Dnslint.exe.

3. At the command prompt, type **dnslint /ql autocreate**.

   When the autocreate parameter is added to the /ql switch, a sample query text file is generated.

4. At the command prompt, type **notepad in-dnslint.txt**.

5. In Microsoft Notepad, in the seventh line from the bottom of the file, change the line from dns1.cp.msft.net to *ComputerName*. **northwindtraders.msft**.

6. In Notepad, in the last four lines of the file, change any instances of Microsoft.com to the name of the domain that you are querying.

7. In Notepad, in the last five lines of the file, change any instances of 207.46.197.100 to the IP address of the DNS server that you are querying.

8. In Notepad, save the file as Dnslintquery.txt in the same directory in which In-dnslint.txt is located, and then close Notepad.

9. At the command prompt, type **dnslint /ql dnslintquery.txt /v**.

   The /ql switch requests queries from the specified list (Dnslintquery.txt). The /v switch requests a verbose response.

10. When the HTML report opens, verify the contents, and then close the report.

11. Close the command prompt.

Using Dnscmd

You can use the Dnscmd command-line tool to perform most of the tasks that you can do from the DNS console. This tool can be used to script batch files, to help automate the management and updates of existing DNS server configurations, or to perform setup and configuration of DNS servers. For example, you can do the following:

■ Create, delete, and view zones and records.

■ Reset server and zone properties.

■ Perform zone maintenance operations, such as updating the zone, reloading the zone, refreshing the zone, writing the zone back to a file or to Active Directory, and pausing or resuming the zone.

■ Clear the cache.

■ Stop and start the DNS service.

■ View statistics.

Dnscmd is provided as a command-line tool for managing DNS servers. To use Dnscmd, you must install Windows Support Tools.

▶ **Installing Windows Support Tools**

To install Windows Support Tools, follow these steps:

1. Insert the Windows Server 2003 CD into your CD-ROM drive.

2. Go to the \Support\Tools folder.

3. Double-click Suptools.msi.

4. On the Welcome To The Windows Support Tools Setup Wizard page, click Next.

5. On the End User License Agreement page, click I Agree, and then click Next.

6. On the User Information page, provide your name and the name of your organization, and then click Next.

7. On the Destination Directory page, type the path to where Windows Support Tools should be installed, and then click Install Now.

8. On the Completing The Windows Support Tools page, click Finish.

▶ Displaying a Complete List of Zones

To display a complete list of the zones configured on a DNS server by using Dnscmd, at the command prompt, type **dnscmd [*ComputerName*] /enumzones**.

Executing Dnscmd using localhost results in the following:

```
C:\>dnscmd localhost /enumzones
Enumerated zone list:
       Zone count = 5
Zone name                          Type      Storage       Properties
    .                              Cache     AD-Legacy
   _msdcs.contoso01.com            Primary   AD-Forest     Secure
   1.1.10.in-addr.arpa             Primary   AD-Legacy     Secure Rev
   computer01.contoso.com          Primary   AD-Legacy
   contoso01.com                   Primary   AD-Domain     Secure

Command completed successfully.
```

▶ Displaying Specific Zone Information

To display information about a specific zone that is configured on a DNS server by using Dnscmd, at the command prompt, type the following:

dnscmd [*ComputerName*] /zoneinfo [*zone*]

Executing the following command results in output similar to what follows:

```
C:\>dnscmd localhost /zoneinfo contoso01.com
Zone query result:
Zone info:
        ptr                  = 00083050
        zone name            = contoso01.com
        zone type            = 1
        update               = 2
        DS integrated        = 1
        data file            = (null)
        using WINS           = 0
        using Nbstat         = 0
        aging                = 0
        refresh interval     = 168
        no refresh           = 168
        scavenge available   = 3529116
        Zone Masters
        NULL IP Array.
        Zone Secondaries
        NULL IP Array.
        secure secs          = 3
        directory partition  = AD-Domain      flags 00000015
        zone DN              = DC=contoso01.com,cn=MicrosoftDNS, DC=DomainDnsZones,
                               DC=contoso01,DC=com
    Command completed successfully.
```

Practice displaying DNS zone information by doing Exercise 4-1, "Displaying DNS Zone Information Using Dnscmd," now.

INTEGRATING DNS ZONES WITH WINS

DNS and WINS integration is the process in which DNS uses WINS to resolve names to IP addresses. DNS is used to resolve host names and services to IP addresses, and WINS is used to resolve NetBIOS names to IP addresses. You can manually configure NetBIOS name-to-IP-address mappings on the DNS server, or you can configure the DNS server to forward the name queries to the WINS server for resolution. Integrating DNS with WINS allows DNS clients to use the existing NetBIOS name entries in WINS for host name lookup. The DNS service provides the capability to use WINS servers to look up names that are not found in the DNS namespace by checking the NetBIOS namespace that WINS manages.

When you configure WINS lookup for a forward lookup zone, a WINS resource record pointing to the WINS server you specify on the WINS tab is added to the zone database. When you configure WINS-R lookup for a reverse lookup zone, a corresponding WINS-R resource record is added to the zone database.

Practice integrating DNS and WINS by doing Exercise 4-2, "Integrating DNS and WINS," now.

Host and NetBIOS names can be the same in Microsoft Windows 2000 or Windows Server 2003, which allows DNS and WINS to work together to resolve names. In some circumstances, it may be advantageous for organizations to use the existing WINS database for host name lookups rather than configuring every client in the WINS database to be in the DNS database.

MANAGING DNS USING ADVANCED DNS SERVER PROPERTIES

Advanced DNS server properties refer to the settings that can be configured in the Advanced tab of the DNS Server Properties dialog box (shown in Figure 4-7). These properties relate to server-specific features, such as disabling recursion, handling resolution of multihomed hosts, and achieving compatibility with non-Microsoft DNS servers.

Figure 4-7   The Advanced tab of the DNS Server Properties dialog box

The server installation settings include six server options, which are either on or off, and three other server features with various selections for configuration. Table 4-3 shows the default settings for all nine features.

Table 4-3   **Default DNS Installation Settings**

Property	Setting
Disable Recursion	Off
BIND Secondaries	On
Fail On Load If Bad Zone Data	Off
Enable Round Robin	On
Enable Netmask Ordering	On
Secure Cache Against Pollution	On
Name Checking	Multibyte (UTF-8)
Load Zone Data On Startup	From Active Directory And Registry
Enable Automatic Scavenging Of Stale Records	Off (requires configuration when enabled)

In most situations, these installation defaults are acceptable and do not require modification. However, when needed, you can use the DNS console to modify these advanced parameters and accommodate special deployment needs and situations.

You can restore these default settings at any time using the Advanced tab. Simply click Reset To Default.

The following sections describe the available installation options in more detail.

Disable Recursion

The Disable Recursion server option is disabled by default (meaning that recursion is enabled). When the Disable Recursion option is enabled, the DNS Server service does not answer queries for which it is not authoritative or which it has not already answered and placed in its cache. Instead, the DNS Server service provides the client with *referrals*, which are resource records that allow a DNS client to perform iterative queries to resolve an FQDN. Do not disable recursion on a server if any other name servers use it as a **forwarder**. Disable recursion when you want to create an authoritative-only name server and prevent cache pollution. Since the server does not query other servers, it does not maintain a cache and is very difficult to spoof (pollute the cache).

BIND Secondaries

The BIND Secondaries option controls whether fast transfer format is used during a DNS zone transfer. Berkeley Internet Name Domain (BIND) is a common implementation of DNS written and ported to most available versions of the UNIX operating system. *Fast transfer format* is an efficient means of transferring zone data that provides data compression and allows multiple records to be transferred per individual Transmission Control Protocol (TCP) message. Fast zone transfer is always used among Windows-based DNS servers, so the BIND Secondaries option does not affect communications among Windows servers. However, only BIND versions 4.9.4 and later can handle these fast zone transfers.

For BIND versions earlier than 4.9.4, DNS servers running Windows Server 2003 can be configured to transfer a zone using the slower, uncompressed transfer format. When you select the BIND Secondaries check box in the Advanced tab of the Server Properties dialog box, no fast transfers are made.

If you know your DNS server will be performing zone transfers with DNS servers using BIND version 4.9.4 or later, you should disable this option to allow fast zone transfers to occur. (BIND 9.1 was released January 17, 2001.)

Fail On Load If Bad Zone Data

DNS servers running on Windows Server 2003 will, by default, load a zone even if that zone contains errors. In that scenario, errors are logged and ignored. Enabling Fail On Load If Bad Zone Data prevents a zone with errors from being loaded.

Reordering Results Sets

Multihomed computers (computers with either more than one network interface card or one network interface card with more than one IP address) typically have registered multiple host address (A) resource records for the same host name. When a client attempts to resolve the host name of a multihomed computer by contacting a DNS server, the DNS server returns a *response list*, or answer list, to the client that contains the resource records matching the client query. Upon receiving the response list from the DNS server, a DNS client attempts to contact the target host with the first IP address in the response list. If this attempt fails, the client then attempts to contact the second IP address, and so on. The Enable Netmask Ordering option and the Enable Round Robin option are both used to change the order of resource records returned in this response list.

Enable Round Robin

Round robin is a load balancing mechanism used by DNS servers to share and distribute network resource loads. If multiple resource records satisfy a query, you can use round robin to rotate the order of resource record types returned to the client.

By default, DNS uses round robin to rotate the order of resource record data returned in query answers in which multiple resource records of the same type exist for a queried DNS domain name. This feature provides a simple method for load balancing client use of Web servers and other frequently queried multihomed computers. The capability to perform round-robin rotation on all types of resource records is a new feature introduced in Windows Server 2003.

> **NOTE   Netmask Ordering Priority**   Local subnet priority (netmask ordering) supersedes the use of round-robin rotation for multihomed computers. When enabled, however, round robin is used as a secondary method to sort multiple records returned in a response list.

Round Robin Example   The Web server named server1.contoso.com has three network adapters and three distinct IP addresses. In the stored zone (either in a database file or in Active Directory), the three A resource records mapping the host name to each of its IP addresses appear in this fixed order:

```
server1   IN   A   10.0.0.1
server1   IN   A   10.0.0.2
server1   IN   A   10.0.0.3
```

The first DNS client—Client1—that queries the server to resolve this host's name receives the list in this default order. However, when a second client—Client2—sends a subsequent query to resolve this name, the list is rotated as follows:

```
server1    IN    A    10.0.0.2
server1    IN    A    10.0.0.3
server1    IN    A    10.0.0.1
```

Disabling Round Robin   When you clear the Enable Round Robin check box, round robin is disabled for the DNS server. If round robin is disabled for a DNS server, the order of the response for these queries is based on a static ordering of resource records in the answer list as they are stored in the zone (either its zone file or Active Directory).

Enable Netmask Ordering   Netmask ordering is a method DNS uses to give ordering and preference to IP addresses on the same network when a requesting client queries for a host name that has multiple A resource records. This is designed so that the client program will attempt to connect to a host using the closest (and, therefore, presumably fastest) IP address available.

When returning more than one IP address to a client when Netmask Ordering is enabled, IP addresses most closely matching the client's subnet mask are placed at the top of the response list. The Enable Netmask Ordering option is selected by default. For example, a multihomed computer, server1.contoso.com, has three A resource records for each of its three IP addresses in the contoso.com zone. These three records appear in the following order in the zone—either in the zone file or in Active Directory:

```
server1    IN    A    192.168.1.27
server1    IN    A    10.0.0.14
server1    IN    A    172.16.20.4
```

When a DNS client resolver at IP address 10.4.3.2 queries the server for the IP addresses of the host server1.contoso.com, the DNS Server service notes that the originating IP network address (10.0.0.0) of the client matches the network (class A) ID of the 10.0.0.14 address in the answer list of resource records. The DNS Server service then reorders the addresses in the response list as follows:

```
server1    IN    A    10.0.0.14
server1    IN    A    192.168.1.27
server1    IN    A    172.16.20.4
```

If the **network ID** of the IP address of the requesting client does not match any of the network IDs of the resource records in the answer list, the list is not reordered.

In a network that uses IP subnetting (nondefault subnet masks), a DNS server first returns IP addresses that match both the client's network ID and subnet ID before returning any IP addresses that match only the client's network ID.

For example, a multihomed computer, server1.contoso.com, has four A resource records corresponding to each of its four IP addresses in the contoso.com zone. Two of these IP addresses are for distinct and separate networks. The other two IP addresses share a common IP network address, but because custom netmasks of

255.255.248.0 are used, the IP addresses are located in different subnets. These example resource records appear in the following order in the zone, either in the zone file or in Active Directory:

```
server1   IN   A   192.168.1.27
server1   IN   A   172.16.22.4
server1   IN   A   10.0.0.14
server1   IN   A   172.16.31.5
```

If the IP address of the requesting client is 172.16.22.8, both of the IP addresses that match the same IP network as the client, the 172.16.0.0 network, are returned to the client at the top of the response list. However, in this example, the 172.16.22.4 address is placed ahead of the 172.16.31.5 address because it more closely matches the network ID of the client.

The reordered answer list returned by the DNS service is as follows:

```
server1   IN   A   172.16.22.4
server1   IN   A   172.16.31.5
server1   IN   A   192.168.1.27
server1   IN   A   10.0.0.14
```

> **NOTE   LocalNetPriority Setting and Netmask Ordering**   Netmask ordering is often referred to as the LocalNetPriority setting. This name originates from the corresponding LocalNetPriority option used with the Dnscmd command-line utility.

Secure Cache Against Pollution

By default, the Secure Cache Against Pollution option is enabled. This setting allows the DNS server to protect its cache against referrals that are potentially polluting or nonsecure. When the setting is enabled, the server caches only those records with a name that corresponds to the domain for which the original queried name was made. Any referrals received from another DNS server along with a query response are simply discarded.

For example, if a query is originally made for the name example.microsoft.com, and a referral answer provides a record for a name outside the microsoft.com domain name tree (such as msn.com), that name is discarded if the Secure Cache Against Pollution option is enabled. This setting helps prevent unauthorized computers from impersonating another network server.

When this option is disabled, however, the server caches all the records received in response to DNS queries—even when the records do not correspond to the queried-for domain name.

Name Checking

By default, the Name Checking drop-down list box in the Advanced tab of the DNS Server Properties dialog box is set to Multibyte (UTF-8). Thus, the DNS service, by default, verifies that all domain names handled by the DNS service conform to the UCS Transformation Format (UTF). *Unicode* is a 2-byte encoding scheme, compatible with the traditional 1-byte **American Standard Code for Information Interchange (ASCII)** format, that allows for binary representation of most human languages. Table 4-4 lists and describes the four name-checking methods.

Table 4-4   **Name-Checking Methods**

Method	Description
Strict RFC **(American National Standards Institute [ANSI])**	Uses strict checking of names. These restrictions, set in **Request for Comments (RFC)** 1123, include limiting names to uppercase and lowercase letters (A–Z, a–z), numbers (0–9), and hyphens (-). The first character of the DNS name can be a number.
Non RFC (ANSI)	Permits names that are nonstandard and that do not follow RFC 1123 Internet host naming specifications.
Multibyte (UTF-8)	Permits recognition of characters other than ASCII, including Unicode, which is normally encoded as more than one octet (8 bits) in length.
	With this option, multibyte characters can be transformed and represented using UTF-8 support, which is provided with Windows Server 2003.
	Names encoded in UTF-8 format must not exceed the size limits stated in RFC 2181, which specifies a maximum of 63 octets per label and 255 octets per name. Character count is insufficient to determine size because some UTF-8 characters exceed one octet in length. This option allows for domain names using non-English alphabets.
All Names	Permits any naming conventions.

Despite the flexibility of the UTF-8 name-checking method, you should consider changing the Name Checking option to Strict RFC when your DNS servers perform zone transfers to non-Windows servers that are not UTF-8-aware. Although DNS server implementations that are not UTF-8-aware might be able to accept the transfer of a zone containing UTF-8-encoded names, these servers might not be capable of writing back those names to a zone file or reloading those names from a zone file.

You should use the other two name-checking options, Non RFC and All Names, only when a specific application requires them.

Load Zone Data On Startup

By default, the Load Zone Data On Startup property is set to the From Active Directory And Registry option. Thus, by default, DNS servers in Windows Server 2003 initialize with the settings specified in the Active Directory database and the server registry.

You can also load zone data using two other settings: From Registry and From File. The From Registry option forces the DNS server to initialize by reading parameters stored in the Windows registry. The From File option forces the DNS server to initialize by reading parameters stored in a boot file. The boot file must be a text file named Boot located on the local computer in the %systemroot%\System32\Dns folder.

When a boot file is used, settings in the file are applied to the server, overriding the settings stored in the registry on the DNS server. However, for parameters that are not configurable using boot file directives, registry defaults (or stored reconfigured server settings) are applied by the DNS Server service.

> **MORE INFO**   *DNS Boot File Structure*   *See the Microsoft Knowledge Base Article 194513, "The Structure of a Domain Name System Boot File." To find this article, go to http://support.microsoft.com and enter the article number in the Search The Knowledge Base text box.*

AGING AND SCAVENGING RESOURCE RECORDS

Traditionally, the DNS administrator manually added or deleted resource records from DNS zone files as required. With dynamic update, individual computers and services are able to automatically add, update, and delete DNS resource records. For example, the Windows Server 2003 and Windows 2000 DNS Client service register their clients' A and **pointer (PTR) resource records** in DNS at start time and every 24 hours thereafter. Dynamic update ensures that the records are up-to-date and guards against accidental deletion of resource records by the DNS administrator.

Over time, stale resource records accumulate in the DNS database. Records become stale, for example, when computers, especially those of mobile users, abnormally disconnect from the network. Stale records provide outdated and inaccurate information to clients, take up unnecessary space, and can possibly degrade server performance. Windows Server 2003 provides a mechanism to remove these records.

Windows Server 2003 adds a time stamp to dynamically added resource records in primary zones where aging and scavenging are enabled. Records added manually are time stamped with a value of zero, which indicates those records should be excluded from the aging and scavenging process. Since **secondary name servers** receive a read-only copy of the zone data from **primary name servers**, only primary zones are eligible to participate in this process. Servers can be configured to perform recurring scavenging operations automatically, or you can initiate a manual and immediate scavenging operation at the server.

▶   **Initiating Scavenging**

To initiate scavenging, follow these steps:

1. Open the DNS management console.

2. In the console tree, right-click the applicable DNS server, and then click Set Aging/Scavenging For All Zones.

3. In the Server Aging/Scavenging Properties dialog box, select the Scavenge Stale Resource Records check box; set one, none, or both of the following; and then click OK:

   ❑ **No-Refresh Interval**   The time between the most recent refresh of a record time stamp and the moment when the time stamp may be refreshed again.

   ❑ **Refresh Interval**   The time between the earliest moment when a record time stamp can be refreshed and the earliest moment when the record can be scavenged. The refresh interval must be longer than the maximum record refresh period.

4. In the Server Aging/Scavenging Confirmation dialog box, select Apply These Settings To The Existing Active Directory–Integrated Zones, and then click OK.

> **CAUTION**   **Proper Configuration of Aging and Scavenging**   By default, the scavenging mechanism is disabled. You should not enable DNS resource record scavenging unless you are absolutely certain that you understand all the parameters and have configured them correctly. Otherwise, you might accidentally configure the server to delete records that it should retain. If a name is accidentally deleted, not only do users fail to resolve queries for that name, but also a different user can create and own that name, even on zones configured for secure dynamic update.

MANAGING THE DNS RESOLVER CACHE

The DNS resolver is a component of the DNS Client service installed by default with Windows Server 2003. It runs within the **SVCHOST process**.

> **MORE INFO**   **What is SVCHOST?**   See Microsoft Knowledge Base Article 250320, "Description of Svchost.exe in Windows 2000." To find this article, go to http://support.microsoft.com and enter the article number in the Search The Knowledge Base text box.

To reduce the amount of traffic to the DNS server or servers, the DNS resolver caches resource records obtained from query responses. These resource records are used to resolve repeated client queries and reduce redundant queries to the DNS server. Each entry in the cache has a specified Time to Live (TTL), typically set by the query response. When the TTL expires, the entry is purged from the cache. When the resolver is unable to answer a query using its own cache, the resolver sends the query to one or more DNS servers configured in the TCP/IP properties of the server. If a **Hosts file** is configured on the client, it is preloaded into the resolver cache.

Practice displaying and purging the resolver cache by doing Exercise 4-3, "Displaying and Purging the Resolver Cache," now.

To view the cache, type the following at a command prompt:

```
ipconfig /displaydns
```

To purge the cache, type the following at a command prompt:

```
ipconfig /flushdns
```

SECURING DNS

DNS is an open **protocol** and is therefore vulnerable to attackers. Windows Server 2003 provides the capability to help prevent a successful attack on your DNS infrastructure through the addition of security features.

This section describes common threats to DNS security and how to determine the level of DNS security in your organization. Default security settings and security features also are discussed.

DNS Security Threats

Table 4-5 describes the typical ways in which a DNS infrastructure is threatened by attackers.

Table 4-5 **Common DNS Security Threats**

Threat	Description
Footprinting	The process by which DNS zone data, including domain names, computer names, and IP addresses for sensitive network resources, is obtained by an attacker. An attacker commonly begins an attack by using this DNS data to diagram, or footprint, a network. For easy identification, DNS domain and computer names typically indicate the function or location of a domain or computer. An attacker takes advantage of these naming conventions to identify the key network resources on the network.
Denial of service	A *denial of service (DoS) attack* is an assault, usually planned, that seeks to disrupt functionality. A DoS attack overwhelms a network resource with bogus requests that cannot be completed. In so doing, it causes the resource to become so busy attempting to respond to the bogus requests that the resource becomes incapable of servicing legitimate requests. In the context of DNS, a DoS attack is one in which an attacker attempts to overload one or more DNS servers by flooding them with recursive queries. This causes the CPU to constantly operate at 100 percent and will render the DNS server unavailable to legitimate requests.
Data modification	An attempt by an attacker (that has likely completed a DNS footprint attack) to use valid IP addresses in IP packets the attacker has created, thereby giving these packets the appearance of coming from a valid IP address in the network. This is commonly called *IP spoofing*. With a valid IP address (an IP address within the IP address range of a subnet), the attacker can gain access to the network and destroy data or conduct other attacks.
Redirection	When an attacker is able to redirect queries for DNS names to servers under the control of the attacker. One method of redirection involves the attempt to pollute the DNS cache of a DNS server with erroneous DNS data that can direct future queries to servers under the control of the attacker. For example, if a query was originally made, for the name example.microsoft.com, and a referral answer provided a record for a name outside of the microsoft.com domain, such as malicious-user.com, the DNS server would use the cached data for malicious-user.com to resolve a query for that name. Redirection can be accomplished whenever an attacker has writable access to DNS data, such as with nonsecure dynamic updates.

DNS Security Levels

DNS security implementations can be grouped into three levels: low, medium, and high. Review the characteristics of each level to determine which level best describes your current DNS security implementation and which characteristics from each implementation should be added to your DNS implementation.

Low-Level Security   Low-level security is a standard DNS deployment without any security precautions configured. Only deploy this level of DNS security in network environments where there is no concern for the integrity of your DNS data or in private networks where there is no threat of external connectivity. Low-level security has the following characteristics:

- If connected to the Internet, the DNS infrastructure of your organization is fully exposed.

- Standard DNS resolution is performed by all DNS servers in your network.

- All DNS servers are configured with root hints that point to the root servers for the Internet.

- All DNS servers permit zone transfers to any server.

- All DNS servers are configured to listen on all of their IP addresses.

- Cache pollution prevention is disabled on all DNS servers.

- Nonsecure dynamic update is allowed for all DNS zones.

- User Datagram Protocol (UDP) and TCP/IP port 53 is open on the firewall for your network for both source and destination addresses.

Medium-Level Security   Medium-level security uses the DNS security features available without running DNS servers on domain controllers and storing DNS zones in Active Directory. Medium-level security has the following characteristics:

- If connected to the Internet, the DNS infrastructure of your organization has limited exposure.

- All DNS servers are configured to use forwarders to point to a specific list of internal DNS servers when they cannot resolve names locally.

- All DNS servers limit zone transfers to servers listed in the NS resource records in their zones.

- DNS servers are configured to listen on specified IP addresses.

- Cache pollution prevention is enabled on all DNS servers.

- Dynamic update is not allowed for any DNS zones.

- Internal DNS servers communicate with external DNS servers through the firewall, with a limited list of source and destination addresses allowed.

- External DNS servers in front of your firewall are configured with root hints that point to the root servers for the Internet.

- All Internet name resolution is performed using proxy servers and gateways.

High-Level Security   High-level security uses the same configuration as medium-level security but also uses the security features available when the DNS Server service is running on a domain controller and DNS zones are stored in Active Directory. In addition, high-level security completely eliminates DNS communication with the Internet. This is not a typical configuration, but it is recommended whenever Internet connectivity is not required. The characteristics of high-level security are as follows:

- The DNS infrastructure of your organization has no Internet communication by internal DNS servers.

- Your network uses an internal DNS root and namespace; all authority for DNS zones is internal.

- DNS servers that are configured with forwarders use internal DNS server IP addresses only.

- All DNS servers limit zone transfers to specified IP addresses.

- DNS servers are configured to listen on specified IP addresses.

- Cache pollution prevention is enabled on all DNS servers.

- Internal DNS servers are configured with root hints pointing to the internal DNS servers hosting the root zone for your internal namespace.

- All DNS servers are running on domain controllers. A **discretionary access control list (DACL)** is configured on the DNS Server service to allow only specific individuals to perform administrative tasks on the DNS server.

- All DNS zones are stored in Active Directory. A DACL is configured to allow only specific individuals to create, delete, or modify DNS zones.

- DACLs are configured on DNS resource records to allow only specific individuals to create, delete, or modify DNS data.

- Secure dynamic update is configured for DNS zones except the top-level and root zones, which do not allow dynamic updates at all.

DNS Objects in Windows Server 2003 Active Directory

In addition to the MicrosoftDNS **container object** in the domain partition that is supported in both Windows 2000 and Windows Server 2003, a MicrosoftDNS container is located in every DNS application directory partition. An *application directory partition* is a new type of directory partition in Windows Server 2003 Active Directory. It can be used by applications to store application-specific data that is of interest in a scope that is smaller than the entire forest or domain. This data can be characterized as either changing frequently (dynamic) or having a short useful lifetime (volatile). For example, Windows Server 2003 DNS can use application directory partitions to store dynamically updated DNS zone data on only those domain controllers that are DNS servers rather than on all domain controllers in the domain, as is required for Windows 2000 **Active Directory– integrated zones**.

The MicrosoftDNS container is the parent object for all zones within the domain or the replication scope, as specified by the DNS application directory partition. A user that does not have read and write permissions on this container is not able to update the zone or create zones or records within zones in that partition.

Each DNS zone is represented in Active Directory by a dnsZone object. Zone objects are the children of a MicrosoftDNS object in the domain or application directory partition. The zone object stores configuration information in the dnsProperty attribute. The DACL on the zone object controls record creation in the zone, and the existing records in the zone may inherit these effects. Zone administration, such as modifying zone parameters, requires a user to have FULL CONTROL permissions on the zone object within the MicrosoftDNS container in Active Directory.

All of the record sets that belong to a single DNS domain name are stored in Active Directory in a single dnsNode object. The access control list (ACL) on this object controls client access.

Securing the DNS Server Service

A DNS Server service may run on a member server or on a domain controller. When the service runs on a domain controller, its security options are far more advanced than the options that are available when it runs on a member server.

Securing a DNS Server that Runs on a Member Server   Table 4-6 describes DNS Server service configuration options that have security implications when the DNS Server service is running on a member server or a domain controller.

Table 4-6   **Security-Related DNS Server Service Settings**

Setting	Description
Interfaces	By default, a DNS Server service that is running on a multi-homed computer is configured to listen for DNS queries using all of its IP addresses. Limit the IP addresses that the DNS Server service listens on, to the IP address that its DNS clients configure as their preferred DNS server.
Secure Against Cache Pollution	The Secure Cache Against Pollution option prevents an attacker from successfully polluting the cache of a DNS server with resource records that were not requested by the DNS server. Changing this default setting will reduce the integrity of the responses provided by the DNS Server service.
Disable Recursion	Recursion can be used by attackers to deny the DNS Server service; therefore, if a DNS server in your network is not intended to receive or perform recursive queries, recursion should be disabled. Note that forwarding is recursive.
Root Hints	If you have an internal DNS root in your DNS infrastructure, configure the root hints of internal DNS servers to point to only the DNS servers hosting your root domain and not the DNS servers hosting the Internet root domain. This will prevent your internal DNS servers from sending private information over the Internet when resolving names.

Active Directory Access Control Settings   The DACL used by the DNS Server service when it is running on a domain controller allows you to control the permissions of the Active Directory users and groups that control the DNS Server service.

> **NOTE**   *Availability of Active Directory Security Features*   The Active Directory security features available to the DNS Server service when it is running on domain controllers are not available when the DNS Server service is running on a Windows Server 2003 member server or the Windows Server 2003 Web Server operating system because these configurations do not host Active Directory.

▶ **Setting the DNS Security Settings for the DNS Server Service**

To set the DNS security settings for the DNS Server service, follow these steps:

1. Open the DNS console.

2. In the console tree, right-click the applicable server, and then click Properties.

3. In the Security tab, modify the list of member users or groups that are allowed to administer the DNS server, and reset their permissions as needed.

> **NOTE** **DNS Server Service Permissions**   The security settings determine who can administer the DNS Server service, but they do not affect the DACLs for the zones and resource records hosted on the server.

Securing File-Backed DNS Zones

DNS security for file-backed zones involves the administration of NTFS file system permissions on the zone files stored on the Windows Server 2003 member server.

▶ **Setting Permissions on a File-Backed Zone File**

To set permissions on a file-backed zone file, follow these steps:

1. Open Windows Explorer, and then locate the zone file or DNS folder in which the zone file is located (by default, all DNS zone files are stored in %systemroot%\System32\Dns).

2. Right-click the zone file or folder, click Properties, and then click the Security tab.

3. In the file or folder properties window, do one of the following:

   ❑ To set permissions for a group or user that does not appear in the Group Or User Names box, click Add. Type the name of the group or user you want to set permissions for, and then click OK.

   ❑ To change or remove permissions from an existing group or user, click the name of the group or user.

4. While still in the file or folder properties window, do one of the following:

   ❑ To allow or deny a permission, in the Permissions For *Object* box, select the Allow Or Deny check box.

   ❑ To remove the group or user from the Group Or User Names box, click Remove.

Securing Active Directory–Integrated DNS Zones

Securing Active Directory–integrated zones involves the additional security options of secure dynamic update and access control.

By default, the dynamic updates setting is Secure Only. This default setting is the most secure setting because it prevents an attacker from updating DNS zones, but this setting prevents you from taking advantage of the administrative benefits that dynamic updates provides. Secure dynamic updates restrict DNS zone updates to only those computers that are authenticated and joined to the Active Directory domain where the DNS sever is located and to the specific security settings defined in the DACLs for the DNS zone.

▶ **Allowing Only Secure Dynamic Updates**

To allow only secure dynamic updates, follow these steps:

1. Open the DNS console.

2. In the console tree, right-click the applicable zone, and then click Properties.

3. In the General tab, verify that the zone type selected is Active Directory–Integrated.

4. In Dynamic Updates, click Secure Only.

The DACL used by the DNS Server service when it is running on a domain controller allows you to control the permissions for the Active Directory users and groups that control the DNS zone.

▶ **Setting the DNS Security Settings for the DNS Zone**

To set the DNS security settings for the DNS zone, follow these steps:

1. Open the DNS console.

2. In the console tree, right-click the appropriate zone, and then click Properties.

3. In the General tab, verify that the zone type selected is Active Directory–Integrated.

4. In the Security tab, modify the list of member users or groups that are allowed to securely update the zone, and reset their permissions as needed.

Zone Transfer Security

By default, the Windows Server 2003 DNS Server service allows zone information to be transferred only to servers listed in the NS resource records of a zone. This is a secure configuration, but for increased security, this setting should be changed to the option to allow zone transfers only to specified IP addresses.

▶ **Modifying Zone Transfer Settings**

To modify zone transfer settings, follow these steps:

1. Open the DNS console.

2. Right-click the applicable DNS zone, and then click Properties.

3. In the Zone Transfers tab, do one of the following:

   ❑ To disable zone transfers, clear the Allow Zone Transfers check box.

   ❑ To allow zone transfers, select the Allow Zone Transfers check box.

4. If you allowed zone transfers, do one of the following:

   ❑ To allow zone transfers to any server, click To Any Server.

   ❑ To allow zone transfers to only the DNS servers listed in the Name Servers tab, click Only To Servers Listed On The Name Servers.

   ❑ To allow zone transfers only to specific DNS servers, click Only To The Following Servers, and then add the IP address of one or more DNS servers.

NOTE   Unsecured Zone Transfer Setting   Changing the zone setting to allow zone transfers To Any Server can expose your DNS data to an attacker attempting to footprint your network.

Securing DNS Resource Records

The access control for DNS resource records stored in Active Directory–integrated zones is managed using DACLs. The DACL applied to a resource record allows you to control the permissions for the Active Directory users and groups that may control the DNS resource record.

▶ **Setting the DNS Security Settings for a DNS Resource Record**

To set the DNS security settings for a DNS resource record, follow these steps:

1. Open the DNS console.

2. In the console tree, click the appropriate zone.

3. In the details pane, right-click the record whose security you want to set, and then click Properties.

4. In the Security tab, modify the list of member users or groups that are allowed to securely update the zone, and reset their permissions as needed.

Securing the DNS Client Service

Whenever possible, specify static IP addresses for the preferred and alternate DNS servers used by a DNS client. If a DNS client is configured to obtain its DNS server addresses automatically, it will obtain them from a Dynamic Host Configuration Protocol (DHCP) server. Although this method of obtaining DNS server addresses is secure, it is only as secure as the DHCP server. By configuring DNS clients with static IP addresses for the preferred and alternate DNS servers, you eliminate one possible avenue of attack.

MONITORING AND TROUBLESHOOTING DNS

In this section, two logging tools and the Replication Monitor are introduced. These tools can be used to both monitor and troubleshoot DNS.

Viewing the DNS Events Log

Windows Server 2003 maintains a separate log for DNS Server events that may be viewed from the Event Viewer and from the DNS console, as shown in Figure 4-8.

Figure 4-8   Viewing the DNS Events Log

If you have problems with DNS, review the DNS Server Events Log for suspicious events. The graphical user interface (GUI) in Windows Server 2003 has been enhanced (see Figure 4-9) to make it easier to configure the level of logging.

Figure 4-9   Configuring the DNS event logging level

To open the DNS Events Properties dialog box, right-click the DNS Events Log in the DNS console, and then click Properties. The DNS Events Properties dialog box contains a General tab and a Filter tab. The General tab, shown in Figure 4-10, allows you to configure the log display name, log file maximum size, and the action to take when the log reaches its maximum size.

Figure 4-10   The General tab of the DNS Events Properties dialog box

By default, the DNS Events Log displays all DNS events. The Filter tab, shown in Figure 4-11, allows you to restrict events displayed in the DNS Events Log by event type, event source, event ID, date, and other parameters.

Figure 4-11   Filtering DNS event logging

Troubleshooting DNS with the DNS Debug Log

In addition to the DNS Events Log, the DNS Server service also maintains a separate log used for debugging called the DNS debug log. This *DNS debug log* is a file named Dns.log that is stored in the WINDOWS\System32\Dns folder. In addition, because the native format of the Dns.log file is Rich Text Format (RTF), you should use Microsoft WordPad to view its contents properly. To view the Dns.log file in WordPad, make a copy of the file and then open the copy.

By default, the DNS debug log contains only DNS errors. However, you also can use it to capture DNS packets sent or received by the local DNS server. To enable DNS packet logging, open the DNS Server Properties dialog box and then click the Debug Logging tab. By default, the Log Packets For Debugging check box is cleared and the rest of the options in the tab are unavailable.

However, after you have selected the Log Packets For Debugging check box, as shown in Figure 4-12, you can configure which DNS packets you want captured to the DNS log.

Figure 4-12   Debug logging enabled

In the Debug Logging tab, you can configure the options and values described in Table 4-7.

Table 4-7   **Debug Logging Options, Values, and Descriptions**

Option	Values	Description
Packet Direction	Outgoing	Packets that the DNS server sends are logged in the DNS server log file.
	Incoming	Packets that the DNS server sends are logged in the log file.
Packet Contents	Queries/Transfers	Specifies that packets containing standard queries are logged in the DNS server log file.
	Updates	Specifies that packets containing dynamic updates are logged in the DNS server log file.
	Notifications	Specifies that packets containing notifications are logged in the DNS server log file.
Transport Protocol	UDP	Specifies that packets sent and received over UDP are logged in the DNS server log file.
	TCP	Specifies that packets sent and received over TCP are logged in the DNS server log file.
Packet Type	Request	Specifies that request packets are logged in the DNS server log file.
	Response	Specifies that response packets are logged in the DNS server log file.
Other Options	Details	Logs all packet details. If unchecked, only summary information is logged.
	Filter Packets By IP Address	Provides additional filtering of packets logged in the DNS server log file. This option allows logging of packets that are sent from specific IP addresses to a DNS server or from a DNS server to specific IP addresses.
Log File	File Name	Specifies the name and location of the DNS server log file.
	Log File Maximum Size Limit	Sets the maximum file size for the DNS server log file.

The following output is taken from the Dns.log file and is an example of a query response. Notice the response flag is set to 1 (true) and the PTR resource record in the Answer section.

```
17:19:33 8C8 PACKET  UDP Snd 10.1.1.200      0001 R Q [8085 A DR  NOERROR]
(3)200(1)1(1)1(2)10(7)in-addr(4)arpa(0)
UDP response info at 007AFE40
  Socket = 372
  Remote addr 10.1.1.200, port 4604
  Time Query=157594, Queued=0, Expire=0
  Buf length = 0x0200 (512)
  Msg length = 0x004d (77)
  Message:
    XID       0x0001
    Flags     0x8580
      QR        1 (RESPONSE)
```

```
      OPCODE      0 (QUERY)
      AA          1
      TC          0
      RD          1
      RA          1
      Z           0
      RCODE       0 (NOERROR)
  QCOUNT     1
  ACOUNT     1
  NSCOUNT    0
  ARCOUNT    0
  QUESTION SECTION:
  Offset = 0x000c, RR count = 0
  Name       "(3)200(1)1(1)1(2)10(7)in-addr(4)arpa(0)"
    QTYPE    PTR (12)
    QCLASS   1
  ANSWER SECTION:
  Offset = 0x0029, RR count = 0
  Name       "[C00C](3)200(1)1(1)1(2)10(7)in-addr(4)arpa(0)"
    TYPE     PTR  (12)
    CLASS    1
    TTL      1200
    DLEN     24
    DATA     (8)acapulco(9)contoso01(3)com(0)
  AUTHORITY SECTION:
    empty
  ADDITIONAL SECTION:
    empty
```

CAUTION   **Enabling DNS Debugging Can Adversely Affect Performance**   Do not leave DNS debug logging enabled during normal operation because it consumes both processing and hard disk resources. Enable it only when diagnosing and solving DNS problems.

Troubleshooting DNS with Replication Monitor

Replication Monitor (Replmon.exe) is a graphical tool included in the Windows Support Tools that allows you to monitor and troubleshoot Active Directory replication. This feature is essential in monitoring DNS data transfer for Active Directory–integrated zones.

You can use Replication Monitor to perform the following functions:

■ Force replication of DNS data throughout various replication scopes.

■ Discover when a replication partner fails.

■ Display replication topology.

■ Poll replication partners and generate individual histories of successful and failed replication events.

■ Display changes that have not yet replicated from a given replication partner.

■ Monitor replication status of domain controllers from multiple forests.

After you have installed Windows Support Tools, launch Replication Monitor by typing **replmon** at a command prompt (or in the Run dialog box), and then press ENTER. After opening Replication Monitor, you must add at least one server to monitor. To add a server to monitor, click Monitored Servers, then on the Action menu, point to Site, click Add Monitored Server, and then follow the wizard instructions. After adding a server, Replication Monitor looks similar to what is shown in Figure 4-13.

Figure 4-13   Replication Monitor console

After you have added the servers you intend to monitor, you can save this console configuration as an .ini file and open the file from within Replication Monitor for subsequent uses.

Directory Partitions and Active Directory–Integrated Zones

For each server listed in the console tree, you can display the Active Directory partitions installed on that server by expanding the associated server icon. Domain controllers that are DNS servers and that host a single Active Directory–integrated zone include a replica of five such partitions by default.

The following list describes these five partitions for an Active Directory domain and DNS zone named contoso01.com:

- **DC=contoso01,DC=com**   The domain partition, which contains objects (such as users and computers) associated with the local domain. Each domain controller stores a full replica of the domain partition for its local domain. In addition, in this partition, DNS data is stored for compatibility with Microsoft Windows 2000 DNS servers. To store DNS zone data in the domain partition, set the zone replication scope in the DNS console to All Domain Controllers In The Domain *domain_name*.

- **CN=Configuration,DC=contoso01,DC=com**   The configuration partition, which contains replication topology and other configuration information that must be replicated throughout the forest. Each domain controller in the forest has a replica of the same configuration partition. However, this partition does not include DNS zone data.

- **CN=Schema,CD=Configuration,DC=contoso01,DC=com**   The schema partition, which contains the classSchema and attributeSchema objects that define the types of objects that can exist in the Active Directory forest. Every domain controller in the forest has a replica of the same schema partition. However, this partition does not include DNS zone data.

- **DC=DomainDnsZones,DC=contoso01,DC=com**   The built-in application directory partition named DomainDnsZones, which is replicated among all Windows Server 2003 domain controllers that are also DNS servers in a particular Active Directory domain. To store DNS zone data in the DomainDnsZones partition, set the zone replication scope in the DNS console to All DNS Servers In The Active Directory Domain *Domain_Name*.

- **DC=ForestDnsZones,DC=contoso01,DC=com**   The built-in application directory partition named ForestDnsZones, which is replicated among all Windows Server 2003 domain controllers that are also DNS servers in an Active Directory forest. To store DNS zone data in the ForestDnsZones partition, set the zone replication scope in the DNS console to All DNS Servers In The Active Directory Forest.

You also can create custom application directory partitions and enlist the domain controllers you choose to store a replica of that partition. In Figure 4-13, Replication Monitor displays such an application directory partition named Custom. To store DNS zone data in a custom application directory partition, set the zone replication scope in the DNS console to All Domain Controllers Specified In The Scope Of The Following Application Directory Partition. Then select the desired application directory partition from the drop-down list.

To find out which Active Directory partition is used to store data for a particular DNS zone, you can either check the DNS zone properties in the DNS console or use the Dnscmd /zoneinfo *ZoneName* command, providing the name of the zone for the *ZoneName* placeholder.

To determine the zone replication scope for a domain named domain1.local, type the following command at a command prompt: **dnscmd /zoneinfo domain1 .local**. Then, look for an entry named Directory Partition in the output. To change zone replication scope, use the /zonechangedirectorypartition switch followed by any of the following switches, as appropriate:

- /domain (for all DNS servers in the domain)
- /forest (for all DNS servers in the forest)
- /legacy (for all domain controllers in the domain)

For example, to set the replication scope of a zone named domain1.local to all DNS servers in the domain, type the following command: **dnscmd /zonechange-directorypartition domain1.local /domain**. If you have proper credentials, you can even use these commands remotely. In this case, simply specify the server name after *dnscmd*.

Forcing Active Directory–Integrated Zone Replication

Once you know the directory partition in which DNS zone information is stored, you can force replication for that zone in Replication Monitor. This procedure can help resolve name resolution problems caused by outdated zone data.

To force Active Directory–integrated zone replication, right-click the appropriate partition in the Replication Monitor console tree, and select Synchronize This Directory Partition With All Servers. The Synchronizing Naming Context With Replication Partners dialog box shown in Figure 4-14 opens.

Figure 4-14   Forcing replication

When forcing a replication, you can use this dialog box to replicate only to neighboring servers, to replicate out to all servers on the local site, or to replicate to all servers across sites.

Searching for Replication Errors

DNS errors in Active Directory–integrated zones can result from faulty zone replication. You can use Replication Monitor to search the domain for such replication errors. To do so, on the Action menu, select Domain, and then select Search Domain Controllers For Replication Errors, as shown in Figure 4-15.

Figure 4-15   Searching for replication errors

As an alternative, you can configure Replication Monitor to send an e-mail to an administrator after a specified number of replication failures. To perform this task, on the View menu, select Options. In the Active Directory Replication Monitor Options dialog box, select the Notify When Replication Fails After This Number Of Attempts option, and then specify the number of failures that you want to trigger an e-mail. Finally, select the Send Mail To check box, and specify an e-mail address in the associated text box.

SUMMARY

- Use tools such as Nslookup, DNSLint, and Dnscmd to manage DNS servers. Use Nslookup in command-line mode or interactive mode to examine the contents of DNS zone files. Use DNSLint to verify the consistency of a particular set of DNS records on multiple DNS servers. Use Dnscmd to help automate the management and updates of existing DNS server configurations.

- DNS and WINS integration is the process in which DNS uses WINS to resolve names to IP addresses. DNS is used to resolve host names and services to IP addresses, and WINS is used to resolve NetBIOS names to IP addresses.

- Use advanced DNS Server settings to disable recursion, increase server interoperability, increase data integrity, and reorder name list responses using round robin and netmask ordering. You also can use advanced settings to secure the cache against pollution, configure name checking, specify from where to load zone data, and enable automatic scavenging of stale records.

- The DNS Client service maintains a local cache, which you can display and purge using Ipconfig.exe.

- Understand various security threats to DNS and prepare for them by assessing the security level of your organization. Based on your assessment, make appropriate configuration changes to restrict dynamic updates, zone transfers, access to file-backed zones, resource records, and the DNS Client service.

- You can use both the DNS Events Log and DNS debug log to monitor and troubleshoot DNS. For example, you can use the DNS debug log to log all dynamic updates received by the server.

EXERCISES

> **IMPORTANT** **Completing All Exercises**   If you plan to do any of the textbook exercises in this chapter, you must do all of the exercises in the chapter to return the computer to its original state for the associated Lab Manual labs.

Exercise 4-1: Displaying DNS Zone Information Using Dnscmd

1. Open a command prompt.
2. At the command prompt, type **dnscmd localhost /zoneinfo** *zone_name* (where *zone_name* represents a forward or reverse lookup zone name) and press ENTER.

Exercise 4-2: Integrating DNS and WINS

1. Open the DNS console.
2. In the console tree, right-click the applicable zone, and then click Properties.

3. In the Zone Properties dialog box, click the appropriate tab:

   ❑ Click the WINS tab if the zone is a forward lookup zone.

   ❑ Click the WINS-R tab if the zone is a reverse lookup zone.

4. In the appropriate WINS tab, select the applicable check box to enable the use of WINS resolution:

   ❑ Use WINS Forward Lookup if the zone is a forward lookup zone.

   ❑ Use WINS-R Lookup if the zone is a reverse lookup zone.

5. In the WINS tab, type the IP address of a WINS server that will be used for the resolution of names that are not found in DNS. For a reverse lookup zone, in the WINS-R tab, type a name in the Domain To Append To Returned Name field, if applicable.

6. In the WINS tab, click Add to add the server IP address. For a reverse lookup zone, in the WINS-R tab, click Use WINS-R Lookup.

7. If additional WINS server addresses are used for a forward lookup zone during WINS lookup referral, repeat steps 5 and 6 as needed to add those server addresses to the list.

8. In either the WINS tab or the WINS-R tab, select Do Not Replicate This Record for this WINS record, if applicable.

   CAUTION   Do Not Replicate WINS Locator Records   If you are replicating zone data to secondary zones on third-party DNS servers that do not recognize the WINS or WINS-R records, select the Do Not Replicate This Record check box. This prevents the WINS locator records from being replicated to other servers during zone transfers. You would select this option when performing zone transfers to BIND servers, because BIND will not recognize WINS locator records.

9. Optionally, in either the WINS or the WINS-R tab, click Advanced to adjust both the Cache Time-Out value and the Lookup Time-Out value.

10. Optionally, in the WINS-R tab, in the Advanced dialog box, select Submit DNS Domain As NetBIOS Scope.

11. In the *Zone* Properties dialog box, click OK.

Exercise 4-3: Displaying and Purging the Resolver Cache

1. Open a command prompt.

2. At the command prompt, type **ipconfig /displaydns** and press ENTER.

3. At the command prompt, type **ping instructor01** and press ENTER.

4. At the command prompt, type **ipconfig /displaydns** and press ENTER.

5. Scroll through the output to locate the London record.

6. At the command prompt, type **ipconfig /flushdns** and press ENTER.

   A message is displayed saying the DNS resolver cache was successfully flushed.

7. At the command prompt, type **ipconfig /displaydns** and press ENTER.

   Note that the London record is no longer in the DNS resolver cache.

REVIEW QUESTIONS

1. What is the function of round robin in DNS?

2. Which feature takes priority—round robin or netmask ordering?

3. Which of the following are valid reasons to monitor the TTL settings on your DNS servers? Choose all that apply.

   a. Query traffic increases as DNS clients request information that has expired from their cache.

   b. DNS clients may be caching outdated records.

   c. DNS clients may not be able to resolve host names.

   d. Query traffic decreases as DNS clients request information that has expired from their cache.

4. What type of test query can be run from the Monitoring tab of the DNS server properties page?

   a. Recursive query

   b. Simple query

   c. Verbose query

   d. Interval query

5. Which of the following approaches provides the best early warning of a DNS service failure?

   a. Create an alert based on the standard performance counters, and set the threshold to notify you if the counters exceed 95 percent of the recommended threshold.

   b. Create an alert based on the counters that you decide are appropriate indicators of a failure, and set the threshold to notify you when it is 10 percent below the baseline.

   c. Create an alert based on the standard counters, and set the threshold to notify you if the counters exceed 75 percent of the recommended threshold.

   d. Create an alert based on the counters that you decide are appropriate indicators of a failure, and set the threshold to notify you when it is 10 percent above the baseline.

6. You are a systems administrator for Contoso, Ltd. Contoso is planning its DNS zones, and you have been asked to recommend the best way to configure the zones on the company's Microsoft Windows Server 2003 computers.

   You recommend using Active Directory–integrated zones. Why do you recommend this configuration?

   Choose all answers that apply.

   a. DNS data is replicated with Active Directory.

   b. You can configure secure dynamic updates.

   c. The DNS load will be shared because the other domain controllers will become secondary DNS servers.

   d. You can configure a replication scope.

7. You are the administrator for Contoso, Ltd., and have updated the IP address for a host by using the DNS console. Assuming it exists, which of the following types of resource records is associated with the host record and must also be updated?

   a. A resource record

   b. MX resource record

   c. NS resource record

   d. PTR resource record

   e. SOA resource record

   f. SRV resource record

8. A client computer on the internal network of Contoso, Ltd., is unable to connect to a file server. You verify the file server is running and are able to connect to it using another client computer on the same subnet. You suspect the client computer that cannot connect has outdated information in its local cache. Which of the following actions would fix the issue?

   a. At the client computer, run the Ipconfig /flushdns command.

   b. At the file server, run the Ipconfig /flushdns command.

   c. At the file server, run Nslookup.

   d. At the file server, stop and start the DNS Client service.

CASE SCENARIOS

Case Scenario 4-1: Enabling Network Users to Connect to Internet Host Names

You are the network administrator for Contoso, Ltd. The Contoso network consists of a single domain, contoso.com, which is protected from the Internet by a firewall. The firewall runs on a computer named NS1 that is directly connected to the Internet. NS1 also runs the DNS Server service, and its firewall allows DNS traffic to pass between the Internet and the DNS Server service on NS1 but not between the Internet and the internal network. The DNS Server service on NS1 is configured to use round robin. Behind the firewall, two computers are running Windows Server 2003—NS2 and NS3, which host a primary and secondary DNS server, respectively, for the contoso.com zone.

Users on the company network report that, although they use host names to connect to computers on the local private network, they cannot use host names to connect to Internet destinations, such as *www.microsoft.com*.

Which of the following actions requires the least amount of administrative effort to enable network users to connect to Internet host names?

a. Disable recursion on NS2 and NS3.

b. Enable netmask ordering on NS1.

c. Configure NS2 and NS3 to use NS1 as a forwarder.

d. Disable round robin on NS1.

Case Scenario 4-2: Implementing DNS Updates

You are the system administrator for Contoso, Ltd. The company has grown rapidly over the past year, and currently Contoso is using only a single DNS zone. Recently, the Marketing department has made several requests for DNS changes that were delayed. Users would like the ability to make their own DNS updates.

What should you do to try to address this problem?

- **a.** Create a secondary server in the Marketing department so that users can manage their own zone.

- **b.** Delegate the marketing domain to a DNS server in the Marketing department.

- **c.** Place a domain controller running DNS in the Marketing department so that people in the department can make changes.

- **d.** Upgrade the network infrastructure to improve network performance.

GLOSSARY

A   *See* address (A) resource record.

access control list (ACL)   A list of security protections that apply to an entire object, a set of the object's properties, or an individual property of an object. There are two types of access control lists: discretionary access control lists (DACLs) and system access control lists (SACLs).

ACL   *See* access control list (ACL).

Active Directory   The Windows-based directory service. Active Directory directory service stores information about objects on a network and makes this information available to users and network administrators. Active Directory gives network users access to permitted resources anywhere on the network using a single logon process. It provides network administrators with an intuitive, hierarchical view of the network and a single point of administration for all network objects.

Active Directory–integrated zone   A Domain Name System (DNS) zone that is stored in Active Directory directory service so that it can use multimaster replication and Active Directory security features.

address pool   The addresses within a Dynamic Host Configuration Protocol (DHCP) scope range of addresses that are available for leased distribution to clients.

Address Resolution Protocol (ARP)   A Transmission Control Protocol/Internet Protocol (TCP/IP) network layer protocol responsible for resolving Internet Protocol (IP) addresses into media access control (MAC) addresses. Address Resolution Protocol (ARP) is defined in Request for Comments (RFC) number 826.

address (A) resource record   A resource record used to map a Domain Name System (DNS) domain name to a host Internet Protocol version 4 (IPv4) address on the network.

AH   *See* Authentication Header (AH).

American National Standards Institute (ANSI)   A voluntary, nonprofit organization of business and industry groups that formed in 1918 for the development

and adoption of trade and communication standards in the United States. ANSI is the American representative of ISO (International Organization for Standardization). Among its many concerns, ANSI has developed recommendations for the use of programming languages including FORTRAN, C, and COBOL and for various networking technologies.

American Standard Code for Information Interchange (ASCII)   A coding scheme that uses seven or eight bits to assign numeric values up to 256 characters, including letters, numerals, punctuation marks, control characters, and other symbols. ASCII was developed in 1968 to standardize data transmission among disparate hardware and software systems and is built into most minicomputers and all PCs. ASCII is divided into two sets: 128 characters (standard ASCII) and a 256-character version (extended ASCII).

ANSI   *See* American National Standards Institute (ANSI).

APIPA   *See* Automatic Private IP Addressing (APIPA).

AppleTalk protocol   The set of network protocols on which AppleTalk network architecture is based. The AppleTalk protocol is installed with Services for Macintosh to help users access resources on a network.

ARP   *See* Address Resolution Protocol (ARP).

ASCII   *See* American Standard Code for Information Interchange (ASCII).

Asynchronous Transfer Mode (ATM)   A high-speed, connection-oriented protocol used to transport many different types of network traffic. ATM packages data in a 53-byte, fixed-length cell that can be switched quickly between logical connections on a network.

ATM   *See* Asynchronous Transfer Mode (ATM).

Authentication Header (AH)   A header that provides authentication, integrity, and anti-replay for the entire packet (the Internet Protocol [IP] header and the data payload carried in the packet).

Authentication Header protocol
See Authenthentication Header (AH).

Automatic Private IP Addressing (APIPA)   A Transmission Control Protocol/Internet Protocol (TCP/IP) feature in Windows products that automatically configures a unique Internet Protocol (IP) address from the range 169.254.0.1 to 169.254.255.254 and a subnet mask of 255.255.0.0 when the TCP/IP protocol is configured for dynamic addressing and a Dynamic Host Configuration Protocol (DHCP) server is not available. The APIPA range of IP addresses is reserved by the Internet Assigned Numbers Authority (IANA), and IP addresses within this range are not used on the Internet.

Automatic Updates   A Windows feature that can be set up to automatically check for updates published on the Microsoft Windows Update Web site. Software Update Services (SUS) uses this Windows feature to publish administrator-approved updates on an intranet.

Background Intelligent Transfer Service (BITS)   A service that asynchronously transfers files in the foreground or background, controls the amount of resources used for transfers to preserve the responsiveness of other network applications, and automatically resumes file transfers after network disconnects and machine restarts.

Applications use the BITS application programming interface (API) to create transfer jobs and to monitor the progress of jobs in the transfer queue. The BITS API is included in the Microsoft Platform Software Development Kit (SDK).

Berkeley Internet Name Domain (BIND)   A popular software tool for administering and maintaining the Domain Name System (DNS) on UNIX platforms. BIND was originally written for Berkeley Software Distribution (BSD) UNIX and is currently maintained by the Internet Software Consortium. Because most versions of UNIX include some port of BIND, it is the most popular DNS server used by Internet service providers (ISPs) for administering and maintaining DNS for the Internet. The DNS Server services on Microsoft Windows NT and Microsoft Windows 2000 are Request for Comments (RFC)–compliant implementations of DNS and are compatible with BIND.

BIND   *See* Berkeley Internet Name Domain (BIND).

BITS   *See* Background Intelligent Transfer Service (BITS).

BOOTP   *See* Bootstrap Protocol (BOOTP).

Bootstrap Protocol (BOOTP)   A protocol used primarily on Transmission Control Protocol/Internet Protocol (TCP/IP) networks to configure diskless workstations. Request for Comments (RFC) 951 and 1542 define this protocol. Dynamic Host Configuration Protocol (DHCP) is a later boot configuration protocol that uses this protocol. The Microsoft DHCP service provides limited support for BOOTP service.

CA   *See* certification authority (CA).

.cab files   Stands for cabinet file and is a single cabinet file that stores multiple compressed files. These files are commonly used in software installation and to reduce the file size and the associated download time for Web content.

canonical name (CNAME) resource record   A resource record used to map an alternate alias name to a primary canonical Domain Name System (DNS) domain name used in the zone.

certificate   A digital document that is commonly used for authentication and to secure information on open networks. A certificate securely binds a public key to the entity that holds the corresponding private key. Certificates are digitally signed by the issuing certification authority (CA), and they can be issued for a user, a computer, or a service.

certificate revocation list (CRL)   A document maintained and published by a certification authority that lists certificates that have been revoked.

certification authority (CA)   An entity responsible for establishing and vouching for the authenticity of public keys belonging to subjects (usually users or computers) or other certification authorities. Activities of a certification authority can include binding public keys to distinguished names through signed certificates, managing certificate serial numbers, and certificate revocation.

checksum   A calculated value that is used to test data for the presence of errors that can occur when data is transmitted or when it is written to disk. The checksum is calculated for a given chunk of data by sequentially combining all the bytes of data with a series of arithmetic or logical operations. After the data is transmitted or stored, a new checksum is calculated in the same way using the (possibly faulty) transmitted or stored data. If the two checksums do not match, an error has occurred, and the data should be transmitted or stored again. Checksums cannot detect all errors, and they cannot be used to correct erroneous data.

class   An administrative feature that allows you to group Dynamic Host Configuration Protocol (DHCP) clients logically according to a shared or common need. For example, you can define or use a user class to allow similar DHCP leased configurations for all client computers in a specific building or site location.

CNAME   *See* canonical (CNAME) resource record.

container object   An object that can logically contain other objects. For example, a folder is a container object.

counter   A representation of an object found in the system. You monitor counters for performance reasons and to help you determine whether processes are running smoothly.

CRL   *See* certificate revocation list (CRL).

DACL   *See* discretionary access control list (DACL).

default gateway   A device on a Transmission Control Protocol/Internet Protocol (TCP/IP) internetwork that can forward Internet Protocol (IP) packets to another network, usually a router. In an internetwork, a given subnet might have several router interfaces that connect it to other, remote subnets. One of these router interfaces is usually selected as the default gateway of the local subnet. When a host on the network wants to send a packet to a destination subnet, it consults its internal routing table to determine whether it knows which router to forward the packet to in order to have it reach the destination subnet. If the routing table does not contain any routing information about the destination subnet, the packet is forwarded to the default gateway (one of the routers with an interface on the local subnet). The host assumes that the default gateway knows what to do with any packets that the host itself does not know how to forward.

demand-dial routing   Routing that makes dial-up connections to connect networks based on need—such as a branch office with a modem that dials and establishes a connection only when there is network traffic between offices.

DHCP   *See* Dynamic Host Configuration Protocol (DHCP).

DHCP audit log file   A Dynamic Host Configuration Protocol (DHCP) audit log file is a log of service related events that occur on a DHCP server. Examples of such events are the stopping and starting of the service, verifications and authorizations, and the leasing, renewal, and denial of Internet Protocol (IP) addresses.

DHCP client   A host on a Transmission Control Protocol/Internet Protocol (TCP/IP) internetwork that is capable of having its Internet Protocol (IP) address information dynamically assigned using Dynamic Host Configuration Protocol (DHCP). The term "DHCP client" can also describe the software component on a computer that is capable of interacting with a DHCP server to lease an IP address.

DHCP client reservation   A process for configuring a Dynamic Host Configuration Protocol (DHCP) server so that a particular host on the network always leases the same Internet Protocol (IP) address. You can create a client reservation on a DHCP server if you want the server to always assign the same IP address to a specific machine on the network. You might do this to assign IP addresses to servers on the network because the IP addresses of servers should not change. (If they do, client machines might have difficulty connecting with them.) An alternative and more common way to assign a client reservation to a server is to manually assign a static IP address to the server.

DHCP lease   The duration for which a Dynamic Host Configuration Protocol (DHCP) server loans an Internet Protocol (IP) address to a DHCP client.

DHCP options   Additional Internet Protocol (IP) address settings that a Dynamic Host Configuration Protocol (DHCP) server passes to DHCP clients. When a DHCP client requests an IP address from a DHCP server, the server sends the client at least an IP address and a subnet mask value. Additional information can be sent to clients if you configure various DHCP options. You can assign these options globally to all DHCP clients, to clients belonging to a particular scope, or to an individual host on the network.

DHCP relay agent   A Transmission Control Protocol/Internet Protocol (TCP/IP) host that is configured to allow a single Dynamic Host Configuration Protocol (DHCP) server to lease Internet Protocol (IP) address information to DHCP clients on remote subnets. DHCP relay agents make it unnecessary to maintain a separate DHCP server on every subnet in an internetwork. You can configure Windows NT and Windows 2000 servers to operate as DHCP relay agents.

DHCP server   A server that dynamically allocates Internet Protocol (IP) addresses to client machines using the Dynamic Host Configuration Protocol (DHCP). DHCP servers perform the server-side operation of the DHCP protocol. The DHCP server is responsible for answering requests from DHCP clients and leasing IP addresses to these clients.

DHCP servers should have static IP addresses. A DHCP server gives DHCP clients at least two pieces of Transmission Control Protocol/Internet Protocol (TCP/IP) configuration information: the client's IP address and the subnet mask. Additional TCP/IP settings can be passed to the client as DHCP options.

Diffie-Hellman key exchange   A cryptographic mechanism that allows two parties to establish a shared secret key without having any pre-established secrets between them. Diffie-Hellman is frequently used to establish the shared secret keys that are used by common applications of cryptography, such as Internet Protocol security (IPSec). It is not normally used for data protection.

digital subscriber line (DSL)   A special communication line that uses modulation technology to maximize the amount of data that can be sent over conductive wires. DSL is used for connections between telephone switching stations and a subscriber, rather than between switching stations.

directory partition replicas   Active Directory objects are logically divided into sets of objects called "directory partitions" (also called "naming contexts"). A directory partition replica is a copy of a set of directory objects in one directory partition as it exists on a specific domain controller. During the process of replication, updates to replicas are synchronized among the domain controllers that store replicas of the same directory partitions. When replication occurs, all current updates to a replica on one domain controller are transferred to the corresponding replica on another domain controller. If more than one replica is shared by the two domain controllers, all updates that apply are replicated.

discretionary access control list (DACL)   The part of an object's security descriptor that grants or denies permission to specific users and groups to access the object. Only the owner of an object can change permissions granted or denied in a DACL; thus, access to the object is at the owner's discretion.

domain namespace   A subset of the Domain Name System (DNS) namespace bounded by a particular domain name. The root of the DNS namespace branches out to a relatively small number of top-level domains such as .com, .org, and .edu. Private companies can register a domain name in one of these top-level domains and then subdivide their branch of the DNS namespace as they desire. This subdivision of the DNS namespace is bounded by the domain name and is called the "domain namespace." For example, a company named Fabrikam might register the domain name fabrikam.com, and then the company might create three new subdomains under it named sales.fabrikam.com, support .fabrikam.com, and hq.fabrikam.com. Specific servers and router interfaces exposed to the Internet might then be given specific DNS addresses to uniquely identify them in the DNS namespace. If you want to locate a particular node in the DNS namespace, you query a name server. The process of locating a particular DNS node and resolving its fully qualified domain name (FQDN) into its associated Internet Protocol (IP) address is called "name resolution."

Domain Name System (DNS)   A hierarchical, distributed database that contains mappings of DNS domain names to various types of data, such as Internet Protocol (IP) addresses. DNS enables the location of computers and services by user-friendly names, and it also enables the discovery of other information stored in the database.

DNS   *See* Domain Name System (DNS).

DNS domain   Any tree or subtree in the Domain Name System (DNS) namespace. Although the names for DNS domains often correspond to Active Directory domains, DNS domains should not be confused with Active Directory domains.

DNS dynamic update   An update to the Domain Name System (DNS) standard that permits DNS clients to dynamically register and update their resource records in zones.

DNS namespace   The entire namespace in Domain Name System (DNS) starting at the root and branching out to a relatively small number of top-level domains (TLDs), such as .com, .org, and .edu. Private companies can register a domain name in one of these TLDs and then subdivide their branch of the DNS namespace as they desire. For example, a company named Fourth Coffee might register the domain name fourthcoffee.com and then create three new subdomains under it named sales.fourthcoffee.com, support.fourthcoffee.com, and hq.fourthcoffee.com. Specific servers and router interfaces exposed to the Internet might then be given specific DNS addresses to uniquely identify them in the DNS namespace. An address in the DNS namespace, called an "fully qualified domain name (FQDN)," maps to a unique node on the Internet. An example might be widgets.support.fourthcoffee, which might map to the address 10.15.6.133. Names of domains, subdomains, and individual hosts are maintained on name servers located at various points across the Internet or within large private internetworks. If you want to locate a particular node in the DNS namespace, you query a name server. The process of locating a particular DNS node and resolving its FQDN into its associated Internet Protocol (IP) address is called "name resolution."

DNS server   A server that maintains information about a portion of the Domain Name System (DNS) database and that responds to and resolves DNS queries.

DNS zone   Also called a "zone of authority," a subset of the Domain Name System (DNS) namespace that is managed by a name server. This administrative unit can consist of a single domain, or it can be a domain that is combined with a number of subdomains. The concepts of a zone and a DNS domain are related: each zone is anchored in a specific domain known as the zone's "root domain."

DSL   *See* digital subscriber line (DSL).

Dynamic Host Configuration Protocol (DHCP)   A standard Internet protocol that enables the dynamic configuration of hosts on an Internet Protocol (IP) internetwork. DHCP is an extension of the Bootstrap Protocol (BOOTP).

EAP   *See* Extensible Authentication Protocol (EAP).

EFS   *See* Encrypting File System (EFS).

Encapsulating Security Payload (ESP)   An Internet Protocol security (IPSec) protocol that provides confidentiality, in addition to authentication, integrity, and anti-replay. ESP can be used alone, in combination with Authentication Header (AH), or nested with the Layer Two Tunneling Protocol (L2TP). ESP does not normally sign the entire packet unless it is being tunneled. Ordinarily, just the data payload is protected, not the Internet Protocol (IP) header.

Encrypting File System (EFS)   A feature in Microsoft Windows Server 2003 that enables users to encrypt files and folders on an NTFS volume disk to keep them safe from intruders.

encryption   The process of disguising a message or data to hide its substance.

ESP   *See* Encapsulating Security Payload (ESP).

Ethernet   The most popular network architecture for local area networks (LANs). Ethernet was originally developed by Xerox in the 1970s and was proposed as a standard by Xerox, Digital Equipment Corporation (DEC), and Intel in 1980. A separate standardization process for Ethernet technologies, known as "Project 802," was established in 1985 in the Institute of Electrical and Electronics Engineers (IEEE) 802.3 standard. The International Organization for Standardization (ISO) then adopted the IEEE standard, thereby making it a worldwide standard for networking. Because of its simplicity and reliability, Ethernet is by far the most popular networking architecture in use today. It is available in three different speeds:

- 10 megabits per second (Mbps), which is simply called "Ethernet"

- 100 Mbps, which is called "Fast Ethernet"

- 1000 Mbps or 1 gigabit per second (Gbps), which is an emerging standard called "Gigabit Ethernet"

event logging   The process of recording an audit entry in the audit trail whenever certain events occur, such as the following events: services starting and stopping, users logging on and off, and users accessing resources.

Event Viewer   A component you can use to view and manage event logs, gather information about hardware and software problems, and monitor security events. Event Viewer maintains logs about program, security, and system events.

Extensible Authentication Protocol (EAP)   An extension to the Point-to-Point Protocol (PPP) that allows for arbitrary authentication mechanisms to be employed for the validation of a PPP connection.

Extensible Markup Language (XML)   A meta-markup language that provides a format for describing structured data. This facilitates more precise declarations of content and more meaningful search results across multiple platforms. In addition, XML enables a new generation of Web-based data-viewing and manipulation applications.

FAT   *See* file allocation table (FAT).

FAT32   A derivative of the file allocation table (FAT) file system. FAT32 supports smaller cluster sizes and larger volumes than FAT, which results in more efficient space allocation on FAT32 volumes.

FDDI   *See* Fiber Distributed Data Interface (FDDI).

Fiber Distributed Data Interface (FDDI)   A high-speed network technology that conforms to the Open Systems Interconnection (OSI) reference model for networking and the American National Standards Institute (ANSI) standard X3T9, which runs at 100 megabits per second (Mbps) over fiber-optic cabling. It is often used for network backbones in a local area network (LAN) or metropolitan area network (MAN).

file allocation table (FAT)   A file system used by MS-DOS and other Windows operating systems to organize and manage files. The file allocation table is a data structure that Windows creates when you format a volume using the FAT or FAT32 file systems. Windows stores information about each file in the file allocation table so that it can retrieve the file later.

forwarder   A Domain Name System (DNS) server designated by other internal DNS servers to be used to forward queries for resolving external or offsite DNS domain names. Forwarders are useful for reducing name resolution traffic and speeding DNS name queries for large private Transmission Control Protocol/Internet Protocol (TCP/IP) internetworks that are connected to the Internet. They also are used to resolve name queries when a firewall between your network and the Internet prevents clients in your network from directly querying name servers located at your Internet service provider (ISP) or elsewhere on the Internet. In this case, a typical location for the forwarder is on the bastion host. (The bastion host is the host running the proxy server or application-layer gateway application.)

forward lookup   A Domain Name System (DNS) query for a DNS name.

forward lookup zone   *See* forward lookup; zone.

FQDN   *See* fully qualified domain name (FQDN).

frame   A segment of data on a network or telecommunications link, generally consisting of a header with preamble (Start of Frame flag), destination and source addresses, data payload, and usually some form of error-checking information. Frames are assembled and generated by the data-link layer and physical layer of the Open Systems Interconnection (OSI) reference model. This assembly process is called "framing." In other words, packets from the network layer are encapsulated by the data-link layer into frames. Data segments generated by higher layers of the OSI model are generally referred to as packets, but the term "packet" is also sometimes used to include frames.

fully qualified domain name (FQDN)   A Domain Name System (DNS) name that has been stated to indicate its absolute location in the domain namespace tree. In contrast to relative names, an FQDN has a trailing period (.) to qualify its position to the root of the namespace (host.example.microsoft.com.).

GPO *See* Group Policy Object (GPO).

Group Policy The infrastructure in Active Directory directory service that enables directory-based configuration of user and computer settings, including security and user data. You use Group Policy to define configurations for groups of users and computers. You can specify policy settings for registry-based policies, security, software installation, scripts, folder redirection, remote installation services, and Internet Explorer maintenance. The Group Policy settings that you create are contained in a Group Policy Object (GPO). By associating a GPO with selected Active Directory system containers—sites, domains, and OUs—you can apply the GPO's policy settings to the users and computers in those Active Directory containers. To create an individual GPO, use the Group Policy Object Editor. To manage GPOs across an enterprise, you can use the Group Policy Management console.

Group Policy Object (GPO) A collection of Group Policy settings. GPOs are essentially the documents created by the Group Policy Object Editor. GPOs are stored at the domain level, and they affect users and computers that are contained in sites, domains, and OUs. In addition, each computer has exactly one group of policy settings stored locally, which is called the "local Group Policy Object."

Group Policy Object Editor The MMC snap-in that is used to edit Group Policy Objects (GPOs).

hash A one-way cryptographic algorithm that takes an input message of arbitrary length and produces a fixed-length digest. Two hash algorithms used by Windows Server 2003 are Secure Hash Algorithm 1 (SHA1) and Message Digest 5 (MD5).

host Any device on a Transmission Control Protocol/Internet Protocol (TCP/IP) network that has an Internet Protocol (IP) address. Examples include servers, workstations, network interface print devices, and routers. The terms "node" and "host" are often used interchangeably in this regard.

Sometimes the term "host" means a device on a TCP/IP network that can both receive data and initiate contact with other devices. For example, a computer configured as a Simple Mail Transfer Protocol (SMTP) host

receives e-mail messages and forwards them to their destination.

Hosts file A text file that provides a local method for resolution of fully qualified domain names (FQDNs) into their respective Internet Protocol (IP) addresses on a Transmission Control Protocol/Internet Protocol (TCP/IP) network. Hosts files are an alternative to Domain Name System (DNS) servers for name resolution on TCP/IP networks. They are used mainly on small networks or when maintaining a DNS server is impractical.

hub A common connection point for devices in a network. Typically used to connect segments of a local area network (LAN), a hub contains multiple ports. When data arrives at one port, it is copied to the other ports so that all segments of the LAN can see the data.

IAS *See* Internet Authentication Service (IAS).

IETF *See* Internet Engineering Task Force (IETF).

IGMP *See* Internet Group Management Protocol (IGMP).

IIS *See* IIS metabase; Internet Information Server (IIS) Lockdown.

IIS metabase A database that stores all of the configuration settings for Internet Information Server (IIS). The metabase is similar to the registry that stores all of the configuration settings for Windows Server.

IKE *See* Internet Key Exchange (IKE).

in-addr.arpa domain A special top-level Domain Name System (DNS) domain reserved for mapping of Internet Protocol (IP) addresses to DNS host names, which is the reverse of the mapping used for standard DNS name resolution.

in-addr.arpa zone *See* in-addr.arpa; reverse lookup; zone.

Integrated Services Digital Network (ISDN) A digital phone line used to provide higher bandwidth. ISDN in North America is typically available in two forms: Basic Rate Interface (BRI), which consists of 2 B channels at 64 kilobits per second (Kbps) and a D channel at 16 Kbps, and Primary Rate Interface (PRI), which consists of 23 B channels at 64 Kbps and a D channel at 64 Kbps. The phone company must install an ISDN line at both the calling and the called "sites."

International Telecommunication Union-Telecommunication Standardization Sector (ITU-T) The standardization division of the International Telecommunication Union, formerly called "Comité Consultatif International Télégraphique et Téléphonique (CCITT)." The ITU-T (also abbreviated ITU-TSS) develops communications recommendations for all analog and digital communications.

Internet Authentication Service (IAS) The Microsoft implementation of a Remote Authentication Dial-In User Service (RADIUS) server and proxy, which provides authentication and accounting for network access.

Internet Engineering Task Force (IETF) An international community of networking engineers, network administrators, researchers, and vendors whose goal is to ensure the smooth operation and evolution of the Internet. The Internet Engineering Task Force (IETF) receives its charter from the Internet Society (ISOC), and its daily operations are overseen by the Internet Architecture Board (IAB).

The work of the IETF is performed by a number of working groups that are dedicated to such aspects of the Internet as routing, operations and management, transport, security, applications, and user services. These working groups interact primarily through mailing lists and are managed by area directors who belong to the Internet Engineering Steering Group (IESG). Some working groups develop extensions and newer versions of familiar protocols such as Hypertext Transfer Protocol (HTTP), Lightweight Directory Access Protocol (LDAP), Network News Transfer Protocol (NNTP), Point-to-Point Protocol (PPP), and Simple Network Management Protocol (SNMP). Others develop new protocols such as the Common Indexing Protocol, Internet Open Trading Protocol, and the Internet Printing Protocol (IPP).

The working groups produce documents called "Internet Drafts," which have a life span of six months, after which they must be deleted, updated, or established as a Request for Comments (RFC) document.

Internet Group Management Protocol (IGMP) A protocol used by Internet Protocol version 4 (IPv4) hosts to report their multicast group memberships to any immediately neighboring multicast routers.

Internet Information Server (IIS) Lockdown A security tool that provides templates for the major IIS-dependent Microsoft products. The IIS Lockdown Wizard works by turning off unnecessary features, thereby reducing vulnerabilities that are available to attackers. To provide defense-in-depth, or multiple layers of protection against attackers, URL Scanner has been integrated into the IIS Lockdown Wizard with customized templates for each supported server role.

Internet Key Exchange (IKE) A protocol that establishes the security association and shared keys necessary for two parties to communicate by using Internet Protocol security (IPSec).

Internet Protocol (IP) A routable protocol in the Transmission Control Protocol/Internet Protocol (TCP/IP) protocol suite that is responsible for IP addressing, routing, and the fragmentation and reassembly of IP packets.

Internet Protocol Security (IPSec) A set of industry-standard, cryptography-based protection services and protocols. IPSec protects the protocols in the Transmission Control Protocol/Internet Protocol (TCP/IP) protocol suite, and it protects Internet communications by using Layer Two Tunneling Protocol (L2TP).

Internet Security Association and Key Management Protocol (ISAKMP) A framework for managing keys within Internet Protocol Security (IPSec).

internetwork A network (usually Transmission Control Protocol/Internet Protocol, or TCP/IP) that consists of multiple networks joined by routers. More generally, an internetwork is any network that consists of smaller networks joined in any fashion using bridges, switches, routers, and other devices. For example, an Internet Protocol (IP) internetwork could consist of a mix of Windows NT or Windows 2000 and UNIX machines distributed over different subnets, connected with standard IP routers from Cisco Systems or another vendor. An Internetwork Packet Exchange (IPX) internetwork could be a set of networks that use Novell NetWare clients and servers running IPX that are connected using IPX-enabled routers.

Internetwork Packet Exchange (IPX) A network protocol native to NetWare that controls addressing and routing of packets within and between local area networks (LANs). IPX does not guarantee that a message is complete (no lost packets).

IP *See* Internet Protocol (IP).

IPSec *See* Internet Protocol Security (IPSec).

IPX *See* Internetwork Packet Exchange (IPX).

ISAKMP *See* Internet Security Association and Key Management Protocol (ISAKMP).

ISDN *See* Integrated Services Digital Network (ISDN).

iterative query A query made to a Domain Name System (DNS) server for the best answer the server can provide without seeking further help from other DNS servers. Iterative queries are also called "nonrecursive queries."

ITU-T *See* International Telecommunication Union-Telecommunication Standardization Sector.

Kerberos V5 authentication protocol An authentication mechanism used to verify user or host identity. The Kerberos V5 authentication protocol is the default authentication service. Internet Protocol security (IPSec) can use the Kerberos protocol for authentication.

lame delegation A lame delegation occurs when one server delegates a zone to a server that is not authoritative for that zone.

LAN *See* local area network (LAN).

Layer Two Tunneling Protocol (L2TP) An industry-standard Internet tunneling protocol that provides encapsulation for sending Point-to-Point Protocol (PPP) frames across packet-oriented media. For Internet Protocol (IP) networks, L2TP traffic is sent as User Datagram Protocol (UDP) messages. In Microsoft operating systems, L2TP is used in conjunction with Internet Protocol Security (IPSec) as a virtual private network (VPN) technology to provide remote access or router-to-router VPN connections. Request for Comments (RFC) 2661 describes L2TP.

Layer Two Tunneling Protocol/ Internet Protocol Security (L2TP/ IPSec) A virtual private network (VPN) connection method that provides session authentication, address encapsulation, and strong encryption of private data between remote access servers and clients. L2TP provides address encapsulation and user authentication, and Internet Protocol Security (IPSec) provides computer authentication and encryption of the L2TP session.

LCP *See* Link Control Protocol (LCP).

L2TP *See* Layer Two Tunneling Protocol (L2TP).

L2TP/IPSec *See* Layer Two Tunneling Protocol/Internet Protocol Security (L2TP/IPSec).

leaf object An element in the directory hierarchy that is the endpoint of a branch and cannot contain other objects like containers can. An example of a leaf object is a mailbox in the directory of Microsoft Exchange Server, which is found within the Recipients container. You can view and manage objects in the Exchange directory hierarchy using the Exchange Administrator tool.

The term "leaf object" can also describe an endpoint of a branch in Active Directory directory service of Windows 2000 and Windows Server 2003. Leaf objects (or terminal objects) are found in containers such as organizational units (OUs), and they cannot contain other directory objects. You can view and manage objects in Active Directory using the Microsoft Management Console (MMC) and by installing snap-ins, such as Active Directory Users And Computers or Active Directory Sites And Services.

Link Control Protocol (LCP) A subprotocol within the Point-to-Point Protocol (PPP) protocol suite that is responsible for link management. LCP operates at the data-link layer (layer 2) of the Open Systems Interconnection (OSI) reference model for networking and is considered a data-link layer protocol. During the establishment of a PPP communication session, LCP establishes the link, configures PPP options, and tests the quality of the line connection between the PPP client and PPP server. LCP automatically handles encapsulation format options and varies packet sizes over PPP communication links.

local area network (LAN) A communications network that connects a group of computers, printers, and other devices that are located within a relatively limited area (such as a building). A LAN enables any connected device to interact with any other device on the network.

Local System account   A predefined local account that is used to start a service and provide the security context for that service. The name of the account is NT AUTHORITY\System. This account does not have a password, and any password information that you supply is ignored. The Local System account has full access to the system, including the directory service on domain controllers. Because the Local System account acts as a computer on the network, it has access to network resources.

MAC address   *See* Media Access Control (MAC) address.

Media Access Control (MAC) address   A unique 6-byte (48-bit) address that is usually permanently burned into a network interface card (NIC) or other physical-layer networking device and that uniquely identifies the device on an Ethernet-based network. A MAC address is also known as an "Ethernet address," a hardware address, a physical address, or a PHY address.

Microsoft Management Console (MMC)   A framework for hosting administrative tools called "snap-ins." A console might contain tools, folders, or other containers, World Wide Web pages, and other administrative items. These items are displayed in the left pane of the console, or the console tree. A console has one or more windows that can provide views of the console tree. The main MMC window provides commands and tools for authoring consoles. The authoring features of MMC and the console tree itself might be hidden when a console is in User Mode.

Microsoft Point-to-Point Encryption (MPPE)   A 128-bit key or 40-bit key encryption algorithm using Rivest-Shamir-Adleman (RSA) RC4. MPPE provides for packet confidentiality between the remote access client and the remote access or tunnel server, and it is useful where Internet Protocol Security (IPSec) is not available. MPPE 40-bit keys are used to satisfy current North American export restrictions. MPPE is compatible with Network Address Translation (NAT).

MMC   *See* Microsoft Management Console (MMC).

MPPE   *See* Microsoft Point-to-Point Encryption (MPPE).

multicasting   The process of sending a message simultaneously to zero or more destinations on a network.

multicast scope   A range of multicast group Internet Protocol (IP) addresses in the Class D address range that are available to be leased or assigned to multicast Dynamic Host Configuration Protocol (DHCP) clients by DHCP.

Multilink   The combination of bandwidth of two or more physical communications links into a single logical link to increase remote access bandwidth and throughput by using remote access Multilink. Based on the Internet Engineering Task Force (IETF) standard Request for Comments (RFC) 1990, Multilink combines analog modem paths, Integrated Services Digital Network (ISDN) B channels, and mixed analog and digital communications links on both client and server computers. This increases Internet and intranet access speed and decreases the amount of time users are connected to a remote computer.

name resolution   The process of translating an Internet Protocol (IP) address, which is necessary in Transmission Control Protocol/Internet Protocol (TCP/IP) communications, into a name that users can remember and identify more easily (and vice versa). Name resolution can be provided by software components such as Domain Name System (DNS) or Windows Internet Naming Service (WINS).

name server (NS) resource record   A resource record that is used in a zone to designate the Domain Name System (DNS) domain names for authoritative DNS servers for the zone.

NAS   *See* network access server (NAS).

NAT   *See* Network Address Translation (NAT).

NetBIOS   *See* network basic input/output system (NetBIOS).

NetBIOS name   A 16-byte name for a networking service or function on a machine running Windows Server 2003. Network basic input/output system (NetBIOS) names are a more friendly way of identifying computers on a network than network numbers and are used by NetBIOS-enabled services and applications.

network access server (NAS)   The device that accepts Point-to-Point Protocol (PPP) connections and places clients on the network that the NAS serves.

Network Address Translation (NAT)   An Internet Protocol (IP) translation process that allows a network with private addresses to access information on the Internet.

network basic input/output system (NetBIOS) An application programming interface (API) that is used by programs on a local area network (LAN). NetBIOS provides programs with a uniform set of commands for requesting the lower-level services required to manage names, conduct sessions, and send datagrams between nodes on a network.

network bridge A connection that makes multiple, disparate networks act as one network.

network ID A number used to identify the systems that are located on the same physical network, which is bounded by routers. The network ID should be unique to the internetwork.

network interface card (NIC) An adapter card that plugs into the system bus of a computer and allows the computer to send and receive signals on a network. A NIC is also known as a "network adapter card" or simply a "network card."

NIC *See* network interface card (NIC).

node A general term for a network device that has a specific physical or logical address or that can recognize addresses. Nodes can be computers, repeaters, bridges, or other devices on a network that can transmit, receive, or process signals. Another name for a node, especially on Ethernet networks, is a station.

Other common meanings for the term "node" include the following:

- A domain or subdomain in the namespace of Domain Name System (DNS)

- An object in the console hierarchy of Microsoft Management Console (MMC)

- In Microsoft Cluster Server (MSCS) terminology, an independent computer system running Windows NT Server or Enterprise Edition that is a member of a cluster

noncontiguous namespace A namespace based on different Domain Name System (DNS) root domain names, such as that of multiple trees in the same forest.

NS resource record *See* name server (NS) resource record.

NTFS file system An advanced file system that provides performance, security,

reliability, and advanced features that are not found in any version of file allocation table (FAT). For example, NTFS guarantees volume consistency by using standard transaction logging and recovery techniques. If a system fails, NTFS uses its log file and checkpoint information to restore the consistency of the file system. NTFS also provides advanced features, such as file and folder permissions, encryption, disk quotas, and compression.

NTFS permissions The settings that administrators apply to access control entries (ACEs) for managing access to files and folders under the NTFS file system. The Take Ownership permission is an example of an NTFS permission.

NTLM authentication protocol A challenge/response authentication protocol. The NTLM authentication protocol is supported in Windows 2000, Microsoft Windows XP, and the Windows Server 2003 family, but it is not the default. It is the default authentication protocol for earlier versions of Windows.

Oakley A protocol used by Internet Protocol Security (IPSec) for exchanging keys securely. Oakley uses the Diffie-Hellman algorithm.

Open Shortest Path First (OSPF) A routing protocol used in medium-sized and large networks. This protocol is more complex than Routing Information Protocol (RIP), but it allows better control and is more efficient in propagating routing information.

Open Systems Interconnection (OSI) reference model A networking model introduced by the International Organization for Standardization (ISO) to promote multivendor interoperability. OSI is a seven-layered conceptual model that consists of the application, presentation, session, transport, network, data-link, and physical layers.

organizational unit (OU) An Active Directory container object used in domains. An OU is a logical container into which users, groups, computers, and other OUs are placed. It can contain objects only from its parent domain. An OU is the smallest scope to which a Group Policy Object (GPO) can be linked or over which administrative authority can be delegated.

OSI   *See* Open Systems Interconnection (OSI) reference model.

OSPF   *See* Open Shortest Path First (OSPF).

OU   *See* organizational unit (OU).

packet filtering   Process that prevents certain types of network packets from being sent or received. This can be employed for security reasons (to prevent access by unauthorized users) or to improve performance by disallowing unnecessary packets from traveling over a slow connection.

permissions   Settings that you establish for a resource to control which users and groups can access the resource and what degree of access they have. Permissions are implemented at several levels in Microsoft Windows operating systems and other Microsoft BackOffice applications. Permissions are implemented in Microsoft systems using discretionary access control lists (DACLs), which are attached to the object they control.

Examples of permission types include the following:

- Shared folder permissions. Can be applied to shared folders on Windows systems to control access to network shares by users

- NTFS permissions. Can be applied to files and folders on NTFS for both local and network control of access to the resources

- Print permissions. Can be assigned to printers to control who can manage printers, manage documents, or print documents

- Active Directory permissions. Can be assigned to objects within the Active Directory directory service of Windows 2000 using Active Directory Users And Computers

- Exchange permissions. Can be assigned to objects in the Microsoft Exchange Server directory hierarchy to control who can administer different parts of an Exchange organization using the Exchange Administrator program

- Public folder permissions. Can be assigned using Microsoft Outlook to files in public folders to control who can read, edit, or delete those files

PID   *See* process identifier (PID).

PKI   *See* public key infrastructure (PKI).

Plain Old Telephone Service (POTS line)   The basic analog telecommunications service provided by a local telco. POTS was the only type of telephone service until the 1970s.

pointer (PTR) resource record   A Domain Name System (DNS) resource record used in a reverse lookup zone to map an Internet Protocol (IP) address to a DNS name.

Point-to-Point Tunneling Protocol (PPTP)   PPTP is a virtual private network (VPN) protocol implemented at layer 2 in the Open Systems Interconnection (OSI) model. PPTP encapsulates VPN data inside Point-to-Point Protocol (PPP) frames, which are then further encapsulated in Internet Protocol (IP) datagrams for transmission over a transit IP internetwork such as the Internet. This means that users can remotely run applications that depend on particular network protocols.

port   In Transmission Control Protocol/ Internet Protocol (TCP/IP) networking, the endpoint of a logical connection between two hosts on an internetwork. Ports are identified by port numbers. A port identifies a unique process for which a server can provide a service or the client can access a service. Ports can be Transmission Control Protocol (TCP) ports or User Datagram Protocol (UDP) ports, depending on the type of service supported.

In general networking terminology, a port is a connector that attaches cables or peripherals to a computer—for example, a parallel port for connecting a printer to a computer or a serial port for connecting a serial mouse or modem to a computer. Connectors on networking components, such as hubs or routers, are also sometimes called "ports," although a better term for a connector on a router is a "router interface."

POTS line   *See* Plain Old Telephone Service (POTS line).

PPTP   *See* Point-to-Point Tunneling Protocol (PPTP).

primary name server   A name server that maintains its own local Domain Name System (DNS) database of resource records. A primary name server has a master copy of resource records for each zone over which it has authority. These records are stored locally on the name server in the form of a text file called the "zone file." All changes to the resource records for a zone must be made on the primary name server.

primary zone   A zone file that contains the master copy of the Domain Name System (DNS) database file.

principle of least privilege   The security guideline that says users should have the minimum privileges necessary to perform required tasks. This helps to reduce the risk of security compromise and, upon compromise, reduces the potential impact. In practice, a user runs within the security context of a normal user. When a task requires additional privileges, the user can use a tool such as Run As to start a specific process with those additional privileges or to log on as a user with the necessary privileges.

process   The virtual address space and the control information necessary for the execution of a program.

process identifier (PID)   A numerical identifier that uniquely identifies a process while it runs. Use Task Manager to view PIDs.

protocol   A set of rules and conventions for sending information over a network. These rules govern the content, format, timing, sequencing, and error control of messages exchanged among network devices.

proxy server   A firewall component that manages Internet traffic to and from a local area network (LAN) and that can provide other features, such as document caching and access control. A proxy server can improve performance by supplying frequently requested data, such as a popular Web page, and it can filter and discard requests that the owner does not consider appropriate, such as requests for unauthorized access to proprietary files.

PTR   *See* pointer (PTR) resource record.

public key   The nonsecret half of a cryptographic key pair that is used with a public key algorithm. Public keys are typically used when encrypting a session key, verifying a digital signature, or encrypting data that can be decrypted with the corresponding private key.

public key infrastructure (PKI)   The laws, policies, standards, and software that regulate or manipulate certificates and public and private keys. In practice, it is a system of digital certificates, certification authorities (CAs), and other registration authorities that verify and authenticate the validity of each party involved in an electronic transaction. Standards for PKI are still evolving, even though they are being widely implemented as a necessary element of electronic commerce.

RADIUS   *See* Remote Authentication Dial-In User Service (RADIUS).

RARP   *See* Reverse Address Resolution Protocol.

recursive query   One of the two process types (iterative and recursive) used for Domain Name System (DNS) name resolution. In this process, a resolver (a DNS client) requests that a DNS server provide a complete answer to a query that does not include pointers to other DNS servers. When a client makes a query and requests that the server use recursive resolution to answer, it effectively shifts the workload of resolving the query from the client to the DNS server. If the DNS server supports and uses recursive resolution, it contacts other DNS servers as necessary (using iterative queries on behalf of the client) until it obtains a definitive answer to the query. This type of resolution allows the client resolver to be small and simple.

recursive resolution   One of the two process types (iterative and recursive) for DNS name resolution. In this process, a resolver (a DNS client) will request that a DNS server provide a complete answer to a query that does not include pointers to other DNS servers. When a client makes a query and requests that the server use recursive resolution to answer, it effectively shifts the workload of resolving the query from the client to the DNS server. If the DNS server supports and uses recursive resolution, it contacts other DNS servers as necessary (using iterative queries on behalf of the client) until it obtains a definitive answer to the query. This type of resolution allows for a small and simple client resolver.

remote access server   A Microsoft Windows–based computer that runs the Routing and Remote Access service and is configured to provide remote access.

Remote Authentication Dial-In User Service (RADIUS)   A security authentication protocol based on a client/server model and widely used by Internet service providers (ISPs). RADIUS is the most popular means of authenticating and authorizing dial-up and tunneled network users. The Routing and Remote Access service that ships with the Windows Server 2003 family includes RADIUS. A RADIUS server, named Internet Authentication Service (IAS), is included in Windows Server 2003, Standard Edition; Windows Server 2003, Enterprise Edition; and Windows Server 2003, Datacenter Edition.

remote computer   A computer that you can access only by using a communications line or a communications device, such as a network card or a modem.

Remote Procedure Call (RPC)   A message-passing facility that allows a distributed application to call services that are available on various computers on a network. Used during remote administration of computers.

Request for Comments (RFC)   An official document of the Internet Engineering Task Force (IETF) that specifies the details for protocols included in the Transmission Control Protocol/Internet Protocol (TCP/IP) family.

resolver   Domain Name System (DNS) client programs used to look up DNS name information. Resolvers can be either a small stub (a limited set of programming routines that provide basic query functionality) or larger programs that provide additional lookup DNS client functions, such as caching.

resource record   A standard Domain Name System (DNS) database structure containing information used to process DNS queries. For example, an address (A) resource record contains an Internet Protocol (IP) address corresponding to a host name. Most of the basic resource record types are defined in Request for Comments (RFC) 1035, but additional resource record types have been defined in other RFCs and are approved for use with DNS.

Resultant Set of Policy (RSoP)   A feature that simplifies Group Policy implementation and troubleshooting. RSoP uses Windows Management Instrumentation (WMI) to determine how policy settings are applied to users and computers. RSoP has two modes: logging mode and planning mode. Logging mode determines the resultant effect of policy settings that have been applied to an existing user and computer based on a site, domain, and organizational unit. Planning mode simulates the resultant effect of policy settings that are applied to a user and computer.

Reverse Address Resolution Protocol (RARP)   A protocol for resolving Internet Protocol (IP) addresses into Media Access Control (MAC) addresses.

reverse lookup   The process of a resolver querying a name server to resolve a host's Internet Protocol (IP) address into its associated fully qualified domain name (FQDN). This is the reverse of the usual host name resolution process, in which a resolver queries a name server to resolve a host name into its associated IP address. Reverse name lookups use a special domain called in-addr.arpa.

reverse lookup zone   *See* reverse lookup; zone.

RFC   *See* Request for Comments (RFC).

RIP   *See* Routing Information Protocol (RIP).

root hints   Domain Name System (DNS) data stored on a DNS server that identifies the authoritative DNS servers for the root zone of the DNS namespace. The root hints are stored in the file Cache.dns, which is located in the %systemroot%\System32\Dns folder.

round robin   A simple mechanism Domain Name System (DNS) servers use to share and distribute loads for network resources. Round robin is used to rotate the order of resource records returned in a response to a query when multiple resource records of the same type exist for a queried DNS domain name.

router   Hardware that helps local area networks (LANs) and wide area networks (WANs) achieve interoperability and connectivity and that can link LANs that have different network topologies (such as Ethernet and Token Ring). Routers match packet headers to a LAN segment and choose the best path for the packet, thereby optimizing network performance.

routing   The process of forwarding a packet through an internetwork from a source host to a destination host.

Routing Information Protocol (RIP)   An industry-standard, distance vector routing protocol used in small to medium-sized Internet Protocol (IP) and Internetwork Packet Exchange (IPX) internetworks.

routing protocol   Any of several protocols that enable the exchange of routing table information between routers. Typically, medium- to large-sized Transmission Control Protocol/Internet Protocol (TCP/IP) internetworks implement routing protocols to simplify the administration of routing tables.

routing tables   An internal table that a computer or router uses to determine which router interface to send packets to based on their destination network addresses. Microsoft Windows platforms automatically build their own routing tables, which are used to determine whether to forward specific packets to the local network segment, a near-side router interface, or the default gateway for the segment.

RPC   *See* Remote Procedure Call (RPC).

RSoP   *See* Resultant Set of Policy (RSoP).

SACL   *See* system access control list (SACL).

SAM database   *See* Security Accounts Manager (SAM) database.

sampling (or sample) rate   The frequency at which a counter is checked to see whether specific criteria are met. The faster a counter is sampled, the more detailed the response. However, the slower a counter is sampled, the less the central processing unit (CPU) must be used.

scope   A range of Internet Protocol (IP) addresses that are available to be leased or assigned to Dynamic Host Configuration Protocol (DHCP) clients by the DHCP service.

secondary name server   A name server that downloads its Domain Name System (DNS) database of resource records from a master name server. The master name server can be either a primary name server or another secondary name server. Primary name servers get their resource records from local files called "zone files." Secondary name servers do not maintain local zone files—they obtain their resource files over the network from master name servers by a zone transfer, which occurs when a secondary name server polls a master name server and determines that there are updates to the DNS database that must be downloaded. This means that the

DNS administrator has to maintain only a single set of DNS resource records (on the primary name server), which simplifies DNS administration.

Secondary name servers are used in DNS to provide redundancy and load balancing for name resolution. On Berkeley Internet Name Domain (BIND) implementations of DNS, secondary name servers are often referred to as slave name servers.

A name server can be a primary name server for one zone and a secondary name server for a different zone. In other words, name servers are defined as primary or secondary on a per-zone basis.

secondary zone   A file containing a read-only replica of the primary zone file.

Secure Sockets Layer (SSL)   A proposed open standard for establishing a secure communications channel to prevent the interception of critical information, such as credit card numbers. Primarily, it enables secure electronic financial transactions on the World Wide Web, although it is designed to work on other Internet services as well.

Security Accounts Manager (SAM) database   The database of user and group account information that is stored on a domain controller in a Windows NT–based network. The SAM database is also known as the "domain directory database," or sometimes simply the "directory database."

The SAM database occupies a portion of the Windows NT registry. All user accounts, group accounts, and resource definitions such as shares and printers have their security principals defined in the SAM database. Because the entire SAM database must reside in a domain controller's random access memory (RAM), it cannot exceed approximately 40 megabytes (MB) in Windows NT, which equals approximately 40,000 user accounts, or 26,000 users and Windows NT workstations combined.

The master copy of the SAM database is stored on the primary domain controller (PDC). Periodic directory synchronization ensures that backup domain controllers (BDCs) have an accurate replica of this master database, so BDCs can also be used for logons and pass-through authentication of users attempting to access network resources.

Security Parameters Index (SPI)   A unique, identifying value in the security association (SA) used to distinguish among multiple SAs existing at the receiving computer.

security template   A physical file representation of a security configuration that can be applied to a local computer or imported to a Group Policy Object (GPO) in the Active Directory directory service. When you import a security template to a GPO, Group Policy processes the template and makes the corresponding changes to the members of that GPO, which can be users or computers.

Server Message Block (SMB)   A high-level file-sharing protocol jointly developed by Microsoft, IBM, and Intel for passing data between computers on a network. Microsoft Windows and OS/2 use SMB. Many UNIX operating systems also support it.

SMB is used between clients and servers to do the following:

- Open and close connections between client redirectors and shared network resources

- Locate, read, and write to files shared on a server

- Locate and print to print queues that are shared on a server

service dependency   A relationship between services in which one service requires that other services are started before it can start.

services   Programs, routines, or processes that perform a specific system function to support other programs, particularly at a low (close to the hardware) level. When services are provided over a network, they can be published in the Active Directory directory service, facilitating service-centric administration and usage. Some examples of services are the Security Accounts Manager service, the File Replication service, and the Routing and Remote Access service.

Server Message Block (SMB).

Security Parameters Index (SPI).

A routing mechanism that Internet Protocol (IP) and manually configured rout-t use static routing Static routers are generally used in smaller networks that contain only a couple of routers or when security is an issue. Each static router must be configured and maintained separately because static routers do not exchange routing information with each other.

stub zone   A copy of a zone that contains only the resource records required to identify the authoritative Domain Name System (DNS) servers for that zone. A DNS server that hosts a parent zone and a stub zone for one of the parent zone's delegated child zones can receive updates from the authoritative DNS servers for the child zone.

subnet mask   A number that, when compared with a network address number, will block out all but the necessary information. For example, in a network that uses XXX.XXX.XXX.YYY and where all computers within the network use the same first address numbers, the mask will block out XXX.XXX.XXX and use only the significant numbers in the address, YYY.

superscope   An administrative grouping feature that supports a Dynamic Host Configuration Protocol (DHCP) server's ability to use more than one scope for each physical interface and subnet. Superscopes are useful under the following conditions: if more DHCP clients must be added to a network than were originally planned, if an Internet Protocol (IP) network is renumbered, or if two or more DHCP servers are configured to provide scope redundancy and fault-tolerant design DHCP service for a single subnet. Each superscope can contain one or more member scopes (also known as "child scopes").

SVCHOST process   A generic host process name for services that are run from dynamic-link libraries (DLLs). The Svchost.exe file is located in the %systemroot%\System32 folder. At startup, Svchost.exe checks the services portion of the registry to construct a list of services that it needs to load. Multiple instances of Svchost.exe can run at the same time. Each Svchost.exe session can contain a grouping of services so that separate services can be run depending on how and where Svchost.exe is started. This allows for better control and debugging.

switch   In the context of controlling data flow within a network, the term "switch" is also used to describe a data-link-layer device that routes frames between connected networks. Data flow switches include the following:

- Local area network (LAN) switches. Used to route Ethernet frames over a Transmission Control Protocol/Internet Protocol (TCP/IP) internetwork. Also called "Ethernet switches."

- Asynchronous Transfer Mode (ATM) switches. Used to switch ATM cells at high speeds over an ATM network.

In the context of high-speed Ethernet networks, the term "switch" usually refers to an Ethernet switch. Thus, the phrase "routers and switches" is understood to mean "routers and Ethernet switches."

The term "switch" can also refer to a device used at a telco central office (CO) for establishing connections in circuit-switched services or forwarding packets in packet-switched services.

system access control list (SACL)   The part of an object's security descriptor that specifies which events are to be audited per user or group. Examples of auditing events are file access, logon attempts, and system shutdowns.

TCP   *See* Transmission Control Protocol (TCP/IP).

TCP/IP   *See* Transmission Control Protocol/Internet Protocol (TCP/IP).

Terminal Services   The underlying technology that enables Remote Desktop, Remote Assistance, and Terminal Server.

TLD   *See* top-level domain (TLD).

Token Ring   The Institute of Electrical and Electronics Engineers (IEEE) 802.5 standard that uses a token-passing technique for Media Access Control (MAC). Token Ring supports media of both shielded and unshielded twisted-pair wiring for data rates of 4 megabits per second (Mbps) and 16 Mbps.

top-level domain (TLD)   Domain names that are rooted hierarchically at the first tier of the domain namespace. They are directly under the root (.) of the Domain Name System (DNS) namespace. On the Internet, top-level domain names such as .com and .org are used to classify and assign second-level domain names (such as microsoft.com) to individual organizations and businesses according to their organizational purpose.

Transmission Control Protocol (TCP)   *See* Transmission Control Protocol/ Internet Protocol (TCP/IP).

Transmission Control Protocol/ Internet Protocol (TCP/IP)   A set of networking protocols widely used on the Internet that provides communications across interconnected networks of computers with diverse hardware architectures and various operating systems. TCP/IP includes standards for how computers communicate and conventions for connecting networks and routing traffic.

triggers   Actions taken when sampled counters are set to go off. Triggers are typically set when a counter rises above a certain value or drops below a certain value.

UDP   *See* User Datagram Protocol (UDP).

unicast   An address that identifies a specific, globally unique host.

user class   An administrative feature that allows Dynamic Host Configuration Protocol (DHCP) clients to be grouped logically according to a shared or common need. For example, a user class can be defined and used to allow similar DHCP leased configuration for all client computers in a specific building or site location.

User Datagram Protocol (UDP)   A Transmission Control Protocol (TCP) complement that offers a connectionless datagram service that guarantees neither delivery nor correct sequencing of delivered packets (much like Internet Protocol [IP]).

user rights   Tasks that a user is permitted to perform on a computer system or domain. There are two types of user rights: privileges and logon rights. An example of a privilege is the right to shut down the system. An example of a logon right is the right to log on to a computer locally. Administrators assign both types of rights to individual users or groups as part of the security settings for the computer.

vendor class   An administrative feature that allows Dynamic Host Configuration Protocol (DHCP) clients to be identified and leased according to their vendor and hardware configuration type. For example, assigning a vendor class of HP to a printer vendor such as Hewlett-Packard would allow all Hewlett-Packard printers to be managed as a single unit so they could all obtain a similar DHCP leased configuration.

virtual private network (VPN)   The extension of a private network that encompasses encapsulated, encrypted, and authenticated links across shared or public networks. VPN connections can provide remote access and routed connections to private networks over the Internet.

VPN   *See* virtual private network (VPN).

WAN   *See* wide area network (WAN).

WebDAV   *See* Web Distributed Authoring and Versioning (WebDAV).

Web Distributed Authoring and Versioning (WebDAV)   An application protocol related to Hypertext Transfer Protocol (HTTP) 1.1 that allows clients to transparently publish and manage resources on the World Wide Web.

wide area network (WAN)   A communications network that connects geographically separated computers, printers, and other devices. A WAN enables any connected device to interact with any other device on the network.

Windows Internet Naming Service (WINS)   A software service that dynamically maps Internet Protocol (IP) addresses to computer names (network basic input/output system [NetBIOS] names). This enables users to access resources by name instead of requiring them to use IP addresses that are difficult to recognize and remember.

Windows operating system kernel   The core (also called the "kernel") of the Windows Server 2003 operating system. Code that runs as part of the kernel does so in privileged processor mode and has direct access to system data and hardware.

Windows Update   A Microsoft Web site that works with Automatic Updates to provide timely critical and noncritical system updates. Updates include security patches, updated drivers, and other recommended files.

Windows Update Catalog   A Web site that lists hardware and software that is designed for use with Windows XP, Windows 2000 Server products, and products in the Windows Server 2003 family. You can use this site to help you decide whether to purchase a particular device or program and help you evaluate whether a particular computer would support an upgraded operating system, as well as for similar hardware and software decisions.

WINS   *See* Windows Internet Naming Service (WINS).

X.25   A packet-switching protocol for wide area network (WAN) connectivity that uses a public data network (PDN) that parallels the voice network of the Public Switched Telephone Network (PSTN). The current X.25 standard supports synchronous, full-duplex communication at speeds of up to 2 megabits per second (Mbps) over two pairs of wires; however, most implementations are 64-kilobits-per-second (Kbps) connections using a standard DS0 link.

X.25 was developed by common carriers in the early 1970s and approved in 1976 by the CCITT, the precursor of the International Telecommunication Union (ITU). X.25 was designed as a global standard for a packet-switching network and was originally designed to connect remote, character-based terminals to mainframe hosts. The original X.25 standard operated at only 19.2 Kbps, but this was generally sufficient for character-based communication between mainframes and terminals.

X.509 v3 certificate   Version 3 of the International Telecommunication Union-Telecommunication (Standardization Sector) (ITU-T) recommendation X.509 for certificate syntax and format. This is the standard certificate format used by Windows certificate-based processes.

An X.509 certificate includes the public key and information about the person or entity to which the certificate is issued, information about the certificate, plus optional information about the certificate authority (CA) issuing the certificate.

XML   *See* Extensible Markup Language (XML).

zone   In a Domain Name System (DNS) database, a manageable unit of the DNS database that is administered by a DNS server. A zone stores the domain names and data of the domain with a corresponding name, except for domain names stored in delegated subdomains.

zone transfer   The process of copying information from the zone file on one Domain Name System (DNS) server to another DNS server.

zone file   A file on a name server that contains information that defines the zone that the name server manages. The zone file is a text file consisting of a series of resource records that form the Domain Name System (DNS) database of the name server. These records identify which name server is responsible for a given zone, timing parameters for zone transfers between name servers, IP address to host name mappings for hosts within the domains over which the zone file is authoritative, and so on.

INDEX

SYSTEM REQUIREMENTS

To complete the exercises in this textbook, get the most out of the Supplemental Course Materials CD-ROM, and install the Microsoft Windows Server 2003 evaluation software, you will need a computer equipped with the following minimum configuration:

- Microsoft Windows Server 2003, Enterprise Edition. (A 180-day evaluation edition of Windows Server 2003, Enterprise Edition is included on the CD-ROM.)

- Microsoft PowerPoint or Microsoft PowerPoint Viewer. (PowerPoint Viewer is included on the Supplemental Student CD-ROM.)

- Microsoft Word or Microsoft Word Viewer. (Word Viewer is included on the Supplemental Student CD-ROM.)

- Microsoft Internet Explorer 5.01 or later.

- Minimum CPU speed: 133 MHz for x86-based computers and 733 MHz for Itanium-based computers. (733 MHz is recommended.)

- Minimum RAM: 128 MB. (256 MB is recommended.)

- Disk space for setup: 1.5 GB for x86-based computers and 2.0 GB for Itanium-based computers.

- Display monitor capable of 800 x 600 resolution or higher.

- CD-ROM drive.

- Microsoft mouse or compatible pointing device.

Uninstall Instructions

The time-limited release of Microsoft Windows Server 2003, Enterprise Edition, will expire 180 days after installation. If you decide to discontinue the use of this software, you will need to reinstall your original operating system. You might need to reformat your drive.